# The BATTERED BASTARDS OF BASTOGNE

Dedicated to the memory of all the defenders of Bastogne and the airmen who provided manna from Heaven and those tankers who provided relief from the south.

# THE BATTERED BASTARDS
# OF BASTOGNE

*A Chronicle*
*of the*
*Defense of Bastogne*
*December 19, 1944–January 17, 1945*

George E. Koskimaki

CASEMATE
*Havertown, Pennsylvania*

Published by
CASEMATE
2114 Darby Road, Havertown, PA 19083

First Casemate edition, 2003
Previously published by George E. Koskimaki in 1989.

ISBN 1-932033-06-8

Map Illustrations by Peter Barnette

Printed and Bound in the United States of America.

# INTRODUCTION

Twenty years after the cessation of World War II, I began research on the actions of the 101st Airborne "Screaming Eagle" Division. My three years in the Army of the United States were spent with the 101st. My basic training was with the 327th Glider Infantry Regiment at Fort Bragg, North Carolina.

After learning the rudiments of soldiering, I was sent to the 101st Airborne Signal Company to begin my training as a radioman. While I became familiar with the operation of several kinds of radio sets, others were training to string telephone lines and run switchboards. Still others were assigned to the message center where they became proficient at encoding and decoding messages.

During July, The Division was moved to Tennessee where we took part in month-long maneuvers. Upon return to Fort Bragg, we received seven day furloughs and then shipped out for Europe from Camp Shanks, New York. About a third of us earned the American Theater Ribbon after we spent a month in Newfoundland, when the H.M.S. Strathnaver developed engine trouble. Our trip lasted 43 days while the other two troop ships carrying our comrades made the crossing in about ten days.

The men quickly adapted to life in England. We were fascinated with the thatched roofs, fish and chips, mild and bitters. We crammed our pockets with candy and gum for our visits to towns such as Newbury, Hungerford, Ramsbury, Reading, Tilehurst and Swindon. We'd have been disappointed if groups of youngsters didn't quickly tail us and call out, "Any gum, chum?"

When the call went out for an echelon of parachutists to be trained for Division Headquarters I volunteered, along with about two dozen members of Division Signal Company. As a result of this qualification, I was assigned as the radio operator to accompany the commanding general, Brig. General Maxwell D. Taylor, on the D-Day mission. (The General received his second star a few days into the Normandy mission.)

The D-Day mission of the 101st Airborne Division became the focus of the first book, *D-Day With The Screaming Eagles* which was published in 1970. It is currently in its third printing. The book is based on the interviews of 518 former airborne soldiers of the 101st. (I wrote to 1,361 of my former comrades.) Each man was provided with a copy of his unit roster, a map of our Normandy action areas and a questionnaire. The lists of comrades shook the cobwebs from the memory cells and triggered recall of actions of that day, now twenty years in the past. Letters, pictures and scrapbooks were dug out of dusty old trunks. Their stories fit together like the pieces of a giant jigsaw puzzle.

Upon the urging of former airborne soldiers and their family members, members of the British airborne forces and airborne history buffs, I took it upon myself to do a second account. This one was the 72-day campaign of the 101st Division in Holland as part of the *Market-Garden* operation. The second account became *Hell's Highway*. A total of 612 individuals provided narrations for this one. Included were stories by parachutists and glidermen of the 101st Division, a member of the British 1st Airborne Corps, pilots and crewmen of the troop carrier planes, glider pilots, members of the Dutch underground and many Dutch citizens who recalled our mission to their land in September of 1944. *Hell's Highway* was completed in 1989 and is now in its second printing. It has been translated into the Dutch language.

Again, on the coaxing of my comrades, I undertook the task of doing a third segment of the division history, part of a trilogy concerning the major campaigns of the "Screaming Eagle" Division. This, of course, is the account you are reading – *The Battered Bastards of Bastogne.*

As was the case in the earlier accounts, this story is a composite of the stories of 530 individuals. I have felt strongly for years that an account of this campaign should provide recognition for those units which fought beside us within the Bastogne perimeter. Other military formations were ordered into the small city of Bastogne. Had it not been for the actions of three combat teams of Combat Command B of the 10th Armored Division who arrived in Bastogne in the late afternoon of December 18, there might not have been a Bastogne to defend. The enemy was already within a few miles of the city when hasty roadblocks were set up at key points east of Bastogne. From the northwest came the men of the 705th Tank Destroyer Battalion. Many of the enemy tanks approaching our lines were stopped by their guns.

To the units which became surrounded with us at Bastogne, it was a new experience. For the sky-troopers it was "old hat," a situation that was common in airborne warfare. The cocky confidence of the troopers rubbed off on the armored and tank destroyer personnel.

After the first four days, when the troops were cut off from the outside world except for radio communication, the arrival of the airlifts with rations, ammunition, gasoline and medical supplies was "manna" from heaven. We owe much to the pilots and crew members of the various troop carrier groups and squadrons. They flew through horrendous flak to drop those valuable supplies to us. The glider pilots, frantic to get out of the streams of flak, watched in horror as the fuselages of their tow planes were eaten away by exploding 20mm and 40mm shells. Their hope was that the tow planes would stay aloft long enough for the motorless craft to reach the safety of the landing zones near Bastogne. Their big worry was that the loads of ammunition might explode as the result of a direct hit or the cans of gasoline being carried might be incinerated by a tracer bullet. We remember those great air crews. Our artillery battalions were down to their last shells when the resupply arrived.

The work of the hard-driving men of the 4th Armored Division in breaking through the enemy positions on the afternoon of December 26 is not forgotten. They lost a thousand men in their drive to provide relief for us.

In the two earlier accounts, our 326th Airborne Medical Company and their attached 3rd Auxiliary Surgical Team had suffered many casualties when their field hospital facilities had been bombed. At Bastogne, over three-fourths of their personnel were lost the very first night west of the city when enemy armor overran the medical set-up. These men spent the rest of the war as prisoners. The regimental and battalion surgeons, dentists and aidmen were called on to perform Herculean tasks in looking after a thousand casualties during the encirclement.

Once the siege was lifted, the defenders were called on to go on the offensive. They became part of the effort to trap the enemy forces which had penetrated far behind Allied lines.

Battling the elements as well as the stubborn troops holding off our attacking forces is also a major part of this account. The weather conditions in the Ardennes during January, 1945 were among the most severe in the memories of local residents who lived through those days with us during the Battle of the Bulge.

Well over 1,300 participants in the Bastogne actions were contacted in this latest effort. I followed the same procedure of providing unit rosters, maps of action areas and questionnaires.

Censorship restrictions were usually lifted within two to three weeks after an action was completed and men were permitted to write in some detail of their experiences. Letters of this nature were found among family artifacts and scrapbooks. While recuperating for long periods of time in military hospitals, some of these veterans wrote long, detailed accounts of the actions. Copies of these letters were supplied.

One soldier, Ted Goldmann, had made a pact with his buddy, John Ballard that if only one lived to tell about their experiences, the survivor was to write or visit the buddy's family and relate what the war had been like for their loved one. As the war came to an end in Europe, Goldmann wrote two long letters to Ballard's parents describing their role in the war. When the soldiers returned to their homes in the United States, Ballard's parents returned the letters. These letters play an important part in this account.

As a highly decorated veteran of the 101st Airborne Division, Robert J. Houston, wrote a book (*D-Day to Bastogne*) about his experiences with 3rd Battalion of the 501st Parachute Infantry Regiment. His widow has graciously consented to the use of selected material in the Bastogne account which helped tie together the stories of several men.

# Introduction

Some men kept diaries or daily logs of actions (including the author) which helped pinpoint specific dates. Unit after-action reports were also used.

Readers should be impressed by the fact that stories have been provided of events which occurred a half century ago and, though most of the participants haven't seen or heard from these old comrades during the interim, the accounts fit together amazingly well.

As was the case with research in Holland for the *Hell's Highway* book, with young Peter Hendrikx doing much "gopher" leg work for me, I have a great appreciation for the efforts of a former Belgian airborne soldier, Andre Meurisse, who interviewed local inhabitants, did follow-up work on communities, made sketch maps of action areas and related his own story. As an eight-year-old fleeing Bastogne with his parents, Andre was wounded by shrapnel from a bomb dropped by an American plane. His story blends in with the accounts of the American soldiers.

There has been much pressure on me to finish this account in a shorter period of time (than the first two narratives) with the admonition from the old veterans – "Get it done so we can read it before we die!"

In most instances, these men are in their 70's now. Fifty of the contributors have already passed on since submitting their accounts and did not read the finished product. For this I am sorry. I am sure family members will be proud of what dad, brother, uncle or cousin did during this major battle of World War II.

George Koskimaki
Northville, Michigan
March, 1994

# CONTENTS

# FOREWORD

The segment of World War II history that follows has never been recorded before. This history of the defense of Bastogne is the product of contributions by 530 soldiers who were on the ground or in the air over Bastogne. They lived and made this history and much of it is told in their own words.

Pieces of a 50 year old puzzle come together in this book, when memories related by one soldier fit with those of another who may have been in a different unit, or when pursuing the battle from a nearby piece of terrain.

The material contributed by these men of the 101st Airborne Division, the Armor, Tank Destroyer, Army Air Force and others, is tailored meticulously and placed on the historical framework known to most students of the Battle of the Bulge. The author, George Koskimaki, has again demonstrated his ability to use recollections provided by soldiers, from private to general, to fashion a narrative that could not be made more exciting by an author of fiction.

There is no evident and repetitious formula, from interview forms, emerging from the introduction of contributors as most works of military history that include personal offerings display. The story is the thing and each individual contribution, by a participant in the defense of Bastogne, is placed in historical perspective and becomes a logical, effective and personal part of this unique history of the men who amazed friend and foe with their tenacious defense of Bastogne.

An additional bonus for the reader is the fact that George Koskimaki was there. He was assigned to Signal Company. He was the Radio Operator for the division commander and he knows most of those who submitted their recollections to be used in the book.

*The Battered Bastards of Bastogne* follows *D-Day With the Screaming Eagles* and *Hell's Highway*, the intimate historical accounts of the 101st Airborne Division's vital role in the invasion of Normandy and the liberation of the southern part of the Netherlands. It completes the trilogy of the most hard fought and bloody battles by the Screaming Eagles in World War II.

*The Battered Bastards of Bastogne* will take you from the peaceful interlude in Mourmelon, where the major action was between the airborne soldiers of the 101st and the 82nd Airborne Divisions on pass to Rheim, to the mopping up operations that followed the resolute defense while enormously outnumbered by German Mechanized and Infantry Armies.

The word that propelled the defense of Bastogne into the media and the attention of the world was NUTS. NUTS was an audacious answer to the Germans demanding surrender. This was a clear indicator of the spirit of the Screaming Eagles and the general disdain for the ability of the German divisions to overrun the 360 degree perimeter.

Many who read about the NUTS answer to the surrender demand did not know the price in life, blood and frozen limbs the men of the 101st paid for their stubborn and arrogant stand against the infantry, tanks, artillery and air bombardment of the Germans.

i

The pages that follow are probably the only chance you will ever have to read, in their own words, how the men who held Bastogne accomplished that momentous task and their feelings about its accomplishment while they were involved in winning one of the pivotal battles of World War II.

Sixty of those who contributed material for this book have died. They leave a legacy of courage and fortitude to all Screaming Eagles who now serve and who will serve in the 101st Airborne Division in the future.

Ivan G. Worrell
Executive Secretary
101st Airborne Division Association

# ACKNOWLEDGMENTS

The material provided by 530 individuals in this *Battered Bastards of Bastogne* account gives us a well-rounded narrative of the many military formations which participated at Bastogne during the month-long fighting on its perimeter. I want to thank all those airborne troopers, troop carrier crewmen and glider pilots and armored force personnel for sending their accounts and those of their comrades.

Special thanks go to the following:

I am so appreciative of the prodding provided by Alex Andros, Col. John T. Cooper, Jr., Michael Finn and Dick Winters. With their assistance, the stories of many former troopers appear in this account which would not otherwise have been included.

Troop carrier group commanders, Colonels William Parkhill, Frank Krebs and Charles H. Young provided materials from their group histories which give us an added aspect of the battle. The P-38 Association, through its newsletter, located the pilot who dropped maps and aerial photos to the troops at Bastogne on Christmas Day. Glider Pilot and author, H. Rex Shama (*Operation REPULSE*) provided valuable information on the glider pilots involved in the December 26 and 27 resupply missions.

Valuable pathfinder materials were provided by Jack Agnew, Glenn Braddock, Gordon DeRamus, George McMillan and Shrable Williams.

Pictures used in the account were provided by Jack Agnew, Herbert Ballinger, my friend Roger Bell in London, John W. Gibson, Carmen Gisi, Cleto Leone, George Rosie, Ben Rous, Richard Rowles and Dick Winters. Some of the photos are rare and were never before used in historical accounts.

The Don F. Pratt Airborne Museum at Fort Campbell, Kentucky, provided photocopies of clippings from newspapers and *Yank* Magazine, copies of small unit after-action reports and the *Narrative - December 1944* which had been prepared by 101st Airborne Division Headquarters at Bastogne.

Excellent excerpts and sections of personal histories were provided by Henry Barnes, H. Lincoln Bethel, Layton Black (deceased before he had an opportunity to publish his memoirs), Richard Bostwick and Donald B. Straith.

Extensive individual and unit accounts were provided by Robert M. Bowen, John Gibson and Bernard J. Ryan who put their experiences on paper while recuperating from wounds suffered in the Bastogne fighting.

Former American Red Cross "Donut Dolly" Helen Briggs Ramsey sent copies of letters exchanged between wartime friends who were recuperating from wounds, and the story of Robert F. Harwick which had appeared in a Gulf Petroleum Corporation newsletter published in late 1945.

Morning reports were provided for "Dog" and "Easy" Companies of the 501st Parachute Infantry Regiment by Robert P. O'Connell while former company commander Wallace A. Swanson provided a similar report for "Able" Company of the 502nd Parachute Regiment.

Sketch maps of action areas were provided by Layton Black, Jr., Robert Bowen, Erminio Calderan, Edward Carowick, William McMahon, Andre Meurisse, Jim Robinson and Ben Stapelfeld.

Diaries kept during combat situations provided excellent recall for Austin Buchanan, George Koskimaki, Donald Woodland and Gerald Zimmerman.

As was the case in our second account, *Hell's Highway*, I am so pleased with the quality of work provided by Sonia Kurtyka of Graphic Touch in preparing the material for the printer.

Many readers wrote to compliment Peter Barnette for the quality of his maps in *Hell's Highway*. I am happy he was able to provide his talents for this third segment of the 101st history.

I may have missed others who had a hand in the preparation of this book and I am truly sorry. The omission was unintended.

# GLOSSARY

| | |
|---|---|
| AA | Anti-Aircraft |
| AT | Anti-Tank |
| AWOL | Absent without official leave |
| BAR | Browning automatic rifle |
| CG | Commanding general |
| CO | Commanding officer |
| DZ | Drop zone |
| EM | Enlisted man |
| F/O | Flight officer |
| GI | Government issue; enlisted man |
| IP | Initial Point |
| LD | Line of departure |
| LMG | Light machine gun |
| LZ | Landing zone |
| MLR | Main line of resistance |
| NCO | Non-commissioned officer |
| OP | Observation post |
| Streamer | Parachute which failed to open properly |
| TCC | Troop Carrier Command |
| TCG | Troop Carrier Group |
| TCS | Troop Carrier Squadron |
| TE | Table of Equipment |
| TO | Table of Organization |

# U. S. ARMY RANKINGS

| | |
|---|---|
| Pvt. | Private |
| PFC | Private First Class (one stripe) |
| Cpl. | Corporal (two stripes) |
| T/5 | Technician Fifth Grade (two stripes and a "T") |
| Sgt. | Sergeant (three stripes) |
| T/4 | Technician Fourth Grade (three stripes and a "T") |
| S/Sgt. | Staff Sergeant (three stripes and a rocker) |
| T/3 | Technician 3rd Grade (three stripes, a rocker and a "T") |
| T/Sgt. | Technical Sergeant (three stripes and two rockers) |
| M/Sgt. | Master Sergeant (three stripes and three rockers) |
| 1/Sgt. | First Sergeant (three stripes, three rockers and a diamond) |
| WOJG | Warrant Officer Junior Grade |
| CWO | Chief Warrant Officer |
| 2Lt. | Second Lieutenant (one brass bar) |
| 1Lt. | First Lieutenant (one silver bar) |
| Capt. | Captain (two silver bars) |
| Maj. | Major (one bronze leaf) |
| LTC | Lieutenant Colonel (one silver leaf) |
| Col. | Colonel (silver eagle) |
| BG | Brigadier General (one star) |
| MG | Major General (two stars) |
| LTG | Lieutenant General (three stars) |
| Gen. | General (four stars) |

# MAPS

*Drawn by Peter Barnette*

vi

# PICTURES

# 1. INTERLUDE

## REAR BASE IN ENGLAND

Many replacements were on the way to the 101st Airborne Division as the fighting was winding down in Holland. The Division had suffered some 3,500 casualties (killed, wounded or injured and captured) during the 72-day campaign.

The experiences of PFC. Donald B. Straith are good examples of what life was like for the average replacement coming to the "Screaming Eagle" Division for the Bastogne operation. Straith had been on the high seas on board the *Queen Mary* headed for a European replacement pool. His shipment went ashore at Gourock, Scotland. From there they traveled by train to Newbury. Straith begins his story:

> From there we went by truck to various small camps, at each of which a few of our group left us. When I was finally ordered out of the truck, I found that I was now part of the rear echelon of the 506th Parachute Infantry Regiment, 101st Airborne Division. I had first seen the Screaming Eagle patch of the 101st back in Anniston and had hoped that I would eventually become a member of that division. Now, at last I had.
>
> Our camp was located a mile east of the town of Hungerford on an estate called Denford Park. The officers were quartered in a manor house while the enlisted men's quarters, mess hall and recreation hall were in Quonset huts scattered among the trees along the driveway. These huts were wartime buildings that looked like half a corrugated cylinder laid on the ground with a door at each end. Assigned to one of the huts, I picked an empty bunk, the bottom of a crude double-decker made of 2 x 4 material and was dead to the world immediately after supper.

Training was rather laid back for the rear echelon people, some of whom had recently returned from extended recuperation periods in Army hospitals. PFC. Don Straith describes a bit of the routine as experienced by a new replacement:

> Time passed slowly while the rear echelon waited to join the rest of the division which was still fighting in Holland. Because of almost constant rain, our officers – Lieutenant Tinsley (company commander), and Lts. Stanley and Stanfield, who had come over with us – couldn't carry on much training. We occasionally did calisthenics, hikes and long-distance runs, but when Lt. Stanley was in charge, he would run us past the first hedgerow outside camp, have us sit down on the far side out of sight and spend the next hour telling jokes.

PFC. Harry Sherrard had received extensive training at Fort Leonard Wood but he wasn't qualified yet for an assignment to the 326th Airborne Engineer Battalion. He wrote:

I was rated as a demolitions or explosive specialist having completed special training at Fort Leonard Wood in Missouri before going to the 101st Airborne Division jump school in southern England. What my "MO" really meant is that I got to carry a lot of Composition 'C' or 'C-2' and a bazooka – which meant outpost duty when we were on the line.

1Lt. Joseph B. Scheiker had been assigned to the 101st Division at Mourmelon in November as the Holland operation came to a close. He was then sent back to England for a quick course in parachute training. He wrote:

I had to return to England to attend jump school. The school was closing as I arrived in Hungerford, England. We had five days of training and did all five jumps in one day to get our wings.

## THE WOUNDED AND INJURED RETURN

Having returned from a hospital stay in England, PFC. Ben Panzarella was sent back to the rear base near Reading to finish recuperating. He and a buddy went to town on pass and got into a fist fight with some replacements for the 101st. He wrote:

I remember still recuperating and getting into a fist fight with some replacements (101st yet)who still had the pre-combat swagger and since we didn't have jump boots or even a division insignia (we got uniforms from the hospital), they took us for S.O.S. troops and got a surprise when we didn't cower. The guy with me was named Ryan and he was recuperating from an appendectomy.

PFC. John C. Trowbridge had spent the better part of two months in a hospital for wounds to the right thigh received in the attack on the town of Schijndel in Holland. He had spent some time at the former training site at Hamstead Marshall. He had boarded a C-47 with several others for the flight to Mourmelon. He wrote:

It was on this flight to Mourmelon that I learned of Colonel Howard Johnson's death. I was devastated! I had lost a lot of friends in Normandy and Holland, but how could we go on without the Colonel!

PFC. James W. Flanagan had been wounded on the morning of September 18 near St. Oedenrode. After being treated in a local Dutch hospital run jointly by Dutch and American personnel, he was flown to England where he spent three months in treatment and recuperation. His story of the continuing saga follows:

Early in December I was still in the 61st General Hospital in jolly ole England. I was in the final stage of recuperation from shell fragments that I had received in Holland. I was getting around real good with lots of exercise and running. I was returned to duty and reported to the 101st Airborne Division rear echelon in the U.K. They were moving to France. I helped them load a C-47 with their files, etc. I climbed into a parachute and went to France with them.

1Lt. William McRae had been wounded on September 22 when he was shot down while observing enemy positions and movements near Veghel in Holland. He was captured by the enemy and liberated the following day by men of "D" Company of the 506th Parachute Regiment. McRae had been taken to England for medical treatment and hospitalization. Upon release from the hospital, he rejoined his comrades in France. He was flying a new observation plane across the English Channel. He wrote: "I was given a new aircraft (L-4 Piper Cub) and flew it to France where I rejoined my outfit at Mourmelon."

Having arrived at the base camp of the 101st as a replacement for one of the anticipated casualties for the Normandy invasion, 2Lt. Everett "Red" Andrews remembers that his assignment continued in England when the 101st Division went on its mission to Holland. He helped close out the rear base camp at a time when he got disturbing news from home. He wrote:

I stayed in base camp and cleaned unit areas for the return of the base to British engineers. Also closed out our PX account and a project as personal effects officer for some 275 casualties the 377th PFA suffered in Normandy.

The last mail call before departure for Mourmelon brought an unpleasant surprise for me. It had my "Dear John" letter in it.

## SETTING UP A NEW BASE CAMP

In preparation for a move to a base camp in France, several of the men were sent ahead to ready the facilities for the troops. One of those men was Cpl. James L. Evans of Division Artillery. He recalled:

In mid-November I was sent on an advance party to the new base camp in Mourmelon-le-Grand in France, probably because of my carpentry work before the war. I thought maybe my first sergeant liked me after that.

Sgt. Reggie Davies was another of the soldiers who left the rain and mud ahead of the troops. He wrote: "I left Holland three weeks before my unit with 1Lt. Charles Disney to help prepare the camp for the arrival of the troops."

After hospitalization for wounds and recuperation in England, PFC. Ben Panzarella arrived at Mourmelon before the troops got there from Holland. He remembers one of the assignments was covering POW work details as they went about making the camp presentable for the arriving troops. Panzarella recalled:

When we got to Mourmelon there were rear echelon troops (some not from the 101st) and 101st replacements in charge of the prisoner work details. Some of the troops who had not seen combat were downright cruel to the prisoners. There was a marked difference between how the combat vets and the replacements treated them.

## DEPARTURE FROM HOLLAND

Without a doubt, all the men of the 101st departing for Mourmelon were extremely anxious to get out from under two months of almost constant rain. During that time any foxhole dug in the saturated soil on the Island in Holland resulted in a mini-sized bathtub within a few minutes. Movement in daytime resulted in mortar or artillery barrages as the enemy had excellent observation from the high hills on the north side of the Rhine River. The positions had become more hazardous since the leaves had fallen from the trees and deciduous shrubs. The natural camouflage was gone.

As his battalion departed from the Island area in Holland after 72 days on the front line, PFC. William J. Stone reminisced on what the scene had been like when he arrived on the continent as a member of a forward observer team attached to the 506th Parachute Infantry Regiment as contrasted to what it was like as they were departing. He wrote:

As we parachuted to earth in September, the skies were blue, the sun was shining, the countryside was shades of green; sturdy houses stood alongside the roads and the fields were carefully tended. There were many people about; some of them assisted us in gathering our equipment while others offered apples which were being harvested then.

Now, in November, as we rolled down the roads off the Island, the skies were overcast, it rained intermittently and the roads were covered with a few inches of water which were pushed aside by the wheels of the trucks forming bow waves as if we had wheeled boats. Much damage had been done to the country. Roofs and sides of buildings had been blown off leaving evidence of the life that had once taken place inside of them visible to all. The fields had been torn up by artillery fire and tracked vehicles and were now fields of mud. Fences had been knocked down, cows and horses were lying dead and bloated in the fields and most of the people had left.

Several of the men commented on their departure from Holland. Two of them remembered comrades who didn't make it and were left behind.

As a veteran of both the Normandy and Holland campaigns, Medic Robert W. Smith had ministered to the needs of the men in his company which had been badly decimated in the sand dunes of Eerde and hit hard again near the dike at Driel. He described what his company commander did for the men who were left behind:

When we were leaving Holland and getting out of artillery range, Capt. (Stanfield) Stach had us stop for a few minutes and say a prayer for those we left behind. He always seemed to be a very caring person.

Captain Willis P. McKee was sad to be leaving two of his close friends behind in Holland as both had been killed when an enemy bomb struck their vehicle at Nijmegen. He was responsible for closing out the area that had been occupied by his company.

Platoon sergeant Frank L. McClure, whose unit had suffered heavy casualties the first night in Holland, remembered the trip from the rain and mud of the Island this way:

The departure from Holland was cold, wet; bedraggled remnants of a once sharp platoon. The British lorry, carrying part of the 2nd Platoon, rolled down an embankment when the driver went to sleep sometime after we left the Island. Miraculously, no one was hurt in the melee of flying bodies and equipment. Sgt. (Bill) Foreman was unaccounted for.

Sgt. Foreman turned up dressed in mostly Canadian uniform and company commander, Captain Frank Gregg, was not pleased.

## ARRIVAL AT MOURMELON

After having lived almost two months in water-logged conditions, a respite in dry quarters was much anticipated by the men. PFC. William J. Stone had this description of what the new situation was like for his group:

The former French Army post at Mourmelon was a welcome sight after the dreary trip from Holland. The barracks were a treat – the best quarters I had in the Army. Each sleeping room had been occupied by 12 French soldiers. However, we slept on double bunks and so had 24 men in each room. Almost all of the members of the Battery "B" detail section were able to sleep in one room. This was the first time since I joined the 321st in September of 1943 at Watcombe Farm that I had enjoyed indoor plumbing and so this was, indeed, a treat.

As we recovered from the shock of not having to go into the cold night air just to use the toilet facilities, we began recleaning our equipment and thinking about passes to Rheims, a nearby city.

On hand to greet the battle-weary veterans were comrades who had recovered from wounds in the earlier fighting in Normandy and Holland. They had been flown to France to help set up the new base camp.

PFC. John C. Trowbridge had learned of the death of his regimental commander, Colonel Johnson, on the flight to Mourmelon. Now he was to learn of the loss of more of his friends but was brightened by the presentation of a special gift from a friend. He recalled:

I was greeted by old friends with a great deal of glee, but when one by one, they listed the casualties, my happiness turned to sorrow. One machine gunner, Oscar Arndt, presented me with a beautiful P-38 luger.

After he returned to the rear base in England, from an extended hospital stay, PFC. James W. Flanagan helped the rear echelon load their files in a C-47 and flew with them to the new rear base in France. He was now back with his buddies in "C" Company of the 502nd Parachute Infantry Regiment. He wrote:

I reported back to the regiment – back to 2nd Platoon of "C" Company – home away from home. Not many of the old hands around – same old supply sergeant with his unbelievable memory. I checked in, checked out my bedding and duffle bag and back to 2nd Platoon with a lot of unfamiliar faces – a few Normandy vets.

Since I had been away since the middle of September I was asked "Why did you come back?" I probably could have gone home, but everything was going so well. The war was about over and I thought I might as well stay. I had not taken my convalescent leave from the hospital and they said I could take my leave to Paris.

S/Sgt. Michael Bokesch was with the Dutch underground for six weeks near Boxtel after his glider aborted its flight far short of the landing zone. By the time the British troops reached them, a group of 120 Allied airmen and airborne troops had been collected by the underground forces and were then able to return to their own units. His group had returned to the rear base in England and then had a plane ride to Mourmelon. Upon his arrival, Bokesch was shown a letter his company commander had just received:

Capt. Clifford Kjell, my C.O., had just received a letter from my cousin, 1Lt. A. Bokesch of the 29th Infantry Division, who assumed I was KIA and wanted the particulars of the event.

The new replacements for the casualties suffered in Holland began arriving on the scene. PFC. Don Straith provides an excellent description of how the men were parcelled out to the various units of the 506th Parachute Infantry Regiment:

Shortly after dark, we pulled into Camp de Mourmelon, a peacetime French Army post and, after dismounting from the trucks, we lined up along our regimental street. An officer counted us off a few at a time and, regardless of our classifications, assigned us to various companies. Being near one end of the line, I – a demolitionist – was with several troopers who went to Company 'A' as riflemen, while Danny, who was farther along, went to Company 'G'. When we reached our company area, a corporal approached us and asked if anyone was from the Detroit area. I and Bill Martin from Dearborn spoke up, whereupon the corporal announced, 'I'll take these two!' and then said, 'I'm Jerry Janes from Trenton and you're in the 3rd Platoon.'

As mentioned earlier, the 101st Airborne Division had suffered the loss of key commanders at the regimental and battalion levels and platoon leaders had to be replaced.

In his book, *The Men of Bastogne,* Fred McKenzie describes how the leadership and equipment had been sorely depleted during the extended period of fighting in Holland:[1]

The Division had spent 72 days continuously on the line in Holland. A fourth of the paratroopers and gliderborne soldiers, including three of the four regimental commanders, were killed or wounded. Much of the equipment and large quantities of supplies were used up or lost and none had been replaced.

As indicated in the experiences of PFC. Don Straith, some of the new replacements arrived at Mourmelon after the troops returned from Holland. Officers were shifted to unfamiliar positions because they brought with them combat experience. Such was the background of 1Lt. Alfred Regenburg who had just arrived from England where he had recuperated from wounds. He recalled:

I had just arrived back in the base camp from England, having spent about three months in the hospital. I had been first lieutenant commanding the machine gun platoon of the 2nd Battalion Headquarters Company of the 327th Glider Regiment. I found that I had been promoted to executive officer of 'G' Company. I only had a speaking acquaintance with Capt. Hugh Evans, the company commander at the time, and the other officers, and very little familiarity with any of the non-coms and other enlisted men.

Platoon sergeant John H. Taylor had lost almost half of his platoon in the 72-day Holland campaign and there had been a big change in the officer staff. He related:

My platoon had twenty new men and the company had many new officers. One of them was a Lt. Bill Robertson from Montana who had played professional football with the Chicago Cardinals. Another was a Lt. Cook from Texas who was gutty but small.

Lt. Colonel Ray C. Allen, commander of the 1st Battalion of the 401st Glider Infantry (which had now become the 3rd Battalion of the 327th Glider Regiment) remembered that one fourth of his men were new replacements.

Sgt. Earl M. Bedwell of "B" Battery of the 907th Glider Field Artillery Battalion remembered a strange group of replacements they got after the Holland mission. He wrote: "I remember getting some replacements that were orderlies from hospitals. They did their best."

---

[1]McKenzie, Fred. *The Men of Bastogne,* David McKay Co., Inc. New York, 1968, p. 13.

## A GRISLY DUTY

Life was almost back to normal in the 326th Medical Company area at Mourmelon. Capt. Willis P. McKee had duty hours at the General Hospital in Rheims and the men were busy planning Christmas parties. McKee's rather sedate life was shaken suddenly with a grisly duty he had to perform. He wrote:

A very depressing event happened at Mourmelon. Early one morning, I was called to Division Headquarters. Colonel Ray Millener, chief of staff, had stood in front of his bathroom mirror, put his service .45 to his mouth and fired. On his bedside table was a copy of *War and Peace*. Perky (my driver) and I took the body to the General Hospital in Rheims where an autopsy was performed. We then spent the rest of the rainy day finding a military cemetery that was open.

In his book, Fred McKenzie wrote about the strain on both body and spirit that had affected many of the men.[2]

Though it showed outwardly only here and there, many of the officers and enlisted men were still beat in body and spirit. Less than three weeks had passed since their withdrawal from combat. In recent days a staff officer and a master sergeant had blown out their brains with .45 caliber bullets. Mental strain and physical drain had caught up with them at last after the haven of Camp Mourmelon was reached.

Colonel Raymond Millener had parachuted into Normandy without having completed parachute school. His stick of jumpers had been dropped many miles southwest of the drop zone and the group had successfully eluded the enemy patrols which searched for them. They arrived at Division HQ six days after the jump. On the Holland mission, the members of his stick of headquarters troopers had jumped through the flames as the pilot sought to maintain level flight so the men could exit successfully. The pilot, Major Dan Elam and his co-pilot died when the plane exploded during an unsuccessful belly landing.

In an entry to a diary he kept during the war, T/3 George E. Koskimaki of the 101st Signal Company noted the tragic passing of Colonel Millener:

December 7, 1944 – Our chief of staff, Colonel (Ray) Millener died early this morning from a self-inflicted gunshot wound. He may have been suffering from combat fatigue.

In his diary a few days later, Koskimaki was to note the occurrence of more suicides:

December 11, 1944 – I don't know what has come over some people. A master sergeant (*David Harmon) in the next barracks shot himself last night. It was the third suicide in four days.

---

[2] ibid.

## BACK TO GARRISON LIFE

Anticipating that he would soon receive his convalescent leave to Paris, PFC. James W. Flanagan felt he could put up with marching and drilling once again. He wrote:

We did some drilling and a short road march – not much as we were not too well equipped at this time. I didn't mind the drilling and marching. I could put up with it until my leave was approved – and that was a sure thing.

Squad leader Jack Hampton remembered they were busy getting the new men oriented and fitted into the squads:

We went back to the basics of drilling and marching just like at Camp Toccoa in 1942. What I learned was that these new guys were aware of the reputation of the 101st and didn't resent the advice and instruction the old guys from Toccoa days laid on them. They were proud to be assigned to the 101st and especially to the 501st PIR and wanted to fit in, which they did.

Whenever army units are in garrison situations there comes the inevitable inspection. PFC. Don Straith describes one such inspection at Camp Mourmelon:

We had the usual Saturday morning inspections in spite of the war. One in particular stuck in my mind. The battalion commander, Lt. Colonel (James) LaPrade, came around followed by our company commander, Captain Meason and a barber. As the colonel walked through the ranks he lifted each man's helmet; if the man's hair was longer than regulation, he was ordered to step forward and have it cut on the spot to a half inch in length.

Pvt. Ted Goldmann was another green replacement who remembered the inspections and the effect it had on veterans of earlier campaign:

On Saturdays we had some very chicken inspections and a bunch of the boys in the platoon resented the treatment to the extent that five of them took off for Paris, AWOL for the weekend. A lot more would have gone but lacked the finances.

Sgt. Donald Woodland describes a Sunday church service while the men were garrisoned in Mourmelon:

Today was an ordinary Sunday in the life of this enlisted man. I recall attending church service in the large auditorium of Camp Mourmelon. We were 'under orders' from Capt. Stach to go to church every Sunday and to pray for our lost men. The captain himself was there in his spit and polish uniform. We sat near him but not with him.

What really made a lasting impression on me was the ceremony at the Consecration of the Mass. Eight paratroopers, immaculately attired in dress uniform, would silently file out and flank both sides of the altar. A quiet command was given and the troopers brought their M1's to 'Present Arms.' At the conclusion of the Consecration, another quiet command was given and the arms were ordered. With rifles 'at the trail' the troopers filed from the altar. Today, on every Sunday that I attend church service, my mind goes back to Camp Mourmelon and the presentation of arms.

## THE 463RD PARACHUTE ARTILLERY BATTALION

The 463rd Parachute Field Artillery Battalion had gone overseas as the 456th PFA Battalion. It had been a part of the 82nd Airborne Division and jumped into Sicily in 1943. It had fought in Italy as one of the support artillery battalions of the 82nd. When the 82nd was moved to England in early 1944, the 456th remained behind as a support group for the first Allied Special Forces and its designation changed to the 463rd. In August of 1944 the 463rd parachuted into southern France and continued in its pursuit of the enemy into the French Alps. In early December it was moved by truck to Mourmelon. Army planners scheduled them to become a support group for an airborne division which had yet to arrive on the continent.

At the time of the alert and departure for Bastogne, the 463rd Parachute Field Artillery Battalion still didn't know its status – would it support the 17th Airborne Division which was scheduled to arrive in France in mid-December, or would it become a part of the 101st Airborne Division.

During the six-day interval when they arrived at Mourmelon and their sudden departure for Bastogne, the 463rd had made an unauthorized change in its TO and TE (Table of Organization and Equipment). Major Victor E. Garrett, the S-3 (Operations officer) for the Battalion remarked:

Colonel Cooper and I decided that since we'd managed to make all of our gun batteries into six-gun units, we'd fight it out with direct fire and indirect fire in case there was ever a break-through on our positions.

During conversations with leaders of the other artillery units of the 101st at meals in the officer's mess hall, the veterans of the Sicily, Italian and southern France and French Alps fighting, related knocking out enemy tanks with direct fire with 75mm pack howitzers. Major Garrett related: "We told them about knocking out a German Mark IV in Sicily. They all doubted us."

Having been designated as the battalion commander after the 82nd Division departed for England, LTC. John T. Cooper, Jr., added to that story:

As you know, the 101st had never heard of the 463rd Parachute Field Artillery Battalion and the members of the officers mess did not care to hear about our war because they had fought the only battles worth talking about.

In a crowd as large as the artillery officers mess it was nigh on impossible to talk at all. But during a little lull in conversation at my table, the question of knocking out tanks arose and I said, 'My battalion has knocked out several German tanks.' That was as far as I got that night as I was told by the other battalion commanders that the General said you could not knock out a tank with a 75mm pack howitzer. You could disable one if you got a lucky hit on a track, but not knock one out. The conversation on Normandy and Holland so overshadowed everything that no further discussion got out. *(Author's note: On Christmas morning, the men of the 463rd were to prove they could knock out enemy tanks with direct fire from the 75mm pack howitzers.)*

## BELATED THANKSGIVING DINNERS

Most units had experienced Thanksgiving dinners of sorts in Holland before departure from the Island. They were promised meals that would be remembered once they got settled into the base camp in France.

What seems to be remembered most is that some of the meals were prepared under less than somewhat sanitary conditions in the new mess facilities. The long awaited Thanksgiving dinner wasn't all it was "cracked up to be" for some of the men.

PFC. William A. Druback remembered "the belated Thanksgiving dinner – a lot of us got the runs!"

In another company but in the same battalion (probably using the same mess hall), PFC. George E. Willey remembered a similar experience: "We had some men get sick on spoiled turkey."

For S/Sgt. Robert J. Rader, it wasn't spoiled turkey but dirty kitchen equipment that caused the problem. He remembered:

My battalion contacted a dirty, filthy hot chocolate vat at our battalion mess and all of us who participated in the hot chocolate came down with the 'Aztec two-step.' The medics fed us a codeine paragoric to stop the spasms of the bowels.

Pvt. Charles D. Cram provided a more humorous detailed account of the problem at the same mess hall though he had been sneaking into another facility for meals:

We were eating in battalion-sized mess halls and the 2nd Battalion facility was across the road at some distance from our barracks. When I thought I wouldn't be recognized by any of the 1st Battalion cooks, I would eat in their mess hall. I did this one Sunday evening and was eyed suspiciously by one of the cooks who had me tagged as being from 2nd Battalion. In any event, I was awakened in the middle of the night by fellow platoon members bailing out of their second tier bunks and tearing out into the company street in a desperate race for the latrines. It soon became apparent that this was a vicious outbreak of the 'GI's' and had infected a large part of the 2nd Battalion. It continued right through reveille with most men dropping their drawers in the company street because they couldn't make it to the latrines, which were already overloaded anyhow. Now comes the good part. Some might even call it poetic justice. Because I hadn't eaten in the 2nd Bn. mess I was one of a few that were unaffected by the outbreak. I was drafted to report out in the company street with my entrenching tool and found myself, along with a mortar platoon buddy, John Joyal, on the first genuine 'shit detail' in my service with the 506th. We proceeded down the company street to clean the piles left by the unsuccessful evacuees from the barracks. The cooks and mess sergeants would have been better advised to concentrate on food preservation rather than checking for imposters like me.

And then there was 1Lt. Everett Fuchs who had been wounded during the early stages of the airborne invasion of Holland and had been evacuated back to England and then returned to the rear base near Newbury. He experienced a rarity in that he enjoyed three Thanksgiving dinners – the first at rear base in England, the second aboard a Navy LST returning to the continent and the third with the 377th Parachute Field Artillery Battalion which had recently arrived at Mourmelon from Holland.

Pvt. Anthony Garcia remembered the Thanksgiving dinner for another reason. He recalled: "being put on night KP during our belated Thanksgiving Day celebration because I didn't turn in my rifle on time."

## DELAYED FOOTBALL SEASON

After two and a half months without sports, other than a make-up volleyball game or two up on the Island in Holland, men were anxious to take part in various sports. One of those was PFC. George Ricker who needed rest from his work with a heavy mortar platoon. He wrote: "I have fond memories of my work with the regimental boxing team and coming football game against other teams within the Division."

Pvt. John G. Kilgore had been a highly-touted football player in Columbus, Ohio and had played in the all-star high school bowl game, the Kumquat Bowl, in St. Petersburg, Florida on Christmas Night in 1939. As a paratrooper replacement, he had been assigned to 3rd Platoon of "G" Company of the 506th Regiment. Kilgore ended up on the regimental football squad. He wrote:

About the third day at Camp Mourmelon, I was sent on a work detail to assist in handing out football uniforms to the players. One of the coaches, 1Lt. John F. Weisenburger, was from Columbus. He recognized me and asked me to play on the team. One of the other players was Pvt. Albert

Gray, who was in my squad. The other coach was 1Lt. Lawrence M. Fitzpatrick.

The fact that one of the football coaches was to be the platoon leader for John Kilgore and Albert Gray would have a bearing on actions in which these two soldiers would have roles.

PFC. Stan Stasica had been an all-state high school football and basketball player at Rockford High School in Illinois and had gone on to the University of South Carolina before answering the call for service. He was part of the 506th regimental football team and had looked forward to the start of a delayed season after Holland. He wrote:

When we came to Mourmelon from Holland, we started to talk about a football game in the 'Champagne Bowl' against the 502nd Regiment.

We were really looking forward to it. We had about four or five practices when the Battle of the Bulge broke out. Everything was called off.

As a former football star at Kansas State University, Capt. Wallace Swanson remembers it wasn't long after the return from Holland that, along with regular regimental training, preparations began for a long delayed football season for the 502nd team. He recalled:

When our regimental training program developed into not only battalion, but company, platoon and squad training, we had some extra time for our own and we took up and trained for a football game to be played in Rheims, France on Christmas Day.

## GAMBLING

Every company had its compulsive gamblers and with the men having just received their accumulated back pay, some lost it all, along with their desire to see Paris while others reaped the extra benefits.

A loser at cards, PFC. Carmen Gisi rationalized about the lack of interest in getting to Paris. He wrote: "I lost all my back pay in a poker game. Never got to Paris and didn't care because I had no money."

T/5 Charlie McCallister did his bit to separate the men from their money. He found that his luck ran true to form:

When we returned from Holland to Camp Mourmelon in France, we were paid up to date, which included some back pay. There immediately followed the usual Army poker game which lasted all night. When it broke up at dawn, I found myself the winner of approximately $1,000 (in French francs).

We had been promised 48-hour passes to Paris, which had been liberated a couple months previously. We would go by battalions and our 2nd Battalion wasn't scheduled until a week or so in the future.

With all that loot though, I couldn't wait and I immediately began to put on my Class A's to go AWOL. Two buddies who had contributed their pay to my good fortune were complaining bitterly and in a moment of generosity, I invited them to go with me and help spend the money. As it turned out, they proved to be excellent help.

So, Jack O'Leary, Bob Cable and I took off and managed to hitchhike on Army vehicles to the City of Light. We were gone three days and, upon our return, I found it necessary to borrow the equivalent of 72 cents for my weekly PX rations.

I remember, among other things, being in the Moulin Rouge night club buying champagne for $22 a bottle (you could get it in the country for approximately 90 cents) and going around with a bottle in each hand filling everyone's glass.

Anyway, upon returning to camp, I was caught. I don't remember if it was a summary court martial – I think it was just company punishment of extra duty, which was that I build and maintain fires in the officer's latrine. The rest of the guys were having it pretty easy as we had begun to receive replacements and renew equipment and really were not yet into a training program.

Sgt. Duane L. Tedrick learned it was not the smart thing to do to gamble on the sabbath once the troops arrived from Holland. He wrote:

I learned never to gamble on a Sunday. I went to the PX and got into a crap game and won $800. On the way back to the company I cut across a field filled with air-raid trenches. I jumped too short and fell in a water-filled hole, lost my winnings, ruined my cigarettes and candy.

## U.S.O. SHOWS

Upon arrival at Mourmelon, preparations were made for unit recreation rooms where the men could relax in off-hours. The Special Service Office of the Division arranged for U.S.O. shows and the Red Cross ladies did an excellent job of providing writing materials. Men scrounged in the country side for quantities of cheap champagne by whatever means. Battalion commander Major John Hanlon related:[3]

At Mourmelon there was no shooting and there were some small pleasures. One of them was the little bar arrangement some of us made. We had taken a vacant room and moved in a table and some chairs and it was our social center, so to speak. Even celebrities came there. One night we had

---

[3] Hanlon, John. *Is That All You Write: One Story a Day?* The Providence Journal Company R.I. 1983. 159-60.

Mel Ott and Frankie Frisch, the baseball people, there. They were on a U.S.O. tour, going around talking baseball to the troops and everyone enjoyed them.

This night, they came to our place after a long day of appearances. At first they were properly circumspect. But then Mel Ott began tending bar and Frisch began his stories. Before they were done, Ott and Frisch were buying and selling each other's ball players, paying for them in loads of worthless German marks they had acquired along the way.

There were the Red Cross girls at our camp and there were sight-seeing trips to Rheims and even Paris. There was something called champagne available in quantities; we were in the champagne district, though few of us realized this was why the stuff was so plentiful. It cost about 90 cents a bottle, as long as you brought along an empty to replace the full one. Only the bottles were hard to come by.

Besides reading and answering long overdue letters and relishing the contents of just arrived packages, PFC. John E. Fitzgerald recalled:

Yesterday we saw our first U.S.O. show in France. Marlene Dietrich had arrived with a large group of celebrities and entertainers. Her show was a big hit with the troops. Mel Ott, my boyhood baseball hero, was shooting the breeze with us. Mel had played for many years with the New York Giants at the Polo Grounds. As a boy, I had tried unsuccessfully to get his autograph. I had it in my pocket now on a dollar bill but for some reason it no longer seemed so important.

PFC. Leonard Swartz remembered that some of the troops of the 502nd Regiment got a special treat when the star dined with them. He wrote:

Marlene Dietrich marched to chow with 'B' Company. The guy behind her 'goosed her' with his mess kit handle. She went up in the air about two feet. The company commander was furious. The guy was restricted to camp.

I can remember the show Marlene put on for us. She had that sexy gown on and on stage she looked like a million bucks.

As one of the youngest troopers in the 101st Airborne Division who had participated in all its campaigns, PFC. Paul Martinez had this memory of Mourmelon: "The thing I remember most was getting to see Bobby Breen and Mickey Rooney with a U.S.O. show in our camp theater."

## FURLOUGHS

As the 72-day campaign came to an end, a limited number of 30-day furloughs to the United States were authorized. Drawings were held to determine the lucky recipients.

Sgt. Richard L. Klein remembered that communications sergeant Chester Wetsig was the lucky recipient of a 30-day furlough. He write:

Call it a hunch or whatever, I gave him my beloved luger to mail home for me when he reached stateside. It never would have made it through the series of hospitals that were to follow.

In an oral taping, S/Sgt. John H. Taylor recalled that in his company certain stipulations were made before a soldier qualified for the 30-day stateside furlough. He related:

One of the men (in a drawing) was to get a 30-day furlough back to the states. The requirement was that it would be one of the only remaining Toccoa men who had made all the missions. Several NCO's, including Sgt. Borden, took their names out of the hat. Clemens got the furlough. It was not the man the company commander wanted to get it but it went that way.

Another platoon sergeant from the same unit, S/Sgt. Vincent Occhipinti, spelled out the requirements in even more detail. He wrote:

Two 30-day furloughs were granted to the 506th Parachute Infantry Regiment during the first week in Mourmelon. Company names drawn out of the hat had given one of these two furloughs to 'F' Company and our company commander and the 1st sergeants and three platoon sergeants were to make the decision of who got the 30 days off – back to the states – to start after arrival at the Port of Debarkation, New York City. One of our 'F' Company members, who was loaded with money, offered to pay almost any price for the furlough. He was serious.

After a complicated method of elimination of persons in 'F' Company, we whittled the list down to about 12 people still eligible to get the furlough. Criteria included: originally with 'F' Company since September 1, 1942; never busted rank for any reason; never in the guard house for any reason; never had VD or similar diseases and a few other insignificant reasons – in other words – a Mr. Clean. The names of the dozen people left were placed in a hat and the final draw was made. It went to PFC. William Clemons of the 1st Platoon. After he got over the pleasant shock, he left for Paris to meet the other lucky winners and eventually shipped to the States.

One of the fortunate winners of the stateside furlough was PFC. Stanley Stasica of "H" Company who got the second furlough issued by the 506th Regiment. He wrote:

I won the 30-day pass for our outfit and Pete Bussone, who had a wife and daughter at home, offered me a thousand dollars for it, which I turned down. Had I given it to Bussone, Pete would be alive and maybe I'd have been killed in his place.

In his diary, T/3 George Koskimaki noted the issuance of 30-day furloughs to lucky troopers:

December 10, 1944 – Spent a quiet Sunday afternoon after sleeping most of the morning. Some boys left for 30-day furloughs to the States yesterday. Butler, of the MP's, was the lucky man in Special Troops.

## ORDERS FROM WASHINGTON

With the battle fronts relatively quiet in the early days of December, General Maxwell D. Taylor had responded to an order to report to General of the Army George C. Marshall in Washington to help resolve some issues that would have an effect on the airborne divisions in Europe. Feeling the 101st Airborne Division was in the good hands of Brig. Gen. Anthony C. McAuliffe, General Taylor had departed. He wrote:[4]

Arriving in Washington with my aide, Capt. Thomas J. White, on December 6, I called on General Marshall and set about carrying out his desires. These included not only discussions with his staff but also visits to airborne activities out of town.

General Taylor also had an opportunity to visit with his family, which he hadn't seen in two years. Capt. Thomas L. White had served as aide to General Taylor in Africa, Sicily, Italy and Normandy. For the Holland operation he had served as a liaison with the parachute artillery assigned to the 506th Parachute Regiment. Capt. White describes how his assignment differed radically from other 101st officers after the return from Holland. He wrote:[5]

A few days after we were relieved of combat duty and were recuperating near Rheims, France, I was ordered to report to General Taylor immediately. Because of our long past association, he offered to take me back to the states for approximately two weeks to brief the Pentagon on airborne operations.

I was thrilled with the idea of being home for Christmas for the first time in many years.

## RELATIVES IN PARIS

Shortly after Paris was liberated and the civilian postal services went into somewhat normal operation in the liberated sections of France, PFC. Walter F. Zagol began to make contact with relatives living in the Paris area. After

---

[4] Taylor, Maxwell D. *The Washington Post*, "3,000 Miles to Bastogne." op. ed. page, December 18, 1984.

[5] From a paper Capt. Thomas L. White wrote for Sarah Lyons, daughter of 1Lt. Joseph Lyons of the 463rd Parachute Field Artillery Battalion as she was preparing a paper for her prep school assignment on the Battle of the Bulge in 1980.

arriving in the Mourmelon area, Zagol requested and was issued a special pass to visit those relatives. Zagol related:

> I met my uncle and aunt for the first time. I could talk a few words of Polish and a couple words of French. My aunt knew a bit of English. I made arrangements to be with my relatives for Christmas.

## PASSES

When the troops arrived on the scene in Mourmelon from the Holland campaign, they were chagrined to find they were restricted from going into town on pass due to the misbehavior of some of those who had arrived earlier.

There had been problems in Rheims and Mourmelon with some of the early visitors from the Division showing too much exuberance when they had too much to drink. In one instance, the first sergeant and all three platoon sergeants had been sacked and sent to other units. They were replaced by a new top kick and three new staff sergeants, all highly respected leaders in their former units.

A machine gunner who was also adept as a rifle grenadier, Cpl. Glen A. Derber, had this recollection of the restrictions:

> I had nothing to do with the fiasco in Rheims so the restriction to our area as the result of it, hurt, after having been in combat so long. They let a few out on pass, starting with the officers and working down through the ranks because they must have realized you can't keep combat vets cooped up.

PFC. Robert W. Smith, who served as a medic for "A" Company of the 501st, remembered that the people of Rheims eventually forgave the troops.

> It seems that the advance echelon that was sent down to Mourmelon to clean up the camp for us raised a little bit of hell in Rheims and got a lot of people upset and so when we got there we did not get a very warm reception. They all seemed to warm up to us later.

It had been a long time since PFC. William J. Stone and his buddies had been to town on pass so their group kept a constant watch on the battery bulletin board as to when passes would become available and the first from the group to spot the listing would sign up each of the men. It didn't turn out to be a big deal for Stone. He remembered:

> When we arrived in Rheims, shortly after noon on the day of our passes, the shops and larger stores had merchandise displayed in their windows and we were anxious to buy gifts to send home. The shops and stores had merchandise but they were closed and would not reopen until 3:00 p.m. We wanted to shop first and then relax in cafes but given the situation, we reversed the order of events and took ourselves to the cafes. None of us had spent much time in cafes during the past three months and so we took

full advantage of the opportunity for food and wine – too much advantage of the opportunity for wine. By the time the stores had reopened, some of us were unable to go shopping. My friends dropped me at the Red Cross where the lovely lady director allowed me to sleep on a couch in her office. By the time my friends claimed me it was time to board trucks for the return to Mourmelon. The trip to Rheims had, for me, been a washout.

When it came time to issue 48-hour passes to Paris, 1Lt. Thomas J. Niland missed out on the luck of the draw but did get one brief pass. He wrote:

We drew straws to see about the rotation of passes to Paris. I lost and wasn't scheduled to go until after Christmas. However, I had one Sunday off and some of us went to Rheims, had a nice dinner, toured the cathedral and walked the streets. This was my one free day on the continent of Europe.

Pvt. Lester A. Hashey had injured his ankle on the September 17th jump in Holland and, although he had been treated in hospitals in England, he was still assigned to light duties. While recuperating, he did manage to have some social life but with a lot of company. He wrote: "I dated a girl in Mourmelon and took her to a movie. Her mother, father and grandmother – the entire family – came along."

PFC. William True was one of the lucky ones to get a pass to Paris shortly after arriving from Holland. He wrote:

'F' Company had been among the lucky units to get 48-hour passes to Paris before December 18 and I recall feeling sorry for the guys who hadn't made it. I met and had a date with Mlle. Helen Dubreuil in Gay Paree and at least had that memory to cheer me.

# 2. THE ALERT

War correspondent Fred McKenzie of the *Buffalo Evening News* had met General A. C. McAuliffe and Colonel Paul Danahy by coincidence in Paris where they were participating in a press conference outlining the 101st Division's role in the Holland campaign. At their invitation, he accompanied the two officers to Mourmelon where he planned to interview western New York veterans of the 101st in their roles with the Screaming Eagle Division. McKenzie had been assigned quarters with the division staff officers. His plans changed suddenly on Sunday evening. He wrote:[6]

On Sunday evening, December 17, there was a suddenly called general staff meeting. Knowing something was afoot, I stayed up until Colonel Danahy returned to our quarters with the announcement, 'Well, Fred, you are going to be with us for a while.'

Then he explained that the division had been assigned a mission and that I must be restricted to camp for two or three days until released.

I knew that Germans were attacking and suspected the division was being summoned to meet the thrust. I knew it might prove to be a dangerous step, but I said:

'How about going along with you, Colonel?'

'We'd be happy to have you,' Colonel Danahy replied.

We didn't discuss possibilities much thereafter. It just seemed I should go along, so we retired. The next day began the most awesome ten days I might conceive in the wildest of nightmares.

The 463rd Parachute Field Artillery Battalion had arrived from southern France on December 12. Veterans of parachute drops in Sicily and southern France as well as supporting roles in major engagements in Italy and in the French Alps, the artillerymen were expecting to join the 17th Airborne Division when it arrived from England. At the moment, they were attached to the 101st Airborne Division only for rations and administrative purposes. On the evening of December 17th, its commander, along with the other major unit leaders, was called to a meeting at Division Headquarters. LTC. John T. Cooper, Jr. describes what happened at the gathering:

A few days later we got the call to meet at Division HQ. Upon arrival, I found a seat with the other artillery battalion C.O.'s and listened to the General explain about the breakthrough and that the 101st would get cracking and go to Werbomont. It was a somewhat lengthy meeting and many questions were discussed and some decisions were arrived at.

---

[6]ibid.

There was a long discussion on how many trucks it would take to move a company, a HQ company, a battalion, etc.

An artillery battalion commander, Carmichael, asked 'how much ammo to take?' The staff, after due consideration, came up with the answer, 'a basic load.'

There was not an officer in the room including all the infantry colonels, their staffs, or any of the General's staff, that had any idea of where they were going or any idea of how many trucks they needed and, to make matters worse, they had never given consideration as to how the trucks were to be loaded once they arrived.

After the meeting broke up, I went in for a private talk with Colonel Tom Sherburne and General McAuliffe. In the hustle and bustle of getting ready to go, the General had forgotten about my battalion and that we were attached only for supply and administration. We were to be assigned to an airborne unit that was scheduled to arrive any day but the General said, 'I wish I could take you, as the 327th needs a direct support battalion.' He asked me how many trucks I would need to make the trip. I told him that I did not need any trucks for the move, but we would need all we could get to haul ammunition.

I left that meeting very much disturbed about the apparent disorganization of the total show and with the understanding that if I chose to go, they would be glad to have us, but I would have to talk to Bud Harper and work out a deal with him.

I went back to my unit and called an officers meeting – all officers. I explained to them what had happened and that we could stay in Mourmelon or go with the 101st to Werbomont. If we go to Werbomont with the 101st, we will have to support a glider regiment.

This sounds silly as hell, but we had jumped into Sicily with Colonel Jim Gavin's regiment and the 82nd Airborne Division. Later, when the 82nd went to England, we were detached (456th Para FA Bn) to stay and support General Frederick and the First Special Service Force through the Italian campaign to the capture of Rome on June 6, 1944, and later combat – teamed with the 509th Battalion for the Southern France campaign up to the French Alps prior to moving from the front line in southern France to Mourmelon.

We had all the parachute bravado and disdain for the glider troops.

Needless to say, our discussion at that meeting of officers lasted as long as General McAuliffe's and we discussed only one thing. Shall we go and support a damn glider outfit or stay in Camp Mourmelon. (As it turned out, the damn glider outfit, 327th Infantry, turned out to be one of the best units that we served with during the entire war!)

I gave the officers all the information that I had. My staff arranged the order of march and the battalion was loaded and ready to move the next morning before the trucks began to arrive for the rest of the division. Some of our trucks were not unloaded from the trip up from southern France.

Capt. James J. Hatch was operations officer for the 502nd Parachute Infantry Regiment. He had gotten back from Paris in late afternoon and felt a bad cold coming on as he hadn't slept much while on pass. He asked Major Doug Davidson, the regimental surgeon, for his best cure for an oncoming cold which seems to have done the trick. He wrote:

I have no idea what it was but I ate an early supper and hit the sack and fell asleep immediately. About 9 p.m., I was shaken awake and told to report to Regimental Headquarters on the double. Since in Paris, I didn't follow any military news and wasn't aware of the big German offensive.

The Division was alerted by SHAEF since we were in SHAEF reserve to be ready to move the next morning, combat loaded to a point to be determined later. I was to assemble the regimental staff plus all the battalion S-3's and S-4's to issue the orders to prepare their units to be ready by 0900 the next morning. We would move by 10-ton trucks plus our organic trucks and jeeps. We decided to take 3 days rations and all the ammo we could carry. It was a very short and limited verbal order and all I can say is Thank God we were now a very mature combat-wise outfit. With those limited words the outfit was ready without panic to board the trucks when they arrived. We had all kinds of conflicting info where we were to go. We were advised where the breakthrough by the Germans was taking place. We had two problems – lack of maps for that area and no winter boots or clothing and here it was mid-December. We finally had a very few maps but the wrong scale. However, they showed the roadways. We were headed for Werbomont.

Platoon sergeant and acting platoon leader Robert M. Bowen describes the assembling of the company officers and top non-coms to hear the reports that had been passed down to the company commanders by the regimental and battalion leaders.

The leaders of 'C' Company assembled in the orderly room. It wasn't a happy gathering. Instead of passes to Paris, we were facing a trip back to the front. Memories were still fresh from the loss of friends in Normandy and Holland. Emotionally and physically, most of us were drained. Months of little sleep, a diet of 'C' and 'K' rations and the gradual diminution of our platoons had had their effect. We were not looking forward to more of the same.

Capt. Preston Towns had led the company since April. He had shown good judgment in all the actions the company had been in, bringing it through with a minimum of casualties.

"I can't tell you a goddamned thing about what we'll be doing except at this time we'll be in Corps reserve," he said in a southern drawl. "That is what they tell me, but I don't believe it. I know you've got men who can't take any more of this shit, so I want you to single them out and leave them behind. Draw ammo and rations from the supply room. Remember, it's winter. Take overcoats, overshoes and extra blankets. We leave as soon as the trucks get here, so get cracking!"

Company 'C' had two officers left besides Capt. Towns. 1Lt. Robert Wagner led the 1st Platoon. He had come after Normandy to replace 2Lt. John Aspinwall who had been killed in action. 1Lt. Martinson was also a replacement after Normandy, taking over for Lt. Armstrong who was seriously wounded in Holland. He became the executive officer and his platoon went to T/Sgt. Larry Donahue, an excellent non-com. However, Donahue had died in action on October 7th and his place was taken by S/Sgt. Grayson Davis.

The two remaining platoons of the company were led by non-coms. As a staff sergeant, I had led the 3rd Platoon since October 8 when 1Lt. Howard Kohl had been killed. T/Sgt. Claude Breeding had led the Weapons Platoon through most of Holland.

All through the Division the hurried wake-up call was being heard and PFC. Harry A. Sherrard, of the 326th Airborne Engineer Battalion, was one of the first to realize something was up at Mourmelon. He wrote:

I was on guard duty the night of December 17th in our area. Through the night there was a lot more 'officer work' in the company and battalion offices than usual. Word filtered down and around that there had been a breakthrough of the American lines in the north around Luxembourg and our people were busy making map overlays of the area.

As a squad sergeant for his rifle company, Sgt. Donald R. Castona had this recollection of what it was like for his men when the alert came to the 101st to get ready for another mission:

I was in charge of quarters on December 18 when we got the news that there had been a German breakthrough some place and we were being sent up to help stop the attack. The officer of the day, 1Lt. Kenneth Holmes, told me to go around and get the guys ready to go. A lot of our guys had been on pass to Paris and got back to Mourmelon a lot the worse for wear. We had to pour some of them on the trucks when we left.

Assigned as a medic to "E" Company of the 501st Parachute Infantry Regiment, Pvt. Anaclete "Cleto" Leone remembered his role in the awakening of the men in the barracks:

I was CQ (charge of quarters) when I received a phone call to get everybody up and ready to move out and the officer repeated the order. I said

'Yes sir!' and ran into the quarters shouting, 'Everybody up! Everybody up! We're moving out!'

I was deluged with a barrage of boots – mess kits – everything imaginable. I was lucky to get out of there alive.

1Lt. Bernard A. Jordan had recently been assigned to the 101st Airborne Division. His assignment early on the 18th was the distasteful job of handling the regimental guardhouse. He recalled:

I was officer of the guard the night the alert notice came for the move to the Ardennes. The phone rang and the captain told me to release all prisoners and have them report to their units.

A warm-up football game had taken precedence over a 48-hour pass to Paris for 1Lt. Bernard J. McKearney of "E" Company of the 502nd Regiment. The game had been called off at halftime so the squad had hurried back wondering what emergency would have caused the game to end so abruptly.

McKearney knew something was seriously wrong when he came upon one of the inhabitants of the regimental guardhouse on the loose. He wrote:

When we got back to the company area I knew something was wrong when I talked to a trooper who had been let out of the stockade. He had beat up an MP. I asked what was going on – he said he didn't know – just to report to his company.

Over in the 506th regimental area, Pvt. Charles Cram was aware that the same thing happened at their stockade. He wrote:

All the bad boys in the regimental stockade, along with the officer's dog robbers, were returned to their units to spend the rest of the night in preparation for moving out.

PFC. Charles Kocourek had just come off a special MP detail at the officer's club in Rheims at 0100. He had just gone to bed when he got a rude awakening:

With only an hour of sleep under my belt, I was awakened by Sgt. Rusin. He told me the company had been alerted to move to the Bulge. I looked out of the window and noted heavy fog. I told the boys, 'We won't be flying anywhere in this weather!' At that time we were told the movement would be by truck.

Many of the soldiers who had been wounded or injured in the Holland fighting had suffered relapses or been reinjured at Mourmelon and were confined in the hospital at Rheims when the alert was sounded.

PFC. Charles W. Hogan of "B" Battery of the 907th Glider Field Artillery Battalion had been injured when an enemy shell hit near a truck load of men returning from Nijmegen, Holland, where they had their first opportunity to clean up in two months. After a two-month stay in a British military hospital he was flown to France to rejoin his buddies at their camp in Mourmelon. The injured leg had not healed completely when it was aggravated by a fall as he raced to get to the head of the chow line. He was sent to the hospital in Rheims because he had difficulty walking. The hospital situation was nice and restful. In a tape which he provided of his experiences he said:

While in bed and reflecting on my situation, I realized what a good deal this hospital was compared to the others I had been at previously – there I was overlooked most of the time because my condition wasn't life threatening. There in Rheims they really took care of us. Every little while they'd come around with juice and they'd check you every little while.

One morning, about 0400, the ward boy came in and turned the lights on. He woke everybody up. Then this 101st officer and a doctor came in. The officer made a little speech. He told us the Division was moving out for combat and everyone who was able was to get back to the unit. There was a truck waiting outside that would take us back. He said, 'I have a doctor here and he will go down the line and check each one over and if you are physically fit we'll send you back to your outfit.' The doctor started checking the guys over. As he started down the line, the fellow next to me and I decided there was no need to wait until the doctor got up to us so we got up and dressed. I had a terrible time getting my boots on as one ankle was still badly swollen. I finally made it. When the truck pulled into the Division area the 907th was almost ready to move out.

Communications sergeant Lloyd E. Jones of "A" Company of the 501st Parachute Infantry Regiment had suffered a setback from the injuries he had received in Holland. After recuperation he, too, had been sent to Mourmelon from England where he had been busy getting his communications equipment in order. The relapse had occurred in the midst of this preparation and he was sent to the hospital in Rheims. In the tape of his experiences he related:

In a few days I was 'chompin at the bit' but they wouldn't release me. We heard that the 82nd had already moved out and the 101st was getting ready to go. All the paratroopers in the hospital were frustrated to be there. I walked out into the ward and happened to run into two airborne officers and two other airborne men were standing there talking to them. One officer said he had gotten some transportation and they were going to go back to their companies. I said, 'Give me five minutes to get ready', and as I was dressing a doctor came in and asked what I was doing. I told him I was going back, that the 'ole man' had no one to run the radios. I was told they couldn't release me. I said, 'the hell, I'm going with or without a release' and I walked out of the room, went downstairs and got in the back of the truck that was there with a bunch of guys and we were on our way.

After returning from the Holland campaign on November 27, Capt. Bernard J. Ryan, surgeon for 3rd Battalion of the 506th Parachute Regiment, was sent to the 99th General Hospital in Rheims on detached service. He recalled a rude awakening:

I was awakened and routed out of bed by the regimental surgeon of the 502nd Regiment, Major Douglas Davidson, at 2 o'clock in the morning. We left Mourmelon that evening for Bastogne.[7]

Still bothered by pain in his back from a poor parachute landing in the Holland campaign, T/5 Richard J. Kazinski was hospitalized for his back problems only a few days after arriving at Mourmelon. There he was told he had some torn ligaments in his back, yet, he was discharged when "word was out that all airborne troops were to receive early release and return to their units."

## ALERT IN PARIS

A hasty call went out through Army channels for the Military Police in Paris to round up all the 101st Airborne Division personnel who were in Paris on 48-hour pass and to send them to Mourmelon immediately.

Recalling the highlight of his stay in the Mourmelon area and the abrupt cancellation of his leave in Paris, PFC. Amos Almeida wrote:

We were given a very much needed rest. We went to Paris and had a ball. While in Paris, the MP's came and called out everyone who was wearing a Screaming Eagle patch, telling us there was an emergency and we were to return to our base at once. At that time I was having dinner and I didn't even touch it. They put us on a truck and took us back to Mourmelon. Our rest did not last long.

Pvt. Charles E. Brown was in Paris celebrating with his new-found friends after having recently been assigned to the 101st Division. He wrote:

The night of December 17th, my buddies and I were just starting to enjoy a few drinks, prepaid, at a Paris bar called the *Ore*. The MP's there told us our division was on alert. They were to drive us back to Mourmelon. Reluctantly, with no refund on our drinks or whatever, we returned to Mourmelon.

For Major Cecil L. Simmons, being assigned as billeting officer to look after the 101st troops in Paris sounded like a cushy assignment. It did not turn out that way when the alert came. Simmons related:

I was sent to Paris as the billeting officer for the Division and had an office set up at the American Express. After I found there were no more trucks for me to send the troops back to Mourmelon and a phone call informed me there were no more troops coming the next day, I asked, 'How come?'

---

[7]Bernard J. Ryan's recollections were sharpened with the rereading of a letter he wrote to regimental surgeon Major Louis Kent from a hospital bed in 1945 while recuperating from his wounds suffered in a battle east of Bastogne.

They said they couldn't let me know over the telephone just what was happening.

I asked, 'Are you moving out.'

The officer said, 'I can't say.'

'How do I get relief?' I asked.

He said, 'You'll have to go to 7th Army to get relief.'

I called 7th Army and asked for relief. They asked, 'Are you an essential part of the Division?'

'Yes, I'm exec officer for the 3rd Battalion of the 502nd,' I responded.

They said, 'OK, we'll send a man down and you meet him at 3 o'clock in front of the American Express.'

I met him and said, 'OK, am I relieved now?'

He said, 'Oh no you don't! Not with all these parachutists in town. They won't pay any attention to me.'

I said, 'You're a major aren't you?'

He responded, 'Yeh, but I don't have a pair of wings on my chest or boots like you're wearing either.'

'All right, but I won't be able to get out of here until tomorrow morning then huh?' I asked.

He questioned, 'How are you gonna get these guys out of here without trucks?'

I said, 'We'll find a way somehow.'

When we had all the people assembled on the spot where they were to wait – there were some of them who were pretty well in their cups and some had women hanging around them. I got some of the people out of the double-decker buses and got the men in and took them over to the railroad station and locked them behind the iron-barred gates and hiked back to the train-master and told him I had to have a train go back to Camp Mourmelon-le-Grand.

He said, 'No you don't – not today!'

I said, 'We're gonna take the train. We've got the men who can run it. Either you're gonna run it or we're gonna run it!'

He said, 'Well, if you put it that way, we'll run the train for you.'

I understand they (the troops) burned up two of the 40 et 8 cars before they finally got to Mourmelon. After that I turned to the major and he said 'OK, you're relieved,' so I got in my jeep and headed for Mourmelon.

PFC. Robert Dunning was one of the more fortunate ones to receive three-day passes to Paris. He was one of the individuals rushed back to camp by the train which had been requisitioned by Major Cecil Simmons. He wrote:

We had not been in Paris more than a couple of days when the MP's alerted us – all airbornes to return to their respective units immediately. After a long, cold train ride, we returned to Mourmelon.

## FEVERISH PREPARATIONS

Companies and batteries were called out for reveille at which time unit commanders and 1st sergeants provided last minute instructions, read the appropriate Article of War and then sent the men scurrying to unit supply buildings. Pvt. Charles Cram relates what happened in his unit:

On the Monday morning of December 18, we were told by our company commander that we were pulling out of Mourmelon and heading north to be put in Corps reserve for a few days, after which we would return to Mourmelon. Shortly after that the company was called to a formation whose purpose was to have our 1st sergeant, Paul Vacho, read aloud to the assembled troops the most appropriate Article of War at the moment which dealt with cowardice or desertion in the face of the enemy, the punishment for which was death, or worse, or such other punishment as the court martial may direct. It became immediately apparent to me that the 506th was just not screwing around and was getting fairly serious.

When the company supply sergeant was admitted to a hospital for the treatment of ulcers brought on by domestic turmoil at home, PFC. Leonard F. Hicks was assigned the job without the rank. When orders came to get the men ready for another mission, Hicks did what he could to see that his unit had enough battle gear. He wrote:

I tried to re-equip 'F' Company with clothing, boots and weapons without any luck. The day we left Mourmelon, I went to supply and the things I had turned in for replacement were still there on the loading dock. I picked up all of this and possibly a few extra items. Even with this, two of our men did not have shoes or boots.

T/3 Charles D. Chapman remembered getting resupplied from the used equipment the men had turned in after Holland. He said, "There was supply sergeant Carl Schwab, sitting on his desk, swinging his feet, and saying "Help yourselves!"

Having just arrived from the hospital in Rheims where the 101st men had left as a group to be with their buddies for the coming trip to the combat zone, PFC. Charles W. Hogan relates what happened to the men of the 907th who had been hospital patients:

We were told to go down to the supply room and pick up our equipment. I had lost all my gear in Holland and was short on a lot of items. The supply room was a mess. The sergeant had already closed it out and all I could find was discarded equipment, but I checked around and got pretty well fixed up. I remember I didn't have an overcoat and didn't find one. I was short on a lot, but I did find enough to get by. What I was really looking for was overshoes. I did not find any. I went out and joined the rest of the battery.

As a medical technician, T/5 Owen E. Miller was usually looking after the needs of others during combat as well as in garrison. This morning he was assisting the battalion surgeon with the daily sick call when it came time for him to get his gear and load up. Miller wrote:

Captain Joseph Warren and I were on sick call December 18th when somebody told us that we were moving out and to get our equipment and load onto trucks. It was late in the afternoon when I went into the barracks and they were empty. I grabbed my equipment – no overcoat – someone else needed it.

Platoon sergeant John H. Taylor had been busy washing his OD's with gasoline as a substitute for dry-cleaning fluid when the alert came. He remembered the sorry state of weapons and ammo.

We were not in good shape here. We had new men. A lot of our weapons had been sent to ordnance. We were short on just about everything. We had so little in the way of 60mm mortars – hardly any .45 caliber ammo.

Platoon leader 1Lt. Al Hassenzahl had apparently not turned in all his weapons which was very fortunate for his buddy, 2Lt. Joe Reed. Hassenzahl recalled:

We were very limited in weapons and ammunition. I recall digging out a Thompson submachine gun from my bedroll and giving it to Joe Reed as he had no weapon. Joe had been our 1st sergeant and had been awarded a battlefield commission. He was now one of our platoon leaders.

PFC. William A. Kummerer knew things were critical when he didn't have to sign for an automatic weapon. He wrote: "Bastogne – the only time that I can recall going into a weapon supply and being given a .45 caliber Thompson submachine gun without signing for it."

Platoon sergeant Vincent Occhipinti recalled that the men had turned in their entrenching tools along with all weapons and ammo. He remembered how critical the shortage was in weaponry and ammunition as the men waited to board the trucks. He wrote:

We had no ammo, having turned it in as soon as we arrived in Mourmelon. I remembered that while we were waiting to load onto the trucks (hurry up and wait!), other buddies came by passing out M1 ammo and grenades and food rations. I had been issued a Thompson sub and they didn't have ammo available for that gadget. I had the good fortune of having seen the old ammo stored in the supply room at one of the barracks and ran in and got myself a half dozen of the long clips of caliber .45 submachine gun ammo and passed the word along to the waiting troops who also ran in and got some of the sub ammo if that is what they needed along with other booty like magnesium grenades.

# 3. THE TRIP TO BASTOGNE

Departure time was fast approaching. As the two chaplains of the 501st Parachute Infantry Regiment were completing the final stages of packing their personal gear, they were interrupted by the sudden appearance of a group of angry troopers. Fr. Francis Sampson wrote:[8]

Chaplain (Kenneth) Engle and I were busy packing when the whole regimental band appeared. They were fighting mad. They had been the butt of constant jibes by the men of the regiment for having missed the operations in Normandy and Holland.

'Father,' their spokesman said, 'we have been ordered to stay behind again. We joined the paratroopers because we want to fight in this war.'

'So?' I said, sensing that they expected me to give them a green light to disobey orders. 'What can I do about that?'

'We thought you might speak to the Colonel.'

'Speak to the Colonel?' I replied. 'He'd throw me out of his office if I bothered him now. Besides, he's up at Division Headquarters, I'm sure, getting his instructions.'

'Well, then, how about our jumping on some of the trucks when they pull out? This might be our last chance.'

I shrugged my shoulders. I was on the spot and evaded the question; but at least I didn't say 'No!' They must have guessed that I personally thought the Colonel would be mighty glad to have a few extra men to bolster our thinned-out companies.[9]

As the unit commanders began loading their men into the semi-trailer trucks, they pondered the effectiveness of going into combat with under-strength companies and platoons. Another worried about how effective his platoon would be with so many replacements with so little training to fill the voids. At least one of them thought the operation would be of short duration.

1Lt. Ralph K. Nelson related the normal make-up of a glider infantry company and what was on hand at the time of departure for Bastogne. He recalled:

---

[8]Sampson, Chaplain Francis L., *Look Out Below!*. 101st Airborne Division Association, Sweetwater, TN . 1989. pp. 102-3.

[9]Sampson went on to say, "Each company in the regiment found a few band members in line with them later at Bastogne and, from all I heard, they gave an excellent account of themselves. Several of them were wounded, but none that I know of were killed. Thus, they regained in full measure the respect of the other men in the regiment."

Normal strength was 150 men and 5 officers but we had 74 enlisted men and officers in 'A' Company to go to Bastogne. Captain Taze R. Huntley, another officer, and half our enlisted men were on pass in Paris, as there was no thought of our being called to the front so soon.

1Lt. Bernard J. McKearney was another officer with an even more shorthanded unit. He relates what "E" Company of the 502nd Parachute Regiment entered the fray at Bastogne with on such short notice: "Aside from the wounded veterans from Holland, all "E" Company men were replacements (63 men). I was the only officer."

Platoon sergeant Stanley B. Clever of "G" Company, 506th Parachute Infantry Regiment was concerned about the new men who had just been assigned to the company. He wrote:

> Due to our hurried departure from Mourmelon, we were ill-equipped and I know the situation was critical. I wondered how our 50 percent green replacement personnel would respond to their baptism of fire in combat.

Sgt. Wilson Boback wasn't certain how the replacements would fit in as the new combat situation began to unfold. He wrote: "I had six men on my roster and didn't get to know them before we loaded on the trucks."

As intelligence officer for 2nd Battalion of the 327th Glider Infantry Regiment, 1Lt. Thomas J. Niland didn't feel the 101st troops would be going into front line positions at this time. He wrote:

> Our numbers were down and we did not get any replacements for our losses in Holland. Most of us didn't take this too seriously and thought we were just going to be back-up. We merely thought we got cheated out of some leave time and we would probably be back in Mourmelon within a week or so.

Though he had gotten his battalion ready for the trip to Bastogne, LTC. John T. Cooper still didn't know if his troops would be going in as support for the 327th Glider Infantry Regiment. It's commander was on a trip to England with Brigadier General Gerald Higgins, the assistant commander of the 101st Division. Colonel Harper didn't know anything about the possibility of an artillery battalion in direct support of his regiment. Cooper describes the situation as the deadline approached:

> Late in the afternoon of the departure date, I finally found Colonel Joe Harper, who just drove up. He had been in England. The 327th was the last regiment out.
>
> I talked to Colonel Harper about two minutes. He said, 'Hell yes, I can use a battalion! Just follow my regiment out.'

Another officer who had accompanied General Higgins and Colonel Harper on the plane from England on the afternoon of December 18 was LTC. Robert Strayer, commander of 2nd Battalion of the 506th Parachute Regiment. He had been in London to attend the wedding of his friend, Colonel Dave Doby, the

British officer known as the "Mad Colonel of Arnhem." The two officers had become good friends at the time 2nd Battalion participated in the extraction of 140 individuals, most of whom were members of the British 1st Airborne Division along with downed airmen and hunted members of the Dutch underground.[10]

Colonel Strayer recalls that he presented a rather odd appearance to his men when he caught up to them in the assembly area near Champs:

> I remember quite vividly my entrance into Bastogne – my battalion was on a modified approach march through the town with me in my Class 'A' uniform.
>
> I had been in London attending the wedding of Lt. Col. Dave Doby, an English paratrooper friend of mine when word reached us to get the hell back to Mourmelon immediately. This I did on General Higgins' plane and my jeep was waiting for me . . . and away we went.

As the last of his men from "A" Company of the 502nd Parachute Regiment were boarding their trucks, Captain Wallace A. Swanson had a surprise waiting for him. He wrote:

> As we loaded onto the trailer trucks with all our men in full gear, an interesting sidelight to this situation – my wife and I were expecting and the mailman came running up and said I had a telegram from the States and it was received just as we were loading onto the trucks. The telegram stated that my wife, Jeanne, had given birth to our first child, Wallace, Jr. He was born on December 13 and I received the telegram on the 18th as we were loading out at about six o'clock in the evening. That gave me a whole new outlook on life, how valuable our living and existing in freedom really was.

One of the smartest moves LTC. John T. Cooper remembers directing in the war was when he followed a hunch that ammunition for his pack howitzers would be in great demand during the campaign so he added to their supply just as the convoys were moving out. He wrote:

> My jeep was number '1' in my column. As we passed the ammo dump I turned and took the whole battalion through with orders to load as much 75mm ammo as we could carry in any vehicle, regardless of how crowded they were.

The time of departure for the advance party and its components, as well as the order of march for the ten-mile long convoy of the 101st Airborne Division, is as follows:[11]

---

[10]A more complete description of the rescue of the Arnhem survivors, downed airmen and Dutch underground is found in *Hell's Highway* on pages 419 to 424.

[11]Headquarters, 101st Airborne Division. *Narrative – December 1944*. March 16, 1945. Copy sent by Pratt Museum, Fort Campbell, KY.

*Troops of 2nd Battalion of the 501st Parachute Infantry Regiment (identified by helmet markings) load the semi-trailer trucks for the trip to Bastogne.*

At 1215 on December 18 an advance party consisting of Company 'B', 326th Airborne Engineer Battalion, 101st Reconnaissance Platoon, and a detachment of Division Headquarters left Camp Mourmelon for Werbomont, Belgium. This town was 137 miles from Mourmelon and contact with XVIII Airborne Corps Advance was to be made there. At 1225 General McAuliffe departed for Werbomont and at 1400 the Division proper began motor march with units in the following order: 501st Parachute Infantry (with attached 907th Glider Field Artillery Battalion and Battery 'B' 81st Airborne AT Battalion); 81st Airborne AA/AT Battalion, 101st Airborne Signal Company, Division Headquarters, Division Artillery Headquarters and Headquarters Battery, 506th Parachute Infantry (with 321st Glider Field Artillery Battalion attached); 326th Airborne Engineer Battalion (less Company 'B'); 502nd Parachute Infantry (with 377th Parachute Field Artillery Battalion attached); 327th Glider Infantry (with 1st Battalion of the 401st Glider Infantry as its 3rd Battalion and 463rd Parachute Field Artillery Battalion attached); 326th Airborne Medical Company; 801st Airborne Ordnance Company and the 426th Airborne Quartermaster Company bringing up the rear.

The strength committed at this time was 805 officers and 11,035 enlisted men.

This was the first time the Screaming Eagle Division would be going into combat by a different mode of transportation than parachuting from C-47 troop carrier planes or riding in CG-4A Waco and British Horsa gliders. OISE Section

Communication Zone was contacted earlier for transportation which was provided mostly as ten-ton open truck and trailer vehicles with some two-and-a-half ton trucks.

1Lt. Alfred J. Regenburg had been assigned to "G" Company of the 327th a few days before departure. Earlier, he had served as machine gun officer for the 2nd Battalion. Unless the officers had seats in the cabs of company vehicles, they rode in the backs of the open trucks with enlisted men. He wrote:

I remember riding for quite some time standing up in a ten-ton truck. Officers were not allowed to ride in the cab because that was for the extra driver. I got a taste of what the enlisted men were going through.

Captain Wallace Swanson described the crowded conditions for the long ride to Bastogne this way:

We were loaded on the trucks, probably 50 or more men to a big semi-trailer with high sideboards and we were standing up – no room to lie down – might be able to push enough to let a few men get some rest.

The situation was so urgent that we travelled all night with head lights blazing. Had the weather broken and the German Air Force spotted us, the results would have been devastating.

As the convoy moved northeast through the night, with no cover over the heads of the men jammed into the trailers of the large trucks, PFC. Charles Kocourek remembered:

I looked back toward the rear of the column and all I could see was bright headlights. I remarked to the man next to me that this must be pretty serious – going into combat with all the lights blazing.

Passing a bottle of champagne around in a crowded truck didn't help when it came time to seek relief as the trucks roared on and on into the night with few rest stops. PFC. Ewell B. Martin remembered:

A bottle of champagne I had bought in Rheims tasted green as a gourd. Don't know whether it was bad or I hadn't acquired a taste for the finer things of life. In any event, it was passed around and gone in short order. The most vivid memory I have of that ride is being packed into this cattle trailer so tightly that there was no way to move to the back of the truck and every time the five-gallon can we used as a latrine got to me, it was full.

S/Sgt. Erminio Calderan had been transferred to "I" Company of the 501st Regiment only a week before departure. He didn't know the men he had been assigned to lead though he had led his platoon in "D" Company through the Normandy and Holland campaigns. Just before the men had loaded onto the trucks, he had asked his signal corporal to step forward so he could be recognized when needed. Calderan worried about the situation throughout the trip. He wrote: "I was scared as hell moving up – not because I was going back into combat but because I was going into combat with a bunch of total strangers."

PFC. William R. McMahon remembered there was a violation of U.S. Army regulations on board his truck. He wrote: "While in the trucks we were ordered to load and lock all weapons, something the Army never does on a movement of this kind."

An opportunity to get better acquainted with the new men in his squad was a memory of Sgt. Jack Hampton of the long truck ride. He wrote:

> We loaded up and began to move out to our unknown destination which would take us overnight on what was to be a bumpy ten-hour journey. Not many slept and we spent most of the hours speculating on where we were going and what role we would play. We got to know some of the new guys better and we talked about where we were from and what we did before entering the service. You would be surprised what you can learn from a bunch of guys on a ten-hour truck ride in the dark somewhere in France.

The feeling was different for T/5 Leon Jedziniak, a combat medic headed for his first assignment. He had this recollection of the damp, cold ride to Bastogne:

> I didn't know anyone around me. They were all strangers to me, as I had just joined the regiment. I was assigned to 'A' Company of the 1st Battalion of the 501st before we boarded the trucks for Bastogne.

For T/5 Owen E. Miller, another medic, late coming off duty for the daily sick call, found most of the men already loaded for departure. Though he was a veteran of both the Normandy and Holland campaigns, he didn't know any of the men on the truck. However, they were men of his regiment. He wrote:

> I loaded onto a truck that had 506th people on it. I don't remember which battalion they were from. Captain Joe Warren said he would see me somewhere down the line at our destination. As we left, it was turning dark.

With the regimental commander in the back seat of the jeep while the driver and Captain Jim Hatch rode in front, the threesome started out ahead of the rest of the 502nd Regiment so they could learn in advance where to position the troops once they arrived. Captain Hatch describes their trip:

> There appeared to be no definite info as to the exact area where the 101st Airborne Division was to locate for deployment let alone the 502nd Regiment. Colonel (Steve) Chappuis told Pat Cassidy he was in charge of the 502nd movement. Since the trucks began to appear, Chappuis and Hatch would move out by jeep ahead in the hope of receiving some positive info regarding our forward assembly area. I don't know how many personnel realize how poorly Steve Chappuis could handle cold weather since he was raised in the warm parts of Louisiana. The best we could do (Hatch and the driver) was wrap Steve up in GI blankets in the back seat of the jeep. That was the last we heard from him until we came to a road stop later in the night. We spent the night going past units of the 101st and did pretty well until we started running into troops and traffic in the passing lane moving away from the front line positions that had been overrun by the Germans.

The rest stops were few and far between, but after many hours men were hungry and relief sometimes came from surprising sources. Such was the case for PFC. Robert A. Crowe. He wrote:

We made a rest stop near a little village in France or Belgium. Ladies from the village came up to our truck with fresh, warm bread and bottles of wine. That sure was good bread!

PFC. Robert Dunning remembered chatting with one of the truck drivers and also recalled taking advantage of some creature comforts at an unscheduled stop in a small village.

For the first time I knew the 101st was not going into combat by air. We were now regular 'straight-leg' infantry. Our truck drivers were 'Red Ball.' One guy said that he was not too thrilled to be hauling 101st Airborne soldiers – 'they go into combat areas!' Ha! He didn't know the half of it!

During the almost non-stop drive to Bastogne, one of the lead trucks skidded off the road in a small town and went through a house blocking the road. As far as I know, no one was hurt. Since we could not get around this wreck, we had a short stop.

Sgt. Gil Morton told us to find shelter as best we could in the local houses. This was great because we were cold. The house that I, Walter Ross, Herb Spence and Jack Manley stayed in was quite nice, as least warm. I'm sure others recall those great big feather ticks. We made good use of them for awhile.

While serving as executive officer for the 2nd Battalion of the 506th Parachute Regiment, Major Richard D. Winters recalled the trip to Bastogne this way:

As the convoy moved along, my job was to bring up the rear of our section and make sure everyone kept the column closed up and in order. When the convoy would stop, it was my custom to get out of the jeep and walk up and down the line. At one point in this long ride, 2Lt. Ben Stapelfeld, one of our replacement officers for the Bastogne campaign, approached me and asked if he should be doing anything. In answer to his query, I said, 'Do you see what the men are doing? (They were sleeping.) You do the same. When I need you, I'll let you know.' (Ben turned out to be an excellent officer.)

As mentioned previously, General McAuliffe had left earlier preceding his troops by almost two hours. He was intent on getting to Werbomont so he would have a grasp of the situation and where he would position his troops in the new defense line. With him in the command car were Colonel Harry W. O. Kinnard, his G-3, and aide, 1Lt. Frederic D. Starrett. When they reached Neufchateau, there was a change in plans.[12]

---

[12]ibid.

At Neufchateau, General McAuliffe was informed by VIII Corps that the Division was attached to VIII Corps with the mission of stemming the German offensive in the vicinity of Bastogne. By means of officer guides, the march objective was changed from Werbomont and the Division was to detruck in assembly areas in the vicinity of Mande St. Etienne.

Just before the 327th Glider Infantry Regiment and its attached units had left for Werbomont, Deputy Commander of the 101st Airborne Division, Gerald J. Higgins and Colonel Joseph Harper, commander of the 327th, had arrived from England. Higgins gathered his gear and sped on forward to catch the leading elements before they reached Werbomont. Before he left Mourmelon, a message had been received alerting the 101st to the change which General McAuliffe had received at Neufchateau.

Sgt. Steve Koper was driving a jeep in the convoy. During the move he remembers a command car trying to pass him along a very congested highway. He recalled:

It was very foggy. Suddenly an olive drab vehicle cut in front of me. I think it was a Packard. It was General Higgins. I almost hit him. He was trying to pass the convoy but a column of trucks was coming toward us.

Captain Jim Hatch of the 502nd remembers there were others in a hurry to get to the head of the convoy. He wrote:

We had a sedan behind us that was giving us a bad time trying to pass us. I finally got out and went back to see what this fellow's problem might be. Guess what? It was General Higgins trying to get ahead of everybody since he had received word before he left that the 101st was placed under the command of the VIII Corps which was located in Bastogne and that was to be the assembly area for the 101st units. Needless to say, we let him pass and now we had positive word as to our next higher headquarters and would head straight to Bastogne. This encounter with General Higgins even got Steve out of his roll of blankets to get the latest word from the General. As we proceeded toward Bastogne, we checked with MP's at crossing sites to ensure they had the correct word as to where to direct 101st units. The MP's were on the ball and we didn't find one without the proper directions.

As the two chaplains of the 501st Parachute Infantry Regiment moved northeast toward Bastogne in Fr. Francis Sampson's jeep, they noted the congestion with vehicles going both ways. Sampson describes the confusion which resulted when a convoy fleeing the Bastogne area was using both lanes of the narrow highway:

A truck company commander, leading his forty or fifty trucks westward had jammed the division's ten-mile long convoy trying to get to Bastogne in a hurry. When General Higgins, our division deputy commander ordered the captain to take his trucks off the road, he refused. General Higgins pulled his forty-five out and ordered the captain once more. This time he saw the wisdom of prompt obedience. Emergency called for emergency measures.[13]

Once General McAuliffe arrived at Bastogne, he went immediately to the Corps headquarters to get the latest word on enemy moves. He left his G-3, Colonel Harry W. O. Kinnard, to be briefed by the skeletal staff of VIII Corps Headquarters while he back-tracked along the highway making plans with his aide, 1Lt. Frederic Starrett, as to the site of the Division HQ and the assembly areas for the infantry regiments and artillery battalions that were following behind. Journalist Fred McKenzie of the *Buffalo Evening News* had been in Mourmelon at the time of the alert and decided to go along. He wrote:[14]

Taking Starrett along, the two rode back into the countryside through which they had come. McAuliffe pointed out an expanse of fields and said he wanted the troops assembled there. A rural settlement of a score or so of buildings situated along a single narrow street off the main highway would be a focal point of this gathering. It was Mande St. Etienne, a village three miles west of Bastogne.

The General then proceeded to designate the bivouac of each of the Division's units. He placed the four infantry regiments so that Ewell's 501st would be near the outskirts of Bastogne, Sink's 506th in line behind it, Chappuis' 502nd next in the order of assembly and Harper's 327th the farthest westward in the Mande St. Etienne vicinity.

As aide to General McAuliffe, it became Lt. Starrett's responsibility to see that the regiments were directed to their proper assembly areas. He had also found a more suitable building to use as Division Headquarters than the farmhouse which had first been selected. Fred McKenzie continued[15]

Starrett's show of initiative had not ended with finding a new location for the C.P. A Signal Company crew had arrived in Kinnard's absence and the lieutenant put it to work stringing telephone lines from the schoolhouse to the Corps headquarters and regimental bivouac areas.

The wire-stringing detail was working at the side of the main road when a jeep carrying Colonel Julian Ewell came along in the darkness. Traveling well ahead of his 501st Regiment, Ewell had turned at the Sprimont road junction, but he was not sure where he was supposed to go from there. He stopped to talk to the wire party.

'You're on the right track, Colonel' said one of the crew after Ewell had identified them as members of the 101st Airborne and explained he was looking for headquarters. 'This line comes right straight out of the Division C.P.'

---

[13]Sampson, op. cit.
[14]McKenzie, p. 21.
[15]ibid.

Ewell followed the wire until he reached the schoolhouse. From there General Higgins whisked him off to Bastogne for a conference with General McAuliffe.

As each of the truck loads of troops arrived at their assembly areas west of Bastogne, they were cautioned to treat the situation as a combat action. S/Sgt. Vincent Occhipinti remembered:

All the trucks, in the portion of the convoy we were in, pulled into a field and we were told to get off. Every truck load was alerted in somewhat the following manner: 'No one knows what the situation is, the enemy can be anywhere; keep all-around protection and move out slowly and carefully.' WELCOME TO BASTOGNE!

If anyone was sleepy because of the arrival time (approximately 0400 hours), the words describing the unknown situation and that the enemy could be almost anywhere was all that was needed to alert everyone and made moving about as quiet as possible.

Very few people in the ten-mile long convoy of the 101st Airborne Division on its move to the Ardennes front were even aware that a change had been made in the assignment of the Screaming Eagle Division. Platoon sergeant John H. Taylor certainly wasn't privy to the information, nor did he know that the Division had been headed for Werbomont. He recalled:

We arrived at 0400 in the morning and unloaded. Didn't know exactly where. We set up a perimeter defense. We knew generally that we were in the Ardennes. More troops were coming in all the time. We could hear artillery and machine gun fire in the distance. It was rumored we were in Luxembourg. We were, but it was the Province of Luxembourg in Belgium.

Upon arrival in the 506th regimental assembly area, Pvt. Charles Cram was put on platoon guard duty at a small farmyard open stable area. He felt he was too excited to sleep anyway. He wrote: "At daylight I asked a young Belgian boy the name of the place where we had stopped and he told me that it was Champs."

It was already daylight when the 463rd Parachute Artillery Battalion, under the leadership of LTC. John T. Cooper, arrived near Mande St. Etienne. As they were directed to their assigned assembly area, Colonel Cooper had a surprise waiting for him. He wrote:

When we arrived at the crossroad to Bastogne, to my surprise, Colonel Tom Sherburne was in the middle of the road directing traffic. He told me to go toward Bastogne and pull off the road some place and wait for orders.

The infantry regiments had arrived earlier and their men and vehicles were scattered about in the various assigned fields and farmyards waiting for their assignments and orders to move out.

As the 463rd Artillery Battalion had followed the 327th Glider Infantry Regiment to Bastogne, they were the last major unit to arrive on the scene of future action. It was already daylight, PFC. Kenneth Hesler describes the scene:

Dawn was gray, dreary, cold and wet. As the convoy stopped once again, troops poured gasoline into puddles along the roadway and warmed themselves or tried to heat canteen cups of water for coffee over flaming C-ration cans partly filled with gasoline-soaked gravel. Small groups of infantry, mostly from the 28th Division, walked single-file along the roadway from Bastogne. Occasionally, someone from the Battalion would shout to them, 'Hey, you fellas are going the wrong way!'

As soon as the troops had been unloaded from the trucks, the officers were summoned to battalion and regimental staff meetings. Squad leaders and platoon sergeants pointed out to their officers that many men in their commands were ill-equipped to go forward into combat. Such was the recollection of S/Sgt. Erminio Calderan of "I" Company of the 501st Parachute Regiment. He recalled:

We bivouacked in an open field and the next morning we left the pup tents standing and pulled out. Only the men who were fully equipped moved forward. Those who needed equipment just fell out. We took the equipment from the green recruits and gave it to the veterans who needed it.

PFC. Donald Woodland had taken a demotion without prejudice when he came on the scene at Mourmelon and joined the men of "A" Company of the 501st Regiment. Old timers in units resented the arrival of replacements who had stripes unless they were regular army vintage and Woodland was not one of the old experienced soldiers.

Upon arriving in the assembly area near Mande St. Etienne, Woodland was to find out he wouldn't be moving out with the members of his battalion or company. He wrote of his experience as the troops readied to move forward to their assigned portion of the defense perimeter:

At 0600, the 1st Battalion was preparing to move out of its assembly area. However, before the move, there was some organizing to do within the company. An inventory of the weapons was taken and machine guns moved around so that each platoon had no more than two light machine guns (the TO provided for three). The shortage of men with rifles was also reported. This was of major concern to Captain Stanfield Stach and, once he had communicated that fact to Battalion, he received orders that no man was to go into action without a weapon. I was one of the enlisted men who was without a rifle. I did have a clandestine pistol, one clip and a pocketful of .45 caliber ammunition that I begged from a corporal with a submachine gun.

Platoon sergeant Lyle Chamberlain huddled with the squad leaders or those who were soon to be squad leaders. The decision was made then and there who would lead, who would be the scouts and who would man the machine guns. The first indication that I would be left behind was when Sgt. Willard C. McIntire came over to where I was reclining on the ground and gave me the word. He also relieved me of my basic load of M-1 ammunition. Finally, another man came over and asked me for my helmet. His helmet liner webbing was broken so there was no support. We exchanged helmets.

Some of the troopers disobeyed the order to stay behind. Having missed the earlier missions because he was a regimental band member, PFC. Julius J. Schrader wasn't going to miss his first opportunity to get into the actions of his regiment at Bastogne. Schrader describes how ill-equipped he was on the 19th of December:

My gear included a helmet steel without a liner, a bayonet but no rifle and no entrenching tool. Fortunately, I did have an overcoat which was to be much needed in the days to come.

We were constantly told that we would be supplied further down the road as we marched toward Bastogne. Of course, the promised equipment never materialized. As we marched out of Bastogne, I found an M-1 rifle along the side of the road with its muzzle plugged with mud.

Another replacement with "A" Company of the 501st was Pvt. Christopher C. McEwan who has this memory of the above assembly and departure for the MLR to be defended by his unit:

When we got to the wooded area we were told, 'Any troopers who didn't have any weapons would stay behind until weapons were brought up to them.' Though I didn't have a weapon, I went with the rest of the troopers. I have wondered how those troopers who stayed behind made out. I later acquired a light, air-cooled machine gun.

# 4. DECEMBER 19

## FIRST ENCOUNTERS

The three Army units which would have the major roles in the defense of Bastogne had all received their marching orders the previous day. The preliminary actions involving the 101st Airborne Division have already been described.

On the first day of the German winter offensive the 10th Armored Division was in a rest area at Remeling, France. It received orders from 12th Army Group to proceed to an assembly point near the city of Luxembourg. The 10th Armored closed in on Merl, Luxembourg at 2155 on the 17th of December. On the following morning, Combat Command B was detached for service with VIII Corps in the Bastogne area. It took the road through Arlon to Bastogne with its commander, Colonel William L. Roberts, arriving in advance of his troops. By coincidence, he arrived at the headquarters of General Middleton about the same time as General McAuliffe.

Colonel Roberts was asked by the Corps commander how many teams he could form from his force. Roberts responded with "three."

Middleton then ordered Roberts to move his teams without delay, once they reached Bastogne. One team was to go to the southwest to Wardin, a second was to go to the vicinity of Longvilly and the third team was to move quickly to Noville. This third team, under Major William R. Desobry, was told to "hold at all costs."

The 705th Tank Destroyer Battalion was in position at Kohlscheid, Germany about 60 miles north of Bastogne when it received its orders to move to Bastogne. Lt. Colonel Clifford D. Templeton's tank destroyers were on the road by 2240 but had to detour around Liege and Houffalize – the enemy was already around Houffalize. Some of Templeton's forces had to fight off small enemy units roving in the area. At the same time, the 705th troops were handicapped in their movements by highways jammed with fleeing troops. After setting up a blocking force against the marauding enemy forces, Templeton moved on toward Bastogne using the Larouche-Champlon-Bastogne road and arrived at his destination at 2030 on the night of the 19th.

The first two combat teams of the 10th Armored Division, "Cherry" under Lt. Colonel Henry T. Cherry and "O'Hara" under Lt. Colonel James O'Hara, got through Bastogne and headed east before darkness fell. It was already dark when the third team under Major William Desobry began its move toward Noville. Desobry was told by Colonel Roberts that it was urgent that he get to Noville before the enemy forces reached that point.

As with the 101st troops, which would arrive on the scene on the morning of the 19th, Desobry was handicapped by the lack of maps. However, the move was completed before daylight and the troops quickly set up road blocks and the tanks moved into strategic locations on the heights and in concealment near buildings within the village.

A few miles to the east and southeast of Noville, German armored forces trapped a large unit consisting of tanks, half-tracks, trucks and jeeps. The history of the 101st Airborne Division, *Rendezvous with Destiny*[16] has the following description of a unit from the 9th Armored Division, along with a small reconnaissance force from Team Cherry being trapped between Mageret and Longvilly:

> The line of tanks, tank destroyers, guns, half-tracks and vehicles stalled along the road made a perfect target for the Germans who got twenty tank destroyers and some 88's onto the targets. Each wrecked or stalled vehicle increased the jam and in a few hours the road was littered with burning or destroyed American armor and vehicles. The survivors, meanwhile, fought their way into Mageret.

The following is a portion of a letter written by a Lt. Rockhammer of the German Army dated December 22, 1944 when the actions seemed to be going in their favor:[17]

> This time we are 1,000 times better off than you at home. You cannot imagine what glorious hours and days we are experiencing now. It looks as if the Americans cannot withstand our important push. Today we overtook a fleeing column and finished it. We overtook it by taking a back road through the woods to the retreat lane of the U.S. vehicles then, just as on a maneuver, we pulled up along the road with 80 Panthers. Then came the endless column, driving in two files, side by side, hub to hub, filled to the brim with soldiers and then a concentrated fire from 60 guns and 120 MG's. It was a glorious bloodbath, vengeance for our destroyed homeland. Our soldiers still have the old zip. Always advancing and smashing everything. The snow must turn red with American blood. Victory was never as close as it is now. The decision will soon be reached. We will throw them into the ocean, the arrogant, big-mouthed apes from the new world. They will never get into our Germany. We will protect our wives and children from enemy domination.
>
> If we are to preserve all tender and beautiful aspects of our lives, we cannot be too brutal in the deciding moments of this struggle . . . .

---

[16]Rapport & Northwood, op. cit. 440.

[17]From a copy of a letter sent by Carl Cartledge who served with the S-2 Section of the 501st Parachute Regiment. The letter was translated by 1Lt. Werner J. Meier of the 501st Regimental PWI team on December 27, 1944.

It is possible that Lt. Rockhammer is exaggerating slightly as to the American losses. The troops of the 501st Parachute Infantry Regiment were to be in action in the Mageret area very soon. The *Rendezvous with Destiny* quotation and Lt. Rockhammer's description may be narratives of the same incident.

## THE 501ST IS COMMITTED

The 501st Parachute Infantry Regiment, led by Colonel Julian J. Ewell, spearheaded the ten-mile long convoy of the 101st Airborne Division to its assembly areas near Mande St. Etienne. The "Geronimos" were assigned the fields nearest Bastogne. As a result, Colonel Ewell's force got the assignment to "go out and find the enemy."

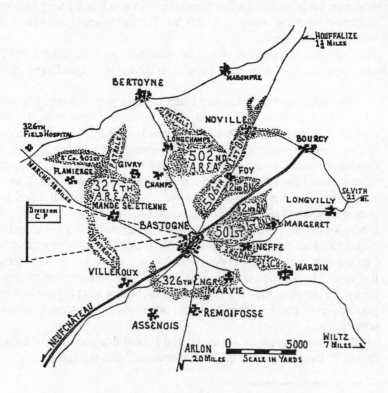

*Deployment of troops on the first day!*
*Map 1*

As mentioned in an earlier chapter, very few maps of the Werbomont and Bastogne areas were available to Division. As Ewell prepared to send his men out at 0600, only a few maps had been obtained from VIII Corps headquarters and twenty of these went to the 1st Battalion Headquarters and to the line company commanders. One map, scaled 1:100,000 went to Lt. Colonel Clarence F. Nelson, commander of the 907th Glider Field Artillery Battalion, which continued to serve as the heavy weapons support for the 501st. This map was all he had from which to prepare his firing data. His staff very quickly prepared sketches for his forward observers. The sketches showed the key features such as crossroads, bridges, woods and towns. These were numbered. The observers knew where the 105mm snub-nosed howitzers were located and so the artillery operation was coordinated.

As 1st Battalion moved out, its commander, Major Raymond Bottomly, was directed not to put out flank patrols as this would delay movement to the front. Contact with the enemy was expected to take place east of Mageret. Long range sightings of the enemy would be difficult with ground fog limiting visibility.

When 1st Battalion moved out from the assembly area and headed east of Bastogne, the S-2 Section men were assigned to the various line companies of the 1st Battalion. PFC. Robert I. Wickham remembers his assignment:

Sgt. Grandin Johnson assigned me, along with another S-2 man, to 'B' Company. I didn't yet have ammo for my carbine or a magazine to put in it. Lt. Stevens came up with a box of ammo for me but still no magazine, which meant that I'd have to use it single shot. (From the stories I heard later, it seems I was pretty well equipped.) We reported to 'B' Company and headed out with their scouts to meet the enemy.

Two jeep loads of men from the Reconnaissance Platoon of the 101st Airborne Division were leading the column. The artillery observers and liaison personnel accompanied the lead unit in the march. The artillery weapons would be positioned about five hundred yards east of Bastogne at the site of the present Mardasson Monument honoring the men who fought in the Battle of the Bulge.

Colonel Ewell left his headquarters in Bastogne an hour after the troops had departed. He found the column moving down the wrong road. The Recon jeeps had made the turn toward Marvie and were headed south. Colonel Ewell recalled the troops by radio. 1st Battalion did an about face and 'B' Company passed through the trailing elements, returned to the intersection and swung right onto the Longvilly road. The Recons had to race through the entire column to get back into their lead position.

As members of the Intelligence Section of 1st Battalion, PFC. Robert L. Wickham and Pvt. Carl Fechtman were moving along in the lead elements of 'B' Company. Wickham has this description of his first encounter with the enemy east of Bastogne on the morning of December 19:

It was so foggy you couldn't see 100 feet. We hadn't gone far when we met a man from the 28th Infantry Division retreating. He had a bazooka which I confiscated, since he obviously had no use for it. He said he had knocked out a tank shortly before and had no more ammo. After begging a round from the 'B' Company bazooka man, we continued our march toward the enemy with the lead scout – then me – the second scout – and then Fechtman.

We were some distance ahead of the rest and I would guess about three-fourths to one mile from the city of Bastogne when a couple of Recon jeeps from the 101st Division HQ went sailing by us and I remember thinking, 'Hell, if those guys are going out like that, the Germans can't be as close as we were led to believe!'

I had not seen a map of the area so we didn't know what we were heading into. On our right was a railroad track and just beyond that, a creek. On our left was a hill. I had noticed that the railroad and road were very close with just a small gravel ridge between them. Ahead of us the road appeared to turn right and I suspected it would cross the tracks. I thought, too, that I would have a better view if I walked along the ridge, which was where I was when the jeeps went by.

We were probably 100 to 150 feet from the curve in the road when the first jeep went around it and right then all hell broke loose. A tank was sitting just around the corner and it opened fire demolishing the first jeep and the second jeep came back in reverse faster than it had passed us just a moment before. I think he escaped unharmed but bullets were buzzing by so thick that I've wondered how any of us managed to get out.

In nothing flat, I had my shovel out and a hole dug in that hard gravel and was joined by the lead scout.

One of the members of the 101st Division Reconnaissance Platoon who was part of the two-jeep group leading the forward elements of 1st Battalion of the 501st toward Neffe was PFC. John B. Moore. He describes what happened to their small group:

A mission was bestowed upon us to go out one of the highways to make contact. The critique informed us the enemy was out two to three miles but moving fast. I was in the first jeep in that recon patrol along with Chuck Tyler (Cincinnati) jeep driver; Tony Benedetto (radio operator) out of Chicago; Rudy Brabec (Browning automatic) also from Chicago. I told Tony to take my front seat in the jeep as he was carrying the bulky radio on his back. I sat on ammunition boxes in the rear of the jeep cradling an M-1 rifle. We made contact only five hundred yards down the road from Bastogne.

There were two pieces of high ground with German machine guns mounted on each. They let us come in and then opened fire. Tyler and Benedetto were killed and Brabec and I were wounded.

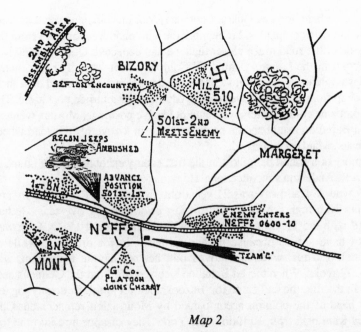

*Map 2*

I managed to crawl back to a medic and got a shot of morphine, then on to an aid station for a number of days.

Out on the point with "B" Company scouts, PFC. Robert Wickham continued his description of the action. He was certain an enemy tank had fired on the recon jeep and was now headed their way. He added to his story:

That tank had come around the corner and was approaching cautiously. I asked the man to load my bazooka and we'd get that tank. He said, 'It's all set to go, don't miss him!' I had never fired one of those things and told him so. He said he had so there was no question at all who should give it a try. WHAM! The damn shell hit about two feet in front of the tank. For some reason, I can't imagine why, the tank stopped. He may have thought he'd hit a mine, but we didn't touch him. He was later knocked out and our main line of defense developed from this spot. To the right of 1st Battalion, across the creek and flat area was the 3rd Battalion and up the hill to our left was the 2nd Battalion, all of us eventually joined up.

As executive officer for 1st Battalion Headquarters Company, 1Lt. Frank L. Fitter was serving as company commander in the absence of Captain Harry Howard who was still in Paris along with several other officers of the company. Before departure from the assembly area at Mande St. Etienne, the men were fed breakfast and then were on their way. Fitter describes the move and the first enemy contacts:

Being a battalion headquarters company, our machine gun sections were attached to rifle companies. I remember the automatic weapons fire from the right side of the road much closer than we had expected. Our company was the second in the column behind 'B' Company. Not long after the enemy patrol was silenced, the recon jeeps passed through and were fired on a short distance in front of us. One was destroyed; the other returned post haste. The rifle companies immediately went into defensive positions. Mortars were set up and Battalion established a command post in a cove off the road where road material had been quarried.

A memory of a friend being lost in the first enemy encounter made up much of Pvt. Carl R. Anderson's recollections. He wrote:

Wayne A. Calloway was 21 years old, from Grants Pass, Oregon, and had married a high school sweetheart just prior to going overseas. He had jumped with the 1st Battalion at Heeswijk, Holland on 9-17-44. Calloway did not have a rifle because he had turned it in for ordnance while at Mourmelon. Thus, when we moved out, he, not having a weapon, was given a bazooka. When the 1st Battalion received fire from the Germans near Neffe in the fog, the call came for 'Bazookamen forward!' Calloway jogged to the head of the column accompanied by Mourmelon replacement Cpl. Stanley Kaminski from Buffalo, New York. They disappeared into the fog and were never seen again alive. (Sometime around New Year's Eve, word came from the unit that took over the 1st Battalion front at Neffe that Calloway and Kaminski were found in some woods near Neffe. They both had been shot with their hands tied behind their backs and their boots had been removed. Thus, they had been captured, hands tied and then killed while being held as prisoners of war.)

As soon as the first enemy fire was received, the two forward companies, "B" and Battalion Headquarters, spread out in defensive positions on either side of the road. Battalion was in position of overall command. Operations sergeant Chester Brooks relates how he was directed to get a machine gun forward to provide supporting fire:

I was with the Battalion command group when whoever was in command turned to me and said, 'Get a machine gun in that woods over there on our left.' There was nothing but bare ground between a ditch our men had jumped into when the firing started and the woods. I grabbed the first machine gun crew I could find and pointed to the woods and said, 'Get your gun over there!' Cpl. Tom Maitland had the crew and he told me later that he thought I was nuts.

This is what he told me when I visited with him in 1958: 'I grabbed my machine gun and told my men to follow me. I was so mad I didn't even take normal precautions but moved swiftly to the barbed wire fence above the ditch. I grabbed a strand and the machine gun opened up on me. It snipped the barbed wire so it hung loose in my hand. I dropped to the frozen ground and sidled back downward to cover. A few minutes later, I heard a horrendous scraping sound and looked below me and one of my men had taken off his helmet and was trying to scrape a hole in the frozen ground.

As mentioned earlier by 1Lt. Frank Fitter, members of the 1st Battalion machine gun teams were interspersed in the line company formations as they moved eastward. PFC. John Trowbridge was one of those gunners. He wrote:

I hadn't noticed the fog so much as we walked through town, but most of the countryside was invisible. Perhaps that's why our 1st Battalion, led by the Recon Platoon, veered to the right at a fork in the road and headed for Marvie.

Not long after being re-routed back to the Longvilly road, whether by chance or design, our squad found itself about 100 or so yards behind the forward elements and began to receive fire from the direction of Neffe. It was the first hostility I had encountered since September 21st in Holland.

Colonel Ewell's jeep had come to a stop about ten feet in front of me, at the sounds of resistance. I had never been that near to the Colonel, nor did I remember hearing his voice before. His calm, cool composure had a reassuring effect on those near him. I can't remember his exact words, as he spoke on his radio, but it meant the same as 'Hold right where you are!'

To the left of the road was a slope rising gradually to a ridge running parallel to the road in an east-west direction and about 30 yards to our front was a house, built into a cove on the left side of the road, protected on the east and west by the terrain. We fell off the road into this cove and set up our machine gun, facing up the slope to the north. We were told that 'B' Company was deployed to our left front.

There was a grove of trees on the ridge about 100 yards to our left front which we assumed was under 'B' Company's control, but we were getting small arms fire and a great deal of shelling on our position. Someone ordered a machine gun up there to clear out the trees. I knew before McDonald yelled that it would be our gun.

We started up the slope on our bellies; Rasmussen on my right, Webb and Thornton bringing up the rear, when 'Jerry' opened up with a machine gun. I saw the dirt exploding between Rasmussen's fingers as he said, 'Let's get the hell out'a here!' We slid back down much faster than we went up. I guess we scared them out, because we weren't fired on again that day.

Sgt. Chester Brooks continued his story, wondering what was happening to their front. As operations sergeant, he needed to be in the know.

However, when things seemed to stabilize, I remember Colonel Ewell came up in a jeep to where we were and I asked him what the situation was and he cooly outlined all that had taken place.

One memory of the Bastogne fighting stays in the mind of PFC. Lawrence C. Lutz who was up front with the forward elements of "B" Company. He wrote:

Just west of Neffe, we were challenged by machine gun fire and we hit the ground. Immediately, a fire fight developed and, after some time, we were ordered to dig in with the 3rd Platoon of 'B' Company on the left of the Bastogne-Longvilly road. We took some casualties in the fighting and one incident in particular stays with me all these years. Sgt. George Adomitis jumped out of his foxhole screaming like he was badly hit. A couple of the troopers knocked him down and shortly after, they took him away. Later I learned that he had died. I was told that Adomitis' mind had taken all the combat it could and that he stood up to end it all. This was just the start of the killing and destruction to take place in the next month.

Pvt. Roy L. Biffle had come to the 101st when they were in Normandy as a replacement and made the rest of the campaigns. He was in on the initial action on the road to Neffe. He wrote:

We made contact with the Germans at Neffe. A machine gun opened up and wounded several before we could get off the road. Ken Casler and I dug in on the ridge and Ken got hit with shrapnel (not seriously) but he had been hit in the shoulder in Holland so it shook him up some.

As a member of the 81mm mortar platoon of 1st Battalion, PFC. George A. Ricker's responsibility was to furnish heavy weapons support to the rifle company commanders. He describes the early morning move toward Neffe:

It was foggy, visibility zero. We came under automatic fire at day light. Although I do not recall the name of the fellow on point or later, I do remember talking with him after the action was over. Since visibility was so poor, he carried an armed grenade in his hand and when within ten feet of a German machine gun emplacement, he escaped by tossing the grenade. I was with T/5 John Riszmiller in the ditch when he took a slug through the wrist.

T/5 Leon Jedziniak had been assigned to "A" Company as a medic just as the men were boarding the trucks in Mourmelon. As a replacement, he knew none of the men on board and now he was on his way to his first combat mission. He was called on by Chaplain Francis Sampson to go to the aid of a wounded man only a few hours after detrucking. Jedziniak wrote:

Just outside of Bastogne, the unit was pinned down by machine gun fire. We crawled to a ravine by a viaduct that had a railroad track. The call 'Medic up front!' came back. I learned a wounded man was lying in an exposed position beside the railroad tracks about 75 yards ahead. Father Sampson, a rifleman, and myself advanced to where the wounded man was lying.

This man was evacuated to the aid station and field hospital. The 101st hospital was overrun by the Germans. A citation for a Bronze Star Medal describing the above action more thoroughly accompanied Jedziniak's story. The citation reads as follows:

On 19 December 1944, in the vicinity of Bastogne, Belgium, Technician 5th Grade Leon Jedziniak learned of a wounded man lying in an exposed position who was reported beyond help. Realizing that the man might have a slight chance of survival, Technician 5th Grade Jedziniak and the Chaplain advanced seventy-five yards under sniper and tank fire to where the wounded man was lying. Finding the wounded man unconscious, they dragged him back in the face of very heavy enemy fire, which necessitated crawling. Although one bullet went through his jacket, Technician 5th Grade Jedziniak continued. Another bullet kicked dust into his eyes temporarily blinding him. He and the Chaplain succeeded in bringing the man to a safe position from which he was evacuated.

One of the actions Chaplain Francis Sampson described in a book of his wartime experiences was the rescue of the wounded soldier as the 501st moved toward its objective on the 19th of December. He wrote:[18]

I attached myself, for the time being, to a company just a mile or so east of the city. A soldier told me that there was a man a couple hundred yards down the road in a culvert by the railroad tracks. He was wounded and had called out for a priest (a rare request under such circumstances, for a man just doesn't count on a priest being on hand everywhere). I asked the soldier to take me to him and grabbed an aid man to help me. A German tank had been knocked out on the road between us and the wounded man, but a German was still manning the machine gun on the tank. As we skirted his immediate area and started to climb through the fence, he let go at us. The soldier leading us had the upper bone of his arm shattered by a bullet. We all three took a dive in that ditch by the railroad track. The wounded soldier pointed out with his good arm where the man I was looking for was located. The medic and I went to him. We were pinned down by crossfire. I lay down beside the wounded man, heard his confession and anointed him. He uttered not a word of complaint but expressed his thanks. He felt everything was going to be all right now. The aid man indicated with a shake of the head that the man didn't have a chance, but we carried him back to our position and some other men took him to the aid station. I never heard whether he lived or not; he was not from our regiment.

---

[18]Sampson, op. cit. 105-106.

After a period of time when patrol activity determined what 1st Battalion was facing, Major Bottomly told Colonel Ewell he felt an enemy force of two tanks and two platoons of infantry faced him.

The 57mm anti-tank guns of "B" Battery of the 81st Anti-Tank Battalion which had accompanied 1st Battalion, could not be brought into play because the road to Neffe ran straight for the last half mile. The enemy tanks had that situation covered.

## 2ND BATTALION MOVES FORWARD

At 1000, Colonel Ewell became convinced his 1st Battalion was stopped so he decided to bring the rest of his regiment out of Bastogne. The 2nd Battalion had to fight its way through the traffic jam of the retreating forces during the next hour. Ewell ordered them on to an assembly area on the reverse side of a gently sloping ridge north of 1st Battalion. They would be in position on Major Bottomly's left.

Colonel Ewell then directed 2nd Battalion to move from its assembly area and seize Bizory. The objective was reached by 1203; no opposition other than some sporadic cannon fire from tanks. He then attempted to seize Mageret from that direction hoping to trap the opposing tanks facing his troops. He also directed Major Sammie N. Homan, commander of 2nd Battalion to send one of his companies to seize the patch of woods directly north of Mageret. This forest plantation was of some very tall spruce trees. Ewell noted that the long ridge running across the evergreen trees dominated Mageret in the valley below. He felt that by putting one company at that height might cover the approach to Mageret.

Major Homan started down the road from Bizory to Mageret but his road march ended quickly. Troops from the Reconnaissance Platoon of the German 26th Volksgrenadier Division were already firmly entrenched in foxholes at the top of Hill 510. Homan took this first setback almost without loss; the enemy wasn't so fortunate. They had left the cover of their foxholes and were coming over the crest when the 2nd Battalion mortars and Nelson's artillery caught them with a full barrage. 2nd Battalion troopers related seeing many of the opposing force fall during the barrage. The survivors raced back to the shelter of their dug-in positions.

As the S-2 intelligence officer for 2nd Battalion in the Normandy and Holland operations, 1Lt. Bill Sefton was always more aware of the bigger picture of the 501st Regiment when it was in action than he was now as a platoon leader in "D" Company on this first day near Bastogne. He has this description of the move up into the Bizory area:

It was a very foggy morning with visibility limited to a few hundred yards. 'Easy' and 'Fox' Companies were ahead of us in the column. Just short of the village of Bizory, we passed a very lonesome platoon of combat engineers dug into a forward slope. To say they were delighted to see the 101st moving past them would be an understatement of impressive proportions.

Up ahead, 'Easy' and 'Fox' had been committed along the rim of a plateau beyond the village which nestled in a small valley. They were engaging approaching German infantry still some hundreds of yards away. 'Dog' Company was halted in defilade where the road dipped into the village. The road there was occupied by twelve or more armored vehicles which had managed to escape the German trap and exfiltrate to that point. The commander was a bird colonel who bore a striking resemblance to movie star Frank Morgan of that era.

Being the senior paratroop officer in the immediate vicinity, I reminded him that his congregation of vehicles was quite apt to draw fire on my unarmored troops and that I'd appreciate it if he would move along in the direction he had been headed. The sounds of the developing firefight apparently made my request quite persuasive, because the little column was soon crawling up the road toward Bastogne.

A single German gun of about .57mm caliber started pecking away at the vehicles from somewhere off on our left flank and our 'Geronimos' were making bets as to which would be the first one hit. Despite the goodly number of near misses, the column was still intact when beyond our sight.

The assignment as platoon leader didn't last very long for 1Lt. Sefton. Later in the day he was called to the company CP and told he was now the executive officer. Sefton wrote:

I was called up to company headquarters to take over as executive officer from 1Lt. Denver Bennett. He was lying on the floor of the small house being used as the command post, his cheek matted with blood and face already the gray-green color presaging imminent demise. An hour or so earlier he had cadged a cigar from me in lieu of a chew of tobacco, biting it in two and tucking half between cheek and molars while pocketing the remainder for future use.

I was surprised that he spoke in rather strong voice, 'Well, Bill, it looks like they got me.' And he was still alive when a jeep arrived to evacuate him. When we heard, two days later, that the division hospital had been captured, we figured Bennett would not have lasted that long anyway. (*Editor's note:* as of 1990, Bennett was still alive.)

Meanwhile, the firefight had stalemated, with both sides digging in as darkness fell. We were told to expect a German armor attack at dawn.

The troops of "F" Company were the most heavily engaged of the 2nd Battalion units as night fell. Major Homan had notified Colonel Ewell that his troops were fully engaged along the 2nd Battalion front. Reaching Mageret at this time was out of the question for 2nd Battalion. The fight would continue for many days.

## MISSION TO WARDIN

With both 1st and 2nd Battalions committed along his assigned front, Col. Ewell wondered why 3rd Battalion hadn't appeared on the scene. He drove back to Bastogne to find that the troops were caught in a huge traffic snarl on the west side of the city. By 1200 they had barely moved at all. As the troops jockeyed to get through the maze of retreating troops, some of the men who were poorly equipped, managed to pick up helmets, rifles and ammunition from those who were bent on departing the fray.

Colonel Ewell ordered LTC. George M. Griswold to move his 3rd Battalion troops to Mont, a small hamlet lying south of the Neffe road. Griswold was also directed to send one of his companies down the Wiltz road to serve as cover for his 3rd Battalion right flank. It was Ewell's plan to send the 3rd Battalion against Neffe from the southwest after it reached Mont but his directive did not include that possibility just now.

To the west and northwest of Wardin were three large evergreen tree lots where enemy troops might be concealed. Company "I" was given the assignment to check out the woods as part of their flank guard assignment. As "I" Company entered its third combat campaign, it was handicapped by a sudden change in leadership. Three of its key officers had been killed in Holland and a few days before departure for Bastogne, the first sergeant and all three platoon sergeants had been 'busted' and sent to other units in the regiment. The new leaders were unfamiliar with the capabilities of their men.

After reporting in to regimental commander Colonel Ewell at 1330 that the three wooded areas were clear of enemy soldiers, Captain Claude Wallace was directed to move into Wardin and make contact with friendly forces which were supposed to be there manning a roadblock.

The actions are described by survivors who participated in the attack on December 19.

There was one benefit from all the foul-up witnessed as the troops moved through Bastogne on their way to the front as remembered by PFC. William B. McMahon of "I" Company. He wrote:

> We did receive one benefit from all this, as our guys got weapons and equipment from the guys who were retreating. We moved down the main street of Bastogne and through to the edge of town. When we came to a halt,

the word came down that 'I' Company was to turn east and search all the woods in its front.

We searched the woods and they were empty. Apparently, we were ordered into Wardin so that is where we headed. Captain Wallace was in command of the company. We could see Wardin across the small valley and everything looked quiet. This valley was approximately five hundred yards across with a stream running through it which was closer to Wardin than to the woods from which we were observing the town.

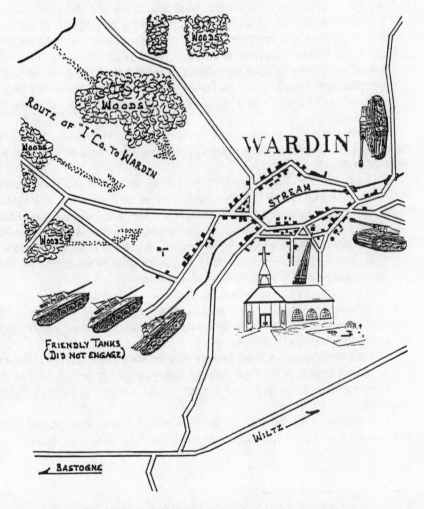

*Map 3 – Company I enters Wardin and is confronted by seven tanks and a battalion of infantry from the 901st Panzer Regiment.*

Platoon sergeant Robert J. Houston had been transferred from "H" Company
to his new assignment. He was a seasoned warrior, having been decorated with
the Distinguished Service Cross for actions in Normandy. From a narrative he
wrote of his wartime experiences,[19] he relates what it was like moving into
Wardin:

> We put scouts in front of the company and hiked along the road from
> Bastogne toward Wardin. After a mile or so, the road slopped down toward
> the village of about a dozen houses and barns clustered around a crossroads.
> We didn't make contact with the combat team of the 10th Armored Division
> but saw them moving back toward Bastogne along the ridge to our right.
>
> Everything was quiet when we arrived at the crossroads at the center of
> the little village. Most of the houses were made of stone and those
> belonging to farms had the barns attached to the houses. Some of the houses
> were deserted. People in this section of the Ardennes had been in the path of
> invasions in both world wars and were evidently trying to get out of the way
> of this one.

In a letter Frank Guzy wrote to Andre and Monique Meurisse in April 1982,
the following information came to light concerning the actions in which he was
involved at Wardin:[20]

> As the SCR-300 radio operator for the company (communications
> between Battalion and 'I' Company), I was unable to reach Battalion
> Headquarters because of the dense forest. When the company started for
> Wardin, I asked Captain Wallace for permission to break away from the
> formation to seek high and open ground. Wardin was in a deep valley.
> Unknown at the time, I was within a short distance of the Germans. They
> were observing "I" Company moving into Wardin.

As a replacement officer in Holland, 2Lt. Leonard E. Witkin was assigned to
3rd Platoon of "I" Company. He describes the arrival in Wardin and a move by
some of the men in the platoon to take a short cut into the area of houses. Some
got wet for their efforts. Witkin wrote:

> As we entered this small town of Wardin, we left the main road and had
> to cross an open field to get into the small village. A stream crosses this
> open field and when men tried to jump across, some of them landed in the
> water.

One of those soldiers who crossed the stream was Pvt. Richard Hahlbohm
who spotted a well as he approached the outskirts of the village. He wrote:

---

[19]Houston, Robert J. *D-Day to Bastogne*, Exposition Press, New York, 1979, p. 93.

[20]From a copy of a letter provided by Ruth Guzy, widow of Frank, written to Andre and
Monique in Bullingen, Belgium in April of 1982.

Half way up to Wardin, I realized my canteen was empty. I asked Sgt. Gus Gaxiola to take my .30 cal. LMG while I ran to a farmhouse to fill it. Me and three more troopers went to get water.

As a member of 3rd Platoon, PFC. William McMahon wondered why American tanks positioned on a hill six hundred yards away didn't give support to "I" Company. He wrote:

The 1st and 2nd Platoons entered the town and we moved in behind them. This is the part that has always mystified me. There were American tanks sitting in the field across the stream. Apparently Captain Wallace made no effort to coordinate with the tanks. We got no support from them though they were less than six hundred yards from the fighting. Maybe the Captain wasn't expecting anything in Wardin or maybe he decided he could handle anything that we would meet. Who knows what's in a man's mind at a time like this.

3rd Platoon crossed the little bridge over the stream and entered Wardin – even today I can see the sign saying 'WARDIN' on the right side of the road as you enter.

S/Sgt. Robert Houston describes how the company was positioned and goes into detail on the way his platoon was placed shortly after arrival:

Our 1st Platoon went out the road running east and the 2nd started out the road to the right, to observe from the ridge. Both of them were to go out a few hundred yards and dig in. Our platoon, the 3rd, set up at the crossroads, with a deserted house on the northwest corner for our CP. The company CP was directly across the road that we had come in on. I took the 1st squad, with Will Gauthier's machine gun, a few yards up to the right and told them to dig in where the gun could cover the crossroads. Cpl. Eldon Crotts set up the 2nd squad behind a house along the east road, where they could be out of the line of fire of Gauthier's machine gun. The 3rd squad set up by the farmhouse to the left of our CP. Everyone was told to dig in and be prepared for whatever the 1st and 2nd platoons found.[21]

As sergeant of the 1st Platoon, S/Sgt. Erminio Calderon's group was most likely the first to receive enemy fire. He describes the positioning of his men:

We moved out to this place called Wardin, getting into town around noon and everybody got off to the right side of the road.

There was a church at the edge of town. We weren't there very long when the lieutenant came back and said he was going to post a squad of men up around the church. Being the platoon sergeant, I wanted to be sure I knew where he'd post these men so I'd know where they would be.

As soon as "I" Company reached Wardin, Captain Wallace sent PFC. Marvin C. Wolfe, one of the combat veterans of both Normandy and Holland, on

---

[21]Houston, op. cit.

a scouting mission. Wolfe was the first to learn of the approach of enemy soldiers. He wrote:

When we reached Wardin, Capt. Wallace sent me and two other men to scout out the enemy. As we entered the village square and using buildings for cover, we noted a large force of Germans with many tanks and men. We immediately started back to report our findings to Captain Wallace, but before we could get back, the Germans started advancing and came across our command post, which they attacked and totally destroyed.

As one of the platoon leaders, 2Lt. Leonard Witkin had gone down to the company CP to get some extra shovels so his men could dig in quickly in their rather open positions. He turned down a coffee break. He wrote:

I was uneasy about being out in the open so I went to the CP to see if I could get some extra shovels so we could start diggin in. My C.O. asked me if I wanted to stay and have some coffee. I told him 'No thanks' and started back to my platoon. As I got half way back, I saw these German tanks come out of the woods and fire point blank into the stone house CP.

Pvt. Richard Hahlbohm had given his machine gun to his squad sergeant so he could more easily jump the stream to refill his canteen from a farmhouse well. He got quite a surprise on his return. He wrote:

I started back to get my machine gun and about that time I heard a mortar shell hit in Wardin. As I reached the edge of town, I asked the lieutenant where my gun was located. He told me 'by the house, the last one on the left'. All hell was starting to break out on the main road. As I rounded the outside of the house I saw a heavy wood pile. I laid behind it and saw Sgt. Gaxiola and another trooper in the middle of a small field with the gun in a shell hole. I thought it was a dumb place to position a machine gun. I called to the sergeant and asked if he wanted me to take over on the gun. He motioned me to stay put.

It wasn't long before Sgt. Gaxiola was hit and he ran to the shelter of one of the houses where a trooper put a bandage on his bullet-punctured buttock. In the meantime, enemy tanks and infantry were appearing in the village streets.

Shortly after PFC. Frank Guzy entered the company CP and informed Captain Wallace that he had been unable to contact 3rd Battalion with his radio, enemy fire hit the building. The enemy sensed it was some sort of command post. Guzy wrote:[22]

Within a minute, there was a large explosion in the living room. The German attack was on. The leading tank sent one shell direct at the target, right through the living room, wounding several and penetrating a second wall, a barn and killing the first sergeant and a cow.

---

[22]Guzy, op. cit.

All hell broke loose, men were coming in and out of the company CP with reports and requests for more weapons and ammunition. We had to leave and go to the back of the house.

From his vantage point out in the street, S/Sgt. Erminio Calderan has this description of how his group just missed being the target of the first volley:

There were 14 men on the road, the lieutenant, 12 platoon members and myself at the rear. All of a sudden, a ball of fire passed over us on the left. Everybody ran to the right side of the road. For some stupid reason, I broke and ran over to a house. I wanted to see where the fire was coming from. I didn't see anything on the road when I crossed but when I got to the house, I looked up and found myself staring down the barrel of an 88 – that S.O.B. had me zeroed in! He must have seen me from somewhere. I did a fast turn and got behind a small outhouse. A shell struck the front. The tank was either in the church or alongside it and the gunner was unable to move his gun to line up with the men on the road. If he had, I wouldn't be here now recording this for you.

I was badly shaken. From this position, I went to another house with a barn attached and the doors were open. There, inside, were a couple of men with a Lt. Mulligan (1Lt. Ray Mulligan) working on a .45 cal submachine gun. I asked a radioman if we had artillery support. He responded that Battalion said we had support. I asked where the hell he was going to put it . . . no answer.

After the tank fired at the men, it fired three times at one individual going zig-zag in the direction from which we had come. I couldn't believe my eyes – three 88mm shells for one man! I don't know how many more shots he fired at the man.

PFC. William McMahon hadn't been in Wardin more than a few minutes when the firing began. He lost a lot of cold-weather gear when he set it aside so he could move about more freely. McMahon added to his narrative:

We were standing in the road waiting for orders when firing suddenly broke out further down the road. I immediately ran into the front yard of a house, took off my overcoat, galoshes and my musette bag – all my dry socks, gloves and rations were in the bag, which I never was to see again.

I got the order to take seven guys to the top of the hill and set up a machine gun as a German company was trying to outflank us. We got to the top of the hill without difficulty and set up the gun covering the flank. Firing was becoming heavier behind us, but we couldn't leave and let them flank us.

The movement of two tanks toward his position now occupied the thoughts of 1st Platoon S/Sgt. Erminio Calderan. He wrote:

By this time I was occupied with Tank #2, which had come down the little road. He was firing at the house on top of the hill and I could see holes appearing in it. If I had had anything to throw at that tank, it would have been very simple for me to put it out of action.

When I took my eyes off Tank #2, I looked up at Tank #1 again. A man was crawling along the road with a bazooka. He got almost beside the tank before he fired his bazooka. The explosion was so great he came tumbling down the hill. I don't think he was hurt because he got up and yelled, 'I got it – I got it!' With that tank out of action, I didn't see anyone come up to push this one off the road.

With Tank #1 out of action, Tank #2 went back. When it came up again, it had infantry support. I'm still down in position #4. I'm looking at the company CP and thinking we should go up to higher ground where the rest of the company is positioned. We were isolated down here. Just then I saw a German stick his head out of the company CP window. I saw that Kraut put his machine pistol to his shoulder and fire. I saw five bullet holes in the door starting from where my belly button would be and going up to my head. I was half in and half out of the door. I know he was aiming at me. The rest of the men were over to my right. I stood there – frozen. The others opened fire and got him.

3rd Platoon sergeant Robert Houston was viewing the various battles from a different perspective. He now needed to check on the positions of the various squads. He wrote:[23]

I was with the 3rd squad down by the barn and decided to go check on Crotts' squad, which was in a spot where the attack would hit us if the tanks stayed on the road. I ran across the road and hit the ground as I heard Gauthier's machine gun open up. Crawling up to the edge of the garden, I saw a tank and German soldiers about 30 yards away, where Crotts and his squad were supposed to be. The tank swung its big gun to the left and fired; Gauthier's machine gun stopped. Other tanks moved ahead. They were in the middle of our company and seemed to have plenty of infantry soldiers with them.

They saw me and began firing, but luckily there was a little swell in the ground between us, so the bullets went over as I flattened myself to the ground. All through training we had been told that our rifles were our best friends, but now a ridge of earth hardly big enough to see kept me alive; the ground was my best friend. My rifle was in my hand but not of any use at that moment.

In a few moments our 2nd Platoon hit them from the other side and that took attention away from me. I went back toward the farmhouse, keeping low for concealment by the bushes in the garden. A tank left the road and started to turn toward me. There wasn't time to get behind the building, so I

---

[23]Houston, op. cit.

pounded on the front door. A man let me in and just as he closed the door, a shell hit the wall behind me. I was thankful for the sturdy stone house. There were a few civilians huddled in the room and since that fleeting glance, I have always wondered if they survived that day and the next two weeks.

I went quickly through the room and out the door into the stable and then out the back door into the yard where the 3rd squad men were right where I had left them. We fired a bazooka shell, which hit the front of the tank where its armor was heavy, so it wasn't knocked out. It moved back around our platoon CP house and stopped with its side toward us. Company 'I', in spite of being outnumbered and outgunned, was stopping this particular part of the breakthrough. We could hear the 2nd Platoon and what was left of the 1st Platoon and our 1st squad, firing from the other side of the road.

Our bazooka man said he could knock out the tank as it was sitting with its side toward us. I told him that the shell would probably explode when it went through the bushes in the backyard between us and the target. Two men volunteered to go with the bazooka, across the yard to where they could poke it through the roadside bushes about five yards from the tank.

The explosion put a hole in the lower part of the tank and we picked off the crew as they scrambled out. There was no way to get an accurate account of what was going on, but we kept firing as long as we could hear the 2nd Platoon firing from the other side of the road. Another tank came up and pushed the one we had knocked out off the road. There seemed to be only three moving around now, which meant 'I' Company had knocked out four of them.

After he and his scouting group had spotted the enemy tanks and troops on the far side of Wardin, PFC. Marvin Wolfe and the others had retreated toward company headquarters to alert them to the danger. The tanks hit the CP before Wolfe got back. He did witness the destruction of one of the enemy tanks. Wolfe wrote:

At that point, we advanced up a high knoll and got behind a large stone building and started returning the fire as the Germans were coming down the road. As the tanks approached, Wilbrod Gauthier ran down to the road with a bazooka and took out the first tank. He was then killed by the machine gun on the second tank. This tank pushed the first tank off the road and the rest of the tanks continued their advance.

Radioman Frank Guzy was with Captain Wallace when the headquarters group was driven from the CP by tank shell fire which killed 1/Sgt. Carl Sargis.

Guzy dumped his heavy radio which had provided no communication when it was so needed at a critical time. Guzy finished his story:[24]

Captain Wallace was one of the bravest officers that I have ever known. His last order to the company was: 'Every man for himself!'

Soon, everyone of our group was gone except me. There was no way to evacuate carrying a big heavy radio (42 pounds) and then I realized that the radio could not receive Battalion headquarters so I dropped it on the ground and double-timed out of there. A short time later, I came upon Captain Wallace and the others.

From his position on the top of a hill, overlooking the small town, PFC. William McMahon's machine gun crew had been positioned so the enemy could not outflank the "I" Company positions in town. He remembered:

Now we began to hear tank bogey wheels behind us and some of the guys thought they were our tanks. The tanks began firing into the houses and we knew our guys had taken cover in the houses so it couldn't be our tanks.

As the British say, 'It's beginning to be a sticky wicket!' and that was an understatement. At this time, an officer came running up the hill yelling, 'Anyone who wants to live, follow me!' My squad was never in the houses.

Several of the buildings were burning and the smoke was dense; the tanks were firing down the road but there was so much smoke, it blocked our vision and allowed us to cross the road. Without the smoke, I don't think any of us would have made it.

With the order being given to pull out, Sgt. Richard "Buck" Ketsdever was still in the village with Captain Claude Wallace and the executive officer, 2Lt. William Schumaker, who had been frantically calling the 3rd Battalion for assistance. He hadn't succeeded in making contact with anyone. Ketsdever wrote:

The lieutenant gave me back my radio and, as we were receiving machine gun and rifle fire from the advancing troops, said we should pull out. He suggested going down the small trail to the gate and getting on the other side of the building to get out of the line of fire. The lieutenant took off first, running. I was behind him and Captain Wallace followed me. As the lieutenant turned into the gate, I thought he tripped because he fell to the ground. I was so close to him by then, I fell over him and Captain Wallace fell on top of me. They had both been hit, either by rifle or machine gun fire, and both were dead. I crawled into the creek and started moving up the hill toward Bastogne.

PFC. Marvin C. Wolfe had witnessed the destruction of one tank by his friend Wilbrod Gauthier and then saw the second tank take him out with a burst

---

[24]Guzy, op. cit.

of machine gun fire. He got word to get out while the getting out was still possible. Wolfe added to his story:

Word spread that we were to return to Division Headquarters in Bastogne. As we started to leave, German fire pinned us down and we hid in and along a creek, just out of sight of the Germans. There we could keep low enough to avoid the enemy fire that was flying overhead. There were large, open fields between us and headquarters so we had to wait until nightfall and the safety of darkness before we could leave the stream bed and return to Bastogne.

Platoon sergeant Erminio Calderan had been shot at by a German soldier firing from a window of the former "I" Company command post. It was time to get out of a tight situation. He closed his account with these recollections:

About this time, I figured I had enough so I jumped over a three-strand barbed wire fence next to the stream and when I hit that water, I lost my rifle. I ran up the hill where I was caught in a barrage of machine gun fire. I threw myself on the ground and yelled. I thought I was alone. I heard someone also on my left. There were two other men going out with me. The one on my right wasn't hit. We just lay there for awhile and played dead. I asked the fellow on my left how bad he was. He didn't think he was hurt bad so I said, 'When I count three, make for the open spot in the hedge.' When I did, we started running. We no sooner got to the open spot when all hell broke loose. There was so much lead flying through the opening that you could plant corn in their furrows without doing any plowing.

Instead of going up, I back-tracked to the wood pile. Unfortunately, the fellow with the head wound never did make it. I don't know what happened to him. We stayed behind the wood pile for probably an hour. Then we made our way along the hedgerow and out to where this house was on the side of the road. At this particular spot, it was all open – there was nothing to hide behind. There were a group of civilians going by. We borrowed some coats from a civilian so we could get out with them. We got about half way up the hill. I guess the Krauts spotted our boots and opened up. I don't know if any of the civilians were hit, but there was a road with high banks. We stayed there for an hour or a little longer.

It was getting dusk and one of the civilians, an old man, came up and I was trying to tell him to keep down. I didn't know what he was trying to tell me. I finally figured he was trying to let me know the Germans were coming up the hill. All I had was a trench knife and I wasn't about to stay there and be shot or captured.

From that point on to the woods, it was about 200-300 yards and both of us started running. Did you ever try to run through a newly plowed field – it was terrible. We got into the woods. It was almost dark and there were noises in the woods. I didn't know what it could be so I pulled my trench knife and challenged. It turned out to be some 'I' Company men picking up stragglers.

Meanwhile, back in Wardin, some of the troopers hadn't gotten a message to pull out or weren't in position to do so. One of these men was replacement PFC. Leo Rozman, experiencing his first day of combat. He wrote:

Company 'I' was ambushed in the town of Wardin. German troops were in most of the attics shooting down at us with burp guns and dropping concussion grenades on us.

Both American and German artillery were destroying the town. I was shocked when I saw the 'entire German army' coming toward me.

However, when one of three tanks fired at my head from a distance of 15 feet, I had all the fight knocked out of me. I was picked up off the ground and became a POW.

PFC. Joseph N. Christman had been in on the action with PFC. Wilbrod Gauthier when he was firing at the tanks with a bazooka. Christman tried to hide from the enemy. He wrote:

I saw Gauthier go down. Rector and I, together, hid in the barn getting into the hayloft. The tank below killed all the livestock in the stable of the barn but they didn't find Rector and me in the loft. We hid under the hay. The German tank crew and infantry stopped, had lunch and drank from the well by the barn.

We thought we could make a try for our lines in the moonlight. We got out from under the hay to make our try when a shell burst in the roof of the barn. Rector was killed. I had shell fragments in my left elbow and both rifles were wrecked. I made a try for our lines the next day but was picked up and captured.

When the enemy tanks appeared at Wardin, the tide of battle turned in favor of the Germans. Those with PFC. Larry Burgoon were trapped in houses and barns within the town. Burgoon wrote:

When the tanks came at us, Sgt. Edgar called, 'We're getting out of here!' But Lt. (Robert) Harrison said, 'Load the bazooka' and took my gun as I wasn't to need it. By that time, it was too late to run – there were Germans everywhere. We went into a farm building with Lt. Harrison and some men went upstairs. Dan Rubenstein, who was a replacement in Holland, hid with me in the attached barn covered with hay in front of the cows. Just before we split up going into the house and barn, a tank shell hit the corner of the house. Sgt. Gus Gaxiola was hit on the cheek of his butt but was still able to walk.

Dan and I heard the Germans taking prisoners from above us but we couldn't see who they were and never saw them again. The Germans set fire to the building and we were flushed out and taken prisoner.

The survivors of "I" Company continued to filter into the 501st command post in Bastogne throughout the night and into mid-morning of the 20th. When a head count was made, a total of 83 men were left of about 140 men who had gone to Wardin the day before.

Had there been coordination between the tank forces up on the hill and the hard-pressed paratroopers down in the village, the results might have been all together different.

## 3RD BATTALION MOVES ON TO MONT

As Colonel Julian Ewell shunted "I" Company off through the woods and to Wardin, the bulk of 3rd Battalion continued on its march toward Mont and Neffe.

As Sgt. Donald Castona and the men of his unit detrucked at Mande St. Etienne, they noted the weather wasn't that uncomfortable so the men began discarding heavy outer gear as they moved east toward their assigned MLR positions. Castona recalled:

We disembarked in a small town. We thought that this was where we were going to fight until we were alerted to get ready to move out. The weather was good and pretty warm and some of our guys conveniently 'forgot' to pick up their overshoes when we got up after our rest breaks. This cost them dearly a few days later when it got cold and snowed.

We walked through Bastogne and passed an awful lot of GI's heading the other way.

There were a few combat engineers set up with their .30 cal. machine guns on the slope before we got to Mont. These were good soldiers and they were prepared to hold their positions.

We set up positions after going through Mont and got ready to meet the Germans. We could hear tanks coming but most of the guys were confident that we could handle things.

As a member of 3rd Battalion Headquarters Company and one of two 81mm mortar platoon section sergeants, Richard L. Klein was in the move to Mont and remembered the officers didn't know any more about what was happening than he did.

The 3rd Battalion marched several miles to and through Bastogne to reach our ultimate destination, which was Mont. No one seemed to know what the situation was. I asked Lt. Horvath where to set up our mortars and he indicated he did not know any more than I did where the Germans were, so put them wherever. We placed one behind a haystack temporarily. Within a matter of minutes, the first shells were coming into Mont from the direction of Neffe. I grabbed a bipod and base plate and sprinted about fifty yards to the cover of a building crossing a tiny creek and a single-strand barbed wire fence enroute. Seemed like an eternity getting there.

Four members of 3rd Battalion remember being involved in a move whereby Colonel Ewell directed that a platoon be sent on a move to the north with a swing to the right to approach Neffe from a different direction. They were to find out how well Neffe was defended by the Germans.

Sgt. Richard Klein was one of the Headquarters Company members directed to join the platoon making the reconnaissance move toward Neffe. He wrote:

On the evening of the 19th, I was told to take Joe Reilly, a radioman, and report to 'G' Company for a patrol. We found that the patrol leader was our former platoon sergeant, now 2Lt. Jim McKearney. We took off almost immediately with no briefing as to where we were going or what the mission was. A couple hours later, I found out we were to see if Neffe was occupied by Germans. As we approached Neffe, along a portion of a sunken road, we ran into fire from our left, in the vicinity of a building that was engulfed in flames. (I later learned that it was the chateau which had been occupied by Team Cherry and later by Lt. Tippit's platoon from 'G' Company.) As we pushed closer to Neffe, we were joined by Tippit and his platoon. It was quite evident that Neffe was firmly held by the Germans.

The position of the lead scout on a reconnaissance mission is unenviable for most infantrymen. Sgt. Donald Castona of "G" Company was part of the platoon making the reconnaissance. He felt sorry for the young soldier who moved out as lead scout.

I remember Pvt. (Daniel) Bazarewski moving out as the lead scout as brave as can be. I never envied those guys their job. Our old first sergeant, now a 2nd lieutenant, (Otis) Tippit, took his platoon and went around the first opposition we ran into and led his men on an assault against the enemy position. Lt. Tippit was wounded in the face in the assault but they picked up several prisoners and stopped the Germans at that point.

Sgt. Wilson Boback was one of the platoon squad leaders involved in the action. It was one of the memorable recollections of his Bastogne area fighting. He wrote:

We made an attack on a small town (Mont or Neffe?). We hit them at night. It was a wild battle – the Germans had two machine guns cross-firing from stone fence lines. Tracer bullets were all over the place. 2Lt. Tippit was a short distance from me. I worked my way on my belly over to one machine gun and tossed a grenade at it. It was silenced. The other one kept firing and Lt. Tippit got hit in the ear. I was going after the other machine gun but Tippit yelled for us to pull back.

As the radio operator for the platoon, Pvt. Walter E. Davis remembers some of the actions which occurred during the move while it was still day light. He wrote:[25]

I was the radio operator and the platoon was the 3rd of 'G' Company. We got heavy machine gun and rifle fire from the buildings in Neffe as we started down the slope leading to the chateau. As I ran across the open ground to where Colonel Cherry's tank was, at the bend in the road, I threw away my extra radio batteries and some other equipment to lighten my load so I could run faster. Colonel Cherry had one tank, one half-track and a jeep at the road block. He could not withdraw during day light and was waiting for dark. The Germans had the high ground under fire from their tanks in Neffe. The best of my memory was there were just a few of us who got down to Colonel Cherry. Our machine gunner was hit just as he set up his gun. He had a bullet in the right shoulder and back.

The fellows driving the jeep thought they could make it up the dirt road, which was partly protected by trees. We tried to tell them to wait for dark but they made a run for it with their jeep wide open. They didn't get fifty yards before both were hit by heavy machine gun fire. They groaned and fell off the jeep. We tried to get to them but could not, due to heavy fire. Both were dead when we got to them after dark.

While waiting for dark, we captured three Germans. Two were wounded. A funny thing happened that almost got us killed. I took the rifle we had taken from the captured Germans by the barrel and broke the stock by hitting a tree. This caused the rifle to discharge and the bullet hit my M-1 rifle ammo in my cartridge belt and set the powder on fire. My clothes were burning and I was trying to get my cartridge belt off and some of the fellows were trying to beat the fire out with their coats. Needless to say, the captured Germans got a laugh out of it. I never broke another rifle without removing the bolt after that.

When the 3rd Platoon ran into heavy opposition on the approach to Neffe, Sgt. Donald Castona was sent back for reinforcements. He ended up leading the original group back to Mont. Castona added:

I was sent back to bring the rest of the company up to where we were but was stopped by Colonel Ewell and told to bring our guys back so we could set up a defense of Mont. I was just told to get them back. We tried to come back the direct way but ran into the heavy sheep fences that were to play such a big part later on. Anyway, we came right back along the road and got back to Mont. I caught a little hell for bringing our guys back along

---

[25]Walter E. Davis wrote a letter to me on April 20, 1966 at the time I was researching *D-Day With The Screaming Eagles*. Something in the roster I sent him triggered a flood of memories of the Bastogne conflict.

the road but we were lucky. It seems that a column of Germans was not far behind us on the same road. By this time, a tank and another armored vehicle had joined us along with the heavy weapons company of 3rd Battalion.

Mortar sergeant Richard Klein remembered the withdrawal and subsequent positioning on a hillside. It would turn out to be a miserable night for him, weatherwise. Fog continued to be a problem the next morning.

We proceeded to pull back toward Mont, crossing several barbed wire fences along the way. For reasons I never understood, we dug in on the reverse slope of a hill, about halfway between Mont and Neffe. We stayed there the rest of the night.

By late afternoon of the 19th, Colonel Ewell had committed all three of his battalions and each had been stopped by tank and small arms fire. The companies had moved into favorable defensive positions and dug in. Ewell felt he needed reinforcements on his right flank and had asked for Division troops to help secure the area through which enemy troops might turn his right flank.

## COLONEL HARTFORD F. SALEE'S 1ST BATTALION

Once the three parachute infantry regiments had departed for their assigned perimeter lines of defense, Colonel Joseph N. Harper and his staff of the 327th Glider Infantry Regiment, took over the temporary command post which Division Headquarters had set up in the school house at Mande St. Etienne. At 1600 hours, the 1st Battalion, less "B" Company, was sent through Bastogne and was attached to Colonel Julian Ewell's 501st Regiment in support of his right flank.

Captain Walter L. Miller, leading his "C" Company of the 1st Battalion, then reported in at headquarters in Bastogne where he was directed to a commanding height near Neffe. Miller relates:

I had reported to Colonel Ewell in Bastogne and he assigned us a hill to his right. We moved up and dug in and I remember it well because I chided my first sergeant about digging such a deep foxhole. When the shells started falling, I jumped in right beside him and was glad he had dug so deep.

During the night, we could hear the sounds of mechanized forces to our front and an occasional burst of a Schmeizzer. The next morning we overlooked a small village and I could see there was fighting as two vehicles had been hit and were in flames.

The stay on the southeast side for the 1st Battalion of the 327th Glider Regiment would be of short duration. After a brief skirmish on the 20th, 1st Battalion and its Headquarters Company would be called back to the west side of

Bastogne. "B" Company would move east on the 20th to serve as flank protection.

## THE ENEMY MAKES ITS DEEPEST PENETRATION

On the evening of the 19th, the enemy would make its deepest penetration into the perimeter defense of the 101st Division at Bastogne. The action is described by a 1st Battalion machine gunner and by 907th Glider Field Artillery Battalion historian Robert Minick.

In a patrol action that enabled the enemy to reach its closest point to the 101st Airborne Division Headquarters, PFC. John C. Trowbridge relates an action that ties in with an event that took place in the "B" Battery (907th Glider Field Artillery Battalion) area during the first night.

I don't know who took over that grove after that, but that night an enemy patrol came within 50 yards of our position when Rasmussen challenged, then fired, along with a .50 caliber from artillery, which was to our left rear. The next morning we found one dead enemy and heard that one was captured.

In a wartime history of the 907th Glider Field Artillery Battalion, which he wrote, Robert Minick provides a more detailed account of the above situation which occurred in the "B" Battery area.[26]

Late on the evening of the 19th, a German patrol of between 20 and 40 men accidentally infiltrated the B Battery position. Having apparently lost their way in the dense fog, the patrol wandered down the slope of a small hill and headed straight for Sergeant McGinnis' gun position. Hushed whispers silently passed the alert down along the line of waiting artillerymen. After a very subdued telephone conversation with Captain McGlone, who was also trying to warn the gun crews of the developing situation, Sergeant McGinnis and PFC. Narcisso Jaso went to work. They acted as decoys while PFC. Stanley J. Vincent and others drove the patrol back up the slope toward one of the .50 caliber crews on outpost guard. With their vision hampered by the fog, the men in pursuit could only listen to the enemy patrol as it scampered back in the opposite direction. In their haste to clear the area and right their course, the Krauts were dropping parts of their equipment as they moved along. When they reached the top of the hill, they received a challenge from PFC. Agapieto Hernandez who was operating the machine gun. When the Germans failed to respond with a countersign, 'Mexican Pete' opened up on them, killing their leader, a young

---

[26]Minick, Robert. *Kilogram* The Story of the 907th Glider Artillery Battalion. (Private Printing), Hobart, Indiana, 1979. pp. 166-167.

lieutenant. The following morning the already frozen body of the German officer was viewed by all who cared to look as he lay there on the frozen ground with a large gaping hole in the middle of his chest. The remaining members of the patrol were driven into the lines of the 327th and captured by the glider infantrymen.

## NOVILLE AND FOY

It had been a long, hard ride for the men of the 10th Armored Division as they moved from their rest area in France to an assembly area near Luxembourg City. At that juncture, Combat Command B, under Colonel William C. Roberts, had been ordered to continue on to Bastogne to be placed under the command of General Troy Middleton and his VIII Army Corps.

Upon arrival in Bastogne on the afternoon of December 18, and after learning where General Middleton wanted hasty defensive positions set up, Colonel Roberts divided his forces into three combat teams. The one of concern here for the Noville operation became known as Team Desobry. It was led by Major William R. Desobry, a tall, six foot four inch, one hundred and sixty pounder who commanded the 20th Armored Infantry Battalion.

Team Desobry was the last of the three combat teams which Colonel Roberts had formed to be positioned at locations to which General Middleton had assigned them to stop advancing enemy forces. Team Desobry made its move after darkness had set in on the night of the 18th.

One of the company commanders in Team Desobry was Captain Gordon Geiger. He was ordered to Noville to set up a blocking force. Geiger began placing his troops and vehicles in positions in and around Noville to stop the Germans from breaking through. He describes the problem he had separating the retreating American forces from the enemy which were reported in the vicinity.[27] All through the night (18-19), American vehicles, with their lights on, moved through Noville heading for Bastogne. Everybody said that more Germans were coming. We knew it and my men were scared. As the Americans came through, they said, 'There are more Germans coming than you have ever seen before. There's no use staying here. They'll run over you in no time!' But my orders were to hold, so that's what we had to do.

---

[27] From an interview of Gordon Geiger that appeared in *The World War II Chronicle*, P. O. Box 68079, Indianapolis, IN 46268-0079.

Finally, my commander ordered me to stop all vehicles going toward Bastogne and take the soldiers off to fill our ranks. They were scared and didn't know me. Some said, "We were given orders to withdraw." But I said, "I'm the one giving orders now. Hold your ground and fight."

The three hundred man force of Team Desobry consisted mainly of the 20th Armored Infantry Battalion and a tank destroyer unit consisting of five TD vehicles. These were augmented by men of the 28th Infantry Division and a few men and officers of the 9th Armored Division who were convinced they could help in stopping the enemy advance.

Shortly before daybreak, the enemy forces were nearing the outskirts of Noville. The men of Team Desobry continued to hold off on their firing as retreating American soldiers sought refuge as they fled into Noville from the north.

Captain Geiger continued his story of how they tried to separate the retreating Americans from enemy forces.[28]

Our men on the outposts didn't want to fire on Americans. The only way they could tell who was there was to holler out and ask if approaching soldiers spoke German. If they did, then they were the enemy.

Captain John T. Prior was a member of the Medical Battalion of the 10th Armored Division and on December 14th had been detached to the 20th Armored Infantry Battalion to replace their surgeon who had been evacuated with pneumonia. Captain Prior was involved with Team Desobry at Noville on December 19, 1944. Part of his story follows:[29]

Arriving in Noville at 0600, December 19th, we found a sleepy little crossroads town. My aid station was located in the pub. I found this type of building always best for our purposes since the large drinking area accommodated many litter patients. Within two hours of our arrival the little town had turned into a shooting gallery featuring small arms, machine gun and tank fire on the main thoroughfare. The large front window of the pub was an early casualty and it was necessary to crawl on the floor to avoid being hit as we treated our increasing number of casualties. Someone had selected our backyard as the 'ammo' dump and this did not boost our equanimity. Team Desobry was ordered to hold Noville at all costs.

The 506th Parachute Infantry Regiment, led by Colonel Robert F. Sink, had arrived in the assembly area near Mande St. Etienne at 0400 on the morning of December 19. The men had a few hours to stretch to get rid of the kinks that developed during the long ride from Mourmelon.

---

[28]ibid.

[29]Prior, John T. *Onendaga County Medical Society Bulletin*, "The Night before Christmas – Bastogne 1944," December 1972. pp. 15-24.

Having accompanied the 506th Regiment to Bastogne to assume its responsibility as the forward observer team of the 321st Glider Field Artillery Battalion, one of the team members, PFC. William J. Stone, remembered that his team leader, 1Lt. Francis Canham, came back from a meeting in the assembly area with the news of the terrible shortage of ammunition in the rifle company to which they were attached for the mission. Stone describes how his team leader tried to alleviate the situation:

While talking with the officers of the company with which we were working, Canham learned that they had no ammunition for their carbines. As artillerymen, we were armed with carbines and had enough ammunition to share with them, which we did. In addition, the riflemen did not have sufficient ammunition for their rifles and there was a shortage of hand grenades and rocket launcher projectiles. This was remedied, somewhat, just as we were entering Noville.

Shortly after daylight on the 19th, and when Division had decided where each of the fighting units was to take its place in defensive positions, the men began their marches east through Bastogne.

With the arrival of daylight, Major William Desobry, in Noville, was able to see periodically into the distance when the fog lifted. He noted that the town was in a pocket with high ground on three sides which made it difficult to defend when the enemy could look down into Team Desobry's defensive positions.

With this observation, Desobry called Colonel William Roberts, commander of Combat Command "B" of the 10th Armored Division at his command post in Bastogne requesting permission to withdraw to more defensible positions. After Colonel Roberts consulted with VIII Corps and 101st Division Headquarters, he was told to keep his forces in Noville and that a battalion of 101st paratroopers was on its way to reinforce his troops.

When Major Desobry learned that 1st Battalion of the 506th Parachute Infantry Regiment was on its way to Noville, he sent a jeep down the road to pick up LTC. James LaPrade, its commander, so the two officers could do a reconnaissance of the area. In this way, LaPrade would know in advance, without an assembly, where to position his men. LaPrade also alerted Desobry to the fact that his men were without adequate weaponry, rifle and machine gun ammunition, mortar shells and hand grenades. Desobry ordered men of his Service Company to rush the necessary armament to the advancing troops. The truck loads of equipment were waiting at the roadside near Foy as the troops came by.

That was the way LTC. Jim LaPrade's troops arrived on the combat scene, ill-equipped to fight a war on the morning of December 19, 1944. They were less than two miles from the enemy forces attacking Noville.

After disembarking west of Bastogne, T/5 Owen E. Miller remembers walking to the east and coming upon a road sign that read BASTOGNE. He remembers Captain Joseph Warren coming by to pick him up in a jeep.

As I was walking through the square in Bastogne in the line of march, here comes Captain Warren in a jeep. He picked me up and had me drive. I asked him where to go and he said just stay on this road. We passed two trucks that had stopped and were dumping equipment along the road. We kept going and came to a small town.

When the assignments were issued in the assembly area, "C" Company was to lead out for 1st Battalion of the 506th Regiment. 1Lt. Joe Reed was in on the action and the first platoon was fortunate to pick up weapons and ammo from retreating troops. Reed wrote:

Company 'C' was the advance party and my platoon was given the point. We were on both sides of the road in the Foy area when we came upon a bunch of friendly armored vehicles withdrawing through us. We were ill-equipped and short of ammo so we asked them for weapons and ammo, which they gladly gave us. We proceeded on up to the Noville area without enemy contact.

For PFC. Robert M. Wiatt, the fighting around Bastogne would be his second combat mission with "C" Company. Near the small village of Foy, his group got some much needed ammunition. He relates:

At this point, we picked up some ammunition. We had no .45 caliber ammo, no machine gun or mortar ammo, but did have some .30 cal. rounds in clips made for the .03 rifle. It was nice to feel, again, that at least we had something to fight with.

PFC. Donald B. Straith of "A" Company was moving into his first combat action and remembered:

A jeep raced up and a crate of hand grenades was unloaded. These were distributed, one to each man, until the small supply was exhausted. Hooking mine to my belt, I listened as we were told that we would move through the town and seize the distant ridge. With that, we were up and moving again.

Though the men in his unit had weapons, there was little ammunition for them so PFC. Robert A. Flory of "B" Company was relieved when ammunition arrived in the nick of time. He relates:

We were pretty well equipped with weapons but had little or no ammo. The closer we got to Noville, the more we could hear the sounds of battle and we were wondering what we were supposed to fight with. Just short of Noville, a convoy of jeeps and 6 x 6's showed up carrying ammo, grenades and mortar shells. We halted and rested. Colonel LaPrade, our battalion commander, had gone ahead to confer with Major Desobry, one of three team leaders from Combat Command 'B' of the 10th Armored Division. We drew our ammo and waited for orders. At about 1300 hours, the 3rd Platoon was ordered to advance up a hill to the west of Noville.

Medical technician Owen E. Miller had been picked up by Captain Joseph Warren, 1st Battalion surgeon and now drove Warren's jeep. They had passed the supply trucks unloading ammunition and were now entering Noville from the south. Miller wrote:

We kept going and came to a small town. I heard loud motors. I told Captain Warren that we had better stop. He asked what for, so I kept going. Then I heard a motor in high rev behind us. It was a tank destroyer and he was really coming up quick. I had to pull over to the side of the road as he went by us. He locked his brakes and kept sliding up the road. He was just past the second house and he backed up between two houses, just as a shell hit the corner of the house where he had secreted himself. I got the jeep turned around pretty quick and came back about a hundred yards to the first house on the right side of the road. We got out and cleared the house to have it set up as an aid station.

With his company at the point of the 1st Battalion move to Noville, 1Lt. Edward Mehosky describes the arrival in the town and the positioning of the line companies:

It was still cold and gray when we arrived in Noville. No Germans were in the village. The place looked battered. The battalion commander had finished his reconnaissance and issued his orders: to effectively defend Noville, the Battalion would have to secure the high ground. 'C' Company was given the assignment to take a wooded ridgeline to the east of Noville. 'B' Company had the other side of the road and were to take the high ground to the northeast. 'A' Company would be in reserve. We moved out by platoons astride the Noville-Bourcy road.

As the morning fog swirled about the Noville area, lifting and again settling to the ground, the two commanders asked for artillery and smoke to conceal the moves of the paratroopers as they advanced toward the high ground which dominated the landscape north and east of town.

As the two commanders watched the movement of the paratroopers, the fog lifted and fell periodically. Major Desobry observed the tactics of these troops. He related:[30]

The paratroopers came on and, instead of going into an assembly area, went on the attack right off the approach march. They hit it just about on the nose in conjunction with the artillery preparation.

They spread out across the fields and those guys, when they attacked, did it on the dead run. None of this fooling around like you see on television – walking and so on. These guys went on the dead run. They would sprint

[30]Astor, Gerald, *A Blood-Dimmed Tide*, Donald I. Fine, New York, 1992. p. 213.

for fifty yards, hit the ground, get up and run, on and on. Our tanks moved out with them.

It wasn't long after replenishing their ammunition supply that the men of 1st Battalion were in combat with the enemy at Noville. 1Lt. Joe Reed was to take his platoon to high ground where he caught some careless enemy soldiers. He wrote:

As we went through Noville, I was directed to take the high ground to the right side of town. As we proceeded to do this, we came up on a bunch of Krauts sleeping in their holes. We started to pop them as we ran along the ridge. Immediately, we heard a bunch of tank motors start up just over the hill in the wooded area. From my observation, there were many, many tanks. I yelled to the guys to get off the hill and fall back to the town, which we did.

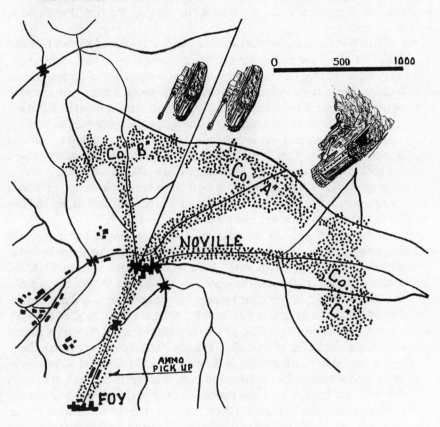

*Map 4*

Company "B" was moving into position on the hills to the west and north of Noville. PFC. Robert Flory describes that move and subsequent action:

There was a much used cow path going up to the top of the hill. The hill top was pretty much wooded but the path we had to take was out in the open. Half way up the hill, we came under machine gun and small arms fire, but we made it to the top with very few casualties. I remember one incident that happened. We had a platoon leader, new to combat, who was not very popular with the men. 2Lt. C. A. Mitchell, who had won his battlefield commission in Holland, had always been a member of the 3rd Platoon and through some pull with Colonel Sink, stayed with his platoon as assistant platoon leader.

As soon as we came under fire, the new platoon leader yelled at 'Mitch' to bring up the stragglers, then he disappeared. 'Mitch' was bug-eyed furious. He yelled back, 'God dammit, the 3rd Platoon doesn't have stragglers!'

Bill Barclay, the 3rd Platoon scout, reached the top of the hill first and yelled for Mitch to come up. He had spotted three German tanks coming our way. We all arrived on the hilltop and spread out in a line of defense. It was useless to try digging in because of the mass of roots. Bullets were cracking overhead and small twigs kept falling on us from being severed by bullets.

Suddenly, one of the tanks was hit by a tank destroyer back in Noville. The other two stopped and another was hit. The third tank turned tail and headed to the rear. There's no doubt in my mind that the TD gunner saved our necks because those tanks were stopped just 300 yards from us.

As a medic, T/5 Owen E. Miller, moved about somewhat more freely than others as he searched for the injured and wounded in battle situations. He had this recollection of what Noville was like the first day:

I remember the bitter cold and fog. I never saw fog like that. It would settle and then rise as soon as it touched the ground, sometimes before it touched the ground. I kept going from the aid station up into town and across about a hundred yards of open space. You had to time it just right. When the fog settled, you started running to get to the other end of the field. I timed it and made a dash just as the fog lifted and a machine gun opened up from the hill on my right side. I beat the bullets and got through a barbed wire fence and ran to a haystack. I thought I could catch my breath there. Just then, the haystack jumped in the air. I thought someone was firing at me. I looked around the haystack and there was one of our tank destroyers that had just fired. Up on the opposite hill, I could see a whole line of German tanks. The TD had just blown one up. I saw him hit another one, setting it on fire. A German tank returned fire and I could see this was no place for Owen Miller and went in the back door of a house into a room full of officers. I said, 'Excuse me!' and went out the front door into the center of town. I went up on the front step of the church to take a good gander. Just then, a shell hit the steeple. I couldn't see why they were chasing me so much. This went on all day in my hunt for wounded, to treat them and to get them to the aid station. There was a barn behind the church and an aid station that had a lot of wounded in it.

Unknown to the Americans, the Germans decided to jump off on their attack toward Noville at the same time. Major Desobry describes that action:

Much to our surprise, the Germans also picked 1400 hours to launch a major attack. So when we came boiling out of town, when the smoke cleared from our artillery preparation, out of the smoke came the Germans over the ridgeline. We were engaged in a head-on clash with whatever was out there.

The fight lasted from 1400 to about 1600. A very desperate flight. Towards the end of it, LaPrade and I realized that even if we did take the ridgeline, we were fighting too big a force to actually hold it. We were taking a lot of casualties with guys exposed out there and the men to the northeast, who had the ridgeline, were radioing they were under severe attack by tanks and panzer grenadiers and didn't think they could hold it.[31]

The combined American force was actually facing an entire German panzer division. The two commanders decided to pull their forces back into the relative protection of the strongly constructed buildings in Noville. The tank destroyers went into action, popping out from places of concealment behind buildings and in haystacks to fire at the enemy tanks whenever the fog lifted.

What T/5 Owen E. Miller had witnessed briefly, when he barged through one of the houses, was the gathering of Team Desobry officers with the line company commanders and their 1st Battalion commander. They had been making hasty plans for the defense of the town as they had been ordered to hold on to Noville.

A description of the "C" Company attack up the hill to the east of Noville, as it stalled, is given by company commander 1Lt. Edward Mehosky:

They were half way up (the hill) when enemy tanks appeared on the ridge and opened fire. My platoons continued to advance up the slope in the face of intense fire. The attack faltered, due to the heavy ground fire it was receiving and the battalion commander ordered a withdrawal to the edge of Noville. My platoons withdrew by fire and movement, leap-frogging back to where defensive positions would be taken.

During the process of withdrawing I observed the enemy following 'B' Company, which was withdrawing under heavy fire. I immediately deployed my reserve platoon along an embankment on the side of the road and hit the advancing enemy units with a punishing enfilade fire that stopped their

---

[31]ibid.

pursuit. They went reeling back to the ridgeline with severe losses. Although we were not able to obtain our primary objective, it was felt that neither were the Germans able to obtain theirs, especially with their numerically superior forces and armor attachments. Once back to our lines, we joined the rest of the battalion and the 10th Armored team in successfully establishing a perimeter around Noville.

Company 'C's' command post was located at the southeast corner of Noville. The company CP's seemed to ring the village while the Battalion CP was more to the center. Later, I was called to a situation briefing at Battalion, along with other company officers. The room we entered was dark because someone had decided to board up the windows and placed a wooden trunk in front of an opening for extra protection.

Major Robert F. Harwick, executive officer for 1st Battalion of the 506th Parachute Infantry Regiment had returned from Paris late on the afternoon of the 18th to find his battalion had already departed for Bastogne. He learned from a supply truck driver the route to use and Harwick left at 0800 the next morning. He traveled the 107 miles to Bastogne, arriving before noon and reported to regimental headquarters in Bastogne. From there he continued on foot to Noville. Dodging from building to building, he finally located the command post after getting directions at the aid station and picking up some necessary equipment. Harwick wrote:

I found our aid post first and picked up a helmet and carbine and directions to the Command Post. There was a continuous fire coming in; and, just after I left the doctor (Warren) to run up the road, he was hit by shrapnel.

The road was partially blocked by a huge fir tree. Just beyond that, a half-track was burning; across the street was a jeep partly buried in a fallen wall. Several houses were burning and beyond another half-track was flaming. The mortar shells kept falling through the smoke and bits of shrapnel and brick and tile whined incessantly. Now and then, a man would make a dash across the street or to one of the vehicles still intact.

The house used for the Command Post was still in good shape. In the living room, the Battalion Commander (LTC. James LaPrade) and a major, who commanded the armor which had been attached to the Battalion, along with the runners, a radio operator and an assortment of men and officers were talking. It seems the Battalion had tried to move onto the ridge, just north of the town, as a German force of 16 tanks and self-propelled guns tried to move into the village. The result was that they had the ridge and we had the town. The trouble was that they could shoot down on us and we had difficulty shooting up at them.

I reported in and started to set up a message center in an adjoining room and, in general, set up for operations. As I did this, a shell came through the window of the Command Post and I found myself in command of the forces in the town.[32]

After observing the paratrooper attack up the ridges to the north and east of Noville and the subsequent appearance of enemy tanks attacking over the crest of the ridges, Major Desobry had hurried back to the 1st Battalion CP in the center of town. The two commanders had been busy pouring over the maps with the assembled company commanders when the maintenance officer of the tank retrieval unit pulled up next to the command post and parked his vehicle there. A short time after the line company officers returned to their own command posts, the building was hit by an artillery shell. The enemy observer up on the commanding heights had apparently noticed the vehicle parked and assumed the building was some kind of headquarters and called down artillery fire on it. The fire missed the vehicle but hit the building. Colonel LaPrade was killed and Major Desobry was badly wounded, being hit in the face, head and one eye.

A seasoned officer and veteran company commander, Robert Harwick had been promoted to battalion executive officer for 1st Battalion at Mourmelon. It didn't take him long to size up the situation he now faced. He wrote:[33]

> There was a quick consultation with the new armor commander. We set up a defense around the town, spotted our tanks and tank destroyers and sent a report to Regimental Headquarters explaining the situation and asking for a doctor to replace the one who had been wounded.

Medical officer for 1st Battalion, Captain Joseph Warren and T/5 Owen E. Miller had been scurrying around giving aid and comfort to the injured and wounded around Noville during the afternoon shelling. Miller describes coming to the assistance of Captain Warren:

> Later in the day, I got Captain Warren when he was hit. He had wounds in both wrists. He told me not to cut his trench coat. I said I can't treat you otherwise. He asked me to take the coat off him and I did this with much difficulty. I got him to the aid station and that was the last I saw of him.

As a surgeon for 3rd Battalion of the 506th Regiment, Captain Bernard J. Ryan had been sent to Noville during the late afternoon of the 19th by General Gerald J. Higgins, assistant division commander, because 1st Battalion was suffering heavy casualties. Using a letter he had written to Major Louis Kent, the 506th Regimental surgeon in 1945, while recuperating from wounds to refresh his memory, Ryan described what happened during the few hours he was with 1st Battalion:

> On arriving in Noville, I took over the 1st Battalion aid station while Captain Joseph E. Warren, the battalion surgeon, proceeded into the town of

---

[32]From an account, *Christmas. . for Real!* written by Robert F. Harwick for the November-December, 1945 issue of *The Magazine of the Gulf Companies*, pp. 2-3.

[33]ibid.

Noville in the midst of a barrage. He was wounded almost immediately. Night was closing in with about fifty 1st Battalion casualties about the town. The battalion C.O., LTC. LaPrade had just been killed.

The line companies now moved into positions of perimeter defense about the town. "A" Company, which had been in reserve, now moved into positions on the north edge of town.

As a member of "A" Company, PFC. Donald Straith's group went into the town and to the northern edge near the cemetery where they set up defensive positions. In a personal account of his military operations in World War II, Straith related his impressions of the first day of combat:

Although I couldn't see enemy troops or tanks anywhere in the fields around Noville, the town was under an artillery attack as we entered. Spread out along the shoulders of the road and crouching low, we approached the crossroads that marked the center of town. Our road was flanked by two wrecked American half-tracks, the farther one still smoldering in front of the burned-out shell of a church, and a two-wheel ammunition trailer blazed in the middle of the intersection. Ahead of me, I could see a familiar knit cap bobbing along. Here we are – going into combat – and I realized that Jack Bram still had no helmet.

We skirted the fire, crossed the intersection and moved into a narrow, inclined lane between two of the buildings on our right. The column came to a stop as word was passed to halt where we were while we waited for the command to attack. We welcomed the brief chance to rest, relieve ourselves and, for some, to light a cigarette, but the command came all too soon. As some men were still trying to button their pants, we set off at a run through the passageway, past a couple of wall-to-wall houses and along the front wall of the town cemetery.

An officer stood at the cemetery gateway waving us in and, as I passed through, I saw ahead of me a low dirt ramp against the far wall. A G.I. stood peering over the wall while motioning for us to vault it at that point. I was only about halfway across the cemetery when the man at the wall suddenly turned and signaled for us to take cover, so I immediately dove between two gravestones and lay there waiting. I could hear heavy firing beyond the wall, and an occasional shell would pass overhead, one striking the side of a small mausoleum nearby. From various shouts I heard around me, I soon found out that those men who had crossed the wall were pinned down in the fields beyond and that forward movement had come to a standstill.[34]

---

[34]Straith, op. cit.

In an article which appeared in his hometown newspaper, PFC. Steve Polander, of the same unit, and probably the same platoon, described his actions from a little different viewpoint in the cemetery:

At 2 p.m. this afternoon, my company is attached to a unit of about 400 men or so as we approach the small village of Noville in double column along the main highway.

Word came down to halt as the front column reaches the base of the hill. An explosion takes place at the front of the column. Someone has stepped on a mine.

The road led up the village hill with houses on both sides and a large red barn at the top on the left side.

Everyone knows something is up. A man about half way up the hill, dressed in civilian clothes, is seen by all as he walks from the left side of a house to the right side, looking down at us. He enters the house as we move in, then all hell breaks loose.

Long range artillery starts pouring in, with precision accuracy. They rake the village hill for about 14 continuous hours and, hidden on the fringes, German tanks pour 88mm timed shells mixed in with heavy artillery.

I find myself lying against a thick concrete wall enclosing a graveyard. A shell explodes on top of it and the concussion knocks me senseless. When I come to, I don't know where I am. I stumble and stagger to get to the top of the hill. I find myself next entering a small chicken coop that seemed to be attached to the barn. Inside sits a young man, on what looked like a block of wood, his back to me. His skull on the upper right side has been totally torn off by a huge chuck of shrapnel. His brains are showing the the medic kneels, dabbing his skull. The village is on fire and we are continually being pinned down, all, that is, except the barn with the cows and horses that lie within, dead and bleeding from shrapnel.

I finally reach an area near the top where I dig in about a foot and a half deep, about 40 yards straight up from the barn. As darkness begins setting in, I lay flat on my stomach and an 88 air burst explodes above me. I feel my head hitting the bottom of the hole. A piece of shrapnel about the size of a quarter tears into the upper backside of my steel helmet, tears up the liner in a circular motion and drops out. It cuts a path in my hair no more than a quarter inch from my skull.[35]

Over in the "C" Company area of the perimeter defense, PFC. Robert Wiatt is sent out to see what his platoon is faced with in that section of the line. He writes:

---

[35]From a story about Steve Polander which appeared in his home town newspaper, *Berwick Press-Enterprise*, dated August 9, 1985.

After a brief pause, we were told to go into Noville and make contact with the enemy. 'C' Company was to be on the right side of town so I and a new replacement, Pvt. Henry Lugo, were sent down the right side of the main street to see what was going on. We went along a stone wall around a church to a corner that went off to the right. By this time, we were drawing small arms fire so we took cover behind a burned-out half-track. At this point, I told Lugo to run back to tell the company what we had run into. As Lugo left the cover of the half-track and started back down the road, he drew a lot of fire. Like most of us, it scared the hell out of him so he turned back to the half-track and threatened to shoot me for trying to get him killed. I had to do some fast talking to make him calm down. Realizing that we could not stay where we were, we went over the stone wall and back to the company which was moving up the right side of town.

When platoon leader 1Lt. Joe Reed, of "C" Company, had been ordered to fall back from the ridge line and set up a perimeter defense at the edge of town he was surprised to learn that they would retreat no further.

The regimental order at that time was to hold Noville at all costs. There would be no withdrawal. We just looked at each other. It was obvious we were very much outgunned. The Battalion went into defensive positions on the edge of town. 'C' Company covered the left part of the Battalion front. My platoon was the left flank of the company at the edge of town.

Due to the fog, sometimes we could see and sometimes we couldn't. It was about this time, two buildings from us, Lt. Colonel LaPrade opened the door and went in. Kraut shells came through a window and killed him. A 705th Tank Destroyer was located with me to help protect the Battalion left flank. The only problem was, he was all out of AP (armor piercing) ammo, only had HE (high explosive) left, which couldn't penetrate the Kraut armor. The Krauts were trying to pull back some infantry way up on a hillside to our front from one strip of woods to another about two hundred yards apart. I asked my machine gunner, Henry Barrett, if he thought he could reach them. In between the fog rolling in and out, he was able to catch some Krauts in the open and laid out about eight or nine or them on the hillside. In the meantime, the Kraut tanks were getting a little aggressive to my front and I helped the tank commander pick targets of opportunity. We were able to knock the track off one tank. It's crew jumped out, but immediately another tank used the disabled tank as a shield and knocked out our TD. The tank commander was on fire when he got out. We put the fire out and a medic took over. My sector quieted down when it began to darken. During the night Krauts tried to probe into town but, due to debris on the road, they had problems. I understand some of our troops were able to knock out a couple tanks for their efforts.

As he traveled back and forth between his company CP and the Battalion Headquarters, 1Lt. Edward Mehosky noted a number of abandoned vehicles of various kinds scattered about Noville and out beyond the perimeter defenses, which had been set up in the late afternoon when the troops fell back from the ridgelines. He was about to get "wheels" for his unit. He wrote:

Having come to and from meetings at Battalion, I passed many abandoned tanks, vehicles and armored personnel carriers. I decided to commandeer the damn things rather than leave them to the enemy. They could be very useful to me, provided I had drivers. The diversity of the airborne trooper was again obvious as I asked for, and got, drivers for these vehicles. 'C' Company now had a jeep, a half-track, a Sherman Tank and a 2-1/2 -ton truck.

An abandoned Sherman tank near their forward position became a prize the new "C" Company commander, 1Lt. Ed Mehosky, wanted his men to retrieve. He had sent a runner to T/4 James J. Cadden's position, asking that he report to the CP. Cadden was asked if he had ever been in the armored forces. Cadden related a weird story:

Not knowing what the company commander meant, I told him so, whereupon he asked me to accompany a 'tank driver' to retrieve an abandoned Sherman tank out in front of the 3rd Platoon sector. With apprehension, I agreed and was escorted outside and introduced to Pvt. Fred Zavosky, of my platoon's 3rd squad, and was informed he would operate the tank. We proceeded to the 3rd Platoon sector, which was being raked with shell fire and observed the Sherman tank, which was sitting about 150-200 yards out in the field. We crouched and crawled toward the vehicle and suddenly were joined by Sgt. Ted Hintz, a squad sergeant in 3rd Platoon. We made our way out to the tank and entered the open hatches. Zavosky jumped into the driver's seat, I into the machine gunner's position and Ted Hintz in the turret. As we were entering the Sherman tank, the Krauts obviously saw us and began firing. (Note: It was at this point that I learned that Zavosky knew nothing about tanks and when I asked him when in the hell he was going to start the tank, he responded that he was familiar with farm tractors and they operated like tanks.)

After flicking on a vertical panel of toggle switches, he probed around and found the starter. The tank started with a roar. Then, Zavosky finally got the thing into low gear and we started jerking and heaving forward. Both Hintz and I commenced yelling for him to turn the thing away from the Kraut tanks and he turned two protruding steering rods back and forth and we made an abrupt turn and heaved and jerked back toward the 3rd Platoon area. The turret cannon was turned at a 50-degree angle and neither me nor Hintz could straighten it to point forward, while we were jerking along.

As we approached 3rd Platoon, Zavosky had lost control of the tank movement and could only direct its steering mechanism. The 3rd Platoon guys scattered in various directions as we came upon them. We knocked over chicken coops and hog pens and then, we drove onto the street with the tank cannon scraping buildings, causing the tank to tilt. Some tankers came out in the street in front of us, pumping their arms up and down, apparently trying to guide us and we almost ran over them. At an intersection, several troopers waved to us to stop and we realized a tank fire exchange was going on between a tank destroyer and a German tank on the intersecting street and we jerked through the intersection. We then rammed head on into a shell-damaged, rock-style house which finally stopped the tank as it stalled out. If we weren't in such a helluva fight, I'd have punched Zavosky in the nose. We could have killed some of the guys, if not ourselves. It was a parallel, with a Max Sennett 'Keystone Cops' caper that you saw years ago in the movies.

Over in the "B" Company defensive positions, PFC. Robert Flory recalled the pullback from the hill and learned a schoolmate had been killed, then to a listening post adventure:

Shortly after that, we were ordered back down the hill and placed in a line of defense in the north part of town. That's when I learned that a schoolmate of mine, Sgt. Johnny York, had been killed. The order came to dig in deep and when the attack came the next morning, we were to let the tanks roll over us and kill the infantry following the tanks. Before we could start digging in, my squad was ordered to move into a barn about 100 yards to our front to act as a listening post. We moved in just before dark and closed the big double doors facing the north. We could see through the cracks and had a good view of what was going on because a German tank was burning just down the road.

At about 2100 hours, we could hear another tank approaching. It pulled up just outside our door, swung that big 88 around facing the barn door and shut his motor off. I swear that tank looked as big as a battleship. We had no bazooka and you just don't fight a tank with grenades and a machine gun. We could hear the Krauts talking inside the tank. I asked Sgt. Lee Rogers what was going to happen. He said, 'Any fool should know that come daybreak, he's going to blow this barn to hell so he can get that tank destroyer up in town.'

I volunteered to leave the barn and go back to the defense line and let everyone know what was going to happen, but Rogers turned me down. All this time, we were whispering. Then something happened that is etched in my memory. We hadn't had anything to eat for over 36 hours and I was famished. Suddenly, I could smell bologna! One of the new men was eating bologna and wasn't going to share it! Later, I found out who it was. To this day, I still crave bologna.

After he returned from his forward post near a burning half-track, PFC. Robert Wiatt got himself another weapon, which he would put to good use. He recalled:

I found an armored infantryman who had a bazooka and some ammunition, which he did not want to use, so I took it because I was sure it would do more damage than my M1. As we worked our way around the left side of town and on towards the high ground beyond, we got some fire from a house on the left side of the main road. Two shells from my bazooka broke that up. As we advanced up the high ground, we came under very heavy fire. We had to back off and dig in.

About this time, we got a very heavy pounding from enemy artillery. I was deep in a hole (as I often was), but wondering if any of the company could have survived. Near dark, things were a bit quiet and we moved into a defensive position at the southern end of Noville. After I got a good, deep hole dug, I was instructed to make contact with the outpost in front of us. I found one group, all new replacements, who were not dug in. I told them they had better dig fast and deep. On my next round, I found that this group of three had dug holes but were not in them because they were wet and muddy. I later found that two of these men were killed by artillery; they were not in their holes.

Platoon leader Al Hassenzahl had passed the house in which 1st Battalion commander LTC. James LaPrade had just been killed. The Germans had counter-attacked and driven his men off the ridge, east of town. He wrote:

We were forced to withdraw to the outskirts of Noville. There we set up a perimeter defense and our orders were to hold Noville at all costs. At this point I began to wonder if any of us would get out of this combat situation alive. But, hold Noville we did. We held it all night.

Members of "A" Company were positioned in the vicinity of the cemetery on the north edge of town. PFC. Donald B. Straith describes what it was like during his first evening and night of combat on December 19th:[36]

As evening approached, activity in the area decreased to scattered, small arms fire and intermittent artillery rounds dropped in and around town. There being no point in lying where we were, Ed Cavanaugh, another 'A' Company man, and I started out to find out what was going on. Several of our men had dug slit trenches in the cemetery alongside a house that formed one wall, then had tilted gravestones over them, against the house, to provide shelter from shell fragments. Although Ed and I did our best to talk our way in with them, they refused our request and, at the same time adding

---

[36]Straith, op. cit.

insult to injury, relayed the latest rumor – that the Germans were taking no prisoners. With our spirits sagging even more from this unwelcome news, the two of us wandered out through the cemetery gateway.

The town seemed almost deserted, but we soon ran into a man from our mortar squad who was out looking for more mortar ammunition. After informing us that Colonel LaPrade, our battalion commander, had been killed by one of the German shells, he asked us to help him in his search. We reluctantly agreed to do so and turned down the same lane we had come up in the afternoon, pausing to make use of an outhouse behind the first house next to the cemetery. It was now getting dark rapidly and, as we started down the lane again, another soldier stepped from a shadowy doorway of one of the houses and told us to go inside.

The house was typical of the area, with the garage and cowshed sharing a common wall. In this latter space, an elderly man and woman and a couple of children had taken refuge. Meanwhile, in the kitchen, two or three women busily prepared bread, butter and jam which they insisted on serving, at a table in the next room, to any of us who happened to enter. As we relaxed there briefly, enjoying our first food since leaving camp, I could not help but be amazed at the courage of these women. I felt that I would be eternally grateful to them for their kindness. This family, the Copines, was left homeless the following night when the house was struck by a shell and burned to the ground. Although uninjured, M. Copine and his daughters (the others in the shed were neighbors) lost everything but the clothes they were wearing.

A short time later we left and, at someone's instructions, made our way to a house on the north edge of town. There we were, teamed up with another young soldier named Cunningham and sent to occupy an observation post a hundred yards or so out in a field. This consisted of a hole about a foot deep and just wide enough for the three of us. With our rifles resting on the edge of the hole, we lay there cold and scared, our nerves taut, staring into the darkness and waiting.

A burning haystack some distance to our left front provided only a slight amount of light. From time to time, we could hear the rumbling and rattling of tanks maneuvering in the night, but the dim light revealed nothing. We grew colder and I regretted having thrown away my overcoat. I had left camp with no gloves, so Cavanaugh loaned me an extra pair of his with the admonition to return them later. This I assured him I would do. Although we were nervous and apprehensive as well as tired, our fatigue caused us to doze off occasionally, waking with a start each time our heads drooped and our helmets hit the ground.

Suddenly, we detected movement out in front of us and, as my heart pounded, I thought to myself, 'Here they come!' In a moment or two, we could make out two helmeted figures crawling toward us. Cunningham and I raised our rifles and, taking aim, were about to fire when Cavanaugh's arm shot out and pushed our weapons down again. He whispered a challenge to the two shadowy figures and, to my surprise and consternation, received the correct reply. We had been a fraction of a second from killing two of our own men. As they crawled on past, they told us they had been a forward listening post, a little fact about which no one had informed us. Because they didn't know what was happening, they had decided to withdraw and, because our condition was the same, we shortly followed their example.

After being directed up a slope and through a low hedge, we dug in for what was left of the night.[37]

## 3RD BATTALION HEADS FOR FOY

It didn't bode well for the 3rd Battalion troops as they moved forward as hundreds of other soldiers were retreating as both passed each other along the highway. There was some indecision on the part of the officers as they neared Foy as to where the defensive positions were to be set. PFC. Guy D. Jackson recalled that first day:

As we proceeded out of Bastogne, heading for Foy, things didn't look too good. Other outfits were coming straggling down the road and we hadn't had much sleep the past night. Everybody was kind of down and out. Foy lies down in a valley. South of Foy there is a rise and there was a little hill. We were stopped there, in the afternoon, deployed in a field to the left of the road, close to some woods. There seemed to be a lot of confusion among the officers, as if they were arguing on what positions to take. For a few minutes, it looked like we were going to dig in the open field and have the woods around us and the Germans could just come up and blow us away. I was kind of uptight about that. They did move us out of there. We wound up more or less in the tree line where you face Foy and have a clear field of fire. From the road to the left, they deployed my company – I wasn't sure if any of the Battalion was deployed on the right side of the road. The 1st Battalion was up there in Noville and heavily engaged.

1Lt. Alex Andros had the 3rd Platoon of "H" Company in the Ardennes fight. He describes the actions in which his group was involved during the day in the Foy vicinity:

We had about 1,500 yards of front to cover as a platoon. We dug our holes 100 to 150 yards apart. The trees were so thick, you could have marched a regiment through the space between two foxholes. Finally, the

---

[37]Straith, op. cit.

enemy started infiltrating through. We did some firing at them but not a lot. We had to move back because 'E' Company, of the 2nd Battalion, was coming through our position. They came through just as we were pulling out. We didn't see a helluva lot of combat that first day – did get to fire at a few guys.

We pulled back to the high ground south of Foy and we were on the left (west) side of the road. On our side of the road was a little concrete house.

1Lt. Harry Begle was assistant leader of 2nd Platoon under 1Lt. Clark Heggeness. The Bastogne mission was the first for Begle, with the 101st Division. He describes his actions for the late afternoon of the 19th:

On the first day, late in the afternoon, when it was getting dark, I cannot remember if we had a password. Clark Heggeness gave me a map and said, 'Find that railroad track and tie in with the 501st.' I had about six men and I was placing them along a dirt road, which was to the right, and I was to the right of Stroud's platoon. I walked up to the edge of the woods some 300 to 500 yards and still didn't see any railroad tracks. We had a big front to cover. I got back and told Clark I never did find the railroad track. It was cold and there was a haystack, so we bedded down for the night in it. The Battalion HQ was in a brick farmhouse about 200 yards to the rear of the haystack.

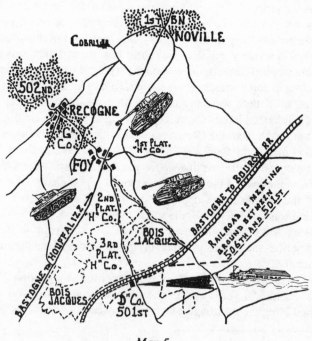

*Map 5*

1Lt. Robert Stroud, of the 1st Platoon of "H" Company was concerned about the expanse of territory his group was assigned to cover. He related:

I deployed my platoon on the right side of the road, just below the heights of a hill. I deployed with Vecchi's squad on the left and Bob Martin's squad on the right. I was told to deploy my platoon to reach a railroad to our right. It was over quite a ways and Bob Martin came back to tell me they were having a helluva time reaching the place. We had Hank DiCarlo's squad in reserve. I had to deploy all three squads on line – we had so much area to cover.

Somehow, PFC. Ewell B. Martin was in the right place at the wrong time, or the wrong place at the right time, as he happened to be near the 506th regimental commander, Colonel Robert F. Sink, on the evening of the 19th. Martin wrote:

On the night of December 19, Colonel Sink picked me up with another 'G' Company man to go into Noville with him. I can recall looking for possible snipers while the Colonel was standing up in his jeep looking around the town from the middle of the street. The town was burning and that smell is something I guess you never forget.

During the days preceding departure for the Ardennes, Pvt. John Kilgore had been practicing for the coming Christmas Day football game against the 502nd Parachute Regiment. Now he was going into combat with a platoon leader who was new to the regiment and knew only two members of the platoon – those two men were Privates John G. Kilgore and Albert Gray, both members of his football squad. The platoon leader was one of the coaches for the 506th team. Kilgore didn't think much of the situation. He wrote:

On the evening of the 19th, we arrived in the piney woods and started to dig in defensive positions outside a cross-road hamlet of Recogne, several miles from Bastogne.

Guess who was the newly assigned platoon leader? Lt. Fitzpatrick! Guess who he knew in the platoon? Right – Gray and Kilgore. Guess who was picked for the patrol the first night – right – Gray and Kilgore. Guess who was picked to spearhead the advance the next day? Right – Gray and Kilgore.

'Jesus Christ, Lieutenant!! Will you please learn someone else's name in the platoon!' He did.

(Albert Gray was taken prisoner while on patrol New Year's Eve and we heard, found shot in the head, execution style, in Germany several months later. 1Lt. Lawrence Fitzpatrick was killed instantly by machine gun fire leading a patrol across a river months later in a different place. John Kilgore zipped when the bullets zagged and came home. He never played football again.)

Members of "G" Company were the first to feel pressure near Recogne, on the 19th, as described by PFC. James H. Martin, who wrote:

The enemy hit the 1st Platoon on our right flank, opposite Foy. They came in under rolling ground fog, early in the evening, with troops and tanks. Our 2nd Platoon was pulled over to help because 1st was getting pressed hard. They (enemy) finally broke through and we were ordered to pull back to a wooded high point to regroup and counter-attack. As we came back, there was Sgt. Stan Clever, all by himself on the machine gun, still stacking them up. He either didn't hear the order or ignored it. I'm convinced that if he had not stayed we would not have been able to repulse the enemy. He got a Bronze Star for the action.

The comment of S/Sgt. Stan B. Clever for the December 19th action was very simply put: "German infantry and two tanks came in with the fog. We fought a delayed action to give the company a chance to dig in on the high ground, south of Foy."

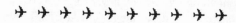

## THE RESERVE UNITS

Accompanied by his regimental S-3, Captain James J. Hatch and his driver, Colonel Steve Chappuis, left early on the afternoon of December 18 so as to be at his assembly area before the troops arrived. Enroute, they had encountered Brigadier General Gerald J. Higgins. The deputy division commander had just arrived from England and was at Division Headquarters when a directive arrived stating that the 101st would go to Bastogne rather than proceed further north to Werbomont.

Their jeep had been passed by General Higgins as he rushed forward to notify the lead elements to move toward Bastogne rather than continue on to their previous destination. Chappuis had been directed to the proper assembly area by the MP's, Colonel Tom Sherburne and General Higgins.

Captain Jim Hatch continues his story of the arrival in the Bastogne area where Chappuis had an opportunity to interrogate the acting 101st Division plans and operation chief. Hatch wrote:

After daylight, we ran into Colonel Harry Kinnard, Division G-3, at Corps HQ. They had already organized advance parties to locate the unit assembly areas. We started on Harry to see what he could do about getting maps of the area. It wasn't long before the 101st troops began arriving.

PFC. Ted Goldmann was getting his first test of combat in the next several days. He remembers the arrival in the Bastogne area as a member of "A" Company:

Just before dawn on the 19th, we disembarked and set out on foot. We could have been in China for all we knew. We hadn't seen any towns, as the men had somehow managed to drop off to sleep. We marched about two miles to a bare hill (it seemed a hell of a place to us) and sat down. We dug shallow holes, filled them with straw, built fires and ate K-rations.

Working with his regimental commander, Captain Jim Hatch was busy during the morning as he and Colonel Steve Chappuis checked out the perimeter area, which had been assigned to the 502nd Regiment. Hatch wrote:

I don't recall any real problem with the 502nd units since it appeared we would be one of the last ones to be committed to action. Steve and I would visit each unit as they were committed around Bastogne and had a pretty good idea of the terrain and what the Germans were putting up in the way of troops and tanks, etc. We could take the battalion commanders with us and they would then take their company commanders around.

Once the battalion commanders knew the extent of their perimeter assignments, there was often some adjusting and moving platoons about. Such was the recollection of PFC. Ted Goldmann. He wrote:

After many stops and starts and at about 11 o'clock at night (darkness at 5), we stopped just outside a small village (Monaville) and were given a squad area and told to dig in and set up the MG and try to get some sleep. We had a tree-lined gulley so we didn't do any digging, threw the MG up on the edge of the gulley, set one at a time on guard and to hell with the Germans – went to sleep.

## A MORTAR OUTPOST

The 3rd Battalion of the 502nd Parachute Infantry Regiment had just arrived in the area assigned to them. Mortar platoon leader, 1Lt. Ray Brock describes his first action:

We moved into the area to be defended by 3rd Battalion in late afternoon and the company commander told me where he wanted the 81mm mortars placed. I told Platoon sergeant Karol Southard to see that the mortars and the men were dug in and I took a corporal and we started stringing communications wire from the position up to the OP, which was a few hundred yards ahead of the mortar positions. It was getting dark by the time we got the OP set up.

A half-track about 50 yards to my right opened fire with a 75mm on some German armored units about 3/4 of a mile away on a ridge. The

Germans returned the fire so the half-track being out-gunned, wheeled, pulled out of position and left.

I was on my hands and knees selecting predetermined targets on my map in the remaining dim light when a shell hit the tree above me. I was knocked down and stunned but fortunately, not hit. My corporal, who had dug a foxhole, was resting in his sleeping bag. I commented, 'That was close!' There was no response so I went over to him and found that he had been killed by the shrapnel from the tree burst. His position was only about ten feet from where I was.

A single, thin communication wire was often the only contact between a forward observer and his back-up forces. One gets a very lonely feeling when nothing is heard at the other end of the line – especially since the line had just been run. A change had occurred at company level while Brock was setting up his OP. He continued:

Later, I lost phone contact with the platoon so I assumed the wire had been cut by shell fire. There weren't any troops around my OP as the rifle companies had selected positions elsewhere and my OP was on the edge of the tree line on a road running from Recogne to Monaville.

I spent the night alone and cold and, as soon as it became light enough to see, started back towards the platoon position, splicing wire as I went. When I neared the platoon position, I was shocked to find no one there except a badly wounded supply sergeant who was unable to communicate. I knew where the Germans were so started in the opposite direction. I had gone about 200 to 300 yards when I met the platoon coming up to look for me. Unbeknown to me, the company commander decided that his position was too exposed so pulled back to a position that could be better defended but didn't feel he could send someone to find me and the corporal in the darkness.

## CHATEAU ROLLE

The headquarters command post for the 502nd Parachute Infantry Regiment was set up in a large 16th century building complex about a kilometer south and east of Champs.

From an excerpt of a V-Mail letter Captain Joseph Pangerl wrote to his parents on December 30, 1944, he describes the setting at Chateau Rolle, which served as the command post during the siege:[38]

---

[38]Though the V-Mail letter had a December 30, 1944 date, it was not mailed until later when censorship was lifted for that period.

Just now, I am in a beautiful 17th century castle which also serves as my home. It has been modernized but, naturally, still has the three-foot thick walls all around and you know what that means in combat dad. In front of this castle is the former castle; this one of the 10th century. The first few days here I spent quite a lot of time going around taking pictures at all sorts of angles. The setting here is much like a Hollywood one. We are on a small hill with hills all around us, covered with pine forests. There are the small lakes and rushing brooks that you always associate with such a setting and the fact that it snowed over a week ago and all the snow is still on the ground makes everything look like a Xmas postcard.

One of the radio operators providing communications at Chateau Rolle was T/4 Robert J. Harle who had a good vantage point from which he witnessed much of the action. He wrote:

As a radio operator, I held forth during the encirclement in the small woodshed. My buddy, Russ Miller, and myself dug in our radio and surrounded ourselves with a low wall of firewood. We each gave up a blanket to be used by the wounded in the stables across the courtyard. On occasion, the Germans would unleash a round or two from what must have been a huge artillery piece and these shells, when they passed overhead, sounded like they were tumbling end over end. Most passed harmlessly over and detonated in the valley to one side of the chateau. Once in a while though, rounds of smaller caliber made their way into the courtyard, causing minor damage and frayed nerves.

From our vantage point, we could keep tabs on all the goings-on in the courtyard. Captain Stone would come and go, twirling his thin, but elaborate moustache. He holed up in a cellar under one of the stone buildings. Communications people occupied every available nook and cranny – barns, attics, basements and haystacks in the compound sheltered a wide variety of troopers. Wounded took up a large area in the stables; S-2 people and demo personnel shared available space with medics and men from the wire gangs. Parts of existing supplies were spread out under tarps on a sloping hillside, just outside the walls. I seem to recall at least one 6 x 6 truck parked just outside the main gates and under it one or two deep foxholes had been dug. Occasional cigarette smoke and muffled conversation would drift out from under there but I never did actually see the occupants. Later on, someone told me that there were two of them and that they weren't from the 101st.

## THE 401ST COVERS THE WEST

The 1st Battalion of the 401st Glider Infantry was given a new designation for the Ardennes fighting. Henceforth, in the official annals, it was to be known as the 3rd Battalion of the 327th Glider Infantry Regiment. Its commander was LTC. Ray C. Allen. During this account, we will continue to identify this unit by its former designation as the veterans of the earlier campaigns are more familiar with "Able", "Baker" and "Charley" Companies of the 401st Glider Infantry Battalion.

In a lengthy story he had written of his wartime experiences in 1946, when the actions were still fresh in his mind, PFC. Richard V. Bostwick has this description of the detrucking of his unit as the 401st was the last of the infantry battalions to arrive on the scene near Mande St. Etienne. He wrote:

We were told the Krauts could come from any direction; the front was everywhere. The company was extended in a ditch, along a gentle rise of slope. This gave us a rise over which we could see without being seen. We dug in much like a bunch of gophers, as the trucks, now empty, circled around in the fields and returned to France. We pulled out from that position before a foxhole could be completed.

Late the same day, we rendezvoused with Company 'C' and set up a road block at an intersection on the 'Red Ball Highway' since this was a main supply route and an open road to France, should the Krauts gain control. I bitched about the poor foxhole location; the bottom of a ravine. Orders were to stay alert – no one was to sleep.

1Lt. Ralph K. Nelson, of "A" Company, had spent 70 days in hospitals in England recovering from machine pistol wounds received on June 7th in the Normandy fighting. He had recovered in time to make the airborne mission into Holland and was wounded again while crossing the railroad bridge at Veghel but recovered in time to participate in the fighting around Opheusden. Nelson describes how his unit brought up the rear as they arrived in the Bastogne area and got into defensive positions:

The 401st was the last battalion to close the ring at Bastogne and my platoon was the rear guard for 'A' Company, which was the rear guard for Battalion. We took up a reverse slope defense so the Krauts could not see us until they came over the brink of the hill. We outposted with a few men to observe the enemy.

As "C" Company moved into its sector of the perimeter defense west of Mande St. Etienne, two of its platoons had non-coms as leaders. No officers had been assigned to them as replacements. S/Sgt. Robert M. Bowen positioned the men of his 3rd Platoon almost immediately after arriving in the vicinity. He provides a detailed description of how he placed his men as well as a description of the company meeting involving the platoon leaders and the company commander:

I saw to the dispersal of my squads and returned to dig in. I studied the surroundings as I dug my slit trench. There were rolling hills, patches of forest and open farm land. To the west was a great hill that ran north and south with a large patch of forest to the east. We were in a valley hidden by the hills but in a poor defensive position. The weather was typically December in a temperate zone, in the forties and overcast. In the not-too-distant hills, sounds of booming artillery echoed hollowly.

A call came over our SCR-300 radio asking me to report to the Company CP. As I hiked up the road, I could see 'A' and 'B' Companies moving out. Evidently, the Battalion had been committed. The CP was in a garage of a small stone house beside the road. Captain Towns possessed the only map in the company of the area. We gathered around him as he pointed out the positions each platoon would occupy. He finished the briefing with: 'There have been reports of the enemy here.' He ran his finger along the ridgeline to the northwest. 'The troops holding the MLR have been routed so look for stragglers filtering back from the north. The 28th, 99th and 106th Divisions were completely overwhelmed. Many of them were captured. We have some reports of German troops dressed in American uniforms. Challenge everyone and make goddamn sure who they are before you let them into your position.'

I returned to my platoon and called the squad leaders. We were to set up a roadblock on a secondary road to the northwest. The 1st and 2nd Platoons set up blocks on the road from Bastogne with the mortars in a wooded area in the rear of the CP. We had too much ground to cover for the size of our decimated platoon. I had Jerry Hans dig his squad in on the road. They overlooked open fields and a distant tree patch. Felker's squad was dug in on a ridge line to Hans' left, with Leamon's men spread out along the same ridge to Felker's left. There was a gap of 400 yards to 2nd Platoon's position, which would have to be covered at night by patrolling. I put Sgt. Andy Mitchell and his 60mm mortar squad in defilade position on a reverse slope overlooking our front. I set up my CP there, also.

The platoon dug in with our one bazooka covering an unimproved road, which led to the northwest. We had three shells for it. 1st Platoon dug in an orchard south of the main road, several hundred yards west of Mande St. Etienne. 2nd Platoon's position was several hundred yards farther west on the same road, entrenched south of the road, also. At its rear, on high ground, was a large stone house with its surrounding out-buildings. Huge fir trees surrounded the house with a wide brick pavement leading from the road to a central court. A 37mm anti-tank gun was stationed among the fir trees, covering the road to the west. A tank destroyer was assigned to the company and took position in the courtyard and a Sherman tank moved up and parked on the east side of the house. It took most of the day to get our defenses in place.

During the afternoon, S/Sgt. Robert Bowen reported to the Company CP to pick up rations for his men. Non-coms from the other platoons were also present for the same purpose. The company commander and his executive officer were in the garage going over the only map available to the unit. Both men had grim, worried looks on their faces. Bowen added:

Captain Towns said heavy fighting had been reported in the 501st and 506th areas and that tanks had been reported heading in our direction. He warned me to be especially alert at night with half the men on guard at all times.

As we settled in for the night, the sound of gunfire was all around us, but most heavy in the north and east. The night was cold with a bitter wind coming in over the valley to our front and into our foxholes. Twice, I left my CP to visit each squad. There were no reports of enemy activity.

The 327/401st glidermen covered a ten-mile front, almost half of the entire defensive perimeter of Bastogne. Patrols were sent out as far as three to six miles to the west and south to probe for German positions and movements. To "B" Company, under Captain Robert J. McDonald, went the long range patrol assignment. From their initial defensive position, southeast of Flamierge, they would be ordered, after midnight, to move west.

## FIELD HOSPITAL CAPTURED

As indicated earlier, in the order of the road march of the convoy of vehicles carrying the 101st Airborne Division to the assembly area near Mande St. Etienne, the 326th Medical Company was near the tail end of the long column.

T/5 George Whitfield remembered the trip to Bastogne as he was driving the jeep for 1Lt. Henry Barnes, the last remaining medical evacuation officer left from the original four who started with the company in Normandy on D-Day. Whitfield describes how their part of the convoy became separated from the lead elements and Lt. Barnes ended up leading the rest of the convoy to the assembly area.

On our way to Belgium, we stopped for a break alongside the road. We expected the truck ahead of us to pull out any minute but they sat there till morning. A jeep came by with one of our surgeons in the front passenger seat. He told Lt. Barnes that most of the convoy had left during the night and he should lead us to where the Medical Company was ahead of us in Belgium.

By the time the remainder of the 326th Medical Company convoy neared the Bastogne area, the on-coming road traffic was sticking to its own side of the road, thanks to the efforts of General Gerald J. Higgins and Colonel Thomas Sherburne. T/5 George Whitfield comments further on the trip:

Every town we went through, the MP's waved us on. We seemed to have priority over everybody going north. Within an hour or so, Major Barfield and the first sergeant came along and led us to where the Medical Company was located. We unhooked our trailers and waited at the company compound till the other drivers made a run out to where the regiments were located. One of the drivers came back for us before nightfall and we arrived at the 502nd.

As the medical evacuation officer of the 326th who was assigned to work closely with the 502nd Parachute Infantry Regiment, 1Lt. Henry Barnes went off immediately to find the location of the 502nd. He wrote:

I left the company there and went on into Bastogne to find the location of the 502nd Regimental Headquarters so I could locate the regimental aid station. In an hour or so, I had located Major (Douglas) Davidson and went back for the balance of my six jeeps and seven trailers.

PFC. Robert "Buck" Barger was assigned to provide evacuation from the 1st Battalion, 506th aid station, back to the 326th medical field hospital as he had done in Holland during that 72-day campaign earlier. The troops of 1st Battalion had left several hours earlier and Barger and his team leader were on their way to catch up with them. Barger recalled:

Upon arrival in the Bastogne area, I was reassigned, along with S/Sgt. Jack Galt, as part of a medical team to the 1st Battalion of the 506th Parachute Infantry Regiment, under the command of Captain Joseph E. Warren, surgeon for that battalion.

We moved up to the town of Noville, in a northeasterly direction from Bastogne – not many miles further. 1st Battalion was going to kick off an attack around 1330-1400 hours.

Meanwhile, back at the site selected as the location for the 326th Field Hospital, work went on quickly to prepare the facilities for the expected casualties, which would begin arriving shortly after the 101st troops had made contact with the enemy.

As a member of the 3rd Auxiliary Surgical Team, T/4 Emil K. Natalle had already participated in the glider landings in Normandy and Holland in support of the 326th Medical Company. Now he describes the beginning of this third venture:

The convoy arrived at the pre-designated area near Bastogne about 10:00 a.m. I was not oriented regarding the area's location in relation to the larger radius.

Soon after arrival, our tent crews hoisted the canvas, mess tent, headquarters tent, surgical tent, ward tents, the works. Meanwhile, during the feverish set-up activity, gun fire was to be heard to the east of us. Most of us had a hunch that we were in vulnerable terrain. Our location was at a crossroads, probably south and west of Bastogne. Our site was totally exposed, no cover, just open space.

As one of the surgeons who had worked long and hard in the 326th field hospitals in both Normandy and Holland, Captain Willis P. McKee was very uncomfortable with the positioning of the field unit so far from the 101st Division, west of Bastogne. He remembered they were receiving casualties by early afternoon. He wrote:

Before long, we were receiving casualties. Sometime around noon, Major (William) Barfield, our CO, left to find an evacuation hospital to which we could evacuate our casualties. Captain Ed. C. Yeary was then in charge. We were aware the civilians were passing our installations with their possessions and assumed that something was pushing them. About 1600 hours, I went into Division HQ and asked permission for us to move into Bastogne, explaining that I thought we were in danger of being overrun and that Division would then be without 3rd echelon medical care. We went into the war room and, after considerable discussion, General McAuliffe said, 'Go on back, Captain – you'll be all right.'

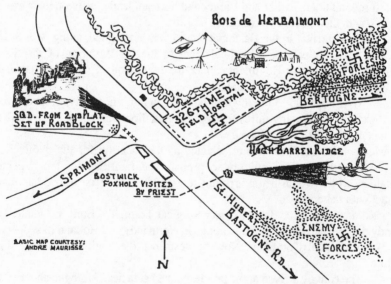

*Crossroads "X" – Site of Division Field Hospital*
*Map 6*

The evacuation team sent to 1st Battalion of the 506th Regiment was busy shortly after the opposing troops began exchanging gun fire. PFC. Robert Barger describes how the 1st Battalion surgeon was among the early casualties suffered that afternoon. He wrote:

There was a very hectic fire fight. I know that upon occasion I walked right by some German soldiers. We set up an aid station in a house. Captain Warren was hit and I evacuated him back to the 326th Field Hospital, west of Bastogne. That trip was made at 1500 hours.

Later on, I was with the chaplain of the 506th and we had loaded two litter cases up on the jeep and about that time a barrage came in and the chaplain and I covered the two litter cases with our bodies until it got so hot we hit the deck behind a brick wall. I guess it wasn't funny but I said, 'Father, will you please pray for us?' He said, 'Barger, I've got enough to just pray for myself, you've got to help a bit.'

About 1700 hours, it was beginning to get dark and we had to move these patients back to the medical company. The regiment was in a poor position and they would most likely have to pull back. There were three jeeps. I had a driver and four walking wounded. The third had a driver and two walking wounded. We took off.

Captain Gordon L. Block had been serving with the 121st General Hospital in England where he had asked for a transfer to the airborne troops. His first move was to the 17th Airborne Division in training in England and then to the 18th Airborne Corps in France. From there he was sent to the 326th Medical Company at Mourmelon in mid-December. After only a few days to become acquainted with the medical personnel, he was enroute to Bastogne. In a letter he wrote in 1945, Block gave a brief description of his experience with the 326th.[39]

We moved into our assigned position – dug our foxholes and set up our hospital tents. I was sleeping, not too peacefully, in my hole that night when the Jerries suddenly opened up on us with 'burp' guns. The firing stopped. I reached the evacuation tent. Machine guns opened up again – tracers tore through the canvas. The wounded lying on stretchers groaned as some were hit a second time with fragments. I remember thinking – Son, you've had it now – what's it going to feel like – come on, let's get it over with. Again, the firing ceased. I crawled to the main tent to find out what was going on. The rank was flat on its collective face. Discreetly, I assumed a prone position. Again, machine gun tracers over our heads – we surrendered. Several vehicles were burning and the road was lined with tanks and armored cars. A great victory – capture of an unarmed medical company!

---

[39]In a letter to a Mr. Orton for a subscription renewal, Dr. Gordon L. Block wrote of his experiences with the 101st Airborne Division and the POW camps on May 19, 1945 while the recollections were still fresh memories.

The attack on the field hospital, west of Bastogne, was the third time that T/4 Emil Natalle had witnessed wholesale violence with his surgical group acting in concert with the 326th Medical Company. The hospital had suffered a direct hit by a large bomb in Normandy and had been hit again at Nijmegen in Holland when a fleeing enemy plane had jettisoned its load of bombs, which unfortunately landed on the hospital and grounds, killing two of the medical staff. Natalle describes the third onslaught:

I was not scheduled for surgical duty so I settled into my foxhole early. We had been on the move for the previous 24 hours. Sleep came quickly but the repose was brief.

About eleven o'clock, out of the dark, broke the light like day. Artillery, mortars, small arms fire, aerial flares combines in a veritable fireworks. German troops and armor were quickly in our hospital area. Firing ceased. The German OIC (officer in charge) asked for the U.S. OIC. Finding the U.S. officer in charge, the German asked for our surrender.

The Germans were all over the area. They hollered, laughed and made noise, just as Germans always do. It was bedlam. And to think that only a few minutes earlier, this place was a peaceful meadow somewhere in the Ardennes.

Captain Willis P. McKee remembered that an anti-tank gun was in defensive position at the cross-roads near the hospital. He recalled how quickly the medical troops were taken into custody:

Just before midnight, there was a sudden outburst of firing. A German motorized patrol in American half-tracks, jeeps and a Sherman tank had knocked out the gun at the crossroads. Then, one operating tent was sprayed with machine gun fire. Captain Charles Van Gorder, a member of the 3rd Auxiliary Surgical Team assigned to us – and of Pennsylvania Dutch origin, who spoke German rather well, yelled that we were medical troops and unarmed. They gave us 45 minutes to load our casualties and ourselves on our own trucks for departure.

T/4 Emil Natalle, who was part of Captain Van Gorder's surgical team, got a close look at the German commander and was asked to check on the needs of men caught in burning vehicles. He wrote:

The officer in command was a typical Prussian. He was wearing well polished, high, black boots and his uniform looked as if he had just come back from a Berlin pass. In his right eye was a monocle. I remember all the details. He was such a contrast with the ordinary fighting men. War is dirty.

Following the surrender order, the German OIC asked for an American officer to accompany him about the hospital area. Captain Van Gorder was designated, because the Captain spoke and understood the German language.

Down at the nearby crossroads, a number of vehicles were burning fiercely. Some of the vehicles surely had men inside for we heard their cries for help. Perhaps they were wounded and unable to escape.

Captain Van Gorder and the German officer decided to send one German soldier and me to the fiery scene and give help. We walked toward the blazing vehicles but could not approach them. The heat was so intense.

Arriving on the scene, with a small convoy of jeeps carrying wounded men from the Noville fighting, PFC. Robert Barger came upon the scene and made the wrong decision. He related:

As we got to the top of the hill west of Bastogne, looking down to the crossroads area where the medical company had set up its tent hospital, we noticed a burning truck right there in the middle of the road and another to the right that was also burning. We stopped at the top of the hill and regrouped, trying to decide whether we should move down there or not. Because of the two litter cases, I made the decision that we would go forward.

Just as we passed the burning truck on the road, a machine gun opened up on us, killing the two litter cases. I was on the floor of the jeep. We got across the road and I discovered there were now only two jeeps. To this day, I don't know what happened to the third. The walking wounded had moved very swiftly into the ditch. I crawled across the road to see what was on the other side of the burning truck because we were going to make a break and go back into Bastogne. Then, I saw a Tiger tank sitting there. I knew we didn't have a chance of making it out that way. I got everybody back into the jeeps and decided to make a break toward Paris. We went down the road fifty yards or so. We were stopped by the Germans who had attacked the hospital and, with their guns pointed at us, directed us up to the Medical Company area.

When I got out of the jeep, I immediately went for my knife attached to my boot and tossed that away because I didn't want to get caught with any weapons, as I had Red Cross arm bands in place. I ran into Captain (Edwin) Yeary, executive officer of my company. I asked him what had happened. He advised me that we were prisoners of war.[40]

Apparently, the three jeep loads of wounded, which were part of PFC. Robert Barger's group heading for the field hospital, were only part of about fifty wounded who had accumulated in Noville by nightfall. Captain Bernard Ryan, who had been sent to Noville from Foy by General Gerald Higgins to assist Captain Joseph Warren with the mounting casualties, had accompanied the convoy as far as Foy and continued on to his 3rd Battalion aid station. Ryan

---

[40]From an oral tape I made with Robert E. Barger on January 29, 1990. He and I had parachuted from the same plane with General Maxwell D. Taylor on D-Day, June 6, 1944.

describes what happened to Captain Samuel "Shifty" Feiler and his group of
medics and the wounded in the trucks.

Just as he (Feiler) arrived at the Division Hospital, he was flagged down
by Germans shooting burp guns. They ordered him into a nearby field. As
he jumped across the roadside ditch, he purposely dropped a fine P-38
German pistol, which I had just loaned him, into a ditch. He proceeded into
that field and saw that the Germans were so absorbed with their booty that
he just kept on going in the dark. He returned through enemy territory to
Bastogne without my pistol. The entire Division Medical Company, with
the Division surgeon and all the officers, with a few exceptions, were
captured at this time.

One of the enlisted medics with Captain Samuel C. Feiler in moving the
wounded to the 326th Medical Company facility west of Bastogne was PFC.
Don M. Dobbins. He had been captured, along with Feiler and others, by
German troops dressed in American uniforms and using American vehicles. He
describes what he saw as an American convoy that was trapped a short time
earlier:[41]

All of a sudden, all hell broke loose. Here is the way the scene was set.
About seven of us were standing behind a truck and along the highway were
twelve trucks on their way back to the Division at Mourmelon to get more
supplies. All of this was taking place at a crossroads. On one side of the
road was a tank destroyer – American, of course. There wasn't anything we
could do about it. The Germans had killed the men in it and were manning it
themselves.

Well, the tracers started flying and hitting everything around there. Why
the few of us behind the truck weren't hit is beyond me. I suppose the good
Lord was with us that night. The bullets were so close that I thought I
would have to brush them off. We all made one big dive for the ditch.

We were having trouble with a trooper who had a head wound and the
medic who was taking care of him told me that he was gone or something
to that effect. I suppose the boy died. There was nothing we could do for the
boys in the truck. To stand up on the road was suicide. The Germans fired
on every truck standing there and set them on fire. I remember a Negro truck
driver in one of the trucks who got up in his cab and blasted away at
Germans with a fifty-caliber gun mounted on his cab. He didn't last long for
the Germans turned everything they had on him. If they had fired a second
longer, they could have cut the cab away from the rest of the truck.

I looked at the trucks and saw every one of them on fire. Our truck was
burning fast because they had fired right into the gas tank. During all of

---

[41]Recollections of PFC. Donald M. Dobbins as they appear in *Rendezvous With Destiny*, a
History of the 101st Airborne Division, pp. 467-68.

that, we didn't hear any outcry from it. I suppose all of them were dead. The guns were trained on them long enough.

While the firing was going on. PFC. Dobbins managed to elude his captors and headed south through the woods. Captains Jacob Pearl and John Breiner, both dental officers, and Captain Roy H. Moore, Jr. also ducked into the woods and managed to get back to Bastogne. It wasn't until after the siege was lifted that Dobbins got back to his unit – or what was left of it.

Pvt. John M. Graham remembered the anxiety of the trip to the Bastogne area. He had been so anxious for rest after the Holland mission. He was able to recall that Pvt. Lester A. Smith was his front-line mate in the Medical Company. They spelled each other on duty hours. Graham wrote:

I had the first twelve hours, while Smith dug our foxhole. I was captured while on duty about midnight, while bringing in a wounded trooper, by the crew of a German tank which had the traditional 88mm gun. Smith was completely missed and completed the campaign.

Pvt. Lester A. Smith was a replacement for the Holland mission. He was one of the few lucky ones when the unit was almost totally captured during the night of December 19. Smith describes his rude awakening and eluding the enemy troops rounding up the unarmed medics:

At the time, I was off duty and was asleep in my foxhole. Upon finding out that the company was being captured, myself and two other friends managed to escape. Others escaped, too, but I don't know how many. Most of the company was captured.

The three of us headed in the direction we thought we might find friendly troops. We had a compass, no guns – being medics, waded a creek, came upon a Belgian home and were taken in and given something to eat and drink. After a short stay, we moved on forward where we thought others from the 101st were located.

Just before dawn a sentry shouted 'Halt!' He asked for the password and, of course, we didn't know it. He had every reason to shoot us, but we finally convinced him we were American soldiers and he let one of us advance. As I recall, this was an engineering company from the Division. We joined them and worked out way into the city of Bastogne. There we joined the few other medical personnel already present.

Over in the 502nd Regimental area, 1Lt. Henry Barnes had experienced two moves until the headquarters finally settled on a command post. Though the 502nd was not in combat yet, there were four patients who needed to be evacuated to the field hospital. To have his sergeant be familiarized with the road network between the 502nd command post and the field hospital, the sergeant was sent along on the truck ambulance. Barnes relates:

With no maps, we couldn't even picture in our minds what area we were in or where, except it was a network of roads on the larger maps.

By midnight, I had four patients, two pneumonia, from our cold all night ride, and two minor gunshot wounds. I sent them back with one of my sergeants so he could know the route, as we had moved twice and I wanted him to know how to get back. Also, since the Medical Company hadn't been dug in at the time I was there, I was afraid they might have moved also.

About two hours later, my sergeant returned, walking and his face ashen. He looked old. He blurted out that the Company was gone. He saw machine gun fire from the woods where they had been left. He had ditched his truck and ran back. No, he didn't know where the driver was. I questioned and questioned him until I put together this story:

It seems just as he drove to the crossroads, he was stopped by an MP directing traffic. The MP asked him where he was going and he pointed out where the Medical Company was located and said he had wounded and was taking them there. Since he and the driver were using a weapons carrier, instead of a litter jeep, for an ambulance the MP went around the vehicle and peeked in under the canvas and looked at the patients and said something in German.

That was when all hell broke loose.

A machine gun started firing from in front of the Medical Company area on the road. A truck mushroomed up in smoke, with the canvas afire. More guns joined the fire. Tracers were shooting out in all directions.

The four casualties, hearing the German words uttered by the MP, jumped up and ran right over him and fled, with bandages flashing white in the lurid flaming light, and headed for the ditches on each side, miraculously escaping. The driver and the sergeant almost beat them to the ditches and also made it except they headed for different sides of the road.

The sergeant was sure the fire was from the Medical Company area and sat staring ahead with a look as though he had caught a brief glimpse of hell.

While these actions were going on at the crossroads, the personnel of the field hospital were quickly rounded up and loaded onto their own trucks to be sent east into Germany and to prisoner of war compounds for the duration.

T/4 Emil Natalle had to suffer the indignity of driving one of the trucks carrying his friends toward confinement. He related:

Meanwhile, back on the hill at the hospital site, the U.S. trucks, trailers and other vehicles had been loaded with all the hospital's equipment and were set to vacate the area. I was told to drive one of the trucks. It was loaded with wounded on stretchers (litters). A German soldier rode 'shotgun' beside me. The convoy of 326th Medical Company POW's headed east from the crossroads site. It was the beginning of the end for the U.S. Army's first ever airborne surgical team and some 150 or more personnel of the 101st's unique surgical hospital.

An ambulance from the 101st Airborne Division had carried Major William Desobry, along with other wounded, back to Bastogne and then continued on to the field hospital of the 326th Medical Company. The armored unit commander had been immediately taken into the operating tent that evening. The last he remembered of that incident was having the anesthesia mask placed over his face. The next he remembered was waking in an ambulance moving down the road, headed for Germany, along with the rest of the wounded and most members of the hospital unit.

The 326th Medical Company was given 45 minutes to load its casualties and personnel on their own trucks for departure. In their small way, the medics got some retribution on the trip toward Germany as related by Captain Willis McKee, who closed his account with this comment:

> The medical officers and dentists were put on a truck loaded with jerrycans of gasoline. We spent the next few hours emptying the gasoline over the side. Also, we emptied a few bottles of cognac that we happened to have along.

The men of the medical facility were on the trucks for several days, moving during daylight hours and being holed up at night in pig sties, barnyards and farm buildings. Later, they joined a larger group of prisoners from the 106th Infantry Division on the march into Germany.

# 5. DECEMBER 20

## WITHDRAWAL FROM NOVILLE

Beginning his first full day as commander of 1st Battalion of the 506th Parachute Infantry Regiment, Major Robert Harwick was pondering what daylight would bring, what with the intermittent nightlong shelling and the sounds of enemy tank movement out to the battalion front. Those minutes before dawn, with each alone in the dark, thinking the thoughts which would be driven from the mind in daylight for fear of discovery by the men next to you. Harwick explains:[42]

Those private minutes – the thought of death, that goes with a shrug. The fear, not of the enemy nor his weapons, but of yourself. What will the fellows think when this is over? Will I be one to give? By God! Not me! And that passes.

How is it at home? I'm glad they don't know the spot I am in. It is about midnight there – all in bed.

Glad I wrote that letter last night. Wish I had some coffee.

Hope those tanks are all set. Wish we had more than six – at least there are nine tank destroyers. But those Krauts sure have a pot full – tanks all over the place.

So it went, thoughts tumbling, but always returning to the attack we knew was coming. The men were tense, staring out into the darkness. They could see nothing, but it was too quiet. The time rolled past the daylight hour and still it was dark. It was unreal. At least you could count on nature being the same. Then, as the black slowly melted into a clinging gray, we saw the reason – FOG!

With the first visibility came the warning shriek of approaching shells. As the men ran for cover, the barrage was upon us. Smoke and dust added to the fog. To see beyond twenty yards was impossible. A warning call came from the outposts. They could hear the German tanks moving.

The battle took on a weird aspect. The country became a confusion of clanking treads, fleeting glimpses of dark hulks and dirty yellow flashes as the tanks fired into the town.

Formations disappeared and each engagement was a tank and a few men probing here, trying there. Our tank destroyers just held position and, at the range of those few yards, the effects of their fire was murderous. Yet the fog was a mixed blessing. German units slipped past and through our defenses.

---

[42]Harwick, op. cit.

One was knocked out just fifty feet from the Command Post by one of the partially disabled tanks which had been placed in front of the building for protection. Firing just rolled on and on. Part of the church steeple came down with a crash of dust and large stones bounded down the street.

Out on the "A" Company front, PFC. Donald Straith had an opportunity to view this part of the battalion perimeter with the arrival of daylight:[43]

When morning came, I was able to survey our position. We were in a small, roughly rectangular pasture area. Through the hedge in front of me, I could see that the field sloped gently downward toward our observation post of the previous night, then leveled out before slowly rising toward the fog-shrouded ridge that had been our original objective. On either side, a roadway angled into the distance. To our right were walled gardens of the village houses. To the left of us were a fence and hedge, beyond which another pasture dropped a dozen feet or so to the main road. The forward corner of the pasture dipped out of my sight, although I assumed it provided access from the road. Beyond this point, the upper story of a building by the road blocked my view. The hedge to the left curved behind us and, beyond it, I could see more houses and the opposite side of yesterday's cemetery wall.

From beyond the building on the road to our left, we once again heard the sounds of tanks. As they seemed to be almost at the hidden corner of our field, I exclaimed, more from the need to release my pent-up emotions than from actual intention, 'If they come in here, I'm going to run like hell!' Our corporal, Jerry Janes, strode over, oblivious to the target he presented, and shouted, 'Like hell you will! You'll stay in your goddamn hole!' He returned to his hole. I stayed in mine and the tanks stayed on the road.

All night we had heard shells passing overhead. Some, which we thought were German 88's, went by with a sudden 'whish-h-h' while others, higher up, made more of a 'whush-whush-whush' sound. But now, a new sound joined the assortment as our artillery dropped several salvos nearby and the grinding of tanks beyond our sight abruptly diminished. This was followed shortly by the almost undetectable 'psst' of mortar rounds as the Germans zeroed in on our position. Frankly, I was terrified. Attempting to flatten myself in my slit trench, I now realized it was not quite long enough and my feet stuck partly out the end. Burying my face in the bottom of the hole, I tried desperately to squeeze all of me into my helmet. Explosions shook the ground and one very close one blew the dirt around my hole back in on my head.

I lay there rigid until there was a lull in the shelling and then gingerly poked my head out. To my right, I saw wisps of smoke curling from a hole next to mine where two of our men had dug in together. My immediate

---

[43]Don Straith revisited that battle site about twenty years later.

thought was, 'My God! They've both been blown to bits!' Later, I learned that, moments before the barrage, one of them had taken the other to the aid station for treatment of a wound.

As our position was in increasing danger, we were told to go through a hole in the hedge and crawl along it to where it ended at a concrete outbuilding behind a house. On reaching that point, I encountered a soldier crouching in a shell hole while behind him lay the corpse of another, its face obscured by dirt. I asked who it was and his companion said, 'Hodge, he got it last night!' (Pvt. Howard P. Hodge is listed as KIA on December 19, 1944.) The name was unfamiliar to me and, instead of being sickened by my first sight of violent death, I felt numb and rather detached. Not having known the man made it easier for me to get him out of my mind and concentrate on my own safety.

Because fire was now being directed into the yards of the adjoining houses, someone told us to return to our previous position. Lying on our stomachs, four of us inched back along the German side of the hedge. As we wormed our way toward the opening, mortar shells once again began falling slightly down the slope from us. We flattened ourselves even more as fragments flew over our heads. I clutched my rifle tightly to my side, telling myself as I did, 'It's not much protection but every little bit helps.' From somewhere across the field, a machine gun began firing and, as more shells exploded, I felt something hit my hand. Thinking that a stone thrown up by one of the shell bursts had struck me, I looked in surprise at the bloody opening between my thumb and forefinger. Where my hand gripped the forestock of my rifle, there was now a hole dead center in the wood and in line with my heart. A machine gun bullet had jammed itself between the gun barrel and the operating rod. Momentarily staring dumbly at my now torn and blood-soaked glove, I thought, Cavanaugh isn't going to want this back now.

PFC. Steve Polander was another member of "A" Company experiencing his first combat in the early morning fight in the cemetery sector. He recalled the morning action:

Just before daybreak, the shelling stops and down in the deep valley north of the village can be heard the rumble of German tanks coming up to clean out what's left of us. An order is passed along to the group and at least ten men are picked for pre-dawn patrol. The men move towards the east, straight out from where I am dug in. No more than five minutes go by when fierce gunfire erupts a short distance away. Word comes back from the few men above that all were ambushed and killed.

As we wait for the tanks approaching the top of the hill, to the north, in this cold, foggy morning of deadly silence, the fog seems to settle the thickest in the valley. As I look about, I see at least fifty tanks and half-tracks with flames flickering and shells exploding within. A nauseating smell of barbecued bodies drifts through the foggy breeze. About 80 yards away, I can see the tanks approach the top of the hill with a grinding, squeaking halt.

At the lower part of the hill, where the tanks stopped, some men are dug in. I do not know how many. The hatch of one of the tanks opens and we are cursed at, but rifle fire soon makes the Kraut drop the hatch.

The first tank slowly enters the positions of the men at the lower end. Death struggle screams can be heard. The men move around the tank as it turns, firing blindly. With a few bazooka shots, the tank is stopped and some rifle fire is heard.

The second tank then starts to make its entry. With no resistance, it starts to make its move toward me and the red barn. Helpless, we watch so as not to give away our position. The tank continues to move slowly toward the front side of the barn at an angle from me. A Sherman tank starts up and moves to the corner of the barn. As it locks the left track, it moves forward a few yards, stops and faces the German tank about 30 yards away. At point blank range, they tear into the hull of each other. The American tank skids back a few feet on each impact. Three times they tear into each other. The Sherman starts smoking, flaming and then explodes. It seems like seconds later the Tiger does likewise. Neither hatch opens as we lay ready. The Third tank then backs off the hill.

Little did he know there were but a few of us left. The clear signal is given. As we walk down towards the barn, there are about ten of us, one in total shock walking like a zombie.

We board the only other tank we had up there. It takes us back down the hill where we came from.[44]

PFC. Robert Flory had been sent to a forward listening post with his sergeant, Lee Rogers, and the rest of the squad. They had spent the night in a barn with an enemy tank parked outside the closed double doors. Flory adds to his story:

Just about daybreak, we took off at a dead run in full view of that tank and made it back to the defense line without a shot being fired. I suppose the tank crew was asleep.

Before 1st Battalion went in on the attack at Noville on the 19th, the "B" Battery, 321st Glider Field Artillery Battalion forward observer team was sent to another battalion at Foy. However, the next morning they were sent back to Noville. PFC. William "Jay" Stone describes the action:

Early on the morning of the 20th, we were ordered to return to Noville and rejoin the 1st Battalion. The Germans were trying to take Noville by

---

[44]Polander, op. cit.

attacking from the east and northeast. When the initial effort failed, the enemy continued to attack Noville while attempting to by-pass the village to the north and south. The Germans moving around Noville to the north were meeting with more success than were their fellows moving south of the village. To the north, there were no American troops. To the south were the 501st and the 506th. The enemy was trying to slip between them and the 1st Battalion in Noville and the going was slow. Within our forward observer party, we knew nothing of this. We only knew that we had to get fire on the enemy north of Noville. To accomplish this, Lt. Canham selected a stone barn on the northeastern outskirts of the village as our OP. He and Bill Plummer went to the second floor from which they could observe through an open window. I set the radio up at the other end of the barn, just outside a door on the first floor, and ran a wire to Canham and Plummer so that we could send fire missions to the Fire Direction Center (FDC) of the 321st in Savy.

At this time, Noville was taking a beating. The Germans were pounding the village (and us) with everything they had. The piercing whistle of incoming projectiles followed by the sounds of their explosions assaulted our ears. Their blasts buffeted our bodies. The sharp, bitter smell of the exploding powder invaded our nostrils. Buildings were blown apart. Wounded were walking or being carried to the battalion aid station. If the enemy could take the village quickly, he would have a straight road into Bastogne provided that he could break through the other battalions of the 506th. Still, the riflemen of the 1st Battalion and the men of Team Desobry, aided by the fires of the 321st, held. For now, there was to be no road through Noville to Bastogne for those Germans. They had to flow around the village in order to continue their advance to the west. The defense of Noville gave the other battalions of the 506th time to occupy and improve their positions astride the Bastogne-Noville road, just south of Foy.

Despite the vigorous German attack, from the narrow perspective of our FO party, the battle seemed to be going well when Plummer called me on the telephone and said that a tank shell had just hit alongside the window from which Lt. Canham was observing and that Canham had been hit. I grabbed the platoon aid man and went upstairs. He said that Canham was dead. I reported this to our FDC which urged Plummer and me to remain in Noville. We, of course, had no intention of doing other than that and were a bit put off by the urging from FDC. Plummer took over for Canham and we continued to direct the fires of the 321st.

During the first hours of combat on the 19th, before the 502nd Regiment had its initial skirmishes with the enemy, T/5 George Whitfield, one of the medevac jeep drivers from the 326th Medical Company, had been sent to do evacuation work at 1st Battalion of the 506th at Noville. Whitfield describes the experience he had on the morning of the 20th when he took a load of casualties from Noville to Bastogne:

> In the early part of the siege, I worked with the 506th. I drove out to Noville to evacuate some casualties and several people climbed on my jeep with my two stretchers. There were seven of us. Between Noville and Foy, as we topped a rise, we saw an enemy patrol ready to cut the highway. I immediately put the jeep in second gear without using the clutch or taking my foot off the gas. I happened to look at the speedometer (it was a straight road) – it showed 55 mph. so we got through. I reported this at 506th headquarters. I tried to get back to Noville but in Foy I got stopped by the enemy occupying the road.

The situation had become critical for 1st Battalion. Major Robert Harwick, the commander, describes the situation as the battle for Noville raged into the morning and mid-day hours.[45]

> Our aid station was full and we opened another cellar. It was obvious that our losses were making gaps in our line, which could not be plugged. The command post personnel, switchboard operators, clerks – also slightly wounded men, were sent to the companies.
>
> There was a lull, but we could see the tanks reforming. We had no communications with Bastogne. A half-track, which contained radio equipment that wouldn't work, was loaded with several badly wounded men who obviously were going to die without attention, was ordered to try to force their way back to Bastogne. The message I sent was 'Casualties heavy – no more armor-piercing ammunition and medical supplies' The vehicle left but did not return.

Major Harwick missed out on what actually happened to the first half-track that was sent out with wounded. This move had occurred before the withdrawal had begun. Captain John T. Prior, the medical officer for the 20th Armored Infantry (part of Team Desobry) was closer to the action which involved the half-track attempting to break through to Bastogne. Prior relates:[46]

> We did load four patients into a half-track at one point and just as it lumbered off, it received a direct hit from a tank and burst into flames. The four patients were unloaded and returned to the aid station; this, under the gaze of the German tank commander.

PFC. William J. Stone, of the forward observer team of the 321st Glider Field Artillery Battalion, describes how critical the situation was without adequate communication to the command elements in Bastogne. The enemy

---

[45]Harwick, op. cit.
[46]Prior, op. cit.

build-up between Noville and Foy had been increasing throughout the morning.
Stone continues his story:

By 1:00 p.m., the 1st Battalion had lost contact with the headquarters of
the 506th and our FO radio was the only means of communication between
the two. The liaison officer from the 321st at the HQ of the 506th had a
radio in the FDC net and he relayed messages from the 506th HQ to our FO
party. We then gave them to the 1st Battalion. It became obvious to the
division commander, General McAuliffe, that the 1st Battalion and Team
Desobry, while they were holding, would soon be surrounded and so he
ordered Colonel Sink to withdraw them. At 1:15 p.m., the order for
withdrawal came down to us on the artillery radio and we relayed it to the
commander of the 1st Battalion.

The German attack around the southern side of Noville was rapidly
becoming more successful. Because of this, the Noville force was in danger
of being cut off from the rest of the 506th and so there was little time to
plan the withdrawal. Shortly after it began, we came under observation and
direct artillery fire by the Germans on the high ground to the east. By this
time, we were traveling with the battalion commander. We told him that we
could get artillery fire from the 321st on the enemy position. He told us to
do so. We sent the fire mission down and the fire was on the way.

Battalion commander Robert Harwick had a brief radio contact with his
regiment during mid-morning but communications were sporadic. He related:

About 10 o'clock, we briefly contacted the regiment by radio. I was
afraid to tell our true situation over the air and the message we received was
'Hold at all costs'.

That cost began to mount then, with a tank attack right down the road.
Part of our infantry positions were lost, but the tank destroyers got their
20th tank, which burned at the edge of town setting fire to one of the few
whole buildings.

The situation was now so acute that I called in the company and tank
commanders. Another attack – surely, two – would end the affair for us. We
drew up plans to fight a withdrawal. A jeep with two wounded men and a
messenger who volunteered was sent down the road. The message was to
General McAuliffe. It just said, 'We can hold out but not indefinitely'. There
was no answer.

The jeep incident just mentioned is related in more detail in an article
written by Collie Small for the *Saturday Evening Post*.[47]

. . .Finally, Captain Rennie Tye, of Memphis, Tennessee, volunteered
to make a suicidal dash through the German-held town. Lying flat on the

---

[47]Small, Collie. "Bastogne: American Epic," *The Saturday Evening Post*. February 17,
1945. pp. 18-19+

hood of a speeding jeep, with an automatic in his hand, Tye raced through Foy, firing until his ammunition was exhausted. One of two wounded men in the jeep was killed by a German machine gunner, but Tye was untouched.

Major Harwick continues his story. With the forward observer team from the 321st Artillery Battalion near him at this time, he may be confused as to the source of messages concerning withdrawals is concerned. He wrote:[48]

> About 1230, a radio operator in a tank picked up a message telling the armored units to assist the infantry in fighting out. I took this as a legal means to do what I knew had to be done in this situation. I ordered a withdrawal at 1330, keeping the message as evidence. (I still have it.)

The withdrawal from Noville, shortly after noon on the 20th, is described by "C" Company commander 1Lt. Edward Mehosky:

> Soon, word came down that we would be withdrawing. It was becoming evident that the Germans were attempting to encircle Noville and that we had to be prepared to fight our way back to the division perimeter. 'C' Company was designated the lead echelon of the battalion and would be accompanied by three tanks of the combat team. My commandeered 'convoy' was positioned to the rear of the tanks as we moved out of Noville. We left, knowing the enemy was moving on our flanks, but didn't know that they had moved ahead of us on our left, and set up a roadblock east of Foy on the commanding terrain that overlooked and controlled the road we were traveling.

Major Harwick continues with his account of the withdrawal from Noville with tanks leading the way, followed by the men of his line companies:[49]

> Of the five tanks remaining, I could find crews for only two. Our troopers took over and drove two more. The disabled one was set afire and a five minutes fuse put on what ammunition was left.
>
> Four tanks and 'C' Company left first, with orders to push and engage any enemy without further orders. Stopping, we knew, would mean the loss of the entire column. The tank destroyers with 'A' Company formed the rear guard to prevent the Germans from following. All of the wounded were placed on vehicles.

A description of the pullout from within the town of Noville is related by war correspondent Collie Small, writing for the *Saturday Evening Post*:

> The rear of the column was still in Noville, where a lieutenant in the engineers waited patiently with his hand on the plunger that would set off the pile of ammunition in the churchyard. Up ahead, the crackle of small arms and a pall of black smoke from burning vehicles marked the battle. Then, into the rain of steel, a cool young captain walked, calmly ordering

---

[48]Harwick, op. cit.
[49]ibid.

the men to double park their vehicles along the road. At Foy, vehicles backed up and at Noville they pulled ahead until the shortened column was halfway between the two villages. The lieutenant in Noville squeezed the plunger. There was a terrific explosion and the church disappeared.[50]

As the medical officer for the 20th Armored Infantry Battalion of Team Desobry, Captain John T. Prior got the order to get his wounded ready for the withdrawal. He describes the situation as viewed from an aid station:

> Upon receipt of the withdrawal order, we were given ten minutes to move out. Since I had no functioning vehicular transportation and no litters, I decided to stay and surrender my patients to the Germans. I asked for volunteers to stay with me but the silence was deafening. It looked as if only myself and the tavern owners (an old lady and her husband who said their rosaries aloud for two days in their cellar) would stay behind. At this point, my first sergeant seized the initiative and ran into the street shouting at the departing tanks to swing by the aid station. The tankers ran into our building and, after ripping off all the doors from the walls, strapped our patients to the doors and tied them to their vehicles. The column then moved down the road toward Bastogne where I assumed there was a hospital and fresh defenders.[51]

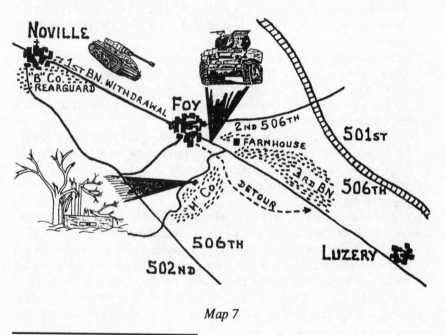

*Map 7*

[50]Small, op. cit.
[51]Prior, op. cit.

T/5 Owen E. Miller had been busy gathering and tending the wounded without respite since arrival in Noville. His load had increased since Captain Joseph Warren had been wounded in the late afternoon of the 19th. He had this recollection of the actions as the troops pulled out:

The next day, I was some place around town. I came back to the aid station (which was separate from the one Captain Prior operated.) It was empty. I went to the door and stood there as vehicles were leaving. A half-track stopped. An officer yelled at me to get my gear and board the vehicle, which I did in a hurry. We were the last vehicle in line. We went about 300 yards and came to a halt. We sat there until word came on the radio to man all machine guns on the vehicle. The men were to keep their eyes on the left bank. On my side of the vehicle was a water-cooled .30 caliber with a big hole in the jacket.

The Germans had cut the road to Bastogne at Foy. As we sat out on the road, a machine gun opened up on the column from our right.

As a casualty from the dawn attack on the "A" Company positions in Noville, PFC. Don Straith ended up in the basement of the 1st Battalion aid station where he had fallen asleep, exhausted, in a potato bin. His story continues:[52]

Sometime in the afternoon, I was awakened and told that the road to Bastogne had been reopened and Noville was being evacuated. Going back upstairs, I found a line of half-tracks standing in front of the aid station. While wounded were being loaded onto the vehicles, the uninjured passed on either side as they headed out of town. I boarded the closest half-track and climbed into the gunner's mount where I could, if necessary, man the .30 cal. machine gun. The fog had lifted somewhat and, as the column slowly moved out, I kept watching the edges of the forest patches beyond the fields, but no Germans ever came into view.

The fog was still patchy and played tricks as has been described in some of the previous accounts. Major Harwick describes how the wounded had been loaded and the forward elements had moved out when the first troops and tanks collided with enemy forces to the south.[53]

Under cover of the now wonderful fog, we took off on time. The men did a brilliant job of changing positions, loading wounded, gathering or destroying ammunition and equipment. The wounded had just been put on a vehicle when sounds of fire told of trouble at the head of the column. I hurried up. The first tank was on fire. But we had to push on – if we did not take losses then everybody would be a loss.

---

[52]Straith, op. cit.
[53]Harwick, op. cit.

From his position in the column moving south from Noville, 1Lt. Edward
Mehosky had this view of the action as it unfolded as his company led the
combined 1st Battalion and Task Force Desobry in the withdrawal:

Noville was now behind us as we advanced toward Foy. The tanks were
in the middle of our column. The other vehicles were strung out in a line
behind us. Men marched in combat formation alert for enemy activity.
Suddenly, there was an explosion as lead elements of the column received
fire. A German tank, supported by rocket launchers and small arms, had set
up a road block on the high ground off to our left.

At the head of the column, leading the withdrawal, was 2Lt. Joe Reed with
his platoon of "C" Company men. He describes how he anticipated where the
enemy would be located if resistance was to be met:

On the map there were two man-made objects (farmhouses) between us
and Foy. I warned the guys to walk softly and quietly and expect most of
our problems there. Due to weather conditions, the Krauts were no different
than us. They sought shelter wherever it was available. We were informed
the 3rd Battalion had been pushed out of Foy but would be counter-attacking
the town to take pressure off us and to retake the town. Our orders were to
fight through, if possible, and not stop.

As we moved out in a column of file on each side of the road, I had my
first scout in front of me. I was next on the left side of the road. Nimmo
was a scout on the right side and Mike Parros, my platoon sergeant, was
behind him. The rest of the platoon was strung out on both sides of the road
behind, including Don Zahn, assistant platoon leader. Fog was very heavy
but it was rolling from time to time. We marched quietly for some time.
All of a sudden, the fog rose and across a ditch from me three Krauts were
setting up a machine gun pointing toward Noville. I was able to dispatch all
three of them – thanks to Al Hassenzahl who had given me a Thompson
sub just before we departed Mourmelon. I yelled, 'Kraut!' and, as I dove for
the ditch, I saw two Kraut tanks setting in the yard – crews half in and half
out of their vehicles.

About that time, a 10th Armored tank with a howitzer-type gun pulled
up on the road beside me. A redheaded captain in the turret leaned over and
asked me, 'What the hell is going on?' I shouted, 'Get the hell out of here!'
Too late, those two Kraut tanks hit him a couple of times and his tank
started burning. He toppled out of the tank on top of me and started crawling
back toward Noville. In the meantime, a heavy fire fight was building up
and the two Kraut tanks withdrew. That was the last I saw of them.

However, there was a Kraut in the upstairs window who was firing a
panzerfaust, continuing to shoot at the burning tank just above me. I kept
trying to pop him but wasn't doing very well, I never did get him.
Eventually, one of his projectiles didn't detonate, glanced off the tank, rolled

over my leg into my crotch and was sizzling. Believe me, all I could think about at that time was the family jewels. In spite of all the fire power going both ways, I got up and ran around to the other side of the tank. Just as I arrived there, my platoon sergeant, Mike Parros, was hit hard and died in my arms while talking to me. It was unfortunate, but we had no orange smoke or identification panels with us. I feel to this day my group got caught in the crossfire in the 3rd Battalion counter-attack.

T/4 Jim Cadden was in the same move as part of Lt. Reed's platoon as it led the withdrawal. His recollections are different as he was further back in the platoon column but he still had some of the same memories.

My squad was on the left side of the road. As we moved out to attack south from Noville, after going about 300 feet, my squad came under enemy machine gun and small arms fire. We all took to the roadside ditch for cover and then all hell broke loose on us. German tanks poured 88mm cannon fire on us and fired into the roadside trees to try getting us with tree bursts. During the fusilade, my second scout was killed; the kid in back of me was critically wounded (he later died) and the first scout (Abrahamson) was hit by small arms fire on the right side of the head and lost his right eye. Both he and the second scout were replacements for the Holland casualties.

We were completely pinned down by a blanket of small arms and tank cannon fire. After a period of time, a Sherman tank came up the road from Noville firing its machine gun and, as it came to within approximately ten feet of my position in the ditch, it was hit broadside by cannon fire and the turret went spiraling in the air and the entire vehicle was engulfed in roaring flames. The cannon broadside explosive impact with the tank rendered me stunned and semi-conscious. However, I was not hurt except for brief hearing impairment. Then, within minutes after the first tank was hit and burning, a second Sherman came lumbering up the road from Noville and when that tank got approximately 25 feet from the burning tank – BLAM! That, too, got hit and burst into flames. As I recall, a soldier in the turret of that tank opened the hatch and tried to get out and suddenly a trooper from the ditch I was in and about fifty feet in back of me, jumped up on the road and hopped up on the second tank and appeared to try pulling the injured tanker from the turret of the second tank. Kraut machine gun fire raked them both and both fell to the ground. (I learned later that the trooper who endeavored to rescue the tanker was my platoon sergeant, Mike Parros.)

Another soldier from "C" Company, PFC. Robert Wiatt, must have been in on this same attack. Again, he views the action from a different angle. Wiatt still had the bazooka he had obtained from a tanker the previous day and he fired his last round into the house which contained enemy soldiers who were keeping the "C" Company troopers in the roadside ditches. By this time, the number of tanks has increased to three, the third was being driven by one of the 1st Battalion paratroopers. Wiatt wrote:

In the meantime, there were three Sherman tanks on the road just short of the house. One of these tanks was hit and disabled. With the road blocked in front of them, the men in the second and third tanks took off, leaving their tanks on the road. My buddy, who had been in the field with me, decided that we should get into one of these tanks since it had armor and a big gun. He said he would drive the tank if I could fire the gun. I had training with the .57mm anti-tank gun so I thought it would work. We started to climb up on the far side of the tank when a shell hit it. I do not know just what took place for a while after that. When I came to, I was by myself in a ditch on the far side of the road. My buddy, whose name I cannot remember, was lying, blown apart, on top of the tank and no one else was around. I took off down the ditch on the right side of the road and found the company just beyond Foy.

Some more light is shed on that action by 1Lt. Joe Reed who remembered the names of two of the men involved in the fight to get to Foy. Both were in on the tank actions:

The Krauts withdrew and we advanced into Foy. I lost five of my men as KIA that I know of on the Noville-Foy road and one of our men, Rosario Rizzo, was killed when he tried to drive an abandoned tank out. (He had special schooling in England.) Unbeknown to me, the Krauts blew two tanks at about the same time. Rizzo was on the second one. Sgt. Eugene Esquible, one of my squad leaders, climbed up on the second burning tank and got the .50 caliber machine gun going. I am told it was a major factor in our favor in the early stages of the fire fight. He stayed on the gun until blown off by enemy fire. After his wounds healed, he was no longer fit for airborne duty.

1Lt. Al Hassenzahl was in on the action, too. He remembered that they brought out all their wounded on a few half-tracks and other vehicles which followed at the rear of the column. He had high praise for Sgt. Eugene Esquible's action in silencing enemy fire so the 1st Battalion troopers could move past the strong point. Hassenzahl wrote:

We had a sergeant, Eugene Esquible, who mounted a Sherman tank and manned a .50 caliber machine gun and, while fully exposed, he so effectively leveled that strong point, silenced their machine gun which enabled us to get across the road and nullify that strong point. I remember seeing Sgt. Esquible knocked off the tank by a round from one of the Kraut vehicles. He was placed in a half-track and evacuated to Bastogne as we went along.[54]

Another incident that happened at the same time and I remember it so vividly was with Sgt. Joe Zettwich. Joe was hit in the chest in this encounter. I remember helping load him into the half-track, telling him he was going to be OK. It was a traumatic experience to learn Sgt. Zettwich had died some time after reaching the aid station.

Medical officer for the 20th Armored Infantry Battalion, Capt. John Prior describes some of the action which took place while he treated wounded in the ditches as the fight was going on around them. He relates:[55]

Even the trip back to Bastogne turned into another fire fight. In a late afternoon fog, the column was stopped by the enemy who knocked out our tanks and harassed us with small arms fire from their tanks. We treated serious injuries in the ditches as we waited three hours for the column to move again. Lying in the ditch and having sniper fire chip away at a fence post beside me was a terrifying experience. I was head to head in the ditch with my dental officer. He did not wear a helmet with the bright red cross and suggested mine was a sniper target and should be shed – a suggestion which I resisted. Many of our enlisted men demonstrated great bravery on the road, pulling tankers from their blazing vehicles, driving jeeps, with the injured on the hood, to our aid station. Many of these aid men were soldiers whose reputations in the unit would have given no clue to the fact that under stress they would meet this challenge. I have often thought I'd still be in that ditch on the Bastogne road if it had not been for the arrival of a parachute battalion from the 101st Airborne Division.

From his position in the column moving south from Noville, 1 Lt. Edward Mehosky had this view of the action as it unfolded as his company led the combined 1st Battalion and Task Force Desobry in the withdrawal. The tank that seemed to follow his moves attracted a lot of enemy attention to the commander and to the tank. Mehosky added to his narrative:

The fire was coming in heavy and too close, so I crawled away from our tank that was drawing all the attention. This developed into a cat and mouse game. I would crawl forward, the tank would move forward; so I would crawl away, the tank would move back – and so on until it burst into flames from a direct hit. I then deployed two platoons abreast to attack the

---

[54]Several years later, officers and men who had served with "C" Company wrote up Sergeant Eugene Esquible for a Silver Star but it was lost somewhere in the Army channels – if ever a man deserved a medal, it was Sergeant Esquible whose actions saved many lives in "Charley" Company that day. (The author located a citation in which Sgt. Eugene Esquible was awarded the Bronze Star for heroism for that action – he deserved better.)

[55]Prior, op. cit.

roadblock. The other platoon and I took cover across the road. The return fire from my platoons and tanks silenced the roadblock. I lost a platoon sergeant, cut down by machine gun fire as he tried to cross the road. A medic was attending a soldier with a head wound. To my left and a couple hundred yards to the north, could be seen enemy armored vehicles advancing toward us. I turned to my right and could see elements of 3rd Battalion counter-attacking. We were not far from the perimeter.

## JOE MADONA'S ROLE

By the time the 101st Airborne Division was relieved from its duties in the Bastogne area in mid-January, "I" Company of the 506th Parachute Infantry Regiment would be down to one officer and nine enlisted men. The reports received from surviving members of that company always had the highest praise of Platoon sergeant Joe Madona, who served as an inspiration to his men. His actions helped immensely in finally breaking the roadblock at Foy which permitted 1st Battalion to complete its march out of Noville. The following statement appears on the citation for the Silver Star which S/Sgt. Joseph Madona received posthumously for the action at Foy:

S/Sgt. Joseph P. Madona, of 'I' Company of the 506th Parachute Infantry Regiment, distinguished himself on the 20th while commanding his squad during an attack against the enemy in the vicinity of Foy. His unit was attacking across open terrain exposed to intense enemy fire. Enemy infantry units, supported by artillery and tanks, were entrenched on the military crest of commanding ground that had to be taken by our forces. Seeing that machine gun fire was hindering the advance of adjacent units, Sgt. Madona exposed himself to heavy enemy fire and moved forward toward the enemy positions. Observing this action, the remainder of his squad and platoon followed him in a swift and victorious attack. On one occasion during the engagement, Sgt. Madona's rifle jammed. Swinging his rifle over his head like a club, he led his squad into and through three enemy machine gun emplacements and captured all three guns and crews intact without losing a single man. His courage and aggressiveness and bold determination, inspired his platoon to a swift attack that ended in opening the main highway and enabled an isolated, friendly force to withdraw down the road with their vehicles and wounded personnel.[56]

---

[56]Headquarters, 101st Airborne Division, Office of Division Commander, G. O. #11, 12 February 1945.

# FRIENDLY FIRE

As had been related by one of his platoon leaders, company commander Ed Mehosky remembers that some of the shooting that was directed at his men was actually friendly fire coming from the guns of 3rd Battalion of the 506th Regiment. He wrote:

I was in a prone position and watching the fire and movement of the advancing company when I saw what reminded me of a 'bee' heading straight toward me. I instinctively turned and rolled away. Then, I felt a sharp, burning pain in my hip. Fearing the worst and afraid to look, I called to a medic to come check me. He couldn't find anything wrong and said I was OK. I discovered something hot had entered the left top part of my trousers and burned my leg. What I found in my pocket was a hunk of lead with a painted black tip. It was a spent M-1 armor-piercing round apparently fired by advancing 3rd Battalion units.

# REAR GUARD ACTION

Off to the rear end on the flank, PFC. Robert Flory, of "B" Company, was with a squad making sure enemy soldiers didn't get into position to put fire on the troops from that direction. He describes the experience of one of the new men in his platoon during the withdrawal:

We were on a slight rise just on the south edge of Noville. I had my machine gun set up facing back towards town. There was a patch of trees about fifty yards to my left. Suddenly, we heard a shot and a few minutes later a fellow from the 3rd Platoon by the name of Lustoff (a new man) appeared holding a German officer by the ear. The man was crawling on his hands and knees. It seems Lustoff was patrolling the woods when all of a sudden this Kraut stepped out from behind a tree. Lustoff had his safety off and his M-1 pointed down. It scared him so badly that he jumped back and pulled the trigger, hitting the Kraut in the foot.

# FINDING COVER

As a member of the forward observer team attached to 1st Battalion, PFC. William J. Stone was still near Major Robert Harwick during the move toward Bastogne. He describes the move, taking advantage of low ground to remain out of view of enemy troops:

The battalion commander ordered the troops to leave the road and continue the withdrawal on the western side of the road, which was low ground – so low that it was not visible to the enemy. The combination of fire from the 321st and the low ground enabled the 1st Battalion and Team Desobry to continue their withdrawal in order to fight another day.

There was considerable confusion once we moved off the road and control was lost. This was certainly undesirable but was not as bad as it might be inasmuch as we were no longer in contact with the enemy. Low ground is often wet and our route was that. By this time, I was riding on a half-track of Team Desobry. The tracks of the rear of the vehicle drove the wheels in the front end into the wet ground and we came to a halt. After we freed the vehicle, I decided that it would be better to proceed on foot and ended up south of Foy and back on the road.

There was no clearly defined front and as I looked at the high ground to the east of the road, three German soldiers emerged from the woods 100 yards away. When they saw me they immediately surrendered. I searched them and took from them their military papers. I later gave them to Captain Joe Perkins, the S-2 of the 321st. It took some time but I finally found someone in the 506th who would take the prisoners from me. The troops of the 506th were busy people, just then, and few of them wanted to have prisoners on their hands.

As one of the walking wounded, PFC. Donald B. Straith had left Noville in the back of a half-track positioned at the mounted .50 caliber machine gun that faced forward. He had a good view to the front. He describes:

The vehicles and the men beside them would move a short distance, then stop, start again, then stop, while the wounded men periodically yelled at their drivers to get moving. From my vantage point, my view reached almost to the head of the column and, as we approached Foy once again, I could see that the first one of three Sherman tanks leading the column was on fire and blocking the road. This was forcing the half-tracks to turn off into a field where they were encountering some difficulty, so those of us who could walk were directed to dismount and go on foot around the cluster of houses. In one field through which we passed, an abandoned half-track stood[57] and near it lay the corpse of a German soldier. Thinking perhaps the man was faking death, I approached the body gingerly and nudged it with my foot. There was no question about it – the only enemy I had seen was definitely dead. We moved on and eventually reached the collecting station in Bastogne in the late afternoon.[58]

Major Robert Harwick summarizes the final actions which took place as his 1st Battalion withdrew from Noville and entered Foy:

---

[57]The half-track is most likely the vehicle which had made the attempt to evacuate wounded earlier as had been related by Capt. John T. Prior.

[58]Straith, op. cit.

I sent a platoon to the left. They ran into heavy trouble but kept pushing. I took a group of about thirty to the right. The Germans had fortified a group of farm houses at a place called Foy. We moved across the fields while a machine gun fired tracers into a large stone barn. The barn caught fire and we caught the Krauts as they ran out. The buildings were captured without loss to our small group. Thirty-two German prisoners, including a major – I did not count the dead. The Germans pulled back and the way was open to Bastogne. Unfortunately, one of the tanks driven by the troopers was lost. There was no pursuit from Noville, as the exploding ammunition moved the remains of the church across the road. All the wounded came out safely.

We had just broken our way through the German ring and the battalion was moving down the road through the few buildings that made Foy. It was no column. The fighting had scattered the groups and they now reformed and filed past me and on into the barn. They were dirty as only fighting men can get – clothing torn and mud-caked. Two day's beard just made them appear dirtier. A few were bloody; all with a shovel or pick or ax, mostly German or taken from the farm. If you don't dig, you die. But happy! I'll say they were. They had been in a rough spot. Through their own strength, they had gotten out. They had done a good job and they knew it. The spring in the step of the tired, dirty bodies and the look in the eyes told that. Almost 600 had gone in. There were less than 400 who came out.[59]

In a letter he wrote to his former company commander, who was recuperating in a stateside hospital, 2Lt. Ted Patching listed the troopers who had served with Capt. Melvin Davis in Normandy and Holland and had become casualties in December. Patching was also in a stateside hospital undergoing extensive treatment for wounds received in Noville.[60]

To get to Bastogne – Captain Meason shot in stomach by explosive bullet – after several emergency calls to the Chaplain to perform last rights, he finally decided to live. He is now in the general hospital in Palm Springs, California.

Joe Hopkins killed instantly – bullet through head. Sherman Sutherland commissioned a few days after me in Holland, died four hours after being shot through the temple by a sniper. Abie Fell died a few minutes after being shot through the stomach. Ollie Barrington killed by a piece of shrapnel in brain; Bill Shearin's whole squad pretty well wiped out when

---

[59]Harwick, op. cit.

[60]From a copy of a letter sent to the author by Joe Powers of "A" Company of the 506th Parachute Infantry Regiment. The letter was written in 1945 while both Capteain Melvin Davis and 2Lt. Ted Patching were recuperating from wounds received in Holland and Noville, respectively.

they were caught in the cross fire of two German tanks – there were only two known survivors but some of the boys seemed to think that Bill might have made it, too. (See comment of Steve Polander on page 108.) Doss had the top of his head blown off and was begging the boys to shoot him. Shoemaker said he was still living 24 hours after he was hit. (See Steve Polander's story on page 81.) Shoemaker was wounded again through the leg and arm; went back to duty, however.

John Powers wounded again (if nothing else, that boy is going to have a nice string of clusters to his Purple Heart).

'Scurvy' Slaton had a big dud land so near to him that it almost covered him with dirt. It knocked him silly and he had to be evacuated. (Steve Polander's story makes mention of this.) Behus was wounded again, badly. Gividen, a squad leader, was put out of action by a house collapsing on him. Tony Borrelli was wounded lightly by shrapnel in the cheek. Rumor had it in the evacuation hospital that Captain Brooks had been wounded lightly and that Captain Kessler had been killed. By the way, Kessler took over 'A' Company after Meason was wounded. Loible's leg tied up on him and put him out of action. Lt. Col. LaPrade killed – his executive officer, Major Harwick, bad stomach wound. I don't know who has the battalion now – the boys said Kessler was really out for blood.

## Revenge

Not all of the civilian population had fled from Noville before the fighting moved into their small farm community. The Allied forces, which had been holding the approaches to the town, finally got word from General A. C. McAuliffe to pull back to the high ground near Foy. Andre Meurisse, who is an authority on the battle actions, which took place around the perimeter of Bastogne, describes what happened to some of the civilians still in town when the enemy arrived:

The 2nd German Panzer Division entered Noville about the noon hour of the 20th of December, just after the joint U. S. Force committed to its defense had left, having received permission to withdraw from General McAuliffe.

Following the main body of the 2nd German Panzer Division, a special German reprisal unit entered the town. Its members had with them photographs showing local area people fraternally celebrating and feasting along with the U. S. troops their country's liberation on the previous September 10th.[61]

## 3RD BATTALION AT FOY

Early morning of December 20th found the 3rd Battalion of LTC. Lloyd Patch along a line which extended from Recogne (where "G" Company was in position) continuing along the Recogne-Foy road and then to the railroad trestle and station (Halte) where the 506th sector ended as it supposedly connected to the 501st at this point. 3rd Battalion troops were in position along the northern fringes of Foy and occupied many of the houses early that morning.

An enemy attack on Foy commenced at 0800, with the movement of tanks and infantry attacking from the northeast. Bearing the brunt of the attack were men of "H" Company.

After spending the first night in a haystack near Foy, 1Lt. Harry Begle and others from the platoon would be sent scurrying from their place of shelter and concealment. Begle related:

On the morning of the 20th, it was cold, foggy and machine gun fire hit the haystack. You never saw so many of us fly out of there at once in your life. The haystack caught fire and I ran up towards a big potato pile covered with horse manure. The machine gun was right after me. It blew a bunch of potatoes at me. I hid there for what seemed like hours (though it was more like a few minutes) and then ran back toward the haystack again. I could hear the tanks. They were so close you could hear the clanking and the Germans started throwing mortars and we could hear the 'thump' and I'd say, 'Oh, oh, here comes a mortar barrage!' Lt. Heggeness ran down and got me and said, 'One of the sergeants had been hit.' We ran to the haystack and

---

[61]On December 21st, they arrested 16 of the villagers and put them in a line alongside the highway. Round about noon, they forced them to remove from the highway all debris of American armored vehicles that had been destroyed during the action that had taken place the previous two days. Approximately an hour later, a German officer ordered that they be gathered again in one line. Facing the line, he took a paper out of his pocket and read eight names. Then he said, "These eight men may go back home." Then the eight men left, including the local priest, were escorted, hands behind their heads, some thirty yards across the highway into a field located some distance away behind the Jacoby family's home. There, three trenches had been hastily dug into the ground. Hands behind their heads, the eight men were lined up right along the edge of these rough graves and then shot down one by one, in cold blood. Father Delvaux,. the priest, first! Eight Belgian civilians had just paid with their lives for expressing joy and happiness at their liberation, which they had shared with the Americans some three months before.

There is a small monument to the martyrs who died by assassination at the site in Noville.

picked up the sergeant. He had been hit in the leg and so we carried him back between the two of us. The enemy was throwing mortars at us.

Clark Heggeness continued on back to the battalion CP and he told me to hold the line as long as I could. Meanwhile, the machine gun was after me again so I headed for my potato pile. We were taking some small arms and mortar fire. Clark had called for artillery fire with a Walkie-Talkie (SCR-536) radio. I had no communication with Heggeness so I told my men, 'Come on – we're gonna pull back a bit.' We pulled back and as we crossed the main road into the woods, I remember Captain Fred Anderson was commanding either 'G' or 'I' Company – he yelled, 'Watch your fire, 'H' Company is withdrawing!' So we withdrew back and I had three or four guys with me. We got back up and I saw Captain Jim Walker, 'H' Company commander yelling, 'Get back down there and line up on that ridge by the main road!' There was a small country road that went behind the pines which were spaced about three or four feet apart. We got in position. We saw another squad crawling on their hands and knees coming up along a fence row across a field. I think it was Wilkinson bringing them up.

A couple of tree bursts hit and someone came up in a jeep yelling, 'Tanks, tanks!'

I ran toward the Battalion CP just as an AP shell went all the way through the house and everyone came tumbling out of there. Then another shell hit the trees. That was all she wrote for me. I was a goner – didn't get back to the outfit until March.

1st Platoon leader Bob Stroud had his men spread thinly over a great distance and below the heights of a hill. Evidently, some of the men were able to get into the houses on the outskirts of Foy. This is what Stroud remembers of that action:

It was fairly quiet the first night and the next morning things really hit. They threw tanks at us and everything else. At that time, about the middle of the morning, we were told to move out to the heights which were directly in back of the town. The heights were covered with quite a few pine trees. There were several elements already up there as we gradually moved into position. Meanwhile, we were catching quite a bit of fire.

I remember well Sgt. Padisak when I pulled our communications out – Snyder, my commo man, and I moved back through Padisak who was firing a BAR from a woodpile in back of one of the houses. He was taking care of quite a few Germans who were trying to push through on our left. We got up into one of the houses and I wanted to check before we pulled all the way back together to see where these Germans were. I went to the attic of a three-story house and knocked out a couple of tiles from the roof and looked down. There was a German tank right next to the little house I had set up as my CP. I went downstairs real quick. We found a bazooka and went back up there. We had a fellow from one of the other platoons feeding me ammunition. He was bringing up one round at a time. I managed to get one round off by poking the launcher out through the hole in the roof and just before I fired I observed quite a few Germans around the tank. I think I hit the tread on the tank. I ran down quick to get another round and meanwhile Johnson was coming up with the additional rocket. I couldn't get off another shot before they started blasting the roof and top of the house.

I came back, pulling my men back to our line on the ridge. After that, we sort of stabilized for a while.

As the company communications sergeant, Gordon Yates witnessed the above incident from his post about a quarter mile away. He remembered:

We had an outpost in Foy in the second story of a house and the men had a sound power phone and I had a wire relay down to the command post. The man on outpost duty kept whistling into the phone, 'Here comes a tank!' and evidently the German tanks were stopping directly below him. The building was right on the road and he says, 'Here comes another one! and another one!' and whoever was on the other end of the line said, 'Well, how many tanks are there?' He says, 'I can piss on nine of them out of this window!' About that time the lead tank started up and came around the corner, firing randomly from left to right and evidently the third round went into a stone building and whoever was in it came out of the back end at the same time. I was about a quarter mile down the road from the outpost and I could see both the outpost and the building and the tanks.

Though most of 3rd Battalion was stopped short of Foy on the evening of December 19th, members of "H" Company moved into some of the houses. Sgt. Charles E. Richards ventured into the first house on the southern outskirts on the 20th. He recalled:

Our platoon's defense was on the edge of the woods, to the left side of the road where the pillbox was located (facing the town of Foy). After dark, Sgt. Hefner and I took some men and crossed the road to the old farmhouse (used as an outpost). This happened on different nights. On one of the nights, two German soldiers were approaching the house. In a short burst of gunfire, one of the Germans was killed. The other got away. We dragged the German into our backyard, took his I.D.'s for our captain and left him lying on his right side with his right arm extended. The weather was cold. In the morning, we turned him on his back to check for unit insignias and he was frozen. His right arm came straight up as we turned him over. From then on, it was a ritual to shake hands with him every time we came or left the house. We figured that if we could shake his hand, we were a helluva lot better off than he was.

Pvt. Guy D. Jackson, of "H" Company, remembers the same incident as was related by Sgt. Richards – even to the date but shaking hands with a corpse wasn't one of the incidents he related:

On the 20th of December, a German scout came down the road, out of Foy. We cut him down. It was half way between our lines and Foy. Later on, we had an OP in a house on a road fifty feet from his body.

In an action which occurred over on the "G" Company MLR, near Recogne, Pvt. Ewell B. Martin had vivid recollections of his first days of action near Bastogne. Combat was new to him as a late replacement:

Our squad was dug in on a line in an open field during the night. I don't recall much of what was happening that night except for the sound of tanks and a wounded German who must have been calling his lieutenant for help for what seemed like hours. Early in the morning the squad member up the hill from me called that we were pulling out. I decided to go down the hill and check to make sure that the squad next to me had also gotten the word. That was a mistake. As I got to the fence I could see that the next squad had already moved out. They had been dug in along a hedgerow. I started through the fence; at the same time, a Kraut machine gun opened up. I jumped into a hole and remember cussing out the digger for not going any deeper. I was trying to get as flat as I could while the tracers were walking toward me, down the hedgerow just above the ground. Had a hole ripped in my pants leg but not a scratch on me. I crawled out along the hedgerow back to the village where I met a 75mm gun crew who had seen me coming in. We tried to search back to the point I had been fired on to locate the tank that was close by but couldn't spot it.

## 2ND BATTALION ACTIONS

Captain Richard Winters describes the confusion which existed in his area on the 20th of December. Though 2nd Battalion was in position, the enemy seemed to move around quite freely – even in the area of the Battalion HQ.

A heavy mist or fog during the night was hanging over the woods and fields at first light of dawn, on the second day. I was standing in the edge of the woods, by a field to the rear of the 2nd Battalion CP. All was quiet and peaceful. Suddenly, to my left, out of the woods walked a German soldier in his long, winter overcoat. He had no rifle, no pack and he continued to walk slowly toward the middle of the field. A couple of men with me instinctively brought their rifles to their shoulders, but by a hand signal, I told them to hold their fire. We watched as he stopped, took off his overcoat, pulled down his pants and relieved himself. After he was finished, I hollered to him in my best German, 'Kommen sie hier!' (Come here), which he did. All the poor fellow had in his pockets were a few pictures, trinkets and the butt end of a loaf of black bread, which was very hard.

Think of this – here is a German soldier, in the light of early dawn, who went to take a crap, got turned around in the woods, walked through our lines, past the company CP, and ended up behind the battalion CP! That sure was some line of defense we had that first night.

Meanwhile, over in the "E" Company area where 1/Sgt. Carwood Lipton was positioned, so he could view actions south of Noville and in Foy itself when the fog would lift, he observed the following through his binoculars:

Noville was outside our defensive positions, however, so that morning the 1st Battalion was ordered to withdraw back through Foy. This was to be difficult as the Germans held Foy and the road between Foy and Noville and the withdrawal became a continuing battle back along the road

The sounds of the fighting came back clearly to me and, from time to time, I could see the maneuvering of the tanks and half-tracks and the slow movement toward Foy.

At the same time, a second battle was underway, in the fairly clear area south of Foy, and I could also watch this fighting through my binoculars. The 3rd Battalion of the 506th was attacking Foy from the south, probably to lessen the enemy pressure on the 1st Battalion and Team Desobry withdrawing from Noville.

As I watched, the German forces began to advance out of Foy against the 3rd Battalion to the south with a tank and infantry. They had gotten several hundred yards out of Foy when a round from a bazooka or an antitank gun hit the tank and damaged one of its treads. The battle continued on while the tank sat there right out in the middle of the open area, unable to move.

Suddenly, out of Foy, another German tank appeared and ran right up to the tank with the damaged tread. A man jumped out of the good tank and pulled out a heavy chain from the rear of it. While the firefight was raging all around him, I'm sure everyone in the 3rd Battalion who could see him, was trying to put a bullet in him; he fastened the end of the chain to the knocked-out tank and jumped back into the good tank. That tank then pulled the damaged tank back through the German positions and probably back to where it could be repaired to fight again.

After that, the Germans south of Foy withdrew slowly as 3rd Battalion advanced against them.

Shortly after that, the 1st Battalion and Team Desobry reached Foy in their withdrawal from Noville. They were stopped there for a time by the enemy forces in and around Foy and by fire from tanks in the woods north of our positions. As they were now closer to us, we could see them quite clearly through binoculars, but they were still too far away for us to give them any supporting fire.

Some of the tanks moved to the right, the west, of Foy while others attacked straight through and the Germans had to give way. Once they started withdrawing to the west, the situation cleared up fast.

In the road was Colonel Sink and he was shaking hands with the men and slapping them on the back in greeting as they came by. He was obviously overjoyed that the men of his 1st Battalion were back.

PFC. Charles Cram, a mortarman with 2nd Battalion Headquarters Company, remembers being in position at the edge of Luzery on the morning of the 20th in an effort to help 1st Battalion. He wrote:

We had some of the 326th Engineers with us and they had a weapons carrier on the road. We had flankers out from our rifle companies that I could see to our right and we had just taken off for maybe fifty yards. We must have been under observation by Kraut tanks because two 88 rounds hit close together right in the column with no warning that comes with incoming artillery. Apparently it was flat trajectory fire from relatively short range. We were all flattened on each side of the road and our platoon leader asked who had been hit. A man on the road said that the weapons carrier driver was killed and Cpl. Wayne Huffman and Sgt. Jack Barickman said they had been hit. My weapon was a folding stock carbine and Huffman gave me his M-1 and told me to be a good soldier, the war was over for both of them.

After a few minutes, our lieutenant said we weren't going to Noville, but were turning 90 degrees east into the field. That was the direction I thought the fire had come from and I thought this was insane. I was shaking badly, thinking I was about to march into cannon fire in which the Krauts were aiming the cannon directly at me. However, the officer was as cool as could be. We proceeded two or three hundred yards up to the edge of a wood where we stayed until the day after New Years.

## CLOSING THE GAP

As has been mentioned by 1Lt. Alex Andros of "H" Company in his earlier account concerning the problem of having men spread too thinly along the MLR so whole platoons and even battalions of enemy soldiers could march through the space between adjoining foxholes if weather conditions permitted, Captain Richard Winters had witnessed first hand an enemy soldier behind 2nd Battalion Headquarter's Company CP. Now in the afternoon of the 20th, he continued to be concerned about the contact between the 501st and 506th Regiments near the railroad which was supposed to be the contact point between the two regiments. Winters related:

Keeping contact with the 501st on our right flank at the railroad station was a running problem. They were there, then they were not there. It made us a little nervous about that right flank.

S/Sgt. Vincent Occhipinti describes the first action in which his unit was involved and how he lost two close friends on the second day while an attempt was made to close the gap between the two regiments near the railroad line running northeast out of Bastogne:

The 1st Platoon of 'F' Company was designated to close the gap between the 3rd Platoon and the 501st PIR on the east of the small railroad station with the railroad track running north and south as the boundary between the 506th and the 501st. Platoon strength at that time was approximately 35 and advance information estimated that only a half dozen Germans were in the area. The action started at about 1600 hours on the 20th of December. Although two days later the entire area would be covered with much snow, the woods and fields were bare at this time and the temperature was probably in the 30's. I attached myself to the 1st Squad because I carried a Thompson sub and the area we entered was dense woods. The firing, if any, would mostly be at close quarters. The area to be cleared with the 501st was approximately 300 to 400 yards.

We had gone about 100 yards, keeping in contact with 3rd Platoon of 'F' Company which was deployed on the small trail running east and west and passing the railroad station at the railroad tracks, which was our contact point with the 501st. Because the woods were rather dense, our platoon proceeded slowly to keep that contact with 3rd Platoon and moved in the general direction of the station. Sgt. Gordon Mather was up front with his scouts, Cpl. George Lovell and one other.

All of a sudden, all hell broke loose as the dug-in enemy opened fire on Mather and Lovell, the first two persons to come into view. (If they had not opened fire for an additional five minutes, they might well have had a field day with 1st Platoon.) As the enemy fire came through our positions (we were too closely bunched), we hit the deck and did not return the fire. The small arms and machine gun fire continued for what seemed like a long time but was probably not more than one minute and I suspect that the Germans realized they might be exposing their positions and they no longer could see us because of the approaching darkness. (It seemed like all of a sudden, it was dark.) During that minute or so, while pressed into the ground, I could see tracer bullets skipping through our positions. No one else was hit but I'll never know why not.

At a distance of perhaps 50 yards, I could hear the Germans make some rude remarks about President Roosevelt and American soldiers in general. I presumed it was all of the choice English words they had learned. We withdrew approximately 50 yards and spread out in a skirmish line, northwest to southwest, still keeping our contact with the 3rd Platoon and providing flank protection for 'F' Company.

The platoon started digging in. Entrenching tools were at a premium, helmets, knives and hands were the order of the night. A runner was dispatched to notify company headquarters and field phones were installed from my position (approximately in the center of the skirmish line) and the right end of the line where we placed one of our machine guns. We also had phone contact with the 'F' Company CP.

Another member of the 1st Platoon, PFC. William True, had a slightly different view of the action. He related:

The 1st Platoon of 'F' Company (my platoon), or at least two squads of it, were sent into a wooded area to see about setting up a line. Gordon Mather's squad was in the lead and my squad was in the rear. Suddenly, a German machine gun opened fire and we all hit the dirt. I recall choosing my landing spot even as I was going down in order to take advantage of a slight depression in the ground. Perhaps four or five inches at most. That very small difference may have kept me from being hit, because the crack of the bullets going over my head was even closer than in training days when we had been intentionally exposed to very close overhead fire as we learned to hug the  ground while crawling on our bellies. None of us ever spotted where the fire was coming from and, after about a minute (or less), it stopped and we were able to move around a bit and assess what had happened.

Apparently, the German machine gun emplacement had simply been an outpost and they had withdrawn after our contact with them. George Lovell, 1st squad scout and Gordon Mather, 1st squad leader, had both been killed. George's position out front as scout had made him an obvious target, of course, and Gordon had been killed as he raised up slightly to turn and call out some orders to his squad and others of us in the rear.

S/Sgt. John H. Taylor had a different assignment with his 2nd Platoon of "F" Company. He related:

We started moving the next morning (20th) toward Foy, crossed a road, started drawing quite a bit of artillery fire. We moved off to the side of the road to our right. This was getting around noon time. We were still in the 'fog' not knowing what was taking place. We moved into some woods where we were held up. That night, we were to outpost an area to our right. We did this. Later found out there was a gap in our lines between us and the 501st. This was in the area of a railroad that went south into Bastogne. There was a place called Halte which was really only a railroad station. There was a stone house. We outposted that area that night. The Germans were moving into the area. We had told the men on outposts to come straight back from their assignments when they were relieved. We had a new man named Ceniceros[62] out in the area with Joe Hogenmiller. It was foggy and misty. Hogenmiller came back. We had another new man named Luke Atkins from Harlan County, Kentucky. He was a crack shot. Ceniceros came back in the fog, dodging from tree to tree. I heard Luke fire. I ran over there and had an idea of what happened. It turned out that Luke had shot Ceniceros. It was an unfortunate thing. It was really Ceniceros' fault as he hadn't followed instructions. We went out and brought him in. Right after this, another company was brought through our position and told to clean it out.

## MARVIE

The morning of December 19 had been a beehive of activity in the Division assembly area as the various units were sent on their missions around the perimeter. Shortly after the parachute infantry units moved out, Division Headquarters moved out from its positions around the little red school house in Mande St. Etienne and headed for the former Belgian army barracks at the north end of Bastogne, which had served as VIII Corps Headquarters.

The 327th Glider Infantry Regiment moved into the brick schoolhouse at 1500 hours and used it as its temporary command post. A few hours later, the 1st Battalion, less "B" Company, was sent east to provide flank protection for the 501st Regiment, near Neffe. The 3rd Battalion (401st) faced its line companies to the west and sent its "B" Company to positions southeast of Flamierge. 2nd Battalion was in bivouac as a protective screen around regimental headquarters.

As the newly appointed executive officer for "G" Company, 1Lt. Alfred Regenburg recalled the first day for the 2nd Battalion as somewhat relaxed at this location followed by an early morning order to move out.

When we disembarked that first morning, we had a defensive bivouac and tried to make life easier and more comfortable with bedrolls and extra goodies that had been stored away in our sleeping bags. Nothing happened that night in our area. The next morning we awoke to shouts of 'Let's get going!' and this time we were going on foot.

---

[62]PFC. Salvadore Ceniceros had originally been assigned to Regimental Headquarters Company for the Normandy and Holland campaigns. He had been a participant in Colonel Sink's wild mid-day ride on D-Day in Normandy as a body guard.

As a member of the last infantry regiment to arrive in the assembly area at Mande St. Etienne, PFC. Donald J. Rich, of "G" Company in 2nd Battalion, had this recollection of a directive issued early on the morning of the 20th that caused problems later:

> We left our packs, overcoats and sleeping bags behind, which we later regretted, because the next three days we almost froze. Later, some coats and sleeping bags were brought to us.

Afraid of falling behind as he struggled to remove his overshoes, PFC. Charles Kocourek of "F" Company finally gave up trying to get them off. He wrote:

> As we marched into Bastogne – the last of the long column to arrive, there was the supply sergeant – he directed us to drop all our overcoats and blankets to lighten our loads and we'd get them back when we got up to the front lines. All I had was my overshoes and the column was moving farther away. I couldn't get them off my boots. I said, 'To hell with it – I'm gonna leave them on.' I kept them on and thank God I did.

During the pre-dawn hours of December 20, Team O'Hara's roadblock, on the Wiltz-Bastogne road, received heavy shelling. At 0645, there was thick fog and little movement could be seen. As day lightened, the fog lifted a bit and the tankers were able to see enemy soldiers attempting to remove the logs and other obstructions at the block site.

The 420th Armored Artillery Battalion was called on to fire on the enemy engineers at the block site. The enemy was driven off with the loss of two killed. The enemy then put up smoke on the position to hide their actions. At this time, they came under fire from O'Hara's mortars and fire from the armored vehicles.

The direction of the enemy assault was then altered and deflected toward Marvie. At 0400 on the 20th, 2nd Battalion, along with the 327th Glider Infantry regimental command post was ordered to move from Mande St. Etienne to Bastogne. The regimental CP set up in Bastogne while 2nd Battalion continued on to Marvie where it took over its defense from troops of the 326th Airborne Engineer Battalion. 2nd Battalion entered Marvie just as the enemy was attempting to break up the roadblock.

Colonel Joseph Harper accompanied the 2nd Battalion troops and joined with LTC. Roy L. Inman, 2nd Battalion commander, in visiting LTC. O'Hara to decide how best to line up the available forces for the defense of the southern perimeter. The troops were then assigned their positions along the MLR.

At 1125, Col. Inman's CP called to report heavy shelling and the appearance of enemy tanks coming toward Marvie, from the southeast.

At that time, Colonel Harper was continuing his inspection of the area and when he got to the top of a rise he turned and saw the enemy tracers streaking toward his troops from the edge of the woods directly southeast of Marvie. The small arms tracers and artillery shells were impacting among the houses in the village.

On the first day, there is often a lot of useless digging in as the officers haven't yet decided on the final disposition of the various units. That is always frustrating to soldiers. PFC. Charles Kocourek wrote:

We got just to the edge of Marvie. We were told to dig in. No sooner did we get dug in than we were ordered to move further south; then 'G' Company took our positions. No sooner do we get situated in our new holes when the sergeant comes along and orders: 'Kocourek – take three men and go out to the edge of those woods. We've got to protect the flank – one guy from each squad.' 1st Platoon was 300 yards to my right. They had a building and a barn. Between us were open fields. The grass had been cut so there was no concealment for anyone trying to sneak up on us between the two platoons. In front of me was a swamp.

Sergeants Mackey and John came out to our position and noted it was well situated so they put up an observation post nearby.

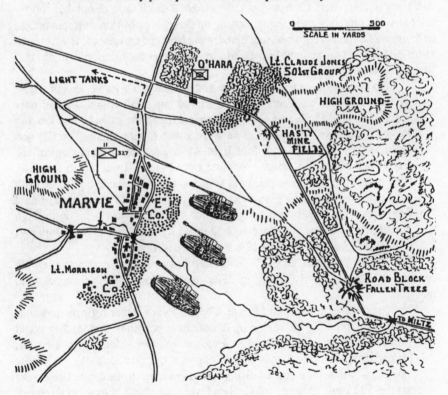

*Map 8*

The move of 2nd Battalion to Marvie was to replace the undermanned troops of "C" Company of the 326th Airborne Engineers which had been positioned at Marvie on the 19th. One of those engineers was Cpl. C. E. "Stub" Storeby who had been on a four hour patrol during the night in which they failed to make contact with the patrol of the adjoining company. His group had spent the night in a hay loft at the edge of the village. He describes the enemy attack on Marvie during the morning of the 20th:

> About daybreak, we lit a fire and had a K-ration. Then the Krauts attacked – came by the dozens – mortars zapped us. The Krauts hit our barn – two guys in my platoon were wounded (Frank Radtke of Milwaukee and Steve Pozar from Orlando). Someone gave word to move out across fields toward a hill and town called Bastogne. Several men were hit as the Krauts took the half-tracks and turned the .50's loose on us. We formed a line on the hill and shelling and mortar fire were heavy.

Meanwhile, "G" Company of the 327th had moved into the positions recently vacated by the "F" Company troopers. "G" Company, along with 2nd Battalion Headquarters Company personnel, got a quick taste of combat shortly after arriving on the Marvie scene. Setting up defensive positions without access to maps was a frustrating experience under the best circumstances. It was much more difficult when actions broke out almost immediately upon arrival. 1Lt. Regenburg recalled:

> No one had any maps of the area and we had just a vague idea of where we were going. Some hours later, we arrived in a small village which I later found out was Marvie. As we were going through the town, I was looking for a CP because I understood we were going to stop there. The CP was close to the road and I saw four light American tanks coming out of the woods hell bent for election – coming right past us. I ran out to the road, fired a shot to get their attention to stop and form a defensive position with us. At least even if their guns weren't heavy, they would provide additional fire power. There was no turning back for them. They just went on through the village. I believe they later hooked up with Task Force O'Hara with part of the tanks from the 9th and 10th Armored Divisions.

PFC. John Sherman, of "G" Company, was in on the early actions. He recalled the officers hastily setting up defensive positions as the action began to unfold:

> I remember going into Marvie. Captain Evans, other officers and non-coms were directing the setting up of defensive positions. Before they could finish, a line of tanks and other armored vehicles, along with infantry, appeared on the ridge across a draw opposite our positions. We no sooner saw them when they started firing and advancing toward us. They were maybe 500 yards away or so. Captain Evans was hit (I believe in the head) while he was directing the guys where to dig in. We could see the infantry

moving toward us alongside the tanks and it looked like the whole German army. The incoming fire was heavy. I think Don Rich and Jim Shaw were in a farm building and got off a bazooka round at a tank that was close by. Their shot was ineffective and the tank gun targeted them. They started to leave the building when an '88 hit the building and blew them out. Neither Don or Jim were hit but Jim suffered severe concussion and had to be evacuated.

After being told that his regiment was to be in reserve and that the enemy troops were still 40 miles away, it was a real shock to PFC. Donald J. Rich to be involved in a combined armored-infantry attack on Marvie when his regiment had just arrived and had not yet completed the job of digging in. He wrote:

The bazooka section had not set up yet when someone yelled, 'There comes a German tank!' I grabbed my bazooka and told one man to come with me. We ran up the street and into a house. I told the man with me to take the bazooka and stay at a window. I went into the next room to watch and told him to wait till the tank went by and then fire at it. He must have stuck his head up before the tank went by because the tanker fired into the house and blew a hole about three or four feet in diameter. I went rolling across the floor. I jumped up to see how my buddy made out. He came staggering out of the room. I rushed him to the medics. I never knew if he had serious wounds or if he made it. I ran back to the house to retrieve the bazooka. It was bent, with the barrel opening sealed. Someone else got the tank further on.

As the intelligence officer for 2nd Battalion, 1Lt. Thomas J. Niland was aware of the importance of defending Marvie as part of the overall defense of the key road network in Bastogne. He wrote:

The 2nd Battalion, after detrucking west of Bastogne somewhere around Mande St. Etienne, proceeded through Bastogne to the area around Marvie to defend the high ground around Bastogne and deny the enemy access to the main road. As we reached Marvie on foot, all hell broke loose and we met the enemy head on in the village and a fire fight developed. They came with half-tracks to Marvie. This is when Colonel Inman was wounded and Lt. Tom Morrison was captured. We soon retook the village and established our defense lines. It was during this action that we were able to free Lt. Morrison and a few men from 'G' Company who were overrun and taken prisoner early in the battle.

Recalling an incident which was humorous to him, Lt. Niland had this recollection of the experience of one of his Intelligence Section men named PFC. Charles Fisher:

After the initial fighting in the village, we had to secure the town because the Germans still occupied some of the houses. We therefore started to clear the village house by house. While doing this I encountered Charles

Fisher, a scout in my unit. He had been sent by Major Bob Galbraith to find the medics for Colonel Inman who had been wounded during the action and needed attention. I warned Fisher that we had not yet cleared out that part of Marvie. He continued on and ran into a house down the street only to face several Germans who were in the house. They apparently were as surprised as he was – no one fired and he fled the house and returned down the street without a shot being fired.

That wasn't the way PFC. Charles Fisher remembered the episode – and he has returned to that action scene on two occasions since the war. This is the way he recalled the incident:

On the morning of December 20, the first day of 2nd Battalion in Marvie – our battalion commander, LTC. Roy Inman was wounded. I was standing guard at the entrance to the battalion CP when someone shouted, 'Fisher, go get the medics. The Colonel has been hit!'

Off I went on the double. I had observed the medics setting up in a barn earlier that morning as we were entering the town so I headed in that direction. There was some shelling and small arms fire so I went a back way rather than down the main street. As I neared the center of town, I walked around the corner of a house just as a German soldier came around the side of a house across the road. I looked at him and he looked at me. We both fired at each other; both missed and ducked behind our respective houses. I determined that this was no time to be out in the open so ran up to the barn where the medics had been located and tried to go in. The barn door was locked so I pounded on it and yelled for someone to open the door. There was no response so I went to a window of the house, attached to the barn, and looked in on a group of civilians. They saw me and began screaming at me and motioning for me to go away. This made me angry so I broke the window, unlocked it and crawled in and started down a hall toward the interior barn door. All this time the civilians were jabbering at me and one elderly woman grabbed by arm and tried to pull me back. I couldn't understand what was going on. I shook her loose, continued down the hall and turned into the barn. It was rather dark in the barn but I could make out silhouettes of people coming toward me wearing long overcoats. I knew that we didn't have any overcoats at the time so I raised my M1 and fired. (I thought I fired one round but when I checked my rifle, later, I had only one round left in the eight-round clip.) I immediately turned, ran down the hall, through the room of excited civilians, dove back out the window and crouched down beside a stone wall while I tried to decide what to do. I saw a GI come around the corner of a nearby house and motioned for him to cover me and off I went, followed by a hand grenade and rounds from a burp gun. I made it to cover with nothing more than a piece of shrapnel in the hand. Then, I took off as fast as I could go back up the hill, toward the Battalion

CP. Enroute, I found the new location of the medics, told them Colonel Inman had been hit (which, by this time, they already knew), had a bandage put on my hand and then back to the Battalion CP where I tried to report what had happened but started to shake like a leaf and couldn't even talk. You've heard the expression, 'scared speechless'. That was me. Later, I was informed that Battalion had known that the medics had relocated before I was sent to get them. I was just part of the ten percent who never gets the word.[63]

With the wounding of Captain Hugh Evans, along with the battalion commander, 1Lt. Regenburg, as executive officer of "G" Company, assumed he was to take over the unit. He related:

I assumed I was to take over. No one disputed that, so I checked to see where the rest of the company was positioned. I found, to my dismay, that the platoon under Lt. Frank Hibbard was attached to 'F' Company, supposedly on our right flank. Communications were difficult and I was very proud of the men of 'G' Company, who seemed to know what they had to do to dig in and set up their defensive lines. Fortunately, 'E' Company on our left had been more cautious than 'G' Company and had dug in. They took the brunt of the attack, for which I was very thankful because of my weakened company strength.

The attack was beaten back by aggressive fighting and the combined effort of Task Force O'Hara, which brought fire on their tanks. One of the incidents that was really a mistake was that there was a half-track belonging to the engineers that was also across the bridge. They started back for cover when the attack broke. By mistake, they were knocked out, I think by either 'G' Company bazooka fire or 81st anti-tank fire. The position of the half-track (knocked out without any serious injury to any of the occupants) was such that it impeded any attempt by the German tanks to get through. One such tank did get through a few days later and Tommy Niland tried to knock

---

[63] At Christmas time in 1951, while stationed in France, I (Fisher) returned to Bastogne, went out to Marvie and to the house where the above incident occurred. As I approached, an elderly woman was sweeping the steps to the house, which had been rebuilt. She looked up, saw me and her face turned pale. She recognized me and invited me in and, over a cup of coffee and cakes, with half the neighborhood present, we reminisced using my fractured French and hand and arm signals. She told me that when the medics moved out of the barn that morning, the German soldiers moved in. The civilians – family and friends – were gathered in one room of the house when they saw me look in the window. They tried to make me understand that the Germans were there and motioned for me to go away but I broke the window and crawled in. As I started down the hall, she grabbed my arm and tried to pull me back but I shook loose and continued. They then heard some shots and I came flying back through the room and out the window. She said her daughter ran over and closed the broken window to slow down the Germans who came running into the room, threw some grenades out of the window and fired at me.

it out with a bazooka and the shell just bounced off the tank. It was later knocked out by Task Force O'Hara.[64]

## COLONEL SALEE'S 1ST BATTALION

1st Battalion of the 327th Glider Infantry Regiment had been ordered to the east side of the perimeter on the afternoon of the 19th when the 501st had experienced heavy pressure in their Mont-Neffe-Wardin area. Salee's men, less "B" Company, had dug in and waited for action on the 501st west flank. The only action experienced had been some rather heavy shelling during the night.

As a platoon sergeant in "A" Company, S/Sgt. Jack Williamson was part of that group sent over to the east side to relieve some of the pressure being felt by the 501st. After experiencing a relatively quiet night, action began to pick up for his group on the morning of the 20th. It is very possible that the Germans he was speaking of are the same ones who were pushed out of the 907th Glider Field Artillery positions. Williamson related:

The next morning (20th), we saw some Germans advancing toward us like a flock of sheep. There was a jump outfit on our flank. When their lieutenant gave the order to run out and surround some Germans, me and another glider trooper went along. About 25 to 30 were captured.

## WILLIAMSON'S STRANGE ENCOUNTER

An encounter with a group of tanks on a patrol during the day of the 20th has left S/Sgt. Jack Williamson wondering all these years. He relates:

An earlier patrol toward Neffe was scrubbed and the second patrol was to go. I looked around for our lieutenant and he had disappeared. He had told me to take the patrol. I asked which way? He said 'about two fingers left of the sun'. So I decided to go somewhere in that direction with about 15 men and we were heavily armed. I started out leading the patrol and, instead of going straight ahead, I eased over to the right and went through the woods instead of over the open fields. The Krauts started shelling the top of the hill about the time we should have been up there if we hadn't changed directions. We came to a clearing in the woods and I was leading PFC. Einard C. Mackey, who was acting as second scout. I got up out about twenty feet into the clearing and spotted a tank with a gun pointed right at me. I froze and, with my right hand, motioned Mackey down and back. He read me right and held

---

[64]See comments of Pvt. Edward Carowick of "B" Company, 326th Airborne Engineer Battalion of page 236.

the patrol back – what to do – either way I felt they would fire the gun at me. Not that I was so brave, I figured my best chance was to approach the tank slowly, which I did. When I got up close, I saw the American star on the side of the tank. Hell, I walked up and saw it was an American tank unit with a captain standing by the lead tank and his jeep.

We started talking and I waved my patrol forward and they came on over. The captain asked me what unit I was with. I told him the 101st Airborne Division. He wanted to know where we were situated. I told him Bastogne. How many men? To boost his morale, I said 'about 80,000 or more in and around town and more coming up'.

They had about ten tanks and were headed toward Bastogne on either side of the road. I told the captain I needed to go and make my patrol. I was to get a prisoner or some German pay books. I said we would be going down the road between his tanks and that we would be safe that far at least. As I left, I suggested he go into Bastogne and join our ranks.

Then, we moved on and there was a soldier standing in the turret of each tank and I waved at each as we went by and said 'Howdy!' Would you believe – not one of those tankers acknowledged me. I told Mackey, 'Them tankers are a weird bunch of bastards!'

We moved along and left the tanks behind a good ways and sat down on either side of the road, in the woods, to take a breather. We saw some Germans in the distance digging in artillery. Coming toward us were three enemy soldiers. They were probably the point of a German column moving our way. I ordered our men to be quiet and pointed toward the Germans. I waited until they got close up so we could capture them.

PFC. Ernest A. Miller was getting his BAR gun in a good position and in doing so made some noise alerting the Germans and the big guy in front gave them the 'achtung' and they spread out like a covey of quail. We opened fire and hit all three. I jumped up and ran out and pointed my empty submachine gun at the big German. I ordered him to spread those hands out and up. I grabbed the grenade from his belt and threw it to the side. I got his binocs and luger and his map and map case. The case held only American cigarettes. He was only hit in one foot – in the heel. The other two didn't make it.

At first, the big German said he couldn't walk. I said, 'Walk or kaput!' and he got up. I had Miller walk behind him to encourage him. I said, 'If he can't make it, shoot him'.

As we started returning to our positions, the Germans started shooting at us with a mortar. The only reason they waited that long was because they thought they had run into our front lines. As we were moving back fast along the dirt road, that mortar was chasing us. I figured they were firing from a map so we headed into the woods, to the left. The road swung to the right. They kept chasing the road. We kept going and came back onto that tank outfit. They were still there.

Once again, none of them spoke to us till we got up to where their captain was out in front. He didn't even ask about the German prisoner we had. He suggested I take him and his driver to our headquarters.

He asked if I knew the password and countersign and I said yes. He said 'Are you sure?' I said, 'Hell, yes!'

He and his driver rode in front and Miller and I were on the back of the jeep with the prisoner. Mackey took the rest of the patrol back and they arrived safely.

As we came into the 327th lines, I was challenged but I knew some of the guys. Some officer came over and looked the situation over and spotted the weapon I had taken. He wanted the German luger I had. He told me his daddy got one in World War I and he always wanted to have one. I told him there were a lot of them out front and that was where he could go to get one. I don't think he liked my response.

We got into Bastogne and found our G-2 office. I told the tank captain 'Here it is!'

Miller and I were standing in the cobblestone street. The tank captain and his driver started moving off real fast. I yelled, 'Don't you want to see our G-2?' He yelled, 'We'll see them later!' At that time, I couldn't figure it out.

We took the prisoner to the G-2 – some Lt. Colonel. If I remember correctly, he spoke perfect German. When he was through questioning the prisoner and me, he said to take the prisoner outside. The German was afraid to go with us but the G-2 colonel insisted we take him over to the church where the wounded were being treated. They had hay on the floor. We let the prisoner lie on the floor – I guess he was hurting a lot. Some troopers at the church relieved us of the responsibility of the prisoner.

We went back to our outfit and they gave me hell for not bringing the prisoner to them but I thought it was the thing to do to get information to our G-2 quickly. I found out later the Germans were using our uniforms. I now believe that tank outfit was German in our uniforms and in our tanks. They were leading the column toward Bastogne. I think it was the 26th Volksgrenadiers.

## "B" COMPANY HEADS EAST

When "A" and "C" Companies headed toward Neffe on the afternoon of the 19th, "B" Company was held back at Mande St. Etienne until it was given a definite assignment. S/Sgt. Paul Slevey would become the acting first sergeant on the following day, in the absence of the regular top kick who was still in Paris, when the unit departed for Bastogne. Slevey traced the "B" Company move to its assignment in the Neffe area:

On December 20, we came across the railroad bridge into Bastogne, passed the Hotel LeBrun and on to the town square, then down the main street, just past St. Peter's Church. We went through the town gate to the next crossroad. We turned to the left and up the hill. This was on the road to Neffe. Near the top of the hill, a lane led off to the right. We went up a short distance and dug in. I dug a foxhole with Sgt. Bob Balchuck and we finished just before it started to get dark. The C. O. wanted Sgt. Balchuck to deliver a message to one of the platoons. He wasn't sure where they were so I said I'd help him find them. On the road, we went up to the fence row that would have led to the platoon but at that time artillery started coming in so we took to the ditches. After the third round, we got up and ran until we heard more coming. This time, when we stopped, I looked over and saw a religious shrine at the side of the road. I laid there and said a little prayers. When the next round came in, I cussed the Germans. Sgt. Balchuck said he was hit but could make it back to our hole. In the slit trench, he laid on his stomach and I lifted his overcoat and with my Zippo lighter, looked to see if he was bleeding. He went back to the aid station and came back the next morning. That night, Pvt. Luke Anderson was KIA. Privates Frank Fetco, John Iski and Jackson were SWA.

## CROSSROADS "X"

Around midnight on December 19th, Division had ordered the 327th Glider Infantry Regiment to Crossroads "X", the site of 326th Medical Company Field Hospital where much firing and explosions had been heard since 2200 hours.

With the platoons of "B" Company of the 401st in defensive positions southeast of Flamierge, being in closest proximity of the road junction, Captain Robert McDonald's men got the move out order at around 0300 on the 20th. The move is best described by PFC. Richard Bostwick who wrote:

About three or four in the morning, we ('B' Company) moved out leaving 'C' Company at the roadblock. We headed west, toward France. The Company had been split up, one half on either side of the road. The road surface was above our heads. We were in the ditches. If the Krauts appeared on the road, we would have the advantage. At one point, we were forced to wade, waist deep, through a swamp that was about fifty feet across.

Time was lost – haven't any idea how long we were on the move. At last a halt was called and it was then that I noticed a weird sound – a low sounding drone resembling the sound of a fog horn. The entire company was now on one side of the road and Captain McDonald clued us in.

In a company history, which he had written before his death and which was sent for our use by his widow, PFC. Marshall E. Griffith describes the movement and actions of his unit upon arrival on the Bastogne scene:

On the 19th of December, we went into a defensive position southeast of Flamierge. At 2300 hours, 'B' Company was ordered to move north to the vicinity of Salle and recapture a truck convoy of the 28th Division, which had been ambushed by the Germans. In a night attack, the mission was accomplished and a road block was set up to protect what we had taken. We secured defensive positions around the road block to repulse any German counterattacks.

Another of the men involved in these actions was PFC. Carmen C. Gisi, who related actions which were very near to the site of the 326th Airborne Medical Company field hospital and clearing station, which was overrun by enemy forces the very first night. Gisi describes the first night's action:

The 3rd Platoon was to the right of the crossroads (X), which was the location of the Medical Company. We were on a ridge. Charles Sawyer and I were sent out in front of the platoon as the 1st and 2nd scouts. When we reached the road, I fired two shots and that was the signal for the 3rd Platoon to move down. Before the platoon reached the road, Sawyer and I heard men running up the road toward us. When they got close to us, we challenged them and they answered in German and we opened up on them, killing some of them. This whole attack took place at night. After it was over, we moved back to our positions on the ridge. At the crossroads, our trucks were burning and the horns were blowing.

In the narrative he wrote shortly after the war, of his experiences, PFC. Richard Bostwick relates how the move was made to the ambush area and also what the troopers found at the scene:

The Krauts had ambushed an American truck convoy and reports indicated the enemy was still on the scene. From this point, the Company proceeded at an angle of about 45 degrees from the road. We proceeded in a zig-zag course up and down the terrain and, all the while, drone became louder and louder. We were soon on the crest of the hill. Several hundred yards below, on a sharp curve, a convoy of trucks was burning – some vehicles in the ditches, some straddled the road. I counted about fifteen vehicles, all in flames. We formed a company-wide skirmish line at the fringe of the area illuminated by the firelight. With our rifles in a ready position, we slowly approached to a point where we hit the ground and waited for the order to move in. The eerie light of the fire and the drone of a truck horn make for a comfortable feeling. Now and then, the guttural shouts of Germans were heard and the clatter of equipment added to the din.

We got to our feet and began to fire as we moved forward. Shouting and screaming followed. The enemy's return fire was a poor example of resistance. They didn't have a chance against the hail of bullets covering them. Upon reaching the trucks, we lobbed hand grenades into the wooded area beyond the road. As far as I knew, there was one casualty on our side. Platoon sergeant Mike Campana was nicked with a bullet-pierced ear lobe.

Bodies were lying all over the place; some American; many German. The continuous drone of a horn was caused by the body of a truck driver draped over a steering wheel. The body was pushed over onto the seat and the sound stopped. The only sound, now, was the crackling of the flames. We regrouped and returned to the top of the hill from which we had attacked.

Anticipating an enemy counterattack after his troops had driven the enemy force away from the blazing trucks near Crossroads "X", Captain Robert McDonald had his men set up an ambush for the enemy. PFC. Carmen Gisi describes that action:

In the morning we caught the German column. The first and last vehicles were knocked out and the rest couldn't move. It was like something out of a movie. After the battle, we moved down to the road, went into the 326th Medical Company area where we found two troopers dead. I also found a camera in the hospital and took a picture of the tents and later on took more pictures of my buddies, on the same film. (Gisi provided a copy of the hospital tent picture for this narrative.)

*The picture was taken by PFC. Carmen Gisi of "B" Company of the 401st Glider Infantry Battalion with a camera found in a foxhole at the site of the 326th Airborne Medical Company clearing station at Crossroads "X". It shows two of the medical tents still standing the following day, an abandoned trailer and the canvas water bag attached to its tripod.*

The morning of the 20th, only a few hours after the ambush, fog was heavy at ground level. More action followed in the "B" Company area, a short distance from the site of the abandoned division field hospital. At his position on the hillside, PFC. Richard Bostwick had just finished digging in when he was surprised by the appearance of a Catholic priest. He wrote:

As daylight began to break, we dug in on the edge of a ravine several hundred yards from the burned out trucks. Directly to my front the ground sloped gently away and disappeared into a thick blanket of fog. Just behind me the ravine dropped away sharply, no telling how deep because of the fog.

I had just finished digging in when bullets began to zip and whine through the area. I strained to see through the fog but everything was obscured. Within a short time, all hell was breaking loose. Artillery shells crashed about us and machine gun fire raked the area. We returned the fire. Suddenly, I was startled when, through all of this, comes a Catholic priest, crawling on his hands and knees; he dropped down beside me and asked if I was Catholic. A most unusual place to hear my confession. What guts![65]

By noon, the fog cleared and visibility was excellent. Our riflemen, who had been out under the fog blanket, began to withdraw through our position. The dead were left in the field. The wounded were being assisted by able-bodied men. Here and there, a Kraut head would pop up and the firing would resume. We were holding our own but ammunition was running low.

Late in the morning, the rumble of a tank was heard. This was one of my greatest fears in combat. There was little defense against them except the bazooka. Fifty caliber machine gun bullets began to chew up the trees around me and I stayed low in my hole.

With dramatic suddenness, the fog dropped over us. The order to withdraw was given. Our squad was picked for rear guard action; while the others withdrew, we would remain to protect their asses. A runner would return when it was time for us to get out of there. It seemed like an awfully long time before it was our turn to leave.

We made our way down into the ravine and came out on the highway. Two or three trucks had been retrieved from the convoy that had been ambushed and this was the means of our departure. Without the fog and the trucks, I'm afraid we would have had it. It felt mighty good to get out of there.[66]

---

[65] A phone call to Msgr. Francis L. Sampson (ret) verified that he probably was the priest who visited with Dick Bostwick as he remembers getting out of the jeep and chatting with the troops at their foxholes.

[66] Bostwick, op. cit.

## FATHER SAM'S ILL-FATED QUEST

On the morning of December 20, Chaplain Francis L. Sampson had just finished a meal with a group of 501st regimental headquarters men and "Doc" Bill Waldmann, one of the surgeons, and several aid men when Warrant Officer Earle Sheen, from communications, came in and excitedly related what he had just witnessed:

'You should have seen what I have just seen!', he said. 'A group of troopers machine-gunned on the road about two miles north of here.' I asked him where the place was . . . perhaps some wounded were left there. No, couldn't explain it very well on the map, for there were four roads going north out of Bastogne.

My driver, Cpl. (Fred) Adams, and I piled into the jeep and went to try to find the place. Since we couldn't find the bodies Sheen had spoken about, I decided to keep going a mile or so farther on to where our division medical company had been captured by the Germans the night before. A few German vehicles, armored cars, etc., had come up from a side road, shot up several American trucks bringing up supplies and captured our whole medical company at the same time . . . Since Doc Waldmann told me that we were getting very short of supplies, I decided to salvage some of the stuff that the Germans had left behind. We loaded the jeep with two chests of much needed equipment and were ready to head back to the regimental aid station.

It is not known if Father Sampson's trip to the devastated field hospital came before or after the men of "B" Company had visited the site at the crossroads. However, the outpost guard should have alerted the chaplain and his driver of the possibility of encountering enemy troops still in the vicinity. Father Sampson continued his story:[67]

However, a soldier on outpost guard told me that there had been quite a skirmish the previous night, on the other side of the hill. He thought there might be some wounded left there. Perhaps that was the place Sheen had referred to, I reasoned. We drove over the hill to see and, just over the crest of the hill, we ran into Germans – hundreds of them. An armored car levelled its gun at me and the Germans jumped out from behind trees yelling something. A light reconnaissance vehicle came up quickly.

'Stop the jeep, Adams' I said. 'I'm sorry I got you into this mess.' We were captured.

---

[67]Sampson, op. cit. 108-9.

## "A" COMPANY

Over in the "Able" Company sector, PFC. Harold R. Hansen, a veteran of all the campaigns, remembered trouble they had with an enemy observation post out in front of their positions. He wrote:

Our defensive position was in a wooded area. 1st Platoon of 'A' Company held it and we were getting shelled. About 300 to 600 yards ahead was another patch of woods on a knoll. It was used as an observation post by Germans. We had orders to take it and did and then were driven back at night by shelling and heavy forces. This kept up until it was taken with the help of the entire company.

## BOWEN'S PLATOON

For S/Sgt. Robert M. Bowen, serving as both platoon sergeant and platoon leader in "C" Company, the 20th brought the sound of tank movement and soldiers moving toward his position whenever the morning fog permitted the sighting. He added to his narrative:

Dawn broke and men began heating a K-ration breakfast on the Coleman stoves. Once more, I checked the squads. Walt Leamon reported that before daybreak he had heard the sound of tanks on the far side of the ridge, facing his position. I checked with my binoculars but, because of the heavy fog, could see nothing. When I got up to my CP, I reported the observation to Captain Towns and then ate breakfast. It was interrupted by a call from Jerry Hans. Men were moving through the woods to his front 600 yards away. I alerted the other squad leaders by sound power phone and hustled back to Hans' roadblock. Through binoculars I could see the men dressed in olive drab and moving south in single file. Hans volunteered to take a patrol and investigate. I called the company CP, asking for fire support if needed and watched grimly as Hans and his men went up a draw and into the woods. Not long after, the patrol withdrew, bringing back a half dozen stragglers from the 28th Division. They had been overrun but managed to escape. They were cold, wet, hungry and terribly demoralized. Most were without weapons or equipment. I directed them to the company CP. It was much the same all day. Hans and his squad guided the stragglers to our positions. The men were sent to Bastogne where they were given weapons and equipment and put in a reserve pool known as 'Team Snafu'.

## THE 501ST FRONT

The awareness of large groups of enemy soldiers operating behind the front lines of the newly arrived 101st troops was related earlier by PFC. John Trowbridge and author Robert Minick.[68]

A large patrol, numbering nearly forty, had infiltrated through 1st Battalion of the 501st Parachute Infantry Regiment and was in among the gun positions of the 907th Glider Field Artillery Battalion when they were flushed out. A captured member of that patrol revealed that their mission was to cut the road to Bastogne, behind those troops, and isolate them from other segments of the defending forces.

As the reserve unit of 2nd Battalion of the 501st, "D" company was given the mission of checking the area which was to serve as the dividing line between the 506th and 501st Regiments.

Also related earlier by Captain Dick Winters, executive officer of 2nd Battalion of the 506th, was the discovery of an enemy soldier relieving himself behind the 2nd Battalion command post, which was a considerable distance behind the front line positions. Officers of "H" Company had also described the spacing between adjoining foxholes which could provide undetected passage between those positions during periods of darkness and fog – and there was plenty of fog during those first three or four days. The total distance to be covered along the MLR was such that individual fox holes were 75 to 100 yards apart.

Action on the "D" Company front, of the 501st, begins with the mission of 1Lt. Bill Sefton, newly designated executive officer replacing the seriously wounded Lt. Denver Bennett, to lead a mine-laying party. An armored attack by the enemy is anticipated in the morning. Sefton describes the mission:

> Meanwhile, the firefight had stalemated, with both sides digging in as darkness fell. We were told to expect a German armor attack at dawn. About 0400, a truckload of land mines arrived and I was designated to take a mine-laying party of one platoon out to 'mine the most logical avenues of armor approach.'
>
> I was supplied with a Belgian highway map and informed there was a combat patrol 'out there somewhere' ahead of me. What with the mines, engineer picks and shovels, plus normal combat equipment, the platoon sounded like a 5 and 10 cent store on the move, as we stumbled our way in the darkness. The Germans were firing one gun with shells that sounded like box cars coming through the air. One such landed a short distance away, spraying the area with clods of dirt as well as shrapnel. A voice behind me cried, 'Lieutenant, I'm hit, I'm hit!' I asked, 'Can you make it back yourself?'

---

[68]Minick, pp. 166-67.

'I think so,' he said. 'Then go back.' My last view of the casualty was a bulky shape making about six feet to the jump on one leg, toward the rear.

A few hundred yards later, a skirmish broke out in the darkness somewhere ahead. The road map was being of no help whatsoever in determining routes of approach. In fact, I hadn't the foggiest idea as to exactly where we were. I called for the platoon sergeant, whom I'd met for the first time, before starting out with the mine-laying party. He was a chemical warfare tech sergeant, obviously brought aboard as a replacement. He didn't answer my summons, but a voice in the night explained his absence: 'He was hit and you sent him back!'

It was wearing on toward dawn. I moved the platoon off to the left from the direction of the skirmish ahead, found a flat piece of ground that might conceivably be of use to an approaching armored column and said, 'Dig the mines in right here.' Within fifteen minutes, the eastern horizon was starting to pale. Now the trick was to get back through our own lines, wherever they might be in relation to our wanderings in the darkness.

The trooper who had guided us out through the lines had long since dropped out of the party. Having veered from the original course to avoid the firing ahead, I could only head for Bizory by dead reckoning, with the skyline behind starting to silhouette us as we came in from the direction of the expected dawn attack. We would not be re-entering our lines at the point we left them.

Concerned for the potential of disaster by 'friendly fire', I preceded the group by some fifty yards, calling out warnings of our approach. I should have been yelling louder. A machine gunner opened up from maybe forty yards ahead, thereby provoking a career act of stupidity. Instead of hitting the ground, I stood there looking down the stream of tracers, which seemed to be passing on both sides of my face, and calling the gunner every abusive name I could recall, plus a few invented in the spirit of the moment. The fact that he stopped firing without hitting me or anyone in the group behind substantiates the adage – 'God rides on the shoulders of the dumb.'

I never did learn of any part the mines we laid might have played in the defense of Bastogne.

During the day, four patrols of "Dog" Company tried to move north along a line west of the Foy-Bizory road but were turned back by fire from the Bois Jacques.

At about the same time that "Able" Company, of the 501st, was ordered to move out to pinch off the pocket of enemy soldiers behind the MLR, Cpl. Frank Lasik of "Dog" Company led an eight-man patrol but altered his course to avoid the fire from Bois Jacques. Eventually, his group pushed as far as the railroad grade, then turned right following a dirt road, which ran parallel to the tracks. He spotted a group of seven enemy tanks and some accompanying infantry moving toward him down the tracks at a distance of 75 yards. Visibility was not good and he was able to slip into the nearby woods and returned to the command post. A call was quickly made to 2nd Battalion, which in turn was to alert "Able" Company of the enemy approach.

With no other map of the area than a Belgian road guide, Lt. Bill Sefton describes the day's activities for the major part of "Dog" Company and his lack of knowledge as to what was occurring on other company fronts.

We spent the day digging in with Dog Company, turning the battalion left flank along the forward slope, short of Bizory. The left flank of the company ended at a woods indicated as a patch of green on my highway map. I had not been advised that Able Company had been attached to our battalion and was holding a position in a woods along a railroad well, off to our left.

Sometime well after dark, Able Company was kicked out of position by a determined enemy unit of undetermined strength. I don't know how far they withdrew. I do know our battalion commander issued an order essentially as follows: 'D' Company will pull back three miles immediately, hook up with 'A' Company and attack two companies abreast through the woods with a rolling artillery barrage two hundred yards ahead, thereby restoring A's original position.'

Brilliant – just damned brilliant! All we gotta do is carry out an impromptu night attack through an unreconnoitered woods against an enemy of unknown strength. Piece of cake – provided, of course, we can survive our own unobserved artillery fire.

Only one patch of woods showed on my map and we were dug in along the edge of it. Ergo, 'A' Company had to have been on the far side, beyond the intersecting railroad bed. So why don't we first send in a recon patrol from our current position and see if the enemy is still right there? If so, we can move out at first light, cutting straight across the front edge of the woods and take 'em on their flank.

Captain Dick Snodgrass, Dog C. O., was even less enthusiastic about the order than I was, so he bucked my suggestion up to battalion headquarters and permission to send the recon patrol was granted.

I sent a lieutenant and four men into the woods with instructions to go as far as the railroad track unless running into enemy dispositions enroute. They returned in little more than an hour to report reaching the railroad without encountering the enemy. Their findings, relayed to battalion, cancelled the night attack order in favor of moving at dawn.

## "ABLE" FILLS A GAP

As the regimental reserve unit, "Able" Company, under Captain Stanfield Stach, was in a wooded area near 1st Battalion Headquarters when it received its marching orders. Stach was ordered to move north to the vicinity of the railroad to plug the gap which existed between the 506th and 501st Regiments.

As runner for his company commander, PFC. Edward Hallo felt their first assignment on the afternoon of December 20th was to probe for enemy positions in an area which had been infiltrated the previous night by an enemy patrol. He related:

Our job was to act as feelers to find the enemy. 'A' Company was sent up along a railroad track. The track bed was built up on a higher level of ground.

The 3rd Platoon was on the left side of the railroad track and the rest of the company was on the right.

As communications sergeant for "A" Company, Sgt. Lloyd E. Jones had a better view of the big picture for his unit than most of the enlisted men in the front line foxholes. He describes the first day's action in closing the gap between the two parachute regiments.

It was late in the afternoon, around 3 o'clock or so. 'A' Company was told to go out toward the railroad tracks as the evening before there had been a contingent of Germans come through this area and the 506th and the 501st were not completely tied in together around the railroad track.

There was an open space and they had gotten 25 to 30 men to come up through there and when they had come over the ridge they had been torn apart by some of our machine gunners. We did know there was a big hole out there and Captain Stach had orders to go out and try to find out where the hole was and get us tied in for at least overnight in case they came through there again.

Bastogne had a lot of trees with lanes going down between the growths. The trees were planted very closely together, mostly pines, not very big around, planted in rows. We got out quite a ways and the 'ole man' had heard noises and he said he wanted us strung out along the side of this forest, just inside the tree line, as there was a field between us and another stand of trees. It was getting pretty dark plus the fact that we had a lot of fog that had settled in that area – you could see about six feet in front of you. As the evening progressed, they started to come up through there. We had orders to let them get as close as possible and then we opened up and they pulled back. I heard it was the 28th Grenadiers. They were exploiting the hole between the lines of the 506th and 501st.

A veteran of the Normandy and Holland campaigns, PFC. Robert W. Smith was serving as a medic for his platoon. He remembered that Sgt. Edward Gullick was the first to spot the enemy. He related:

We had gone down through these areas and Ed Gullick went through the next clearing and into a wooded area ahead of that and discovered a large German force ready to jump off. With this news there was only one thing to do, that was to spread out and wait for them to come across the clearing. When they got close enough, our men started firing into them. This, no doubt, got them completely by surprise. There was a heavy exchange of fire but I think the Germans had an advantage over us because they had more heavy weapons than we had.

The actions of December 20th for "A" Company, of the 501st Regiment, are well remembered by 1Lt. Joseph B. Schweiker, who was serving as executive officer. He described the move near the railroad track where they made the initial contact after being in battalion reserve:

We were called from reserve to fill a gap. As we moved into position from one tree grove to another, with the railroad tracks on our left, we spotted the Germans to our front and coming at us. It was dusk and getting dark. Soon a fire fight began. As it built up, we were stalled and so were the Krauts. It appeared the Germans were firing tracers about 4 to 5 feet above the ground and ball ammo 2 to 3 feet – several of our guys were hit right in the neck or chest. Captain Stach realized the situation was somewhat different than expected. The gap could have been 500 to 1000 yards, with the railroad thrown in on our left.

Captain Stach and Lt. Monk Mier moved one squad over the railroad track with Sgt. Chamberlain to protect our left flank. As the darkness moved in, the firefight increased and we were at a standstill. Captain Stach sensed the situation and directed me to hold our position, since he couldn't contact Battalion by radio; he had to find his way back to their location and report our situation. Captain Stach told me to hold our position until he radioed me and stated 'W'. This meant to pull back to the higher ground where we came from.

With 3rd Platoon moving up along the left side of the tracks while the rest of "A" Company moved forward along the right side in a spread formation, PFC. Ed Hallo's group hadn't received the warning yet of the approach of enemy soldiers. He describes actions involving his small group of men:

We started moving up and just as we got past the second grove of trees, we could hear voices and it was late in the afternoon. Dusk was setting in. We decided to stay near a stand of trees and every platoon member got behind a tree to wait for something to happen. As the voices got louder, platoon sergeant Lyle Chamberlain, who was acting first sergeant at the time, ran over the railroad tracks to warn us, 'Don't fire until we give the signal!' and then ran back.

Lying down on the ground, you couldn't see over the railroad grade and you didn't know what was on the other side. Herman Bebe was with me. I always considered him the mascot of the company – a little guy. He had a grenade on the end of his carbine. Bebe asked, 'What is the signal?' I said, 'He didn't say what the signal was – just pass the word down the line and we'll play it by ear.'

It was getting dark fast – you could hear the voices getting louder and louder – then we spotted the Germans coming across this wide open field toward us. They were taking their sweet time in spread formation. I'd say the Germans were about seven to ten yards in front of us and Bebe says, 'I'm not going to wait any longer!' and he fired the grenade at a German and all hell broke loose. The company fired, too. I had the second tree. Lt. Monk Mier was behind the first tree and he turned and said, 'Hallo, have the MG section aim down and cover the railroad tracks. Bebe was left of me and I had a tree between me and the enemy. Bebe must have blown the German apart with the rifle grenade. We all had a target. We just kept firing for a time and lay there waiting to see what would happen.

As a replacement, Pvt. Christopher McEwan joined "A" Company as a machine gunner. With many of the heavy weapons being turned into ordnance for inspection and cleaning, as a newcomer, McEwan faced going into combat without a weapon. Rather than wait at the assembly area until weapons could be found, McEwan went forward with his unit, hoping to pick up a weapon along the way. During the first night near the front, a machine gun was found for him so he was ready to participate the next morning. McEwan relates his first combat experience:

The next day, with a belt of machine gun bullets wrapped around my neck, we headed east down a road. We stopped and laid in a ditch. A Tiger tank fired a shot at us but it hit the roof of a barn. We moved out along a single-track railroad. I was told to set up my machine gun at the edge of a wooded area. I had a large, open area in front of me. I was on the right flank of my outfit. I had no one to cover my right flank, which I felt very uneasy about.

Suddenly, I heard firing off to my left. Thinking now that my buddies needed help, I picked up my machine gun and took off to the left, running up the side of the railroad track. As I crossed over, the machine gun belt, which was dragging along the ground, got caught between the rail and ties. I was left standing in the open trying to free the belt. I could hear bullets whizzing past my head, like angry bees. I finally got it loose and ran down the other side of the tracks and got into the fight. It finally quieted down. I laid there, behind my machine gun, for quite a while. I didn't know where the others had gone, so I started moving forward. I moved for quite a distance.

Over on the right side of the tracks, where he was more or less in the center of the extended formation of the remaining two platoons of "A" Company, 1Lt. Joseph Schweiker recalled that it was decision time. The enemy was moving around 3rd Platoon in a flanking maneuver. He wrote:

As time passed, the Germans seemed to be gaining on our left flank, across the railroad track. I checked with Monk Mier and he felt the same way. 1Lt. Jimmy Murphy hadn't felt the pressure as much on our right. Since we had no contact with Battalion or Captain Stach, we decided to pull back in order to prevent the Germans from getting around us on our left flank and establishing our position on higher ground. We had the machine gunners fire for a minute or so with riflemen protecting them; during the period, we pulled back. It worked out fairly well and we dug in for the night.

Back on the left side of the track, PFC. Ed Hallo and his machine gun team was ordered to provide cover so the rest of the company could fall back to more advantageous positions. He continued his story:

By this time, it was getting pretty dark and Monk Mier came up and announced, 'We're gonna pull back to the group of trees behind us. Hallo, you stay here with the MG section and stay as long as you can while the rest of the company pulls back.'

The company moved back and there was a lull. Then, all of a sudden, there was a lot of noise and it was coming from down along our left flank. I said to the guys, 'We'd better try to get out of here. I think the Krauts are going to move down to our left flank and set up a machine gun and we're going to catch it sure as hell.' It was so dark that we held hands with the free hand and I looked up to see the sky between the rows of trees. We ran through the woods just as fast as we could – carrying a machine gun you really can't run very fast! We got beyond the clearing and made contact with the company. We stayed there that night.

Pvt. McEwan hadn't heard the order to pull back and, consequently, was out by himself. Darkness set in. Unknown to him at the time, he was well behind the enemy lines. He had never been in a combat situation before. McEwan continues his story:

It started getting dark and foggy. I set up my machine gun and laid down behind it, ready for action. I couldn't see very well and started hearing some noises up in front of me. As the sound got closer, I knew then that it was Germans. I could hear them talking and their cannisters were making noise. They were committing the unforgivable, thinking there was no one there. They came closer and closer until they were almost on top of me. I could not see their faces, but I saw their silhouettes. I opened fire, raking my gun back and forth. The burst of machine gun fire picked up the first two Germans and slammed them to the ground. I continued to fire about six inches off the ground because I figured they were going to hit the ground and it would be able to hit some of them. They really panicked. I heard someone shouting orders to try and control them. I heard some of them moaning – then it went quiet.

As "A" Company fell back to the higher ground in another tree line, the medics were busy treating wounded. As a platoon medic, PFC. Robert W. Smith was at his usual position, slightly to the rear and center of his group. He had already treated Pvt. George Loies for an arm wound. He continues his account:

Ed Poznek came back with a wound to the upper part of his body. As it was dark, it was a bit difficult to dress his wound and note if there might possibly be two holes – where the bullet went in and a second where it came out. Firing started to ease up and we crossed back over the railroad track and walked him up the hill and placed him alongside a dirt road and tied a piece of bandage on a bush so he could be seen and picked up. I found out later, a medical jeep picked him up. I started back down to see if there were any more wounded and I ran into Billy Daniels. It was a damn good thing, as the company was pulling back. If I had not met Billy there, I could very well have been killed or captured. We were ordered back almost to the hill where we had started. I teamed up with another trooper and started digging a foxhole.

Communications sergeant Lloyd W. Jones remembers the pullback and the heavy shelling they experienced. Still handicapped from the injuries that had put him in the hospital in Rheims, Jones was called on to evacuate one of the wounded. He wrote:

As we pulled back, we experienced one of the worst nightmares that an infantryman encounters – they started throwing many, many 88 shells into the trees and, of course, there were the tree bursts. For a while, we just fired blindly back into them and it didn't do much good. We were being cut to ribbons. Captain Stach gave the orders to pull back into the next area behind us. I had a problem coming back from the hospital and not knowing the replacements. This guy, who I didn't know but evidently he knew me, had been hit in the lower part of the body and he pleaded with me not to leave him. I just grabbed him and picked him up and, amid the tree bursts and the darkness, literally fled with this man on my back toward the rear along with the rest of my comrades to set up new positions in the next tree line. We finally ran into a jeep that had come up to pick up the wounded. After I put him on the jeep, that was the last time I saw him.

## MONT

Sgt. Donald Castona had been a part of the patrol which had gone to Neffe on the evening of the 19th, to check out the size of the enemy force in place in that small community. After asking for reinforcements when they were involved in a firefight, the troops were ordered back to the 3rd Battalion positions at Mont. Castona had planned to lead the men back through some fields which were partitioned off with barbed wire but opted for returning along the road. Those same fenced-in areas proved to be a very fatal hazard for enemy troops who tried to cross those fields on the night of the 20th. Castona continues his story:

It seemed that a column of Germans was not far behind us on the same road. By this time, a tank and another armored vehicle had joined us along with the heavy weapons company of 3rd Battalion.

It started getting dark and we went to work digging in around and about the little town of Mont. Before we did much more than a shovel's depth deep, we were hit by a very heavy barrage. A lot of the shells landed right about on our positions but we didn't get very many casualties and the enemy rolled their barrage behind us. One shell – looked like a 155mm – landed right beside the hole Aloysius Riley and I were trying to dig. Luckily, it was a dud.

The Germans followed the barrage with an infantry attack just after dark. It was supported by a couple of tanks. Our machine gunners and our tanks fired tracers into a haystack; just at the crest of the hill the Germans were coming over. This haystack caught fire and left the German tanks and infantry silhouetted and in plain sight. The tank supporting us knocked out the German tank and made even more fire behind the German infantry. That is when they ran into the sheep fences I had mentioned earlier. Those poor guys were trying to get over, under, or around the fences and made good targets for our guys. They got shot up really bad, even though some of them got almost to our lines. Some of them were killed by the heavy weapons company with their .45's. (At this point Castona stopped, adding, 'I'm kind of running out of gas now. Remembering this stuff gets me excited and poops me out.')

Mortar sergeant Richard L. Klein was in on the same action as a member of the heavy weapons company referred to by Sgt. Donald Castona earlier. He had discarded his galoshes and overcoat to increase mobility while on patrol the night before and would pay for it as the evening of the 20th approached. Klein recalled:

After darkness had set in, we returned to Mont barely returning before the Germans launched an attack on the night of December 20th. It was during this attack that I was hit. This attack was the most intense that I had ever experienced. The artillery bombardment was extremely heavy along with a large volume of machine gun and small arms fire. Obviously,

Colonel Ewell's defensive deployment was outstanding. The 501st stopped the attack cold without giving up an inch of real estate.

More than once I've reflected on the December 20th attack. Thank God, it was launched on the 20th and not December 19th and thank God the Germans didn't attack an hour earlier. If they had done either of these two things, those two platoons of 'G' Company, plus Reilly and Klein, would have been history.

A description of the overall action that took place near Neffe is provided by the authors of *Rendezvous with Destiny* as follows:

Between 1900 and 1930 on the night of December 20th, the enemy struck through the fields lying between Neffe and Mont, advancing against Colonel Griswold's left. The presence of the tank destroyers had intimidated the German armor. It took refuge in a little wooded patch lying just to the west-southwest of Neffe and from the grove it shelled Mont. The German infantry advanced under this fire. Enemy self-propelled guns moved along the railroad line next to the highway from Neffe a short distance and went to work on the same target. These two lines of fire converged on Griswold's positions at almost right angle. The men in the forward line had to give ground, falling back on the village. The most forward of the tank destroyers, commanded by Sgt. George N. Schmidt, became their rallying point. Schmidt unloaded most of his crew and told them to join the fight with small arms. He then joined the infantry machine gunners who were already searching the bottom slopes with every automatic weapon the Battalion could bring to bear. In the next few minutes, he threw 2,000 rounds of caliber .50 at the enemy. Lt. Andrews used a radio-equipped jeep as his command post and central control station. He used his security section as ammunition carriers to feed the stuff up to whichever tank destroyer was calling for it most urgently. The other three tank destroyers, under Sgt. Darrell J. Lindley, were shooting at the railway line. They tried, at first, to spot the self-propelled guns by firing at muzzle blasts. When that failed, they put flares up over the valley. The fighting died down about 11 p.m. By that time, the three self-propelled guns were out, the defenders of Mont had no clear idea of why their automatic fire had made such a clean reaping of the German attack or of where the attack had broken. But, in the light of the next morning, December 21, they could see what had happened. The hillside between Neffe and Mont was crossed in both directions by barbed wire fences, spaced between 30 and 50 yards apart with five or six strands in each fence. In ordinary times, they were used for cattle. With the tank fire behind them, the Germans tried to come right through this fenced area without first destroying the fences in any way or equipping infantry to cut them. On coming to the fences, they tried to climb through but the spaces were small and their individual equipment bulky. Griswold's men had perfectly clear fields of fire and so did the tank destroyers supporting them. The fences were as effective as any entanglement. The evenly spaced lines of dead told the story. They had charged right into a giant mantrap.[69]

## AN ACCENTED OUTPOST

Being assigned to outpost duty, in front of the MLR, is not a choice assignment and having a partner who spoke with a heavy accent didn't help when it came to returning through the line from that duty. PFC. Robert I. Wickham relates what happened one night, a few days after the initial contact with the enemy was made:

One memory that I always get a kick out of was a night on outpost with Herman Koeppl. We were manning the outpost that had been set up on the hill above where we first encountered the tanks. In daytime, the post was on the front line but after dark we moved to a foxhole about a hundred yards forward. My watch ended about 0300 and I woke Koeppl and told him to get me up before daylight so we could move back to the line under cover of darkness. I then went to sleep. I woke up in broad daylight and knew immediately that something was wrong. I was alone and no one in sight. Moving back across that field, I felt so naked that I shudder, even now, to think of it.

I came across the first machine gun emplacement and asked them if they had seen anything of Koeppl. They didn't know him but asked me if he spoke with a heavy accent. When I affirmed that he did they said, 'Yeh, we captured him but when he said he was with you, we let him go and he headed back to you about an hour ago.'

Now what? I started down the line toward 2nd Battalion, asking each man I met if anyone had seen him. But no one had. Then I saw six or seven men coming toward me. They were from 2nd Battalion and they had 'captured' my man. We all got a kick out of it and even Koeppl laughed.

Herman Koeppl was born in Germany, of Jewish parents. He left Germany in 1936, I believe, and lived in New York City until the war. He came to us in 1st Battalion S-2 as a replacement while we were in Mourmelon. In my opinion, he was a good soldier but he had a problem with the English language. It was difficult to understand him. Sometimes (jokingly), we would use Fechtman as our translator.

---

[69]Rapport and Northwood. pp. 478-79.

## DWINDLING ARTILLERY AMMUNITION SUPPLY

After a day of heavy firing in support of the 501st Parachute Regiment, its artillery support battalion, the 907th Glider Field Artillery, found its supply of ammunition for the snub-nosed 105mm howitzers was running dangerously low. The 907th Glider Field Artillery Battalion History records the following action to find further ammunition sources for its 105mm guns.

At 10:30 (December 20), five GMC trucks were sent to ASP (Army Supply Point), in the vicinity of St. Hubert, with instructions to bring back either M2 or M3 ammunition. These trucks returned about 1700 with 1500 rounds of M2 ammunition and stated that they had been under tank and small arms fire. At about 1500, Assistant S-4 was still trying to locate ammunition dumps with M3 ammunition. The only ammunition available at that time was 105mm M2 but the 105 M3, which was used by our type howitzer, was expected in. The maximum range with M2 is 4400 yards (charge 3) while a range of 7500 yards is considered effective with the M3 ammunition.[70]

PFC. Charles W. Hogan was one of those men sent on the mission to find an ammo depot to replenish the fast disappearing stock of 105mm artillery shells. At the time he walked out of the hospital at Rheims on December 18th, he was still not one hundred percent fit for full duty. However, he felt he could handle the resupply mission. He recalled:

We decided to go for ammunition. We had very little ammo for the 105's, just a few rounds per gun. They asked for volunteers to go on this ammo detail. There were two or three from each of our batteries who went along. The only other one I remember from my battery was Cpl. Dwight Spotts. The trucks that were taking us to pick up the resupply of ammo were the same ones that brought us in. They were from a Quartermaster Truck Company stationed in Paris. The ammo dump was sixty to seventy miles from Bastogne. The weather wasn't too bad when we started out – kind of dreary and foggy. That was one reason why I wanted to go on the detail. Anytime I could get away from the battery, I went. I liked riding around the countryside. We took off and headed for the ammo dump. We didn't have any trouble getting there. Everything was in kind of a mess. No one seemed very excited. We asked for a certain kind of ammo and the fellow in charge said, 'We don't have any shells that are suitable for your guns – only type we have is for the regular 105.' We, in the 907th, had the snub-nosed or short-barreled gun.

---

[70]Headquarters, 907th Glider Field Artillery Battalion, *After-Action Report, December 1944*, 7 March 1945.

The ammo available had seven powder charges whereas the 907th guns had only four charges. The shells could be fired in the snub-nosed gun but three charges had to be removed. PFC. Hogan continues his story:

We decided to get regular 105mm ammunition and we could tear off three powder charges and go ahead and use them. Our guns weren't safe to shoot seven charges. The guns could blow up or tear up the recoil mechanism. We picked up all the regular 105 ammo we could find and started back to the Battalion. It seems to me we had to take a different route and did a lot of detouring because the Germans were between us and Bastogne.

It was getting dark and the small arms fire was something terrific and the engineers were blowing down trees across a highway as we came back in. I remember one place we stopped – it was late at night and there were some boys from one of the infantry regiments who ran down the road and crawled in the back of the truck with us. They were stocking-footed. One of them asked, 'Where's George?' Another responded: 'That crazy SOB stayed to put his boots on!' They hadn't taken the time to put their boots on and had come down the road stocking-footed and carrying their boots. They had a roadblock and they were staying at a house. They had all bedded down but one or two and the rest were out there in the road directing traffic. They said tanks were coming up the road and one of the fellows said he was out there directing which way the tanks should go and they wound up being German tanks. He took off in a big hurry.

We got into Bastogne and it was real late. We stopped at Battalion HQ and they said we couldn't go through Bastogne with the ammo as the Germans were shelling the town so bad and they didn't want us to lose any of the ammo. We bedded down in a house. In a little while, they came and woke me up. They said, 'Captain McGlone is out of ammo – we're going to have to risk taking one truck through Bastogne and get to the gun positions with the ammo.'

I hadn't been paying much attention to directions as we rode in the back of the supply truck. I didn't know the location of the batteries. Ole Spotts was a-laying there fast asleep and I kicked him awake and said, 'Spotts, wake up – Captain McGlone said for you and me to bring one load through Bastogne to the gun positions!' I knew ole Spotts would know the way. He just got up and never said a word and away we went. About every foot of the way, through Bastogne, the shells were landing every place. I've never seen such a barrage and somewhere near Bastogne there was a bridge and a shell had hit there. A fellow lying along the road there with his head cut off.[71]

---

[71]Several men have mentioned passing the decapitated soldier near the bridge while relating their stories. Some thought it was a German soldier; other failed to mention an identity.

We got to the battery position and reported in to Captain McGlone. He said, 'Boy, am I glad to see you! We are clean out of ammunition!' We explained to him that the ammo was not the type used for our guns and that the shells had seven powder charges and three had to be removed before they were fired through the howitzers.

## A Trip to Find Gasoline

Besides the scarcity of artillery ammunition at this early stage, the leadership was already sensing that additional gasoline would be essential in case the troops became surrounded. Gasoline was necessary for the tanks and other armored vehicles (which had to race from one hot spot to another), jeeps, trucks, ambulances and the portable generators for making electricity throughout the command posts within the perimeter.

As a member of the wire communication platoon of the 101st Airborne Signal Company, Cpl. Joseph Gambino had this recollection of the importance that fuel for the vehicles played in the total picture of actions in and around Bastogne. He was driving one of the trucks sent out on the 20th to find gasoline supplies. He wrote:

I feel I was the last guy to get gasoline before we were completely cut off at Bastogne.

With a 6 x 6 truck – don't ask where I went because I don't know, but I was sent down a road and through the woods to a supply area – filled the truck with five gallon cans of gas and came back through the woods – no roads – just followed tank tracks. I was stopped a couple times by the 327th boys. They said, 'Step on the gas and don't stop for anything else'. Shortly after that, all hell broke loose.

## Engineer Actions

As dawn broke on the morning of December 19th, PFC. Harry Sherrard and a small group of engineers had been supplied with plenty of ammunition, hand grenades and bazooka shells. They had been whisked off in the direction of Neffe and Mont where they were posted at an intersection of dirt roads. A long vigil had followed. Early on the morning of the 20th, a vehicle came on the scene and transported them to the road perimeter positions being held by "A" Company of the 326th Engineer Battalion. Sherrard wrote:

We were dropped off in an area south of Bastogne where 'A' Company was starting to dig in some positions between the road to Neufchateau, across and just east of the dirt road to Assenois.

I was positioned at an outpost at the end of a woods on the east side of the road with Eugene Walters, my ammo carrier. I had a bazooka and an M1. There was about a ten foot road cut so we dug in about five feet from the edge of the cut with a V-shaped foxhole. We placed some trip flares in the woods to the south and east of us. . .maybe thirty feet from our hole. It was still daylight. A command car[72] came up to us from Bastogne and went on toward Neufchateau. Later, a jeep with a machine gun mount along with a recon car came to our spot in the road, stopped and the officer in charge said they would let us know how far out they saw anything on their way back. A few minutes later, we heard some small arms fire down the road. Then we heard the two vehicles racing toward us on the road. They sped on by us without stopping, right on back into town. We wondered if they really saw anything.

Later, another recon group did the same thing – we waited but no one came back.

A single railroad track paralleled the road. It was about fifteen feet on the far side of the road from us.

We heard artillery fire to the north and west of us but I think that died down on the second day. We had a telephone hook-up between our outpost and 'A' Company's CP. Our CP was not more than 100 yards in front of the company line and the company CP was not very far behind it just over the dome of the rolling hill.

The first night our trip flares went off. However, we didn't see who or what set them off. They were set with the trip wires only about a foot off the ground. We guessed some animals had tripped them. They were reset the next day, a little higher.

## FORWARD OBSERVERS

The 377th Parachute Field Artillery Battalion served as the support group for the 502nd Parachute Infantry Regiment in Normandy and Holland and would continue to serve in that capacity at Bastogne. The group had arrived at Bastogne behind the 502nd and, after a night of digging in the 75mm pack howitzers and preparing shelters for the gun crews, the forward observer teams needed to be assigned to the various battalions.

As a forward observer, 1Lt. James A. Robinson was assigned to the 1st Battalion of the 502nd at its OP from December 22 to January 3. He has this

---

[72]The staff or command car was probably that of General McAuliffe on his way to Neufchateau to meet with General Middleton of VIII Corps.

description of the strategic post and its importance to the planners at Division Headquarters:

This OP was the most exposed infantry outpost on the Champs defensive perimeter. It was also the most forward of any position from the MLR (about 250 yards). Here, both the 502nd PIR and 377th PFA were busy around the clock, reporting on enemy activity. With the stronger radio, the artillery observer was in contact with his own battalion artillery S-2 and S-3, as well as the artillery liaison at the 1st Bn., 502nd PIR CP, Capt. Marv Richardson.

Since there was such a dire lack of artillery ammunition, normal massed concentrations of artillery fire in the American manner had to be held in abeyance or eked out under the strictest control. The many targets of opportunity coming into plain view further aggravated the frustration being felt not only by the artillery observer but by battalion and Division staffs astounded at the large accumulation of reports on such a wide variety of intense enemy activity. The OP offered a broad picture of three sides of the outlying bowl-shaped landscape about Champs. A commanding sweep of the countryside, coupled with the wide choice of available targets within normal range, had never been experienced before. So much so, that it was only from this place that the Division staff could gain clear observation on troop movements on the important Bertogne-Sprimont perimeter road.

Very often, as many as ten vehicles could be seen on a half-mile stretch of road and several times as many as fourteen tanks, armored or other vehicles were reported. On looking north onto this Bertogne-Sprimont road, one could see at shorter ranges and at lower elevations the villages of Rouette and Givry, German strongholds where the enemy even held staff conferences in open view and troops could be seen milling about and tending to their daily ablutions, to use an English term. As one looked right or eastward, much of the Champs-Rouette road could be observed. This main approach, from the north, lay in the extreme eastern section of 'A' Company and ran straight through the company positions, becoming, itself, the village main street going past the church on the left and, after a little rise, it passed the company CP on the way toward the 502nd Regimental Headquarters at Rolle.

Between the OP and that main road lay a broad expanse of barren ground descending for more than 600 yards. Having great depth, this snow-covered field separated much of the company's forward elements from the enemy positions.

For 1Lt. Jack J. Price, the assignment for his forward observer team began the very next day after the firing batteries had set up their guns in and around Savy. The team had to pick up an intelligence sergeant from Regimental

Headquarters and then head out to where a patrol had spotted vehicular movement the very first night. Price wrote:

Early the next morning, my FO team was sent to the 502nd to pick up an intelligence sergeant and he was to take us up where we could fire on some Germans. We started north, passed the 502nd outpost and continued for about two miles. There was nothing moving in the area until I saw a man behind a building, about 100 yards off the road. I stopped the jeep and we all hit the ditch. Six men came out from behind the building with their hands up. I halted them at about 25 yards. Strange – three of these guys had on 1st sergeant stripes. As my team covered the men, I went out and checked them. Sure enough, they were legit. They were 106th Division troops. The 1st sergeants were experienced vets and, when they were overrun, they were smart enough to escape and brought the other soldiers with them. I sent them on the road to the 502nd outpost.

We continued further north where we contacted a 502nd patrol, near Longchamps. We left our jeep and went on foot forward to see the target. It was a road running east-west, north of Longchamps. There were lots of German vehicles and troops on the road; lots of captured American vehicles, also.

As we went up the westerly road, there suddenly appeared a big Kraut tank on the east road. If it got to the town before we could get back, it would cut us off from our jeep. We ran – I mean really ran – we made it and got out of there fast.

Incidentally, the 502nd intelligence sergeant was outstanding. He looked like a high school kid but was very professional. I might add that the Germans on the road were out of range of our 75's so we did not fire.

Having spent the night in the hayloft of a barn, attached to a good-sized house, Cpl. Walter "Putt" Murphy describes his assignment for the 20th of December:

In the morning, 1st/Sgt. Fitzgerald sent Sgt. Bob Clifford and me, with an officer up front, as FO's. I had a radio in a jeep and was going through a field parallel with the road. We were getting artillery fire from the Krauts and two or three shells landed near us and you could hear them hit the ground. Thank God they were duds. One was not, though, and it hit a barn in back of us and set it on fire.

This forward observer team was apparently accompanying a segment of the 502nd which had been called to go to the assistance of the 1st Battalion of the 506th Regiment but had then been turned around after being notified that their help wasn't needed. This was one of those moves the average rifleman never knew the whys and the wherefores but just plodded from one position to another. Cpl. Murphy continues his story:

At this point, we turned around and headed the other way. The infantry stopped and dug in at the base of a big hill and we went to a big white house about half way up. It was the CP. I was not getting very good reception on the radio (in the house now) so I took a piece of wire and was climbing up the side of the house (vines) when I heard someone call me. I looked down and there were a couple of GI's with M1's pointed at me.

I had a cap on my head and they thought I was a Kraut. I did some fast talking and they backed off.

The perimeter held by the 502nd Parachute Infantry Regiment remained the quietest of them all for the first several days. Actions were restricted to patrolling out away from the front lines. There was a shifting of the front line troops.

# 6. DECEMBER 21

Out beyond the western perimeter, Captain Robert McDonald and his Baker Company of the 401st Glider Infantry continued to discourage any moves by the enemy to push closer to Bastogne from that direction. They were still out about three to four miles west of the positions of Able and Charley Companies.

Action was beginning to pick up in the roadblock areas of Able and Charley in the Mande St. Etienne part of the perimeter.

As "B" Company, of the 327th, moved from an overnight position, near Neffe on the east side, they were hit by an artillery barrage as they passed through the western end of Bastogne. The remainder of 1st Battalion was undergoing heavy shelling in the Senonchamps area as the enemy moved in closer from that direction.

A concerted effort was on in the area between the 501st and 506th regiments where the enemy had infiltrated a force of over two hundred men so as to be a real threat to Bastogne. Elements of that enemy force were within a mile of Bastogne. The actions would involve Companies "A" and "C" of Major Bob Harwick's 1st Battalion of the 506th with "A" Company of 1st Battalion of the 501st and, to a lesser extent, "D" and "F" of 2nd Battalion of the 506th and "D" Company of the 501st.

Over in the "E" Company area of the 501st, three of the participants have recollections for actions in the Bizory area on this day.

Service Company of the 501st Regiment is ordered to move southwest of Bastogne to get out of range of the constant shelling. A real problem develops when Service Company, along with a group from Division Recon and an armored artillery battalion are trapped by an enemy armored force.

## THE WEST PERIMETER

The roadblock set up by "Baker" Company, of the 401st, became an objective of the enemy force still in the area just east of the captured field hospital site. "B" Company historian Marshall E. Griffith recorded the actions:

At 0800 on the morning of the 21st, it was 'B' Company's turn to set an ambush. The prize included nine half-tracks pulling artillery pieces, plus other small vehicles. Also included in the prize were enemy dead, wounded and captured Germans.

Two other attacks were broken up at the road block that day. On the third counter-attack, one enemy tank was knocked out and one captured along with more prisoners. The company was ordered to move back three miles to the MLR. This was accomplished on our newly acquired transportation.

At daybreak on the 21st, two tanks supported by German infantry tried to outflank the "B" Company position where PFC. Carmen Gisi was positioned. These troopers managed to cripple one of the tanks and the other withdrew to safety. Gisi's recollection of the action is as follows:

The tank was knocked out by Pvt. George Karpac. That action took place to the left of us and I wasn't there but we all knew of this. He laid on the road and knocked the tank out with his bazooka. On the attack of the crossroads, my buddy Frank Alamovich was shot in the ear by one of our own machine guns and a few days later he was KIA.

When we searched some of the dead Germans, we found American candy and cigarettes in their pockets.

## A COMBAT PATROL INTO A TOWN

In an action filled with a surprising amount of detail (having written it while memories of the actions were still fresh in mind in 1946), PFC. Richard V. Bostwick was a member of "B" Company, along with S/Sgt. Roger Seamon, PFC. Carmen Gisi and PFC. Marshall Griffith. The mission of his squad was much different as Captain McDonald sent the group into an unnamed town, which the author assumes was Flamierge. Bostwick wrote this detailed account:

In the morning, Captain Mac summoned our squad to the CP. It seemed that our squad's number had been coming up too darned often. When there was a dirty job to be done, we were the ones to do it. Mac didn't waste any words and we were soon preparing to go to the village on a 'combat patrol'. This meant being prepared to fight. (A scouting patrol goes after information and avoids any encounter with the enemy.)

A light tank was assigned to us. It carried a 20mm cannon and a .50 cal. MG; additionally, an armored car with a .50 cal. MG and two jeeps were added to the array.

Our caravan started out with every man riding on one or the other vehicles. I was perched on the rear end of the tank while others clung to the front and the sides. Riding space was scarce because six men had been added to the squad. It was a rough ride as the tank lurched along the road. I suspect it was WW I surplus.

Just as we entered the outskirts of the village, the sharp staccato popping of a Kraut MG had us all in the ditches on either side of the road. The jeep that was leading our parade was hit and the driver wounded, maybe killed. He was hanging half out of the jeep on the driver's side, some forty or fifty feet in front of me. The driver of the second jeep risked his life when he raced up alongside the disabled jeep, driving in almost a prone position, loaded the wounded man into his vehicle, made a U turn and got the hell out of there. During the rescue, there wasn't a shot from the enemy gunners.

Blimp and I watched from the ditch as the tank waddled forward with its guns blasting at targets unseen by us; turning a corner, the tank was out of sight. We crawled along the ditch to the corner where the tank had left our view. There sat the monster in the middle of the roadway, blasting away at every building in sight.

As we passed in front of the house, Blimp shouted that he had seen movement through the front window. The structure was about thirty feet from the road. Blimp pulled the pin from one of his grenades and gave it a mighty heave. It hit the house and rolled back in our direction. I crawled into my helmet again. There was one helluva 'WHAM'. Neither of us were scratched. We moved on.

The Krauts began lobbing mortar shells, which were exploding all over the place. I could hear the hollow 'choonk' sound of the shells leaving the mortar tube, indicating that the Krauts weren't far from us. When the barrage ended, we got up and continued into the town. I could still hear the tank, somewhere in the town, firing away at wood frame buildings.

Entering a part of the town that contained a greater number of houses and buildings, we watched carefully for snipers. I fired at a cat sitting inside a window, the shot shattering the pane and probably missed the damn cat. I don't think the echo of the rifle shot faded away when five German soldiers walked out of the house with their hands above their heads.

Blimp, using his limited knowledge of German, succeeded in having the prisoners point to one of the houses, indicating that there were troops in the basement. While others guarded the prisoners, I explained the situation to the driver of the armored car, who pulled alongside the house several feet from the basement window. The gunner in the armored car opened fire and sprayed MG bullets through the window, into the basement. After several MG bursts, I pulled the shattered window screen aside and chucked a grenade into the darkness. The explosion was deafening. The process was repeated several times. MG fire followed by a grenade. Following the explosion of my last grenade, I heard the sound of crying and a woman screaming. I ran into the house, to the head of the stairway leading to the basement and held my rifle ready as the sounds of footsteps ascended the stairs. Sgt. Watson and some of the others joined me just as an old man and three women, all civilians, appeared. Two of the women were elderly and one appeared to be about twenty years old. The old man had a terrible gash over his right eye and the skin was hanging down over the eye. My grenades had done this.

The young girl asked if we were Americans; we assured her that we were. She bawled and bawled and kissed every one of us on the cheek. The old man was attended to by the medics. They were loaded onto a vehicle and returned to our lines.

Blimp and I followed Watson to the basement, he with a flashlight that threw about as much light as a match. Groping in the semi-darkness, we found an opening in a concrete wall that led into a room that measured approximately 12 x 12. I suggested throwing a grenade in before entering but Watson didn't like the idea.

Watson had guts. He entered the room with that stupid flashlight throwing a feeble glow before him. Suddenly, the light fell upon a German uniform. It was incredible. There were seven others, fully armed, standing with their backs to the wall, standing in the darkness, with their hands over their heads.

The prisoners were herded outside without incident. We lined them up and searched each one. Watson was the smart one, he picked out the officer and relieved him of his Luger. For my part, I got a P-38, 9mm pistol and a small Belgian hand gun, as well as binoculars. One Kraut objected when I took a rosary from him. He repeated, 'Mutter, Mutter.' I returned the rosary to him.

We had been in the village several hours. Our tank had run out of gas and had used up its ammunition. A phosphorus bomb was placed in the tank's engine to immobilize it.

Blimp had returned inside the house and had gone upstairs when he called, excitedly, for me to join him. When I reached him, he pointed out of the window where we saw a wide skirmish line of Krauts approaching the village from the opposite side from which we had entered. Using the binoculars taken from the prisoner, I could see that they were enemy and they were well armed. We spread the alarm. When viewing the surrounding terrain, I spotted a truck, some 500 yards away in a small grove of trees, unloading more Germans. I hollered down to the armored car driver and pointed in the direction of the truck. The gunner attempted to bring his cannon around to fire but the turret had frozen solid.

Watson ordered the armored car to shuttle as many men as it would hold back to our lines. In the meantime, the prisoners were herded into the stable attached to the house. While in the stable, I stood between two horses and was surprised at the heat given off from their bodies. It was a bitterly cold day. From my position, I could see out through a small rear window. Now and then, a German would be seen running across the open ground some distance from where we were

The armored car returned for another load. It had encountered small arms fire during the round trip but no damage done; taking on another load, it was gone. Mortar fire began falling on our position.

The armored car returned for another load. It would be the last one because enemy rifle fire was very heavy and mortar shells were tearing chunks out of the buildings. It was a possibility, and a damn good one, that we would be taken by the Krauts. A sniper killed one of our men. Time had run out. Time to go. I discarded everything I had taken from the prisoners except the hand guns.

We prepared to make a run for it. I ordered the prisoners to line up in a column of two's. They didn't understand. I physically stood two of them side by side and motioned for the others to fall in behind in like manner and then they understood. The Krauts were stepping up the tempo of their attack and it was a matter of grave concern.

They were still several blocks away. Houses and buildings obscured the view and they were not yet in position to fire directly at us.

This was it. A half dozen of us, together with the armored car and twelve prisoners, made a run for it. We ran and ran. The crossfire was murderous. Tracer bullets cut red patterns all around us, some bounced off the armored car. Mortar shells exploded both in front and behind us. One soldier made the mistake of climbing atop the vehicle. A single bullet through his head and he toppled without a sound into the ditch. One of the prisoners was shot through the jaw; he didn't make a fuss, just kept on running.

After running the longest three miles of our lives, we literally stumbled into the company area. The prisoners were turned over to the Captain. I had to dig a new hole because of the change in the company perimeter defense. Blimp and I collaborated and dug a two man hole overlooking the ground that sloped away toward the village we had so hastily departed. The Krauts hadn't followed us but we remained on alert. Gathering straw from a nearby barn, Blimp and I made our hole as comfortable as we could. The experience of the day left me limp. Blimp kept on the lookout and I dozed.

The weather worsened on the 21st, with the temperature dropping sharply. There was a feeling of snow in the air. Over on the "C" Company perimeter, S/Sgt. Robert Bowen was in the company CP when he got an order to provide support for another unit. He wrote:

I went to the company CP in the early morning. Captain Towns told me to take a squad of men and support 'A' Company, which held a roadblock near the hamlet of Mande St. Etienne. There were about a dozen houses around a courtyard in the hamlet and one on the main road between 'C' Company and Bastogne. I withdrew Felkner's squad, spread Leamon's and Hans' to cover their spot and headed for the roadblock. 'A' Company had two squads dug in around a big stone house and barn with a machine gun covering the road. Their left flank was vulnerable so I put Felkner's men there, dug in around the base of a row of great fir trees with a 180 degree field of fire. As I headed back to my CP, snow began to fall.

Time passed slowly. The snow came down faster, covering the ground with its whiteness and the chill wind whipped it into drifts. Many of the troops had no overcoats or overshoes and were protecting themselves from the bitter cold with blankets and shelter halves. Bowen had his men disassemble their weapons and remove all the oil as the weapons began to freeze up.

## TEAM O'HARA STRONG POINT

Actions at the Team O'Hara roadblock would have a bearing on members of "C" Company of 1st Battalion as they passed just to the north of this position on the morning of December 21st. As a member of a small twenty-man group which had been left behind when 1st Battalion of the 501st had headed east through Bastogne on toward Neffe, PFC. Donald L. Woodland and others had come as far as Mande St. Etienne without weapons. (See account on page 40.) He was now at a strong point with Team O'Hara not far south of the positions occupied by 1st Battalion. He had just been briefed about a tank assault on some Germans by Sgt. Lester Wynick, another member of his group; then the position came under an artillery barrage. Woodland related how the two controlled troops from abandoning positions.

Sgt. Wynick now came over to the position and began to brief me about the tank assault. He said that they came out of the fog and surprised some German vehicles, which they promptly shot up. They all got back except for the tank that became stuck in the mud. Suddenly, our front line position came under rapid and intense artillery fire. This unnerved some of the stragglers that were occupying part of the line. Some yelled in panic-filled voices, 'The Germans are attacking!' A few of the men climbed out of their foxholes, abandoning their weapons. Sgt. Wynick and I instantly sized up the situation and we drew our pistols. Wynick ran to the right and I ran to the left towards the men, urging and forcing them back into the line and to man the guns to beat off any German infantry attack.

Then I remembered the machine gun that had been overhauled that morning and decided to put it into position to be able to fire down the road. The location selected was on the left side of the small stone building (most likely used as a field tool storage shed.) Blackie and I were setting up the gun when Lt. Jones came running up. He said to us, 'Very good!' and then he ran around the stone shed to his right to check the line. The next salvo of artillery fire found him exposed and he was mortally wounded. I rolled over and around the building and Lt. Jones was lying on the ground, face down. I saw his Colt with the lucite grips and the picture of his loved ones.

The German artillery fire that had mortally wounded Lt. Jones also found their targets on several other men on the MLR. Another of our 1st Battalion group was killed. I do not recall his name. Sgt. Wynick was all business. He carefully wrote down the names of the KIA's in a little book and removed one of the dog tags.

Another member of the small band of 1st Battalion (501st) troopers who had been left behind because he had no weapon was Pvt. Duane Harvey who, in a normal situation, would have been operating as a member of the S-2 Intelligence Section for Headquarters Company. He lost a friend in the barrage that took the life of 1Lt. Claude Jones. Harvey related:

> The next morning (December 21), our positions received heavy artillery fire and one of the 501st fellows came over and said, 'Don Fair and the lieutenant had been killed over by the block house.' Don Fair was a Fort Benning replacement and we had come from England together. The war was very brief for him, killed the first time he came under fire. After the shelling, we stayed in those positions until later in the day when we moved back to a small village (Senonchamps). There we set up in a house which was the last one on the road.

As a member of "C" Company of the 327th Glider Infantry, PFC. George K. Mullins had been rushed to the 501st sector to fill a gap in the perimeter defense on the afternoon of the 19th. After a relatively peaceful stay in the area, interrupted by intermittent shelling, Mullins and his buddy, H. C. Parker moved out toward the enemy early the next morning only to be called back to move to another threatened spot on the west side of Bastogne. Mullins recalled:

> We were just getting acquainted with this foxhole when we got orders to move outwards to where I could hear a battle going on just over the hill. We hardly made contact with anyone when we were rushed to the west side of this town (Senonchamps).
>
> We stopped for a few minutes when a chaplain priest showed up. The Catholic troopers hurriedly followed him to the side of a hill for Mass. Hell is near, just around the corner, I knew. I've seen this situation before.

An artillery barrage that caught his unit along a road as they were in the process of moving from the Neffe area to Senonchamps, on the west side of Bastogne, is a vivid memory of PFC. George M. Kempf of "C" Company. He wrote:

> PFC. Joe Carpenter and I were company scouts. We were leading our group to new holding positions when artillery caught us. Joe was killed. I was missed but everyone behind us was killed or wounded. I believe Joe was from Binghamton, New York and was married and had two children.

What PFC. George K. Mullins is about to relate ties in with what acting sergeant Donald Woodland of "A" Company of the 501st Regiment stated earlier about his lieutenant being mortally wounded near the Team O'Hara roadblock.

We moved out to the top of the hill. It was timber area with some open spots. I had two mortar ammo bearers with me and we moved out ahead. We came upon a paratrooper covering his platoon leader who, a few minutes earlier, was killed by an incoming shell.

The artillery barrage, which had been described by PFC. George Kempf, is the same one which Sgt. Donald Woodland and PFC. George Mullins are about to relate, though neither of them has ever spoken to the other about the action.

Woodland continues with his description of the incoming barrage at the time a company from the 327th Glider Regiment happened to be passing the position he had been at since the 19th:

To our rear, we noticed that a company from the 327th Glider Regiment was moving down the road toward the MLR. As the point of the company reached the MLR, the German artillery shelling increased in violence. Some of the shells were air bursts in the trees. It seemed as if the shrapnel would follow the tree trunks. The infantry hit the dirt and several were wounded.

One of the wounded riflemen almost fell on top of me. He had been hit in the neck and I laid on my back to administer first aid. He asked me if his jugular vein had been hit. I told him that I did not know. He then asked if the blood was coming out in spurts or in a steady flow. I answered his question. I took his M1 for my personal use, but neglected to remove the ammunition from his belt so that I had only the clip in the gun.

A short time later, Wynick received his 'million dollar wound.' Now I was in charge of the remaining men from 1st Battalion. Some of the troopers said that they were taking off for the outfit, but I decided my place was here and would attach ourselves to the 327th.

PFC. George Mullins of "C" Company of the 327th was one of the men who was hit by the barrage in the vicinity of Donald Woodland's position. He wrote:

I heard tanks on a ridge below. One of our tanks rolled up behind. He stopped about 100 feet to our right. Immediately, he took a round from a German tank that I heard from the ridge below. The tankers wasted little time bailing out of that big hunk of steel.

The next round was meant for us. I dived for a low place in the ground with the two ammo bearers on top of me, one being a large man, the other was a man named Johnson, from Indiana. The tree burst was too close for comfort. The explosion was terrific. Everything seemed to be dark and hazy, although I could feel blood trickling near my face. Both men were mumbling prayers. I am sure I owe my life to these two troopers, their bodies being my only protection against the shell fire.

Mullins ended that narration with "I now found myself in a cathedral being used as an aid station. Many soldiers lay wounded. A doctor and two medics were busy operating, taking a bullet from a soldier's head."

Apparently Pvt. Duane Harvey and acting sergeant Donald Woodland joined Captain Walter L. Miller and his "Charley" Company on the move west. The "C" Company commander failed to mention the shelling in his story. Miller describes the move to Senonchamps:

At that time, I received an order to go cross-country to Senonchamps to protect the 10th Armored Division artillery located in that area. I can remember going by the Chateau Ile-le-Hesse on the way to Senonchamps.

I met there with a Colonel Browne who commanded the 10th Armored Division artillery unit. He was killed that day or the next by a shell fragment as he walked in the village. A Lt. Col. Crittenberger took command. We moved to the far end of Senonchamps, taking positions to the right and left of the road. We could see the Germans moving from a woods on our right front to a woods on our left and we engaged them with fire. We also had the support of 'Choo-Choo' artillery of the 10th Armored Division who would throw a shell in among the enemy.

## "B" COMPANY HIT

Companies "A" and "C" of the 327th moved out first on the 21st followed by "B" Company, which had arrived near Neffe only the day before. When "B" Company got its marching orders to move to the Senonchamps area, they used a different route to avoid shelling. It didn't work. They were hit as they moved along the outskirts of Bastogne. S/Sgt. Paul Slevey describes what happened to "B" Company. One shell did a lot of damage. He wrote:

On December 21st, the company was moving from the edge of Bastogne down through an open area in town and we were caught in an artillery barrage. McMinn was KIA and Stanley was SWA. Walt Dazkowski was SWA – he lost part of a leg. Ernie Schneider was lightly wounded; the SCR-300 radio he was carrying kept him from being hurt bad – the radio didn't come out so good – it was junk.

These guys were wounded as the result of one round. When I walked by Stanley, he held up his bag and said, 'Here, you're the first sergeant now!' The bag contained the company records as they would be with us. We went past the town square. After we crossed the railroad bridge, we went to the left, passing the water tower. About a mile further, we stopped in a patch of woods that was next to the railroad tracks and here we dug in.

## SENONCHAMPS

As a replacement in "B" Company of the 326th Airborne Engineer Battalion, Pvt. Kenneth K. Knarr was experiencing his first combat action near the western outskirts of the small village of Senonchamps with other members of his platoon. His group had been assigned to the position on the 20th. He wrote:

> The first or second day our platoon was in a garage and we were being shelled constantly. One of our men had a grenade in his left shoulder pocket. Somehow he pulled the pin. It exploded, blowing off his right hand and left shoulder. I heard he died but don't remember his name.[73]

The next day Rip Reardon had his feet propped up as he was making pancakes on a cast iron stove. At that time, a tanker from an armored outfit walked in the front door looking for his unit. Just then, some large shells hit the building. Some of us dove into the cellar. A few minutes later we went back up and found Rip Reardon unhurt and the tanker badly wounded.

Pvt. Duane Harvey of the 1st Battalion of the 501st Regiment experienced the same shelling. He remembered a Sherman tank parked in the yard behind the house and recalled a shed in which two Belgian civilians, killed by the Germans, had been placed until they could be buried. (See the story of Countess Rene Greindl for more details of this story on page 371.) At the time of the shelling, Harvey was patrolling the grounds near the house.

> During the night, I was patrolling outside the house while the others were inside. The Germans started shelling our positions. When it started, I stepped inside and stood up against the wall between the door and the window. A shell hit outside and the blackout shutters fell off. A wood stove in the corner fell over, spilling the supper of several GI's on the floor. We all thought it was from shell concussion but the next morning we found a dud 75mm shell under the stove and the wooden window casement had a half-moon crease along the side where I had been standing.

With the last road out of Bastogne being cut the night of December 20th, it became very important to beef up the defense lines to the southwest. In his book, *BASTOGNE, The First Eight Days*, Gen. S.L.A. "Slam" Marshall wrote:

> Later in the morning of December 21, Team Pyle – 14 medium tanks and 200 infantry, mostly from the 9th Armored – moved to the vicinity of Senonchamps to assist the 420th Armored Field Artillery. LTC. Barry D. Browne, in command of the 420th, had received reports that Sibret and Morhet had fallen into enemy hands. He figured that he was out on a limb and that the enemy might come upon him from either flank. So, he turned one of his batteries to fire on Sibret and rushed a forward observer out to

---

[73]The soldier was Pvt. Nick Prato who died of his wounds on December 28th.

adjust on the village. At that moment, he saw the motorized column of the 333rd Field Artillery group as it came speeding up the road out of Sibret. Another column came driving hard behind the 333rd – men in American clothes and riding American vehicles. They got fairly close to Senonchamps, then stopped, deployed and opened fire with an M8 assault gun.

Even as Colonel Browne realized they were Germans, they started side-slipping off into the Bois Fragotte, which lies south of Senonchamps. Team Pyle got there in time to help Browne fill those woods with fire; one battery from the 420th Field Artillery Battalion and one from the 755th Field Artillery Battalion (155mm's) also engaged in this action. The infantry and tanks moved west into the woods. Almost immediately, one of the tanks knocked out an enemy 75mm self-propelled gun. The force then advanced into a large clearing in the center of the forest. While crossing the clearing, one of the tanks was disabled by a shell from a high velocity gun somewhere in the woods. The tank lost a track. A smoke screen was laid in an attempt to cover its withdrawal, but the tank would not budge and had to be destroyed.[74]

Part of "A" Company of the 327th Glider Infantry Regiment was sent down to the area of Villeroux to check out on friendly troops and find out if it was still in friendly hands. This occurred on the 21st of December. One member of that patrol, PFC. Willis F. Rohr, describes the experience:

Our squad made a patrol down the road south from Ile-le-Pre to contact American troops in a town to the right and about two or three miles out. No opposition was met that night. We managed to get hot water and our food heated in one of the houses at the crossroads.

Captain Walter L. Miller describes the situation in Senonchamps after his men had moved into the area on the 21st of December:

While in Senonchamps, we did not use the houses except at night when we would bring in our weapons for cleaning and oiling so they would not be frozen in the early morning attacks by the enemy. One of the replacements I picked up going into Senonchamps was from a disorganized unit. He was found frozen to death in his foxhole, inasmuch as he had been afraid to move during the night. We did have several stragglers assisting us there from other units but they were taken away from us when we returned to the lines.

In Senonchamps, we were very low on ammunition and living on one-third of a K-ration a day and with no dry socks. The artillery battalion only had about 39 rounds of ammunition with which to support us.

---

[74]Marshall, Gen. S.L.A., *BASTOGNE, The First Eight Days.* Infantry Journal Press, Washington, D.C., 1946. p. 113.

## PINCHING THEM OUT

Over in the 506th sector, 1st Battalion commander Major Robert Harwick felt his men deserved a rest from the arduous two-day battle at Noville and Foy but it was not to be. The men had slept in the hay barns of Luzery and in the morning of the 21st, Harwick had to call them out for another mission. He wrote:[75]

The Germans were far from through. They moved back into Foy that night. Worse of all, they broke through our defense perimeter, leaving nearly 200 Germans holding a section of woods inside our defenses and within a mile of Division Headquarters. At 0700, I received an order to get them out.

1Lt. Ed Mehosky's "Charley" Company was one of those selected for the clean-out mission on the 21st. He remembered:

1st Battalion was in Division reserve in an area near the village of Luzery, located just north of Bastogne and west of Foy. On the 21st of December, we got word that there had been a penetration by German forces along the Bourcy-Bastogne railroad tracks between the 506th and the 501st sectors, southeast of Foy. 'C' Company and 'A' Company were given the job to eliminate the threat. After a meeting with the Battalion commander, I briefed my platoon leaders on the mission. By 0900, we were heading in the direction of Foy. The morning was cold. A misty fog blanketed the gray landscape. We marched northeast on the Bastogne-Foy road. From the road, we turned southeast into a sparsely wooded area, mostly evergreens. The deeper we advanced, the thicker the woods. We came to within a couple hundred yards of the tracks where we thought the German positions would be. We were south of the Halte railroad station and parallel to the Bastogne-Foy road.

Major Harwick added to his account with a description of the wooded area through which the attack was being made:

One company was put between the woods and Bastogne. I took Meason's company and Mehosky's and carefully started through the woods to try and chase the Krauts into the waiting company.

The woods here had been planted. The trees were pine and fir, in neat rows and with no underbrush. It was like a tremendous hall with a green roof supported by many brown columns.

We moved very carefully and slowly, feeling out each section of the forest. We were especially careful at the fire gaps and boundary roads that divided the woods into planting sections. There was some German artillery falling, the shells hitting in back and to our left, but nothing disturbed the

---

[75]Harwick, op. cit.

quiet of the woods. The men moved softly, orders were whispers or motions.

*Map 9*

Over on the "C" Company front, company commander Ed Mehosky directed his platoons to make their moves toward the enemy positions. He added to his story:

> Reconnaissance completed, 'A' Company moved off to the left, 'C' Company to the right. I deployed two platoons and engaged the enemy. The other was held in reserve. My two platoons soon drew fire. Forward movement became very difficult. Heavy small arms fire was pouring in and artillery bursts exploded in the tree tops. My platoons were temporarily stalled. The enemy had the advantage of well-concealed positions. They had dug in and were using fields of fire cleared through the low hanging tree limbs.

Action now began in front of Major Harwick's position. A rifle shot put the troops to ground. Harwick added to his story:[76]

> Then the rifle crack from in front, just over there! There was no one standing, but helmets peered around trees trying to spot the source. Just

---

[76]ibid.

where did that come from? Then another, and now a burst of machine gun fire, the tracers bouncing from tree to tree like a pellet in a pinball machine.

Pvt. Steve Polander was one of the members of "A" Company who took part in that fighting. He gives his version of the action from his position out in front where the action was hot and heavy:[77]

> Rifle fire starts coming off the hill above us, ricocheting all around. We quickly regroup, about 40 able-bodied men in all, and head straight up the hill where German infantry is dug in beyond a strip of wooded area, not too deep. We move among the tall timber and some men drop.

Captain Richard Meason, who had been a platoon leader under Bob Harwick in Normandy, was now commanding "A" Company. The Ardennes campaign was to end his combat experience in World War II on the morning of the 21st. He wrote:

> We pulled out immediately thereafter and attacked the Germans through a woods at approximately noon of the morning of the 21st. During this attack, I was hit in the abdomen by an explosive rifle bullet. This fight was short, furious and successful.[78]

The description of the 1st Battalion actions in this fight were written by Major Harwick less than a year later so he provides more detail in his report than the others but surprisingly the stories tie in so very well. Harwick continues:

> But 'A' Company had them spotted. A few low mounds of freshly turned earth marked the outer foxhole line. The fire is returned and now a few greenish figures bound up and move forward, running crazily, then they are down again and have disappeared. 'C' Company on the right had stopped at the shots on the left, but they now moved forward again. 'A' Company continues to work forward and now the first call for 'Medic!' 'C' Company hadn't found anyone yet. I worked past Zahn[79] and his reserve platoon to be sure that 'A' and 'C' didn't become separated. But there it was, 'C' had made contact. A long burst of machine gun fire. Again it rattles and bounces through the trees and the men on the right go forward in dashes. Rifle fire was now heavy and crackled continuously. I pass the boy who caught that first shot, face down, still holding his rifle, his helmet a little off to one side.[80]

Situated in the middle of his platoons, 1Lt. Ed Mehosky moved along with his men of "C" Company. He added:

---

[77]Polander, op. cit.

[78]Taken from a long letter Richard Meason wrote in 1947 while still recuperating from his war wounds. Copy of letter sent by his widow, Norma. Also, see comments of Captain Barney Ryan, 3rd Battalion surgeon who describes the seriousness of Meason's wounds on page 249.

[79]Zahn was formerly Harwick's platoon sergeant in "H" Company.

[80]Harwick, op. cit.

Seeing the situation, I then deployed my reserve platoon around my right end on the flank of the enemy pocket. I quickly followed the platoon on the run, constantly advancing with fire and movement. The Germans could see we were flanking them and started to move from their positions. This coordinated movement between the two lead platoons and the maneuvering platoon enabled the attack to continue with sufficient fire power to cause the enemy casualties and to withdraw into a crossfire from 'A' Company and other elements of the regiment. Many were killed, others captured. A bunch of them were chased over into the 501st area.

As the two companies charged forward, enemy soldiers in the forward-most foxholes panicked. Some fled. A few surrendered. Harwick continues his narrative:[81]

Two prisoners come back. They were terribly scared and kept ducking their heads as the bullets buzzed and whined. Finally, a close burst and they dove for a foxhole. The guard took no chances and threw a grenade in after them. He walked up to the hole and fired four shots from his carbine and returned to the fighting in front. Cruel? No. Calloused? Maybe. But the penalty for a mistake here was death. If you are a prisoner, you don't run, if a guard, you don't take chances.

The fight was not long, but it was hard – it was bitter, as all close fighting is. A wounded man lay near to where I had moved. I crawled over. He needed help badly; beside him was an aid man, still holding a bandage in his hand but with a bullet through his head.

Out front, with the attack platoon of "A" Company, Pvt. Steve Polander describes the final rush and the result of their actions:

We made a second lunge with fierce small arms firing and more men drop as I see tracers fly by me. At close range now, only about 20 yards now, we make the final dash and more men drop. Many Germans lay slumped dead against their foxholes.

In 15 to 20 minutes, the bloody ordeal is over. We have punched a hole in the lines at this point. We lost about 15 dead and about 10 wounded, some seriously. I would guess the Germans lost twice that many dead and 20 surrendered.[82]

A terrified prisoner and a scornful enemy lieutenant are part of Major Harwick's continuing description of the action of the 21st:

Prisoners are coming in. One, terrified, kept falling on his knees, gibbering in German, his eyes continually here and there. Finally, in English he kept repeating, 'Don't shoot me!' He finally fell sobbing on the ground and screamed as we lifted him. The rest had an attitude between this

---

[81]ibid.

[82]Polander, op. cit. (In a later action, Polander lost a leg.)

man and the coldly aloof lieutenant who was so aloof that somehow, somewhere, he got a good, stiff punch in the nose. His dignity suffered as he nursed the injured member.

We had these prisoners carry our wounded back. In all, there were fifty-seven.

'C' Company was still working on a group. When they finally quit, there were about thirty more prisoners. There were fifty-seven German dead scattered through the trees. Most had been shot as they climbed out of their holes and ran to others further in the woods. The fifty-fifth German was made sure about this time when one of the 'dead' Germans was found to be trying to operate a radio on which he was lying.

Not all were accounted for, so we reformed and began sweeping the woods toward the waiting company.

We soon found them. Having reached the edge of the woods, they were afraid to take to the fields. Hastily, they tried to dig in. They fired on our scouts. One squad worked around their flank. The fight was sharp and quick. Four Germans dead, three wounded and one prisoner. The fight was over, with none of our men hit in this last fracas.[83]

"C" Company commander Ed Mehosky summarized the 1st Battalion actions in the following manner:

The enemy was written off by 1600. The line was restored. We killed 65 enemy soldiers and had taken 80 prisoners. The 501st captured 85 of the enemy who withdrew into their sector. We later learned we were up against 1st Battalion, 77th Regiment, 26th Volksgrenadier Division. This battalion-size force, had it not been stopped, could have opened the way for panzer divisions to enter Bastogne and cut the 101st in half.

## "A" COMPANY OF THE 501ST

Pvt. Christopher McEwan hadn't been aware that his company moved back from their position along the railroad the night before. During the night, he had moved further west through plantations and clearings. He heard the sound of voices and clinking cannisters. Dropping to the ground, he had positioned his gun in the direction of the approaching soldiers. Listening closely, he determined the language was German. He had fired into a group of enemy soldiers. Afraid to move, he had laid behind his machine gun in the same position all night. With the approach of daylight on the 21st, he was able to survey the scene in front of his position. McEwan added to his story:

---

[83]Harwick, op. cit.

The next morning when I could see, there were dead bodies all over. I realized then, that I was behind the German lines by myself. While I was wondering what my next move would be, I heard firing way behind me and to the left. I assumed it was my own unit firing at the enemy. I then circled to my left. I finally came up behind the enemy soldiers who were battling 'A' Company.

As darkness turned to daylight on the 21st, PFC. Edward Hallo was out in the forefront, along with scouts out on his right. "A" Company was returning to the same action site from which they had withdrawn the previous night. Hallo recalled:

The next day, we got the orders to move up again to see what the situation was. The whole company was on the right side of the railroad track. I don't think the company realized the Germans were closer to us, the 3rd Platoon on the left, but still on the right side of the railroad grade. We moved up to the area we were in the night before. The scouts were out. They were more or less to the right. I stayed ahead of Capt. Stach and we were moving up and I was closer to the track. As we moved up, the very tree behind which our MG had been the night before, there was now a German. I raised my rifle in the air in the 'enemy in sight' signal and everybody went down. I don't think the scouts on the right side knew we were moving up and this German started to aim from behind that tree so I quickly took aim and fired and saw him pitch forward. I don't know if I killed him or not. At the same time, I crawled forward and took out a grenade and threw it as hard and as far as I could over the railroad track and crawled back. The firing started on the other side of the track – I don't know what was going on over there.

As a disciplinary measure for not heeding a warning to get rid of his German motorcycle, which he used to scrounge the countryside near Mourmelon for wine and champagne, Pvt. Michael J. Caprara was sent to Company "A" a few days before departure for Bastogne. Consequently, he didn't know any of the men with whom he was entering battle. Caprara reminisced:

The first trooper I got to know was Pvt. John W. Conn in 'A' Company. He and I became a team as we were vets as far as combat goes. He was much younger than me – also, a very good soldier. We fought side by side in a winning way. One day, we were in a wooded area and just got there about dawn. The Germans opened up with 88's in this area, hitting trees and completely saturated the area. 'Billy' is the name he went by and that is why I remember him, because of a prize fighter named Billy Conn.

Me and Billy were under a large tree and shrapnel from the 88's came in on us. Billy was unlucky that day and was killed. I asked him where he was hit and the only response I got from him was a gurgling sound. We were lying in a prone position at the time and I called out for the medics but never saw any.[84]

The same artillery barrage that snuffed out the life of Pvt. Billy Conn took out Medic Robert W. Smith as he hastily dug a foxhole. He related:

The next morning, our people got some heavy stuff in the form of artillery. I was only there a couple minutes when another trooper came to me with an arm wound. I put a dressing on him and sent him to the battalion aid station. I went back and told Lt. Jim Murphy where I would be digging in. I think I had dug a couple of shovels of dirt when I got hit from a tree burst overhead – caught a piece of shrapnel in the butt and started back to the aid station to see if they could get it out. Sgt. Johnny Hughes followed me part way up the hill and asked me to lend him my boots, in case I didn't come back. Hughes later lost a leg in action. He was a good man. The battalion aid station could do nothing for me and sent me to the next place.

The enemy soldiers in the woods to "A" Company's front were now being squeezed by "A" and "C" Companies of the 506th Regiment, "D" Company of 2nd Battalion of the 501st while "F" Company of the 506th and Captain Stach's "A" Company were in position to trap the retreating enemy forces.

Having roamed around, lost behind enemy lines during the morning, Pvt. Christopher McEwan was in position to block one of the last escape routes open to the enemy. He wrote:

I set up my machine gun in a position of the only retreat the Germans had. I opened up and was delivering some real effective fire. The enemy had nowhere to go. They must have called for some supporting fire to knock me out. Rocket and artillery fire started knocking down the trees around me. Branches were hitting me in the back. The concussions were awful. There was yellow sticky stuff coming out of my eyes, nose and ears.

The fight ended with the remaining Germans surrendering. As we gathered the prisoners to bring them back to Bastogne, one prisoner made a run for it. A short, stocky trooper ran after him and shot him[85]

A summary of the day's actions is provided by 1Lt. Joseph B. Schweiker who wrote:

The following morning, 'A' Company went right back to our position of the night before. The Germans were across the tracks and somewhere to

---

[84]Records indicate Private John W. Conn was KIA on December 21, 1944.

[85]In checking through a list of men who received the Silver Star and Distinguished Service Cross awards in World War II while serving with the 101st Airborne Division, I noticed the name of C. C. McEwan as the recipient of the Silver Star. I called him in November, 1992 and asked if the award was made for the above action, which he affirmed. McEwan went out with frozen feet a week after the action and never returned to the Screaming Eagle Division. The award was mailed to him after the war.

our right. We fought a good part of the day until contact was made with the 506th. Then the squeeze was initiated and it was too much for the Krauts and the fight and attack ended. The German casualties were high, bodies all over the place. Our lines consolidated. Company 'D' tied in with the 506th and we in 'A' Company were pulled back closer to town in reserve.

The woods into which the 1st Battalion of the 506th Regiment was sent on the 21st were the same plantation growth into which S/Sgt. Vince Occhipinti and his 1st Platoon of "F" Company (506th) had reconned and lost two of his key personnel. He had been told only a few Germans were positioned there. The process of clearing the wooded area on the 21st proved there were far more enemy soldiers involved. S/Sgt. Occhipinti added to his narrative:

The following morning (21st), the unit in reserve for the 506th and units from the 501st on the east went through the woods that we were originally selected to secure and in the ensuing morning fire fight over 200 Germans were killed, wounded or captured. During the fire fight, our platoon took several prisoners who had escaped in the wrong direction.

Regimental headquarters instructed me by phone to bring in all prisoners for questioning to determine the forces against us. As all telephone conversations were being monitored by other units, a sergeant from another unit ran up to my position to relieve our platoon of the first two prisoners we had acquired. I didn't like the look in his eyes and told him we'd see that the prisoners would get back to regimental headquarters. (Can't blame the sergeant – he had seen a good buddy killed right next to him and didn't feel we should keep prisoners.)

Snow fell on the night of the 21st. Everything turned white. The frost penetrated deeper into the ground. S/Sgt. John H. Taylor describes action which took place at the Halte railroad station:

Later that afternoon we went down. We tied in again with the 501st at this railroad station. That night, it snowed. We had people in the railroad station house. It was set out in a clearing and our main line dropped back around the edge of the woods. We had good fire across the open area to protect this outpost. We dug in there and stayed several days in this position. We went around to our right and tied in with Occhipinti's 1st Platoon, which had been shifted around in there. There we tied in with the 501st.

We had a little trouble. The Germans would try to take the station. They dropped mortar fire on the house and then the fire would be moved to the back of the house. They tried this two or three times but the house was strongly built. The men could tell when the fire shifted and they'd be ready for the infantry attack and halted it with automatic weapons fire. The enemy got to the door and around the house but they never got in it. They lost some people there.

Another unit which went into a blocking position near the railroad track was Captain Richard Snodgrass and his "D" Company of the 501st Parachute Regiment. The company executive officer was 1Lt. Bill Sefton who recalled the final phase of the "squeeze" operation this way:

Later that day, a battalion of the 506th attacked along the other side of the railroad from the back end of the woods. From our side of the track the firefight sounded like a gigantic popcorn popper as they wiped out the enemy unit that had dispossessed 'A' Company. A few of the enemy fled across the tracks into our area as the assault reached a crescendo, only to be killed by 'Dog' Company.

## TOM BUTCHER

It wasn't until near the end of the war that PFC. Anaclete Leone learned why he was always invited to share foxholes with others. The men of his platoon wanted him nearby when they were wounded so he could patch them up. He recalled an action near Bizory on the 21st of December that would cost the life of his friend, Tom Butcher, the following day. Leone related:

It was getting near dusk and we were told to dig in along the road. The ground was frozen. The shovels would just bounce off that frozen dirt. I remember some 88's coming in and the ground 'seemed to melt.' Sergeant Butcher came over and asked if I knew anything about a .50 caliber machine gun. 'Yes, I knew something about a .50 cal.' I had training in intelligence and the medics. I joined the paratroops in England where I had my training in heavy weapons.

There was a .50 caliber on a knocked-out half-track and I told Butcher I could take it apart and put it back together. He took off like a bunny and came back lugging this big weapon. I showed him how to load and operate it. I asked him where he wanted it zeroed in. He showed me a line that he wanted to fire on. He was absolutely fascinated by the butterfly trigger but the tracer bullets brought in mortar rounds and I told him to leave it alone and get some sleep. It was very dark by now. I took off up the road to my hole just on the other side of the line. I was passing Shuler and Calahan. 'Hey Cleto, no sense going any further, stay here with us!' They had a hole dug there nice and neat, lots of room for me.

Later that night, I heard the pumping of that .50 caliber machine gun. Then I hear some mortar rounds. Next morning we learned Sgt. Butcher was killed.

Describing the early actions in and around Bizory where the 2nd Battalion was positioned, Pvt. Henry DeSimone related the action in which he lost his close friend:

On the 21st in Bizory, we made a tactical withdrawal back about 1,500 yards to the next high ground. We were digging in. Sgt. Tom Butcher, who was my squad leader, and I were dug in next to each other along the bank of a road into Bizory. We dug all night. When daylight broke, I was down in my hole and Tom Butcher was putting a roof on his foxhole. I told Tom the Germans were dropping artillery to the left of us about 150 yards and he'd better get down in his hole. He replied, 'Those god-damn Krauts can't hit me!' and with that I heard this tremendous explosion and saw the shrapnel coming off the opposite bank. It picked him up and threw him down like a rag doll. He was dead. The next shell threw stuff into my hole. At this period in my life (three seconds), I saw my whole life pass in front of me. I don't know what happened. I jumped out of the hole and took off. I ran into Sgt. McClure and told him, 'They got Butcher!' This was one of the worst things that ever happened to me as a soldier. I saw one of my best friends get killed.

*Paratroopers from "Easy" Company of the 501st Parachute Regiment took over a half-track which was abandoned by retreating soldiers. This is the vehicle from which Sgt. Tom Butcher retrieved the .50 caliber machine gun for added fire power at his foxhole position. (Photo from collection of T/4 Richard C. Rowles.)*

## IT'S ALL IN FRONT OF YOU!

An enlisted man on a mission with an officer may have an altogether different idea of what is being sought than the officer in whose company he is traveling. Such was the case for Sgt. Arthur Parker who thought he and his lieutenant were out looking for target areas inasmuch as they had very few maps of the Bastogne area. Parker wrote:

We tried to get maps of the area but none were available at that time so we could not run a survey for locating exact positions of guns and possible target areas. We took off the next morning (December 21st) and headed southeast out of Savy and tried to find just where the front lines were. We got close to Marvie where we were stopped. Some 327th infantry men told us that this was the end of the line. Everything else in front of us was held by the Germans. We returned to Savy and Lt. Shaw reported to Colonel Elkins what we had found. Shaw then told us we were out looking for some supply trucks that were trying to find us but they never made it and were probably captured by the Germans.

A sudden change in gun firing direction ordered by superiors caught gun sergeants by surprise. Two of the former members of the 377th Parachute Field Artillery Battalion relate such experiences.

Sgt. William D. Gammon of "Baker" Battery, a veteran of both Normandy and Holland, describes his experience:

We began fire missions. I was chief of a gun section. We received a deflection shift over the phone. I asked the battery exec officer (1Lt. Jim Denning) to repeat the last deflection, which he did. I responded to him, 'that we would be firing behind us!' He said, 'Sergeant Gammon, there is no behind us – it's all in front of us!' We were surrounded.

Sgt. Bernie Palitz was on duty with "Charley" Battery at Savy about a mile north of Bastogne. He remembered when he got an order to make a 180 degree swing to face in the opposite direction.

My howitzer was directly in front of a row of trees, fairly tall and fairly close together.

I was the 'adjusting gun' and, late that night, about midnight, we were roused with the command, 'Fire Mission!'

All six guns reported in and the very first command was, 'Adjusting gun – Right!' (I'm not sure, but it was an enormous shift and it required that the gun itself be physically turned.) I had two men on the trails shift the gun completely around; laid back onto the aiming stakes, looked up and saw the damned trees directly in front of me and yelled out immediately, 'Number One Gun out – adjusting gun out!'

It was training that made my #2 man not ram a round into the howitzer. I had stopped him in time.

Because the town of Bastogne was almost directly in back of my gun, it's probable that we were among the first to realize that something was terribly wrong.

An officer came to my position to verify the facts. I don't recall moving the gun, but I was unable to fire at all during that mission.

Major William E. Brubaker, S-3 for the 377th Parachute Field Artillery Battalion, remembered an unusual report which was just related by Sergeants Gammon and Palitz, who were members of firing batteries. He verified their reports with these comments:

One very important mission by the 377th – our normal gun positions were oriented in the area assigned to the 502nd Infantry – we were a combat team – our mission – direct support. The trails of the howitzers were dug in to fire in this area – and sometimes to fire in support as called for by Division Artillery. In one heavy action, we (377th) were called to support one of the regiments fighting 180 degrees from our normal zone of fire. We had to swing the howitzers around and fire without the trails dug in. I don't know about our accuracy, but we accomplished what I thought was impossible, the capability to give fire support.

## SERVICE COMPANY TRAPPED

As commander of Service Company of the 501st Parachute Infantry Regiment, Captain Eber H. Thomas had been ordered by the regimental S-4 officer to move his unit west of Bastogne several miles to a site which would be away from the shelling. Captain Thomas recalls the action:

During the afternoon of the 21st, Major William H. Butler, regimental S-4, visited the Company area. He informed me that the plan was to move out of Bastogne to the west. He instructed me to relocate Service Company about 8 to 10 miles west of the present location. I was to unload the trucks and return to Bastogne to assist in transporting the troops to the new location. I sent 1Lt. Bill Jones down the road to Sibret and 1Lt. Frank Sheridan down another road to the west to see if the roads were open. Both returned and reported the roads blocked. I assumed the penetration was from the Arlon-Bastogne highway side so I took the convoy along the Bastogne-Marche road for a few miles and then turned southwest on a smaller road which headed in the direction of the town where the S-4 had instructed me to relocate the company. The convoy proceeded along this road for about one to two miles and ran up against other U.S. units blocking the road.

During the time the convoy was halted, Cpl. Eugene Flanagan, of Service Company, came to me and stated he saw a German soldier in the woods along the branch about 200 yards to the right of the road. He wanted to take a few men and go after the German. I doubted his observation and instructed Flanagan to remain with his vehicle as the convoy might start moving at any time.

After waiting for awhile without any movement, I started walking up the column of vehicles. Immediately in front of Service Company was the 101st Division Reconnaissance Platoon commanded by a Lt. (Powers) Thomas. I requested that he contact 101st Division HQ as his platoon seemed to be equipped with a large radio. He advised that he had been unable to contact the Division. I continued walking up the column. The next unit in the column was the 58th Armored Field Artillery Battalion. I requested the location of the 58th commanding officer and was guided to a house where the CP was located. There I met and talked with a Lt. Col. Paton, the battalion commander. I requested that he contact the 101st Division HQs, but he stated he had been unable to contact the headquarters of the unit in Bastogne. LTC. Paton then informed me that he had two of his tanks knocked out by Germans located up the road leading out of the village to the southwest. He felt there were strong German units ahead.

At dusk, I pulled the 501st convoy off the road and parked in the rear of a house. 1/Sgt. John Cederburg posted the guard. 1Lt. Jesse Tidwell was with me and also assisted in posting the guard.

The 58th FA Bn. posted guards on the roads leading into the village. A 105mm howitzer was set up on the road we had traveled.

Around 0200-0300, a German tank accompanied by a patrol (we could hear them talking) came up the same road we had used to enter the village. The 58th FA guard fired the 105 howitzer at the tank but apparently did no damage as the tank fired its machine gun which did no damage either.

I immediately went to LTC. Paton's HQs to see if he had knowledge of the situation. He stated he had received a message relating that a U.S. armored column was coming through to clear the area. This didn't happen. I talked with him for a while and then returned to Service Company (which consisted of about 30 men – Company HQ, cooks and part of the motor pool).

At daylight, I returned to the 58th FA Bn. HQs, but there was no news. At this time, the German tank was visible in the field and located near the edge of the woods about 300 yards. I informed LTC. Paton that I was taking my men and heading for Neufchateau. We could not get the vehicles out as all roads were blocked. Each 501st man had only a few rounds of ammunition and there was one bazooka with two rounds.

I then contacted the platoon sergeant of the 101st Recon Platoon. We looked at the map and I asked him to lead us cross-country to Neufchateau – no towns, no crossroads – just cross-country.

By this time, the fog had set in and we marched to Neufchateau in about three to four hours. The Recon Platoon was with us and the 58th Field Artillery Battalion also followed us. I never saw them again after reaching Neufchateau.

After arriving in Neufchateau, Captain Thomas reported in to the 28th Infantry Division Headquarters. In checking his personnel, he found only one man from his group was missing. Thomas and his men were placed in charge of outposts leading into Neufchateau from the east and north.

# 7. DECEMBER 22

The damp, misty and foggy weather conditions changed somewhat during the early morning hours of the 22nd when snow began to fall. Visibility would still be limited during the day as the snow continued off and on throughout the day.

Much of the battle action was occurring in the 401st Glider Battalion area where "A" and "C" Companies would experience most of the day's fighting.

Shortages in food and ammunition were beginning to show up and examples of "make-do" will be illustrated in this chapter. The snow became a problem as the troops lacked camouflage and their dark green uniforms stuck out like sore thumbs.

During a night of heavy shelling, several officers positioned at the Division command post lost their lives when an artillery shell exploded in the room in which they were sleeping.

During the day, enemy parliamentaries come through the lines to negotiate the surrender of the Bastogne garrison. There is some wariness after the truce ends but the fight goes on.

## THE 401ST AT MANDE ST. ETIENNE

The action was now picking up in the Mande St. Etienne area where the 101st Airborne Division had assembled on the morning of December 19th. As day broke on the 22nd, S/Sgt. Robert Bowen was called to the company CP. On the way, he could hear the rattle of small arms fire from the direction of the "A" Company roadblock. The company commander notified Bowen that the road to Bastogne had been cut and he was to get over there as fast as possible to appraise the situation. Bowen wrote:

I plowed through knee-deep snow to the road block. A fire fight was raging. The Germans had moved into Mande St. Etienne during the night, blocking the road with farm vehicles and cutting us off from Bastogne. They had dug in around the houses and along the main highway.

I stopped at 'A' Company's position first. The platoon leader told me he had been sending a two-man patrol down the road to the battalion CP every two hours. On it's return, it was fired on just before daybreak near the hamlet. One patrol member had been wounded but the other had helped him back. Germans had moved into the hamlet during the night, blocked the road and dug in. They estimated there were at least a platoon of them.

I decided to check with Felker next. To reach his line of foxholes, I had to cross forty yards of open farm yard in perfect view of the enemy. I made a mad dash through the snow, bullets flicking the snow and taking needles off the fir trees when I got that far. Felker had dug a BAR position. I let out a yell to let them know I was coming and dove into it. Smith, the lanky Tennessee gunner, and Felker made room for me. Felker pointed out the German positions.

They were dug in by a wooden shed and some big mounds of potatoes, which had been covered with dirt. There was at least a squad. I could see foxholes and a machine gun position by the road and panzerfausts. Lying on the road, near the farm vehicle, were two screaming, wounded Germans. Any attempt to retrieve them by the enemy brought a hail of fire from 'A' Company foxholes.

I passed the word to cover me and made a run for the rear, bullets zipping around me. The only reason the Germans could've missed me was they were as cold as we and couldn't aim properly. I made a detailed report and was sent back to my CP. I no sooner arrived than Captain Towns was on the phone. As the conversation ended, he turned to me and said, 'Bowen, Colonel Allen (Battalion C.O.) wants that roadblock taken out. Take a squad from 'A' Company and Hans' squad and see what you can do. Hans is on his way up.'

I looked over the situation. A mad dash down the road or across the fields was out of the question. I was saved from the dilemma by the rumbling of a tank coming from 2nd Platoon. It stopped by me and a stocky sergeant got out.

'Colonel Allen told me to run down the road and shoot up those houses,' he said in a quiet drawl.

I pointed out the panzerfausts. 'With those there? How far will you get?'

'What do you suggest, then?'

I told him I was going to send a squad down each side of the road. If his tank could support them with his 75mm cannon and .50 caliber machine gun while Felker's squad provided enfilading fire from the left flank, the plan might work. He agreed and I ran to Felker's position to direct their fire. I gave a signal and all hell seemed to break loose.

The tank cannon began to bark, it's machine gun blazing. 'A' Company's machine gun and riflemen added to the din and Felker's men raked the German foxholes from the side. The two attacking squads took off with yells, dodging from tree to tree along the road and firing at the foxholes in front of them. The Germans panicked as the 75mm blasted them out of the houses and our enfilading fire kept them down in their holes. They hardly fired a shot in return.

I was in an end slit trench with Felker. Our weapons were hot from firing clip after clip. The Germans around the shed and potato mounds had enough. They began to pull out. Only a few made it and soon their bodies littered the snow in bloody heaps. I hit one and he went down and began to scream. We brought him in later with a gaping wound from knee to hip. He was barely eighteen and scared to death. We dressed his wound and evacuated him to Bastogne with the other German wounded.

The action ended, having taken about a half hour. Cries of 'Kamerad! Kamerad!' meant it was over. I went back to the tank on the main road. The tank sergeant was exhuberant.

'By God, I've been in this mess since D plus twelve and I've never seen anything like this. You're a crazy gang,' he said.

The squads were checking the houses when I joined them. Hans lay on the road, shot through the calf. He was our only casualty. Our medic dressed his wound, wrapped him in a blanket and I called for a medical jeep.

The enemy roadblock was destroyed. Twelve of their dead were put in the courtyard, a half dozen more lay in their foxholes by the road. Thirty were taken prisoner, including their wounded. Some had escaped to a nearby stand of trees and began to snipe at us. I called for the tank and a few bursts of its .50 caliber sent them flying. Most of the prisoners were young and wore parts of American uniforms, overcoats, overshoes, sweaters, knit caps and gloves. Evidently they were having the same problems with the cold weather. Some begged for mercy, thinking we were going to kill them. Felker spoke German, assuring them they were prisoners of war and would be sent to Bastogne to a prisoner camp. In retrospect, they were the lucky ones because the Germans took horrendous losses during the battles around the city.

I got Captain Towns on 'A' Company's phone and reported the outcome of the engagement. He asked me to bring the POW's to the CP. On the way, I met the first sergeant and some men. I turned over the Germans to them and went back to the roadblock.

I got back in time to see a jeep pick up Hans. I wished him good luck and waved good-bye as he left. We had been close friends since I joined the company eighteen months before, being in the same squad, then the same platoon until that day.

Shortly after the action ended, General McAuliffe visited the roadblock. We had met once before in Holland when he visited my platoon when it was on the MLR on the Neder Rhine. He recognized me immediately and, while inspecting the scene of the battle, congratulated individually the men who had fought in it. He was an extremely gracious person who was loved by his troops.

# THE PLIGHT OF AN EIGHT YEAR OLD REFUGEE

As an eight year old boy, Andre R. Meurisse was forced to flee from the family home in Bastogne. The family, with other neighbors, had first gone to Hemroulle where the horse and cart were left. The horse was too frightened to pull their belongings further. The Meurisse family had moved on toward Champs but again the artillery bombardment was bad. The father had then changed their course for Mande St. Etienne and on toward Namur and Brussels. However, the small arms fire and artillery was too much for the refugees and they turned back to Mande.

All of this travel took place on December 22nd and the family took refuge in the last house in town. Andre Meurisse describes their plight:

It was the Dominique house. Rushing to get into it, I ran over two German bodies which were lying on the frozen ground just in front of the doorway to the house. We ran down into the cellar where we found the owners already huddling in one corner. Not a word was said between my parents and the owners. We sat there and listened. In about five minutes, two American GI's ran down the cellar stairs and joined us. They were out of breath and I watched them as they sat there sweating profusely from fright and fatigue.

When the shelling let up some, these two Americans got their equipment together and left us. One of them dropped some loose cigarettes from his pocket. My father and the owner of the house greedily picked them up and each one lit one. My father said, 'What a Godsend!'

When we left the cellar and the house to go outside again it was late in the day, darkness was about to come so we turned around and went back to the center of the town. There we went to the farmhouse located right at the cross roads in the center which belonged to the two Cawet brothers. There we stayed the night along with other refugees. All together there were about twenty people in that house, which, because it was an old house, had no cellar. We were fed some food that the brothers had and then we all went to the stables where we made beds out of the straw and hay. Outside it was dark by now and the opposing weapons had almost stopped their firing. As they were used to doing every day, the two Cawet brothers, along with some of the refugees, started milking the cows which were in the stable. All of us then drank that wonderful sweet milk, the only good thing I can remember of those first days; five or six buckets full of milk were placed along the stable's back wall so anyone could take some any time it was wanted.

The rumors of where the combat was continued to whirl around us, each new refugee had a different report on just what was happening 'outside'. I remember looking from time to time to the attractive buckets of lukewarm milk aligned along the wall. We didn't know if we should try to take that liquid food with us or not. Then the children were given a second cup of milk and the adults finished the rest of the bucket with the cups the children had used. We all then tried to sleep. Outside, it was nighttime and complete darkness had fallen on the fighting armies as well as on those fleeing those armies.

All of a sudden, the firing of machine guns woke us. It was now close to us. Now I could hear the running of army boots past our stable. The wooden door to the stable was suddenly kicked open. There stood two German soldiers with their Schmeissers (automatic weapons) pointed at us. They stopped cold in their tracks and looked at us who in turn were looking at them in utter hopelessness as we were unarmed and helpless. The only light was a weak petroleum lamp but it was enough for the Germans to recognize the young and the old of our group as just helpless refugees. I thought this was going to be the last moments of my young life. The two Germans came closer, walking cautiously in an awkward manner. . .they were drunk! Every one of us was frozen to the spot. I was frightened of those submachine gun muzzles that kept swinging in my direction as they would walk around the stable looking at us.

Then one of the Boches spotted the remaining buckets of milk along the back wall of the stable. While the other drunk soldier held us at gun point, the first soldier undid his trousers and urinated in each of the remaining buckets of milk. He didn't miss one. They were both laughing when another German voice from outside the stable called to them. The two damned soldiers then ran out of the stable and disappeared into the night as quickly as they had appeared just a few minutes before. What a relief, after having been suspended between life and death! The milk was poured into the manure drain and we sat there in the semidarkness, relieved, but still too shaken to resume sleep.

After warming himself at the big stone house near the roadblock, S/Sgt. Robert Bowen returned to the company CP to draw rations and to inspect Tom Leamon's squad on the windswept ridges. The cold wind was swirling the snow over the men's foxholes. Without overcoats and overshoes, many of the men were suffering terribly. It was one helluva night for the men. Bowen would add more to his story the following day.

## COPING WITH SHORTAGES

Shortages were becoming a problem by the third day at Bastogne. From the Division "Narrative - December 1944", this description is provided for the 22nd of December:

By this time, food supplies as well as ammunition had become critical. It was necessary to requisition food from civilian sources. An abandoned U.S. Army bakery in Bastogne was also a source of considerable amounts of flour and lard. A Division hospital had been set up in Bastogne and was operated jointly by several of the unit medical detachments. Fortunately, an abandoned U.S. Army medical dump was found also in Bastogne and this was of great value to the hospital. During this period of encirclement, snow fell in the area and our troops were at a distinct disadvantage due to lack of snow capes. Only about one half of the Division had overshoes. All available white cloth was requisitioned for camouflage purposes and burlap bags were found and used to keep the men's feet warm.

The 907th Glider Field Artillery Battalion commander's office reported the following as a time when the "fortunes of war smiled upon the men of this battalion" in a narrative of its December activities:

The selection of the above command post (a chateau one mile west of Bastogne) appeared to be one time in which the fortunes of war were in our favor. This chateau had been formerly used as a headquarters for the American Red Cross clubmobiles in this vicinity and there was a considerable amount of sugar, donut flour, butter and other edibles stored in the buildings adjacent thereto. This food supply was shared with other units in our area and it proved to be invaluable later inasmuch as it was flour to make hotcakes for breakfast, donuts for dinner and hotcakes for supper until other rations arrived.[86]

The troops had been issued a basic load of K-rations and that supply was gone by the third day. However, the discovery of the large supply of flour in one of the warehouses provided for pancakes as a staple food. A bit of warm food does much for the morale of a front-line soldier. 1Lt. Robert P. O'Connell describes such an occasion:

While on the MLR outside of Bizory, our food was K, C and D rations. This was adequate – we were making do. However, on two nights we got word that just before daybreak some hot food would be at a road junction but to be quiet and not stir up the Krauts. We were to go to this spot one at a time. At the site, there was a marmite container full of warm pancakes, king size. Weapon in one hand, we reached in and grabbed a couple (no syrup or butter) and back to the foxhole. Not a big thing, but a morale booster. It was not so much the hot food, it was that someone back there was thinking of us. The MLR can be a lonely place!

When the Division pulled out of Mourmelon on the 18th, the basic issue of rations would take care of the first few days. It was assumed that once the men

---

[86]From the *History of the 907th Glider Field Artillery Battalion* as prepared by Captain George McCormack in 1945.

were positioned, the regular G-4 channels of the Division would provide additional supplies. However, for all intents and purposes, roads leading into Bastogne were cut on the night of December 20. Food supplies, or lack thereof, became a major problem. Captain Jim Hatch remembered how very concerned regimental commander Colonel Steve Chappuis was for the well-being of his men concerning food. Hatch recalled:

Steve Chappuis gave an order that we in Regimental Headquarters Company would eat only two parts of a ration a day and send the extra one to the front line companies. That afternoon, after we pushed the extra rations to the front line units, I went forward to visit those groups. To my surprise, here were units eating steaks and French-fried potatoes. Our extra rations were still in the supply room. Division had passed down the order that units could give a hand receipt to owners of livestock and stored potatoes and proceeded to set up company kitchens in their buildings and were eating first class.

Remembering an impulsive act he did in tossing away food that he did not particularly like, Pvt. E. B. Wallace recalled:

On the first day, I threw away a can of K-ration cheese. When I became very hungry three days later, I crawled in the snow that covered the ground and found that cheese. The first cooked food we had was sprouted bean soup from dried beans someone found in a shack by the railroad.

Recalling the days when food was in short supply, S/Sgt. Tom Alley may be remembering the same supply of dried beans briefly mentioned by Pvt. E. B. Wallace when he wrote:

We had very little, if anything, to eat and I recall someone found a bag of beans in a farmhouse and they or the cook had made a large pot of bean soup. At night, they dragged the pot from foxhole to foxhole and gave each man some soup in his canteen cup. I never tasted anything better.

For several days, fog was a major problem for the men. Snow began to fall on the night of the 21st. Men often became lost and confused when confronted by fog on patrol or on a scrounging mission in search of food. PFC. John E. Fitzgerald remembered such an incident:

The morning of December 22nd brought dense fog. The problem of food was becoming acute. During the night, in an attempt to find something to eat, two men from 'G' Company decided to search a small village to our front. They went through one of our outposts and were gone for several hours. On their way back, they became lost in the fog and wandered too far to their left. As they approached our lines, they were cut down by one of our machine guns. Later that morning when the fog cleared, someone spotted their bodies. A detail was sent out to bring them back in. As we watched them being placed onto a jeep, we could see some potatoes rolling from their pockets onto the ground.

Operations sergeant Chester Brooks remembered a story his friend Cpl. Tom Maitland had related to him on a visit a dozen years after the war about being offered some fresh boiled chicken soup at a time when he was in need of sustenance. Brooks related:

Food was scarce from the kitchen. Machine gun sections and squads were always attached and more often than not, attached units got less or felt they did. Anyway, it was a dark night and two men came carrying a marmite can and whispered to Maitland, 'Get your men – this is not from the kitchen.' They made a big point of saying it was chicken the company was providing. Evidently someone had raided a chicken coop and had boiled some chopped up chickens. Maitland got his men and they stood around the chicken pot and the 'caterers' said, 'Help yourselves!' Each man took off his jacket, rolled up his underwear or whatever and reached down into the deep can. Each man came up with a wing. Maitland said he had been gradually losing his appetite and knew after that pot had gone down the whole line there were only chicken wings left. The 'caterer' said, 'Help yourself!' but he said, 'No thanks – I'm not that fond of chicken.' They then looked around to make sure none of Maitland's men would hear them and said, 'Get your canteen cup and you can have some of the broth!' Maitland said that he visualized a reinforced company of men who hadn't washed in a week reaching down in that can sloshing their dirty hands around trying to find a drumstick or a breast and really had no appetite for the broth either.

As a substitute supply sergeant in his company at Bastogne, PFC. Leonard Hicks remembered the scrounging that he did upon arrival to compensate for the lack of overshoes for his men:

I was told to set up company supply at the small military post on the north side of town. Having no supplies, it didn't take long. Then Edgar Bishop and I got busy. Before the day was very old, we had discovered a storage building packed with burlap (gunny) sacks – probably 2,000 to 3,000 of them. I told Bishop 'these are more valuable than gold!' We loaded all we could on the truck and headed for 'F' Company where they had dug in on a rise to the southeast of Foy. I explained and demonstrated to enough guys to wrap their feet with two or three bags per foot – great for keeping feet warm and dry, also to line their fox holes with bags. Anything left over was passed along.

One of the soldiers from a neighboring unit who received gunny sacks for footwear, Pvt. Anthony Garcia wrote: 'Burlap sacks were issued to us in place of overshoes, which would keep the feet warm only while standing still but would be left behind like foot prints when you tried to walk even using the string supplied to tie the sacks on . . . a laughable situation."

## SHELTER FROM TREE BURSTS

The problem with artillery tree bursts was an extremely serious one – especially with the men dug in the relative concealment at the edges of the various tree plantations. PFC. Leonard Hicks describes how the men in his unit coped with the tree-burst problem:

'F' Company was set up in a patch of woods about a mile south of Foy. While some were trying to dig foxholes, others were felling and bucking six to eight-inch diameter logs to cover their foxholes. None of them could dig any deeper than a few inches – solid rock. They pulled out of there and left all those logs. I was sure they would need them at their next position. I discussed this with Edgar Bishop. He agreed that if we could get a truck driver to go, we would take a load of logs to 'F' Company. We really had a load when we finally arrived where the men were diggin in. The first person I met was Colonel Sink. He wanted to know what in hell I was doing with a truck up there. I said, 'Sir, I have a load of logs for 'F' Company.'

His answer was, 'Dump them over here for 'D' or 'E'.' My answer was, 'No sir – we gathered these for 'F' Company and they will need them!'

His response surprised me a little. 'Get you a detail from 'F' Company and get this truck out of here!' We did. That night, we were hit hard by tanks, anti-tank guns, some got close enough to overrun some emplacements but when it was over the German Army had lost another battle. Several of the men thanked me for the logs saying, 'Without them, most of us would not have survived.'

Communications sergeant Hugh Pritchard describes the hole which became the sanctuary and command post for "Dog" Company of the 506th Parachute Infantry Regiment in the woods near Foy:

For the company CP, we dug a hole approximately eight feet square by four and a half feet deep, cut pine logs to lay over it, covered the logs with a tarpaulin, then piled all the loose dirt on top. This became home for Captain Joe McMillan, our company commander, 1Lt. John Kelly, 1/Sgt. Robert Shurter, Sgt. Allen Westphal and myself. As communication sergeant, I ran telephone lines to 2nd Battalion, all of our platoons and outposts. We also had standby radios so our company CP was in touch with all necessary echelons at all times.

With the shortage of fighting equipment available to the front line troops of the 101st Airborne Division, it wasn't above them to appropriate equipment from those who didn't seem to be using it against the enemy. T/Sgt. Frank A. Palys relates such an instance:

We were in Luzery and there were times when we just sat around. About the main excitement we had was stealing a jeep from some major who was high-tailing it out of Bastogne. We helped steal a half-track with quad-fifties on it, but someone from Division HQ took it away from us.

## THE 502ND FRONT

From their first defensive position at Monaville, "A" Company made its first move to Champs. PFC. Ted Goldmann describes the move and the way they were positioned in a perimeter defense:

At 2 a.m., the 22nd of December, the first snow fell and it came down off and on from then until nightfall. At 0700 we got up, finished the food we had obtained the night before and moved out with all our load. We had picked up the packs and overcoats when we went into the woods. The first village we had been in was Monaville, now we moved from the woods to Champs, a slightly larger village. We dug in on the northern outskirts and then started hunting for food which the civilians of Champs had very little of but shared willingly – again, bread, butter and chicory (coffee substitute).

Patrols went out from the front line companies and from the various S-2 sections within the regiment. Some were successful and others were not.

As a member of the S-2 intelligence section, Cpl. Newman L. Tuttle was involved in a lot of patrolling. It was a little different in Bastogne with the snow, cold and constant threat of enemy soldiers appearing in American uniforms and with the fog playing tricks, rising and then sinking quickly. Tuttle recalled:

On a night patrol in the cold and snow, I remember watching German tanks coming up a road and stopping at a road junction about one hundred yards down the hill from us. We sat quietly in the snow in our white camouflage and listened to the Germans. We counted the tanks and vehicles to report back to Regiment to the S-2 officer. We did not open fire on them. Our orders were to only gather information. This was several days before Christmas. When we approached our lines, we had to give the sign for the evening and wait for the countersign. Also, we had to have our left hand on our hip. I had a nervous feeling and hoped none of the new replacements in the company would have 'itchy trigger fingers.'

Another patrol that went out from "A" Company was not as fortunate as the S-2 patrol from Regimental Headquarters. PFC. Ted Goldmann describes what happened to some of their men on the night of December 22nd:

That night, a six-man patrol from our platoon went out with Givry as its mission and we never saw them again. In March, one of the men, Cpl. Jim Goodyear, escaped and said they had become lost on the return trip and veered too far west (of Champs) and on Christmas Day had been captured when they fell asleep from exhaustion in a house.

## THE NEED FOR SHEETS

In an article he wrote for *Readers Digest*, John Hanlon, former commander of 1st Battalion of the 502nd Parachute Infantry Regiment, described the sudden need for camouflage material to counter the new snow which had fallen at Bastogne:[87]

The paratroop battalion I commanded, some 600 strong, was ordered into Hemroulle, a little village in the Ardennes about two miles northwest of Bastogne. It didn't look like much of a place; two dozen farmhouses and as many cow barns, about 100 inhabitants in all; a small church with a perky spire; one dirt road and a couple of byways – all of it sitting rather bleakly in a dip in the terrain. We were short of food, low on ammunition and outnumbered. Six inches of snow had just fallen and we were without camouflage – our soldiers in their olive-green paratroop uniforms were sitting ducks against the white background.

At my headquarters in house billet No. 13, I called a meeting of my staff. Someone suggested bed sheets. But how on earth could we get hold of that many sheets in a hurry?

I sent my executive officer, Capt. Edward Fitzgerald to ask the burgomaster if there was any chance of our borrowing some sheets. 'Tell him,' I said, 'we'll return them when we can.'

The burgomaster was Victor Gaspar, a man in his seventies with a round red face and a large mustache. Twice in Monsieur Gaspar's lifetime, in 1914 and again in 1940, the Germans had invaded his village. When Fitzgerald told him of our needs, he did not hesitate. 'Come,' he said and led the way across the road to the village church. There he unwound the belfry rope and began tolling the bell. 'The people will know,' he said. 'The ringing is a signal for them to come.'

As the first sound of the bell floated over the village, a surprised woman poked her head out of her cottage door and listened. She wiped her hands on her apron, threw a coat over her shoulders and started for the church. Others followed. Singly or in small groups, some accompanied by their children, most of the villagers were soon scurrying along the road to the church.

As they arrived, Monsieur Gaspar gave them instructions. 'Bring your sheets,' he said. 'The Americans need them for camouflage. And be quick!'

A few could not come. Mme. Eudoxie Collard, for one, was too busy cooking a meal for 60 people who had taken refuge in her cellar and she couldn't leave her stove. But the burgomaster called personally on those who

---

[87]Hanlon, John. *The Readers Digest*, "A bell rings in Hemroulle," December 1962, pp. 8-10.

did not answer the bell's summons. At the church, meanwhile, the villagers were beginning to return with their precious bundles. In half an hour, 200 sheets were stacked in the church vestibule. There was never a word about my promise to return them.

Quickly I had the sheets distributed to the men – and a few minutes later I realized the folly of that promise. The soldiers were making proper military use of their camouflage; they tore out square pieces of the sheeting and made them into coverings for their helmets; they cut strips and laid them across the machine gun barrels. For their own covering, the men slit openings in the sheets and slipped them over their heads, pancho-fashion. When the job was done, they were a weird and ghostly lot but they were well concealed.

Apparently the requisitioned sheets that were available for camouflage purposes to conceal troops on the MLR were often given to members of S-2 patrols on a priority basis. They were not always a welcome addition to their gear as is related by T/Sgt. Frank Palys of the S-2 Section of the 506th Parachute Regiment. He wrote:

On those patrols that the S-2 made, we had some white sheets that were given to us to wear while on patrol. I sure as hell didn't want to wear them because when they got slightly damp, they would rustle as they froze and the sound would carry for some distance.

## SNOW AND SHELLS

In a diary he kept while serving with Signal Company in both Holland and Bastogne, T/4 Gerald Zimmerman made the following notation:

<u>December 22, 1944</u> – Snow began to fall and the fir trees by our radio set look beautiful. The first real snow I've seen since I've been in the Army. Shells still falling and three officers were killed by one.

The scariest night of the war for PFC. Charles Lenzing, of Signal Company, occurred on the night of December 22 when a large shell hit the building in which many of the Division Headquarters personnel were quartered. He wrote:

I remember the night of December 22nd when Sgt. Iving Schmidt and I took refuge from the weather in an empty room on the opposite end of a building in which Division HQ men were housed. The night was cold and blustery. As we were falling asleep on the ice-cold floor, some incoming mail began to rain down on us. We immediately grabbed our helmets and rifles and ran down the long hall that went from one end of the building to the other. We stopped at the center entrance and knelt next to the opening. Outside the doorway, lying prone, was Tommy Younger and another

Signalman. A shell landed in the middle of the narrow street and went
bouncing down toward the cemetery. Thank God it was a dud. Schmidt and I
started to stand up inside the hall preparatory to running for the German
constructed air raid shelter. The shelling was reaching saturation
proportions. A very large shell zipped over our heads, penetrated the roof and
ceiling on the opposite side of the hall's brick wall and exploded, killing
three Headquarters men. The blast blew a triangular section of the brick wall
all over the heads and shoulders of Schmidt and myself, knocking my
helmet off and almost driving me to my knees. In the dark, I felt with my
feet and hands for my missing helmet but to no avail.

Schmidt and Lenzing fled for the cover of the earth–covered air raid shelter
where they spent the remainder of the night. In the morning, Lenzing returned to
the building to seek out his helmet but had to be content with head cover of a
stranger, one of those who died as the result of the shelling. He never did feel
right about wearing a dead man's helmet.

## THE SURRENDER ULTIMATUM

From his position on the flank of his platoon, PFC. Charles Kocourek of
"F" Company of the 327th Glider Regiment wittnessed the approach of the
German parliamentaries and felt it strange that enemy soldiers would surrender
after being fired on from a distance of many hundred yards. He related:

While we were standing around, we heard some firing and I walked over
to those positions and asked, 'What for?' The men said, 'Germans – way out
there!' Off in the distance were four Germans with a white flag coming down
the road. One guy says, 'Three shots and we've got four Germans – not bad!'
I said, 'Why would four Germans at 400 yards distance from our positions
want to give up? It doesn't make sense.'

The soldier who made the first contact with the emissaries was S/Sgt. Carl
Dickinson of "F" Company. At 11 o'clock on the morning of the 22nd, he had
spotted the Germans carrying a white flag, coming down the road toward his
position. He had gone out to meet them. He describes the encounter:

I went down and met them below our line and one of them who could
speak English said, 'According to the Geneva and Hague Conventions, we
have the right to deliver an ultimatum' and asked to be taken to our
commanding officer.

They each carried handkerchiefs for blindfolds and the German major
blindfolded the other officer and I, in turn, blindfolded the German major. As
soon as this was accomplished, our company medic, Ernest Premetz, not
knowing if any of the Germans could speak English, came down as he could
speak German. We left the other Germans with PFC. Leo Palma in a BAR

position at the side of the road and Ernest Premetz and I started back to the CP where Sgt. Butler and Lt. Smith came to the door to learn what was going on. When we asked what to do with the two German officers, they told us to take them to the Company CP where they stayed until their ultimatum was delivered to General McAuliffe in Bastogne. Colonel Harper returned them to us after receiving the famous 'NUTS' reply. They then went back to their own lines.[88]

Lt. Colonel Ned D. Moore was acting chief of staff for the 101st Airborne Division at Bastogne. He was on duty when the call came from "F" Company of the 327th that some parliamentaries had come through the line under a flag of truce to negotiate our surrender. General A. C. McAuliffe had been up all the night before and was sacked out in deep sleep in his basement cubbyhole, next to the Division Command Post in the cellar. Colonel Moore went to General McAuliffe and shook him awake, saying, "The Germans have sent some people forward to take our surrender."

Still half asleep, the General muttered "Nuts!" and started crawling out of his sleeping bag.

While the General was getting up, Colonel Moore got back on the phone and told the troops at "F" Company to keep the enemy confused as to locations so they'd have no knowledge of where the various command posts were situated.

When the actual ultimatum for surrender was delivered to the Division command post, the staff had already heard from Colonel Moore what the General's response had been when he was so rudely awakened and told of the ultimatum. It may well have been that the famous "NUTS" response can be attributed to G-2 Major Paul Danahy who was very clever at coining phrases when sending out situation reports to the regiments positioned out on the front line.[89]

Fortunate to be on the scene when the headquarters staff pondered what reply to send in response to the ultimatum which had just been received, PFC. James Oleson of the G-3 Section wrote:

> Sgt. Tom Bruff was the one who actually typed the reply to the German commander. I thought it was a strange reply but we had been taking what they could send in. We waited – thinking we would be getting greater activity after they got the reply but it didn't really change.

With the Division message center and switchboard located in an adjoining room of the cellar, members of Signal Company were pretty much aware of events as they occurred throughout the stay at Bastogne. T/3 William C. McCall was on duty when the surrender ultimatum came in. He recalled:

---

[88]From a letter Peter J. K. Hendrikx received from Carl E. Dickinson dated July 13, 1985.

[89]Material gathered during a phone conversation with retired General Ned D. Moore on November 17, 1991.

On December 22nd, while on day shift duty in the Message Center, the Germans brought the surrender ultimatum or be annihilated boasting of the units surrounding us. The commander of Combat Command B, 10th Armored Division, sat there in the Message Center and read this ultimatum out loud to us. Don't know how the others felt but it scared the heck out of me.

General McAuliffe's response to the surrender ultimatum had already been sent by the messenger who delivered it when T/3 George Koskimaki came in to deliver a coded radio message. He wondered why there were so many grim faces in the assemblage in Message Center. He wrote:

I had just received a coded message by radio for Headquarters and it needed decoding so, consequently, it ended with Message Center. Noting the grim appearances on the faces of the men, I wondered what kind of news they were privy to. 'Haven't you heard that we've had a surrender ultimatum from the Germans?' one of my friends asked.

When it was explained, and looking at my watch, the deadline was fast approaching. I headed for my little nook in an earthen air raid shelter where I dug out my log, which I recorded on the onion skin sheets found at the backs of Signal Corps message books. If the shelling got bad, I wanted those notes in my possession in case it became necessary to eat my evidence.[90]

As executive officer for the 463rd Parachute Field Artillery Battalion, Major Stuart Seaton had arrived at Division Headquarters just after the surrender ultimatum had been delivered to General McAuliffe. He had this recollection of the event:

I vividly recall the day I took our battalion's plan of perimeter ground defense in to Division Artillery Headquarters. When I got there, the first thing I was greeted with was a comment by Colonel Sherburne. He told me that General McAuliffe had just received a surrender notice from the German commander. Colonel Sherburne gave me a copy of it. After reading it, I noticed that if Division didn't surrender by 4 o'clock, they would level the town. I think it was then about two o'clock. After getting our plan checked, I wasted little time getting out of the city and back to the Battalion.

From his outpost position, PFC. Charles Kocourek observed the actions from a distance of several hundred yards and, once the emissaries returned to their

---

[90]Whenever we returned to base camp from the combat zones, I would then transcribe the notes in my regular diary. After the war, while enrolled in college, I received a request from the officers chosen to write the 101st history, for the loan of my wartime diary, which they used quite extensively in the preparation of *Rendezvous With Destiny*, the wartime account of the actions of the Division from activation to deactivation.

lines, word was brought out to the positions from the platoon CP. Kocourek adds to his story:

Some time later, a trooper came out of the CP and explained the German surrender ultimatum. We were being given two hours to surrender. If we didn't give up, they would shell the hell out of us and come and wipe us out. During the two-hour lull, we got all the extra ammo we could find, dug some extra holes right next to Sgt. John. We had an L-shaped position.

When the two-hour cease fire ended, PFC. Charles Kocourek and his friends watched as a group of Germans moved across their front without any appearance of caution. They probably figured the Americans would surrender. Kocourek describes the following action:

About 20 minutes to three, we moved into our defensive positions. At 3:00 nothing happened. In about five minutes, I heard voices to my left and I could see Germans coming out of the woods. I counted 23 of them. In their midst was a civilian with a horse and two-wheeled cart. They were crossing in front of us. They were so non-chalant, rifles on shoulders and the civilian pointing to something in the distance. I kept cautioning the men – 'Don't shoot – let them come down.' I think the enemy soldiers were totally convinced we were going to give up. They were moving toward a clump of trees that would provide concealment and then we wouldn't see them to shoot at. I had a German machine gun in my foxhole, along with two rifles. I opened up with the German MG and the damned thing jammed. Then everybody started shooting. I worked frantically with the machine gun and could not clear the jam, so I picked up a rifle and started banging away. The enemy was firing back at us with snow and ice kicking up into our faces.

When it was all over, there were seven of them lying out there. One was wounded pretty bad as he was moaning loudly. The next morning, when we got up – they were all gone.

Company and platoon runners often ran into dangerous assignments as they carried messages to and from outpost positions. PFC. Kocourek describes such an incident that occurred on the night of December 22nd:

That night, a runner came through and I thought here comes a German and I let him come through the heavy marsh – it had to be an enemy – no American would be out in front of us. I was just ready to pull the trigger when someone called out. Oh, oh, a German wouldn't be hollering like that. As the man came closer, he called softly, 'Kocourek, Kocourek!' He was a runner looking for me. I asked, 'What the hell are you doing out in front of our position? You almost got yourself shot!' He said he had lost his way.

# 8. DECEMBER 23

## S/SGT. BOB BOWEN'S PLATOON

As platoon sergeant and leader, S/Sgt. Robert M. Bowen of "C" Company of the 401st Glider Infantry Battalion had his hands full on the 23rd as he battled both the weather and the enemy which was now appearing in front of his roadblocks and outposts with considerably more strength than had been displayed in the first three days at his positions along the main road to Marche. Bowen relates:

The night passed like a nightmare. My foxhole was like a freezer. No amount of exertion could warm my feet or hands and, as we had gotten orders for a minimum of movement during the night, I was unable to warm up by checking my squads. Dawn came like a blessing.

But the blessing was short-lived. A heavy ground fog had settled over the area cutting the visibility to nothing. From 1st Platoon's outpost came a burst of small arms fire, M-1's and machine pistols. The outpost withdrew as planned but, in the mad dash over the snow to the MLR, PFC. Ernest Howard and PFC. Steve Horkay, veterans of 'C' Company, came under heavy small arms fire. Howard was mortally wounded and Horkay lost a thumb. About the same time, cannon and small arms fire broke out in 2nd Platoon's area. The men at the roadblock had been told to watch out for tanks of Patton's Third Army, which were on their way to relieve the 101st. Hearing the roar of tank engines in the dense fog, 2nd Platoon thought them to be Patton's. Too late, they were identified as German. A spirited fight developed.

I checked the squads of my platoon at daybreak, returning to my foxhole by the stone house on the main road. I was eating a K-ration breakfast when Pvt. Norman Labbe, my radio operator, called me to the set. It was Captain Towns.

'Bowen, 2nd Platoon's under heavy attack. Take two of your squads up there right away and support them. Lt. Bob Wagner will meet you on the main road and guide you up there,' he directed.

Hans' squad was now led by Sgt. Joseph Kluckowski. I roused both squads, his and Felker's, and we set off to meet Wagner with a cold, biting wind whipping over the snow like ocean foam. We couldn't use the main road because Germans in white snow suits were just to the south of it advancing toward 1st Platoon. However, the road was raised five feet or so above the surrounding terrain, providing some cover. We plowed laboriously through the snow, weighed down by our arms and ammunition and breathing like exhausted athletes at the end of a contest. Wagner appeared out of the mist and told me to follow him. He took off at a fast pace, too fast for my men to keep up. We reached an elevated road bisecting 'C' Company's sector, dashed over it and into the open field beyond. Small arms fire and mortar shells swept the area. Several hundred yards ahead was the stone house behind 2nd Platoon. Wagner had picked two men from his platoon, Sgt. Joseph Damato, an old friend, and PFC. Frank McFadden, another old timer. Wagner and his men took off as fast as they could go. My men were exhausted from the dash to the road. I called to them to follow me and took off with bullets flicking the snow and mortar shells tearing black holes wherever they hit. Added to the din were the sharp cracks of tank cannons. But I was oblivious to everything but running as fast as I could. I reached the out buildings around the house, dropping against the wall of the house, totally exhausted. When I finally caught my breath, I took stock of the situation. Only Sgt. Joe Kluckowski and PFC. Harold Zimburg had made it from my platoon. (I learned later, after the war, that Captain Towns had changed his mind and sent someone to stop my platoon from crossing that open field, so most were back at the elevated road. Labbe, my radioman, was with them, so I had no contact with the CP.)

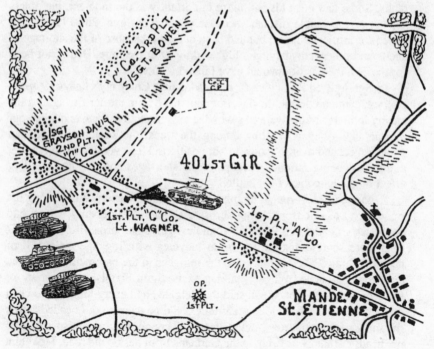

*Map 10*

The situation at 2nd Platoon's roadblock wasn't good, as Wagner and I soon found out. The tank which had supported my platoon the day before had been moved back to its former location and been knocked out, the burly sergeant painfully wounded in face and hands. He had been firing the .50 cal. machine gun at the advancing infantry when a tank shell hit the turret under him, spraying him with shrapnel and wounding others in his crew. He was moved to the basement of the stone house which was being used as an aid station. In the basement, also, was a group of civilian refugees who had been fleeing ahead of the Germans and caught up in the action. They were crying, praying and generally making things more difficult for everyone. The .37mm anti-tank gun on the ridge overlooking the road was out of action, also. It's wheels had frozen to the ground and the gun couldn't be moved enough to fire at the tanks. The men in the 2nd Platoon foxholes were taking a terrible beating with many dead and wounded. The only bright spot was the tank destroyer.

The TD was commanded by S/Sgt. Chester Sakwinski. His platoon leader, Lt. Gwyn, had just been commissioned in the field and joined Sakwinski's crew that morning. Under Gwyn's direction, Sakwinski maneuvered his TD up the sloping courtyard to take shots at the attacking tanks. Some had been hit but, more importantly at the moment, the others kept at a respectable distance because of the TD's gun. 2nd Platoon had called for artillery support but had been denied it because of the shortage of shells and other units having a higher priority at the time. Had it not been for the TD, the position would have fallen by noon.

S/Sgt. (Alfred P.) Schwartz, of Headquarter Company's heavy weapons platoon, came up during the day, directing his 81mm mortar fire against the enemy infantry. Many were in a wooded area to the left flank and when our mortar shells began bursting among the trees, the screams of German wounded echoed over the snow to our positions. However, the 81mm mortar ammo was being rationed because of the shortages and this had a telling effect on the outcome of the battle.

The men I had brought up, plus Wagner's, had taken position along the raised road to our front, firing across the field at the enemy, which had continued to bathe 2nd Platoon's foxholes with small arms fire. Along this road were scattered some ten or so bicycles with luggage racks full of personal things. They belonged to the refugees in the basement. One of the civilians approached Wagner, talking excitedly in Flemish. Wagner spoke some high school French and said the Belgians had everything they owned on the bikes. He asked me to see if they could be recovered. I headed across the snow to the main road, bullets from the enemy in front whispering past my head. Damato was firing at the Germans from beside the road. I told him what I had been asked to do. He pointed out the bikes scattered along the road in plain view of the Germans who were shooting at anything that moved. I returned to the basement and told Wagner that nothing could be done to retrieve the Belgians' personal possessions. My news was greeted with a chorus of crying howls.

Some medics from the battalion aid station managed to slip across the field to our rear. There were five, I believe, led by T/Sgt. Bonner and Sgt. Bell. They set up an aid station in the basement and began treating the wounded who, at this point, had received battlefield first aid. One of our .30 caliber MG positions had taken a direct hit from one of the tanks. Two men, Pvt. Lorne Torrence and PFC William Epson, were killed instantly. There were other wounded from the weapons platoon, including S/Sgt. Oakley Knapp, who had been thrown from an MG emplacement by an exploding shell. In a mad scramble for cover, a bullet had pierced his ankle. He was in great pain.

There were other wounded lying in the snow along the MLR, some screamed in delirious agony. I asked T/Sgt. Bonner if anything could be done for these men. He said it would be suicide for anyone to try to help them under the circumstances. I said I would try if a medic would go with me. Pvt. Everett Padgett volunteered.

We crossed the main road and started down the slope to 2nd Platoon's foxholes, wriggling through the snow on our stomaches. As soon as the Germans spotted us, their volume of small arms fire dramatically increased with bullets ripping through the snow around us. We got up and ran back to the cover of the road, the screams of the wounded ringing in our ears. Padgett told me to stay put, perhaps the Germans would respect the Red Cross on his helmet and arm band. Then he went back.

It was one of the bravest acts I ever witnessed in combat, characteristic of our medical section and one which, to my knowledge, was never recognized for an award. With German bullets tearing up the snow around him, Padgett got to the wounded, checked each one and made it back to the road. He told me there was no point in trying to bring them in, as two had been shot through the head and were brain dead. The other was so mutilated that any effort to move him would be fatal. One of them was Pvt. Joseph Cammarata. We called him 'Peppernose.' The other two were Sgt. Robert Rehler and Sgt. Fred Poling.

The second TD attached to the company started up the main road to help 2nd Platoon. As it tried to rotate its gun turret, it couldn't. It was frozen in place. The commander decided to find a safe area to thaw the turret, turned and made off in the direction of the battalion CP. It came under German tank fire immediately and, as it reached a rise of ground, a shell grazed the back, sending blanket rolls flying. The TD wasn't damaged, but never rejoined the fight that day.

The day dragged on with 2nd Platoon's fire gradually diminishing. I
went to the aid station and talked to the wounded tank commander telling
him something had to be done or else the roadblock was doomed. I said I had
some artillery training and could probably operate the 75mm gun on his
tank if someone could get the tank from behind the house. He said it wasn't
possible as the turret was jammed and the gun was out of commission.

Wagner, Gwyn and I had a meeting in the courtyard, agreeing that
something must be done to keep the German tanks at bay. The TD was
nearly out of ammunition and was drawing a hail of cannon fire each time it
came up the courtyard ramp for a shot.

As we talked, I noticed a half-track from 10th Armored nearly hidden in
the big fir trees to the rear of the courtyard. It's crew was in position along
the main road. On the side of the vehicle was a bazooka and a canvas pouch
holding three rockets. I suggested that I take the bazooka and try to get a
shot at one of the German tanks which had come within a hundred and fifty
yards of the MLR where it fired point blank into 2nd Platoon foxholes.
Wagner gave the okay, so we loaded the bazooka and I headed for the
elevated road. I could see a part of a tank which was in a defilade spot with
just the turret showing. I set the sights, took careful aim and fired. The
rocket left the tube with a blast which singed my face. The rocket grazed the
turret without exploding. Hearing the blast of the bazooka, the tank
hurriedly backed below the rise and out of sight. I went back to the house.

'Save the other rockets, we might need them later!' Wagner said, after
witnessing the withdrawal of the tank. The other tanks were too far away for
an effective shot.

2nd Platoon was taking a terrible beating. Had it not been for the TD,
their foxholes would have been overrun by the German tanks. PFC. George
Kalb had fired every clip of BAR ammo he and his assistant possessed, then
watched helplessly as the Germans inched forward. When darkness fell, he
managed to withdraw with PFC. Frank Marino, a stocky Philadelphian.
Once clear of their foxholes, they made a mad dash over the deep snow to
the rear. But the night was bright and clear with the moon shining like a
giant spotlight. Marino was killed while climbing over a wire fence by
bullets which miraculously missed Kalb.

2nd Platoon was nearly in a state of chaos, although we didn't realize it
from our position in the courtyard. A direct hit by a German tank had blown
up the CP, nearly tearing the shoulder off S/Sgt. Grayson Davis, the acting
platoon leader. Ammunition was low and casualties were mounting. Wagner
had requested more artillery support but the appeal went unanswered. Every
shell was being rationed. Gwyn continued to direct Sakwinski's TD. The
house, outbuildings and huge fir trees were hit, scattering debris in the
courtyard in a rain of rubble. S/Sgt. Louis Butts, squad leader in the 2nd

Platoon, who had taken over for Davis, managed to wriggle up the snowy slope and into the courtyard. A stunned expression was on his face. Short and rotund, he was a veteran of Normandy and Holland and knew what he was doing.

'Half my squad is dead or wounded and the rest of the platoon is no better. I think we should pull back,' he said, not too coherently.

Wagner was on the spot. Like me, he had been sent by Capt. Towns to help 2nd Platoon. But what help could we give without more support from our heavy weapons? I think he realized, also, that by withdrawing now would only mean more casualties. Any withdrawal would have to wait until dark and then only if Capt. Towns gave the order.

Wagner looked sympathetically at Butts. 'My orders are to hold this position, Sergeant. If there is a change in that order, I'll let you know immediately.'

Butts stared at us with disbelief on his face. He was too good a soldier to argue with an officer, although, under the circumstances he should have. Getting all his men killed wasn't going to save the roadblock. 2nd Platoon needed help. Anger flooded Butts' face. He gritted his teeth, turned and headed back for 2nd Platoon's foxholes. Somehow he made it.

The tempo of the battle increased, as the Germans sensed the resistance against them was crumbling. Tank and mortar shells were exploding with regularity around our stone house. I watched a huge fir tree near us disintegrate after being hit, showering us with bark and needles. It should have been a warning, sending us to cover, but we ignored it, as we discussed the situation. Sgt. Joe Damato had come back from his position on the elevated road, telling us that 2nd Platoon couldn't hold out much longer. Then, the world seemed to blow up around me. I found myself on the ground, choked by acrid fumes and my ears ringing. A shell had dropped less than ten feet from us, throwing me against the side of the house and bowling over like ten pins, Wagner, Gwyn and Damato. My chest and stomach were on fire and my right arm hung limp. Gwyn lay in a crumpled heap, having taken most of the force of the blast. Wagner and Damato limped toward the cellar as a medic rushed to help us.

Gwyn was the most seriously wounded, having shrapnel shards throughout his body. He was placed on a litter, sedated and moved into the aid station. Wagner had a foot wound which, although not serious, later became infected and caused him to be sent to the hospital. Damato had a wound the size of a silver dollar in his left thigh. I was lucky, my web equipment stopped the shrapnel from tearing deep into my torso, but a big piece was buried to the bone in my right wrist. The medics took us inside, gave us morphine and dressed our wounds. For us, the battle was over.

It was nearly dark. Wagner had been treated and was outside somewhere trying to round up stragglers from 2nd Platoon and men from the half-track which had dropped back from the main road. I understood him to say the wounded would be evacuated when it was fully dark, but time passed and only random shots were coming from in front of us. Joe and I limped to the doorway of the basement and went outside to see what was happening. We thought Wagner had gone to 2nd Platoon, as no more stragglers were coming back. A full moon in a cloudless sky made the scene around us look like a postcard picture.

Joe looked across the moonlit field behind us and said, 'I think we ought to try making it back.'

I looked at the distance we would have to cover and Joe's gimpy leg and knew he would never make it. Going back the way we had come was out of the question. Small arms fire had broken out along the road in 1st Platoon's area, the route we would have to take. More importantly, I wasn't going to leave until Wagner said the aid station was going to be evacuated. 'C' Company had never before left its wounded behind in any withdrawal. It was a decision that was to plague me for years later, but one which I was to finally rationalize later as the right one under the circumstances.

I helped Joe back to the basement, which had become a scene out of the 'Inferno.' The civilians were hysterical, crying and praying loudly and couldn't be quieted down by the medics. Our wounded were in such pain, despite the morphine and solace of the medics. Joe and I went to a corner and waited for Wagner to arrive with orders to evacuate the place, not realizing 2nd Platoon had withdrawn as best it could, leaving the MLR unoccupied. Wagner had been cut off by infiltrating Germans and was unable to return to the aid station. There was nothing to stop the Germans.

The civilians had some candles, the only light in the basement. I took my .38 Smith and Wesson from its shoulder holster and held it in my lap, as one of the medics went to the doorway and looked out. When he shouted to someone, 'All verwunded. Das ist gute!' I slid the pistol into the sling holding my wounded arm, as Germans poured through the doorway.

One of the medics spoke German. He talked with the Germans for a few minutes, then told us we were being taken prisoner. I wasn't sure because we had heard about the Americans who had been murdered at Malmedy. However, the medic said that we would be treated as prisoners of war and that the Germans wanted all the wounded who could walk to leave the basement. As I got up, I slid my pistol under some straw, deciding to take my chances with the rest.

'Hande hohe!,' a burly German said to me. I painfully raised my arms. He motioned for me to lower the wounded one. I did so, gratefully.

The ambulatory wounded were marched through the snow to the area from where the enemy tanks had been firing. Our watches, rings and other valuables were quickly snatched away while our captors complained about 'under kamarades kaput!' and 'verdammen Amerikaner swinehund.' It was a ticklish moment and I was sorry I had left my pistol behind because the Germans seemed that mad. However, cooler heads prevailed and the verbal storm blew over.

While this action was going on during the night of December 22nd, "B" Company of the 401st had been ordered to pull back from its forward positions out in front of the main body of its battalion so as not to be cut off by the enemy, which was now threatening the positions of Companies "A" and "C". The move was made during the night with "B" Company appearing on the scene at first light.

PFC. Carmen Gisi of "B" Company remembers the incident of the bombing by American planes on the first morning when the weather cleared. He wrote: "I remember Company 'C' being hit by our own planes and, after that, we had to put color panels in front of our foxholes."

## A MISTAKEN TARGET

Meanwhile, down the road a few hundred yards, eight-year old Andre Meurisse was about to become an innocent victim of the heavy fighting which had engulfed S/Sgt. Robert M. Bowen and his "C" Company comrades. During the sleepless night, another group of German soldiers had come to the house in Mande St. Etienne, gotten one of the Cawet brothers to hitch up his horses to pull their truck out from where it was mired in mud. The fighting intensified with the coming of daylight on the morning of the 23rd. The Americans were now attacking the village and pushing the enemy soldiers out. Andre Meurisse continues his story:

After waiting a while, my father and mother took me to the main stone farmhouse and there I was given some food. My father was talking to one of the Cawet brothers. I remember him saying that things would be better now. It was December 23rd and, now that the village was back in American hands and the Americans had pushed the Germans some distance back toward Germany . . . suddenly, terrific explosions, one after another, ripped through our location. The farmhouse building jumped under my feet, bowls on the shelves flew in every direction. Plaster fell from the ceilings, window glass flew everywhere. I ran out of what was left of the doorway, toward the stables. My father told us all that the cows stable was probably more strongly constructed and we would be safer there. He must have been right because the people who had been in the stable were unhurt, but a few of those who were in the house with me had been wounded by flying glass and some others were almost crushed when a portion of the house collapsed.

By now we could hear airplanes some distance away and the explosions had ceased as suddenly as they had started. I looked out of the stable through a dormer window in the doorway and saw a large strip of red canvas rolled out right in the middle of the main street next to our building. A few American medics were carrying litters past the adjacent barn with wounded soldiers on them. The portion of the building used for their living quarters by the two brothers was almost leveled to the ground. A putrid smelling smoke was drifting through the air, coming from the burning manure pile nearby. Two more buildings had been hit, one was burning, all of that done with just two or three bombs.

It wasn't until sometime later, after the shock of the building coming down around the heads of Andre Meurisse, his parents and the other civilian refugees in Mande St. Etienne, that Andre realized he had been injured during the bombing. He remembered:

It was sometime later that I began to feel a pain in my right shoulder. Slight at first, but growing worse with each minute as time was passing. Finally, I told my father about it. He thought, at first, that I had banged my shoulder against the wall when the bomb had blown out the house. But the ache became so intense that he finally took off my shirt and heavy winter clothes. As my underclothes were being taken off, they saw that all the under garments were soaked with blood. It had been an hour or so since the bombing and the blood was matted and coagulated now. So, he got some water and cleansed the wound. I was not crying, nor afraid, so I was sure that my father knew all the right things to do to protect and care for me. Also, as I was barely eight years old and had no idea of what was really happening in the world. After the wound was cleansed, I could see my shoulder. There was a bloody hole just slightly larger than my thumb. My father made me move over to the window where the light allowed him to look at the wound more closely. He knew that there was a piece of metal there in my shoulder for there was no exit hole, so that piece of shrapnel was still there. I could still move my arm somewhat so he felt that at least my arm was not broken. He took and opened his pocket knife and passed the blade through an open flame and very carefully tried to contact something metallic but to no avail. He told my mother, who was standing there expressing more anguish than me, that she clothe me while he went out to search for help. He came back about fifteen minutes later with an American medic, who applied a sterile bandage dressing to the seeping wound. My father tried to explain to the American that his son must be taken to a hospital but the medics said that my father could not go along, only wounded were allowed there. My father got mad and yelled at them. The medics finally agreed to let only my father go along with me; my mother had to remain behind. So I was loaded into the rear of an uncovered GMC truck and, with my father, we left my mother and went to Bastogne. (Even years later, when I think of that parting from my mother, tears come to my eyes, not for me but for her.)

I was taken to the military compound in Bastogne that the American Airborne Division was using as headquarters. The only thing that took my mind off of my pain was watching from the truck as an American dispatch rider, riding his motorcycle through the front gate of the compound suddenly slip and fall on some ice patch. With all the excitement of the last few days, I was worried about that unnamed rider lying there on the ice, but he got up under his own power and was all right.

## SENONCHAMPS

With the arrival of the larger enemy force to the woods to the southwest of Senonchamps on the 21st, the positions of "C" Company and the other defenders came under heavier artillery bombardment, most likely from the enemy tanks hidden in the woods.

This was the morning when there were several casualties from one of those artillery barrages as will be related by both Captain Walter Miller and Donald Woodland. Both also remembered the use of a "quad-fifty" that brought in artillery responses. Captain Miller related:

The 'Choo-Choo' artillery also provided us with a quad-fifty which we would run up from defilade and catch the enemy in the open. This technique lasted only a few days – on about the third day they were laying for us and they threw a shell and hit the end building where I was standing with two observers from the 10th Armored Division. It killed both men, one of whom had been all through Africa and Sicily. I was totally paralyzed temporarily by the explosion and was taken to the 10th Armored Division aid station in the village but returned to my unit.

Acting sergeant Donald Woodland had been out at a machine gun position and, after being relieved, had returned to the house to warm himself and get something to eat. Just as he got near the house, a shell hit between him and a tanker who was trying to thaw out the turret on his tank. Woodland wrote:

I was just inside the door with most of my body shielded by the stone masonry of the door jamb. Out of the corner of my eye, I observed the tanker who had been working on the frozen turret, slowly collapse. His body had received most of the shrapnel, but I was hit in the left side of the face, arm and wrist.

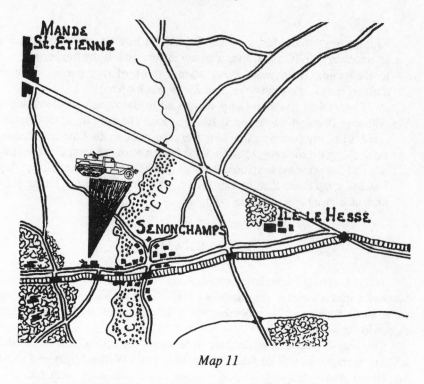

*Map 11*

My mind told me to get away from the house and back to the machine gun position; I believed that an attack was underway. I crawled over toward Blackie. The blood from my wounds was dripping in the snow. More shells landed on the position.

A team of medics soon arrived to evacuate the dead and wounded. I followed them on foot up the road to the aid station. They had me wait in a farm building. I went inside and reclined on the dirt floor. Across from me was a dead tanker from the 9th Armored Division. The two medics soon returned and stripped the tanker of everything of value. His personal effects were placed in a bag along with one of his dog tags. Then his body was carried outside and placed in a small shed on top of a half dozen other bodies.

After being treated for his wounds, Donald Woodland returned to his machine gun position near the western edge of Senonchamps where he had an opportunity to view the "quad-fifty" in action at close hand. The multi-purpose gun moved forward to take care of the enemy machine gunner who was harassing the troops. Woodland added:

A short time later, an M16 multi-gun motor carriage (probably from 'B' Battery, 796 AAA AW Bn of CCB 10th Armored Division) moved down the road to the roadblock position.

There was a short conference with the patrol leader and then the guns were loaded. Next, the motor carriage was backed down the road an estimated 125 yards. The guns were pointed in the direction of the machine gun in the woods and then fired.

It was a spectacular event with the tracers converging on the German machine gun position. The fusilade of .50 caliber bullets impacted in the forest. I could hear trees being felled, chopped down by the fire. Once the ammunition was expended, the motor carriage returned to the roadblock position, reloaded and repeated the action.

Then it went deadly silent. After a short time, the German gunner fired a short burst from his gun to let us know he was still alive. Our position then came under intermittent artillery fire for the remainder of the night. I believe the fire was from tanks in the woods.

PFC. George M. Kempf of "C" Company remembers the vehicle as being a tank, little realizing it had been moved from elsewhere with the Sherman being immobilized with a frozen turret. He was directing some of the men from the Snafu group which had been made up from the retreating forces.

Behind us was a Sherman tank hidden in front of the house, but all it had was .30 caliber ammo for a machine gun.

On December 23rd, the tank was moved forward between the house and my men who were mostly non-coms, about 25 or 30 from all groups. Why we weren't warned that they were going to move the tank and fire the .30 cal. machine gun up at a point in the woods above us I don't know. If we had known, we could have moved from the down slope to the back of the hill ahead of us but we didn't. They pulled the tank back to where it had been. Then we caught hell from the German artillery.

The memories of Pvt. Duane Harvey sum up many of the actions that took place over the first few days at Senonchamps. He remembered much of what the others had recalled in bits and pieces. Harvey wrote:

A little after daylight, we once again received artillery fire on the house. The first salvo killed a tanker sergeant. I left the house for the security of a foxhole across the road. The shelling was heavy and during one lull an AAA-AW half-track backed down the road and emptied its ammo drums into the woods and then pulled back. I think the Germans were in the woods, preparing for an attack. As the result of the half-track firing, we came under heavy artillery fire again. Things then quieted down for the rest of the afternoon and that evening we pulled out of Senonchamps and set up on a small ridge just outside of the village.

Enemy activity increased in the Senonchamps area and, as had been stated by Brig. Gen. S.L.A. Marshall, troops which had defended Sibret and Morhet, had barely reached the shelter of the woods and houses at Senonchamps ahead of the hard-driving German forces. Captain Walter L. Miller describes some of the actions which eventually led to the pull-out from the village:

> The Germans continued their activities in the woods to our front, gradually working to the one on the left and finally, about the 22nd or 23rd, forced themselves upon the 10th Armored and I was informed they were withdrawing to the perimeter inside Bastogne. We stayed and covered the withdrawal, finally returning to the line and crest above Countess Rene Greindl's chateau. We could not defend this line from the crest as it was covered by heavy enemy fire and we conducted a reverse slope defense with listening posts on the crest so we could determine enemy activity. The company CP was located in the barn of Countess Greindl's chateau. It was in defilade so shells passing overhead crashed to the rear. There was an artillery outfit without ammunition located there and I remember them streaming into the basement of the chateau when the incoming fire was received and then returning outside when the fire had lifted. About this time, two tanks from the 9th Armored Division, CCR, trundled into our lines. These two tanks were commanded by two lieutenants, Pulsifer and Terrell. They were two brave men. They would load up their tanks and charge down the hill into Senonchamps, spraying the Germans with machine gun and cannon fire and undoubtedly disrupted any attack from that direction.

In one of his experiences on the line at Senonchamps, Pvt. Duane Harvey may very well be relating an action which involved those two tankers. He wrote:

> I remember two Sherman tanks entering our lines from the direction of the village. We were in our foxholes. The tanks stopped and one lowered its cannon and the turret turned, like they were getting ready to fire into our positions. I think they realized we were not the Germans and drove on toward the rear.

When the withdrawal to shorten the lines was made in the Senonchamps area on the evening of the 23rd, Donald Woodland and his buddy Blackie had just begun to enjoy the comforts of a house where they had found a ham and were in the process of cooking it. Woodland describes what happened when the order came to pull back:

> The pullback of the 327th Glider Infantry Companies was made in good order. Two medium tanks leap-frogged each other to cover our road march. Machine gun squads took up positions on both sides of the columns and stayed in position until the last man had cleared the location. Then we heard the sound of aircraft engines. Bombs were dropping on Bastogne. The ground shook where we were. It must have been hell in town.
>
> The other company of the 327th that was pulling back, and was on the right flank, came under heavy enemy fire which seemed to be coming from the woods. A sharp fire fight developed and I had the feeling that we would have to be committed, but that did not happen.

Captain Walter Miller continued his story, praising the engineers who were in position on his flank and added a humorous story at the same time:

My right flank was tied in with the 326th Engineers who fought both as infantrymen and as engineers and did a terrific job of blocking the enemy from coming down the main road.

An amusing incident I remember at the Chateau Ile-le-Hesse was when several of the men, to avoid the cold, cut arm and leg holes in their sleeping bags and ran around looking like giant green beans.

## THE PATHFINDERS

As he left the battle zone in Holland, 1Lt. Shrable D. Williams, along with several other 506th Parachute Regiment troopers, was placed on TDY to the 9th Troop Carrier Command Pathfinder Group and flown to England.

Another officer who continued his assignment with the pathfinders was 1Lt. Gordon DeRamus, who had led his stick into Holland on September 17, 1944. He remembered:

We stayed at base camp until right before the Ardennes when pathfinders were sent back to school at North Witham, near Nottingham – I suppose this was the long range planning on proposed jumps across the Rhine in the spring of 1945.

Not all of the 101st Airborne Division pathfinders were assigned to a particular mission as an entire group. Also, they were not a permanent part of the 9th Troop Carrier Common Pathfinder Group. From a report to the commanding general of the XVIII Airborne Corps, the following information was extracted:[91]

Airborne pathfinders participating in this operation are not permanently assigned to IX TCC Pathfinder Group but were on temporary duty while attending school for a period of two weeks. It was merely a coincidence that sufficient airborne pathfinders to accomplish the mission were available at this base at the time the mission was received.

For those pathfinders not assigned to the mission to drop near Bastogne, teams were sent to the continent to be ready if needed. 1Lt. Gordon DeRamus added to his story:

Just as we got to Pathfinder Camp, the Bulge came up and four sticks of us were sent to a French airfield camp in Chateaudon – stayed on 30 minute alert for several days to drop around Bastogne for resupply missions but were not called.

---

[91]From a report of Airborne Pathfinder Operation "NUTS", to commanding general, XVIII Airborne Corps on January 7, 1945.

When a request had come from the 101st Airborne Division for resupplies after the roads to the city had been cut from all directions, a hurried plan was developed to use pathfinder teams to direct an aerial resupply as quickly as possible. The Troop Carrier report to the Commanding General of XVIII Airborne Corps continues:[92]

The first decision was to commit one stick (one officer and nine enlisted men) to mark the DZ. Due to the fact that the DZ was known to be surrounded by the enemy and considering the effect of small arms fire on C-47 type aircraft at jump altitude (400-600 feet) the Exec-Officer, IX TCC Pathfinder Gp and XVIII Corps (Airborne) Pathfinder Officer felt that two identical teams should be committed. A telephone (scrambler) request to commit two teams was approved by IX Troop Carrier Command.

The orders for the mission arrived on such short notice that it was impossible to develop the plan for the mission in time for a December 22nd drop in which the aerial resupply would have occurred during night-time hours. The pathfinder report to the commanding general of XVIII Airborne Corps continues:

Airborne Pathfinder Teams were equipped with weapons and combat equipment by the Group S-4. Smoke and panels had been predrawn and were available in the XVIII Corps supply room. Radar equipment was set up and checked. Due to limited time all enlisted men belonging to the Airborne Pathfinder teams were dispatched to the Dispersal Areas to load at 1330. Officer jumpmasters reported to Group Operations for Pilot-Jumpmaster briefings at this time.[93]

One of the jumpmasters, 1Lt. Shrable "Willie" Williams remembered the briefing and dry run on December 22nd. He wrote:

We were told that the 101st Airborne Division in Bastogne was surrounded and didn't know if they had been overrun by Germans. We were to parachute in and set up our equipment if we landed in friendly territory and prepare to guide resupply missions into Bastogne.

We were loaded into the aircraft and were ready to take off with the motors running when the mission was cancelled. We went to the briefing rooms and they said they had reports that the 101st Airborne was overrun by Germans but we were to be ready to leave the next morning if the situation changed. Intelligence reports were not too good at this time.

Information continued to trickle in from Bastogne during the night and additional maps (1:50,000) were found and distributed to the pathfinder teams. Further briefings were held and the flight was scheduled for 0645 on the morning of the 23rd. Because last minute intelligence reports were not available for the Bastogne area, it was decided to drop one stick and wait for a predetermined

---

92ibid.
93ibid.

signal (orange smoke grenade) before dropping the second stick in case the first group fell into enemy hands upon landing.

Jumpmaster Shrable Williams couldn't recall why his stick was picked to lead the two-plane mission. He describes the trip:

We were called early the next morning and told the mission was on again. I do not remember why my pathfinder team was picked to fly in the lead aircraft. I think we cut cards to see which team would jump first, mine – or 1Lt. Gordon Rothwells'.

One plane, the leader, was to fly over Bastogne and drop the 101st Airborne pathfinders and, if they landed in friendly territory, they would throw out a smoke grenade. The other plane would circle and wait for the proper signal before it dropped the other pathfinders. If the first plane dropped in enemy-held territory the other plane was to continue looking for members of the 101st Airborne Division before they made their jump. We picked up fighter support over France and they stayed with us.

One of the team members of 1Lt. Shrable Williams' stick was PFC. John Agnew who described his experiences in the newsletter of the IX Troop Carrier Pathfinder Command Association:

Take-off time was 0645, 23 December 1944. I was in the lead aircraft (#993) piloted by LTC. Joel Crouch. We were followed by a second aircraft (#681) piloted by 1Lt. Lionel Wood. The flight from Chalgrove to Bastogne was uneventful but as we approached the 'DZ' and the red light came on for 'hook up!' tension mounted and you got a lot of funny feelings. Suddenly, there was a burst of ground fire and you could see the tracers go by. It came from a German gun emplacement directly in front of our flight path. Quickly, Col. Crouch dove the aircraft directly at the Germans (we were looking down the barrels of their guns), who, thinking they had shot us down and we were going to crash on top of them, jumped out of their gun emplacement and ran for safety. The colonel then pulled the aircraft back up to jump altitude. However, since we were all standing (loaded with heavy pathfinder equipment), the suddenness of the maneuver caught us by surprise and most of us sank to our knees due to the 'G' force exerted. Luckily, we all recovered our balance just as the green light came on and out the door we went. Upon landing, George Blain signalled the second aircraft to commence their drop.

After the shock of my chute opening, I looked around to orient myself and saw what I thought to be a German tank. I started loosening my 'Tommy' gun in anticipation of a fight. Suddenly, I hit the ground in what I think was the hardest landing of my career as a paratrooper. My tommy gun slammed into my face and I became a bloody mess. A medic quickly patched me up and, after assembly, we sought shelter in an old metal building which the Germans quickly blasted to get us out. Next, we tried the basement of a damaged building but the Germans zeroed in on us again. We lost some of our equipment this time and some of our people were trapped in the basement for a while but John Dewey and I managed to get them out.

As jumpmasters of the two teams, Lieutenants Shrable Williams and Gordon Rothwell had to determine where the 101st Division wanted the resupply drop to take place. Lt. Williams wrote:

The drop was successful. Both teams landed OK. Upon landing, Lt. Rothwell and I went straight to 101st Division Headquarters to see where they wanted the resupplies dropped. We went to the designated DZ and LZ in a low place almost in town. We set up our electronic equipment and in less than an hour later the planes were contacted and were homing in on our signal and the resupply mission was history. We were located on the highest ground in and around Bastogne so we had a front row seat.

When the pathfinder officers returned and ordered their teams to the proper location, the equipment was readied in anticipation of the arrival of the resupply planes. The homing devices did attract unwanted attention. PFC. John Agnew concludes his story:

*A pathfinder team member monitors a homing beacon on brick pile near Bastogne on December 23 as resupply planes approach to drop bundles. Team members stand in shelter provided by the bricks.*

Finally, we took shelter in Mrs. Massen's house and across from her place, on high ground, was a big brick pile. (See picture on previous page.) We set up our equipment (CRN's) there and waited for the first sound of incoming aircraft. We didn't dare turn on the sets until the last minute because the Germans would have 'homed in' on us and blasted us to bits. Shortly, the sound of approaching aircraft grew louder and louder so we turned on the CRN-4's. Even though the Germans started firing at us, the sight of the aerial armada distracted them and we suffered no casualties. The air drop was a great success and a Christmas present that the beleaguered troops at Bastogne wouldn't forget for a long time.[94]

The first forty aircraft arriving with supplies were from the IX Troop Carrier Command and all were carrying maximum loads of supplies to be dropped to the hard-pressed troops.

In short order, four of the planes were shot down and 35 of the surviving 36 aircraft received battle damage. Six of the aircraft were so severely damaged that they had to make emergency landings at bases other than Chalgrove, England, their home base.[95]

Records indicate that 234 planes from Troop Carrier Command took part in the December 23rd resupply operation. Three planes turned back and did not drop their supplies. Another group of three dropped their loads three to four miles off the DZ while another group of three missed the DZ by a mile and a half. These bundles were recovered. The rest landed on the drop zone and were quickly recovered by troops on the ground.

## MANNA FROM HEAVEN

Following closely behind the pathfinder planes was Lt. Colonel William H. Parkhill and planes from his 441st Troop Carrier Group. He describes how they became aware of the resupply mission and the route they would follow:

On December 22, 1944, a fighter pilot was sent to our base to describe what he had seen around Bastogne the previous day. We received orders to load up 21 C-47's with 66,800 lbs. of ammunition, 15,600 lbs. of rations and 800 lbs. of medical supplies. We also received a route map and pathfinder signals data. The route took us from Dreux (SW of Paris) direct to the Initial Point about 60 to 80 miles due west of Bastogne. The weather couldn't have been worse. A great frontal storm was moving slowly westward over all of northern Europe. The next morning when we took off,

---

[94]From a copy of an account John Agnew sent to the editor of the newsletter of the 9th Troop Carrier Command Pathfinder Association, Vol. I, No. 4.

[95]Airborne Pathfinder Operation "NUTS," op. cit.

the clouds were right down to the ground. We flew in a column of 3-ship V's right through the tree tops. We managed to stay together and turned at the IP heading due east to Bastogne. About 40 miles from target the weather broke and we were out of the weather front. You could see for a hundred miles in all directions. There were no other aircraft around. We stayed on the deck but had to cross a series of low hills running north and south. In the valleys, there were roads loaded with German armor and other vehicles bumper to bumper moving north. When they heard us coming, but couldn't see us because of the low hills, they ran away from their vehicles. When they saw what we were, they ran back and started shooting. They knocked down our last three aircraft. We went on to the target, got all the right signals, dropped our loads and climbed out right over Bastogne. As we climbed and turned, we could see over the weather front to the west and saw hundreds of bombers and fighters climbing out of England making contrails on their way to the battle areas.

Stating that he felt his plane and crew were among the first eight to go to Bastogne, 1Lt. Art Feigion was with the 1X Troop Carrier Pathfinder Group. Feigion describes his flight:

I like to think my crew was among the first eight planes into Bastogne. We took off from England in instrument weather. In pathfinder we flew a lot of our missions on instrument, when the weather was so bad 'even the birds were walking.' We handled our formation by altitude separation. And, believe it or not, we all broke out of the weather over France and within sight of each other.

We went in pretty low over the snowy fields in France. Before we got to Bastogne we must have flown over some German areas; we were all hit by small arms fire, but nothing serious. One of those bullets came up through the belly of the plane, right through the navigator's seat, and missed his 'dinkus' by about an inch. The bullet then buried itself in the radar control box. We didn't find out where the bullet had ended up until we got back to England.[96]

Aboard one of the early planes as a radio operator for the craft, T/Sgt. Martin Wolfe describes the loads they carried and what the Bastogne area looked like from on high during those cold winter days:

On December 23, the first day of aerial resupply, 260 troop carrier planes, including seven from our squadron, flew in 334 tons of supplies to Bastogne. This, and our subsequent resupply missions into the Bastogne area, were so straight forward they seemed almost cut and dried – except that, unlike noncombat supply missions, we now flew as part of large

---

[96]Wolfe, Martin. *Green Light*, University of Pennsylvania Press, Philadelphia, PA. 1989, p. 348.

formations, dropped our supplies with pararacks and parapacks instead of landing them and came back with a mess of bullet holes. No fancy tactical planning, no elaborate flight paths this time. Just straight on in, jettison your loads over the position markers west of Bastogne and get the hell out of there. In our squadron we carried mostly ammunition, but also K-rations and Signal Corps equipment. We took off from Membury shortly after noon each day and flew the long (three hour) trip to Belgium at 1,500 feet.

The first thing you saw, coming toward Bastogne, was a large, flat plain completely covered with snow, the whiteness broken only by a few trees and some roads and, off in the distance, the town itself. Next, your eye caught the pattern of tank tracks across the snow. We came down lower and lower, finally to about 500 feet off the ground, our drop height.[97]

*Elated troops of the 101st Division drag equipment bundles and resupply parachutes off the snow covered fields northwest of Bastogne.*

[97]ibid.

On board another plane from the 81st Troop Carrier Squadron was S/Sgt. Ben Obermark, the crew chief, who wrote:[98]

When we were flying over the Bastogne area I couldn't believe an army of men could be trapped down there in what looked like nothing but wide fields of snow. At first, I couldn't see any men at all. We pushed out the parapacks through the open door and then I lay down on the floor looking out the door and sort of squinting against the glare of the snow; that way, I could see men running toward the stuff we had dropped and dragging it away to their still invisible foxholes.

Down below, waiting in the snow-covered fields for the critically needed resupply of ammunition, food and medical supplies, PFC. Kenneth Hesler had this description of the arrival of the first resupply planes:

. . . hearing the drone of those C-47's around noon on December 23rd, 1944, as they came over the cemetery at Bastogne and out toward Hemroulle, cheering them wildly as if at a Superbowl or World Series game – a sensation yet remembered when that scene is replayed from newsreel tapes.

For PFC. Ben Rous, the planes brought something to be used to protect those frost-bitten feet. He wrote:

Finally, on the 23rd, the sun came out and Glory be – the sky was full of our resupply planes. What a relief! What a blessing! Watching those bundles of supplies and ammunition drop was a sight to behold. As we retrieved the bundles, first we cut up the bags to wrap around our feet, then took the supplies back to their proper areas. What a great feeling to have warm feet!

The 435th Troop Carrier Group which flew Division Headquarters into both Normandy and Holland, was on hand to drop much needed ammunition to the men at Bastogne. The group history describes the experience of one of its veteran pilots:[99]

One of the most harrowing individual experiences was that of Capt. Paul W. Dahl, of Los Angeles, Calif., who was leading the second element of his squadron. Four minutes from the drop zone, two shells burst through the plane, wounding Dahl, his co-pilot, Lt. William Murtaugh of Chicago and navigator Lt. Zeno H. Rose of Suffolk, Va. simultaneously. The first burst had sheared away all the instruments on the co-pilot's board and half of Capt. Dahl's panel, but the crew managed to maintain the plane in formation, sluggish as she was. They arrived over the target, dropped their supplies and made the turn to get out. As Capt. Dahl took a new heading, a

---

[98]ibid.

[99]Gilmore, Maj. Lawrence J. and Lewis, Capt. Howard J., *History of the 435th Troop Carrier Group*. Greenville, S.C. 1946.

burst of flak caught the lumbering plane flush in the nose, setting fire to the pilot's compartment. Capt. Dahl gave the order to bail out and, after setting the plane in a gradual glide, left the cockpit to jump himself. He attempted to find his chest-pack chute, but was unable to do so. Going back into the main cargo cabin, he did find an extra seat-type chute, but was unable to fasten it properly because of his arm wound. 'At this time, the rest of the crew had already left the airplane,' Dahl later stated, 'so I placed my arms through the shoulder straps of the seat-type chute and jumped and hung on by my arms until I reached the ground. At the time I left the plane, it had stalled out on its left side and was beginning to dive toward the ground. Due to the fact that the plane had stalled just before I jumped, I believe the air speed was at an absolute minimum, which resulted in very little opening shock from the chute. It was my opinion the only reason I was able to hang on the chute straps by my arms in descent.' Luckily, Capt. Dahl landed in friendly territory and was given immediate first aid. His co-pilot, navigator and door-load man were all brought to the same place. The radio operator and crew chief were apparently lost. Their chutes were riddled by machine gun fire.

The 438th Troop Carrier Group participated in three aerial resupply drops during the time the 101st Airborne Division was surrounded at Bastogne. On the 23rd and 26th, the drops were over Bastogne while the one on the 24th was near Morcouray, outside the Bastogne area. 1Lt. Austin Buchanan has this description of the first day mission:[100]

December 23, 1944. After we went to bed last night, the Group C.O. received other orders for today. The planes were unloaded and parapacks were installed. When we awakened this morning, we were told to dress for a combat mission – to relieve the beleaguered 101st Division at Bastogne. Went to a briefing after an early mess. The major briefed us and we were in our planes by 11:00. Were delayed for a time by new orders but at 12:40 hours, started engines and took off at 13:00. Our load consisted of six parabundles and four door bundles.

Flew to A-91, near Sedan, which had been designated as the IP. As we turned to our next course of 58 degrees, we could see heavy black puffs of smoke to the right of course. This, we knew, was the flak – the fire from the hated German 88's. Fighters were all around us and we could watch as they dive-bombed German tanks, half-tracks and gun positions. Our course continued on for forty miles to the DZ with only intermittent flak and some small arms fire to bother. Heard one fellow say that he had been hit but after the Holland missions this one was fairly easy. Dropped our bundles on a

---

[100]From a wartime diary kept by 1Lt. Austin Buchanan at his home station at Greenham Common in England.

large field at the edge of the town of Bastogne, where the 101st Airborne Division was so heroically fighting off an immensely superior (in numbers only) foe. We could see furious fighting going on below and were glad to see G.I.'s race out to retrieve the bundles we had dropped. As we turned away, I saw one of our planes leave the formation suddenly, nose downward and blow up as it hit the ground near the DZ. Upon return to the field, we discovered that it had been Lt. Roberts' plane. He was a pilot in the 88th Squadron.

The trip back was without incident until we hit England. Ran into bad weather and lost formation but turned on the compass, picked up G.C. and rode in on the beam.

## GROUND TO AIR COMMUNICATION

The work of Capt. James Parker, Capt. Charles Cherle and 1Lt. George B. Woldt in providing communication with the fighter bombers sent in support of the ground troops at Bastogne is described by Meyer Levin:[101]

Great quantities of German armored equipment was smashed and thus prevented from dislodging the American ground troops from Bastogne. This was done when the two captains and Lt. Woldt operated a switchboard and, by various types of radio-to-plane systems, contacted the Thunderbolts and sent them on their murderous missions against the Nazi tanks.

After the battle, Capt. Cherle told Levin, 'I would have bet three years pay the planes couldn't work over the enemy so close to our troops.'

At one point in the battle, according to Capt. Cherle, the telephone rang and a Thunderbolt pilot came in with 'Kingfish leader here, Kingfish leader here, See armor in woods. Is it ours or Krauts?'

Capt. Cherle replied, 'I don't think we have anything there but hold on until I check the position.' Picking up another telephone, Capt. Cherle made sure the armor was part of an enemy force.

He shouted to the pilot, 'Buzzard calling Kingfish. Go ahead and shoot them up.' A moment later, four planes dove out of the sky with machine guns chattering to knock out the tanks.

The tank switchboard was set up in the first few days of the battle for the important Belgian road hub. The air liaison team was made up of officers from various land units, in addition to Capt. Parker who is a pilot with three Zeros to his credit in the South Pacific.

---

[101]From a newspaper clipping of a story written by Meyer Levin of the Overseas News Agency that appeared in a Staten Island, New York newspaper, January 2, 1945. Clipping sent by George Woldt.

Capt. Parker went into Bastogne with essential radio parts bulging his pocket. In short order, the switchboard was set up and soon the team was directing artillery fire as well as the Thunderbolts.

'Once we saw some planes sneak up on our boys who were bombing the German tanks,' said Capt. Parker. 'We called our planes and warned them and in a few seconds they wheeled, caught and knocked out the would-be attackers,' he declared.

During the three days of good flying weather as many as 19 squadrons circled Bastogne and sometimes the switchboard gave directions to as many as five of them at once. The Germans made every effort to hide their tanks but the planes attacked anything that looked as if it were a good hiding place and caught many of the enemy that way.

Capt. Parker described one typical dawn mission. The enemy, he said, was barely more than 1,000 yards away and the switchboard man could hear their tanks clattering away in an attempt to move out and go to work.

The switchboard, he declared, would immediately contact the Piper Cubs and order them to watch for fresh tank tracks in the snow and telephone back the position. Then, the Thunderbolts would get their instructions to go out and wipe out the tanks.

'The beautiful teamwork of this tank switchboard group, which underwent severe shelling but never stopped talking to the fighter-bombers, was one reason why the German attackers kept butting their heads into a stonewall,' Capt. Parker said.

## WRONG TARGET!

Before the air-to-ground communication was fine tuned, there were some problems on the first day when air support could be provided. PFC. Charles Lenzing of the 101st Signal Company remembered watching the planes dropping supplies for the first time on December 23. He also wrote of mistaken targets:

I was watching a C-47, it's cargo door open and the right engine on fire, sputter past us and, just before it cleared out of my view, I saw two parachutes come out of the plane. The plane then crashed out of my view.

Just then, a flight of two P-47 fighter-bombers came low from the left over the cemetery and down the valley toward enemy territory. One dipped a wing – I think he was trying to mark a chute gone astray. Seeing the wing dip, the other pilot, looking around to his left, saw only our pack howitzer in the edge of the trees on the opposite side of the valley. Thinking it was German, he wheeled his plane up and to the left coming around he dove at the unsuspecting men with the artillery piece, firing all of his wing guns. I saw the light and dark green evergreens and the leafless trees of winter shake from the hail of bullets. Pieces of branches went flying off. The second P-47 followed suit and a terrible thing was happening right in front of me and four or five other guys. The planes came around for a second pass and, as they started dropping their wing bombs, an unseen machine gunner near the field piece opened fire on them. I could see the tracer bullets penetrating the right wing next to the body and my thoughts were with those poor guys on the ground as I kept repeating to myself, 'Aim a little more to the right!' then I realized I was shouting at the top of my voice, 'Kill that son-of-a-bitch!' The other guys were also screaming obscenities.

At that moment, a man came running up to us shouting, 'Where is the main radio?' I instantly pointed the way. He was the air to ground coordinator. After that, the P-47 planes withdrew. Can you imagine how those pilots must have felt, knowing they had machine-gunned and bombed their own men!

Over at the Fire Direction Center of the 377th Parachute Field Artillery Battalion, Sgt. John Kolesar was in the target area when the strafing and bombing attack occurred. He recalled the incident:

I don't recall the date, but the skies cleared and, to keep me sane, T/Sgt. George Barnett handed me an axe and he and I started chopping wood for the stove in FDC. All of a sudden, a Headquarters Battery machine gun began firing at a low flying plane. This plane was American and we knew we were in trouble. The plane flew upward and circled around, came back over and dropped a bomb near us. You could see a manure pile, straw and many other items going skyward. T/Sgt. Barnett pushed me aside, ran into the FDC and returned with orange panels. He ran across the road into an open field and began to display the panels to let the pilot know that we were Americans. Meanwhile, the rest of us near the machine gun section swore we would kill the next man who shot at that plane. Thank God, the pilot spotted Barnett and the panels, tipped his wings and went on.

During the time the weather turned from damp, foggy and cold to snowy and bitter cold, Cpl. Robert T. Romo, a member of "C" Battery howitzer crew, developed trenchfoot. When he took off his boots to put on dry socks, his feet swelled and he was unable to put the boots back on. He cut pieces from one of his blankets and wrapped them around his feet and inserted them into his galoshes.

On the 23rd of December, the gun crew was eating a meal of hot cakes beside a small fire near a local barn and about 20 feet from his foxhole when the men noticed four P-47's flying low and strafing German positions. Cpl. Romo picks up the story:

We cheered when they swooped down and fired their machine guns at the Germans. Suddenly, one P-47 turned and came straight at us, firing it's MG guns at us. What a terrible and helpless feeling to see your own planes coming at you, firing their guns. We made a mad dash for our foxhole. I was spinning and wheeling, trying to move up a little icy incline with no help from my galoshes. All I remember are the bullets hitting close by as I dove into my foxhole and curled up into a little ball and started praying. McCullough stuck his head into the foxhole and kept asking if I was alright. I finally hollered at him, 'Can't you see I'm praying!'

He jumped into the foxhole just as the P-47 made another pass and this time he dropped a bomb on our position. One of our officers finally jumped out into an open area and kept waving our identification panel. The pilots acknowledged and then flew to other targets.

The strafing by friendly planes was a lasting memory for Sgt. Steve Koper of "Baker" Battery. He wrote:

The day the fog cleared for the first time, I was assigned to take the jeep out to the drop zone to pick up resupplies. I jumped in the jeep and headed for the DZ. As I hit the road, our P-47's came behind me, strafing the road. I turned the jeep into a snow bank and ran for the open field. When I returned to the jeep, it had three holes in it but was not hit in a vital spot. I drove to the drop zone and it was being shelled. I threw six cases of K-rations into the jeep and got the hell out of there.

The strafing reports by our own planes came, for the most part, from men of the 377th and 463rd Parachute Artillery Battalions. PFC. William Kummerer from "Dog" Battery of the 463rd had this report:

A disconcerting moment – when a P-47 red-nosed fighter strafed our machine gun position. Seeing wing guns flashing at you from one of your own is depressing. When his first pass was completed, I ordered the gunner, Colombus Frazier, to fire on the Thunderbolt should it attempt a second pass. It did and we fired up, passing his nose and seeing red tracers (the Germans used green) he aborted the attack.

## ENGINEER REINFORCEMENTS TO MARVIE

Division Headquarters, sensing that a major build-up was taking place on the southern perimeter, ordered one of its engineer platoons from the Ile-le-Pre and Senonchamps front to move to Marvie to support 2nd Battalion of the 327th. Describing their roles as members of 3rd Platoon of "B" Company, Privates Edward Carowick and Kenneth Knarr were part of this move. When the snows came to Bastogne, Carowick had used his G.I. ingenuity. He found a loose piece of roofing tin and fashioned it into a toboggan-like sled to which he attached a tow rope of communication wire. This way, the men were able to move their heavy machine gun and ammunition boxes from place to place along their assigned perimeter.

By the time 3rd Platoon was ordered to Marvie, it was already 11 or 12 men short. Carowick remembered how care was taken in positioning the men in strategic positions:

On the eve of December 23, the commander of 'B' Company received orders for our unit to be attached to the 327th Glider Regiment in an infantry role.

The 3rd Platoon was ordered to prepare, assemble and depart for Marvie, to assist in its defense along with 2nd Battalion of the 327th. We were to leave as soon as possible. It was pretty dark when we arrived.

Lt. Robert Coughlin went immediately to Marvie to reconnoiter the platoon sector that would be assigned. He took along the three squad leaders with him so they would know their assignments.

Lt. Steinhaus, his assistant and S/Sgt. Ferra were to bring the platoon to the triangle where Lt. Coughlin would take us to our assigned squad sectors.

There were some buildings burning in Marvie and, due to the snow on the ground, the area was pretty well lit up.

As we started out to the assigned sectors by squads, we began receiving some artillery and mortar fire but it was more or less to our left rear.

On the way to our squad sector, we ran into ten or twelve men from the 327th. I remember two men told me they were from 'G' Company. Also, I recall a few who stated they were from 'E' Company. They were moving north into Marvie. We tried to get them to accompany us to our positions but a few stated, 'We have been fighting this armor for three days and don't think it can be stopped here now.'

Apparently a lot of research had gone into Carowick's report as he had contacted a number of men from his platoon to get their recollections of the actions. These were accompanied by a map on which their positions had been marked and where the actions had taken place. The reader need only refer to his map, following his coded references. Carowick wrote:

The 3rd Platoon took up positions on an east-west line north of a small stream (#3 on map). The 1st and 2nd squads had a fence row along the small stream (which was covered with snow) and the banks along the stream were such that tanks could not negotiate them along our two-squad front. Also, there were foxholes on the two-squad front that had previously been dug so we were very fortunate for this.

Crew served machine guns for 1st and 2nd squads were set up at approximately position #4 on the map. Each of the rocket launchers (bazookas – #4) were positioned at the large half culverts which were at least 4-1/2 feet high. The culverts had stone walls for guard rails.

I remember, after setting up my air-cooled machine gun, I could hear tank traffic on the road to my front (#6 on map). They were moving quietly as the engines were not revved up. The bogie suspensions were not making any noise.

Then, about fifteen minutes later, a flare went up and the area was lit up. I saw the three tanks (#7) and also saw infantrymen with the tanks. (They were clad in snow suits.)

It seemed like everyone saw these developments about the same time as they all opened fire.

MG's #2 and #3 (indicated by #4 on the map) were water-cooled weapons. Privates Mason and Murry from the 1st squad, and Privates Becerra and Reardon on #3 were firing at the infantry. When tanks #2 and #3 saw the two positions, they fired simultaneously at the machine guns. I saw the bursts of shells exploding above them when they struck the small trees in the fence row.

Mason and Murry stopped firing (later said to 'have the enemy think we were knocked out'). Becerra and Reardon continued firing. They received another round into their position. (This was probably from tank #3 as they were moving more rapidly now.) Due to the fact my MG was behind the view of the tanks, I did not receive any fire from the tanks. Also, I took out the tracers where I had a tracer every 15 rounds instead of five.

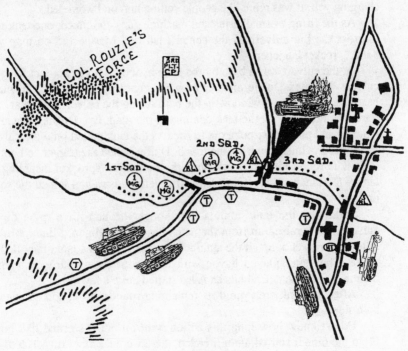

*Map 12*

S/Sgt. Ferra thought MG's #2 and #3 were firing at the tanks. He sent a runner (crawling) to tell MG #2 to stop firing at the tanks. As the runner was crawling to within a few feet of #3 gun, he was killed by the second round fired at Becerra and Reardon's position. I don't remember the names of the men on #4 gun in the 3rd squad.

Pvt. Kenneth Knarr was in on the same actions but viewed them from a different position on the line. His recollection of that incident is as follows:

I remember one night when the Germans attacked us with infantry and four tanks. Duffie knocked the track off one tank and stopped it. At the same time, Manuel Becerra, with Paul Borkowski as his loader, opened up with his light .30 caliber machine gun on one of the tanks. Just then a sergeant, who was an Indian, was crawling to Becerra to get him to stop firing at the tank when it opened fire with its 88 and killed the sergeant. Borkowski was deafened for a while. Becerra was not hurt and received the Bronze Star for his action.

Pvt. Edward Carowick continues his story in what was an action-packed span of time. He wrote:

After the flare went off and the platoon fire power of six machine guns and M1's cut loose, the enemy infantry began yelling. It didn't sound like a charging yell. It was more like people getting hurt and wounded.

As the firing of small arms and machine guns continued, one tank tried to cross the big culvert on the center road into Marvie (#5 on map with #2RL – rocket launcher.)

At the culvert was a barn by the stream, about four to six feet from the culvert. Privates Duffie and Knarr were guarding this approach with a bazooka. There was a window in the barn facing the culvert. When another flare was lit, they saw the tank coming up the road. Pvt. Duffie opened the window and put the bazooka out to fire. As the tank pulled onto the culvert, Knarr barely finished wiring the round. Duffie pulled the trigger and got the tank. The round hit and demolished the right front sprocket disabling the tank (#8 on map). Both Knarr and Duffie left the barn and joined the squad on line.

Suddenly, the tank commander thought he had hit a mine on the culvert. As he raised up from the hatch he yelled, 'Minen, Minen, Minen!' After the crew shot up all the ammunition that was in the tank, they fled the scene. They sure played havoc with Marvie as they destroyed a lot of buildings with the A.P. shells and also started quite a few fires.

After the tank crew fired its remaining rounds, all action stopped on both sides.

I don't know how long this action went on but it seemed like hours. From the time it started, until it ended, there were no more than 125 to 135 yards of movement from when we first saw the tanks to the one that was disabled.

## LT. NILAND'S MEN

The men from "B" Company of the 326th Airborne Engineer Battalion had no knowledge of what was going on in other sectors of Marvie. Their concern was the area at the bridges over the stream at the southern end of the village.

The decimated platoon, led by 1Lt. Tom Morrison of "G" Company, was dug in around a building on Hill 500, just to the south of Marvie. Morrison was about to be captured for the second time in four days. A platoon of Company "C" of the 326th Engineers led by 1Lt. Harold Young would be forced to withdraw. Some of its members were captured. With that strong point taken out, the Germans approached "B" Company positions near the bridges with some of their tanks. Others had used different routes to get into town to assault 2nd Battalion's command post.

During the evening attack on Marvie, 1Lt. Thomas J. Niland, intelligence officer for 2nd Battalion, played a key role in stopping the attack. The enemy had succeeded in penetrating the center of the battalion, opening a passage to the battalion command post and Bastogne. Realizing the seriousness of the situation, Niland immediately organized intelligence, supply men, cooks and other command post personnel. Under very heavy enemy tank and small arms fire, he established a defense by placing these men in key positions. Continually exposed to heavy shelling, Niland guided and placed into position two Sherman tanks which greatly assisted in repelling the German attacks. Lt. Niland then led a patrol to contact friendly forces which reinforced nearby positions.[102]

The most vivid action for 1Lt. Tom Niland in the Bastogne campaign took place on the evening of December 23. He describes the furious fighting that involved troops of "G" Company as well as members of 2nd Battalion's Headquarters Company:

The enemy overran Lt. Stan Morrison's place at the outer edge of Marvie (called Hill 500). We, in Battalion headquarters, supported by two tanks from Team O'Hara, were able to stop the attack in Marvie by this action. The Germans were denied access to the main road to Bastogne and forced to withdraw. The S-2 squad played an important role in this action. Panik and Feeney killed a German machine gun team that had infiltrated Marvie when the attack began. It seemed like we knew exactly what they were trying to do and positioned ourselves to stop them at all costs.

---

[102]From citation for Silver Star awarded to 1Lt. Thomas J. Niland dated 27 October 1945.

We had two 37mm regimental anti-tank guns that were under the direction of 1Lt. Neil J. Fahey. He and most of the crew were killed during the mortar and artillery fire in the attack on December 23.

In on the same actions was PFC. Harry W. Bliss from the heavy weapons platoon. When the enemy attacked the positions of his unit, his machine gun section was assigned the mission of supporting the withdrawal of the command post. Realizing that one gun was disabled, PFC. Bliss, under heavy artillery, mortar and small arms fire, moved his gun to a new position to support the withdrawal. When the enemy tried to penetrate the line again, PFC. Bliss killed all but one of the enemy with his machine gun fire and killed the remaining enemy soldier with a hand grenade.[103]

Closing out his narrative, 1Lt. Niland wrote: "Our previous battle experiences were of great value to us. We could anticipate the situation and did not panic when it happened. Everyone took it upon themselves to stop the attack. I quote the old adage, 'Having the right people there at the right time.' "

---

[103]From a citation for an Oak Leaf Cluster to his Bronze Star for PFC. Harry W. Bliss, awarded posthumously, dated 30 March 1945.

# 9. CHRISTMAS EVE

## "FOX" COMPANY OF THE 327TH

There was a continuing action in the 2nd Battalion sector of the 327th Glider Infantry Regiment on Christmas Eve. After the successful enemy attack on Hill 500 south of Marvie during the evening hours of the 23rd, part of the German force was shunted to the left toward Remifosse and the positions of "F" Company.

Over in the 501st sector, Company "A" had been ordered to send a platoon to the Marvie sector to assist 2nd Battalion in resisting the assault that was threatening to overrun completely the positions in and about the small village. Upon arrival at the northern outskirts, Captain Stanfield Stach's men had been directed to the area of "F" Company which was now feeling the force of the tank and infantry assault.

After two relatively quiet days, action picked up for "F" Company in the western end of the 2nd Battalion sector. PFC. Charles Kocourek had this recollection of the actions of the night of December 23rd. He was still on outpost duty on the flank with two comrades. He related:

We had it all cleaned out there – it was pretty quiet. Nothing much was going on until night – 10 to 11 o'clock. Then all hell broke loose. The shooting broke out on the right side – then the left side, but none of it came out by me. There was noise behind us, too. I told the other two guys to stay put. I was going back to the main line to find out what was happening. As a parting shot, I said, 'If I don't come back – you guys pull out and move straight back to Bastogne.'

So I went cautiously off to the left and was challenged. The guy says, 'You almost got shot – there are Germans all over the place!' He added, 'Go back and get the other two guys' and I did and they gave me a neighboring foxhole. I got in that hole and fell asleep. Someone woke me and said, 'Let's go – we're gonna withdraw!' This is when I discovered my rifle was useless – riddled and bent. I was told we were shelled furiously and yet I didn't hear any of the shelling. I was so tired. We started moving back toward Bastogne. I didn't have a rifle and I was the second to last in line. We had only 15 left of the 33 who started out in Mourmelon. The medic was behind me. As we moved out in the dark, I could hear the Germans digging foxholes in the same woods we had recently used as our CP.

A house-barn combination a half mile northwest of Marvie would become an unlikely meeting place of members of "A" Company of the 501st and PFC. Charles Kocourek of "F" Company of the 327th as the night of December 23-24 wears on. 1Lt. Joseph B. Schweiker, executive officer for "A" Company, is confused as to the time and the date (after 48 years) as he describes being part of a force to assist the 327th Glider Infantry Regiment at Marvie.

On Christmas Eve about 8:00 p.m., 'A' Company moved up to help stop the breakthrough at the town of Marvie. When we arrived, we were setting up road blocks in around the high ground as directed. I can still see Colonel Harper moving about with an M-1 rifle in the dark, setting up a defense against the Germans. Captain Stach and Colonel Harper set up 'A' Company's headquarters in the farmhouse overlooking the town of Marvie with the rest of the company dug in around the farmhouse. What sticks in my memory was in the basement of the house. There was a room with several women huddled in that room, fearing the return of the Germans. This never happened, but we spent Christmas Eve and more in that position. The enemy kept trying to break through our defense while we were covering the 327th moves. The enemy was not successful.

At the time "A" Company of the 501st was called over to help reinforce 2nd Battalion of the 327th, Pvt. Christopher McEwan was confused about the location as the troops were sent from one section of the MLR to another. The town he describes in his story is not Bizory but Marvie, over in the 327th sector. He wrote:

We later moved to another defensive position. I believe it might have been on Hill 510. We dug a foxhole, another trooper and me. It was very cold and blowing snow. I believe the town of Bizory was off our left. It had been burning furiously all night and day.

From my position, I could see five German tanks pounding that town with fire. I wished that I had an anti-tank weapon so that I could have gone down there. I had a good opportunity to hit them all from the side. We were short of weapons and there weren't any available.

## "HEY, WE'RE AMERICANS!"

It was now early morning of the 24th. Moving about on the MLR at night is extremely hazardous. Two soldiers from different units wrote about the same action which turns tragic. PFC. Charles Kocourek continues his story of pulling back from the forward positions as the enemy attacks northward during the night:

We started moving up the hill behind us. Division sent a bunch of paratroopers behind us to back us up. As we were going up the hill, all of a sudden, a machine gun opened up on us. I remember I dove in a water-filled ditch and we all started shooting back toward our rear. Pretty soon someone yelled, 'Hey, we're Americans!' A guy out there says, 'Americans – get up here fast because we're gonna start mortaring that area!' Sure enough, as soon as we cleared, a barrage came down. One guy said, 'What the hell are you shooting at us for?' The machine gunner said, 'I was digging a foxhole and I looked out there and saw all those tanks. I continued digging and then saw something moving and jumped on the machine gun and opened up!'

'Without challenging?' We were mad. We lost two good guys – Dennis, a bazookaman, and a guy named Cy.

As a machine gunner in Company "A" of the 501st Parachute Regiment who had accompanied his platoon to Marvie to support the 2nd Battalion of the 327th Glider Infantry, Pvt. Christopher McEwan describes what happened as troops were falling back on the positions being prepared by his platoon:

One night we thought we were getting a frontal attack just over a little ridge. There was a BAR man off on my left flank. Someone raised a white parka in the air and started waving it. The BAR man shouted, 'It's a trick!' and opened fire. I then started firing with the machine gun and raked the top of the ridge because I couldn't see them. We later found that it was some glider troopers. I think they were 327th. One of them died.

A trip through a water-filled ditch on the way back from his outpost position had left PFC. Charles Kocourek soaked so he needed to get some place where it was warm so he could dry out. He headed back to the shelter of a building. He added to his story:

We went back and joined the paratroopers. I think Captain Stach was in charge of those guys and Colonel Rouzie was back there about fifty yards from our lines. There was a building and we'd go in to get warm. There was a fire. I was soaked to the skin and shaking. A woman was there and she saw me shaking and went and got me a blanket. Boy, did that feel good! I stayed in the barn until I got fairly dry and then went back to the front lines.

The same night that PFC. Kocourek and his fellow "F" Company glider troopers were driven from their positions to the west of Marvie, the men of "A" Company were now in position around Colonel Rouzie's headquarters. Pvt. Christopher McEwan describes an attack on the house by a German tank:

That same night, a Tiger tank came out of the woods on our right and fired three rounds. He didn't see us but one of the rounds hit a hen house off to our right. It sent the chickens flying about fifty feet in the air. They were making all kinds of racket and flapping their wings like mad. Well I tell you, they were the highest flying chickens that I have ever seen.

## ENGINEERS OF "ABLE" COMPANY

Situated in position to cover the secondary road that led to Assenois and the railroad track that wound to the southwest, PFC. Harry Sherrard and his fellow engineers continued to maintain their positions in the vicinity of the small concrete blockhouse. These positions would become the meeting place between the engineers and the 4th Armored Division tanks on the 26th of December.

On the 24th, "A" Company was experiencing some of the same pressure that "F" Company of the 327th was getting. In the case of the engineers, there weren't tanks involved in the attack. Sherrard wrote:

> After a few days, it snowed. One morning, early, we looked out to the southwest of our positions across the road and tracks and the field beyond to the next tree growth. It looked like the snow was moving. It was German troops in white camouflage outfits getting ready to assault our positions hoping to move past us along the tracks and into town. When they got close enough, we fired with our M-1's but that's all it took – they had us zeroed in and with machine guns and burp guns had us pinned down during the attack which we repulsed. Each time we moved, it seemed one or two Krauts were just across the road to blow trees apart just above us. I don't believe there were any tanks involved in this attack.

Relief eventually came to PFC. Sherrard after several days of MLR duty when he and his partner got an opportunity to get some rest in Bastogne. He wasn't far from Division Headquarters, which was across the road from the town cemetery. Sherrard adds to his story:

> Walters and I were relieved from this OP position and were sent into Bastogne for some rest in some row houses in the east end of town, just west of the cemetery from the Belgian army camp which Division had taken over for headquarters.

After a night in which Bastogne was bombed on two occasions, Sherrard and Walters were anxious to return to the relative safety of their front line positions the following morning.

## LT. O'HALLORAN'S PLATOON

On the 23rd of December, strong enemy forces, supported by tanks, had driven "C" Company of the 401st Glider Battalion from their roadblocks west of Mande St. Etienne. S/Sgt. Robert Bowen and others had been taken prisoner along with several medics and members of the 705th Tank Destroyer team when the enemy overran the aid station. Captain Preston E. Towns had been ordered to pull his men back so as not to be outflanked. On Christmas Eve, his unit was in battalion reserve near Colonel Ray Allen's command post.

The hilltop position occupied by Captain Robert McDonald's "B" Company enabled his men to observe enemy soldiers moving into a farmhouse complex on the far side of the valley. Artillery fire called on the position did not move the enemy from the position. Several of the "B" Company men witnessed a platoon attack on the farmhouse from their positions on the hillside.

S/Sgt. Roger Seamon remembers the attack ordered by the company commander to get the Germans out of the farm buildings because those troops were a potential threat to the 401st positions. Seamon wrote:

The next day, we observed a large number of enemy troops entering the farmhouse and barn across the valley from us. We got some artillery fire on them but it didn't seem to bother them much. Captain McDonald figured they were going to attack us so that afternoon Lt. O'Halloran led a platoon backed up by a TD in an attack on the buildings. The platoon advanced to about 100 yards from the house, laying down a heavy fire as they moved up. The barn was soon burning. After about a half hour, the platoon moved back to our positions and we received no attack as the Germans withdrew that evening. S/Sgt. Joseph Sopczyk was killed in this operation. Sgt. Tom Leamon of 'C' Company was also in on the action.

From these same positions, we got a lot of long range shooting at small groups of Germans who would come across the far side of the valley not knowing we were there. We would fire at them and they would hit the snow and lie there all day, either wounded or afraid to move. At night, German ambulances would come down and pick them up. We could see the crosses on the trucks, plainly.

Also in position to observe the action from the same hilltop area, PFC. Carmen Gisi relates what he witnessed:

Our 1st Platoon went out on an attack on a farmhouse. A tank from the 705th TD was with them. I could see the action from my foxhole. The house was being used to direct fire on us. The platoon had to withdraw because of heavy German fire power. We lost some people. Norman 'Blimp' Blimline was hit and was left there but managed to crawl back to our positions and was sent back to the rear.

In the "B" Company history, which he had written, PFC. Marshall Griffith had this brief description of the action involving 1Lt. John O'Halloran's platoon:

On December 24th, after observing the Germans moving into a house, the C.O. ordered Lt. John O'Halloran's platoon, supported by a TD, to attack and wipe out this strong point.

As one of the actual participants in the platoon raid to rout the enemy troops from the farmhouse complex across the valley, PFC. Richard Bostwick had recorded the actions in 1946 when memories were still fresh. He wrote:

I should judge two hours of daylight remained when our platoon was summoned to the CP for a patrol briefing. Blimp always groaned when he shouldered his BAR – the thing seemed to weigh a ton. The Captain was generous. He passed around a bottle of cognac. I hadn't had a drink for some time. The liquor burned all the way down. We were briefed concerning a Kraut observation post believed to be in a farmhouse directly to the right front, beyond the crest of the rise above the water hole.

We filed out of the CP and entered the firebreak in single file, near the well, and started up the draw toward our objective. The snow was deep. I was ahead of Blimp and I heard him cussing the snow as well as his heavy load. We followed a route that gave us the maximum protection from being observed; however, we were out in the open and vulnerable to artillery.

Near the crest of the draw, we held up for last minute instructions. Sgt. Watson called for a skirmish line as soon as we came into view of the farmhouse. There were about twenty of us, including Lt. O'Halloran, a freshman officer; probably his first combat assignment.

As soon as we came out onto open ground in view of the farmhouse, we formed a wide 'kick-off' formation and advanced at a slow pace with rifles ready. Several hundred yards away stood a farmhouse above which was a haymow. The upper end of the structure had been blown away earlier and a great bunch of hay was hanging out. Two small buildings covered by tin flanked the main building. I was in the middle of the formation. We had to cross a barbed-wire fence and there was cussing that went with torn garments. It was too damned quiet; the only sound was the crunching snow under our boots.

Near the farm buildings Watson barked, 'fire and movement'. Firing from the hip and spacing shots, we walked forward. Suddenly, a figure darted from the farmhouse, running straight across in front of us. He spun crazily with his arms flailing as he was hit by a storm of bullets. The shot that I sent after him was a tracer bullet that seemed to curve gracefully as it passed through his body and into a nearby tin shack.

Instantly, an MG opened up on us and took down about six men on my left. The rest of us made a wild dash to the barn and stood there against a stone wall, out of the gunner's sight. The enemy fire appeared to come from one of the farmhouse's basement windows. Blimp and I became separated; he was on my right flank. He called to me but I couldn't see him because of a row of shrubs. While running, my thought was to put the farm building between myself and the gunner. There I stood, wild-eyed and hay hanging above my head. O'Halloran asked if I had a tracer bullet left. He wanted to ignite the hay. In the absence of tracers, I hoisted the lieutenant high enough to touch a match to the hay.

As the fire began to gather speed, we could hear German voices above us. Several concussion grenades were thrown from the hayloft but no damage was done.

Blimp gave out a yell to warn of reinforcements coming over a hill behind the farmhouse. He began firing the BAR and our light MG joined in.

I was looking in the direction from which the sound of Blimp's voice had reached me when the chatter of a machine pistol sent a stream of orange tracer bullets at the area from which Blimp had been firing. Blimp screamed,

'Oh my head, my shoulder, my arm!' The Krauts had hit him. I wanted to go to him but enemy small arms fire was showering the area. From the protection of the brick wall, I continued to fire at anything that moved.

It was getting dark and the flaming farmhouse lit the area. I continued firing at shadows as the Krauts dashed across the field behind the building. I suddenly found myself to be alone. Looking around, I discovered our men had taken to the foxholes that had been dug by the Krauts. They were directly behind me. I made a mad dash for a black spot in that sea of trampled snow; not much of a hole but it was better than no hole at all.

The burning building continued to cast weird shadows on the snow. Bullets were flying and hand grenades were exploding. The Kraut MG continued to blaze away. The word was that we were badly outnumbered and the odds weren't getting any better.

It was becoming darker as the fire began to burn itself out. From out of the darkness, an American 75mm mobile cannon appeared. It could have run right over me but stopped when it's front wheels were about ten feet from my hole. The gun barrel was right over me when it began firing. The noise was deafening. Pieces of the stone wall were flying like shrapnel. The big gun withdrew and left us alone in the darkness. The tempo of battle was more intense; all hell was breaking loose and there we were in the middle of a roaring farmyard.

The Lieutenant had had enough and above the unbelievable noise came the order, 'Every man for himself!' It was the first and only time I was to hear such an order during my days of combat. It was getting so bad that I didn't dare look over the edge of my hole but for an instant. I felt sure at this point we would be overrun. I unhooked my gun belt, which by this time was empty, and removed my overcoat. If I was going to run, I didn't need anything but my rifle.

I am sure I was holding my breath as I lunged from the hole in the ground. Expected to feel a bullet at any time. Through all that hell, I ran as though possessed – I bobbed, weaved, fell down, rolled, got up, stumbled, fell down. I had a helluva time!

What was left of our group reorganized when we reached the shelter of the draw. We had lost a dozen or more men, including Blimp. Poor Blimp!

It was a sad looking group that straggled into the company area. Capt. Mac was very displeased. The lieutenant reported to the captain. I returned to the hole that Blimp and I had dug.

It was midnight when O'Halloran checked the troops to see if there were any wounded men. I asked him if we could form a patrol and go back for

Blimp. The Krauts hadn't followed us and it seemed as though two or three men could return without too much of a struggle. No way![104]

## AID STATIONS

The 326th Airborne Medical Company field hospital, with its attached 3rd Auxiliary Surgical Group, had been captured on the night of December 19 at its site about eight miles west of Bastogne. With the loss of about 150 medical personnel, the defenders of Bastogne were in tough straits when it came to providing proper care for its wounded, injured and those suffering from the extreme cold weather with pneumonia, bronchitis and frozen feet.

Aid stations were set up at various locations including garages, riding halls, a seminary, St. Peter's Church and private homes. Eventually, the facilities were taxed with 1,500 casualties before the siege was broken.

Medical officer for the 20th Armored Battalion, Captain John T. Prior had evacuated his patients from Noville on December 20th when the combined 10th Armored and the 1st Battalion of the 506th had pulled out to more defensible positions. Prior was now in Bastogne, He wrote:[105]

Bastogne, on this date, was an intact but somewhat deserted city. The sight of the residents dragging their belongings with them on little carts, leaving as we entered, was recognized as a bad omen – rats leaving a sinking ship. Many of these people faced the difficult decision whether to retain the American flag over their doors or to put the Swastika back up. My aid station was initially in a garage on one of the main streets. Two days later I had to move into a larger area in a private three-story home as the casualties increased and because I could not heat the garage adequately – the weather was very cold and there was about a foot of snow on the ground. My diary indicates we worked twenty-four hours a day in the Aid Station, that the plasma froze and would not run, that we had no medical supplies and that the town was continually shelled. It was a major decision to run up the street one block to the Battalion Command Post. German artillery fired propaganda leaflets into the town, urging us to surrender. These were regarded by the GI's as humorous and were collected and swapped like baseball cards. One of these had a photograph of a little girl and her letter to her daddy.

In regard to the care of the wounded in Bastogne, I have always believed, and still do, that this did not constitute a bright page in the history

---

[104]As mentioned in PFC. Carmen Gisi's brief report, PFC. Norman "Blimp" Blimline managed to stagger into the command post under his own power.
[105]Prior, op. cit.

of the Army Medical Department. I operated the only aid station for the Armored Division Combat Command (in Bastogne) although there were at least three other battalion surgeons with the armor. I was holding over one hundred patients of whom thirty were very seriously injured litter patients. The patients who had head, chest and abdominal wounds could only face certain slow death since there was no chance of surgical procedures – we had no surgical talent among us and there was not so much as a can of ether or a scalpel to be had in the city. The extremity wounds were irrigated with a preciously low supply of hydrogen peroxide in an attempt to prevent gas infection. I attempted to turn my litter bearers into bedside nursing personnel – they were assisted by the arrival at our station December 21st of two registered female civilian nurses. One of these nurses, Renee LeMaire, volunteered her services and the other girl was black, a native of the Belgian Congo. She was 'willed' to me by her father and when we eventually left Bastogne, he was most distraught with me for refusing to take her along. They played different roles among the dying – Renee shrank away from the fresh, gory trauma, while the Congo girl was always in the thick of splinting, dressing and hemorrhage control. Renee preferred to circulate among the litter patients, sponging, feeding them and distributing the few medications we had (sulfa pills and plasma). The presence of these two girls was a morale factor of the highest order.

This decaying medical situation was worsening – with no hope for the surgical candidates and even the superficial wounds were beginning to develop gas infection. I never did see any tetanus develop during the entire siege. It was at this point that I visited the acting Division Surgeon of the 101st Airborne Division and requested he make an effort to bring medical help to us.

I had not visited the Airborne area up until this time, December 23rd. Their headquarters and hospital were in a former Belgian army barracks compound. Major Douglas Davidson, their surgeon, listened as I detailed our hopeless situation and he assured me it was impossible to bring a glider surgical team into the area because of the weather and because the Germans would knock down anything that tried to fly in. He also stressed the fact that his paratroopers were used to being cut off (Normandy and Holland) and this situation was the expected. He then brought me to a riding hall where I saw the unbelievable! There, on the dirt riding floor, were six hundred paratroop litter cases – I cannot recall the number of walking wounded or psychiatric casualties. These patients were only being sustained, as were mine. I did see a paratroop chaplain (armed with a pistol and shoulder holster) moving among the dying.

*Members of the 101st receive emergency treatment in an improvised aid station in a riding stable.*

Gas gangrene was rampant there, aided and abetted, I am sure, by the flora on the dirt floor. Major Davidson did drive into the German lines, later, with a white flag in an attempt to arrange a truce for medical evacuation. He proposed to take out one German to two Americans but it was refused by the ranking German medical officer.[106]

The loss of the 326th Airborne Medical Company field hospital the first night left the whole medical set-up in chaos. Describing the situation at the 101st facilities in Bastogne, Captain Bernard "Barney" Ryan, surgeon for 3rd Battalion of the 506th Parachute Regiment, had this recollection of the situation:

The second echelon medical set-up collapsed completely. The next day, we were completely surrounded and there was no evacuation of wounded out of Bastogne. As fast as men were wounded in the fierce fighting on the perimeters, they were brought into the town where places were found for

---

[106]That statement is in conflict with the 101st history, *Rendezvous with Destiny*, which states it was Major Martin Wiseley, surgeon of the 327th Glider Infantry Regiment, who made the proposal.

them in warehouses and cellars. Captain S. C. Feiler organized the walking wounded department and cared for several hundred wounded men in an empty warehouse with parachutes (resupply chutes) for warmth until the siege was lifted. (He never got proper recognition for this feat, by the way.)

Seriously wounded and litter cases were treated here and there throughout the town of Bastogne, wherever warmth could be afforded. One of the depressing experiences was 'making rounds' on these patients during trips into town and seeing so many in need of definitive surgical or medical treatment which was, of course, unavailable.

Captain Richard P. Meason, of Tucson, Arizona, was a very good friend whose face I shall never forget as he lay on a litter with a full blown acute peritonitis secondary to a bullet of the abdomen incurred three days before. Surprisingly, he lived to be evacuated and recovered probably because he did have penicillin and sulfadiazine by vein from the beginning. He was operated on later. I never expected to see him alive again.

We have viewed the aid station situation through the eyes of medical personnel. The following are recollections of officers and enlisted men who visited at least some of the facilities or were there for treatment of wounds or frozen feet.

Platoon leader 1Lt. Robert Stroud of "H" Company of the 506th Regiment was hit by shrapnel in the shoulder on the second day and was evacuated to Bastogne. He wrote:

I hung around as part of the walking wounded in the center of Bastogne for a few days and was taken care of by Captain 'Shifty' Feiler, the dentist, who did a beautiful job. He organized crews when they made drops of supplies and gathered parachutes for pallets for the wounded and put them in the barracks there at Division Headquarters.

Platoon leader Robert P. O'Connell was put out of action at 0400 one morning when a large enemy patrol came through the positions. He was hit with a burst from a Schmeizzer burp gun and grenade fragments. He was first treated at the platoon level and then sent on to Bastogne. He wrote:

I was treated by Captain Louis Axelrod in the battalion aid station and carried back to St. Peter's Church in Bastogne where the 501st casualties were being treated. We laid down in pews and on the floor where we were helped by Belgian nuns and sisters (nurses). Very devoted people to share our hardships.

Next, we were housed in warehouses – all casualties waiting to be evacuated. It wasn't too bad there – not much to eat but we had a lot of body warmth.

PFC. Donald B. Straith had been wounded early in the morning of the 20th of December. He was among a large group of wounded that came out of Noville during late afternoon of the 20th. His experience in one of the aid stations in Bastogne left him with a bad taste in the mouth. He wrote:

The collecting station was housed in an abbey that dominated one end of town. Inside, the stone floor was crowded with casualties, many of them lying on stretchers. Stepping carefully among them, I recognized one as a man named Straitiff from Company 'A'. He was delirious from shell shock and every minute or two would sit up and start yelling that someone was stealing his boots. Several times I reassured him that he was still wearing his boots and got him to lie down again. Then, tiring of this, I left him and moved on.

As evening came, a chow line was set up at one side of the room. Since leaving Mourmelon forty-eight hours earlier, all I had eaten was the bread, butter and jam given to me in Noville the preceding evening, so the aroma of hot food smelled particularly good. Several of us joined the growing line and worked our way forward but, on reaching the serving table, we were asked 'Where are your mess kits?' When we said we had lost them, the reply was, 'Sorry, we can't serve you unless you have a mess kit.' After directing a few choice obscene epithets at the mess personnel, we withdrew to a drafty hallway where we curled up on the cold stones and, tired and hungry, gradually fell asleep.

Sgt. Paul Bebout suffered from trench foot. His feet had already started turning black. He was sent back to the Bastogne aid station for a respite. He wrote:

The lieutenant told me to go back and report to the medics in town. I did. I saw a few of the dead American soldiers along the way. That kind of bothered me. I had seen more stacked up in Normandy. The medic was a dentist and this was in a rifle range (indoors that the enemy had set up). I spread my blanket out and we got one ration a day. I was there for a couple days.

## THE LITTLE OLD LADY OF CHAMPS

Recalling days of hunger at Bastogne, when the supplies dropped by air were not enough to sustain the warriors positioned along their perimeter defenses, PFC. Ted Goldmann remembered:

After a couple of days of sweating out artillery barrages and patrols, Christmas Eve rolled around. Several other soldiers and myself came off standing guard duty on our positions about five o'clock in the morning and went into the house across the road where we knew a fire was burning. The snow was fairly heavy and the weather generally miserable. This particular home was the only structure with a cellar in which the Belgian civilians living in the immediate vicinity could stay in some degree of safety from the barrages which came over intermittently. There were 18 civilians in this group which, with the lone exception of one old man, were all women and children. They had been feeding us since the 22nd because we had no Army rations at that time and our aerial resupply had just started. As we entered the kitchen, we found the Belgians in various stages of slumber as they had just come up from the basement. In a few minutes, the old grandmother of the house and one of the other old ladies got up and started to mix the flour which was in a long trough-like bin in the corner. I didn't think much about it except to watch with no little fascination since she had to obtain additional wheat from the barn which adjoined the house. After several minutes, one of the younger women, who was talking to one of the boys in from guard, told him that this was the first time in her sixty years that the old lady had ever worked on Sunday, which was the day Christmas Eve fell on that year. She made fourteen loaves of whole wheat bread that morning, which went to feed the 18 civilians and 20 odd soldiers.

I sincerely believe that I have never eaten anything that tasted as wonderful as that bread which a sweet old lady broke her life-long religious belief to make for us. I shall always remember 'the little old lady of Champs' as one of the people I gladly risked my life for during those miserable days.[107]

## A CHRISTMAS TREE

It doesn't matter where American troops are stationed – out in a desert, in a jungle, wherever – they are bound to improvise with a tree of some sort so as to remember Christmas occasions that were celebrated in family situations during happier times.

The resupply missions of December 23 and 24 provided materials with which to trim a tree as well as furnished much needed material to cover boots to aid in the prevention of trenchfoot. The outer padded covers in which the supplies were wrapped were used to line foxholes and provide padding to the cold floors on which the wounded lay in the various make-shift aid stations. PFC. Ben Rous provided a picture and a story of the preparation of a Christmas tree and a display of their new footwear. Rous wrote:

On December 24th the Germans didn't throw as much artillery at us, so we decided to trim a Christmas tree. We picked up any bright-colored bits we could find – mostly the chaff the airplanes dropped out to foul up the

---

[107]From a letter Ted Goldmann wrote to the editors of *Readers Digest* on April 25, 1947 while attending Texas A & M University on the G.I. Bill.

enemy radar and some full and empty ration boxes to represent presents – even used a couple of live mortar shells. Through all of this we were not bothered by German artillery. They were saving all their ammunition for the next day to give it to us for Christmas presents.

We really enjoyed December 24th – it was sunny and warmer and a fellow from Regimental Headquarters Company came along with a photographer who took a couple pictures of us and our Christmas tree. These pictures show how we wrapped our feet with the bag material.

*Men of the mortar Platoon of 2nd Battalion Headquarters Company of the 506th Parachute Infantry Regiment celebrate with their decorated tree on Christmas Eve. Note the special wrappings on some of the feet.*

## A BOOST IN MORALE

Life on outpost duty, in cold weather and without adequate clothing, and at Christmas time, when a mans thoughts are about home and loved ones, more-so now than at other times, company commanders are often called on to do counseling – especially of men for whom outpost duty is a whole new ball game. 1Lt. Al Regenburg provides such a recollection:

This was a time of survival. You either took care of yourself or you were in trouble. No one really had the time or strength to mother them. And yet, at night when things were quiet, a young private was admitted to the CP. He told the corporal that he wanted to talk to me. He had gotten permission to see if I could help him out. He was feeling homesick and lonely. He had pictures of his wife and baby. We ended up splitting a couple ounces of cognac. I showed him pictures of my wife and baby. He showed me pictures of his wife and baby and once he found out there were a lot of people in the same boat as he was, he seemed to perk up and feel that I really helped him. The thing he didn't realize was that he had helped me too.

## LIPTON, YOU'RE STANDING ON MY HAND!

Cpl. Walter E. Gordon, a machine gunner for "E" Company of the 506th Parachute Regiment, remembered that his battalion was deployed behind a narrow road leading to Foy on Christmas Eve. He wrote:

Snow was on the ground and Christmas Eve arrived. I had managed to brew a canteen cup of coffee with my little gas stove when Sgt. Amos Taylor asked me to man the machine gun. It seems the outposts had returned with some news that the Germans were advancing through the woods. As I was brushing off the weapon, I was shot in the shoulder by a rifle shot and removed to the rear and later to the church in town.

1/Sgt. Carwood Lipton remembered the incident moreso as Walter Gordon went into shock shortly after being hit. Lipton wrote:

When Gordon was hit, I was not far away. I yelled at Alley and Rogers to pull him out and get him back and someone else helped, though I don't remember who. They brought Walter back into the little cleared area close to the path that ran behind our positions and laid him on a shelter half in the snow with a blanket and a shelter half over him.

I didn't get back there right away as there was an attack by the Germans just getting under way against us, although it seemed to be concentrated more to the right of our company front. When I did get there, someone had mixed up some plasma – probably one of the medics. We had dried plasma in one bottle and sterile water in another with a way to get the water into the plasma bottle while keeping everything sterile.

The plasma seemed to be flowing into Walter's veins very slowly and I thought it might be starting to freeze in the plastic tube from the bottle. I took the bottle from the man holding it, opened my jacket and put the bottle under my arm to keep it warm, standing right over Walter as I did it.

He was lying sprawled out under the shelter half and blanket and he looked almost dead. His face was gray, his eyes were closed and he was barely breathing.

Suddenly, he opened his eyes. I said, 'Walter, how do you feel?' He said, in a surprisingly strong voice, 'Lipton, you're standing on my hand!' I jumped back and saw that I had been standing on his hand, which was partly covered by the blanket and shelter half.

Shortly after that the medics brought a jeep with stretchers along on each side, up the path behind us and took Walter back to Bastogne.

## CHRISTMAS EVE – 1944

Memories of Christmas Eve in and around the Bastogne perimeter were recalled by a number of soldiers. Thoughts of his wife and children were on the mind of a German soldier as he penned a last letter to his wife before the big battle.

The following is a translation of a letter written on Christmas Eve, 1944, by a German soldier outside the perimeter facing Bastogne:

Dearest:

Against expectations, the planned Christmas Eve attack did not come off. The whole front is quiet. I suppose that the Americans will be equally glad that everything is so peaceful on the most beautiful and sacred evening of the year. They feel the cold even more than we for they are lying in their holes without having been issued winter clothes and that is no pleasure in this weather, I assure you.

This Christmas Eve is probably the quietest I have spent since coming into the Army. No tree, no carols, nothing Christmacy. Tomorrow evening there's supposed to be a simple ceremony. But, meanwhile I expect this attack to come off.

The boys have gone to bed, but even if its only in my thoughts, I'd like to spend part of this festive evening with you and the children. Darling, I suppose it is hours since you lit the candles on the tree. Little Hannelore has gazed at the sparkling thing with her childish eyes shining and happy. Probably she has found more than one little present under it, and you Darling, have certainly been thinking of me – what I am doing, whether I am well or perhaps already wounded. Yes, my dear Bertile, this is another serious Christmas. Many families of boys in our company are receiving the worst news that could hit them. Destiny is hard and cruel to many. Last year we were sure we would meet again in a very short time. How happy we were then, and of course little Walter owes his existence to that short reunion.

I haven't sent you anything in a long time. May God grant that I shall be able to make up to you one day for everything that you have missed.

Another hour and I shall be able to go to bed. It's eleven now. God knows what terrible things tomorrow may bring.

Dearest, I am thinking of you with longing and great love. I can imagine that in a corner of your heart you must have hoped I would come and hold you in my arms tonight. You'll have to go on dreaming, Darling.[108]

Father

## CHRISTMAS EVE AT ROLLE

The traditional Christmas was missing, for the most part, at Bastogne and its environs but the troops still had a way of celebrating. The following is a memory of Captain Joseph Pangerl after he reread a letter he sent to his parents on December 30, 1944:[109]

I can just vaguely remember the Christmas party for the kids in the Chateau Rolle through one of my letters where I wrote to my mother that I was able to contribute as she had sent me Christmas presents wrapped in Christmas paper and string which arrived just a day before we left Mourmelon. I hadn't even unwrapped them and in Rolle gave them to the Countess so she could wrap a few things for the children.

As operations officer for the 502nd Regiment, Captain James J. Hatch had this recollection of a Christmas Eve party that the men in Headquarters had planned:

I recall an event which went from a moment of joy to sadness and took place at the 502nd CP at Rolle, a small castle-like home belonging to a Count. We brought in a small Christmas tree and invited the families with children to come down from the upstairs where they had been living so they could decorate the tree and open their Christmas presents.

Several of the staff members recalled the Mass celebrated on Christmas Eve at the Chateau Rolle. This is how Captain Joe Pangerl described the scene:

Christmas Eve we had a midnight Mass in the chapel which is in the tower of the castle. The chapel is round, like the tower. It had rough, stone

---

[108]Copy of the above letter was sent by Carl Cartledge of the S-2 Section of the 501st Parachute Infantry Regiment. The letter was written at 8 p.m. on Christmas Eve. It was translated by 1Lt. Werner J. Meier. The notation at the bottom of the letter read: "This letter was written by a German soldier on Christmas Eve. It is believed that the soldier is dead as this letter was found among some other documents turned in to PEW."

[109]From a copy of a V-Mail letter Joseph Pangerl wrote to his parents from Chateau Rolle dated 29 December 1944.

walls and was fitted out with rustic but beautiful furniture and had pine
boughs all around. The Chaplain was our own and we filled the chapel. In
fact, there were many who couldn't get in. The family of the house was also
present, of course. I thought about you at home . . .[110]

Captain Hatch continues his story and relates how the party was disrupted
by artillery fire:

They (the children) were having a great time until about 10 p.m. The
Germans were getting ready to attack our positions and they were throwing
artillery rounds to include our C.P. We had to break up the Christmas party
and sent them to the basement for protection.

## CHRISTMAS EVE IN HEMROULLE

As executive officer and S-1 for the 463rd Parachute Field Artillery
Battalion, Major Stuart Seaton recalled the Christmas Eve service at the little
town of Hemroulle:

One could hardly forget the night before, Christmas Eve. The Division
chaplain came out to our town for a Christmas Eve service. We had the
service in a stable. Somehow that service had a distinct significance. A
rather humble setting, somewhat reminiscent of an event some 2,000 years
previous. I have often thought back to that night and that service.

PFC. Gordon Bernhardt of the same battalion remembered the Christmas
Eve service also. He wrote:

I remember going to a barn on Christmas Eve with other men. A
chaplain was there and we had a church service with the familiar 'Silent
Night,' of course. I was thinking of everyone at home.

## CHRISTMAS EVE ON OUTPOST

Christmas Eve is memorable for PFC. Leland G. Jones of Headquarters
Company of the 401st Glider Battalion because rations from the previous day's
drop of supplies hadn't filtered down to his outpost. Jones and the men with him
were making the best of it. He recalled:

On Christmas Eve three of us melted a roll of Life Savers to make a
cup of 'hot soup' – all we had left. But we three then started singing
Christmas carols, every one we could remember and we talked of
Christmases we recalled at home with our families. Today, still, all good
Christmases, before and since, seem to be lumped together. I remember only

---

[110]ibid.

that horrible Christmas at Bastogne. I cannot listen to 'I'll be Home for Christmas', 'White Christmas', or 'Silent Night' without choking up.

*Catholic Christmas services being conducted in one of the Division Command Post buildings by Chaplain McGettigan. Note the heavy drapes over the large windows so as to adhere to blackout conditions.*

Before General Patton's troops joined the beleaguered troops at Bastogne, thoughts of Christmas and home were on the minds of front line troops on both sides. Pvt. Mike Zorich describes what he witnessed and heard while on outpost duty Christmas Eve:

We were dug in on a bald hill overlooking the Germans who were in a patch of woods 200 yards to our front. I was sent on outpost duty with Herman Sheets and we managed to crawl out to this little patch of trees for cover, overlooking the Germans who had their two men out for duty like we did. The Germans started singing Christmas songs, one of them being 'Silent Night.' It was strange. It was unbelievable that we were lying on that cold snowy ground, teeth chattering and trying to sing 'Silent Night.' We were keeping it to ourselves, afraid to let the Germans know we were there.

They didn't mind. They were very strong with their voices. That's how strong Christmas is to soldiers out in the field.

Acts of thoughtfulness on the part of one's peers was greatly appreciated – especially at Christmas time. Company commander Al Regenburg had such a recollection. He wrote:

The attacks of about two a day continued to Christmas Eve. I was instructed to go to 1st Battalion to relieve 'A' Company, which had been cut up pretty badly. When I assembled all of 'G' Company, I had only 44 men, including Lt. Hibbard's platoon. We spent the night in the woods. The trees were too thick and the ground was too hard to dig a foxhole. While we were waiting to go to relieve 'A' Company, I heard a voice calling, 'Regenburg, Regenburg, where are you?' I guided the person to me, to find lovable warrant officer O. P. Adams, who had left the sanctity and warmth of regimental headquarters to bring me a bottle of wine to celebrate Christmas Eve. That made me feel so good to think that anyone would do that for me.

## TERROR IN AN OUTPOST

Sgt. Duane L. Tedrick of "D" Company of the 506th Regiment describes an action at a forward listening post on Christmas Eve when the slightest sound created a feeling of panic:

Our Company 'D' was dug in along a road with the 3rd Platoon on the left flank. We had a listening post near the center of a band of trees. Don King, George Guckenberger and I were in that post. There was a little wind and snow would fall from the trees and make some noise. We were all feeling sad at having to spend Christmas Eve in a hole in the ground. We had been there several hours when suddenly there was a noise of metal striking metal. It was quite loud and we were all shook up thinking the enemy had gotten that close to us. 'Gook' got down in the bottom of the foxhole and I piled our blankets on top of him so he could call the company on our sound power phone. Somehow the phone came unhooked and 'Gook' could not see to reconnect the line. We decided that King would throw a grenade; I would empty the BAR and we would run down the strip of trees and turn left and head for the road. I had just released the safety on the BAR when a Battalion mortar fired a flare right over the open area to our front. As the flare came down, it lit up our area. King kinda giggled and said, 'It's a little mouse in the ration cans in the trash hole!' We rehooked the soundpower and made a commo check with the company BUT did not report the 'terror-producing mouse.' King had a watch with a luminous dial and he leaned over and whispered, 'Hey guys, Merry Christmas!'

## BOMBERS HIT BASTOGNE

The entry in T/4 Gerald Zimmerman's diary for this date covers some of the highlights for Christmas Eve as Bastogne received its first aerial bombing:

December 24, 1944 – Another clear day - our air support and more supplies by air. Shells going in and out. I went to bed about six in the shelter but was awakened about eight when we received our first bombing here. It was a living hell. We have no ack-ack or machine guns to hinder them. They (enemy) come over, drop flares and then take their time dropping their 'bundles'.

When war correspondent Fred McKenzie volunteered to go on the mission with the 101st Division, he never dreamed just how hectic life would be for him and the others. The first aerial bombing of Bastogne is etched in the memories of all who had to withstand the sounds and explosions as the enemy planes flew unmolested over the city. The action is described by McKenzie:

Most of us were underground when the first German aerial attack was launched at 8 o'clock Christmas Eve. Our cellar heaved and trembled from blasts 150 yards away.

'Steady men, keep calm and don't crowd,' said Lt. Col. Ned D. Moore, the chief-of-staff and there was no disorder.

About that time, little Cpl. Daniel Olney of Tucson, Arizona and I got the same urge to find foxholes. We dashed out into bright moonlight. I, with a feeling of exhilaration.

It was cold but the fresh air was invigorating after the fetid atmosphere underground. I decided 'to do my dying' above ground and did not again seek shelter in a cellar.

On leaving the cellar after the air raid, I went to the police barracks and there found an empty bunk whose occupant had taken refuge underground.

Bastogne was lighted by flames from the bombing, garish in bright moonlight. A division officer came by the police station enroute to the fire and we went together.

Now and then, a shell whined over and we hugged walls until after the bursts. The streets were deserted but we were frequently challenged by sentries until we reached the fire. An aid station, housing wounded, had been hit by a bomb.

There seemed nothing to do so we turned back to headquarters and subsequently I went to bed in the police barracks where Pvt. John Connolly was sound asleep.[111]

---

[111]McKenzie, Fred. Correspondent for *Buffalo Evening News*, January 18, 1945 (delayed) column in *The Detroit Free Press*.

As commander of "B" Battery of the 81st Anti-Tank Battalion, Captain A. G. Gueymard's troopers were attached to the 501st Parachute Infantry Regiment. Thus, his battery command post was in the same building that housed the regimental command center in Bastogne.

One of the most memorable experiences Gueymard had during the war was on Christmas Eve during the first enemy attack by bombers. He wrote:

On Christmas Eve, German bombers were roaming around above the town. We heard a few bombs drop nearby and were naturally a bit excited. All of a sudden, we heard a tremendous crash – not an explosion – and then all was quiet. The bombers departed and we all turned in for the night. The next morning, upon arising, we investigated as to what had caused the crash the night before and found that in the next room to where we were, a 500 pound bomb had fallen into the room – not exploding – but splitting open like a watermelon and covering several tons of coal stored there. The powder was green so that the coal looked green also. Needless to say, had the bomb exploded, many of us would not be here today.

## AID STATION HIT

Captain Gordon Geiger of the 20th Armored Infantry Battalion of the 10th Armored Division had been hit by shrapnel as the armored troops and the 1st Battalion of the 506th Parachute Infantry Regiment had battled to maintain their foothold in Noville on December 19. He was evacuated to the medical facility of the 10th Armored Division in Bastogne.

On Christmas Eve the Germans shelled Bastogne with a vengeance and bombed the town twice during the night. It was the first time Geiger had ever been bombed and shelled. He wrote:

They hit our first aid station, which caved into the basement. We went over and tried to get the men out. A lot of mattresses had caught fire, as well as other things. One boy was pinned down by a beam on his leg. Someone found a saw and began to cut at the beam to free him. The boy was saying, 'Shoot me! Please shoot me!' But we said, 'You'll be all right!' We were able to cut him out of there.

Others weren't so fortunate. Only about half of the soldiers in the aid station survived. Included in the casualties was a young Belgian girl named Renee LeMaire, who had volunteered to care for the wounded.

She was a very beautiful eighteen year old girl who had been taking care of our boys. When the bomb came in, she was killed. My doctor was there and he sat down and cried like a baby. He had a daughter about the same age and the Belgian girl's death really got to him.[112]

A move to return to his make-shift hospital to write a letter to the wife of a young officer was interrupted by an invitation from one of his men to share in a Christmas Eve drink may have saved the life of Captain John T. Prior. He wrote:

> At 0830 p.m. Christmas Eve, I was in a building next to my hospital preparing to go next door to write a letter for a young lieutenant to his wife. The lieutenant was dying of a chest wound. As I was about to step out of the door for the hospital, one of my men asked if I knew what day it was, pointing out that on Christmas Eve we should open a champagne bottle. As the two of us filled our cups, the room, which was well blacked out, became as bright as an arc welder's torch. Within a second or two, we heard the screeching sound of the first bomb we had ever heard. Every bomb, as it descends, seems to be pointed right at you. We hit the floor as a terrible explosion next door rocked our building. I ran outside to discover that the three-story apartment serving as my hospital was a flaming pile of debris about six feet high. The night was brighter than day from the magnesium flares the German bomber pilot had dropped. My man and I raced to the top of the debris and began flinging burning timber aside looking for the wounded, some of whom were shrieking for help. At this juncture the German bomber, seeing the action, dropped down to strafe us with his machine guns. We slid under some vehicles and he repeated the maneuver several times before leaving the area.
>
> Our team headquarters, about a block away, also received a direct hit and was soon in flames. A large number of men soon joined us and we located a cellar window. (They were marked by white arrows on most European buildings.)
>
> Some men volunteered to be lowered into the smoking cellar on a rope and two or three injured were pulled out before the entire building fell into the cellar. I estimated that about thirty injured were killed in this bombing along with Renee LeMaire. It seems that Renee had been in the kitchen as the bomb came down and she either dashed into, or was pushed into, the cellar before the bomb hit. Ironically enough, all those in the kitchen were blown outdoors since one wall was all glass. I gathered what patients I still had and transported them to the riding hall hospital of the Airborne Division.[113]

---

[112]Geiger, op. cit.

[113]Prior, op. cit.

*These ruins are believed to be the remains of Captain John T. Prior's 20th Armored Infantry Battalion's aid station in Bastogne.*

## SECOND STRIKE

Whether the onset of the 0300 attack on the western perimeter and the second bombing strike of Bastogne at the same hour was a coordinated attack on the part of the enemy wasn't known to the participants on the receiving ends.

War correspondent Fred McKenzie managed to get some sleep in the police barracks after the first bombing attack but finally awakened to the chill in the room. He continued his story:

I awakened about 2 o'clock and felt cold. The feeble fire was almost out, so I poked it hopefully and went outside to talk to soldiers guarding the gate.

The Germans, I learned later, were preparing one of their biggest attacks. It came against our lines and by air at 3 o'clock. The drone of planes was the first warning.

I told myself they were friendly planes. It couldn't be that Christmas morning would bring new horror in the defenders of Bastogne. Hadn't they passed through the crisis enough?

The scream of descending bombs answered us. Down, down they came and one of the sentries cried, 'In here, sir!' As I plunged into a foxhole where they stood guard with .30 caliber machine guns, bombs burst everywhere, but we were unscathed.

I don't know how many bombs fell, but none of us was fear-stricken and all were very angry. After a while, I climbed from the foxhole and we talked, but I don't remember the substance of the talk.

A third soldier joined us. Then shells began to whine. This time, there were four of us in the foxhole.

We could hear machine guns chattering and mortars coughing in the battle begun on the southern boundary of the defense perimeter. The soldier came back into the bivouac area and disappeared.

A plane droned over again and this time flares came down and hovered many minutes, lighting so brilliantly you could see far across Bastogne and out on the plain.

We saw sparks like tracer bullets off to the west, but instead of going up from the earth they started in midair and streaked parallel to the ground. They must have been fired from a plane, but that eerie sight in the sky served to unnerve me more than crashing bombs and shells.

We went to the other side of the barracks and then there were more planes overhead and screaming bombs. I remember huddling in a foxhole just big enough to squeeze into and the cold earth seemed furry and soft and it seemed my helmet came down to cover even my knees that were tucked under my chin.

Here was the supreme moment of apprehension for me at Bastogne. A bomb fell 70 yards away beside the cemetery where Sunday they had buried our dead.

A shell struck a pole on the other side of the barracks, broke it off and shattered bricks and windows, but no one was hurt.

By this time, I had reached the limit of self-reliance and as shrapnel from shells and bombs tinkled around I was physically and spiritually folded in one little knot of thought which ran something like this: 'Thy will be done – for how long, I do not know.'[114]

Captain John T. Prior ended his account of the bombing episode wondering how the pilot picked his hospital as the particular target or was it the fact that the streets were so full of vehicles which offered such a wealth of "easy pickings."

At about 3 a.m. Christmas morning, the bomber returned and totally destroyed a vacant building next to the smoldering hospital. I have often wondered how the pilot picked this hospital as a target. There were no

---

[114]McKenzie, op. cit.

external markings but, as some of the men said, the bomb must have come down the chimney. Many tanks and half-tracks were parked bumper to bumper in the street in front of the hospital so it seemed probable he simply picked an area of high troop concentration.[115]

## A TRAGIC SHOOTING

Two soldiers relate the story of a tragic shooting at an outpost position in the area of Senonchamps on Christmas Eve.

Other than some sporadic shelling, the Senonchamps area probably experienced one of the more quiet Christmas Eves around the perimeter. On duty at the Chateau Ile-le-Hesse to patrol the grounds, Pvt. Duane Harvey remembered a report of a tragic shooting:

When we were on the ridge outside of Senonchamps, a sergeant would make a check of the foxholes during the night. One of the fellows said, 'the sergeant was shot last night by a replacement when he came by on his nightly check'.

S/Sgt. Robert G. Salley of Headquarters Company of the 326th Engineer Battalion, whose unit was part of the western defense line, related a story which may fit the action recited by Pvt. Harvey but it wasn't the sergeant who got shot. Salley wrote:

During the night of December 24th, I was on guard duty with PFC. Tony DiSalle on top of a hill on the edge of a woods. We had been there all night and just as it was getting light, Captain William J. Nancarrow sent two men up to relieve us.

Our replacements were from the 9th Armored Division engineers, who were with us temporarily. Tony and I, being on top of the hill, were easily discernable by these men as they came up to us.

I could see them coming up the grade and they were running from tree to tree and bush to bush. About that time, Tony stood up to stretch the kinks out of himself.

I told him to get down but before he could do that one of these men, probably nervous as we all were and not being sure who we were because the area had Germans dressed in our uniforms, shot Tony in the stomach. Tony died where he fell. In the turmoil that followed, I never did learn who these two men were. I'm sure this same sort of thing happened many times during the various conflicts our country has been in.

---

[115]Prior, op. cit.

# 10. CHRISTMAS DAY

Reconnaissance of the area west of Bastogne had convinced Division that the next major attack along the perimeter would come from that direction and most likely it would come on Christmas Day.

The thinly held line was outposted by men of 1st Battalion of the 401st Glider Infantry with Companies "A" and "B" on line and Company "C" in reserve around the Battalion command post on the outskirts of Hemroulle.

The brunt of the battle in the initial stages was to be borne by 2nd Platoon of "A" Company. The pre-dawn attack by 18 enemy tanks would come through their foxhole positions.

World War II historian, Brig. General S. L. A. Marshall provides this description of "A" Company's readiness to do battle on this day:[116]

Perhaps the best measure of the fighting elan of this unit is that on the morning of the attack they were covering their ground with five .50 caliber machine guns and two light MG's in excess of the two light guns allowed by the tables. They had scrounged this extra weapon power and were quite happy to carry it along. This was a general characteristic of the 101st Airborne Division; it's men never overlooked a chance to build up weapon power. They would pre-empt armor and work it, if they could get their hands on it.

There were 77 men in the Company under 1Lt. Howard G. Bowles in the hour of the action. They were holding a sector approximately 1100 yards in width, organized generally along a ridge line, with a large pine plantation on the Company right and a small forest lot in the center ground in which the CP was established. Two tank destroyers of the 705th TD Battalion were in position in a forest patch directly behind the CP and two others were in tree cover farther up the hill, well to the left. Company A's machine guns were disposed so as to tie together the general front defended by the glidermen and the destroyer crews.

Reconnaissance had already convinced Division that this was the most likely avenue in the whole defensive circle for a thrust by enemy armor. The men knew this. Moreover, late on Christmas Eve, they had heard armor out beyond their horizon; the noise came from the forward elements of 15th Panzer Grenadier Division, which were just entering the battle.

At 2200 on Christmas Eve, on order from Division, 1Lt. Jack Adams commanding the 3rd Platoon, was given ten picked men by Bowles and told to work out through the fog and dynamite the culvert short of the village of

---

[116]Marshall, Colonel S. L. A. *Armored Cavalry Journal*, "Men Against Fire". May-June, 1950, pp. 5-7.

Flamizoulle, where the sounds of activity were coming. The patrol had gone five hours. The fog had enabled Adams to make his approach safely, but it had also slowed his progress. He got to the culvert, drilled a few holes, put in the dynamite, then he heard the tramp of German infantry marching along the road and coming toward him; he had to withdraw before completing his mission.

He brought this word back to Bowles and told him that there seemed to be 'plenty of armor' in the village. Bowles at once asked for an artillery shot on Flamizoulle and got it. But it was too late to be effective. Almost coincidentally, Pvt. Allie Moore got back from the 2nd Platoon outpost and told Bowles that a considerable force of infantry and 'many tanks' were coming directly on his front.

Bowles ran forward to the outpost on his left flank. He reached it just in time to see the tanks come on; the armor was in column, moving on a line which would take it directly between his left flank (2nd Platoon) and the Company CP. Bowles doubled back to the main position.

Awakened from a sound sleep in an upstairs room of his command post near Hemroulle, LTC. Ray Allen, commander of the 401st Glider Infantry Battalion, was told a long column of tanks was headed toward the positions of his line companies covering a ridge southwest of Champs. Asked by his staff officers if the men on line should commence firing, he had told them no. It would be better to determine at what point the enemy was moving through the line positions and order those men to move out of the path of the armor.

The tank column accompanied by white-capped infantrymen, some riding on the backs of the tanks, came through the positions of 2nd Platoon of "A" Company. Knowing that to stay in their foxholes would mean certain death, the glider troopers moved out of their positions and joined 3rd Platoon up on higher ground.

In an interview with his son-in-law, Colonel Allen described the action that occurred as the enemy forces came through the abandoned positions:

The column of 60-ton German tanks began moving into Company A's positions with their flame throwers blazing. Each tank had 15 or 16 infantrymen, wearing white sheets, riding on it and some infantrymen were walking behind the tanks. They were firing rifles and flame throwers as they came into the 2nd Platoon's positions. The Germans were probing, trying to find my front-line positions. As soon as the last tank rolled through 2nd Platoon's position, about 30 minutes later, the men of the 2nd Platoon simply climbed out of the 3rd Platoon positions and went back to their own positions, closing up the front line. No one told them to do it, they just did it and not one man failed to return to his position. Now they were behind the tanks and in front of the approaching infantry.[117]

PFC. Harold R. Hansen was a veteran of all the campaigns and served with Captain Taze Huntley in "A" Company of the 401st. On this occasion, 1Lt. Howard Bowles was commanding the unit while Captain Huntley and half of the unit had missed out on the trip to Bastogne as they were in Paris. Though he doesn't remember the exact battle site, it was west of Bastogne and southwest of Champs. This is his memory of the attack on Christmas morning when the enemy tanks came through the positions of his platoon:

> We had a close call in a wooded area when a flame thrower came in but luckily it didn't flame but quite a few men got burned from the hot fuel oil.
>
> An enemy tank rode over our foxhole in which my buddy and I squatted down, hoping it would keep going. It did, but destroyed my M-1 and our bazooka. My buddy's helmet got smashed. I think the tank was captured by 'E' Company.[118]

Hidden by the military crest of the hill on which 2nd Platoon was dug in, the defenders hadn't been seen yet by the forward elements of the enemy armor. Colonel Allen continued his story:

> One of my men on the far left flank began firing a .50 caliber machine gun, but no one else did any firing. This added to the deception. The German tanks thought they had just passed a weak outpost and kept on going. They didn't know they had passed through a well-fortified front line position.[119]

In the meantime, the tank destroyers which were attached to the 401st were concealed from view in the evergreen plantation. They, of course, couldn't see the enemy tanks which were approaching the position at an angle. Allen added to his story:

> They (TD's) were in the woods, 200 yards behind the CP and couldn't see the German tanks until the tanks were right beside them. As the German tanks slowly rolled past them, one of the tank destroyer crews was cursed for 'dallying' by a German tank commander who thought they were part of his force in the darkness and the heavy fog. No one answered him, no one fired and he moved on. The German tanks slowly rumbled toward Company C. The tank crews thought they were well on their way to Bastogne. As soon as the tanks had moved past them, the two tank destroyers pulled out of the trees and joined the other two tank destroyers on the left flank of the area.

---

[117]Martin, Darryl R. *Military History*, "Unexpected Trap for Panzers," December 1988. p. 51. Copy sent by Robert C. Bowen.

[118]Not so. Koskimaki is sure the tank Hansen is referring to is the one which was captured by T/4 "Booger" Childress and his tank stalking party from "B" Battery of the 463rd Parachute Field Artillery Battalion.

[119]Martin, op. cit.

No one told the men to do it, they just did it. It's important to point out that no one was giving any orders at this time. You can't tell someone what to do in a situation like this. The men were acting completely on their own.[120]

*The tree plantations around the Bastogne perimeter had received a heavy snowfall for Christmas Day. (Photo by Mike Musura, courtesy of John Gibson.)*

The only infantry troops accompanying the tanks were the ones riding on the backs of the white-washed tanks. Following five hundred yards to their rear came the white-capped infantry troops. Colonel Allen continues:

They were still marching in formation in the field below the ridge. They were wearing white sheets, screaming and firing their rifles into the air. In the early pre-dawn light and the heavy fog, they looked like ghosts floating across the snow covered field. They didn't know they were just minutes away from their doom. They were heading to our well-hidden, machine gun final protective line on the ridge and my men were becoming angry as they watched the hundreds of screaming German infantrymen coming toward them, but they stayed low, waiting for the Germans to get into range. Their plan was working. The German tanks were separated from

---

[120]ibid.

the infantry and infantry still didn't know where we were dug in. It was almost dawn and my men, four tank destroyers, our bazooka teams and Colonel Cooper's 463rd Artillery team were all in position. Waiting – patiently, quietly waiting.

No one told them to wait. They knew if they made a mistake they were done for. Then suddenly, the front line roared as my men began firing every gun they had and our machine gun final protective line went into full effect. The surprised German infantry was trapped in the flat, open field and were being cut to pieces by the cross fire from our machine guns.[121]

The column of enemy tanks was headed in the direction of Colonel Allen's battalion command post and the positions of the 463rd Parachute Field Artillery Battalion pack howitzers. The four tank destroyers from the 705th TD Battalion followed along at the rear of the column. Colonel Allen describes how they attacked from the rear:

The four tank destroyers had avoided a direct frontal fight with the tanks because of the thick armor plating on the front of the German tanks. When the first shot rang out, the tanks were still in a column moving toward my command post. Instantly, the four tank destroyers raced into position behind the tanks and opened fire. Five of the tanks exploded as their thin, unprotected backsides took direct hits.[122]

With the arrival of the first dim light of morning, the artillerymen of the 463rd could now distinguish the first of the enemy tanks standing still, presumably waiting for their infantry to catch up, orders were given to commence firing. The same held true for the men of "C" Company, which had been in reserve near Battalion Headquarters. Colonel Allen added:

'C' Company was dug in and they were not going to budge one bit. Someone said they shot at anything and everything that could be German. Colonel Cooper's 463rd Artillery was so close to the tanks that they had to level their muzzles and shoot almost straight across the ground to hit them. They fired point blank and said it was like 'shooting fish in a barrel.' Now the tank column was being bombarded by fire from every direction. The column was surely staggered. Then, to escape the furious fire that was pounding them, it split up. Some of the tanks started racing toward Champs, two miles north, and six of them sped toward my CP in Hemroulle, two miles west of Bastogne.

My CP was beside the road leading from Champs to Hemroulle and on into Bastogne. It was about 7:15 a.m. now and Captain Preston Towns, the commander of Company C, called to warn me about the tanks speeding toward my CP. I asked him where they were and he said, 'If you look out

---

121[ibid.]
122[ibid.]

your back window now, you'll be looking right down the muzzle of an 88.'[123]

When Colonel Allen looked out the back window, he was spotted by the gunner in the tank who began firing armor piercing shells into the house, easily penetrating the brick walls and setting the building on fire. Allen and the remainder of his staff and enlisted personnel fled toward the woods. Several shells were sent after the fleeing commander but he managed to elude them and reached the safety of the woods.

## "C" COMPANY AND THE 705TH

Darkness had settled in on Christmas Eve. 2nd Platoon of "C" Company of the 502nd Parachute Regiment was positioned at Hemroulle. The weather had turned colder and to provide his men more comfort, S/Sgt. Curtis DeWitt had sought out an old wood barn with a hayloft. Except for those on guard duty, the others bedded down in hay in their sleeping bags, covering themselves with loose hay which provided added warmth.

There wasn't much sleep for any of them. At 8 o'clock, the enemy bombed Bastogne. The old barn shook after each blast. Peering through the cracks in the end wall, the men could see the flares floating slowly to earth and the flames from the burning buildings were easily visible.

After some fitful sleeping, the men were awakened at 0330 and ordered to get ready to move out. "A" Company was being attacked by a large enemy force.

DeWitt's 2nd Platoon moved onto the road that led north from Hemroulle at 0400, still in the dark as to where they would move. The move was made up the road with the troops now standing on the highway across from Colonel Ray Allen's 401st Battalion command post. Here they stood about, waiting for what seemed like hours. With little or no movement, the body begins to feel the cold and dampness of the morning.

In the 401st command post courtyard, a fire was lighted. Platoon members of "C" Company edged over there to capture some of its warmth and to heat a canteen cup of coffee.

Squad sergeant Layton Black set up a machine gun facing to the west just in case an attack came out of the fog from that direction. It seemed odd to be standing around a fire in another battalion's courtyard. Black wondered why they were being permitted to stand around. He soon learned the answer. He wrote:

Suddenly, the answer was there. Hell, this battalion CP was leaving. We didn't start the fire. They did, to burn maps and papers! Talk about real action – that was the most action by a group of officers and their men I was

---

[123]ibid.

ever to see. It was at this point that I saw the Colonel. He was leaving on foot for somewhere else!

It was at this point that the cry, 'German tanks!' rang out loud and clear. All hell broke loose.

Looking for the biggest gun he could find, Sgt. Black turned toward his machine gun only to see it blown to smithereens. It was the first round fired by an enemy tank at "C" Company. As Sgt. Black related, "Eighteen German tanks had caught us standing flat-footed on that 'cold road' near Hemroulle, Belgium."

With eighteen enemy tanks looming out of the fog, 2nd Platoon was directed to head for the cover of the nearby woods. As one man, "C" Company raced for cover.

The tanks began to fan out in different directions with some going in the direction of Hemroulle to the south, others headed toward Champs to catch "A" Company from the rear and seven of them headed for "C" Company which was, at that moment, gaining the cover of the wood lot.

The 1st Battalion of the 502nd Regiment had its command post in Hemroulle as did the 401st troops and Colonel Cooper's 463rd Parachute Artillery.

Pvt. Memphis E. Nixon was a 1st Battalion Headquarters Company mortarman who happened to be in the path of the tank force which was moving toward the north in the direction of Champs and Rolle after breaching the lines in the 327th regimental sector. Nixon's most memorable action occurred on the morning of Christmas Day. He wrote:

About 0200 on Christmas Day, we were moved out toward Champs and halted at a crossroad. I went out on flank guard with Pvt. Arthur Hunt to the west of the Champs road.

As dawn broke, we were sitting against a haystack facing north when we saw a lieutenant from the 327th crawling toward us down this road lined with hardwood trees. When he got close enough, he said there were enemy tanks right there, pointing behind the haystack. Sure enough, there were three tanks less than 100 yards away. Hunt and I started crawling with him – no hole – no cover. After about 10 to 15 yards of crawling, a tank fired its 88mm into the trees not more than 20 feet above us. Evidently the hedgerow was too low as he fired again and about ten yards further on. Both times, sticks and limbs fell over us, but miraculously none of us were hit. Those 88's exploded so close to us that things didn't register for a few seconds. Up to this point, the two 88 rounds aimed at us were the only fire.

Then all hell broke loose as 'C' Company engaged them and diverted their attention from us. By now, we had crawled to the Hemroulle-Champs road. With no more cover, we jumped up and ran, expecting to be mowed down by machine guns on the tanks. It never came.

Company "C" had been in reserve in Hemroulle on the morning of
December 25th as related by Sgt. Layton Black. They had been prepared to move
to the north to reinforce "A" Company when 2nd Platoon was caught in front of
the 401st Battalion CP with the appearance of the enemy tank column moving
up from the west. As a member of "C" Company, PFC. James W. Flanagan
was about to lose his soft reserve duty. He wrote:

Early Christmas morning, the Germans became very active at Champs
and by 0400 we were alerted to get ready to move as 'Able' Company was
under heavy attack. Company 'B' was sent up the road toward Champs with
'Charlie' Company to follow. We were on the road strung out in column of
two's at just about daybreak when the German tanks and infantry that had
broken through the 327th came charging over the snow-covered hill. 'C'
Company was broadside to this mess and we were ordered to fall back to the
woods on the east side of the road. As we were being shot at by rifles,
machine guns and cannon, we expedited the withdrawal to the woods much
better than at Olympic time.

I was passed by a trooper with an officer's marking on the back of the
helmet. Of course, he wasn't loaded down as I was. He swerved to go around
a large tree. I swerved to go around on the opposite side. An 88mm HE
from a German tank passed between us blowing the tree off its trunk about
three feet above the ground. I didn't get a scratch but I don't know if he did. I
continued to run out from under the falling tree, dodging a couple of large
bushes. All of a sudden, I was running in midair – my feet not touching the
ground. I sailed out over a ditch and dropped. With snow on the ground, it's
difficult to tell your altitude. I hit bottom – right through the snow. A
couple inches of ice with a foot or so of water. By the time I extricated
myself, I was wet up to my gut and I could feel the water in my boots. I
was in a bit of trouble to say the least. The Germans were behind me and I
was wet to the waist in that damned cold weather. I worked my way up the
bank to see what was going on. The Mark IV's and SP's were still out there.
The infantry that was with them were taking a beating and about this time I
noticed that the tanks were getting shot up by our TD's and Shermans and,
as my trusty M1 was frozen up due to my dunking, I couldn't do much more
than act as a cheerleader.

During the surprise appearance of the enemy tanks with their riding infantry
at the courtyard entrance, part of 2nd Platoon of "C" Company was trapped and
captured. Those not captured, joined the rest of the company in the race to the
tree line. Out of nowhere appeared the company commander, Captain Cody who
put a halt to the rout. Sgt. Black relates what happened:

I remember we were half way up this long hillside, already out in the
open past the tree line, when I looked up and there stood Captain Cody with
his arms raised on high. He said, 'Hold up right there! This is as far as we're

going to run. Turn around, we are going back to get the bastards!' You know something? For a moment there, he looked a lot like Jesus Christ to me.

Company "C" started back to the location from which they had fled. Sgt. Black noted that about half the men were missing from 2nd Platoon. The thought that the missing were either killed or captured spurred the company on its mission. Along the way, the company was joined by two 705th tank destroyers in the woods.

When the lead elements got within two hundred yards of the vacated 401st command post, the lead scouts spotted enemy tanks parked near the entrance with enemy infantry milling about in the courtyard. Sgt. Black picks up the action:

The time could have been about 0800 hours, but I knew no one who was looking at his watch. We were all engaged in a dead serious act now. Some of the Jerries were cooking their breakfasts and we caught them by surprise. They had made the mistake of not coming after us; and, at least they should have been ready for a counterattack.

We all opened up at once. We poured all the rifle fire into that old farmhouse. Suddenly, all four tanks took off going straight north, down the road toward Champs, one behind the other. Now they were on the run, as if they were only saving the tanks.

The German infantrymen ran out from the farmhouse in a rush to catch a ride on the tanks. Many of them were cut down by our rifle fire which now had become a cross-fire of 2nd, 1st and 3rd Platoons of 'C' Company.

I was walking along near the edge of the clearing in line with a potato pile by now. Walking next to me, among the large hardwood trees, was S/Sgt. Don Williams. He was a platoon sergeant in 'C' Company of the 705th TD Battalion. Two of his TD's were following along behind us at a slow pace. The platoon sergeant asked me to hold back my men, while he 'taught the Germans a small lesson in tank warfare.'

Sgt. Tony D'Angelo from Wellsville, Ohio, was the commander of the nearest TD and was walking in front leading his destroyer around the big trees. Tony stopped his driver right beside me. I heard him say to his gunner inside, 'Take the last tank first and then one at a time right up the line. Fire when ready.'

He fired point blank into the side of each Mark IV tank. The last tank first, and so on up the line, was hit and caught fire. The TD next to me (D'Angelo) fired six shots. Two shots hit big trees, four shots hit tanks and four were knocked out. It was absolutely the best I have ever seen.

As for the German infantry, not a man got away. In the end though, there was a big surprise waiting for the men of 2nd Platoon.

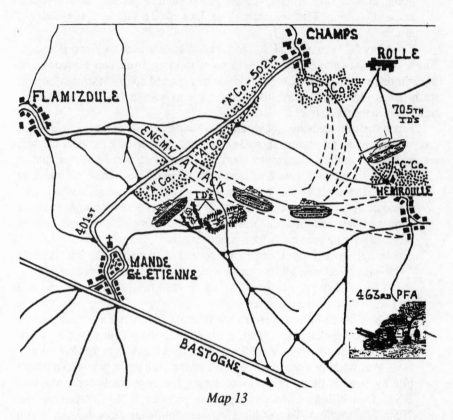

*Map 13*

Some of our men were still pouring rifle fire into the farmhouse when, all of a sudden, a white flag began to wave back and forth at the front door. We stopped firing and out stepped Cpl. Milligan, from my squad. The fighting ended and all of our 2nd Platoon troopers who had been captured by the Jerries, came running out of that old farmhouse. They certainly were a happy bunch and the victory had come just in time. That old house was now on fire, blazing into the sky.

We in 'C' Company captured 35 prisoners and killed 67 Germans for our part in the Christmas morning fight. The real glory to save the front lines and stop a major breakthrough belongs to our own 'A' Company of the 1st Battalion in their defense of Champs.

## LET IT HIT THE FAN!

The actions at Bastogne were the first experiences of the 463rd Parachute Field Artillery Battalion in working closely with the 101st Airborne Division in a combat situation. It's commander, Lt. Colonel John T. Cooper, Jr., wrote about the activities of his battalion and how they prepared for the actions when they learned the Division was surrounded:

The days prior to Christmas began to pass about like all the others we had been in for the past year. Each day presented its targets and we fired our missions. From these positions we fired 6,400 mills (around the total circle).

As it began to snow and ammo decreased to critical conditions, we organized our battalion for the possibility of 'stand and fight,' for there were no other places to go. We posted, dug in out-post guards with telephone communications to Battalion HQ as well as to the battery they represented. Our guns were mutually supporting. Banking on the fact that a tank will attack a gun head on, we had another gun that would have a side shot at the tank.

We had 20 rounds per gun of hollow charge anti-tank ammo that were never used or counted in ammo reports except to be used for direct fire.

The preparation for the tank attacks we received on Christmas Day had been planned and set up for several days. Snow had covered the gun positions. All we had to do was move our gun sections and start shooting.

Sgt. Joseph F. Rogan, Jr. was serving as forward observer on an outpost with "A" Company of the 401st Glider Infantry Battalion. He was the first to alert the 463rd Parachute Field Artillery Battalion that an attack was headed in their direction. The S-2 Report for the 463rd states:[124]

During the early morning, a strong enemy attack developed along a line from Champs to Flamizoulle. The battalion forward observer, Sergeant Joseph F. Rogan, Jr., adjusting indirect fire in support of the 327th Glider Infantry Regiment, notified the Battalion S-3 by radio, that he and his supporting company had been over-run by tanks and that the tanks were moving in the direction of the firing battery positions.

Major Victor E. Garrett was the S-3 (Operations) officer for the 463rd. He describes how the actions involving the 463rd evolved during the night and early morning of Christmas Day:

On Christmas Eve night the Germans broke through our front lines. I had many intelligence reports all night about the situation.

---

[124] S-2 Report of the 463rd Parachute Field Artillery Battalion for December 25, 1944.

About daylight, Captain Ardelle E. Cole advised me by radio that there were four tanks lined up on a ridge above us. I asked, 'Do they have muzzle brakes?' His reply was, 'Yes.'

The 463rd had knocked out several tanks in the earlier fighting in Sicily and had participated many times after that in Italy and southern France against armored vehicles with much success. Now it was early Christmas morning. Colonel John T. Cooper describes the developing situation:

I was awakened by my S-3, Victor Earl Garrett from the Operations Room across the hall in the house we were using as our CP.

He told me that eleven tanks had moved in on Sgt. 'Booger' Childress's 'B' Battery. Some four tanks had stopped so close to him that he might be discovered if the soldiers moved around very much. He could hear the other tankers and they had gotten out of the tanks and were waiting around. He had to whisper. Snow was about a foot deep all over the place.

The Germans got out of their tanks and made coffee and sat around waiting for daylight. They did not know that while this was going on, they were being observed through the tube of a 75mm pack howitzer, which would soon be loaded with hollow-charge ammo, probably the only such ammo in the (European) theater and they had parked in front of the only guns that had the ammo.

I told the S-3 to alert all the batteries and for them to stay in their sacks, except for the C.O.'s and executive officer and gun crews. Movement in batteries are to be kept at a minimum. No lights. No one was to fire a round until we gave the order: 'Let the shit hit the fan!'

As it was still dark and as the word got out, our gunners had occupied their gun pits and other outposts were able to see the tanks, we had a good view of what we had to do.

You will remember how I was greeted for several days by 'How many tanks did you knock out today?'[125]

I was now determined to be able to give Elkins and Carmichael a damn good answer. I was also sure that Patton's tanks were in the vicinity and I was damn sure we were going to shoot German tanks. I told the S-3 that we would not shoot until he could see the muzzle brakes on the guns or the Swastika painted on the tanks.

As the Germans began to make a move, we could see the muzzle brake on the guns. The S-3 gave the order: 'Let the shit hit the fan!'

Having refreshed his memory by rereading a letter he sent home in late 1944, PFC. Walter J. Peplowski, a member of the #3 pack howitzer for "B" Battery, has a vivid description of the Christmas morning action:

---

[125]See page 10.

The number 3 pack howitzer with Wolfenbarger, Silvas and Peplowski as a full gun crew was used. If it wasn't for powerful George Silvas, I don't know if we could have made it up hill through the soft snow to the gun pit.

Now the howitzer is in the pit – all ammo is taken out of the cases. The bare shells are lined up in perfect order: HE, WP, HE, WP, etc. The barrel is traversed to the tanks on the extreme left. We wait, knowing to fire now would invite disaster, powder snow, smoke, a real give-away.

The enemy infantry action to the right indicates that a tank swing to the left is inevitable to make a fire team.

The snow is melting as we kneel this Christmas morning. My knees are wet. We talk about the range and decide that a lead of 2-1/4 to 2-1/2 tank lengths would be just right; also, to drop rounds, aim lower so there would be no overs.

The leading tank swerves, others follow just like in the book. We joke a little – the tension is broken. We know soon firing will commence and will move like hell. Wolfenbarger is gunner, a cool, calm, efficient and accurate one.

The action comes fast – last tank first, every shell a hit – one – two – three tanks on fire, one in the woods. This is for certain.

PFC. Joseph F. Callahan was the cannoneer on Sgt. Derwood Parker's gun in the same battery on Christmas morning. This is his recollection:

When word was received about the German tanks, I don't think we used the eye scope but just fired. And we saw the first tank, but we shot and hit the second one. We went to the tank that afternoon and there were two bodies inside it and one body lying outside.

Cpl. Nicholas Bellezza was on a .50 caliber machine gun with PFC. Al Fredericks and a raw recruit in the "B" Battery sector. They were covering the right flank. Bellezza related:

Snow kept filling our gun pit at which we stood guard 24 hours every day. On Christmas Day, at daybreak, I noticed through the haze, approximately 350 yards, the outlines of tanks which were located directly in front of my position. I immediately called the switchboard for a verification to find out if they were our tanks. The response was negative.

Noticing movement around the tanks, I opened fire. German fire was returned (white tracers) at my position. The recruit said, 'Don't fire – they may see us!' He was so scared that he left the gun position leaving Fredericks and me to keep firing. The barrel got so hot we had to stop and change it. Fredericks, in his haste, grabbed the barrel without using asbestos gloves. However, his burns were minor.

By the time we were to refire, the tanks had moved. I remember that one of the battery's guns was moved to give direct fire at the tanks.

PFC. Gus Hazzard was one of the men on forward outpost duty as part of T/4 Corsen "Booger" Childress' team. He provided his recollection of the early action:

> In the pre-dawn hours of 25 December 1944, T/4 'Booger' Childress, Joe Pimlott and myself were assigned as supporting infantry. We were lying in an open, snow-covered field waiting for the dawn as directly to our front tanks were moving about. When dawn broke, all hell broke loose. After the small arms quieted down and the smoke cleared, we advanced forward to an idling tank. There was one German still alive sitting with his back to a tree. The prisoner, along with others, and the tank were driven back to our lines by Childress, Pimlott and myself.

The S-2 Report for the 463rd sent by PFC. Ken Hesler, continues with its description of the early hours of the attack and lists the make-up of the stalking party:

> During the fire fight in the battalion's northern sector, at approximately 0730 hours, the western tank defenses engaged four medium enemy tanks – destroying two and damaging one to such an extent that it withdrew to a hull down position where it was captured by Battalion Tank Stalking Party consisting of Tec 4 Corsen H. Childress, Pvt. August F. Hazzard, Pvt. William L. Justice, Pvt. John T. Paris, Pvt. Stanley M. Levandosky, Pvt. Gordon L. Ballenger and Pvt. Joseph W. Pimlott under the command of 1Lt. Ross W. Scott.[126]

The S-2 report sheds further light into the actions of this tank stalking party and another small patrol:

> This same party also captured two officers and twelve enlisted men on this same patrol. Sgt. Thomas J. Spivey, with PFC. Charles Johnson, Pvt. Gunther F. Winter and Pvt. Gloden E. Oglesby, engaged a German machine gun with small arms fire killing one and capturing eight enlisted men who were turned over to the 502nd Parachute Infantry.

Though he was not a member of a gun crew, Pvt. Merle W. McMorrow had this report of the action:

> I was not in a gun section but we got a message by phone that Germans had broken through the defenses of the 327th Infantry. I ran across the road to where one of the howitzers was partially dug in on a small knoll. It must have been somewhere between 0700 and 0730 a.m. and the rumbling of the approaching tanks could be heard in the semidarkness. I recall there was more excitement than fear in the group. We usually never had an opportunity to see the enemy we were firing at. Three or four tanks were in our immediate front at about 300 yards distance. There were scattered patches of woods located within the field. German infantry was following

---

[126]463rd S-2 Report.

beside and behind the tanks. It involved direct fire and the gun had to be moved down the slope slightly to get the tube depressed sufficiently to get the tanks in the gun sight. A .30 caliber usually stopped them (infantry) before they got into the cover of the wooded area. The other tanks continued to be fired on and it soon became obvious they were no longer advancing toward our position. I remember a number of fellows ran out to the tanks – whether they were guessing that it had just been abandoned or found that out after they got there, I don't know. I do know they drove it back with a great deal of pride.

Battalion commander John T. Cooper was justly proud of his men and hoped by calling higher headquarters he could prove once and for all to the "doubting Thomases" that tanks could indeed be knocked out with direct fire from pack howitzers. He wrote:

> I picked up my telephone to Division and reported the attack on the 463rd. 'We would like some help but would stay in contact and not give ground. Our HQ was being attacked.'
>
> 'Cooper, are you making this up?' someone asked at Division.
>
> 'Hell no – look out your window and you will see five smoke columns each of a burning tank. No – make that six, there goes another one!'
>
> 'We will get Task Force Cherry down as soon as possible, out!'

*This German Tiger tank was knocked out near Bastogne. A grenade was exploded in the barrel of its 88 by Germans to keep it from being used against them. (Photo by Mike Musura, courtesy of John Gibson.)*

In the first 15 minutes we had disabled 8 tanks, hit ten tanks, the one close to Childress on the turret, killed two inside and one getting out. Childress called and said he had dragged the man off the track and got the two dead men out. I told him to sit tight, but put a white undershirt on the tube and wait for me.

By this time, about 45 minutes had passed. Walter Scherl, my driver, and I drove out and led the tank, driven by 'Booger' down a draw into our HQ area and parked it outside my CP. I called Headquarters to tell them I had a present for them.

In a letter Colonel Thomas P. Sherburne had written to George Koskimaki while the latter was serving as executive secretary of the 101st Airborne Division Association in 1980, Sherburne responded to an item which appeared in the newsletter about his old friend, Colonel John T. Cooper. He wrote:

I remember when, on Christmas Day at Bastogne, he (Col. Cooper) called up and announced he had a Christmas present for me, but I had to come and pick it up. It was a German tank no less; this his doughty battalion had shot up (but still ran) when we rushed them out to use direct fire at the tank breakthrough. No Boche foot soldiers got through them.

In a letter Cpl. James L. Evans had written to Col. John Cooper in recent years he described having accompanied Col. Tom Sherburne on the inspection trip to the 463rd sector shortly after the battle ended. Evans had been on duty at the Division Artillery switchboard when he got the assignment to accompany the artillery commander. Evans wrote:

Soon after I arrived at my switchboard, Colonel Sherburne appeared to pick me up to ride as security for him. (This he did several times during the war, always having me use proper procedure in getting permission from my captain, R. Wilson Neff.)

We proceeded to your location at the scene of the battle which had just ended. You and Colonel Sherburne talked and I kept my distance (as a corporal should).

Colonel Sherburne and I then proceeded to examine the tanks. You followed us at a close interval as you could hear Colonel Sherburne if there were any question or remarks made. I am the one who asked, 'What gun hit this tank?' I knew it showed my ignorance when I said it.

I then went around the first tank, which had burned. There was a German tanker burned to a crisp hanging upside down on the right side of the tank. His foot was caught in or near the opening on the top of the tank. There was a brown leather suitcase strapped on the right front of the tank that had not burned.

The other tank that I remembered made a mad dash into a thick patch of pines to escape. The trees were 6 to 8 inches in diameter. The tank plowed into the woods 75 to 100 yards, making a swath about ten feet wide until it hit a bank about 4 feet high at a 45 degree angle. I understood that your men captured the tank crew.

Colonel Sherburne and I then left. We went through the village and we inspected the tank you had captured. We then went out of the village toward Bastogne about 150 to 200 yards where we met General McAuliffe in his jeep. The jeeps stopped side by side while the General and the Colonel talked it over. It was decided that we would turn around and go back to the battlefield and show the General what we had seen.

Before we could turn, a flat trajectory shell came directly over the jeeps from the direction of the knocked-out tanks, crossed the road at 90 degrees and hit or missed one of the village houses about 200 yards away. We all hit the ditches. Then another shell came over. General McAuliffe had Sgt. Brown turn his jeep around and the General, Colonel Sherburne, Sgt. Brown, Colonel's driver and I went back to Bastogne. (The jeeps were driven by two Browns.)

A special commendation letter was sent by Colonel Thomas Sherburne, acting commander of the 101st Airborne Division Artillery to LTC. John T. Cooper, Jr. and his men which the 463rd Artillery commander was to show to the "doubting Thomases" of the other division artillery units who had derided the statements of Cooper and his officers concerning destruction of German tanks with a 75mm pack howitzer. The letter reads in part:

. . . During this action, your battalion can be officially credited with having: (1) Destroyed with AP and WP two medium enemy tanks, proved by line of hits and ricochet marks in the snow direct from your positions. (2) Captured in running condition one medium tank, crew having given up when a round from one of your pieces struck the vehicle and injured the commander. (3) Killed with HE and MG fire two enemy tank crew members who left the tanks. (4) Captured fourteen assorted enemy infantry and tank crew members . . . [127]

## DESTROYING SECRET EQUIPMENT

The unit history of the 463rd Parachute Field Artillery Battalion states the following:

In the 463rd Command Post, all classified documents as well as the M-209 crytographic machine were destroyed. By about 0830 hours, enemy infantrymen had approached within 200 yards of the CP and were taking it under rifle and machine gun fire.

---

[127]From a copy of a commendation letter written by Colonel Thomas Sherburne to LTC. John Cooper and the men of the 463rd on December 25, 1944.

Out in the "Dog" Battery area, its commander, Captain Victor J. Tofany was prepared to destroy personal belongings. He related:

It all started with an all-out German attack designed to wipe out the 'doughnut'. Everyone was prepared for the worst. The barracks bags with our belongings were piled ready to be burned and the cannoneers were oiling their rifles and carbines in case we were overrun by the enemy. General McAuliffe had told them Nuts and they were going to finish us off. In the ensuing battle, many of the 463rd men fought as infantry and helped to halt the German advance.

## A PLAY BY PLAY REPORT

1Lt. Everett Fuchs served as executive officer for "A" Battery of the 377th Parachute Artillery Battalion. His group was positioned in the small hamlet of Savy, a short distance from the 463rd batteries at Hemroulle. On Christmas Day he was able to give a "play by play" description of the tank attack which he witnessed from his position. He wrote:

On Christmas Day, our battery position was at Savy on a hill west of the road to Longchamps. We had a good view of the whole area east, northeast and north. In the early morning of the 25th, we heard heavy activity over in the 502nd area. We were called for some missions and were on the alert. As day broke, I was scanning this whole area with glasses when I picked up tanks all over the area. Some were heading in my direction. Most looked like they were in the 463rd area. I called my Battalion Fire Direction Center and reported this and I warned them of the approaching tanks and said I was going to position my guns to take on the tanks if they got through the 327th and 463rd. Battalion was unaware of these tanks and questioned me. I was talking with Captain Aldrich and told him to open his back door – he would see the tanks. Just at that time, two tank destroyers which had pulled up and took position near Battalion started firing. Both scored direct hits on the tanks. At the same time, the 463rd had taken tanks under fire. In that area there seemed to be about eight tanks. None of the tanks got through – destroyed by the 463rd and 327th so I was not able to get into the fight. I assumed the 463rd took care of most of the tanks because near their area I saw many smoldering remains of tanks. All this time I was describing the whole series of events to our battalion fire control center. A short time later all tanks being destroyed, crews killed or captured, everything quieted down about 0900 to 0930.

## SUMMARY OF 463RD ACTIONS

As the day wound down in the 463rd area, Pvt. Merle W. McMorrow had this observation about the prisoners captured by his unit:

Prisoners were rounded up and brought into our area for holding until consolidated with others. Many were young 15-year olds. They wondered why we were putting up so much resistance – didn't we know we were surrounded?

Operations officer, Major Victor Garrett summarized the actions that played such a big part in the 463rd area on Christmas Day:

Our command post and fire direction center was in Hemroulle, near Bastogne. We were in a house and the aid station was in a chapel across the road. On Christmas Day we kept our prisoners in the stable to the left of the C.P.

Ever since Sicily, we carried extra armor-piercing and phosphorus ammo (as per Col. Cooper's orders). Some say the armor-piercing did the job and some say the phosphorus caught them on fire.

There was now a respite in the 463rd area as far as defending their own positions were concerned. The 4th Armored Division of the 3rd Army broke through the enemy lines south of Bastogne on the evening of the 26th.

## PARKER TRIES FOR ANOTHER

The same enemy attack which hit the 463rd Parachute Artillery Battalion as well as the 502nd and the glidermen of the 401st, also got to the 377th Parachute Artillery area at Savy. Sgt. Arthur Parker hoped that the opportunity would present itself so he could get some more tanks with his bazooka. He wrote:

The next morning the Germans broke through the lines somewhere and our headquarters came under attack by one tank and some infantry. Everybody was out in the snow to fight off the attack. I was out in the open with my bazooka and wondering if I could be so lucky as I was in Holland when I got two tanks.[128]

This tank was coming straight on with no chance to get a side shot. Trying a frontal shot is like committing suicide. Off to our right a tank destroyer came out of the woods and put a round into the tank and it went up in smoke.

---

[128]Koskimaki, *Hell's Highway*, pp. 315-16.

## CHRISTMAS DAY ATTACK ON CHAMPS

Frontal attacks by the enemy on the positions of the 502nd Parachute Infantry Regiment began with the shelling of the forward positions of "A" Company in the Champs area. The situation is described by the company commander, Captain Wallace A. Swanson:

On December 25th, Christmas morning, shelling started about 0300 and we had well over three to five minutes of continuous shelling. All of our communications were destroyed from our CP to the platoons. The only way we could get messages in or out was by runner – and that was dangerous because of the barrages but that was something we had to keep doing out of necessity.

The enemy attacked our forward positions in the eastern and northern edges of Champs between the 1st and 3rd Platoons. We had street fighting throughout the night with hand to hand, door to door fighting. The CP of 2nd Platoon had been set afire during this action. We now encountered large enemy forces in and around our front lines and behind it. The tank destroyers were committed to help clean out some of the enemy elements. This was going on around 0315 to 0400 in the morning.

As the assistant platoon leader for 2nd Platoon of "A" Company, 1Lt. Al Wise relates what happened shortly after midnight on Christmas morning in the platoon command post:

The CP of the 2nd Platoon with 1Lt. John Harrison (I was assistant platoon leader) on December 24, 1944 was situated in a farmhouse on the outskirts of Champs. Our men were dug in about 150 yards in front of the CP on the reverse slope of the crest of the hill which was about 300 yards in front of our front lines. The 1st Platoon CP was in another farmhouse on our right flank.

We stayed up until midnight Christmas Eve to wish each other a 'Merry Christmas' and then turned in. About 0225 our area came under very heavy shelling, lasting approximately 15 minutes. During a lull in the shelling, one of the men from our forward outpost came running into the CP requesting a medic, as one of the men on the outpost had been severely wounded in the back by shrapnel. As the medic and Lt. Harrison started to leave, they noticed some white-clad strange figures surrounding our CP and also the 1st Platoon CP. At approximately the same time a German machine gun, situated about 20 feet from one of the windows of our house, opened the attack by firing directly through the window into the house in which we were standing. At the same time, a machine gun on the opposite side of the house, fired alongside our house, preventing our using the door. The machine gun firing through the window hit our stove, upsetting same and setting the room on fire. About that time another Jerry team, using their bazookas, let go at the walls. We returned the fire but as we could see very little, the fire was out of control and smoke filled the entire house. We had to get out.

(A point of information – all this happened as I mentioned above, about 150 yards behind our front lines and, therefore, we did not know at that time whether our front lines had been overwhelmed or not. It so happened our lines were spread so thinly, as it was so bitter cold and dark, that Jerry had little trouble infiltrating behind our lines and seemed to know exactly where the platoon CP's were located.)

We went into the barn, which was attached to the house, as most barns are in Belgium, letting out the cows and saw that they were not fired on. The smoke, by this time, made observation nigh impossible so we made a mad dash for the hedgerow roughly 25 yards away. Luckily, seven of the men from the CP made it, but minus everything we owned – coats, gloves, bedrolls, blankets and grenades, with the exception of our rifles and ammunition.

We reorganized in the hedgerow and saw there was confusion all about. In the dark, it was impossible to tell enemy from friend. However, by this time our CP was a blazing mass and from the light it caused we could see the Jerries attacking the 1st Platoon CP. Lt. Harrison, with a couple of runners, went on ahead trying to locate our remaining squads, and seeing where our front lines were, if any, while we fired at the Jerries attacking the 1st Platoon CP trying to distract the enemy.[129]

For Sgt. Louis Merlano from the same platoon, there were several skirmishes – the most memorable being the December 25th battle. He wrote:

Company 'A' had the responsibility of protecting the Champs area. The 1st Platoon was on the right, 2nd Platoon was on the left and the 3rd was left of the 2nd. The outstanding parts were that 3rd Platoon covered one knoll and 1st Platoon covered the knoll on the right, out in front of the church and schoolyard. I happened to be up on the line with the mortar squad and the machine gun squad which was manned by Tippins and Sirocco. The rest of the 1st squad had foxhole positions along the line. We had several men in a house resting and warming up, taking turns and sending 4 to 5 people back and forth. Lt. (Maurice) LaGrave was back further, closer to the village of Champs and he had kept in contact with us by runners.

Along about midnight, I was going back to the house to check to see if some of the men were ready to come out on the line. I got caught in a terrific barrage and I had instructed the men that it sounded like we were in for an attack and asked them all to hustle up. As I was coming out of the

---

[129]From a letter Albert J. Wise wrote to Major Ivan G. Phillips at Fort Benning, Georgia on June 29, 1948.

cellar, I ran into several Germans. I jumped out through one of the windows. The men were all shooting as they were getting out of the doors. We were being overrun. I got back to Tippins and Sirocco and we fired as much as we could.

At that point, it looked like we were totally overrun and our hopes were shattered until we saw one machine gun over on the left – Fowler's weapon, had kept pace with what was going on so it was our intent to fire alternately with them although they didn't know if we were still around or who it was that might be on the right.

This went on through the night. After being overrun, we turned our guns around back toward Lt. LaGrave who then met the Germans head-on and now we really had them in a pincers.

PFC. Werner C. Lunde remembered that his company didn't see much action until Christmas morning and then the roof fell in on some of them. He was one of those who were asleep in that platoon command post. He wrote:

I should have gotten back to our line. I feel real bad about that. I still don't know how so many Germans could get past our guard posts without being seen. By the time the guys on guard woke us up, we were completely surrounded. There were several tanks right outside the door. That was the beginning of the worst four months of my life.

## CPL. FOWLER'S GUN

A weapon that receives proper maintenance is the one that performs best when its use is critical. That is what Cpl. Willis Fowler wrote about concerning actions which took place on Christmas Eve and Christmas Day. He is the machine gunner referred to by Sgt. Louis Merlano in his earlier narration. Fowler describes the action:

The afternoon of December 24, I decided to clean my machine gun. I took it apart and cleaned it thoroughly – put it back together and set the head space. I was pleased with the sound of the head space on that gun.

That night, we went to bed. This included our squad leader, Sergeant Charles Asay and others. We were with our squad in a potato shed alongside of a road near Longchamps.

About 0230 in the morning of the 25th, the Germans attacked with artillery. The shelling woke us up and Sgt. Asay took the rest of the squad across the road from the potato house. I stayed with Pvt. Bill Emerson, who was my assistant gunner. He was on the gun at the time. I awoke and went out to where he was in the gun emplacement. He hadn't been firing the machine gun and I needed to get that gun in action.

As I began to fire the machine gun across the opening in front of us, we could hear the Germans hollering as the bullets hit them. My machine gun was the only one that was firing at the time. I had cleaned it and had it in good working order. The other machine guns were froze up. They were stuck, unable to operate. Some of the men were urinating on the guns to unfreeze them. Since my gun was the sole MG firing, other people began to bring me ammunition. From the time the attack started until daylight, I was on the machine gun, firing out into the area to our front. I don't have any idea how much ammo I expended from then until daylight.

As a member of Sgt. Charles Asay's squad, PFC. Ted Goldmann was jarred awake by the noise of artillery explosions and machine gun fire heard in the potato shed where he and others were sleeping in the hay. Bastogne was his first combat experience. He wrote:[130]

A little after 2 a.m. on the 25th, we were awakened and told the 2nd Platoon outpost reported tanks and half-tracks moving up the road toward us. Our only heavy weapon was the TD which came up at dark each evening and withdrew at dawn each morning. We ignored it until it actually happened and at 3:15 it did happen. All the artillery the Germans had, broke, and we scurried for our holes. The squad on the right side of the road wasn't so lucky. Four men were in the house with the barn and two men were in a haystack when the Germans infiltrated. Only two men were on their MG. The Germans brought up two tanks to the outpost along with infantry and, since there was no telephone, they had no orders to withdraw. Anyway, the tanks had them covered. The corporal, Jimmy Goodyear, who escaped in March, said these six men on the outpost were also captured, that he had seen them all, which substantiated our beliefs.

Our squad was ready and God was with us and the Heinies started doing stupid things. They shot flares into a totally dark sky and we took advantage of them. They fired haystacks and then got in between us and the blazes to form perfect silhouettes and down they went. Fowler was a miracle man with that LMG. He deserved all the credit he got along with the Silver Star.

The TD opened fire on the two tanks by the outpost as soon as they got on the crest of the high ground and knocked one out with the first shot and damaged the second with the following shot. The Heinies managed to pull both back before dawn. The Germans, in their eagerness and self-confidence, even set up an aid station in the house with the barn attached. Sgt. Asay

---

[130]Privates John Ballard and Ted Goldmann had made a pact earlier that if one or the other survived the war to tell about it, the survivor would write to the other's family, describing what life had been like for them in combat and the action in which the one had lost his life. This description is part of a letter which Ted Goldmann wrote to the father of his buddy, Johnny Ballard in June of 1945.

threw grenades right into their midst and scattered them like a busted vase. He was wounded in the jaw by a piece of his own grenade. That house was an odd one – four Americans hiding upstairs, a German aid station on the main floor and 18 Belgian civilians hiding in the basement. The Germans kept taking it on the chin and getting nowhere.

S/Sgt. Robert Barnes of "A" Company remembers an incident in which enemy soldiers used white snow gear to camouflage their approach to his machine gun position. He wrote:

It was a cold winter night. Sgt. Everett Brown and I were taking our turn on a .30 caliber machine gun. It was time to be relieved so I went and aroused the two who were supposed to take over. After being relieved, I went to my slit trench which had straw and was partially covered and started getting in my sleeping bag. The bottom third was frozen from getting into it with wet shoes and I had a tough time getting my feet to the bottom. This was the type of bag that some of the men who didn't have overcoats, cut off the bottom half, cut slits for arm holes and used them for coats.

Suddenly, I heard what sounded like a moan from the direction of the machine gun. I looked over and saw a figure in white making arm motions. I ducked down in the foxhole, not knowing if other Germans were around. I heard another moan that was real low. My first thought was that a bayonet or knife was being used. I suppose this helped put me to use as I raised up, pointed my rifle, could not see the sights, and fired. The figure in white fell and, at the same time, a grenade went off. Shots were fired at me from my flank. Four or five shots were fired and then all was quiet. I went over to the machine gun and the figure in white was a German officer, shot in the head. The grenade was a concussion type and was dropped by the officer when hit. As there were only two, I assumed that it was a reconnaissance patrol trying to pick up a prisoner. The two men on the machine gun received slight wounds from the grenade but didn't put them out of action, which was good as we only had 17 men left in the 2nd Platoon at the time. The German who fired at me from the flank made a getaway. With all the firing and grenade exploding, only Fred Terwilliger on the radio heard anything. The men were that tired and exhausted. The two who were on the machine gun had agreed that one would rest while the other stayed awake. The only trouble was he dozed off, also. When confronted by the German, he tried to holler, but nothing came out, only moaning sounds. All's well that ended well.

While Cpl. Willis Fowler was busy keeping the German infantry on the ground to his front, his sergeant, Charles Asay wasn't far off directing the remaining members of his squad. He wrote:

The Germans hit us on Christmas Eve. We fought an all-night action at Champs. The squad on the right was overrun. I spent the night directing fire and throwing hand grenades on the right to keep the Germans off our flank.

We had no wounded or dead. I like to think I took good care of my men. I had the only squad left on line in the platoon.

The continued involvement of 2nd Platoon in the actions is described by Lt. Al Wise, the assistant platoon leader. He wrote:

At about 0400, there was another lull in the firing and at this time Lt. Harrison, having again reorganized his platoon, returned knowing approximately where most of the men in our platoon were located.

Privates Mullen and Terwilliger, a medic and myself, decided to try going forward to our advance CP and see if we could aid the wounded man who was still up there. We climbed the ridge without incident, except for scattered rifle fire, and found the CP still intact. The medic, with another man from the outpost, carried the wounded man back to our lines and I remained at our outpost with Pvt. Grosvenor for the remainder of the night.[131]

With the sounds of heavy action coming from the "A" Company sector, 502nd Regimental Headquarters wanted to know if reinforcements were needed. Capt. Wallace Swanson was concerned with all the movement going on in front and behind him. He felt friendly troops coming in as reinforcements might be fired on in the early morning darkness. He wrote:

During the early morning hours of the 25th, the regimental command wanted to know if we could use additional help. I informed them that even though there was lots of action going on in Champs, I did not feel as though any more troops should be sent in because of the darkness. There was no need to send 'B' Company down in the woods because we couldn't know who was enemy and who was friendly. So they sent 'Baker' Company to a road block area between our positions and the regimental command.

Captain Swanson went on to cite the bravery of one of his machine gunners on outpost duty who did so much to keep the enemy from making further inroads into his positions. He added:

One of the mainstays who helped turn the tide in our favor was Cpl. Willis Fowler, a machine gun corporal who had taken over the machine gun because he had to have more effective fire power on the enemy that had come down from the higher ground. From the hillside that was out in front of us, the enemy had overrun the outpost on top, and came down the side which was a trail-like road. The enemy tanks were sitting up on the hillside just back of the ridge and blasting our positions down in the village of Champs. The tanks did not move into our area, but the infantry did and, with Willis Fowler handling the machine gun in such a magnificent way, stopped the enemy infantry from advancing with a large additional force.

---

[131]Wise, op. cit.

Many of the enemy were wounded or killed because of Fowler's action on the machine gun along with the work of other riflemen taking position and picking off others in the enemy advance.

In his forward machine gun position, Cpl. Willis Fowler had continued to beat the enemy infantry to the ground through the pre-dawn hours. As the first faint streaks of dawn appeared on the eastern horizon, there was a brief respite before the enemy attacks were renewed. Fowler describes a situation in which he became the target of one of the tanks:

As darkness waned, action slowed down somewhat. We had a little breather but just after daylight, to our front, there was a ridge and up over this ridge came four German tanks. They got to the top of the ridge and stopped. They just sat there and I told Emerson that we'd just stay down in our hole which was beside the potato house. We'd be very quiet and inconspicuous. I'm sure the tankers could probably see us but whether they did or not, I was looking at them when a column of German soldiers came up behind the tanks. They started down the ridge toward our location. I told Emerson to stay low; I was going to fire on them and then the tanks would open up on us.

I caught the column from front to rear and every man fell. I'm not sure whether I killed every one of them or not but I'm sure I killed some. While I was firing, I saw a muzzle blast from one of the tanks. I immediately dropped down in the hole. The projectile went over our heads and hit the corner of the potato house where we had dug in – just above our heads. The explosion and concussion of the shell shook us all around that hole and, after we regained our composure, we checked each other for wounds. We were both okay. I said, 'We'll stay down in the hole – if they see any movement, they'll fire again.' We stayed down in that hole – I don't know how long. I cautiously peeked out from the edge, having removed my helmet so just my eyes and the top of my head were exposed. It was then I discovered the projectile had damaged the machine gun. I peered up at the ridge and the four German tanks were still setting there. There wasn't any action. We stayed down a couple minutes longer and I decided to take another look. As I peeked over the edge this time, I noticed the tanks started moving back down the ridge from which they had arrived earlier. I learned later they didn't advance because they had lost their supporting infantry.

## ENEMY TANKS HEAD FOR ROLLE

As was the case for "C" Company of the 502nd Regiment, which had been in the process of moving north to help "A" Company, "B" Company got the word to move toward Longchamps from Hemroulle in the pre-dawn hours. Part way during the move, one platoon of the company was recalled and ordered to set up a blocking position south of Champs facing the direction of the attack which was coming through the positions of the troops of the 401st Glider Battalion. PFC. Amos Almeida of "B" Company remembers the move and the resulting action:

> We had been going back and forth, relieving one unit after another. On Christmas Day we were called to go toward the town of Longchamps. On the way over, we were shelled. Some of the unit had to keep on going, but we were called back to stop a tank attack which consisted of six enemy tanks and a company of infantry. We didn't have time to dig in so we just stayed down in a ditch. We had two bazookas, a machine gun and some riflemen. There was no time for us to position ourselves before we were attacked. About that time, two of our tank destroyers came out to help us as the enemy attacked in full force. Tanks were firing their artillery and machine guns – their infantry was firing at us. We held our fire until the last moment. We knocked out five tanks and killed all the men in their infantry. We lost one man and two TD's.

After word of the German attack in the vicinity of Hemroulle and Champs had been received at Regimental Headquarters, Captain Joseph Pangerl, the prisoner interrogation officer for the 502nd, had gone forward in the early morning darkness so he would be near the first enemy troops to be captured so he could interrogate them right on the scene of the actions. He has this description of what could have been a fatal action on his part:

> I went over the bridge between Rolle and Champs in the dark on December 25th to interrogate PW's before dawn. Our dug-in troops wondered why we didn't blow up as they had mined it without telling HQ – and the mines were within our lines. (We later found out that after they had laid the mines, it had snowed, gotten warm during the day and the melting snow later froze and made the mines inoperative. Thank God!)

While at a location near Champs, which had already been hit by tank and infantry attacks in the pre-dawn hours, 1Lt. Samuel B. Nichols, intelligence officer for 1st Battalion, spotted enemy armor and infantry moving along a ridge as dawn was breaking. They seemed to be headed toward Rolle. Nichols raced ahead on foot, arriving winded, he announced to regimental commander Colonel Steve Chappuis "there are seven enemy tanks and infantry coming over the hill to your left!"[132]

For a short period of time there was turmoil at the Rolle chateau as cooks, clerks and radiomen were collected under Headquarters Company commander Captain James C. Stone. They were rushed west to the next hill which was a dominant feature and took up positions close to the road.

---

[132]*Rendezvous with Destiny*, p. 550

One of the communications men who rushed forward into the defensive position was S/Sgt. Kenneth H. Garrity. He remembered seeing one of his friends stop a tank with a bazooka. Garrity wrote:

Early in the morning of Christmas Day, orders came for all personnel to 'get out on line' – meaning cooks, truck drivers, communications men, walking wounded, etc. German tanks were approaching the chateau. I saw Sky Jackson with a bazooka crouched behind a stone wall. Don't know how many tanks he got that day but he was awarded the Silver Star for the feat.

The earlier shelling before midnight had been enough to send others scurrying to less exposed shelter but PFC. Leonard Swartz, the regimental mailman, had placed two full ten gallon water cans at the head end of his sleeping bag and had gone to sleep, unaware of the shelling until wakened by his buddies. He remembered:

All of a sudden, I heard these guys laughing. I looked up from my sleeping bag and there were all these rocks and rubble on the bag. I glanced around and there was a big hole in the wall. The guys said, 'Boy, he can sleep through anything!' They yelled, 'Germans are coming – we've got to go out and dig foxholes and get ready to fight a war!'

I went out there and it was like digging in cement. I got next to a hedge. Four Mark IV's came and a couple of TD's knocked out some of them and the rest were disabled by bazookas. The Germans piled out of the tanks and they were mowed down. It was just red blood on the snow.

As a member of the Demolitions Platoon of the 502nd Regiment, Sgt. "Sky" Jackson won his second Silver Star on Christmas Day in front of the regimental headquarters when he disabled an enemy tank, part of the attacking force which was threatening to overrun that command post. It was extremely cold when he and his fellow troopers were rushed out to set up a hasty defensive line. Jackson recalled:

What I remember was hearing the shells from the tank guns and the mortars dropping. It was so cold – the temperature had dropped 22 to 23 degrees in a day.

We had mined a bridge leading to the chateau, but it was so cold that everything froze and we couldn't blow it up. One tank stopped right in the middle of the bridge and we couldn't blow it up.

I ran out of the door and saw five tanks coming through the snow with the German infantrymen riding on them. I ran and got a bazooka as the rest of our guys ran out and reinforcements started coming in from the town. I hit the first one in the track and knocked it out. Then we got the others – killed all the infantrymen.[133]

---

[133]Ferretti, Fred. *New York Times* writer, interview of Schuyler Jackson in *Stars and Stripes*, August 8, 1984.

1Lt. Henry Barnes, a medical evacuation officer from the 326th Airborne Medical Company had returned during the night from Bastogne where he had transported wounded to the Division medical facility. Now he was back at the 502nd aid station in the barn. He wrote:

I dozed sitting on a parachute in a candle-lit barn while talking to the wounded. At dawn, most of them had drifted off to sleep.

I awoke when someone shook me and whispered that enemy tanks were crossing a mined bridge and told me further that the mines didn't detonate as the batteries were low. Not knowing anything about mines, I tried to figure what he meant by batteries. Someone else ran up and said we were going to be captured.

I thought of stories told by other medical officers who had been captured. One had had a German run up, point a tommy gun into his ribs, pull the trigger and laugh while holding up the magazine in the other hand. Another told me he wasn't even bothered as long as he was treating wounded Americans and Germans. I remembered we had no German wounded here.

The noise of firing, explosions and shriek of incoming shells increased with daylight. A medical officer ran over to me and told me to get ready to burn all our medical books of tags so the enemy couldn't know how many men we had lost. Everyone was running around; suddenly the courtyard was cleared and most of the able-bodied personnel followed a captain down the road and took up defensive positions along another road.

Here it was Christmas morning in a Belgian chateau with a room full of wounded and outside all hell was breaking loose. I glanced at the wounded and smiled comfortably and went outside behind the chateau and relieved myself.

I came running back picturing myself walking along with my arms over my head, a prisoner of war, when I ran into the room we used for our dressing room. The shooting was just outside the wall and the sound of grinding tanks could be heard. Someone shouted, 'Burn the tags!' and I started a small bonfire, watching the smoke curl up. We heard there were seven tanks outside with about a company of infantry.

I rushed in to comfort the litter wounded and gave one a rifle to calm him. A shout caused me to run back into the aid station and, on our walkie-talkie, a shrieking voice shouted in German, filled the room with discordant sound. One medical officer listened in disbelief and said that it must be one of the tank commanders outside giving orders. It shut off and left us bewildered.

Back to the wounded I went and told them what was going on and said I would stay with them when someone ran in shouting, 'We're getting them!' I whooped with delight and ran down the slope. Four German tanks were in sight, smoking and the ground was strewn with bodies, some clothed in white.

One soldier pounded me on the back, kept shouting that he had hit one tank with his bazooka, but in the excitement had not armed it and all that happened was a loud clang when it hit the tank.

Intelligence section member, Cpl. Newman L. Tuttle remembered that even in the heat of battle there is one wisecracker who comes up with a relaxing remark. He wrote:

On Christmas morning practically all of the personnel from regimental headquarters of the 502nd were in foxholes waiting and ready for the Germans. After a rather fierce encounter, several enemy tanks were burning. I could hear some of the enemy wounded screaming in burning tanks. If one thought of trying to rescue them, he would probably be killed in the attempt. Along about 0930 or so in the morning, my good buddy Louis Migliarese poked his head out of his foxhole and yelled over to me, 'Tuttle, this is worse than a snowball fight in south Philly!' That really made me laugh and broke the tension of the encounter which had just ended with our having stopped the Germans once again.

Captain Jim Hatch, the regimental operations officer had this description of a frustrated attempt to stop the remaining tank which had not been put out of action in front of Rolle:

After the fire fight, most of the infantry on the tanks were KIA. The tanks started to pull out. All but one were knocked out. I figured it would head for the road leading to Champs, which would be the shortest route back to their front lines. There was a short bridge on the road which our demolitions people had prepared to blow up if needed. I got the demo man and we ran to the bridge and got there before the tank and we hid in the stream bed and had the two wires ready to rub together when he hit the bridge. Sure enough, the tank was headed for the bridge. Just as he got there, the demo man put the two wires together and we expected the tank and bridge to go up together. Needless to say, the snow-ice for some reason had shorted out the demolition and the tank went over the bridge and the span remained solid. All we could do was cry!

## THE FIGHT CONTINUES IN CHAMPS

The appearance of the enemy tanks on the hilltop in front of Cpl. Willis Fowler's machine gun position on the "A" Company front heralded the start of the daylight attack which is described by 1Lt. Albert Wise. He had stayed at the outpost with Grosvenor and others. He wrote:

At about 7:30 a.m., I was relieved and returned to the platoon. About 0800, Pvt. Grosvenor and the remainder of the outpost were dislodged from their position by a Jerry strike which signalled another major German push on our whole line. At this time, it was light and naturally we could see the Jerry infantry and tanks coming over the hills and could prepare a reception for them.

On the Christmas Day attack I believe the Jerry attack would have penetrated our lines, as they had the commanding heights of the hill to fire down upon us. They had my section of the platoon pinned down. However, a forward observer from the artillery crawled up to me and said that all they had were six rounds of 105mm, which they would fire. He mentioned something about a new type magnetic fuse which would explode when the shell was in the vicinity of the target. He also mentioned that these shells had not been used before now as intelligence had not wanted any duds falling into enemy hands. I have an idea these might have been the first application in the ETO of the radio proximity fuses, used so successfully in the Pacific.

We fired one round for range, which by luck was excellent and fired four rounds for effect. I never saw a more beautiful sight; all four bursts detonated approximately 100 feet over the Jerries and I guarantee the hill was cleared. At this time, I took one squad of men and went up the hill, taking same with no casualties. We did inflict several on the Jerries.

The balance of Christmas Day was quite uneventful except for rooting out any Jerries remaining in the village houses. The remainder of the subject is history.[134]

Because 1st Battalion of the 502nd Parachute Infantry Regiment spent considerable time in the Champs area, PFC. Ted Goldmann was able to sketch the battle area which he included with his letter to the parents of Johnny Ballard. Using his sketch, he related how the action unfolded. The appearance of the tanks on the hillside, as mentioned earlier by Cpl. Willis Fowler, comes into his continuing narrative. Goldmann describes:

At 0700 or a little earlier, four tanks appeared on the high ground to our left flank and two opened fire on the TD which they soon disabled (knocked out the motor rendering it useless for the remainder of the battle but injured none of the crew). As you can tell by the map, their line of fire was directly over the position occupied by our squad. The shack marked 'X' received four direct hits which ruined it along with three chickens we had killed and plucked for Christmas dinner. Fowler could have touched the side of the building from his hole and so could Johnny. The shells hit only a few feet away. Even the shoulder rest attachment on the back of the LMG was riddled with shrapnel. Lenz's and William's rifles even blew up and still the squad

---

[134]Wise, op. cit.

was unscathed except Asay's jaw. Call it luck or what have you, we call it God's will. Although six men in the other squad were surrounded by the Germans, when daylight came and the Germans were forced to surrender or withdraw, those six came in unscratched also. Only the outpost was missing.

Those four tanks were driven off by aerial bursts from the hoarded supplies of artillery ammo, which we had practically none of, and the appearance of four P-47's. Lovely artillery, beautiful TD's, wonderful Air Corps; we had been hurting for sure and now we had won.[135]

Before daylight arrived on Christmas morning, many of the infiltrating enemy soldiers were in and among the farm buildings, some hidden in wood piles and others in haystacks. The church, a place of prominence, had been searched, but not too thoroughly as will be related.

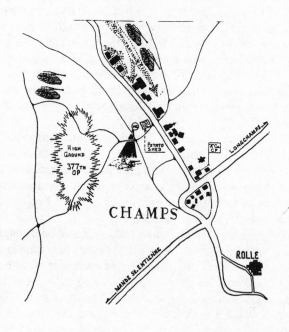

*Map 14*

---

[135]Goldmann, op. cit.

Sgt. Charles Asay remembers the assignment of going through the area to check it out for hidden German soldiers. He related:

Sgt. Zweibel and I were cleaning out houses. He went in the back door while I was backing him up. A sixth sense turned me and I was face to face with a German sergeant 25 feet away. I told him 'Hande hoch!' and, after what seemed like an eternity, he laid down his Schmeizzer. I had a rifle. He walked forward and 17 or 18 followed him out from behind a woodpile. I still have his Iron Cross (medal) dated 1939.

Near the church, Sgt. Louis Merlano found even more of them. With their capture, the attack was halted. He wrote:

At the crack of dawn we had quite a number of them in a haystack beside the church. When dawn came about, they all surrendered – a total of 80 prisoners which Captain Swanson came up and noted their number. It now appeared that we had finally squelched the action.

As the enemy soldiers had roamed almost at will through the "A" Company area in the early morning darkness, it was logical that they seek vantage points from which to view American positions when daylight arrived. Captain Wallace Swanson describes the action:

In an interesting action in Champs, the enemy had used a church steeple which was the highest point in the town to observe the action. We had men go up there to flush out the snipers and observers. These were some of the men we captured. After I asked the sergeant if every place in the church had been secured, he assured me that it had been done. I went up to see what I could view from the highest vantage point. As I was going up, I ran into a curve in the stairway and steps and as I was moving I happened to glimpse out of the corner of my eye the movement of a white sheet lying in the corner of the floor area behind some paste board and boards leaning against the wall. Realizing something was different, I told the object to come out, not realizing what, if anything, was there. Speaking in German, what little I knew of the language, I ordered 'it' to come out. The object under the sheet moved again and it turned out to be a German officer who had been in command of some of the troops who had entered Champs. I retrieved a pistol which he had in his hand and told him to move on down stairs. As I came out of the church doorway, the sergeant who had told me everything was clear, was almost flabbergasted when I brought a German officer from that church steeple area.

With this action, the men and officers of the different platoons searched out the buildings and barns, anything that might be a hiding place. Around noon time and early afternoon, everything was back to normal.

The sheets that had been provided for the troops of 1st Battalion of the 502nd Regiment a few days earlier when the snow fell, now proved their worth on Christmas Day. Major John Hanlon, battalion commander, describes the action:

The fighting that followed was the most vicious I ever knew. It was close in, immediate; once I was able to read the markings on an enemy tank and many times I could clearly make out the features of a dozen or so Nazi soldiers. At one point I met one of my men, draped in his sheet, standing at the corner of a house with his eyes fixed calmly on six Nazis approaching from the rear.

'How do you suppose they got inside our circle?,' I asked.

'Beats me,' he replied casually, 'but they'll have a hell of a time getting out.' And so they did. That private had the stuff of which good soldiers are made.

Our improvised camouflage was paying off everywhere. One bazooka team stationed at a crossroads watched a tank close in. The two men waited until the tank was within 50 feet of their position. Then, with one perfect shot, they knocked it out.

Suddenly, almost as if on signal, the fighting ended; and eerie calm broken only by the crackling of burning tanks, came over the field. We had a bag of 50 prisoners and there were many enemy casualties. Our own losses were light.[136]

In citing the actions of others who provided much assistance to the men of his unit, Captain Wallace Swanson singled out the artillery observers and the men of the 705th Tank Destroyer group. He wrote:

During this Christmas Day encounter with the enemy, the field artillery observer, 1Lt. Jim Robinson and his radio operators gave me terrific support by calling in the needed artillery shelling on the advancing enemy. As daylight came to our area, men of 'A' Company were able to pick off a lot of enemy infantrymen who were moving towards our line.

The other action that helped out was by the tank destroyers which were called on to help rout the enemy who had infiltrated into several homes and buildings. Sgt. Valletta took his tank destroyer forward and blasted into where our men knew the enemy had taken refuge. Sgt. Ted Beishline, our first sergeant, helped him move in the right area and showed where the enemy was holed up as stated by our men. We were able to stop further advances by the enemy during this encounter by using the tank destroyers direct firing into the enemy position even though close in contact with our men.

---

[136]Hanlon, op. cit.

## THE MAVERICK TANK

It is still a mystery where the maverick tank had been hiding. The tank battle had ended about 0930 with the last ones being destroyed in the Rolle vicinity. But, as mentioned by Captain Jim Hatch in his story, the demolition charge which was to have blown the bridge and tank skyward, was a dud. In mid-afternoon, a lone tank suddenly made an appearance from the direction of Bastogne and headed in a northerly direction.

In the "A" Company CP, Captain Wallace Swanson was being visited by S-3 commander Jim Hatch, Major John Hanlon and Captain Joe Pangerl when the officers were surprised by a commotion. Swanson wrote:

As the day continued on with fighting in and around Champs, the regimental S-3 officer, Captain Jim Hatch came forward to my CP and while we were talking over the situation, he asked how we were holding up. We heard a loud rumbling noise outside the house we were using as the company CP. We wondered what was going on out there. We both went to the front door and, as we opened it, we saw this German tank go by from our rear toward our front lines. We realized we had no weapons that would do any good. We shut the door and Hatch said, 'This is no place for a pistol!' That tank went out through our position in Champs. As it was clearing our front line area, Pvt. John Ballard, using his bazooka, knocked out the tank. He did it with two hits. Other elements, anti-tank 57mm guns and others may have fired but it was the Ballard bazooka that knocked the tank out and destroyed the tank crew by small arms fire by our men.

As the prisoner interrogation officer, Captain Joe Pangerl was on the "A" Company field phone in conversation at the time. In a V-Mail letter to his parents, Pangerl describes the tank incident:

The first I knew about it was when I was telephoning with my back to the door, looking out of the window. About four men, including one of my majors, climbed over me to get out of the window. The last one said 'Scram – there's a German tank outside the door!' In my imagination, I could see the 88mm gun pointing through the door ready to fire so, needless to say, I went out that window, telephone and all. Nothing, however, happened so I went around the front of the house and saw it disappearing up over the hill with men running after it shooting but of course not doing any damage. We finally got it with a bazooka.[137]

It was now mid-afternoon. The men were busy cleaning weapons and looking for additional ammunition and the troops were hungry. Pvt. Ted Goldman describes the situation:

---

[137]Pangerl, op. cit.

Food and bragging and post mortem of the battle were the order of the day now. Cleaned weapons and hunted ammo. My rifle – I traded off for another at supply. It had stuck at a crucial time and my hand was raw from beating back the bolt so I could load and extract rounds by hand.

Our chickens gone, the civilian houses all severely damaged more or less, we salvaged one loaf of bread and used some butter taken off the prisoners when we searched them and they were left with nothing but their uniforms, smelly German cigarettes and pictures.

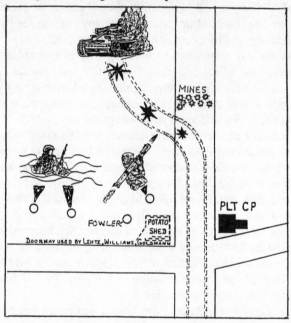

*Map 15*

Johnny was in his hole cleaning his rifle; Fowler and Curry in theirs. Lenz, Williams and I were slicing bread with a bayonet. I had a slice fixed when Johnny yelled to ask me to fix him one, which I started doing. I never finished. Fowler yelled, 'Here comes a German tank behind you!' Sure enough, a light-medium tank was coming up behind us with its machine gun blazing away. We ducked behind what remained of the potato shack doorway (Lenz, Williams and myself). On the enclosed map, you can find the location in relation to the other one. At point #1, tank ran up against Pvt. John C. Ballard, Jr. Here he shot the one remaining Heinie hanging on the outside. #2 marks where he hit it with the first round high on the back of the motor, just under the turret. #3 is where he hit it with the second bazooka round solidly in the motor. It stopped dead and was burning furiously. The crew came piling out to be met by a volley of lead from all of us. No more tank and all the crew was killed except one who had a radio on his back that Sgt. Bud Zweibel wanted to get intact. He was lying wounded and our men picked him up, his pants shot off and the radio ruined.[138]

At close hand to witness the final demise of the maverick tank was Cpl. Willis Fowler who was sharing a foxhole with Pvt. Harold Curry and verifies the action just described by Pvt. Ted Goldmann. Fowler wrote:

> In the middle of the afternoon, there came a tank out from the direction of Bastogne. It went past our position and cut off the road just after it got by us. Our bazookaman, Pvt. John Ballard, grabbed his bazooka, which was lying near him, and fired one round into the back of the tank and it stalled. He quickly reloaded and fired another round into the rear and it caught fire. The Germans began coming out ;and were picked off as they ran for cover.

The attack by the enemy soldiers advancing under cover of darkness on the "A" Company positions north and west of Champs had swept the outposts and forward observer position off the prominent hill where they had excellent observance of enemy activities in the distance. As the action areas in town had quieted with the capture of many of the enemy troops, the dominant hill position was still held by the enemy that afternoon.

"Baker" Company of the 502nd had been called back from its move toward Longchamps and ordered to retake the high ground (tree patch) west of Champs. PFC. Amos Almeida was a member of the one platoon which had been placed in a blocking position in front of Rolle beside the regimental headquarters personnel. When that action had died down, Almeida's platoon had joined the rest of "B" Company in the hill action. Almeida continued his story:

> From there we went to the top of the hill where the rest of the company was engaged in a battle with the enemy. We lost a few men there, among them Lt. Porter C. Little. We had set up a defensive line and were engaged with the enemy until dark.

All efforts by "Baker" Company to drive the Germans from the heights which provided such excellent observation of enemy movements to the north and west had failed. Now it became the task of forward observer Lt. Jim Robinson of the 377th Artillery Battalion to move the enemy off that piece of real estate. 502nd troopers kept up a steady stream of small arms fire which was only an annoyance to Germans who had taken over the observation post as well as the infantry foxholes dug on the heights. Lt. Robinson called for the fire mission just before the maverick tank went roaring up the road in Champs. Both events were very successful in their outcomes. Robinson wrote:

---

[138]Goldmann, op. cit.

Obviously, now we could be sure that no friendly troops were nearby. Earlier in the week, we had taken great care in registering an artillery concentration 75 yards to their rear to defend the OP. So now, no preliminary firing was necessary and the 75-yard adjustment was made as 'fire for effect' was called for. Like giant thunder claps 'Battalion – four rounds!' of time fire enveloped the dugouts and foxholes of our old OP. Gone for the moment was the pent-up frustrations of days of counting our scant ammo supply as massed artillery converged on the target.

As the barrages were ending, I heard a heavy rumbling to the rear followed by shots and blasts ringing out and I looked back to see one of our men with arms extended high in the air exulting in the sight of a burning tank with soldiers scrambling to get out of the hatch. Thinking it was our tank, I became momentarily alarmed that maybe he had become mad until I saw that the men crawling out were wearing German field uniforms.

These two events happening at the very same time are remembered as the change of momentum in the battle for Champs on Christmas Day, even though the battle did rage on.[139]

## SENONCHAMPS

The 1st Battalion of the 327th, along with the members of a "Snafu" force were now positioned between Senonchamps and Ile-la-Hesse with outpost lines extending almost to Mande St. Etienne. Acting sergeant Donald Woodland was now in charge of a group of soldiers from various units which had fled as the German armor had scattered their groups. His position was now near the location which had served as his battalion assembly area on the first morning on arrival in the Bastogne area. He describes the developing situation:

There were some stragglers in the group from some of the smashed outfits that had moved through Bastogne. I was wearing the overcoat with the 9th Armored Division shoulder patch so one of the enlisted men buddied up with me to share my foxhole. I took over a squad and deployed the men behind the MLR that was along the rim of a stone quarry. The ground was semi-frozen so that I had a difficult and painful time from the wrist wound.

There were two haystacks near our position, so we went over and took several arms full of hay to the holes. Several of the stragglers talked about sleeping in the haystacks but I vetoed the idea. A light machine gun was placed on our right flank with a field of fire to the open space on the slope below. Our left flank was a bazooka manned by a gliderman from the 327th.

[139]General Order Number 11 from Headquarters of the 101st Airborne Division dated 12 December 1945 cited 1Lt. James A Robinson for his actions with the award of the Silver Star.

Immediately to our rear and dug into the rear slope was an artillery unit with 155mm howitzers.

Several hours before dawn, our sector of the front exploded with a heavy concentration of artillery fire and what sounded to me like nebelwerfer (smoke mortar) shells. None of the shells were impacting in our immediate area, but the noise was disturbing. It was still dark when our line came under machine gun fire. The German machine gun was located below us and at a distance of approximately 250 yards. I fired a clip of rifle ammunition at the machine gun, carefully spacing the shots to achieve a spread of several yards. Our machine gun also opened up. The fire was right on target, but the tracers were ricochetting off the target. Not being able to see the target, I called for a cease fire so as to conserve ammunition.

With the first light of dawn, the intensity of the fire increased. From my vantage point on the rim of the quarry, it was possible to observe the action below. The glidermen of the 327th were moving into position in the open and placing machine guns and mortars into action. I could not see any of the German infantry, but the return fire was intense.

From his position at Ile-la-Hesse, Captain Walter Miller had this comment about the two 9th Armored Division tank commanders he had spoken about earlier:

I am sure these men also accounted for many German tanks on Christmas Day's breakthrough toward Bastogne. They were on the flank and had direct fire into the sides of the German tanks as they passed by. When they ran out of ammunition I requested resupply and when Division realized I had tanks, they were taken from my command and I did not see them again.

The left flank of "B" Company of the 327th Glider Regiment was adjacent to the positions of "A" Company of the 326th Engineer Battalion. In a major action for "B" Company, which occurred on Christmas Day on the southern perimeter, S/Sgt. Paul Slevey describes the enemy moving in on the "B" Company positions from the direction of Senonchamps and the woods to the south and west:

On December 25, early in the morning, a group of Germans came across the tracks into our area. They were pushed back into the patch of woods they came from. Pvt. Thomas McNamara took a Walkie-Talkie radio to the high ground next to the tracks and called the range back to the gunners on the 60mm mortars set up on a fire break. We also had a light tank in the woods with us and it was firing also. Further back, Headquarters Company set up their 81mm mortars. Twenty-one prisoners were taken.

A respite from front line duties had sent PFC. Harry Sherrard and Pvt. Eugene Walters to Bastogne on Christmas Eve. When the town was bombed twice during the night, the men were happy to be ordered back to their outpost duties on the road to Neufchateau. Sherrard added to his story:

Our outpost position on the road to Neufchateau had been abandoned – too far out, I guess. We took over some positions to the west of the road to Assenois, maybe 120 yards north of the cement pill box or guard house. We had a machine gun which we felt at the time as being a terrific amount of fire power. There were three of us in the position and I was on the gun just after dark when some movement was noted about 100 yards east and below our position. I couldn't see what it was and one of my 'hole mates' said it was two Krauts crawling along a fence line. He shot his M1 to show me their position. I fired with the machine gun but was too high. He fired a positioning shot again. The machine gun was too far back of the hill line so I moved it out as far as I could then started to dig up the dirt in front of our position with continuous fire until I could rout out the fence line where the two Germans were.

Ray Stockstill was in a foxhole with a machine gun, just east of a hedgerow. After the second day of attacks, I found out that Ray was either picked off with a shot in the head by a sniper who was near the little cement pill box or from a lucky shot in the attack.

To the left of the position of PFC. Harry Sherrard and his 'A' Company engineer buddies, PFC. Charles Kocourek was still on line with the troops of 2nd Battalion of the 327th. These troops were on a ridge northwest of Marvie. The action quickened pace once more. Kocourek related:

On Christmas morning, I was with Major Galbraith when shooting started up and I got to my foxhole. One of the guys hollered, 'The Krauts are dressed in white!' Most of the shooting was on my left. I couldn't see them. Us guys who were beside the road could not see them. Pretty soon the Germans gave up. There were 23 of them. One of our guys, Jimmy J. Gee, was in a foxhole and he saw the Germans coming up in the white uniforms. He opened up. If it hadn't been for Jimmy, we'd have been hurting. With the 23 captured, another 7 were killed. The Germans had American gloves and American overshoes.

There were some buildings right in front of us. When we looked in them we found a German officer with a P-39 in his hand. He was frozen but still barely alive. We took him into Bastogne but I doubt that he made it.

## MAPS AND AERIAL PHOTOS

The map situation was critical at Bastogne from the time the 101st Division arrived on the 19th of December through most of the month. Artillerymen had difficulties pinpointing targets. Appeals went out by radio to higher headquarters requesting maps and aerial photos of the Bastogne area.

The 10th Photo Group usually worked with General George Patton's 3rd Army and with the 4th Armored Division closing in on Bastogne. Patton, as well as the beleaguered troops, needed the photo maps to pinpoint the locations of the latest enemy concentrations.

Captain Rufus Woody of the 10th Photo Group drew the Christmas Day assignment to drop maps and aerial photos to the troops in Bastogne. He recalled 'receiving the request for updated photo reconnaissance so the artillery would know where the targets were hidden from our guns.'

Captain Woody describes the way the aerial photos and maps were to be delivered and what the conditions were like over the drop zone:

> The 9 x 9 inch aerial photos on a scale of 1 to 10,000 were packed in padded material and placed in a hinged, detachable gasoline tank like those used on long range missions and then jettisoned when empty. The day was overcast. I made one pass, looked for smoke and came down to 100 feet, dropping the container with the aerial photos.

> The vehicle of delivery was a P-38 Lightning twin-boom fighter plane. A second delivery was attempted the following day by Lt. Lanker and Capt. Woolcott as they were to drop updated aerial photos to the men at Bastogne in the same drop spot. However, both planes were shot down, never reaching the target area.[140]

Pathfinder records provided by PFC. John Agnew indicate that a P-38 did drop aerial photos on the drop zone at 1225 on the afternoon of December 25 with smoke being used for guidance.

## GENERAL MCAULIFFE'S CHRISTMAS MESSAGE

The following message was distributed to the troops at Bastogne on Christmas Day by Division Headquarters over the signature of Brig/General A. C. McAuliffe:

MERRY CHRISTMAS!

What's Merry about all this, you ask? We're fighting – it's cold – we aren't home. All true but what had the proud Eagle Division accomplished

[140]By coincidence, Rufus Woody had just returned from a reunion of his World War II fighter group the week before and his memories had been refreshed during the visits with his old friends. The above information was obtained during a telephone conversation with Woody on the evening of September 28, 1992. It was also learned that the plane losses on the 26th were due to friendly fire. The ground troops had not been alerted to the flight path and at that time, enemy fighter planes were making sneak sweeps of the Bastogne area. The anti-aircraft gunners took no chances.

with its worthy comrades of the 10th Armored Division, the 705th Tank Destroyer Battalion and all the rest? Just this: We have stopped cold everything that has been thrown at us from the North, East, South and West. We have identifications from four German Panzer Divisions, two German Infantry Divisions and one German Parachute Division. These units, spearheading the last desperate German lunge, were headed straight west for key points when the Eagle Division was hurriedly ordered to stem the advance. How effectively this was done will be written in history; not alone in our Division's glorious history but in World History. The Germans actually did surround us, their radios blared our doom. Their Commander demanded our surrender in the following impudent arrogance:

December 22, 1944

To the U.S.A. Commander of the encircled town of Bastogne:

The fortune of war is changing. This time the U.S.A. forces in and near Bastogne have been encircled by strong German armored units. More German armored units have crossed the river Ourthe near Ortheuville, have taken Marche and reached St. Hubert by passing through Romores-Sibret-Tillet. Libramont is in German hands.

There is only one possibility to save the encircled U.S.A. troops from total annihilation: this is the honorable surrender of the encircled town. In order to think it over, a term of two hours will be granted with the presentation of this note.

If this proposal should be rejected, one German Artillery Corps and six heavy A.A. Battalions are ready to annihilate the U.S.A. troops in and near Bastogne. The order for firing will be given immediately after this two hour's term.

All the serious civilian losses caused by this Artillery fire would not correspond with the well known American humanity.

The German Commander

The German Commander received the following reply:

22 December 1944

To the German Commander:

N U T S !

The American Commander

Allied Troops are counterattacking in force. We continue to hold Bastogne. By holding Bastogne, we assure the success of the Allied Armies. We know that our Division Commander, General Taylor, will say: 'Well Done!'

We are giving our country and our loved ones at home a worthy Christmas present and being privileged to take part in this gallant feat of arms are truly making for ourselves a Merry Christmas.

/s/ A. C. McAuliffe
/t/ A. C. McAuliffe
Commanding

## MEMORABLE CHRISTMAS MEALS

1Lt. Robert I. Kennedy will never forget the meal the men had been promised for Christmas. He describes the situation and the content of that meal:

Then there was the hot meal we were promised while the task force was in the line in the 327th sector. Due to heavy concentrations of artillery fire, the arrival of the meal was four or five hours late. It arrived in the middle of the morning on Christmas Day in marmite cans and consisted of one can of hamburger patties and one can of mashed potatoes so cold they were almost frozen but a welcome sight. No one had any mess kits or any utensils so each man reached dirty, bare hands into one can for one patty and with the other dirty hand for a fist-full of mashed potatoes – so I never forget my Christmas dinner of 1944.

At times food supplies were critically short. There were chowhounds who got more than their rightful share. Captain Dick Winters related his experience:

In the field, officers are the last men to go through the chow line. All enlisted men think that is one of the best rules ever set up in the officer code manual.

Chowhounds can finish off a canteen cup of beans in quick order and, in the dark on Christmas night, they could easily slip back in line for a second cup. That night, I was the last man to get to the container of beans – I got about a half canteen cup of bean soup. I guess that's why I've been trying to make up for that skimpy meal every Christmas since then.

That supply of bean soup must be the same batch S/Sgt. John H. Taylor recalls for his Christmas meal. He wrote:

I think it was Christmas night when we got word there was some hot food up there for us. We had to come and get it. That was no problem We got there and found it was nothing more than a marmite or utile food container holding bean soup with very few beans and some bread. It was the first hot food we had since arriving.

# 11. THE SIEGE IS BROKEN

The 26th of December would be a memorable day for the besieged soldiers in Bastogne. It would be remembered by the tankers of the 4th Armored Division as the day they were able to forge a path to the beleaguered garrison. The day promised to be another good one for the fighter-bombers of the Allied Air Forces in their missions to knock out the enemy armor hidden in the forests around the perimeter. The fighter-bombers of the German Air Force were up in considerable numbers strafing and bombing the front line positions as well as Bastogne. Cargo gliders would be utilized in limited numbers to bring in critically needed medical personnel with their equipment, along with some gasoline and ammunition.

In the 501st regimental sector, the enemy undertook an aggressive nighttime action in the 2nd Battalion area. West of Bastogne, the enemy made another attempt at breaking through the lines of the 327/401st Glider Infantry and 1st Battalion of the 502nd Parachute Regiment. On the southwestern sector the troops of the 326th Engineer Battalion were anticipating a breakthrough some time during the day.

## AN ENEMY PATROL IN THE CP

Patrolling behind enemy lines is an essential phase of warfare. As in the earlier campaigns, much of this activity on the part of the 101st and its comrades from the other units was of a defensive nature. With the enemy attempting to find openings into Bastogne, the Germans resorted very often to offensive (aggressive) patrolling. A good example of such an activity is provided by Pvt. Henry DeSimone and 1Lt. Robert P. O'Connell, both of whom served as members of "E" Company of the 501st Regiment.

Pvt. Henry DeSimone describes how the selection of a sleeping place for security was a smarter move than being near a source of heat. He wrote:

We had moved out there and were getting set up. We were getting Christmas carols (by the Germans) three hundred yards to our front.

We were supposed to maintain a patrol from 'D' to 'E' Company. There was a defiladed area between these two companies. In headquarters, when the officers overheard them talking, saying 'We can't maintain a patrol through there, we'll just have to take a chance that nobody comes up through that defiladed area.' It was to the right side of 'E' Company's main line of resistance.

A fifteen man combat patrol came through there late on December 25th. They broke through at about 0300 in the morning. In the meantime, this house – most of us had trench foot – we had this nice house and a beautiful, warm stove. Everybody was saying, 'Ah boy, this is great – we can sit next to the stove and thaw out our feet.'

It was a one-story house and out under the porch was a potato cellar. I convinced the guys that the cellar was where we ought to go, not next to the stove.

Everybody was taking turns on the phone. We would get the messages, checking in on the MLR and sending the word back to HQ. I had taken my turn on the phone, laid down on top of the potatoes in the bin and fell asleep. An hour and a half went by and I was shaken by one of my friends who said, 'Listen!' I could hear, in broken English, 'Hello!' and then the machine gunning of the door. They kicked the door in. Just imagine, if we had been lying next to the stove, we'd have been dead.

As the result of all the racket and turmoil, the enemy had captured one of the machine guns on the end of the MLR and put it up on the porch and were having a skirmish with our troops. This battle went on for about 45 minutes. 60mm mortars were coming in at them and the enemy was firing the .30 caliber MG off the porch back and forth. Finally, everything got quiet. Those of us down in the potato cellar finally got enough courage to come upstairs. We walked outside and it was daylight. We could see ten dead Germans lying around the grounds. This was how I spent Christmas night in Bizory in 1944.

Platoon leader, 1Lt. Robert P. O'Connell must have been Pvt. DeSimone's commander. He remembered that December 26 was the last day of combat for him in the war. An enemy patrol had infiltrated through the positions. O'Connell recalled:

On December 26th, about 0400 in the morning, my platoon of Company 'E', 501st, was on OPLR in the Bizory area when I was hit. My platoon sergeant, Dale Smith, was hit with me. It was pitch dark and a 40-man Kraut patrol had infiltrated into our lines. I was hit first with a Schmeizzer (machine pistol) burst and a while later with a potato masher grenade. Smith had a hole through his arm. We were such sad sacks we got to laughing about it – this was back at the platoon CP. We made enough noise so that the Krauts eventually pulled out. We held our lines.

The most memorable recollection of the Bastogne experience for PFC. George Willey occurred on the same night. He was in a different platoon of "E" Company and his actions fit in with the stories just related by DeSimone and Lt. O'Connell. Willey wrote:

After arriving in Bizory, we dug in behind some barbed wire where we could cover the road with fire. After five days we turned our positions over to 3rd Platoon. That night, Germans attacked us in a snowstorm and hit 3rd and took prisoners and killed and wounded others and set fire to the 2nd Battalion command post. We left our positions on a hill a quarter mile from Bizory and went into the village to drive attackers off but the Germans had already left.

## CONTINUING ACTION NEAR CHAMPS

On the 26th of December, "B" Company of the 401st Glider Infantry was again called on to defend against an enemy attack consisting of tanks and infantry. Company historian, PFC. Marshall Griffith recorded the actions:

At 0400 on the 26th, the Germans again attacked with tanks supported by artillery and infantry that penetrated the woods held by 'A' Company on our left flank. 'C' Company in reserve, immediately counterattacked with the help of our 705th TD and drove the enemy back.

Everybody, including the supply sergeant who was manning a .30 caliber machine gun, got an opportunity for revenge for the short rations of Christmas Day. The 2nd Platoon and the LMG section had a field day that evening. Bazookamen PFC. Marshall Griffith, PFC. William Star, PFC. John Volachin and PFC. Follman accounted for three vehicles. One of the vehicles produced a Lt. Colonel, a Major and a Lieutenant. These officers gave the Division valuable enemy information. A short time later, the 2nd Platoon and LMG's got three more vehicles.[141]

About five hundred yards to the northeast of the 401st Glider Battalion positions, men of the 502nd were alert for a continuation of German attacks. They had been hit hard in their positions before daybreak on the previous day.

"Able" Company of the 1st Battalion of the 502nd Regiment had been replaced by "Baker" Company in its former outpost positions northwest of Champs. The 3rd Platoon was sent out near midnight to set another outpost further west at a "Y" junction of two farm roads. PFC. Ted Goldmann, having made the parents of Pvt. Johnny Ballard aware their son had already destroyed one enemy tank with a bazooka, relates how they missed several golden opportunities the following day. The actions tie in with those just described by PFC. Marshall Griffith of the 401st. Goldmann wrote:[142]

We dug in by 0200 and went to sleep, two men on guard for two hours at a time. Next day we had things quiet enough, being an isolated target, we attracted no artillery. We spent the day watching a tank battle to our

---

[141]Griffith, op. cit.
[142]Goldmann, op. cit.

southwest and P-47's going into dives on tanks in the distance. We had front row seats to it all.

Also watched C-47's drop supplies and tow in gliders. After dark and we had settled down, we were told we were going up on the hill top again. This was way past where we were shot at the night before. Leery as heck, we went out and found nothing so we picked out our positions along the side of a woods and started back to the road for our MG, bazooka and our personal equipment.

Half way there, we saw a light tank come racing past the 401st headed for Champs. It got about two hundred yards past our 'Y' position and turned around and took off the other way only to be met by a hail of steel from two TD's, which left it burning. Our chance gone because we had just moved. Back at the holes at the 'Y' we found the tracks of tanks that were less than 18 inches from the side of Johnny's and my hole. Curses – foiled again!

Up the hill we returned only to witness four repetitions of the same event by two German jeeps, a captured U.S. command car and a half-track. One of the jeeps managed to get away. By now, we were thoroughly disgusted with having to move and missing our best opportunity, but we dug in.

The action which Pvt. Ted Goldmann and the members of his squad had witnessed from their hilltop position on December 26th is described in this G-2 report from Division Headquarters:

At 0430 and continuing until approximately 0930, an attack with infantry and armor of battalion strength was launched against our western perimeter in the vicinity of 513598 (map coordinates). The attack succeeded temporarily in penetrating the MLR but was quickly restored by counterattack and close-in fighting. In this same area, throughout the remainder of the day, the enemy continued his offensive effort which amounted to reconnaissance in force. At 2030 tonight, the enemy concentrated approximately 200 men and seven tanks in this area but the impending attack was broken up by particularly accurate artillery fire on their assembly area. At 2300 the enemy regrouped and was again dispersed by artillery fire. The northern, eastern and southern sectors were generally quiet throughout the period. However, the enemy continued his normal patrolling activities against our lines in these areas. The friendly air cover flew missions from daylight to dusk and their action confined the enemy's activity chiefly to passive resistance and prevented concentration of troops in any area within the immediate vicinity.[143]

---

[143]The above item was taken from G-2 Periodic Report #8, dated December 26, 1944 from the office of assistant chief of staff, provided by Captain Joseph Pangerl, prisoner interrogator of the 502nd Parachute Infantry Regiment.

## MEDICAL HELP AND GASOLINE

In his book, *The Glider War*, author James E. Mrazek describes a critical operation of getting medical personnel and supplies into Bastogne as the casualties continued to mount with no relief in sight. Division commander, General Anthony C. McAuliffe of the 101st had radioed an urgent request for such assistance. Mrazek wrote:[144]

Anxious for his wounded, McAuliffe radioed a request that surgeons and medical supplies be flown in by glider, the only possible way any surgeons could get to the 101st. Apparently about this time, (perhaps on the suggestion of the division commander, McAuliffe's G-4), LTC. Carl W. Kohls radioed the Air Force to try to get ammunition in by glider, as supplies going in by glider needed no such special packaging as was necessary for a parachute drop. The Air Force had retrieved gliders from the Holland operation and had hundreds sitting on French airfields and it remained now to load them and take off.

The Army sent out a call to its area field surgical units for doctors and technicians for volunteers to go into Bastogne with medical supplies. The requests were sent over rickety telephone lines deep into mountains and to the tents of these units. Officers listened and pondered and many said no, for reasons that those who have been to war surely understand. But by the 25th of December, a group of eleven stepped forward and said they would go to Bastogne to save those who could be saved.

'This was something we felt we absolutely had to do,' says Dr. Lamar Soutter of Concord, Mass., who, as a major, was the ranking surgeon on that mission. Soutter was with the 4th Auxiliary Surgical Group attached to General Patton's 3rd Army. Plans were discussed in Metz, where Soutter had been stationed throughout Christmas Day, about how best to get into Bastogne. At first the group was going to parachute in, then it was decided they would go by glider. The volunteers thought this was an unnecessary touch of drama, as none had ever been in a glider before.

On December 26th, the group left Metz in an Army truck heading for Thionville, France, where their flight would begin. 'We were supposed to drive over this one bridge, but the Germans had knocked it out,' says Soutter. They had to take another route, finally arriving at Thionville at 4 o'clock in the afternoon. On a chilly runway, the trench-coated medical officers loaded their supplies into the glider. The C-47 that would pull it by rope sat on the runway. They boarded the glider, five doctors and four technicians. There seemed little to talk about. A pilot and co-pilot entered

---

[144]Mrazek, James E. *The Glider War*, St. Martin's Press, New York, 1975, pp. 224-228.

the cockpit. Bastogne was 100 miles away. By now the casualty count had reached 1,500.[145]

The pilot for the glider was 1Lt. Charleton W. Corwin, Jr. of the 96th Squadron of the 440th Troop Carrier Group. He provided a brief description of his role in this "mercy" flight.

I believe that the glider flight into Bastogne, carrying the medics, was not only the only single glider combat mission in World War II, but also may have been the only glider to have landed twice on the same combat mission. We took off at Orleans, France. Benjamin F. Constantino was my co-pilot; the trusty towship, a C-47, was piloted by Captain Raymond H. Ottoman. . .

We landed on the fighter base strip at Etain, France. It was a thrill to bring that glider down on that P-47 strip.

While we were again briefed at the operations office at Etain, the medics loaded the glider. The briefing was an exact repeat of an earlier briefing we had at Orleans in the presence of Colonel Krebs, our group commander. Some fighter pilot captain conducted the briefing. It was a relief to know that we could have an escort, or support of four P-47's.[146]

A trip into a combat area at Christmas time came as a surprise to the glider pilots. At yule time, reports from the battle areas were still heavily censored so glider pilots and their ground crews had an opportunity to celebrate on Christmas and many were sleeping off the effects. Mrazek had this description of the experiences of one of the eleven glider pilots who participated in the December 26th glider mission:[147]

It was the 26th of December and still dark outside. At one base in France, 1Lt. O. B. Blessing was sleeping off the Christmas holiday. A crew chief yelled, 'Hey Lieutenant, they want to brief you!' He did not hear the first call, he was sleeping so soundly. The sergeant came over and shook him and repeated the message. Blessing went to the briefing shack as fast as he could throw on his clothes, with no inkling of what was 'cooking'. At 1432, he was in the air with a load of ammo, the most surprised glider pilot alive. Everything had happened so fast he was not yet fully about his wits.

Blessing's glider was one of eleven winging to Bastogne. In the mist ahead, several gliders flew with surgeons and aid men, jeeps filled with litters, surgical kits, ether and other medical supplies. These gliders landed

---

[145]Fourth Armored Division Association Newsletter, *Rolling Along.* "A Special Christmas Issue," 1985. pp. 51-53.

[146]From a copy of a letter written by Charleton W. Corwin, Jr. to W. H. Horn, editor and publisher of *Silent Wings* the official publication of the Glider Pilots Association, July 15, 1977.

[147]Mrazek, op. cit.

before the Germans encircling the division caught on that gliders were coming in. During the same December 26th operation in which Captain Raymond H. Ottoman towed 1Lt. Charleton W. Corwin, Jr. with his glider load of surgeons and medical assistants to Bastogne, another group of gliders was winging its way to the same landing zone from another airfield in France. An account of their actions is described in the 440th Troop Carrier Group History:

At about the same time that the first lone glider and tug were winging their way toward Bastogne, a second group of ten aircraft and ten gliders loaded with 2,975 gallons of 80-octane gas had taken off from Orleans at 1500 and were on their way in. Taking advantage of the early winter dusk, they flew in low over the enemy lines. However, the Germans had been alerted by the earlier plane and glider and they threw up a screen of small arms and machine gun fire at the formation from positions along a railroad about two miles from the town.

In spite of the fire, the tow planes held on course, cutting off the gliders directly over the landing zone at 17:20. The altitude at cut-off was approximately 600 feet.

As the glider pilots swung into their patterns and dove for the comparative safety of the ground, the tow ships pushed their engines to the limit and hedge-hopped out of the area, still followed by enemy fire.

Although the glider-borne gasoline took care of the most urgent need, the general supply situation was still inadequate. Troop carrier planes took off from bases in the United Kingdom and flew on instruments to carry 320 tons of food, clothing and ammunition into Bastogne. This material was put to immediate use by the 101st and other units.[148]

During periods of emotion and stress, the human body seems to reach back and provide for the moment when one needs extra strength. Such was the experience of PFC. Kenneth Hesler of "D" Battery of the 463rd Parachute Field Artillery Battalion when he was nearby to offer assistance at the glider landing fields. He wrote:

A medical supply glider landing in the open near the FO with incoming mortar fire in the area and being told, along with others, to get it unloaded and never before or after, lifting such heavy objects alone or carrying them to cover with such dispatch.

During the same day, other planes dropped bundles from bomb racks and equipment handlers pushed four or five bundles out through open doorways. A bundle sometimes strayed into an open area between the lines. These were contested for by the adversaries. Recovery of bundles was like finding Christmas presents – if you didn't understand the color-coded parachutes, one might be

---

[148]*DZ EUROPE. The Story of the 440th Troop Carrier Group. pp. 80-82.*

surprised as to what the heavy padded canvas container held in store. Pvt. Mike Zorich was on hand to get to a wayward bundle. He has this recollection:

Not too long after that, the skies opened up and the C-47's came over in formation, dropping huge bundles with parachutes. One bundle came down right in front of us, ready to land in German-held woods. A couple of the men and I decided to attack the woods, knowing that the Germans would be excited to see some crazy guys running across the snow toward them. They managed to get away and we sort of 'captured' this big bundle that dropped from the sky. Quickly, we opened it with our knives only to find hundreds and hundreds of packs of Old Gold cigarettes! That was something to remember. There weren't any medical supplies, ammo, or food – just Old Gold cigarettes! When we got back to the lines, we really caught hell from the C.O. and Sergeant Houston.

*101st Division command post personnel watch as resupply planes drop bundles on December 26. The antennae extending above the trees are part of the radio equipment of the 101st Airborne Signal Company. (Krochka photo)*

## DELAYED GLIDER FLIGHTS

Other gliders had been scheduled for tow to Bastogne from the air base at Chateaudun on the 26th but the weather conditions were poor. A veteran of three glider missions behind enemy lines, Flight officer Case Rafter made his only flight in support of the 101st Airborne Division at Bastogne on December 27th after a delay of one day. His first recollection is of a group of paratroopers from the 17th Airborne Division. They had been flown to France from their bases in England and were scheduled to move to the front shortly. Rafter wrote:

After Christmas, 1944 and before New Year's, evidence of the Battle of the Bulge began to be seen at our field. One group of paratroopers in planes had stayed overnight. They were heading for the front and the idea was to have them sleep in the C-47's down at the field. Most of the glider pilots and power pilots and enlisted men went down to the planes and invited the paratroopers up to sleep in our warm tents. The troopers were glad to do this and also appreciated the drinks that were handed around as there was plenty of liquor in the camp after the liquor ration had been started.

After the paratroopers had gone on, all the glider pilots were called out to the company street and informed that an airborne division had been surrounded by Germans and that they had to be resupplied from the air by gliders. Captain John Neary, our immediate commander, called out the names of the pilots who had volunteered to go on this mission. As I had only flown one mission, that to Holland, I was one of the volunteers and, in general, it was considered fair to even up the missions so those of us who had only one mission were sure to go into Bastogne. We went down to the flight line where the gliders had been loaded and lined up with the 91st Squadron first and the 94th last. I dressed in officer's shirt and trousers and with winter flying gear, which was leather with a wool interior and very warm and comfortable. I went down to the plane and got into the seat of the glider to which I had been assigned. This glider was filled with 155mm ammunition. I asked the men who had packed the glider if it would explode if it were hit. One said 'yes' and the other said 'no' and explained that he had stored all the detonating devices near the tail. This was very encouraging because the detonation – if it went off, would not set off the ammunition. On the other hand, it occurred to me that it would not have a very beneficial effect on the way the glider would fly. Since there was not very much I could do about it, I merely climbed into the glider, fastened the seat belt and my friends who had accompanied me from the tent – Horace Saunders, John Schumacher and Reggie – helped me to place a flak suit over my winter flying gear. At this point in the proceedings, I felt a cold breath of air in the rear and found that my shirt tail had come out. Nothing could be done about this and it was at this time that Schumacher said to me, 'Whatever you do,

Rafter, don't let the Germans capture you.' Thinking that he had some inside information on Germans treating glider pilots as 'franc tireurers,' I asked him why I particularly shouldn't allow the Germans to capture me. He replied that, 'if the Germans get you, they'll know we're at the bottom of the barrel.' This was an encouraging remark for my takeoff but, actually, I thought it was pretty funny and remember it to this day.

The day that we had been selected and sent down to take off on the mission into Bastogne, a freezing rain was falling which turned ice on the gliders and on the planes. We had already had one plane, which had not been properly maintained, dive into the ground just outside Chateau-dun and it was decided that, due to the weather conditions, it was impossible to fly the mission that day.

## CONTACT WITH THE ARMOR

The men of PFC. Harry Sherrard's platoon were in position a short distance from the enemy-held concrete pillbox which was about a hundred yards south and east of their foxholes and on the secondary road that led north from Neufchateau past Assenois and Clochimont. Help arrived to push the enemy out of the positions to the south and east of the "A" Company positions. Sherrard wrote:

The next morning things were pretty quiet. However, the Krauts still held the pillbox and the woods. Then a squad or platoon from 'C' Company (326th Engineers) came up behind us to help clean out the area. We fired and kept the pillbox covered until they advanced beyond our positions and routed out six Krauts from that position.

On the 26th of December, General George Patton's troops had reached the small hamlet of Clochimont. It was another clear day for air support and there were enemy aircraft overhead as noted in the diary entry of T/3 George Koskimaki positioned at Division Headquarters where he listened for messages from the approaching armor. Koskimaki noted:

December 26, 1944 – We had another clear day for air support. German fighters were up this morning and our planes shot down two of them. I watched one particular ME-109 lose its wings directly over our heads. Its momentum carried it well beyond our area where it crashed in flames. I saw no parachute. Another resupply was dropped. The 4th Armored Division is only two kilometers away this afternoon. I picked up a radio message asking our troops to be on the lookout for their advance elements.

The following item is from a copy of a letter which was written by 2Lt. Charles Boggess, commander of "C" Company of the 37th Armored Tank Battalion of the 4th Armored Division. A short time earlier, he had received a battlefield promotion. Boggess describes the approach and contact with the defenders of Bastogne. He mounted the tank of his battalion commander, LTC. Creighton Abrams, for his instructions:

I mounted his tank that afternoon and we studied a well-worn battle map. He decided that 'C' Company would take a little known secondary road leading from Clochimont, through Assenois to Bastogne, a distance of approximately 3-1/2 miles. He explained that there had been no recon work done on the road, but it was known that all this area was held by the enemy. If we could get through on this road, it might work well for a surprise attack. He gave me his familiar short and explicit order, which was simply, 'Get to those men in Bastogne.'

I called Lt. Wrolson and the seven tank sergeant commanders together, and the following plan was employed: As company commander, I would be in the lead tank (Cobra King) and I would set the speed of the attack – I would fire straight ahead. Lt. Wrolson would be in the second tank firing to the right, the following tank to the left – and so on down. Each man was given the route and the objective – each tank was to continue the attack to the last tank, if necessary, and with that, we were ready. Colonel Abrams gave us the familiar hand signal and we started to roll toward Bastogne.

It isn't possible for me to remember the names of all 45 men who made that run. My own tank crew consisted of Hubert J. J. Smith – driver, Milton Dickerman – gunner, Harold Hafner – bog gunner and James G. Murphy – loader – all battle proven veterans. I was told later that Company 'C' carried a 46th man with them on the run. One soldier returning from the hospital, on a supply truck, jumped off, ran, caught the last tank and managed to wedge himself in it. Where they found room inside a tank for him, I'll never know. I guess he just got there in time to see his company moving out and didn't intend to be left behind – such was the spirit of the 4th Armored man.

We moved at full speed, pumping heavy fire straight ahead and to the right and left of the road. As soon as my tank cleared Clochimont, I called for artillery fire on Assenois – almost immediately, the town seemed to erupt. Following directly behind our tanks was Captain Bill Dwight of the 37th Tank S-3 and the 53rd Armored Infantry. Still maintaining fire and speed, the column neared Assenois and I called Battalion for them to raise the artillery fire 200 yards. Due to the speed of the tanks and the time lapse of getting the command to the gun crews – our tanks entered Assenois under our own artillery fire. This allowed the momentum of the attack to continue. After clearing the town, the first four tanks ran into enemy resistance coming from both sides of the road. The other five tanks, along with Captain Dwight, were slowed briefly because of the resistance. Teller mines were thrown in the path of our oncoming tanks and half-tracks. Captain Dwight dismounted and personally directed the clearing of the road, thus allowing the five 'C' Company tanks to get through. Mopping up operations were continued in Assenois by the 53rd Armored Infantry.

*Map 16*

I saw a large pillbox ahead and ordered Dickerman to throw several rounds into it – it was demolished. I saw the enemy in confusion on both sides of the road. Obviously, they were surprised by an entry of this road, as some were standing in a chow line. They fell like dominoes. As we cleared the woods, we came upon a small, open field, where we saw multicolored parachutes – these had been recently used to drop supplies of food and ammo to the 101st Airborne Division. This meant that we were near the line defending the town. I slowed the tanks down and we cautiously approached what seemed to be a line of foxholes, spaced about 50 feet apart. Out of each hole, a machine gun was leveled at my tank, with a helmeted figure behind each gun.

*The small concrete pillbox southwest of Bastogne serves as a memorial to Lt. Charles Boggess and his men and the troops of the 326th Airborne Engineer Battalion through whose defenses the 4th Armored Division entered Bastogne on the afternoon of December 26, 1944.*

The men of the 101st knew full well that the enemy had been using American uniforms and equipment during the past few weeks and they were taking no chances. I called out to them, 'Come on out, this is the 4th Armored!,' but no one moved. I called again and again and finally, an officer emerged from the nearest foxhole and approached the tank. He reached up a hand, and with a smile said, 'I'm Lt. (Duane) Webster of the 326th Engineers, 101st Airborne Division – Glad to see you!' He was no more glad to see me than I was glad to see him! As I shook his hand, I knew that Company 'C' of the 37th Tank Battalion, 4th Armored, 3rd Army, had broken through the bulge and that the siege of Bastogne was over.

A few minutes later, Captain Dwight and Colonel Abrams met General McAuliffe. All nine tanks, with their crew of 45 (or 46) men, had made the drive successfully and Patton had missed his boast by only a few hours – his 3rd Army was in Bastogne. Time – 1640.[149]

The machine gun outpost position of PFC. Harry Sherrard happened to be in the location of the actual link-up with the armored troops fighting their way to Bastogne from the south. Sherrard describes the action leading up to the meeting of the two forces:

The next real excitement in this sector came on the day the 4th Armored came through Assenois to our lines. Our CP had apparently been in touch with them because we knew they were the cause of all the noise in Assenois on the other side of the woods about mid-afternoon. Besides, Lt. Webster was in one of the foxholes close behind our position. Late afternoon or early evening, just before dark, we saw the half-tracks and a tank or two coming up the slight hill with their .50's blazing and lighting up the snow around us. We just hoped they saw us in time to shut it off. They even took a couple shots with the 75's at the little guard house-pillbox to our left front. Then they stopped right by our hole and yelled that 'All is OK!'

That night, we ate their 'C' rations, drank some of their wine, had a bonfire and thought that maybe I should write home so my mom wouldn't have to worry about me. (She saved that letter for me.)

## AN UNCOVERED LIQUOR CACHE

Bastogne was bombed for the first time on Christmas Eve and the second time at 0300 on Christmas morning. The contents of buildings and basements were exposed to the elements and to opportunists.

Several soldiers recalled that the explosion of a bomb had ruptured the wall of a building revealing a hidden storehouse of wine, beer and liquor.

Sgt. Arthur Parker, a member of an artillery survey team, happened to make a big find the day after Christmas that would help make the holiday season a bit merrier. He wrote:

The day after Christmas I found a tavern in Bastogne that had been bombed. I found I could get into the basement where I located a full barrel of beer and it was a big one. I managed to get it out of the cellar and started rolling it back to Savy. I knew that I could not get it back there by rolling it so scouted around and found a manure wheelbarrow and got the barrel aboard and pushed it right by Division HQ and back to our area. I set the

---

[149]From a copy of a letter Lt. Charles Boggess wrote of his experiences in 1974 of the final rush to get into Bastogne. He had written the letter on the urging of his friend William Dwight. A copy of the letter was sent by Peter Hendrikx of Eindhoven, Holland, whose historical interest is General George Patton and the 101st Airborne Division.

beer barrel in the kitchen of the Battalion HQ and asked Colonel Elkins if I could get a jeep to go back and get a spigot so we could tap the beer. I also told him I could get some whiskey that was in the tavern. He gave the use of a jeep and I went back to Bastogne in style. I found about a dozen bottles of booze and a spigot and headed back to Savy. Colonel Elkins confiscated the booze for the officers but said the enlisted men could have the beer.

Pvt. Albert Gramme of the same battalion remembered that men of his battery "rescued" some beer and liquor and surprised one of the glider pilots who had just flown through heavy flak and machine gun fire to bring relief to the beleaguered troops at Bastogne. He wrote:

> Prior to the arrival of the gliders, some of us had gone into town and rescued a keg of beer and returned with it to our gun positions on the perimeter. As the gliders were landing, we were standing around drinking some beer. One of the gliders landed near us, smashed through some fences and came to a hard stop in the grove of trees where our guns were positioned. The pilot, slightly hurt and not knowing exactly where he was, staggered out of his glider, pistol in hand, looking for trouble. We immediately offered him a mess cup of beer. I'll never forget the look on his face. He had just flown over a hundred miles to bring supplies through enemy flak and machine gun fire, landed in unknown territory and remembering all the horror stories he had heard about how desperate we were and now, there we were, standing around drinking beer.

When General Middleton's VIII Army Corps pulled out of Bastogne as the 101st and other defenders arrived on the scene, a large cache of liquor was left behind. Division Headquarters located the one storage site and the second was exposed when an enemy bomb took one wall off its hiding place. Most of the liquor was placed in the hands of the medical personnel who were supervising the emergency medical set-ups in the rifle range and other buildings in the community. Colonel Ned Moore, the Division chief-of-staff stated: "There was enough liquor available that we were able to provide a bottle to every two wounded men. There wasn't much else with which to overcome pain at that stage of the game."[150]

It is uncertain whether gunner sergeant William D. Gammon got into the supply mentioned by Colonel Moore or the cache which had been located by Sgt. Parker and mentioned by Pvt. Albert Gramme. Gammon's mission was to scrounge for items which would make living conditions more tolerable for the men in his battery. He wrote:

> Some days later, after the German Luftwaffe had bombed Bastogne a few times, PFC. Martindale and I took a jeep and trailer into town to find stoves, timbers, quilts, etc. – anything to help keep us warm.

---

[150]Moore, op. cit.

We found a building blown open by the air raids. Lo and behold – it was full of booze. I thought at the time the Belgians had sealed it up to prevent the Germans from finding it. I was surprised to find some of the bottles were American brands – also a lot of Havana cigars. We loaded up and took it back to our unit and it was enjoyed by all.[151]

---

[151]At a Talon Chapter (101st Association) meeting in Fort Worth, Texas 40 years later, Bill Gammon learned "the rest of the story". He wrote: "I was relating the above story at the bar. Colonel Weldon M. Dowis, who had been with G-2, Special Troops HQ, listened intently, then said, 'We often wondered what happened to the corps liquor.' "

# 12. DECEMBER 27

## AERIAL RESUPPLY CONTINUES

The freezing rain and sleet at the Chateaudun air base where the 439th Troop Carrier Group was stationed on December 26th had caused postponement of additional flights of gliders. As was the case with F/O Case Rafter, another pilot was caught up in the operation officer's mission to get "volunteers" for the flight. F/O Herbert W. Ballinger has this story of flying to Bastogne with a load of artillery ammunition:

> The first that I learned about the Bastogne mission was when the operations officer came through the glider pilot's area asking for volunteers to fly supplies into Bastogne. Since I had nothing better to do, I agreed to fly the mission. We were scheduled to take off on the 26th of December but for some reason it was delayed until the morning of the 27th. The glider was loaded with high explosives (artillery shells) with the fuses removed and packed in the back next to the battery box. We were also issued a parachute but were not assigned co-pilots. I was assigned glider number "35" in the 50 to be flown from the 439th TC Group. The tow pilot was from another squadron in the 439th Group and I did not know him.

On the home field of the 439th Troop Carrier Group at Chateaudun, Colonel Charles H. Young was on hand checking out the gliders on the morning of the 27th. The 439th would provide the fifty gliders for the mission while 37 of the tow ships would be his and the remaining 13 would be provided by the 440th Group. Colonel Young describes the activities taking place and the last minute problems developing:

> I was out on the runway at Chateaudun checking last minute details of the marshalling and I recall that it was cold and that I was worried about a rather heavy coating of frost on the aircraft, especially on the cockpit windshield of the gliders. Some of the glider pilots had only small holes melted or scraped through the frost layer to see through.
>
> While I was checking the frost on one of the gliders, an officer in a jeep slid to a stop beside me to tell me that the co-pilot on one of our 91st C-47's was very sick. I went immediately to the airplane and found that he really was sick and throwing up. I told the first pilot that I would fly as his co-pilot, then sent my driver, Cpl. Collen R. Connell to get my parachute and flight gear.
>
> I continued with my inspection of the gliders and about that time another jeep stopped abruptly beside me and in it was Captain Pat Maloney, our assistant group intelligence officer (Major John L. Yaple, our Group S-

2, was on leave), Captain Maloney said 50th Wing A-2 had just called with this message – and I remember the exact words – it said, 'You might want to consider changing the route into the LZ,' and gave some suggested navigational fixes. I asked Captain Maloney, 'Why would I want to consider a change in route?' He said, 'I don't know – they didn't say,' and he repeated the message word for word.

The crews were already in their airplanes and gliders, it was almost engine start time; there was no time to re-brief the pilots and most important in my estimation was that a delay would make us miss our fighter protection. This was not expected to be a difficult mission, however, as we knew that other groups had previously used the same route we were briefed to fly and they had experienced no enemy action of consequence. We discussed the situation briefly and I said, 'We'll go as planned.' I was expecting to go on the flight myself at the time this decision was made.

*Flight officer Herbert W. Ballinger stands beside his glider shortly before takeoff for Bastogne on the morning of December 27, 1944.*

Then it was time for me to go to the airplane, but when I got there a stand-by co-pilot was already in the seat. He had been rushed out to the plane from the 91st Squadron area, so I was not needed.

Concerning the route our formation was to fly, General McAuliffe's message about a suggested change was evidently sent to SHAEF Headquarters in Paris the night before our mission. What its original content was, or why it was not received before time for take-off, I have never learned. What I do know and remember distinctly is what the message contained when it reached me, as noted above.

Answering nature's call when one is occupied with controlling a glider in flight when there isn't a co-pilot on board becomes a problem. Such was the situation for F/O Herbert Ballinger. He wrote:

Early on the morning of the 27th, the resupply mission became airborne. The air was full of ice crystals which rattled against the windshield as we flew. I did not have a watch so could not tell how long we were on tow before reaching the front lines but it seemed like a very long time. The glider would not trim properly and had to be constantly maneuvered to hold position. Besides becoming tired, I also needed to relieve myself from that morning cup of coffee. Since there was no one to hold the wheel, I could not go to the back to use the relief tube. I also had on a lot of clothes as well as a flak suit and I could not go on the floor. I also knew if I went in my pants, I would freeze when I got on the ground. However, about this time we reached the front lines and the flak was so bad that I forgot all about having to go until late in the afternoon. The flak looked like a large black cloud that extended far above our flight formation. I saw some tow ships go down as well as gliders. Two friends, Dick Blake, who lived in our tent, and Charles Brema, next door, were behind me and I kept wondering how they were making out.

I remember very clearly watching the Germans shooting at my tow ship with flak and I remember praying that they would not hit it. I know that if the tow ship went down I would also go down. They finally hit the tow ship and blew a rather large hole in the left aileron. Shortly thereafter it appeared that they quit shooting at the tow ship but left the gun firing which followed the tow line back to the glider. One round burst in front of the glider with some fragments penetrating and making small holes in the left windshield and a crack in the right. However, I was either not hit by any of the fragments or they were stopped by the flak suit. The next round hit the back in the door area between the fuses and ammunition and the last hit was on the elevators which I felt through the controls. I was not aware that the windshield had been penetrated and cracked and that I had been hit in the door area until we started unloading the glider. I took a lot of small arms fire, especially after I released and the glider slowed down.

2Lt. John D. Hill piloted the glider which was towed by 2Lt. Joe Fry, also of the 91st Troop Carrier Squadron of the 439th Group. His recollections of the flight are as follows:

About eight miles from the DZ, we started getting small arms fire and something turned loose underneath us. It sounded like large antiaircraft fire. The tow ship then caught fire under the belly and it blazed up suddenly over the whole back end. We flew for about three or four miles further with the blaze getting larger all the time. It looked as though the tow ship would blow up any minute. It was burning furiously. Flames were leaping back half-way down the tow rope. Just as we got inside the LZ, which would be about four miles from the DZ, two chutes came out through the flames. After about one more mile the third chute came out. About this time, I thought I could make it into the LZ so I released and cut across to the LZ, never seeing the fourth chute open.

After I landed, I talked with a paratrooper lieutenant who stated he saw only three chutes get out of the ship before it crashed. I later found the pilot, Lt. Fry, at the aid station getting his face burns treated.[152]

Tow ship pilot 2Lt. Joe Fry related his story to Milton Dank on January 29, 1976. Dank was a glider pilot in the same squadron and is the author of *The Glider Gang*.[153] Fry's story is as follows:

I was flying the last position in the squadron, number 13. The flight was uneventful until just prior to reaching Bastogne. We had six parapacks of ammunition on the belly of the aircraft and were towing a glider piloted by the 'Abilene Kid,' John D. Hill.

Just prior to reaching the drop zone, we sustained a direct hit just aft of the trailing edge of the wing in the belly of the aircraft. Evidently the hit penetrated the wing tanks because we had quite a fire going. Immediately upon realizing the severity of the fire, I ordered the crew to bail out. The radio operator and crew chief immediately bailed out; however, George 'Weapons' Weisfeld told me (and I will never forget), 'Joe, I'll stay with you until you're ready to leave.'

We managed to continue flying until J. D. Hill cut loose his glider. At that point, I jettisoned the para-packs and told George 'let's get out of this SOB before it blows up!' George went out the back hatch and, from what he told me later, darn near didn't make it. By the time I got the aircraft stabilized and the automatic pilot on, put my chest pack on and opened the cabin door to leave, I realized I had to find another departure route as by that

---

[152]Statement made by 2Lt. John D. Hill, from 93rd Troop Carrier Squadron. Received from Colonel Charles H. Young, 439th TCG commander.

[153]Dank, Milton. *The Glider Gang*, Philadelphia, J. B. Lippincott, 1977. Copy of material sent by Colonel Charles H. Young.

time the cabin section of the aircraft was nothing but a mass of flames. I closed the cabin door, went back to the cockpit, jettisoned the top hatch and climbed out, hoping I wouldn't fall into the props . . .

I landed about fifty yards from a trench occupied by members of the 101st Airborne Division, who immediately came out and dragged me into their rifle pit. I received severe burns about the head and knocked my right leg out of kilter when I hit the ground. The GI's who picked me up were very generous with their liberated cognac, of which I partook very generously.

This spectacle was witnessed and recorded by two soldiers of the 101st Airborne Division. Their observations were made after the glider release.

PFC. Bruce Middough of the 463rd Parachute Field Artillery Battalion had a good view of the scene through binoculars. He wrote:

During the resupply mission, one C-47 had been hit by antiaircraft fire and the whole tail assembly was engulfed in flames. The plane was flying on a course from west to east about a half mile south of Hemroulle. I watched the plane as it approached and saw one, then another, and the third crew member bail out. Their chutes all opened near 'A' Battery's gun positions. The plane continued on for a few seconds but was losing altitude rapidly. Then the fourth crew member bailed out. He didn't wait for the count of four but pulled it (ripcord) immediately upon departing the plane. His chute was just beginning to deploy when the tail assembly of the aircraft broke off and the plane went straight in, exploding upon impact. The crew member's chute opened okay and he came to ground on the hillside just southeast of Hemroulle.

I watched him through binoculars and observed that he just lay in the snow without moving. Shortly thereafter, two troopers went down the hillside to where he lay. They stood near him for a few minutes. Then one of the troopers cut his parachute off, bundled it up and both returned to their positions. I continued to watch the crew member who was still lying in the snow, but thought he must be dead. Thinking it odd that the troopers didn't carry him back toward their positions, several of us in the farmhouse were a little upset at the crew member being left in the snow and as we were talking about it, the crewman got up out of the snow and started walking toward the direction the troopers had come from.

Viewing the above spectacle from another angle, PFC. Edward Carowick of the 326th Airborne Engineer Battalion witnessed the departure of the fourth man. He wrote:

When the plane was directly over us, we saw movement and then we saw white silk/nylon coming out. The silk flew back and got hung on the tail (left section). The crewman also came out and was being dragged behind the burning plane. The plane continued on its course for five to fifteen seconds more. When the fire burned through the fuselage behind the wings, the wings plunged to the ground. When the wings fell free, the remainder of the fuselage seemed to stop in mid-air, then after a split second the forward end started to drop first. As it dropped the parachute fell from the tail section and opened fully. Then it disappeared completely from our sight due to the surrounding terrain.

I know the airman landed in friendly territory and was in the hospital near Bastogne because at the time we had someone in the same hospital from our platoon and the airman had been admitted for shock and burn treatment.

For the first airmen who departed from that burning aircraft, they got instructions from the soldiers waiting on the ground. PFC. William Kummerer wrote:

During the resupply, a C-47 was forced to come down near our gun emplacement. The crew, sans the pilot and co-pilot, bailed out. As they descended, one would think it was a scene at Fort Benning with instructors issuing directions. The troopers on the ground, mindless of the incoming enemy fire, were standing up shouting as to what position the descending flyers should take – relax, bend your knees as you hit the ground – tumble, get off your god damn feet! I'm pleased to relate three crew members hit the deck with nothing more than a few bruises.

In the interrogation Check List for Glider Pilots, which was filled out after a completed mission, 2Lt. Albert S. Barton included as part of his summary the following description of his landing site and how the Airborne soldiers got the glider unloaded:

I was forced to land in a field two miles west of Bastogne. The landing was good; I was within friendly lines. The airborne met me and we pulled the glider three-quarters of a mile nearer Bastogne to an area more protected from gun fire than where I landed. They unloaded and proceeded to the ammo dump.[154]

In the meantime, how had 1Lt. Ernie Turner fared at the controls of 2Lt. Albert Barton's tow ship? As a 94th Squadron power pilot, 1 Lt. Turner has this account of his landing in the Bastogne area:

As we passed over a wooded area we, and everyone else behind us, got clobbered. It seemed like the whole German army was in this wooded area. We were hit with .50 caliber machine gun fire. They started hitting us in the left wing across and through the cockpit and into the right wing and they wouldn't let up. The left engine quit and we continued on with the glider

---

[154]The Interrogation sheet was dated 30 December 1944 and the copy was provided by Colonel Charles H. Young, wartime commander of the 439th Troop Carrier Group.

until the right engine quit. We then cut the glider loose and I gave orders for everyone to bail out. I told my co-pilot, Casey Narbutas, to leave also.

We were losing altitude and were down to about 500 feet when the crew chief, who I thought had already left the plane, came back and asked me if I was going to jump. I yelled at him something to the effect that I wouldn't have time and for him to get the hell out. I then told Casey to get going and he said that he would ride it down with me.

The terrain was rolling ground and snow covered. I glided as far straight ahead as I could, then made a 90-degree left turn, clipping the tops of a clump of trees and set it down in a field. It was a very smooth wheels-up landing but because of the snow, I couldn't stop the plane. We ran out of field, came off the edge of a hill and over a road that was down below that soldiers were moving on and came to rest in a creek. We ran out of the aircraft thinking it was going to blow up.

*Both engines of this airplane were shot out on the glider re-supply mission to Bastogne, 27 December 1944, and the pilot, Capt. Ernest Turner, 94th TC Sqdn., belly landed it in the LZ. L-R: Capt. Turner, 2nd Lt. Keistutis J. Narbutas, co-pilot, and S/Sgt. Richard G. Whitehurst, radio operator. The crew chief, T/Sgt. John E. Douglas, was hit on a leg, but not badly wounded, and was at the aid center when this photo was made. (Photo from John L. Hoskins.)*

When I looked around, there was my whole crew. When I asked them how come they were there, they told me that when I said that I would have to stay with the aircraft to be sure they got out, they decided to stay with me in the plane.[155]

At the time 1Lt. Ernie Turner's "Ain't Misbehavin" came in for its belly landing, 2Lt. Everett "Red" Andrews was on the landing zone gathering equipment bundles for the 377th Parachute Field Artillery Battalion. He wrote:

I was in Savy watching a drop when 'Ain't Misbehavin' was hit over the flak belt. You could see the engine on fire and the plane gradually losing altitude. We all knew it was going to belly in onto the field right behind the 377th and near the 463rd PFA. The plane skidded in without mishap and was moving at a good clip, angling toward a road where a 2-1/2 ton truck was moving toward Savy. The driver had no idea he was about to be hit by the left wing of a C-47 and he skidded around. Ernie Turner was the pilot and he has told me all the weird things of the flight.

Also observing the belly landing of the aircraft was Captain Victor Tofany, commander of "D" Battery of the 463rd Parachute Field Artillery Battalion. He had a different angle in viewing the close-shave of the airplane with the truck. He wrote:

When the C-47 landed, it came across the road very close to the ground. As it crossed the road, a truck was passing under it. The tail wheel of the plane caught the back of the truck and spun it around 180 degrees. The truck driver, finding himself suddenly going in the opposite direction, jumped out and ran toward Bastogne – not knowing what had happened.

Several of the artillerymen of the 377th rushed to the plane site to provide assistance to the crew. They invited the air crew to stay with them rather than stay at Division Headquarters, which was under nightly attack by enemy bombers. Turner added to his story:

We were met by an Airborne colonel and some of his men who came running over to the aircraft. The colonel told me that we would have to report to Headquarters in town and they would want us to stay there (at Division Headquarters) overnight. The colonel said, 'Don't stay there, come back and stay with us in the farmhouse where we are staying.' He stated that Germans came over every night and bombed Division Headquarters.[156]

Another crew member who had an unusual experience on the 27th was 2Lt. Richard Fredrickson, serving as co-pilot for 1Lt. Martin H. Skolnick. He wrote:

Three miles from the LZ our aircraft was hit in the tail section by a blast of flak which cut the elevator control cables. The aircraft started into a

---

[155]From a copy of a letter Colonel Charles H. Young received from Ernie Turner dated 11 March 1981. Copy supplied by Colonel Young.
[156]ibid.

dive after which the glider cut loose. 1Lt. Skolnick, the pilot, ordered the crew to bail out. By the time the crew chief, radio operator and I reached the rear door of the plane, we were too low to jump. I believe that our combined weight in the rear of the aircraft may have helped Lt. Skolnick bring the plane out of the steep dive. Skolnick, using the throttles, was trying to bring the nose up. He kept the plane in the air using bursts of power until he saw we were over friendly territory and saw a suitable place to crash-land. We hit the top of a hill at very high speed and bounced back into the air. The second time we hit, we dragged the right wing causing us to come to rest in the LZ, 180 degrees from the direction we were originally headed.[157]

Several of the glider pilots described how the ammunition-starved soldiers approached their gliders to remove the vital artillery shells.

A veteran of the glider landings in Holland, Bastogne and Operation Varsity over the Rhine, F/O David H. Sill remembers his assignment to fly in a supply of artillery ammunition to Bastogne's beleaguered troops with these comments:

I landed on the north side of Division Headquarters. I stopped at a fence along a road. Some troops were on the other side of the road and came running over. Some kissed and patted the glider. I had ammo in my glider and it was the size and kind they needed at their emplacement. The troops got some and started hauling it across the road.

Flight officer Herbert Ballinger landed only 300 to 400 yards inside friendly lines and the glider was struck nose first in the snow which made unloading difficult. He wrote:

The airborne came over with a jeep and trailer to unload the ammunition. Off-loading the glider was more difficult than normal because we could not get the nose out of the snow and had to unload through the back door. We were also occasionally harassed by artillery and heavy machine gun fire, even though we were out of sight of the German lines. Whether it was meant for us or for 'to whom it may concern', I will never know. Before we finished unloading the glider, another jeep showed up which took me back to headquarters.

1Lt. Charles Brema had trouble braking his glider in the snow-covered field. He got a different kind of response from the airborne troops as was described by James E. Mrazek.[158]

Nearby, men from the 101st rushed toward the glider and pulled open the door. Brema thought they wanted to see if he was still alive, or perhaps congratulate him for making it without getting killed. Instead, they started pulling and hacking at the lashings, binding the ammunition to the glider

---

[157] 93rd Troop Carrier Squadron History sent to Colonel Charles H. Young by Colonel Robert A. Barrere on 30 October 1987. Copy sent by Col. Young.

[158] Mrazek, op. cit. p. 226.

floor, and ran off with it, leaving him unceremoniously to his own devices. He took a little time to check the glider. Not a bullet hole could he find, nor had the glider suffered any damage on landing. He felt let down.

Other gliders were on their way down and, realizing that the pilots would get little more help than he did, he ran from one glider to another as each landed, to give what help he could to each glider.

*Troops from one of the airborne artillery battalions rushed across the road and over a fence to retrieve artillery shells from the recently landed glider. Some of the shells in their protective cases can be seen piled at the fence line.*

Glider pilot Charles Brema may not have had the kind of greeting from the troops at Bastogne that he had hoped for, but others remembered the warm welcomes and expressions of appreciation bestowed upon them. One of them was F/O Case Rafter who wrote:

I got out of the glider all by myself with no other gliders around and a paratrooper came walking over to me with the insignia of the 'Screaming Eagle' of the 101st so I knew which division had been surrounded by the Germans. I asked him how things looked and he said that since that morning things had looked good but it had been a real tough fight. He explained that Patton had gotten into Bastogne that morning. I asked him if there was anywhere around where I could get a drink and he gave me a bottle of fortified wine from North Africa which I tucked in the pocket of my flying jacket and had a few swigs when I got into town.

With tow ships shot down before the safety of the Bastogne perimeter was reached, the gliders landed in enemy-held territory. By the time the tail end of the column reached and passed over the enemy gunners, the anti-aircraft soldiers had tow ships and gliders zeroed in. Such was the lot of F/O Mike Sheff. He wrote:

I was the last glider off. As we neared Bastogne, we ran into a wall of flak. My tow plane was hit and I released and landed in an open field of a densely wooded area. I was shot at as I landed in the snow. I was wounded in the left forearm. I put my hands up and three German soldiers came out of the woods. They searched me – fought over my gun. I was taken prisoner. It made me mad because they took my six packs of cigarettes.

The tow plane which pulled F/O Harold K. Russell's glider was hit near Sibret, many miles southwest of Bastogne. Two crew members parachuted safely, a third man died when he suffered a streamer and the pilot went down with his plane. After Russell dropped his tow rope, his craft suffered three hits with one bullet passing through his thigh. He managed to get out of the glider but in his wounded condition, chose not to oppose the enemy soldiers approaching his position. Russell wrote:

Since I was unable to move around, I thought it inadvisable to fire at them. When they spoke to me in German, a language I understood, I learned they were German soldiers and they wanted me to go over to the command post before visiting the aid station. They helped me over to the CP where an officer attempted to interrogate me. I resisted the interrogation and gave only my name, rank and serial number. I was treated courteously and not pressed for information. They were surprised when I sprinkled sulfa in my wound and seemed to have no knowledge of its use.

I was taken to the aid station about 500 yards away, which was in a farmhouse, half of which served as a communications office. There were no other wounded in the station and the doctors took care of me immediately, stating that the wound was not too serious. I laid on the straw covering the floor. It was now about 1400. I remained there listening to the conversations of members of the medical and communications sections – their morale seemed very high and they seemed to think that the big push in the Ardennes was the beginning of the fight to drive the Allies back into the sea. The men in the aid station were well equipped and had good clothes. They offered me tea, coffee and cigarettes and did not confiscate any of my possessions except the helmet, arms, bedroll, trench knife and musette bag.

About 1800 hours of the same day, the Germans began looking out the window and making preparations for a withdrawal. During the excitement and hasty activity, I was left unguarded and hid in a potato bin in one of the rooms of the house. When they were ready to leave, they made a quick search but seemed more interested in getting out than in finding me. They soon left and, after a safe interval, I crawled into the hayloft and spent the night there.[159]

The next morning the farmer in whose loft F/O Russell spent the night, found him and told him there were Americans in the neighborhood and so Russell was returned to his unit to glide another day. His glider had come down near Sibret and troops of General Patton's 3rd Army were busy widening the corridor from the south.

Flight officer Pershing Y. Carlson had been busy tuning his motor bike when he got the call to get ready to fly a glider to Bastogne. His load consisted of artillery ammunition. He didn't make it to the proper landing zone and spent seven days eluding the Germans before being captured. He wrote: "I was captured a week after being shot down and spent the rest of the war as a POW at Barth, Germany."

## 440TH HIT HARDEST

On the final day of aerial resupply for the 101st and fellow defenders, the 440th Troop Carrier Group was once again called on to provide tugs and tows to assist the 439th which provided the bulk of the gliders and tows of the 50-plane group. The historian describes the 440th role:[160]

On the morning of December 27th, the 440th was given another glider mission and at 10:39, eight C-47's and eight gliders of 95th Squadron and five planes and gliders of the 96th Squadron took off from the air strip at Chateaudun. These 13 aircraft and gliders formed the last element of a 37-plane serial operated by the 439th Troop Carrier Group. The 440th gliders were loaded to capacity with high explosives.

The weather was good and the run into Bastogne was made without trouble. The job looked easy when, almost without warning, the 440th planes collided with the most withering hail of anti-aircraft fire ever encountered by a 440th formation during the European campaign.

Apparently the German ack-ack gunners had gotten the range as the first elements of the 37-plane formation came over and as the thirteen 440th planes and gliders swung over the target they were blasted with unprecedented fury.

---

[159]Summary of Interrogation Check List by F/O Harold K. Russell, 93rd TCS glider pilot. Retyped by Col. Charles H. Young from a barely legible copy from National Archives provided by Col. Robert Barrere.

[160]440th TCG History.

Although intense fire had been observed reaching out at 439th planes at the front of the serial, the 440th aircraft held a steady course and cut their gliders as scheduled although explosions were already knocking the tugs from side to side and shells were starting to hit home with disconcerting frequency.

One glider completely disappeared in mid-air as a high explosive shell hit the cargo of TNT. The others cut their approaches as sharply as possible and dived for the ground with their pilots using every form of evasive action to dodge the upcoming stream of fire.

Before cutting off their gliders the tow planes held steady courses and were unable to make any attempt at evasive action. Sgt. Robert J. Slaughter, radio operator of a 96th Squadron ship, was in the astrodome when the right engine of his ship was hit. At the same time, he saw three different planes hit, catch fire and start to fall.

A few moments later, there was a tremendous explosion in the tail and fire broke out. The bail-out signal was given but only the crew chief was able to get through the cargo door before fire blocked it.

Their only hope was for a successful crash landing and the pilot, 1Lt. Billy J. Green, managed to bring the ship down although most of the controls had been shot away. Upon hitting the ground, the roof of the cockpit caved in and caught Lt. Green behind the control panel. Although expecting an explosion at any moment, Sgt. Slaughter battered the escape hatch open and managed to drag Lt. Green from the burning ship.

In the air over Bastogne other 440th aircraft were taking equally severe treatment. As the leading part of the serial pulled away, all of the German fire was concentrated on the 440th ships as they cut their gliders and turned back. It was all over in a few short moments but in those moments the 440th sustained 42 percent of its combat losses during the entire period of the European campaign.

Of the eight ships from the 95th Squadron, five were shot down with every member of their crews either killed or captured by the Germans. One managed to get back over friendly territory before making an emergency landing and only two made their way back to the home base at Orleans. Both of these planes were so badly damaged that ground crews found it hard to understand how they had remained airborne.

Of the five 96th planes, three were shot down with seven crew members killed and two taken prisoner. Both of the 96th planes that managed to get back to Orleans were also heavily damaged. The pilots of both of these ships attributed their safe return to their split-second decision to turn right out of the landing zone instead of to the left as briefed.

Most of the gliders had managed to land with their cargoes relatively undamaged and the ammunition and explosives were immediately put to use by the hard-pressed troops around the perimeter of the town.

## AN AIRBORNE GREETING

As the process of unloading the gliders was taking place, the pilots were driven to Division Headquarters where they reported in. This is when they learned which of their comrades had come through the fire safely, which planes and gliders they had seen going down prematurely, etc.

F/O Case Rafter had been given a bottle of wine by an airborne soldier and stuffed it in his jacket pocket. It wasn't long before he ran into one of his close friends. Rafter wrote:

I ran into a friend, Tom Longo, from the 440th. He thought it was hilariously funny that I had a bottle sticking out of the pocket of my combat jacket and he was in high spirits, explaining that he had come in the day before with doctors and medical equipment in his glider.

Before the airborne troops had finished unloading his glider, a jeep had appeared to take F/O Herbert Ballinger to Division Headquarters. His story continues:

When I arrived at Headquarters, I joined the other glider pilots who got through and some power pilots who were shot down but still made it to the intended area before bailing out or crash landing.

At their foxhole positions on the Champs perimeter, PFC. Ted Goldmann and members of his squad had been watching since mid-morning as the planes and gliders had appeared from the west and southwest. As some of the aircraft were forced to crash-land or the gliders abort before reaching the proper landing zone, the ground troops were determined to go out beyond the foxhole positions in an attempt to rescue downed airmen. Goldmann related:[161]

On the morning of the 27th more C-47's, both with and without gliders, were coming in again. A flight of six came in north and west of us right into the thick flak belt which shot down five planes and all six gliders. Some of us went out to see if we could rescue some of the pilots who might have landed safely. We had about nine men, half of whom were from 'C' Company but ran into Germans about three hundred yards out and, after a brief fight, we returned with one boy shot in the arm. Had shot three Germans, though. Everything settled down to normal again but that afternoon as Johnny, Asay and I were sitting by our hole talking, Johnny

---

[161]Goldmann, op. cit.

and Asay had their backs to the enemy. I said, 'Here comes someone through
the woods!'

A figure was about 100 yards off. We yelled, 'Halt!', and while Johnny
covered us, Asay and I went out to see who it was. He turned out to be a
glider pilot (a North Carolina boy) shot down behind the enemy lines on the
day after Christmas and who had been wandering around since then. We took
him back to the CP.

## EVACUATION OF THE WOUNDED

A large fleet of ambulances had followed the forward elements of the 4th
Armored Division into Bastogne. With over a thousand wounded and frostbitten
individuals in desperate need of more advanced medical procedures, the first
critical cases were sent out late on the night of December 26th. Most of the
wounded were evacuated on the 27th.

Among the first wounded to be evacuated on December 27th was eight-year
old Andre Meurisse who had been wounded on December 23rd at Mande St.
Etienne when American fighter-bombers hit some of the houses, not realizing
civilians and American soldiers were in the buildings. Meurisse had a large piece
of shrapnel which was festering in his shoulder. He describes a dangerous
ambulance ride out of Bastogne:

The day after the tanks broke through to Bastogne, the convoy of
medical ambulances, which had arrived with the armored force, were loaded.
Around 11 o'clock that Wednesday, December 27th, the U.S. medics formed
a convoy of wounded and, as the fighting still raged, the ambulance convoy
left Bastogne for the rear area hospitals. I was one of the wounded who were
riding in that convoy.

As I was a small boy, the medics put my litter at the top level of the
ambulance. There I laid, my stretcher hanging from straps attached to the
roof of the ambulance.

We had left the shelled and bombed ruins of the town buildings and the
seminary school which had been my hospital and quickly drove out of town
heading south. We had been gone from the town about ten minutes when
machine gun fire from close range hit the ambulance I was in along with
my father sitting next to the back door of the patient compartment. The
bullets pierced the thin sides of the ambulance between where my body was
and the top of the roof, missing me by just a few inches. I had heard the
sound of the burp gun but didn't see the holes until some time later when
we halted for a while and my father showed them to me and to the others in
the ambulance. Then I realized that for a second time in just a few days
time, I had narrowly escaped death.

By the time ambulances further back in the convoy had reached the point where the above vehicle had been attacked, the enemy threat had been eliminated. Others who were evacuated have not mentioned being fired on as they were moved south.

One of the airborne soldiers being moved back, with multiple wounds, was 1Lt. Robert P. O'Connell who remembered the compassion of the ambulance drivers who assisted in handling the litters. He wrote:

We were relieved by the 4th Armored Division. In their wake were streams of ambulances. For the most part, the drivers were negro soldiers and I was greatly moved and have never forgotten the compassion of these men in helping us. Many of our 101st men were in poor shape from their wounds. I remember how these black soldiers picked us up and carried us with words of encouragement, 'You're going to be all right now – I'll take care of you men,' etc. It made me feel strong just to be around them.

Suffering from an acute case of trench foot, Cpl. Bernard Stevens had this remembrance of the sensitivity of the affected members of one's body that had suffered from prolonged exposure to frost bite. He wrote:

When we were being evacuated out of Bastogne, a rather funny incident happened. As all who have trench foot know, you cannot have even the slightest thing touch them. As a result, all of us on stretchers, with trench foot, had our bare feet uncovered. The German prisoners were used as bearers. When the trooper next to me was going to be moved, the Germans bent over to pick up his stretcher. The one at his foot end, as a sign of compassion, pulled the blanket over his feet. The trooper was in such pain that he struck straight up at the poor German at his head end, knocking him over backward. There was a great deal of laughter, swearing and confusion before the medics were able to explain to the prisoners what happened.

At first, Stevens was to lose his left leg but the operation was delayed and when the doctors saw the condition had improved, there was no need to amputate it. Stevens returned to his unit several months later.

As the day ended, a total of 652 wounded were moved back to Army hospitals in the XII Corps area. The evacuations were carried out by the 64th Medical Group. The last stretcher case from those accumulated during the siege was transported to the rear on the 28th. By this time, the number had reached a thousand.

## ESCORTING PRISONERS

A very elated F/O Case Rafter had been driven to Division Headquarters before his glider had been completely unloaded. He had met his friend Tom Longo and other glider pilots and tow plane personnel who had been assembled, ready for evacuation. Rafter provides a brief description of the move to the rear: "When the airborne decided to evacuate us, they loaded us onto trucks and all the German prisoners on other trucks and we escorted them to the rear areas through the opened corridor."

Flight officer Charles F. Sutton had served as co-pilot on one of the eleven gliders flown into Bastogne on December 26. He remembered that the glider had been loaded with fifty-five 5-gallon cans of gasoline for the hard pressed troops.

Sutton has a vivid recollection of his trip out of Bastogne when the glider pilots were evacuated along with the 700 enemy soldiers who had been captured. He wrote:

> After the highway to the rear was opened, we were to escort German POW's to the rear. Blessing, Hammargren and I were assigned to the last truck carrying about 25 POW's. Blessing and I were sitting on the tailgate; Captain Hammargren was in the cab. The driver got too close to the edge of the road and the truck slid down an embankment and tipped on its side. The POW's were returned to the holding area and we three glider pilots were placed in an uncovered truck which rejoined the convoy. On the way, we passed a group of Belgian farmers who had been throwing rocks at the POW's as the trucks passed. A rock was thrown at our truck and immediately the thrower saw that we were all Americans in the truck and his actions indicated he was sorry. The rock hit me on the left eyebrow, cutting it and blood ran down my cheek, making me look like a casualty. I was patched up at the aid station when we arrived at the village where we turned the POW's over to the MP's. The medics wanted my name, rank and serial number – they said I was due a Purple Heart. I wouldn't give them the information – not when others gave their lives.

## AERIAL OBSERVERS

An unheralded group of pilots arrived from England with their Piper Cub L-4 planes on the day the Division departed for Bastogne. These were the flyers whose job it was to fly above the front lines looking for enemy gun positions and concealed armored vehicles. They had a dangerous assignment. Two of their planes had been shot down in Holland with two occupants in one plane dying when their craft burned on crashing.

The pilot of the second downed plane, 1Lt. Bill McRae, had been shot down between Veghel and St. Oedenrode while observing enemy traffic and was rescued the next day from captivity by men of the 506th Parachute Regiment.

He had flown into Mourmelon on the day the Division departed for the Ardennes. He remembered the pilots who made the flight to Bastogne a few days later: "Major Shannon Powers, 1Lt. George Schoeneck and I are the only people of the 101st who went into Bastogne airborne. We flew in with our Piper Cubs."

As an aerial observer with Headquarters of the 463rd Parachute Field Artillery Battalion, 1Lt. Ben F. Wright remembered that the L-4's didn't accompany the division as it moved out on December 19. He wrote:

When we got to Mourmelon with our L-4's, the Division had just departed for Belgium. I was an observer, not a pilot, and flew in over the Krauts with 1Lt. George Schoeneck, who was killed later over Bastogne.

When the movement orders were given to proceed to Bastogne, most of the L-4 pilots and crew members were in Paris on 48-hour pass. 1Lt. Jack Washishek describes how most of his small segment of the artillery wing made their way to the fighting front:

A number of the pilots as well as crew members were on leave when the call came for Bastogne. These were mostly in Paris. The troops were all back in time for the move to Bastogne. It was decided, since we knew nothing of the area (didn't know yet that it was Bastogne), to send a pilot and all the crews to Bastogne with the Division. The pilots and planes would follow once the air strip was established.

The Division had been in Bastogne for several days and in the midst of heavy fighting when the three small planes were flown into Bastogne. The arrival is described by 1Lt. Bill McRae:

They shot at us as we approached the town and as we circled looking for a place to land. The flak was extremely heavy against our three little planes. Lt. George Schoeneck was later killed in the air.

Apparently in the observer's seat of one of those planes, 1Lt. Jack Washishek didn't sense the ack-ack coming up at them was that serious even though there were lots of holes in the planes. He provides more detail of the landing strip and its previous occupants:

Surprisingly, the ground fire was not as intense as we expected. Most of the planes were hit but none seriously. Holes through the fuselage or wings by small arms was not too serious – just scared the hell out of us. As we neared Bastogne, we saw the panels indicating our landing strip. We landed and found we were on the strip just abandoned by the previous air section. I'm not sure who we replaced but, due to the fog, they could not fly out and burned their planes on the strip. We were about a mile east of Bastogne.

For the first several days that the L-4's were in the air to provide eyes for the artillery, the information obtained by the observers provided more frustration than satisfaction. Lt. Jack Washishek continues his story:

Since we had very little artillery ammo, our principle job was recon. We tried to keep everyone alert to troop and tank movement. We could have directed the killing of a good many of the enemy if we had all the ammo needed. There were targets everywhere.

The failure of relieving forces to reach Bastogne on Christmas Day was a big disappointment to General McAuliffe. His frustration may have shown when aerial observer 1Lt. Ben Wright came in to report on his information obtained while flying over the western perimeter during the major attack on Christmas Day. Wright wrote:

I was sent up once with 1Lt. George Schoeneck and thought that my mission was to mark a map and report to General McAuliffe. I went to his headquarters in Bastogne and started a long dissertation on every position. The General said, 'Hell, I know that! I want to know where the 4th Armored is!'

To have a ringside seat to an aerial dogfight is one thing; to have that same seat at eyeball level was something else. Lt. Ben Wright describes the action which occurred over the battle areas the following day:

Another time, it was like an air show or chapter out of WINGS, when the P-47's took on the Kraut planes which were shooting up our resupply C-47's and gliders. We watched it all from an L-4 right in the middle. They all flew right past us like we weren't there. One liaison pilot described a similar situation as a 'Box seat over Hell'.

As the temperatures dropped dramatically at the end of December, the cold weather had an adverse effect on the engines of the small observer planes. Like a family car on a particularly cold frosty morning, it was very important to get that engine going early in the morning. Lt. Washishek relates:

The pilots stayed in a small house at the southern edge of the airstrip while the crew stayed in town. Since it was so cold, the job of starting and keeping the planes going was a helluva job. Plugs had to be pulled in the morning and heated before they would start. The engines had to be kept warm so the crews came up with all kinds of great ways to keep them warm. Almost as soon as you took off, you were within range of small arms fire. Surprisingly, we were not hit often. Perhaps because so many other targets were available.

Mentioned previously by fellow L-4 pilots and observers, 1Lt. George Schoeneck was shot down with his observer (2Lt. Jack S. Terry) while watching enemy tank and infantry movements during the battle in which the troops of First Army moved south and the 101st and other divisions moved north, closing the gap and finally sealing off the Bulge on January 16. According to former officers of the 463rd Artillery Battalion, the L-4 and its occupants were hit by a 105mm shell fired by friendly forces when the plane flew into the path of the shell.

# 13. CALM BEFORE A STORM

## DECEMBER 28

It was a misty day. Our fighter-bombers failed to show up but enemy observation planes made runs over the Bastogne sector. There were two small probing attacks in the 401st Glider Infantry area which were quickly repulsed.

Convoys continued to arrive from Mourmelon with ammunition and gasoline. The first mail arrived for the troops. This included a huge amount of Christmas packages which, for the most part, were shared by the troops with their buddies.

Additional anti-aircraft gunnery units arrived and were put under the command of LTC. X. B. Cox of the 81st AA and AT Battalion of the 101st. These guns would keep the enemy bombers at greater heights decreasing their accuracy.

With the arrival of the commanding general, Maxwell D. Taylor, from his abbreviated trip to Army Headquarters in Washington, the 101st commander was quickly appraised of the dangers in Bastogne with the continued shelling and the regular appearance of enemy bombers during the night. For this reason, the Division Headquarters became three segments. A forward element remained at the cellar headquarters in Bastogne; a rear echelon was moved to Sibret about two miles southwest of Bastogne, and a third group moved to the chateau at Ile-le-Hesse to establish a night-time command post. This was done to decrease the possibility of an enemy shell or bomb wiping out a major portion of the command elements of the 101st Airborne Division.

In his diary entry for December 28, T/4 Gerald Zimmerman of the 101st Airborne Signal Company describes a move of his high-powered radio transmitter truck to Sibret. It was his final entry into a diary he kept during the Bastogne fighting. He also offered praise for the units which fought side by side as part of the defensive team at Bastogne. Zimmerman wrote:

<u>December 28, 1944</u> – No air support today but we got plenty of shells. Today I moved with the rear CP a thousand yards from the front lines where it was safe. The forward CP took a beating after that. This ends the so-called story of Bastogne . . . take it from the Battered Bastards of Bastogne, the boys of CCB, 10th Armored and the 705th TD Battalion are tops. It would have been a lot worse without these gallant men.

As a member of the radio platoon of Signal Company, T/3 George Koskimaki was sent with his team to provide night-time radio communication for the Division command post at Ile-le-Hesse.

## CHATEAU ILE-LE-HESSE

This large manor home is located a mile west of Bastogne at the juncture of the Bastogne-Marche highway and a lesser road which led to Senonchamps. The property was the estate of Baron and Baroness Greindl. During the German occupation, the Baron had received the temporary appointment as governor of Luxembourg Province of which Bastogne was a part. When the Allies began their march across western Europe, Baron Greindl had been dismissed. As American soldiers neared Bastogne in September of 1944, he was seized after the German SS learned he had been working with underground forces. He was sent to Germany as a political prisoner at Buchenwald. He was executed on February 20, 1945 leaving the Baroness to rear their twelve children.

The first troops to occupy the chateau were the artillerymen of the 420th Armored Field Artillery of Combat Command "B" of the 10th Armored Division. These groups were followed by 1st Battalion of the 327th Glider Infantry with Captain Walter L. Miller and "C" Company using the garage as their command post after withdrawing from Senonchamps.

Captain Walter Miller's "C" Company was given the assignment of providing security for that division command post. Miller was able to keep General Taylor posted on the up-to-the-minute actions going on around the division perimeter. Miller added to his account:

As an ex-communications officer, I had tied into the artillery line and pretty well knew what was going on around the perimeter of Bastogne and briefed General Taylor who had moved the Division CP to the chateau at that time. We remained in the vicinity of Ile-le-Hesse until the evening of January 3rd.

Baroness Rene Greindl was sheltering her large family, some young boys, their teacher and a group of civilian refugees in the cellar of the home while the military occupied the upper floors. The communications personnel occupied the furnace room along with its coal storage area. Baroness Rene Greindl describes how life was lived in the cellar during this time period in December 1944:

Here is an idea of what the cellar was like: a flight of eight steps led to the landing, where stood our sentry; near the staircase was a cellar 22 by 25 feet. Next came a vault 6 by 6 feet. Then a sort of larder of 6 by 9 feet. The children christened the vault 'Vincent Dormitory' because a refugee couple from Bastogne came there to sleep every night, while the larder was 'St. Thomas Dormitory' because they said it was impossible for eight people to sleep there, which nevertheless they did, over a long period of time. On the other side of the passage was a vault coming downward in an arch, provided with an opening to the outside air. I took up my abode, with the two babies, to one side of the opening and my corner was called 'Spiros Dormitory'. On the other side, the Abbe made himself overseer of all this improvised sleeping space and nipped in the bud any tendency to indiscipline amongst all these children. Our passage was out diagonally by another (way) which, in turn, came on to the central heating cellar which, in spite of being encumbered by a large furnace, was the American combat post during the battle of Bastogne.[162]

(Author's note: Although my family and I had been guests at Ile-le-Hesse in 1967 on my first research trip, and revisited again in 1984, it was not until 1989 that I got to enter the cellar where I had spent about ten days providing communication for 101st Airborne Division Headquarters. A change I noted was the coal furnace had been replaced by a smaller and more efficient oil heating unit. I pointed out to my wife where we had placed the 9-foot long radio antenna so it protruded for most of its length outside a small basement window.

When Christmas packages arrived from home once the highway was reopened, I shared many of the goodies with Baroness Greindl's young children.)

## AN "UPSTANDING" COMPANY COMMANDER

PFC. John "Wilkie" Wielkopolan remembered that "G" Company had received a replacement company commander fresh from the states. As an old timer, Wielkopolan was not anxious to expose himself to enemy fire while serving as runner for his gung-ho commander. He wrote:

His name was Captain Shay and he was from New York. My platoon leader, Lt. (Jesus) Cortez had sent me to be his runner. That didn't go over too well with me because I had all I could to take care of myself. This captain did not believe in hugging the ground like I did. He was always standing up everywhere we went. It seems that he was always looking for something. It was about the 28th of December and we were out front checking our outpost positions. He was standing up in the middle of the road. That was when a sniper opened up. I was on the side of the road, standing in a ditch. I didn't know just where the sniper was located at the time. I looked over at the captain. When I glanced at him, he was still standing in the middle of the road – the sniper was still firing at him. I could see the bullets hitting the road. I guess the captain didn't know where to go so that was when I rushed out and pushed him off the highway. We both landed in the ditch. That was when I noticed that he had been hit in the neck. After we took care of the sniper, I led the captain back to the aid station. The doctor found it was only a flesh wound.

---

[162]Greindl, Countess Rene. *Christmas 1944 at Ile-le-Hesse*, Bastogne, Belgium, 1965. p. 32.

## WIDENING THE CORRIDOR

Still on line along the ridge northwest of Marvie, after one road had been opened to Bastogne by tanks of the 4th Armored Division, PFC. Charles Kocourek remembers the approach of tanks up the same road along which the German parliamentaries had approached on December 22nd. He recalled:

A couple days later we saw four or five tanks coming down the same road along which the four German soldiers had approached with their surrender ultimatum. These tanks were off the road about 20 yards traveling parallel with the roadway. There was a building about 250 yards in front of us. I said, 'Oh, oh! those are German tanks!' The tanks that had supported us earlier were not with us now. One of the approaching tanks shot at the building and put a hole in the roof and hit it with at least three more shells. Then I saw them throw or shoot a red flare into the woods. Then the American planes came in and strafed those woods. We knew then that the tanks were American. That was the first time I had seen airplanes work closely in support of infantry. It sure was beautiful to watch.

The tanks finally came up to our position and we were one happy bunch, shaking hands with those guys and pounding each other on the back.

The tankers were part of a force in the process of widening the corridor from Neufchateau to Bastogne. It would now be safer to travel.


## DECEMBER 29

Daybreak brought a bright clear day. Men of 2nd Battalion of the 327th had an opportunity to watch an armored attack which was coordinated with the efforts of fighter-bombers on their front to the south of Bastogne as the corridor was widened. After the armor reached the men of the 327th, "F" and "G" Companies were moved into Division reserve at the northwest edge of Bastogne.

Convoys continued moving up the corridor from Mourmelon with the trucks of the 426th Airborne Quartermaster Company bringing in rations, many of them being the popular Ten-in-One type. Overshoes and overcoats arrived for the poorly clad troops. Another convoy brought in one hundred members of the 506th Parachute Regiment and fifty men of 2nd Battalion of the 501st Regiment who had been in Paris at the time the Division left for the Ardennes. These men were experienced and well-trained soldiers who were welcomed with open arms by their units which had been decimated in ten days of fighting.

The trucks returning to Mourmelon carried out the first mail which the soldiers had written. The unit censors made sure the letters revealed nothing of military value should the packets of letters fall into enemy hands.

Observation planes as well as fighter-bombers reported extremely heavy enemy anti-aircraft fire whenever they made passes over the perimeter to the north and northeast. Something was going on in those regions which were shielded from view by the heavy forestation.

A first sergeant on a line company front provides a story of a soldier in his unit who exhibited sharpness of vision to point out one of the enemy batteries which was harassing planes which flew near that location.

The day would also find recently-returned Major General Maxwell D. Taylor visiting his front line commanders around the perimeter.

Descriptions of actions in retrieving the bodies of fallen comrades are provided by two soldiers.

Acting first sergeant Paul Slevey got a shock when he spotted his countenance in a mirror.

A diary entry recorded by T/3 George Koskimaki fits in with the night's activity as described by a front line machine gunner on security duty in Bastogne.

## A TREE THAT WASN'T THERE

The keen observation of a front line soldier resulted in an enemy anti-aircraft unit position being taken out. 1/Sgt. Carwood Lipton relates the story of one of his men gifted with sharp vision:

One of the men in the 3rd Platoon of 'E' Company had excellent vision and he was also an outstanding marksman with a rifle. He was PFC. Darrell C. 'Shifty' Powers, a tall part-Indian from Clincho, Virginia.

It was on December 29th that his eyesight paid off for us. We were in our strong defensive positions in the woods southeast of Foy, able to see the town below us and Noville across open fields and along the road about a mile and a half to the north.

Shifty came over to me that morning and said, 'Sergeant Lipton, there's a tree up there towards Noville that wasn't there yesterday!' He had no binoculars, but I did. He showed me how to find the tree that he had been looking at. It was by the road up towards Noville and I located it through the binoculars.

It was not an isolated tree as there were a number of trees along the road, but he insisted that it had not been there the day before. As I continued looking through the binoculars, I saw some movement under other trees around it. Then I saw gun barrels – anti-aircraft guns by their appearance as the barrels were elevated – and Germans moving around. We could see that they were setting up an anti-aircraft battery around and under the trees and had put up the tree that 'Shifty' saw as part of their camouflage.

We had a forward observer for the 105's that were back in Bastogne on call and I got him on the radio. He was there in just a few minutes and when he saw what we had, he had no trouble getting approval for full battery fire.

To zero his battery on target, he first fired only one gun at a position he could locate on his map, about 300 yards to the right of the trees. When the shells from that one gun hit right on that position he shifted its aim to the left by the distance that position was right of the target and called for all the battery's guns to lay in on the same azimuth and range. In that way, he got all his guns laid in on the target without alerting the Germans that he was zeroing in on them. When that was done he had all his guns fire for effect, several rounds from each gun.

The shells landed all around the enemy position, as we could see through our binoculars, knocking down trees and enemy guns and putting the German position out of action. Their activity after that was to get out of the area and we could see them getting their wounded out and salvaging what they could of their equipment. By the time an hour had passed, there was no one there.

It all happened because 'Shifty' saw a tree almost a mile away that hadn't been there the day before.

## WATCH THOSE WOODS!

Upon his arrival on the Bastogne scene, General Taylor was apprised of the fact that the enemy held the dominant ground to the north and northeast of Foy and Noville. Before those towns could be taken and held, the heights had to be secured. An early trip to the front line units was then made. One of those who was stung by a remark made by the Division commander on his first trip to the MLR near Foy was Major Dick Winters, executive officer for 2nd Battalion of the 506th Regiment. He wrote:

After General Taylor returned from Washington, D.C., he paid us a visit. He inspected the front lines very briskly. His instructions before leaving us were, 'Watch those woods in front of you!' We didn't appreciate that! What the hell did he think we had been doing while he was in Washington!

## RETRIEVING FALLEN COMRADES

Retrieving the bodies of dead comrades who had been killed when they ran into an enemy machine gun nest while on a night patrol is a lasting memory for PFC. Carl H. Cartledge of the 501st regimental S-2 section. His dead comrades were PFC's Norman D. Blanchette and Arthur Teichman. The two soldiers died on December 28 and the retrieval party went out after them the following day. Cartledge related:

It was just after Christmas when our team moved out beyond the front line to bring their bodies in – two of the greatest fighting men ever to give their lives for their country – Arthur Teichman of Philadelphia and Norman Blanchette of New Bedford, Mass. Their night patrol had run square into a German machine gun road block with supporting infantry. They had been the lead scouts. Their battle had raged for most of the night. It was heard all around the front.

We fanned out on either side of the roadway, following it down to where it split two rolling hills. The snow had stopped. We could see no movement out front and drew no fire.

Blanchette lay on the left side and Teichman on the right. It had been a helluva fight. Empty shell casings were all around them in the snow. On the left hilltop was what had been the machine gun emplacement. Eight leather harness straps lay cut away from their wounded. Their KIA's were marked by blood patches in the snow. They had been battered and had pulled out.

We carried the frozen bodies of our own back through our lines on stretchers. Counting our losses – for Normandy the 501st Regimental S-2 recon teams had jumped with twenty-four men. Of those, we were down to eleven. Six had been killed – men we would never forget: Blanchette, Gardner, Palmer E. Smith, Stiles, Beamsley and Teichman. They were our lost brothers-in-arms. There would be no shaking of hands with the enemy when the war was over. This was a sad, sad day.

An incident involving the recovery of fallen comrades is remembered by Pvt. Michael Zorich who had returned from an extensive recuperative stay in a British military hospital after being wounded in Holland. He had arrived at Mourmelon just in time to make the trip to Bastogne. He related:

We were moving through the woods and came upon a little road with trees on the right and left. From our front approached a jeep pulling a trailer so we had to get to the side of the road. On the trailer were frozen stiff, dead soldiers. It was sad. One piled on the top of the other. As they passed our position, one of the bodies slid off the pile and hit the ground like a slab of concrete and was lying at my feet. God, I lived with that for many a night – it was a young, blond lieutenant wearing a brown tanker's jacket. His arms were in a surrendering position, frozen stiff and it looked like he was covered with melted sugar. Sgt. Houston ordered me to pick him up and put him back in the trailer. I refused. He ordered someone else – I was too disturbed. The two guys in the jeep had to go pick him up.

## A LOOK IN THE MIRROR

The extremely cold weather that gradually encompassed the Bastogne area in December and January meant that personal cleanliness suffered greatly. S/Sgt. Paul W. Slevey remembers well the shock he received the first time he happened to look in a mirror. He wrote:

On December 29, arrangements were made to have ten men at a time leave the area and go to a chateau near by and clean up. We had been out for ten days and hadn't been inside a house or building in that time. I took one group over and knocked at the back door and opened it a little. I could see a G.I. lying on the floor getting the last rites. We went to another door and it led into a large room with a fireplace. As I walked past the big mantel there seemed to be a small window at one end of it. My eye caught the image of a bearded, dirty face. I stopped, went back for a better look and I was peering at myself in a mirror.

In the room was a stove from a field kitchen; on that was a clean garbage can full of hot water. Each G.I. got one-half helmet full so we could brush our teeth, shave and take a bath. We didn't get a change of clothes. I wore my O.D. shirt for 59 days until I got a new one.

## BOMBING AND STRAFING

The diary of T/3 George Koskimaki fits in with the account of PFC. John C. Trowbridge who had been sent to Bastogne from his front line position to provide security for armored units which served as "fire brigades". These vehicles were rushed to threatened points on the perimeter. The notation in the diary for December 29 reads as follows:

<u>December 29, 1944</u> – German bombers dropped some heavy stuff as well as butterfly anti-personnel bombs early this morning. The Krauts hit one building in our area and also strafed a little. Hazy weather. The German counter-offensive has stalled.

As a member of a machine gun team from 1st Battalion of the 501st, PFC. John Trowbridge was sent to Bastogne when the fighting in his area quieted down. He describes what happened one moonlit night:

We took over prepared positions, which had both foxholes and deep slit trenches, some with thin covering, which were better for sleeping. We felt safer here away from the front lines, until one moonlit night when Jerry came over bombing and strafing. We were enjoying the fireworks, watching the anti-aircraft tracers filling the sky until a bomb exploded a few yards from our hole. We didn't know we were being strafed until daylight, when we saw where the 20mm shells had exploded in the snow all around us.

# DECEMBER 30

As the 30th day of December dawned, added reinforcements from other divisions were moving into the fray. One of the soldiers of the 6th Armored Division describes a trip to Bastogne where they were positioned in the Wardin-Neffe area.

With the decrease in enemy activity in the 501st perimeter in front of Neffe, Colonel Julian Ewell ordered a patrol into town to check out the presence of German troops.

This was the day General George Patton visited various units of the 101st and soldiers provided their recollections of his visits.

## 6TH ARMORED DIVISION MOVING UP

As a member of one of the divisions moving into the Bastogne area in a supporting role, Sgt. David Reich of the Reconnaissance Platoon of the 44th Armored Infantry, 6th Armored Division, remembers the trip to the Bastogne area. The weather was both a hazard and a help. He wrote:

Near noon on December 30, one of my pals volunteered me for a patrol to Bastogne. We were to find march routes and recon assembly areas for a move and an attack on December 31 towards Wardin and Neffe. We contacted units of the 101st and the 4th Armored Divisions before returning to our unit.

Near dusk on the 30th, with a light snow falling, we began to lead our combat team toward Bastogne. A tank was our lead vehicle to set the pace as roads were so slick. When darkness set in, the storm became a gale with very heavy snow and tanks were slipping and sliding into our jeeps on the grades.

Late in the evening, our route was blocked by the 11th Armored Division marching across our front. We found a back road way to Bastogne and continued on our march. We gave thanks for the storm as it was the best cover ever.

## HAVE THEY PULLED OUT?

A request had come in from 501st regimental commander Colonel Julian Ewell to find out if the Germans were still in strength in Neffe, or had they pulled out. The assignment went to the S-2 team of which PFC. Carl Cartledge was a veteran member. He wrote:

On one of the last days of December, Sgt. Jim Ganter called me on the field phone. Colonel Ewell wanted a daylight patrol into Neffe to determine if the Germans had pulled out. We had reported for several days the reduced activity and yesterday had observed no enemy movement at all.

We moved out early that morning – Becker, Collins, Brown, Chief Sayers and myself. Brown took the point and we fanned out about a hundred yards apart, taking advantage of the clumps of fir trees for part of the way. The snow made the going tough at times, but finally we reached the farm houses. It appeared the Jerries had pulled out.

It was time to hunt for German stragglers or food. We knew all the secret places – behind the doors at the side of the fireplaces, the trap doors, the attics. Somewhere there might be a ferocious 'wild chicken,' a discarded cured ham or bottle of pears, cognac or anything to drink. Even some ersatz coffee would be great.

Collins and I advanced on the nearest farm building. I opened up with a burst from my Thompson on the wooden slab door and exploded into the room. No one was inside. Collins quickly ran through the other rooms, but I had spotted the trap door in the floor. There had to be some food down there. I leaned over, took the ring in my hand and flung it open.

There were three German soldiers waving white handkerchiefs frantically while one bleated out breathlessly, 'Nicht schiessen – Ich haben cousin in Chicago!'

## GENERAL PATTON SHOWS UP

Memories of the surprise visits of General George Patton to various locations around the perimeter of the 101st are related by three troopers. Two were at 502nd Parachute Infantry regimental headquarters when the general arrived to award its commander a DSC and to inspect enemy tanks which had been knocked out near the chateau. Another soldier was surprised to have the general appear at his artillery forward outpost in the midst of a firing mission.

In a V-Mail letter to his parents dated December 30, 1944, Captain Joseph Pangerl described the visit of General George Patton to 502nd regimental headquarters at Chateau Rolle for the purpose of decorating the regimental commander, Colonel Steve Chappuis:

It is almost eight o'clock in the evening. Not much has happened since then and it is very quiet. This afternoon we had the pleasure of General Patton's presence. He came right to our castle and pinned a medal on our Colonel for we were the regiment that finally stopped the last big German effort. I was waiting for him with my camera outside and as I took his picture he walked over to me and said, 'Now get a good one!' I took one only a few feet away and then one of him pinning the medal on the Colonel. That really tickled me. I can't wait to have the picture done now.[163]

Medical evacuation officer Henry Barnes was at the Chateau Rolle when General George Patton appeared on the scene to decorate two of the officers involved in the fighting. Barnes wrote:

It was on December 30th that I saw General Patton himself at the Chateau Rolle. He was wearing his famous white-handled revolvers and gave both General McAuliffe and Colonel Chappuis, the 502nd Parachute Infantry commander, the DSC medals. He must have liked the tanks he saw burned out around the chateau.

I heard him shouting over a field phone. He had a high-pitched voice and he was bawling out the division commanders of the units on his flanks. At their protests his answer was the same – 'I am up here. Why aren't you?'

*Lt. Gen. George S. Patton, Jr., (right) chats with Brig. Gen. Anthony C. McAuliffe and Lt. Col. Steve Chappuis (center), after awarding them both the DSC for their defense of Bastogne.*

---

[163]Pangerl, op. cit.

## DAMN IT – STAY DOWN!

Captain Donald N. Martin was serving as liaison officer to the 327th Glider Infantry Regiment from the 463rd Parachute Field Artillery Battalion. He had gone out to the positions of 2nd Battalion of the 327th a few days after the breakthrough. The glidermen were under attack from a mixed armored infantry group. He wrote:

We were getting another attack from that direction and I only had one forward observer with them so he needed some help. By the time I arrived the infantry battalion commander had been hit. I went on past Battalion Headquarters to a long sloping hill that was very bare of vegetation and set up an OP where I could observe from and see the enemy real well.

There were several tanks down in the valley before me. I am sure these were a part of the tank unit that had attacked the 463rd earlier. I called Major Vic Garrett and told him what I was seeing. He gave me one gun to adjust on them. That gun was from 'B' Battery. The Germans discovered me and my radio operator there so every time we moved, they would fire at us.

Suddenly, I glanced around. Some people were coming up the hill behind us. I yelled for them to stay down. They paid no heed, just kept walking. Well this really infuriated me so I started yelling some real Sunday school words at them. Cpl. Scrivener nudged me and said, 'Sir, you better stop yelling like that – it is General Patton! I had been so intent on firing on the tanks that I had not tried to identify the approaching party when I had glanced back but just got the word to them to stay down.

Just as they arrived, I had finished my adjustment on the tanks and was asking for 'fire for effect'. Battalion gave me all they had. I remember one round went right into the hatch of a tank and it exploded the ammo within. General Patton, with his way of speaking, said, 'Now by God, that is good firing!' We knocked out two of them and the rest moved out. We had no further trouble from that group of tanks. By this time, the attack on 2nd Battalion had subsided and I returned to Bastogne.[164]

---

[164]The above material was excerpted from a long letter Donald N. Martin wrote to the daughter of Joseph Lyons (executive officer for "B" Battery of the 463rd). Sarah Lyons was preparing a paper for her prep school class.

# 14. DECEMBER 31

## A TREE PATCH OUTPOST

A growth of evergreen trees, divided into sections by fire lanes, was located at the top of the highest point of ground west of Champs. It was the location of 1Lt. Jim Robinson's artillery outpost during the fighting at Christmas time when "A" Company of the 502nd Regiment occupied the positions. The Germans had driven the observers and outpost members from the heights during the early morning fighting on Christmas Day. Robinson had worked his way back toward the abandoned outpost while "C" Company went about trying to wrest the valuable position from the enemy in position up there now. After calling a heavy artillery barrage down on the enemy, Robinson had sent the enemy soldiers scurrying to their former positions north and west of the hillside. By the end of the day, the OP was back in friendly hands though much the worst for wear.

## "OSCAR"

Continuing in his role as artillery observer for the 502nd Regiment's 1st Battalion, Lt. Robinson was now with "C" Company which had relieved "A" Company in the positions west and northwest of Champs. Robinson describes the appearance of the hilltop after the heavy shellings and an unusual way the men had of placing position markers out in front of the foxholes.

On the 31st of December, the date of the attack on Sgt. Black's Company 'C' position, the OP position would clearly show the bullet-torn tree trunks, broken limbs, and mangled underbrush resulting from enemy mortar and artillery fire, as well as from fire fights involving small arms and grenades. Such actions against this position had also occurred daily during Company 'A's' occupation of the OP December 22nd through December 28th prior to Company 'C' taking over the area. Retaking the CP on Christmas Day had been a substantial undertaking. Therefore, it was plain that the enemy also prized what this location had to offer and wanted it badly. The frozen enemy dead accumulating on the small space in front had been pre-arranged in the still of the night to serve as directional markers. One was stood upright in a foxhole, pointing skyward and was called OSCAR in honor of the paratrooper's mascot jumping dummy. OSCAR held the central point of the little snow-covered field of fire and, when darkness came in close around and suspected infiltrators could not be located in the fog, one could always whisper to a buddy, 'He is to the left or right of 'OSCAR'. After many hushed exchanges, artillery fire could then be placed in that direction and onto the pockets hidden from view. Then, if harassment continued, one or two guns shooting time fire could be brought in as close to the edge of the thicket as safety would allow. Enemy positions were so close that the artillery radio picked up German transmissions quite clearly.

On New Year's Eve, Sgt. Layton Black's "C" Company squad was up there as the snow continued to fall. It was the kind of night when an enemy patrol could probe the area and possibly make an attempt to recapture the location. All the while an artillery barrage was coming over the hill with most of the shells landing among the houses in Champs. During moments of extreme tension, the senses tend to be overly acute. The eyes play tricks and sounds are magnified.

In their two-man foxhole situated near the hilltop, Sgt. Layton Black and Cpl. Marvin Milligan were anticipating an attack at any moment. Black wrote:

Back in our foxhole at the machine gun, the two of us were certain now that we saw something move out in front of us. The words 'Open fire!' were only a breath away from my lips. All that held me back from saying them was that we both didn't see it at the same time. It was like Milligan saying, 'Black, did you see that?' 'No, where?' – 'There!' 'What was it?' 'Something moved!' – 'I didn't see anything, can you still see it?' 'No.' Then it was my turn to see something. 'Hey Milligan, what was that?' – 'Where?' _ 'Over there!' – 'You mean, right there?' – 'No, over more to my left' – 'Oh! That's that bush again – I think.' – 'Did you hear it, or did you see it, Sergeant?' 'I thought I saw something. It must have been that bush. Yeh, that's what it was. Man, I almost pulled the trigger on this air-cooled baby that time!'

During the night of sporadic shelling by the enemy, "C" Company's commander called his outpost, manned by Sgt. Layton Black and Cpl. Marvin Milligan, asking where the 88mm shells were landing in Champs and particularly how close the explosions were to the command post. With the snow and foggy conditions at the time, the two outposted soldiers had no idea as to where the shells were exploding. The inquiries from the jittery commander had been going on ever since the barrage started earlier. The two men were worried about the possibility of enemy soldiers trying to sneak up on their position.

When soldiers want to communicate with the sound power telephone between two positions, they often whistled into the phone to get the attention of the person at the other end. The whistling sound carried long distances at night.

The two soldiers were acutely aware of the possibility there was an enemy soldier close enough to their position to actually hear the whistling sound coming from the other end of the line and could thereby determine the exact location of their foxhole.

By midnight, Sgt. Black was all talked out and turned the phone over to Milligan who had already become extremely annoyed listening to his sergeant having to respond to every artillery explosion that landed in Champs – and there was no way of knowing where those hits were occurring in relation to the buildings. Milligan allowed his annoyance with his captain to show. Black wrote:

Let me say a new voice must have been a very welcome sound to everyone back of the line. Everyone who was tuned in to us got the message except the company commander. The message, of course, was that we did not want to make a sound, let alone have to talk. Hell, we were faced with the real threat of a German patrol which was just counting on us to make some kind of noise.

But to the captain, who had set up 'C' Company's CP in one of the better houses (still standing) in the center of Champs, our 'tree patch' outpost was 'his' listening post and by God he was going to use it as such – and did so.

Milligan had been on the phone for over an hour responding to the query of his commander, who asked, 'Where did that one hit?' after each explosion.

Suddenly, out of the dead silence, came the damndest whistling noise I have ever heard. It came blaring out of our foxhole. It made the hair stand up on the back of my neck. I am sure that the Germans heard it in Givry (small town to the north). All of my men heard it all the way to the haystack. That was the straw that did it!

That was it. With the question repeated three times, Corporal Milligan sat up still and straight as a board and, speaking as clearly as I've ever heard anyone talk, stated 'Right on top of the damn Company CP!'

While the company commander screamed into his phone demanding to know who was giving him sass and smart-ass responses, the questioning was cut short when Sgt. Black ordered his men to commence firing. The order to start firing was in response to Milligans answer to the commander's last question. Black wrote:

I pulled Milligan down into the foxhole and yelled, 'Open fire!' With that, I held the trigger down on the machine gun. As I did, everybody else opened up. I threw several hand grenades and so did everybody else.

I don't know how long we had been firing when Cpl. Milligan came to his senses and asked me, 'What in the hell happened?' I said, 'That last batch of 88's hit the company CP, so I opened up on these damn Germans!' Cpl. Milligan said to me, 'Are you shitten me Sergeant – the Germans hit our Company CP?' 'Hell yes, I'm sure,' I said. 'How the hell do you know?' he asked. 'By God, because you said so!' I replied.

In between laughing, firing and throwing hand grenades, no Germans got through to us in our 'tree patch' on this night. We must have kept firing for a half hour. Then, all quiet until 0400 hours.

We used up two boxes of machine gun ammo; all of our hand grenades and half of our rifle ammo. However, we had yet to fire our bazooka. We had made it through that German attempt to capture us, but I was sure daylight would bring worse.

Suddenly, it was quiet for the men of Black's squad. They needed the next two hours of quiet. They had spent the night peering ahead as the wind drove the snow into their faces. The conditions had been ideal for an enemy patrol to sneak up to their positions. They hadn't seen a soul out to their front. Nobody got any sleep though the men were dead tired . . . Black explains why:

Sleep would have come if it had not been for the sound of a wounded German soldier's moan. Out in front of us, so very close, he was to die slowly. Yet, in so doing, he surely saved my men's lives. He was the only proof we had that the Germans had been out there on this night, for we were yet to see them.

After continuously shelling the village for many hours, which was most likely diversionary so as to allow their snow-caped patrols to penetrate the 'C' Company outposts and positions along the hilltop, heavy shelling of the entire 1st Battalion front began before daybreak. One of those shells severed the telephone line from Black's position to the platoon sergeant in Champs. Leaving Milligan on the machine gun, Black started back along the wire, tracing it to its break. The break was such that the two ends couldn't be pulled together and spliced. He had to go all the way back to the command post. Black continues his story:

The platoon sergeant told me to go by way of the company CP and pick up an artillery lieutenant from Division Artillery. He was going with me to the 'tree patch' as the observer for the 377th Parachute Field Artillery Battalion.

As I went by the CP, picking up a Lt. James Robinson, I saw the first sergeant, Robert Grotjan. I said to him, 'I heard that the Jerries landed a direct hit in here last night.' All he answered was – 'How in the hell do you know about that?'

As Sgt. Black, accompanied by Lt. Robinson, returned to the tree patch position, he pondered the news he had received about Sgt. Bill "Big Holly" Hollingsworth's squad which was now being reported as missing. He had also learned of the death of another company favorite and learned of the other company casualties and the discovery of additional dead enemy soldiers found in front of the positions. Black continued his story:

On the way up the hill, I kept thinking about Holly and his squad. I had also been told about Haddick's death. Sgt. Howard had said that he hadn't heard from any of Holly's squad since last night. I quickened my steps up the hill now for the thought of those three dead German soldiers came back to mind. I remembered, too, those last words about our losses (one officer and two EM's dead – four wounded). I wondered if Holly had trouble. But, try as hard as I could, I didn't remember hearing any small arms firing from over on my left flank. I was almost running up that long hill west of Champs now. I heard someone behind me say, 'What's the big hurry Sergeant?'

When I reached Sgt. Griffith's mortar dugout, Sgt. Howard told me that Holly and his whole squad were gone. 'Damn it Black, they ain't there!' He had taken a look and found no one in their foxholes. I was stunned. I had to look for myself. It was true. No one was left.

What had happened? Everything was still in place around each foxhole. Even rifles and machine guns were still in place. All the ammo, plus their bedding, was still in each foxhole. It looked like they had just crawled out of their sacks. Hell – they had all been captured in their sleep!

If so, I was mad. 'Damn it!' Cpl. Milligan, Sgt. Bird and I, with all of our men, had fought all night – well, not in the true sense. But we had been under the gun and we damned well hadn't shut our eyes. I'll be a son-of-a-bitch if I hadn't lost three men while these guys were asleep! My mind raced on for the answer and I was mad.

By the time I reached the tree patch outpost, the artillery officer had already set up his big radio. He had started to call in the big stuff – even the 155mm stuff. From the hill at our tree patch we could see some of the German soldiers on foot moving off this hill way down in front of us. They were off to the left of us somewhat but very much in our view. While the lieutenant was still talking, over went the barrage. Man, that was something to watch. The 377th troopers sure let those Krauts have it. While this was going on, our platoon medic was taking care of the wounded. Some would be done with war.

The enemy artillery barrages which had been hitting the 1st Battalion positions in and around Champs were not the only positions on the 502nd perimeter being hit. In the Longvilly area where he was busy evacuating wounded in the woods as the result of the shelling, 1Lt. Henry Barnes has this recollection of how an incoming shell can have a surprising effect on a soldier who is screaming and crying in pain. As the medical evacuation officer from the 326th Medical Company attached to the 502nd, Barnes was attending the wounded man in the woods on New Year's Day. He wrote:

New Year's Day brought on a new reaction. We started on the attack. We spent most of our time in dense pine woods. I don't know where we were most of the time. I remember once trying to calm one man who was screaming and crying. I was sitting on him, straddling him, trying to inject some morphine with one of our syrettes when an artillery short whistled into the trees above us. You could tell by the erratic whistling, it wasn't a good one. Next to us was a dugout built underground with pine log cover.

There was a 16-inch opening through which this soldier disappeared as the shell exploded. He must have scared the hell out of the soldiers he dove on. He certainly was faster than I who was left sitting in the snow. These upset men seemed to sense danger sooner and reacted faster.

Back at the tree patch area, Sgt. Black had gone to look at the empty foxholes in Sgt. Hollingsworth's sector. He tried to figure out what had taken place. He also stopped by Sgt. Willis O. Bird's machine gun position and learned of action which occurred at the time he was tracing the broken telephone line. Black added:

As I came from Holly's position back to my tree patch outpost, I stopped by Sgt. Bird's gun crew to see how he had made out. They had a close call sometime after the haystack had burned out. It must have been about the time I reached Sgt. Howard's foxhole.

As near as Bird and I could put the pieces together, this is what happened to him. Those Germans who had slipped to the far left of my tree patch, because of the haystack fire no doubt, had then come upon Holly's squad. Finding them easy prey, the Jerries became even more bold. But, they ran into Griffith and Howard next, and they were not so easy. Three dead so quick must have forced them to think about saving their prisoner catch. Thus, they started back down the hill toward their lines. But, one Jerry came too close to Bird's gun crew.

Over in the tree patch where Cpl. 'Jump Knife' Milligan was then alone, he saw the Jerry at the same time as Sgt. Bird. He ran and jumped into Bird's foxhole (with him) to help out. Sgt. W. O. Bird yelled to his machine gunner to swing his gun to the rear and open fire. The boy was a new trooper named Kelley. He turned in plenty of time to see the German bearing down on him. Kelley froze and did not fire. Bird and Milligan did. But, it was too late for Kelley. He was wounded. The rest of the Jerries hurried off with their prisoners.

Back at the tree patch outpost, Cpl. Hartman was putting in my new telephone line. He was also running new wire from Sgt. Griffith's post on down into Champs to our platoon CP. Still coming over my head was the good stuff of the 377th. Now Lt. Robinson was giving the Germans hell all over the valley out in front of me. He certainly had them on the run and was paying them back double for last night.

While moving around investigating his squad members on the outpost and checking the phone line to see it was clear to platoon, Sgt. Layton Black was called by Lt. Robinson to come up to his OP position. Black wrote:

It must have been some time after 1000 hours (New Year's Day) when the artillery officer called me to come back to the top of the hill where he was located. As I reached the top of the hill near him, I heard some rifle fire off to the south. It was more over in Sgt. Hollingsworth's area than mine, or where he had been. It was a single rifle firing – Pow-Pow-Pow! I asked the lieutenant what was going on. He told me to look down there and pointed to one trooper seated in the snow down the hill.

That long range rifle marksman was none other than Sgt. William T. "Big Holly" Hollingsworth who had somehow eluded the enemy and was now firing at the last retreating form in the distance. Black continues describing the marksmanship he witnessed:

> The officer then let me use his powerful field glasses. I saw clearly that Holly was firing at a German soldier who was at least six hundred yards away.
>
> I watched at least five shots through the field glasses as they hit on either side of the German. The German was down in the snow. One of Holly's shots would land to the left and the German would roll over to his right. The next shot landed right and the German rolled back left; so on it went for those five shots.
>
> I handed the glasses back to the lieutenant and a short time later he yelled, 'He got him, he got him, men!' Then a cheer went up from everyone on our hillside.

Sgt. Black then walked part way down the hill, calling to Holly to get back up to the platoon positions. Then Black got a surprise. He wrote:

> With the sound of my voice, he stood up and said, 'That you, Black? I thought they got you too!' As he came near me I saw right away what was wrong – hell – Holly had been drinking! I knew Holly better than anyone else and something had to have happened to him for him to take that kind of a chance with his own life. He had to be drunk – and he was.

Sgt. Hollingsworth was drunk but not bad drunk. He went on to relate how the enemy had taken his squad with no shots being fired. Sgt. Black adds to the story:

> I asked, 'Where are the rest of your men?' He started in slowly, 'Those damn Germans walked right up to each one of my foxholes and stuck their bayonets in on us. We didn't have a chance Sgt. Black. We couldn't see them – they were all wearing white uniforms. You know it was still snowing, not quite daylight.' I said, 'You guys must have been asleep. Couldn't you hear them coming?' 'No sir – they did not make a sound. It's damn scary the way they can creep up,' said Holly. 'Why didn't they take you?' I asked. 'They did,' he said.
>
> Holly said that about a squad of big German S.S. soldiers started to take them back down the hill toward their lines. 'For some reason, the Germans stopped for a while.' (My feelings have always been that maybe they stopped to await the burning down of the haystack fire because of its flare-like glare.)

Holly went on to say that after they moved out again and were part way down the long hill, they were stopped again. This time it was by our 101st artillery. He said it came right in on top of them and everybody hit the ground. Holly saw a bush near by and dove under it for protection from the shelling. It was devastating and seemed to last a long time.

'When our guns let up, the Germans all jumped up and started to hurry off the hill. One of them who could speak good English told us GI's to get up and hurry down the hill before more shells came in on them. Everyone but me got up and ran down the hill with the Germans. They never missed me for some reason,' Holly said. 'I guess they couldn't count too good,' added Holly as an afterthought.

When Hollingsworth was certain there were no more Germans in the vicinity, he headed back up the hill toward his own position to retrieve his rifle. His arrival at his foxhole had occurred in the nick of time for Lt. Jim Robinson who had gone forward from his observation post to get a better look. His vision was being affected by snow squalls.

## A HEAD-ON ENCOUNTER

A description of a head-on encounter between Lt. Jim Robinson and a German officer is related first by Robinson and then by the trooper who came to his aid in the nick of time. First by Robinson:

Off and on we were getting snow flurries and now they had increased somewhat. Dressed in full-length white shroud-like sheets and almost invisible in the snow, I felt I could use the cover of the snow storm to advance unobserved. I left my radio operator at the dugout position, elated with the chance to punish the people to our front, and I made it to the top of the ridge, crossed it and went downward into a small saddle-shaped swale where I could shoot observed fire on the enemy-held positions. The snow fall had become heavier, or perhaps it was the sensation of the hillside funnelling the breeze upward and seemingly carrying the soft snow flakes almost parallel to the ground and right into my eyes. I was making haste, for no artillery observer holds up a battalion radio network on an approved fire mission. I had a cloth sling over one shoulder carrying an extra battery for my radio. I was moving downhill with momentum and wham!, as in basketball, I made a stand-up offensive body block against a German officer coming up the hill. We met head on, helmet to helmet, breast to breast. He, too, was dressed in the fashion of the day – solid white covering. The impact and the imbalance of the spare battery versus radio turned me completely around, facing the rear with my arms flailing about, catching myself in a crouch.

Some distance away, a G.I. wearing the old familiar Army O.D. wool knit cap, without a helmet, went down in kneeling position. As the shot rang out, the German appeared to bow deeply at the waist and slid silently, feet first, into an abandoned foxhole. I slipped a newly knit wool balaclava from his head and a belt from his waist. Of all things, I needed a belt – a converted German rifle sling, leather, with leather-covered buckle. The balaclava I immediately put on against the bitter cold.

The battalion gave us massed support on the hill, on the slopes and onto the fields beyond. The snow flurries were timely, but Sgt. William T. Hollingsworth, with the wool knit cap, from Horseshoe, North Carolina, had made the difference.

The story of the above incident as experienced by Sgt. William T. "Big Holly" Hollingsworth was related to Sgt. Layton Black a few hours after the episode as the two men trudged up the long hill. Black wrote:

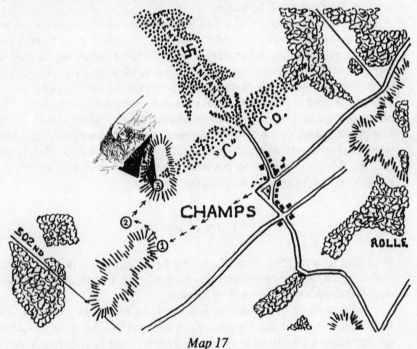

*Map 17*

*The moves and actions of forward artillery observer Lt. Jim Robinson are provided to illustrate the actions which took place on New Year's Eve in the Champs area. #1 is his move to a position near Sgt. Layton; Black's squad on the hillside. #2 is approximate location of his encounter with the enemy officer. #3 is his move to the original "tree patch" OP from which he calls down artillery barrages on targets of opportunity.*

Sgt. William T. Hollingsworth then told me of an unusual happening as he wound his way back to our lines. Since the German attack was still in progress, and he could see a stray Jerry on the hillside here and there, Holly made his way to his foxhole for his rifle. He then worked his way back over to the tree patch area. As he came by a small drop-off area, (mound of dirt) Holly ran smack into a German soldier with his rifle aimed at a fellow trooper. Sgt. Hollingsworth was to fire first – the German fell dead. (The American whose life was saved, I learned forty-two years later, was Lt. James Robinson of the 377th Parachute Field Artillery Battalion, the same officer I had accompanied up the hill earlier.)

After the heavy fighting they had experienced in and around Champs on Christmas Day, the men of "A" Company had been relieved by "C" Company at the tree patch site. Lt. Robinson had continued to observe from the "C" Company positions on the hill top. Captain Wallace Swanson of "A" Company also provides verification of the story:

> Our forward observer, 1Lt. Jim Robinson, moved back up there with 'C' Company along with his radio operators. The team tried to pick out enemy targets that they put artillery on. Lt. Robinson moved out forward of the 'C' Company positions to get a better view of the enemy area. He headed for a clump of trees in a ravine that was toward the enemy lines. As he entered the trees in the ravine, he encountered a German soldier in the same clump of trees and the enemy soldier had the drop on him and was taking him prisoner. One of the 'C' Company men had a good view and he was a good marksman. He took aim and shot the German. Robinson cleared the area quickly and returned to the team position and continued to call for artillery support from this vantage point.

## SCHNAAPS

Returning to his earlier story of meeting Sgt. Hollingsworth after he had returned from his sniping episode far down the hillside, Sgt. Black sensed that his friend was drunk and asked for an explanation:

> I said to Holly, 'You must have stopped at a bar on the way back.' He said, 'Yah, in a way I did. Here, have a drink!' and he handed me a German canteen filled with Schnaaps (which is a very strong German drink made from potatoes).
>
> As I took a drink I asked Holly, 'Where did you find this?' He said, 'Over in front of your tree patch outpost! Those dead German soldiers lying over there had their canteens filled with Schnaaps!' then continued, 'They sure were not going to need it anymore and it seemed a shame to see it go to

waste. I brought back three full canteens. See them down there in my foxhole?' he said, pointing down into his hole.

I took another drink from Holly's canteen and remarked, 'Well, its no damn wonder those Jerries came up that long hill straight at us into Bird's and my great field of fire, with as strong as Schnaaps is, a few drinks and a soldier wouldn't care if he lives or dies.'

## BILL HADDICK IS DEAD!

As a sergeant in the 1st Platoon of "Charley" Company, Kenneth Kochenour was also in position along the MLR on New Year's Eve. He spent a lot of time on a .30 caliber machine gun and, as previously mentioned by Sgt. Willis Fowler in describing Christmas Day actions, machine guns tended to freeze up in cold weather. Kochenour also remembers the day as one of his close buddies was killed on the 31st of December. He tells his story:

The day PFC. William F. Haddick was killed, the 1st Platoon was on line just west of Longchamps. My squad was down to five men and we dug two-man foxholes. I was teamed with a new replacement. We had part of our implacement covered with logs and earth. We were manning a .30 cal. light machine gun on a small hill top. The platoon was standing two-hour shifts during the night. I took over just about dawn and as I was wiping the sleepy dirt out of my eyes, looking at the vast snow-covered no-man's land, a platoon of Kraut infantry was advancing on us. They were just about a hundred yards out. I was no longer cold, the blood was rushing through my body as I grabbed the handle of the machine gun and started firing. The Germans seemed to be surprised and ran in many directions. The gun froze up and stopped just as my buddy came crawling out of his sack. I hollered, 'Piss on it!' and he did. The gun started spitting out death again till I expended the better part of 250 rounds. Only a few stray shots of small arms fire hit around our position. I expected some 88mm shells or at least some mortar fire. Company 'B' was on the 1st Platoon's right flank in the town and the Germans were able to infiltrate during the night.

At daybreak they started their attack and Bill Haddick was firing on them with his machine gun when he was hit in the head. He was killed outright. It wasn't until nightfall that I found out he was dead. He had taken basic with me at Camp Wheeler, Georgia. Somehow, we never expected him to get it.

With Sgt. William "Holly" Hollingsworth back with members of his own platoon as the only one who had eluded the enemy patrol which captured them earlier, Sgt. Layton Black wondered if it was time to break some bad news to "Holly". Black added to his story:

I told 'Big Holly' that I was truly glad he had made it back to our lines and very sorry that his men had not. I even said, 'With all the old timers gone now this war isn't going to be any fun'. Then I thought about the loss of William Haddick, which Holly didn't know about yet.

I sat on the edge of the big sergeant's foxhole and wondered if now was the time to tell him. The two men deeply liked each other. They had been together as far back as basic training and had come into the 502nd PIR back in the Alabama days. Both had been machine gunners and two of the regiment's best. They were two of 'C' Company's best liked men.

I decided now was the time to tell Holly. I thought about how to do it. Suddenly he said to me, 'What's the matter with you Sergeant Black? You look like you need another drink.' (He always liked to get me drunk.)

At last I said, 'Yes, I do. I've got to tell you something. Take one more drink with me.' We drank one last drink together, (and I remember how awful it tasted).

'Okay, I'm ready – tell me the bad news. I can tell when you're not kidding,' Holly said.

I began, 'We in 'C' Company lost two of our best men today – one from the 1st and one from the 2nd Platoon. We here in the 2nd lucked out. We got you back. But the boys over in the 1st were not so lucky. They didn't get a second chance. William Haddick died today Holly – shot straight through the head. He didn't know what hit him. It was a clean shot, they said. We can thank God for that.'

It was a terrible blow to Holly because they had been such good friends. I just didn't know how else to tell him about Haddick. Tears streamed down 'Big Holly's' face and he said only, 'Not Haddick, Black – not Haddick – not William Haddick – oh God, not Haddick!'

I got up and walked back to my foxhole in the tree patch outpost. It would surely be a sad New Year's Eve for Company 'C'.

## "ABLE" COMPANY

Company "A" had been relieved on December 28 from the tree patch position by "C" Company and was now enjoying the relative warmth in some of the less damaged houses in Champs on New Year's Eve. Sgt. Louis Merlano recalls experiencing the heavy artillery shelling which the "C" Company commander had been so concerned about. Merlano describes the action which took the life of one of his friends:

We now had solidified our position around Champs and along about the 28th of December, we were relieved by 'C' Company and took positions in a wooded area and had four houses in which we could shelter some of the fellows. I recall that the house I was in was hit with many artillery shells and we were in the back trying to get out. At one point, John Kleinfelder was in front of me and attempted to make a dash through the door when a shell hit right smack in front of him and it was sickening to see and he died in my arms. I believe that was December 31st.

After a period of relief in town, as was described by Sgt. Merlano, men in "A" Company were rushed forward to fill a gap in the "C" Company lines. Pvt. Ted Goldmann continues his story:

> On New Year's Eve a strong German combat patrol overran and knocked out the center of the middle platoon of 'C' Company on the hill directly under the high line and about half way between our positions of December 25th and 26th. The remainder of 3rd Platoon was elected to plug this gap. Our major order at night was to have one man of each two-man foxhole awake at all times. We moved up under a mortar and 20mm barrage on the position. The holes were one-man trenches and we enlarged them as best we could. Some of the holes had dead Germans lying right beside them but they were frozen so nobody paid any attention. Nothing much happened except more snow and bad weather and a lot of barrages which were very irritating but hit nobody. It scared one boy when the cable on the high line came down with a crash across his hole. Luckily he was lying down and it didn't touch him.[165]

## REPLACEMENTS

Arriving with the first group of replacements after the highway to Bastogne was reopened, Pvt. Gerald B. Johnston was back with his old unit in the 1st Battalion. He had been wounded during the first hours of the assault on St. Oedenrode in Holland on September 17. He had arrived at Mourmelon too late to be part of the December 19 move. Johnston wrote:

> Several of us were delivered to 'C' Company in Champs, a tiny village of stone buildings with several tanks parked on the backside of the buildings. Here I joined up with 2nd Platoon again. Troy Wall was still the platoon leader. I was assigned to Sgt. W. O. Bird's squad again, just as had been the case in Holland. The village was behind and below the foxhole line. Men were coming down from the line to warm up and heat their K-rations. I specifically remember 'Holly' Hollingsworth being there because he was talking about his escape from the Germans who attacked the hill above the town the night before, or perhaps the previous night. Apparently Holly's squad occupied the front slope of the hill and most of them were

---

[165]Goldmann, op. cit.

captured, including Holly. While being marched back to the German lines, Holly decided to make a break for it and ran back through the darkness to our lines, a clean escape despite being shot at. (One of the men captured was recovered later by the American advance in February or March and was at Mourmelon in March when we returned from Alsace.)

W. O. Bird took me up on the hill and showed me the positions and foxholes, all just on the back of the crest. Everybody was already doubled up in foxholes so I got my own private one, just down a hedgeline from the machine gun. We dragged the German body away and there I was, back in the war again. At this time it was totally quiet, no booms or bangs. It was hard to believe this was the front except for the bodies and Holly's story indicating anything could happen here at any time.

## 44TH COMBAT TEAM

After slipping and sliding over snow-slick by-ways, the 44th Armored Infantry Combat Team of the 6th Armored Division arrived in the 501st Parachute Infantry Regiment's Neffe perimeter. Their trip had been impeded by a heavy snowstorm and crossing paths with elements of the 11th Armored Division south of Bastogne.

Sgt. David Reich of the Reconnaissance Platoon has always remembered the welcome given his group by the cooks at a battalion kitchen. He wrote:

At first light, we were entering Bastogne under cloudy skies. Cold, tired and hungry, we were approached by a man from the kitchen of the 501st and he invited the fifteen of us from the Recon Platoon to share in a pancake breakfast.

The old farmhouse sat on the backside of a knoll and as we approached, the odor of hot coffee and food filled the air. We were warmly greeted and mess kits were filled to overflowing with the best darn pancakes I've ever eaten.

While waiting in line by a window, I could look out onto a large field where our mortar platoon was digging in at the time. As I stood there, a mortar round landed and killed a man I knew only as Littlejohn. The round landed far from him but the ice-hard snow caused the rounds to cover a wide area.

Near noon the 44th Combat Team moved out on the attack. Division Artillery of the 101st provided support. The 44th suffered heavy losses but the objectives were all taken. Neffe was taken but the woods southeast of Wardin were still in German hands.

## NEW YEAR'S GREETINGS

A surprise visit to the front line posts of the troops by the regimental commander was a pleasant encounter for sergeants Sam D. Hefner and Charles E. Richards. Hefner wrote:

Charles Richards and I were in our foxholes when a jeep pulled up. In it was Colonel (Robert) Sink and he said, 'Back home in North Carolina on New Year's Eve we always celebrated with a drink.' He gave each of us a bottle for our squad. That was a morale booster – even if some of the guys were afraid to drink it.

# 15. JANUARY 2, 1945

The new year arrived with a little fanfare from either side. All of the artillery pieces of the 3rd Army units positioned on either side of the German salient spoke as one voice in ushering in the new year. A few enemy bombers appeared over Bastogne to drop missles, which did little damage. The 101st Division artillery fired throughout New Year's Day in support of the 6th and 11th Armored Divisions which were moving up on the flanks.

On the morning of January 2, in an effort to widen the corridor leading south, the last threat to vehicular movement along that route was removed. The men of "F" Company of the 327th Glider Regiment were attached to Team Cherry of the 10th Armored Division for a sweep of Senonchamps, the small village two miles west of Bastogne.

One of the local residents came out of Senonchamps with a horror story as will be related by Baroness Rene Greindl.

The 501st Regiment was preparing to go on attack in an area which included a railroad trestle between Foy and Bizory. Two troopers will tell of their actions. Another soldier was held back by his company commander from an attack scheduled for the following day.

## CLEARING SENONCHAMPS

After a few days of rest from the hard fighting south of Bastogne and northwest of Marvie, the men of "F" Company of the 327th were moved by trucks to the Senonchamps vicinity for an effort to drive the remaining Germans from those positions. PFC. Charles Kocourek describes this action in which they had an opportunity to work with tanks for the first time:

The next day they drove us down near Senonchamps in trucks. We were to try taking it. Two earlier attempts had failed. Sgt. Francis McCann went on a patrol into the town and returned saying it was pretty quiet. He related: 'It doesn't look like there are any Germans in there.' We had three or four tanks with us. We hadn't fought with close tank support before. I asked a tanker what do we do? He said, 'Take care of enemy bazookas (panzerfausts). You can ride on top or follow behind us.' We started, guns blazing. We saw a couple soldiers race away. We let them go. We got all the way to the other side of town. There were two or three American tanks still burning – no bodies. The troops continued on, going toward a hill and shooting like mad. There was no firing coming in our direction.

We came to what looked like a chicken coop. There was a whole pile of dead Americans inside, piled on top of each other – at least 15 to 25 of them in that little building.[166]

We left that building and went down to the road, crossed over and there was an American half-track, slightly burned. I looked up into it and there was a gunner slumped over his .50 caliber machine gun – lots of shell casings strewn on the floor. He must have put up a helluva fight. One other soldier lay dead on the floor and a third man was lying beside the half-track.

We made a circle around and came back. In the meantime, the tanks came back. They had a couple prisoners.

## DECEPTION TURNS BRUTAL

An added story of enemy brutality toward the civilian population is related by Baroness Rene Greindl whose home at Ile-le-Hesse was being used as the nighttime 101st Division command post at this time. Team Cherry and "F" Company of the 327th had just cleared the remaining enemy soldiers from the village of Senonchamps. She wrote:

On the 2nd of January, to our surprise, the Americans brought us back from Senonchamps, Mademoiselle Vernel. She told us about the terrible time she had in that neighboring village, taken by the Germans before Christmas, after a battle from house to house, in which 17 out of 25 houses were destroyed. That tiny place had been the scene of horrifying events. We had seen from the chateau the terrible bombing attacks by which the Americans intended to destroy every German sheltered in this village.

Two men were murdered by the Germans under particularly horrid circumstances. They were father and son, and lived in the last house of the village towards Chenogne. The following details were clearly established thanks to the testimony of the next door neighbor's child, young Picard, age ten. The boy had his evening meal at the neighbor's house, when the village was still in the hands of the Americans. Suddenly, a jeep stopped outside the door and five Americans entered. They spoke French and seemed famished. They ate three loaves of bread and two pounds of butter. This detail alone should have struck any observant person. The Americans, well fed at the beginning of the battle, were always extremely loathe to accept the peasant's food; in addition, few, if any, spoke French. The good peasants, overtrustful, spoke openly and made no secret of their feelings toward the enemy and openly boasted that they belonged to the White Army and had

---

[166]The chicken coop is the same one referred to earlier by Duane Harvey and Donald Woodland, who had been fighting at Senonchamps earlier as part of 1st Battalion of the 327th.

helped to feed it. The guests left during the night and the child went to his own home. The next day, the murdered bodies of father and son were found in their house. The truth was not far to seek. Once more stood revealed German treachery; the guests were not Americans, but Germans in stolen uniforms, who had come to examine the neighboring woods. They had come back during the night to wreak their vengeance on these innocent people.

Mademoiselle had spent the last days in the stables of the principal farm, the only shelter left standing and where the sixty remaining villagers had also taken refuge. She had seen the enemy tanks firing on each other from a range of 100 yards. A man had fallen mortally wounded beside her and another had died in the battle. In this humble village of twenty-five houses, seven men were killed, apart from those already mentioned. . . .[167]

## ACTION NEAR THE RAILROAD TRESTLE

One of the actions that stands out in the memory of Pvt. James Jacobsma is an experience he had at a railroad trestle which occurred on January 2nd. He wrote:

On or about the night of January 2nd, the platoon was a little northeast of Bastogne underneath a railroad trestle. We had set up or dug holes with two .30 caliber machine guns when the Krauts put on their biggest and last counter-offensive against us. We put out anti-personnel and anti-tank mines. The first German tanks were stopped at the bridge and that is where we held them. They halted on the grade and we kept them there all night. I fired the machine gun for two, maybe three hours. The gun got hot. Others passed me rags to keep from burning my hands. I don't remember who was firing the other gun. When daylight came, we couldn't believe that we had stopped so much armor and infantry. We had held them back. We felt proud and very tired.

A machine gunner from the weapons platoon of 1st Battalion of the 501st, PFC. John C. Trowbridge was also in the action near the railroad trestle. He describes his part in the action:

The lowly private first class is never fully informed of the battle situation and rarely is he certain as to who is on his right and who's on the left flank. Seldom does he know the enemy's position and strength. So it was on this day.

My understanding was that our 1st Battalion would relieve 3rd Battalion on the line in the Bois Jacques the night before the attack. Next day, after

---

[167]Greindl, pp. 49-50.

what little rest they could get, 3rd Battalion would advance through our lines. Then 1st Battalion would pull back and remain in regimental reserve.

The attack never got underway on the 2nd as planned. The only action that I saw that day, but never fully understood, was a half-track and a jeep with mounted anti-aircraft guns making dry runs down the slope toward the railroad tracks, then back up again.

That night, January 2nd, our squad went forward to outpost a bridge where the Foy-Bizory road crossed a railroad which ran northeast out of Bastogne.

At this point, the rail bed laid about 20 feet below the actual lip of the cut. The woods at our rear had trees planted in straight rows, like you would plant corn. The branches of the trees were so weighted down with snow that they nearly touched the snow-covered ground beneath. This muffled the sound of gun fire to the extent that one never knew who was firing at whom.

We set up the gun about 50 yards to the right of the bridge, with a field of fire directly across the railroad into another woods, more dense than the one to our rear. Although we couldn't see the road as it approached the bridge from Foy, we could cover it with fire.

We arranged for two men to man the gun for a two-hour watch, while the other two tried to keep as warm as possible with one blanket and an overcoat in the nearby dugout. Without a doubt, this was the most frightful, the most desperate situation, it seemed to me, that I had faced up to this time.

We only had three grenades and it should be mentioned here that, a few days before, Rasmussen has traded his Thompson for an M1 rifle. That turned out to be a big mistake. That very night, it could have made a big difference in the German casualty list.

Sometime during the night, while Rasmussen and Thornton were on watch, an enemy patrol made its way along the tracks to a point directly below the gun. It was impossible to fire without the gunners exposing themselves. They dropped the three grenades and yelled for Webb and me to get out there and help. By then, it was our carbines against their grenades and machine pistols. As the patrol disappeared into the night, I wondered what that Thompson might have done.

## A "DEAR JOHN" LETTER

Mail call is always awaited with great anticipation – and even moreso after a unit has been isolated and in continuous combat for a long period of time.

Sometimes the news wasn't good. PFC. Seth O. Berry describes such a piece of mail:

When Patton broke through to us and we received our mail, there was a letter from my wife's aunt to the effect that my wife had started living with a man who was married and had four children. She had broken up his marriage. Two days later, I received a letter from her asking me to get a divorce from my wife. I took this letter and went back to company headquarters. I let Captain (Harry) Howard read both of the letters. I also told him that if I was killed that I sure didn't want my wife to get my insurance. We went back to personnel and he typed up a letter to this effect. He told me that it was not legal to do this, but to send all of this to my mother in case she (my wife) tried to collect it and go to court. He didn't think there was a court in the United States that would let her have it. Captain Howard and I went back to company headquarters. We were supposed to jump off in an attack the following morning. He looked at me and told me to stay there with him and the first sergeant. I looked at him and said, 'Captain Howard, if you think that I am going to commit suicide, you are mistaken'. He looked at me, grinning, and said, 'No, I don't think so, but I won't take the chance so you just stay here with me'.

# 16. JANUARY 3, 1945

On this day the fighting would be particularly fierce in the 2nd Battalion of the 502nd Parachute Regiment front at Longchamps where the enemy attempt to move south was stopped by the combined efforts of infantry, anti-tank, armor and artillery. The most valuable prisoner of war taken by the 101st during any of its campaigns is part of this chapter.

To the east, in the Bois Jacques (Jack's Woods), a unit of the 506th was hit hard by a heavy barrage as it returned to its former positions. Several key non-coms were lost and the company commander showed the first signs of cracking from the strains of battle.

Using American uniforms and driving a jeep, enemy soldiers penetrated the lines of the 501st and hijacked an armored vehicle.

Troops of the 501st Regiment were locked in several fierce battles as the troops attacked and retreated, fighting from one plantation to another.

## 2ND BATTALION HIT HARD AT LONGCHAMPS

To the northwest of Bastogne, along a 7,000 yard arc running outward from the villages of Champs, Longchamps, Monaville and Sonne-Fontaine, the 502nd Parachute Regiment was holding with all three battalions on line. As has been extensively reported thus far, 1st Battalion was on the left in the Champs vicinity; 2nd Battalion faced north in front of Longchamps and Monaville while 3rd Battalion covered the area northeast from Monaville to Recogne where its troops tied in with the 506th Regiment.

In the 2nd Battalion sector, Captain Earl Hendricks, with "F" Company, was in reserve. Additional support for 2nd Battalion was provided by "C" Battery of the 81st Anti-Tank Battalion of the 101st with five 57mm guns. Also in a supporting role were troops of the 705th TD Battalion with eight of its tank destroyers.

The description of the action beginning on what looked like a quiet day is found in the division history, *Rendezvous with Destiny* of the fighting taking place on the 2nd Battalion front:

It was looking like the beginning of a quiet afternoon on this front when, at 1310, the phone rang in the CP of the 502nd's Company D. 'I hear something.' It was Sgt. Lawrence J. Silva calling in from the outpost line. A few minutes later he called back. 'I can see fourteen tanks.' Then there were eighteen. Then there were twenty. Then more. Finally, his voice came: 'I can't tell you any more.' 'Why not?' 'There's a tank right over me. I'm lying flat on my stomach.' A day or two later he was found that way in his hole, dead.

The attack was not unexpected; for several days patrols had been returning with reports of an obvious buildup, chiefly in the section north and northwest of Longchamps, which was the center of the 502nd position and was held by 2nd Battalion. Heavy traffic had been observed on the main east-west highway between Compogne and Bertogne within mortar range of the front lines. But when 2nd Battalion got Sgt. Silva's first report they could only estimate, due to the heavy fog, the strength and intentions of the enemy force by sound and not by sight.

The first report received by Division twenty minutes after the tanks were heard on the 2nd Battalion front, said that there were fourteen enemy tanks in front of Lt. Bud Rainey's Company D and asked for tank destroyers. Actually, an estimated thirty to forty tanks, mostly Mark IV's, and a battalion of infantry were there in the mist.

The enemy armor had come down the road which runs south from Compogne to Longchamps. On reaching the crossroads north of Monaville and just beyond the 2nd Battalion's lines, the tanks had fanned out for the attack. In a well planned maneuver six of the tanks moved west across the front of Company D, crossed the Bertogne-Longchamps highway and, from the west side of the road, set up and maintained a base of fire throughout the attack. Their fire was very effective against both the anti-tank guns and automatic weapons defending the sector. Meanwhile, five other tanks moved to a point approximately four hundred yards northwest of Longchamps in front of Company E, went into position, and added to the fire of the six tanks. Though these eleven tanks never moved forward the fire from their cannon and machine guns, spraying over the 2nd Battalion area, kept the paratroopers down in their foxholes and handicapped their efforts to do anything about the main attacking force.

Some of the officers who had fought since Normandy thought the afternoon set a high in courage. The Germans had enough tanks to use them to shoot or rout or gas out individual riflemen. Tanks would stop over foxholes and pivot with the hole as the point of the pivot. Often, the hardness of the frozen ground and the depth of the hole would thwart the tank's action; then the man would rise and fire on the following German infantry. Sometimes the tank would return and park over the hole and gun its motor, flooding the paratrooper with carbon monoxide. The man could only lie and take it; but if he was still living when the tank finally went on, he would again get up and look for targets against which his rifle might be effective. It was a day productive of fear, frustrations and bravery. PFC. Bruno J. Mecca of Company D, whose hole on the outpost line was early overrun, came back to the CP that night with tears in his eyes: 'I'll fight any son-of-a-bitch, but I can't fight those goddamn tanks with a carbine.'

There was one man on the Company D front that day who did not stay in a foxhole. He was Warren Cobbett, a medic attached to the company. All afternoon Cobbett moved about in the open, picking up and bringing in the wounded. To many a man there, he was the hero of the day.[168]

On a day when "F" Company would suffer staggering losses, there was one soldier at a bazooka position who gave the Germans all they could handle and then some. PFC. E. O. Parmley relates the story of how his buddy, Pvt. Ray "Calfboy" Blasingame earned his Silver Star at Bastogne:

It is daylight, January 3, 1945. An order is shouted and relayed all along the 'F' Company line – 'All bazooka teams on line – a tank attack is imminent!'

The ground is covered with four to six inches of snow. 'Calfboy' looks for a position of concealment. There is none – the ground is flat and treeless. He spies a mount of dirt about 50 yards in front of the 'F' Company line. It is a square hole about three feet wide and three feet deep – a previously dug German hole. Calfboy says, 'they dig square holes to match their helmets. We dig round ones, not so much work.' He heads for the hole. Ray Gary, the pack mule for the bazooka, follows.

It is about noon when the monotonous funeral music of tank motors is heard. They come into view slowly, four abreast parallel to the line. The turret guns fire as suspect targets appear on the line. The tank nearest our lines is coming directly toward Calfboy's hole as they are fifty yards in front of the line. Concealment is the only chance for them. A shot to the front of the tank is useless. With its slow pace, the tank is thorough in its search for targets or possible danger spots. Calfboy's position is spotted when the tank is forty to fifty yards from them. The first shot explodes behind them. The next one hits the front of the mound, blowing them, along with a large amount of dirt, halfway out of the hole. Gary yells, 'we've got to get out of here! We've got to get out of here!'

Calfboy yells, 'We stay, get back in the hole!' The tank continues its agonizing crawl, possibly its commander was thinking the occupants of the hole are out of action. The tank passes within ten to fifteen feet of the hole.

Resting the bazooka on the edge of the hole, Calfboy fires when the rear of the tank is exposed. The tank goes up in flames and smoke. Two men emerge. No one seems to know what happened to them. There are other tanks to attend to. Calfboy fires five more shells. One hits a tank but does not explode. Gary failed to pull the pin, although after each shot Calfboy yells, 'Pull the pin!' There are three hits on the remaining tanks. One shot is

---

[168]Rapport & Northwood, 622-624.

a miss. Calfboy is credited with half a tank on the three remaining, which
are knocked out also. The battle lasted thirty to forty-five minutes. A new
battle line is formed as German artillery will try to avenge their four lost
tanks.

Sgt. Burt Ellard was in the same squad of the 2nd Platoon with PFC. E. O.
Parmley and Ray Blasingame. Ellard claims he activated the first round for
Blasingame's bazooka before "Calfboy" headed for the foxhole in front of the
company's positions. This is the way he describes the bazooka action:

At the same time that Blasingame was after the lead tank, the others had
moved on by the foxhole position with their infantry and isolated a large
segment of 'F' Company. Blasingame got the one that had advanced over the
ridge. The others did not advance as far and they are the ones that captured
our men. 1st Platoon was the group captured. Sgt. Howard Matthews was
one of them. Our platoon was in reserve. 1st and 3rd Platoons were on line.

After the company was pretty well annihilated, my squad was taken
back and we were sent to regimental headquarters and went out on combat
patrols to get info on the enemy.

One of the men who was with the company commander as his radio operator
when 1st Platoon was trapped by the tanks was PFC. Walter F. Zagol. He has
this memory of the fierce battle in which his company was involved that resulted
in the loss of nearly fifty men. Zagol wrote:

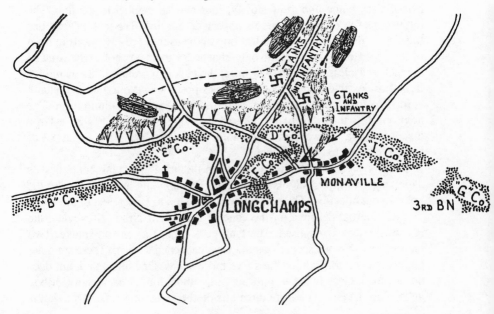

*Map 18*

Our company was situated on the outskirts of Bastogne near the town of Longchamps. 'F' Company was caught in the open by the German tanks and infantry. We took a terrible beating, losing 47 men including our company commander and two other officers and nine non-coms in one day of fighting. My company commander put up the white flag on his submachine gun and surrendered his men as the German tanks started to mow down our men in the hedges we were in. I crawled back and managed to escape.

## 81ST ANTI-TANK GUNNERS

Attached to Company "D" was the anti-tank gun team of Sgt. Joe O'Toole of "C" Battery of the 81st Anti-Tank Battalion of the 101st Division. The main function of Sgt. O'Toole's section was to protect a roadblock in the 2nd Battalion sector near Longchamps. This was a continuing action as described by a gun crew member, PFC. Edward Peniche, who wrote:

In our deployment toward Bastogne, our AT squad was assigned to Company 'D', 502nd Parachute Infantry Regiment. By dawn on Wednesday, December 19th, we had taken defensive positions in the outskirts of the village of Longchamps. We emplaced our 57mm AT gun on a knoll overlooking a valley. We were covering one of the main roads leading into Bastogne. Our main mission was to protect the roadblock on that road. We had piled all the plows and other farm implements that we could find in the area to set up the roadblock and we felt that we could defend and hold that position against any German attack. We had dug in, until the barrel was just barely visible above the snow. Down in front of us was 'no-man's land'.

## MAD MINUTE AT LONGCHAMPS

The role of Sgt. Joe O'Toole's gun crew of that anti-tank section is described vividly by PFC. Edward Peniche in an article he wrote:[169]

On January 3, 1945, the 502nd Parachute Infantry Regiment was attacked in force and its MLR was overrun by enemy armor. The action began around 1330 hours. The enemy armor came down the road which runs southward from Compogne to Longchamps. In a well-planned maneuver the German tanks, about 15 to 17 of them, fanned out for the attack. They were being followed by infantrymen and panzer-grenadiers. It was a fierce and determined attack against our front. As the German tanks and infantry began to advance against our position and towards the road block, our squad leader,

---

[169]Peniche, Edward. *Military*, "Mad Minute at Longchamps". April 1985, pp. 15+

Sgt. Joe O'Toole, gave us orders to engage the enemy – the enemy fire was effectively raking our positions.

I was sure that at that moment everyone was as scared as I was – PFC. Alfred Stein was ready to load the piece again as PFC. Darrell Garner, our gunner, was finding the range.

I quickly moved two more AT shells to the gun position, making sure that they had AP fuses (SABOT), a new type of high velocity shell.

Several airbursts exploded between us and the road block, our machine gunners to our right, were keeping the grenadiers from reaching the road block. As a Mark V Tiger tank approached that point on the road, we hit it twice; the second shot took its turret off and, as the crew was leaving the burning tank, they were riddled with machine gun fire – our SABOT ammunition was proving very effective AT ordnance. Behind our position one or two armored vehicles, either U.S. TD's or half-tracks, sporadically came up the ridge to lob a shell or two against the attacking force. The German 88's were proving to be accurate and devastating – shells and bullets were spraying our emplacement. In reality, once an AT gun is committed to battle, its position is easily spotted and the situation becomes one of do-or-die. There are no avenues of retreat nor room for maneuverability.

I crawled back to our ammo dump to bring more AT shells.

As we destroyed a second tank, all hell broke loose around us. We were determined to offer a heavy resistance, but the German gunners zeroed in on our emplacement; we were being hit with everything that the enemy could fire. It was the hour of the mad minute. It was that terrifying moment when all the weapons on the line seemed to explode violently all at once. The incoming shells were so numerous that the ground felt tremoring. Our gun took a direct hit and was destroyed. All three of us, O'Toole, Garner and myself, were hit by shrapnel. The battle raged on all around us; the TD's and our mortars were hitting the Mark IV German tanks which were not advancing but were continuing their murderous fire. The mad minute was upon us at Longchamps.

By this time, I crawled to assist O'Toole who had been severely wounded. He had been hit in the hip and leg; he was bleeding profusely and looked like he was going into shock. To mitigate the pain, he had given himself a shot of morphine. Garner was hit in the face and shoulder; my left leg was numb above the knee, but my knee was hurting a lot. I looked down and saw the blood on my muddy trousers. Voices and moans of some other men could be heard. I remember praying in both English and Spanish. As I crawled on the snow toward the ridge, I heard the bullets and shrapnel cutting the air above me, but I needed to reach our CP just behind the knoll. We needed medical attention.

The entire episode could not have lasted more than 15 or 20 minutes – I finally reached the CP and reported what had happened and was happening.

## OTTIE BROCK'S GUN

Along the same front in the Longchamps area, Sgt. Ottie Brock was in charge of another of the anti-tank guns and pointed out the superiority of the British six-pounder over the American version of the 57mm anti-tank gun:

I can recall that our men on the British 6-pounder anti-tank gun were attempting to eat their dinner when we received word over our sound power phone, messages from a paratroop outpost that a tank was approaching. The anti-tank men were immediately warned. In the meantime, the outpost man's warning was increased as the number of tanks increased one by one until it finally reached about 17. Also, the men on the anti-tank guns were changing tank targets as more came into view. Finally, the 'commence firing!' order was given and the action was furious. Snow and dirt was thrown in the air and a nearby haystack caught fire so that visibility from our position was poor. A tank got right in front of our gun and Durwood McDaniel put it out of action. It was a good thing our anti-tank guns were the British 6-pounders instead of the 57mm guns the Americans generally used. Our guns had a double shield in front, which gave us more protection than did the U.S. 57mm gun. Also, the muzzle velocity was about 6000, giving us a greater advantage over the 57mm shell. Anyway, the German tanks were stopped although most of their tanks were retrieved later by the enemy. Sgt. O'Toole in our section, was injured and evacuated to England. O'Toole told me his weapon was hit so hard that the muzzle was pointing almost straight up.

## SERGEANT FORD CREDITED WITH 7 TANKS

Sergeant Edward E. Ford of "C" Battery of the 81st Anti-Tank Battalion was in position with his British 6-pounder weapon on the morning of January 3, 1945 when a large group of enemy tanks approached his position. He had moved up to the position during the night, dug himself a good, deep foxhole and waited for enemy armor that might come his way. He recalled:

Shortly after noon, I saw this column of enemy tanks followed by infantry approaching our positions. I was amazed to see so many infantry men popping up in their holes and firing at the oncoming enemy vehicles and foot soldiers. I hastily got on the phone and called my battery commander, asking for all the artillery we could get.

We got two rounds. When the tanks were within 800 feet of my foxhole and moving across my front, I started picking them off, one by one. Sgt. Edward Ford was credited with destroying seven enemy tanks on this date. He was awarded the Distinguished Service Cross for heroism.[170]

The unit history of the 81st Anti-Tank Battalion provides a brief description of the hectic actions which took place in the vicinity of Longchamps involving Battery "C". Captain George McCormack wrote:

The 502nd Para Inf was attacked 3 January 45 and its MLR was overrun by an armored attack. Btry 'C' lost five guns but managed to destroy ten enemy Mark IV's. Sergeant (Edward) Ford being credited with seven tanks destroyed.[171]

## ACTION ON THE MLR

After a two-week period of relative quiet in his sector, Pvt. Robert L. MacNaughton and his "D" Company buddies were in the thick of the actions on January 3 and, like "F" Company, they took heavy casualties. MacNaughton wrote:

We had not had too much direct contact except a few patrol probes by German infantry (panzer grenadiers). However, on the 3rd of January, the Germans launched an all-out attack on our sector, trying to breach our road block and defensive position on the ridge at Longchamps. During the late afternoon, a Mark IV tank and a Tiger tank broke through and most of 3rd Platoon was captured. The tanks were shelling our CP and it burned. It was about this time that 1st/Sgt. John Woolen was KIA. I helped carry him to the aid station in the church just below the crossroad.

On returning to the CP, a Cpl. Flaig (not of our outfit) was there with a bazooka and four rounds of ammo. We worked in close to the tanks and 'killed' one of them, which lost a tread or track. We fired on the other tank, which withdrew, and it did not return.

The remaining tank, although disabled, was still shelling and machine-gunning us. Flaig was killed. It was getting dark about then and I managed

---

[170]In a telephone conversation with former sergeant Edward Ford on September 13, 1990, the author learned Ford had never received the medal. He may have missed out on the award ceremony as he was sent stateside on a 30-day furlough to promote the sale of War Bonds. I wrote to his local congressman asking that the oversight be corrected. Nothing came of it.

[171]*Small Unit History of the 81st Airborne Anti-Tank Battalion* which was compiled by Captain George W. McCormack. Copy was obtained from the Fort Campbell museum courtesy of Paul Lawson.

to get in close and, when the tank commander opened his hatch, I dropped a phosphorus grenade inside and the tank burned all night.[172]

As a replacement in "E" Company, and getting a taste of combat for the first time, Pvt. Alfred Harrison remembered what happened to a fellow replacement. He wrote:

I recall Pvt. George F. Nordberg, who was a member of my company. He was killed on January 3, 1945 during a major attack by the Germans. As I understand it, he was standing up in his foxhole shaking his fist, yelling at the Germans when he was struck by fragments from a tree burst overhead. I'm sure those who came in contact with him remember him well as he had an enormous chip on his shoulder and had a hostile attitude that found him fighting, verbally and physically, with members of our own units, even when we were in action against the Germans.

In describing the attack on January 3 when "F" Company lost so many men during the enemy assault on the 2nd Battalion sector, Captain Robert S. Dickson of "E" Company wrote:

'Easy' Company occupied a sector wider than could be considered most efficient with foxholes in some areas but not mutually supportable. That, plus the openness of the frozen, snow-covered terrain, made camouflage exceptionally difficult. The men prevailed however, and several days passed before the first artillery fire of any consequence hit us. This was the beginning of the German attack in the northern sector that involved 'D' and 'F' Companies so drastically. The openness of the terrain in front of 'E' Company was not favorable for an enemy advance. Some tanks did get fairly close, but their infantry was too vulnerable in that environment. Consequently, 'D' Company, whose lines ran through a wooded area, received the brunt of the German attack.

If I may say a word about the 'F' Company counterattack that resulted in so many casualties, years later, (Captain) Earl Hendricks and I talked about this and agreed that rushing into an ongoing fight against German tanks by parachute infantry, with their paucity of anti-tank weapons, was asking for trouble. I remember seeing 'F' Company walking across open, snow-covered terrain on their way to counterattack and thinking they had better get under cover of trees soonest. The final result however, was favorable as the Germans were stopped and made to withdraw.

There is always a soldier in a period of extreme tension who has a way of easing the strain with a light remark. Such was the case with this action provided by T/4 John Seney, operations sergeant for 2nd Battalion:

---

[172]After a period of 47 years, Robert L. MacNaughton was surprised to hear from former Sgt. Carl Robare of his unit. MacNaughton could have sworn he helped stuff the remains of Robare into a mattress cover on the day of the heavy shelling at Longchamps.

I don't remember the area but we had a Robert McGinley in our outfit who would and did drink anything. His most important contribution was during a terrific shelling when you couldn't raise your head and all of us were becoming addled. Suddenly, it got real quiet. McGinley stood up and in a loud voice said, 'A guy can get killed around here!' It broke the tension – you could hear chuckles and remarks – crazy bastard, etc.

## A POW SPILLS THE BEANS

As a member of the jump band of the 502nd Parachute Infantry Regiment, Pvt. Lincoln H. Bethel had participated in both parachute drops in enemy territory and then served as a body guard for the staff officers. At Bastogne, he was on the front line as a member of a machine gun crew. He describes his experience in the third person:

The miserably cold, snowy night of 3 January '45 found the private with a corporal he didn't even know, huddled in a shallow hole on the military crest of a hill located somewhere north of the outskirts of Bastogne near Monaville. Their .30 caliber light machine gun was set up to traverse down this long hill which ended in a valley with woods on the other side. The temperature was down to zero degrees Fahrenheit and a light snow was adding to that already fallen – in some places waist deep, but on the wind-swept hill, it averaged some six inches.

The machine gun platoon of HQ Company, 2nd Bn., of the 502nd was attached for this engagement to 'D' Company. Their only contact with anyone was with Sgt. Reggie Davies who constantly checked on his forward outposts. It seemed to the private, with the very limited visibility, that they were alone on this hill.

Sometime during the night, on one of his contact checks, Davies decided to probe further down the hill and the private accompanied him. They took off from the machine gun emplacement, keeping as low as possible, slipping and sliding in the slippery going. After reaching almost the bottom of the hill, they could see about 14 German tanks across the clearing. They crept close enough to hear the guttural voices and see and smell the vile smoke of German cigarettes.

Deciding discretion the better part of valor, Davies decided to return up the hill and report this information. The return up the hill was uneventful – again leading the private to believe they were alone on the hill. Upon reaching the gun emplacement, Davies advised the corporal and private that the shallow hole should be twice as deep as dawn might show the tanks a perfect target.

The private placed his tommy gun to the rear of the hole, away from the enemy tanks, and immediately began to hack and chisel the frozen earth. After about 20 minutes of very little success, having worked up a cold sweat in digging, the corporal got in the hole, started digging and our private stood with his back to the tanks, sweating and breathing heavily from his exertion.

Suddenly, a jab in his back and the guttural query of 'Vas is das?' assailed his senses. In a complete reflex action he whirled, grabbed at the pistol with his left hand and decked the sheet-covered apparition with a swinging right hand to the jaw. Down they both went, with the private on top and by the time the corporal scrambled out of the hole to assist, it was over – as events were to prove, the private had captured one of the most valuable captives the 101st Division ever took.

Hearing this commotion, Sgt. Davies came hurrying over and personally escorted the German to the 101st interrogators. With little regard for his fellow soldiers, this German runner carried detailed information about concentrated attacks scheduled for early that morning and maps that he carried pinpointed locations of armor designed to be probably the heaviest the Division would ever face. After spilling his guts to Sgt. Schmidt, the 502nd interrogator, who after initially suspecting a plant, it was decided to believe the information and all remaining artillery in the area concentrated on the information as described by the runner.[173]

Responding to a request from Lincoln Bethel for verification of the action for which the Silver Star was being requested, Rene A. Schmidt, who had served as the interrogator of German prisoners for 2nd Battalion of the 502nd Regiment, sent this response to Bethel:

As soon as I read your letter, the incident you mentioned came to mind. I heard the same account of the capture of this prisoner, however, not having a personal knowledge of this, I doubt it would stand up in an affidavit.

Link, here's another angle to this incident that I do have first-hand knowledge of. Remember we had been in heavy combat since about noon of that day and the losses to our battalion were staggering. Our lines were non-existent in places. I was awakened some time during the night – don't remember the time. At first I said No! What's one more Kraut. Let him go

---

[173] On page 627 of *Rendezvous with Destiny*, appears this item: "Shortly after dark that evening – January 3 – occurred one of the incidents which change the course of battles. A German soldier came up to the machine gun nest of Corporal Davies of Headquarters Company, 2nd, tapped the corporal on the shoulder (mistaking him for a fellow German) and asked directions. The lost German was personally escorted to the 101st interrogators and turned out to be as valuable a captive as the Division ever took. He was a runner from the 19th SS Grenadier Regiment of the 9th SS Panzer Grenadier Division; he was delivering messages to company CO's and he had detailed knowledge of another concentrated attack scheduled for early that evening."

until morning, but they insisted. So, reluctantly I went over and interrogated this prisoner. Yes, he was a runner and at the time of his capture he was rounding up elements of an armored infantry unit that was scheduled to mount an attack on our positions at I believe four a.m. through Monaville – remember that name?

At first we thought this man was a 'plant' and while we were concentrating on his information they would hit us somewhere else.

However, it was decided that in our weakened condition we had no choice but go for broke. We called Division and gave them the grid coordinates (which he obligingly pointed out on the map) of the alleged assembly area. Here again, DivArty was reluctant to fire this mission because artillery stocks were very low, but in the end decided to go along.

Sometime around daybreak after the prisoner was taken and confirmed the information we had received they were about to attack when the artillery hit them and 'scattered them like leaves'.

I am convinced if that attack had taken place, our battalion and possibly the 3rd Battalion on our right would have been ground to pieces.[174]

## THE BOIS JACQUES SHELLING

1st/Sgt. Carwood Lipton of "E" Company describes the terrific shelling inflicted on his unit on January 3 when it was part of a large-scale attack through the Bois Jacques woods:

After clearing the woods and holding them the night of the 2nd, we returned to our old defensive line in the wooded area southeast of Foy. Our positions there had been occupied by another unit while we were in the attack. When we got back we saw that the Germans had zeroed artillery in on them. There were a number of shell holes and branches from tree bursts. Tree bursts in wooded areas are especially dangerous as the only protection against them is overhead cover. We had covers of logs and dirt over our foxholes. We could see that the German fire had been from heavy caliber guns so everyone dropped his equipment and began working in strengthening his foxhole cover. I grabbed an axe and ran over to some smaller trees about fifty yards from my foxhole to cut more logs to put over it.

I had no sooner gotten there when I heard the German guns open fire in the distance. There wasn't time to get back to my foxhole, but I saw a small open foxhole that someone had started to dig and then abandoned and I

---

[174]From a letter to Lincoln Bethel written by Rene A. Schmidt October 19, 1980. Schmidt was the 2nd Battalion interrogator.

jumped into it. Everyone else was also jumping into whatever cover they could find.

The foxhole that I had jumped into was so shallow that when I crouched down as low as I could into it, my head, from about my nose up, was above the ground, so I saw the shells hitting into the trees and into the ground. The sound was deafening and the ground was rocking and pitching like an earthquake but, for some reason, I didn't feel afraid or even nervous.

After several long minutes the shelling stopped and I came out of the foxhole. The area was a shambles and men were yelling that they were hit. I ran back to my foxhole for my rifle and heard someone yelling from a foxhole close by that had been caved in by a round that had hit into the base of a tree right by it and had knocked the tree down across it. My recollection is that the man in the foxhole was William 'Shep' Howell.

Although other men were yelling, 'Shep' was the closest and I started trying to dig him out. The tree across the foxhole blocked my way and I put my shoulder to it to move it although it was a whole tree and it was at least 16 inches in diameter. Of course I couldn't budge it, but with the help of some other men who were unhurt we dug him out around it. He wasn't hurt either.

Then I heard the German guns open up again and jumped into my own foxhole. This was something that both sides did. After a first barrage, there would be a pause to let the rescue efforts on the wounded begin and then a second barrage would be sent in to get the rescuers.

After several more minutes the second shelling ended and I came out of my foxhole, still unhurt. As I was trying to see what our situation was, expecting that there would be a ground attack into our position after the shelling, I heard Lt. Dilke. I can still hear him with that deep voice of his. He was about 25 yards away, without his helmet or a weapon.

'Sergeant Lipton!' he yelled at me. 'You get things organized here and I'll go for help.' And with that, he left.

I started rounding up the men who hadn't been hit, some close to breaking and some amazingly calm, to help the wounded men and to organize against the German attack that I felt sure was coming. Several men had been killed and many badly wounded. One of my closest friends, platoon sergeant Bill Guarnere, had a serious leg wound and when I walked over to him he looked up at me and said, 'Lip, they got ol' Guarnere this time!' It was the end of the war for him as he lost the leg. I put Sgt. Malarkey in charge as platoon sergeant. Little Cpl. Hanson was one of the calmest. He came to me and said that he had his squad and its light machine gun in position in case there was an attack.

Squad sergeant Joe Toye had been hit in the wrist by a bomb fragment from an enemy raid on January 2. He had been evacuated back to the aid station in

Bastogne where he was treated and spent the night. Toye has this recollection of his return to the unit:

> On the morning of January 3rd, I returned to Captain Dick Winters. At this time, Dick was the battalion exec. Captain Winters told me where I could find Company 'E'. They had been ordered to clean out the pockets of Germans on the front of our lines. I joined them and took over my job as squad leader in the 2nd Platoon.

Captain Dick Winters remembered when Sgt. Joe Toye had been hit and sent to the Bastogne aid station. This is his recollection of Toye returning to his unit:

> While I was at the battalion CP, I looked out across the field to our left flank and saw Joe walking back from Bastogne, up the road and across the field, his arm in a sling, heading back to the front line. I walked out to meet him and asked, 'Where are you doing? You don't have to go back to the line.' Joe answered, 'I want to go back with the fellows.' Joe and Bill Guarnere got caught in an artillery barrage and both men lost a leg.

Sgt. Joe Toye continued his story describing how he was caught in an exposed position and was hit. Platoon sergeant Bill Guarnere had come to his aid and he in turn was hit.

> Late afternoon on January 3rd, we were ordered back to our original positions. It was just getting dark as we took up our position. The Germans opened up on us with their artillery. Since I was a squad sergeant, I had to position my men. That's why I was caught standing up. They always said if you can hear the shells, you'll be okay. I did not hear the shell that put my lights out. The last thing I remember was asking if someone could drag me into a hole. Platoon sergeant Bill Guarnere tried to get to me, but did not make it. He lost his leg trying – I lost my leg, was wounded in the stomach, chest and both arms. That was the end of the war for me.

> Bill Guarnere risked his own life to save me from being hit with more shrapnel. Bill never made it to me, but he tried and it cost him.

Also injured in the same shelling was Pvt. Lester A. Hashey who recalled being near S/Sgt. Bill Guarnere. His platoon sergeant didn't realize his wound would be so serious it would result in an amputation.

> Sgt. Bill Guarnere lost a leg saying 'that is a million dollar wound!' We took the worst shelling outside of Foy that I ever experienced. I got hit from a tree burst. The wound was in the right shoulder and penetrated my lung. The medic told me to go to the rear and I would find the battalion aid station. With jacket cut off, I walked through the snow. A jeep came by loaded with wounded. I hung on to the rear tire with my good arm and through the hills and woods we went.

# THE ATTACK ON BOIS JACQUES

The attack on "Jack's Woods" was another of the military moves that a private first class doesn't understand nor is the strategy explained to him before the attack unfolds. This is PFC. John Trowbridge's story:

The next day, around noon, on the 3rd of January, the long awaited attack began as the 3rd Battalion crossed the tracks and immediately came under fire.

We waited and waited, but our lieutenant never came, so we decided it was high time to get out.

We had gotten about 75 yards toward the rear, in the clearing at the edge of the woods, when shells began exploding all around us. As we ducked into the woods, I saw a shallow slit trench and made a dive for it. I landed in the trench with my back toward the clearing and was immediately hit with what seemed like ten pounds of searing hot shrapnel, all along my exposed left side, from head to foot. Most larger pieces entered my chest cavity. I heard Thornton yell 'Medic!' then saw him running off into the woods. I thought at the time, 'How heroic of him!' I learned later that he had taken a bad hit. Perhaps from the same burst. Rasmussen and Webb were unhurt.

I knew my war was over and I suspected that my life was too, in just a matter of time. The enemy had counterattacked on the 2nd Battalion's unprotected right flank, rendering our position untenable.

I asked Webb to give me a shot of morphine and advised him and Rasmussen to get the hell out, or they'd get it too.

In the meantime, Rasmussen had gotten the gun set up and began to fire on the enemy formation of platoon strength, in the direction we had been headed, at a distance of about five hundred yards.

He sent them scurrying back to cover when the gun jammed. He kept working the bolt, but to no avail.

My back was towards the clearing and I couldn't move, but I knew that 60 yards across the clearing was another grove of trees that bordered the tracks and ran in a northeasterly direction.

Since I couldn't look in the direction of the clearing, I don't know exactly what happened, but two vehicles from an armored unit had been knocked out and were burning. Even with the sounds of battle, the exploding ammo had its own particular sound.

A captain and an enlisted man from the knocked out vehicles ran to our position. I don't know how many men the captain lost in those vehicles, but he seemed berserk when he joined us. At the same time, Rasmussen was telling me to hang on while he and Webb went for help. Until the captain found out that the gun wouldn't fire, then he too left, with little concern for me, the fallen warrior.

Shortly after that, four troopers came from across the bridge and stopped forty yards from where I was lying. One of them spotted me, raised his M1, aimed and fired point blank at my face. I had so many wounds already, I don't know whether that bullet hit me or not. The four of them made their way off through the woods.

Five minutes later, a jeep came roaring up to the edge of the woods, not ten feet from my feet; the driver jumped out and ran hell bent into the woods. Then I became aware that the enemy was moving into the adjoining woods just sixty yards behind me.

I felt I had seen it all and wasn't too surprised when I heard the crunch of foot steps in the snow and, through my one good eye, saw a Kraut looking down the barrel of his machine pistol, pointed at me, less than nine feet away. Yet I wasn't prepared, not knowing that there were two of them, to hear the jeep crank up, the gunmen jump in and speed away.

In the meantime, Rasmussen and Webb had reported my position to an evacuation team and sent them in my direction. The afternoon was rapidly fading away when they found me.

I could never adequately express my gratitude to the men of that team, but I have spent most of my days since then, thanking God. I thank Him, too, for permitting me to serve my country among the finest, bravest and most caring men one could ever know.

## SUPPORT UNITS

Cpl. Glen A. Derber was a day late getting back from his pass to Paris and the troops had already departed when he got back to the 501st regimental area. His most memorable actions occurred after the New Year. He wrote:

My most memorable actions occurred on January 3rd. It started the night before actually, with the following events: an LMG crew of four men was normally attached to an infantry company as it was SOP to stand our own guard duty. This meant two hours on duty and six off, but we only held to that schedule through the hours of darkness. It was my assistant gunner's turn for his two-hour shift starting at midnight and he had relieved me. I told him to wake me if he got sleepy. Some unusual noise startled me about 0100 hours and I was immediately wide awake. The first thing I learned was that my assistant gunner had dozed off – great! Then the noise of a motorized vehicle, probably a half-track about 200 yards off to my right, was heard. We were deployed along the edge of a woods with a half mile of open ground in front of us. There was some shooting and the half-track retreated toward the German lines. I figured it was a probe and expected an attack the next morning.

The sounds of vehicular movement which Cpl. Glen Derber heard was the commotion created by enemy soldiers moving about behind the 2nd Battalion front lines and capturing one of the armored half-track vehicles as noted in an S-2 report for the 501st Parachute Infantry Regiment.[175]

At 0230 this morning, an enemy patrol dressed in American uniforms, driving an American jeep, penetrated our lines a distance of 300 yards; came upon a half-track, killed the driver; took the half-track and shot their way back through our lines. This entire action took place at approximately 599600. (The numbers pertain to the map coordinates.)

While the battalion machine gun teams were assigned to the various line companies along their perimeters, the 81mm mortar tubes were nearer to the battalion headquarters. On the 2nd of January the mortar platoon had moved to another location and it was felt a patrol out to the front was in order to see what the enemy was up to out in that direction. So, while the enemy had moved around furtively behind the 2nd Battalion lines and captured the half-track and raced back to their own positions, Sgt. Ahzez Karim and his section leader were scouting out enemy positions. Karim related:

Late one day, Lt. Alton Phipps wanted me to go with him past our front lines, up the valley, as close to the woods where the Germans were thought to be planning an armored attack. We were slowly moving up the hill and a few hundred yards from the woods. I stopped and said, 'Lt. Phipps, if we keep going any farther, we'll walk into a German outpost.' Phipps said 'Yes, I think you're right.' So we stayed there for about two hours, listening for sounds of tanks and vehicles. Toward the end of the second hour, we heard a lot of low rumbling of tank tracks. Lt. Phipps said, 'That's what we came for. Sounds like they are grouping for an attack – let's get back!'

It was dark now but light enough to follow the way back. Now it was dangerous going down and up the hill into our own lines. The guys at the outposts knew we were coming back. When we spotted them, we stayed down until we used the password. We now felt safe, moved up to the top of the hill toward our mortar positions. Two medics were carrying one of our guys. He had been hit by machine gun fire. They had a fire fight down the hill to the left of us. He was in tremendous pain. He asked a couple guys who were walking along with him to shoot him. He kept begging his buddies, 'Please shoot me!'

Anticipating an enemy attack through the 2nd Battalion positions, the Mortar Platoon officer, 1Lt. Alton Phipps, called all of his non-coms to a meeting. Sgt. Ahzez Karim relates what plans were made:

---

[175]From *S-2 Periodic Report 15* for Headquarters, 501st Parachute Infantry Regiment dated 3 January 1945.

The next morning Lt. Phipps called all of us sergeants to a meeting. S-2 had made some prisoners talk and verified that a tank and infantry attack was coming from the woods and up the valley. So we were to move all our 81mm mortars to the left a few hundred yards, directly across the woods. All the companies were to move and get set for the attack. Phipps told us to have all the men dig our foxholes deep enough so if the German tanks overran us we were to keep all of our weapons at the bottom of our foxholes and to get all the hand grenades and ammo into our holes. Phipps said the plan was if the tanks overran our positions, we were to stop the infantry. We picked up our 81's, moved and started digging in at our new positions. Most of us dug 3 to 4 foot deep when all hell broke loose. Grogan, Baker and myself were standing in number 1 gun pit, a 4 x 4 we had dug. I was talking when Grogan grabbed me by the jacket and pulled me down with him. A German mortar shell hit about a foot or two from the edge of our gun pit. We looked at each other, asked if everyone was okay. We laughed. We looked so pale, white as ghosts. The shell had exploded as my head was below the level of the ground. There was a piece of steel about two inches long and one eighth-inch in diameter, very jagged looking – it had penetrated my combat jacket collar and rubbed against my neck. That was close! I give Grogan credit for quick thinking. That action saved my life.

In a few minutes we had all four 81's firing. We zeroed in on the incoming attack. The Germans seemed to have our number, too. They were hitting up and down our lines with 88's, 120mm mortars and some direct attacks from German tanks. I called for more ammo. We had dug shallow holes around our gun pits to store 81mm shells. One soldier, Pvt. Jose Jimenez, did more to brave the incoming hell and deliver ammo to my 81. Pvt. Peyton Griffin and John Grogan, gunners of guns #1 and #2, kept their cool and adjusted according to my commands that came from the outpost. Right in the middle of a command, the line from the guns to the outpost went dead. Lt. Phipps ordered one of the staff sergeants to send someone out to repair the line. The sergeant said to Phipps, 'I can't – it's suicide to send someone toward the outpost!' Phipps turned to me and said, 'Karim, get the line repaired!' I called to Pvt. George Root to follow the line and fix the break. Root told me to do it myself. I picked up my M1 and looked down the barrel, aimed it at his chest and said, 'Get the hell out there and fix that line!' There was a stand-off for two or three seconds, then Root put his two hands on top of the hole and hopped out, went down the hill, line in hand. I thought if he didn't make it back I would have to send someone else down the line. The four 81's were blind without contact with the outpost. We had been firing area targets into the coming German attack. Each gun would put nine rounds in the air before the first round hit the ground. In any event, we put a lot of kill power in the air. One salvo could cover a couple football fields. If anyone, a German, was standing, walking or running, chances are he would be hit. Then, suddenly, the phone came to life. A few minutes later here comes George Root into his foxhole swearing. I thought that was one of the bravest actions of the battle.

Just after Root made it back, the battle reached its peak. Some Sherman tanks moved up alongside of our gun pits and started firing. A captain was standing in one of the turrets of a tank next to our holes directing fire. The tank fired a few rounds but I thought they were staying in one place too long. I hollered at the captain, 'Get that tank out of here! You're going to get hit!' As I tried to get his attention, suddenly, the sound of an 88 hitting the side of the turret was heard. It must have hit the very edge or side of the turret. You could hear it when it made contact, then flipped end over end as it went across the sky. The captain and crew of that tank were lucky. They backed up, went about a hundred yards to our right and started firing again. I guess it was payback time for tankers. They took it from the Germans a few days before. They were giving a good account of themselves. The 10th Armored Division and the 705th Tank Destroyer Battalion helped back us up.

The artillery, mortar, machine gun and rifle fire had stopped as quickly as it had started. The medics were carrying wounded to the aid station. Some of the troopers who had light wounds were also heading to the aid station. Once again, the medics showed a lot of courage in picking up wounded comrades under these extreme conditions. The call for 'Medic!' kind of sticks in your mind – something you never forget.

The view from a machine gun outpost was much different. The mortarmen used the forward observer on outpost duty to serve as their eyes, while the machine gunner viewed the whole panorama to his front. Cpl. Glen Derber relates:

Morning came and nothing unusual happened, just the normal artillery exchanges and far off noises of battle. In the early afternoon, however, my fears were confirmed when we saw some armored vehicles followed by infantry on foot pull out of the tree line across the opening we were facing. They came from our left and were proceeding at right angles across the opening to our front. The closest one, which I estimated to be 400 to 500 yards away, had a large barreled assault gun mounted on it and I could see the operator alongside working his aiming controls.

Cpl. Derber had a reputation for being a crack shot with a rifle and he had done a lot of sniping up on the Island in Holland only two months earlier. Now he had an opportunity to do some long range shooting again. He added to his story:

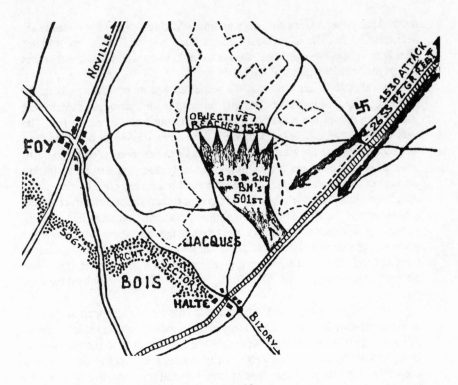

*Map 19*

I had saved two incendiary (blue tipped) bullets from a belt of aircraft ammo which somehow got sent to us in Holland. My thought was to use them, if the opportunity arose, to shoot an enemy in the helmet. I ended up putting them into the engine compartment of the half-track. They made a nice blue flash when they hit and confirmed my range estimation but did no harm to the vehicle. Being as how they were designed for thin-skinned aluminum aircraft, I didn't expect much. Then I concentrated on the operator of the assault gun and toppled him backwards off his position. Another man took his place and got the same treatment, but he didn't seem to be as hard hit. This left nothing but the infantry following along behind so I started picking at them. One dropped in his tracks, another fell and was helped up and into the back of the armored half-track. I wounded one more before they caught on to where the shots were coming from and the half-track made a 90 degree right turn and that big barreled assault gun was aiming right at us! When all this started, I had informed my assistant gunner to catch the empty clips from my M1 and reload them with armor piercing ammo from our machine gun belts. When the shells started coming in we both hugged the bottom of our foxhole and only peeked out now and then to make sure the infantry didn't overrun our position. Right then I thought this was going to be how the war ended for us. It got so bad they called in a reserve rifle company and, as they came up to the MLR from our rear, I looked up to see a rifle bullet go right through the shoulder stock of our LMG. Good God! I thought, now we are getting it from front and rear! The attack was repulsed, of course, with casualties to another gun crew which had set up in a shell hole out in the open field and been over run. The only casualty near me was Manuel Dandis who had been hit in the buttocks with a 20mm shell.

The actions of 2nd Battalion in the Bizory area are remembered by PFC. George E. Willey of "E" Company. He was involved in the same action just described by Cpl. Derber. Willey wrote:

I remember the 10th Armored Division tanks at Bizory. When we went through 'Dog' Company, which was dug in along the railroad and occupied the woods, we received heavy 88mm barrages and after they lifted about five German half-tracks tried to flank us but tanks and our machine guns stopped them.

For 2nd Platoon of "D" Company, the action began to heat up after the first of the year as related by Sgt. Jack Hampton:

We pulled out of our defensive position and began an attack through some woods the enemy was holding. It turned out to be the bloodiest operation we had since arriving in Bastogne. In our 'D' Company sector, 2nd Platoon, we had four casualties in about 15 minutes. One of the new guys caught a bullet in the head. One of our veterans had a chunk of shrapnel catch him just above the wrist. He was in very bad pain and I pulled his medicine pack off and gave him a shot of morphine. A medic arrived and poured sulfa over the wound. I am sure he lost his hand. Another took a big chunk of shrapnel in the leg, just below the knee, which tore out most of the leg muscles. I am sure he lost that leg below the knee. During another phase of clearing those woods, we knocked out a German tank that had been harassing us. In a skirmish we routed the Germans out of their positions and caused them to make themselves visible. It should have been like shooting ducks in a barrel but the temperature had dropped several degrees below freezing. Even with our woolen gloves on it was difficult to squeeze off rounds fast enough to take advantage of our opportunity. I have never been that cold before in my life nor have I since.

Though American medics don't carry weapons (whereas the British and Germans did), PFC. "Cleto" Leone had obtained a hand gun in Holland when he has stumbled on some enemy soldiers in a house near his position. He was carrying it in the heat of battle when one of his comrades asked to use it. Leone describes the incident:

I was in a foxhole in some woods with Shuler and Calahan when some German tanks appeared with infantry behind them. We started firing mortars, bazookas, machine guns – everything we had. All of a sudden, we were just overrun with German infantry. Shuler managed to set one of the German tanks on fire. They had some nets on the backs of them for camouflage purposes I assume and, with tank grease, that is what set the tank on fire. We were told to get the heck out of there – so we did. S/Sgt. McClure came up and said, 'Let me use your Luger!' I said 'Okay'. That was the last time I saw McClure. We were supposed to traverse a large field and get into some woods. The Germans were starting to pour into our woods and the tanks were shooting and we were being shelled. We just ran across that field. I would call it a rout but we did make it to the next woods.[176]

Platoon sergeant Frank E. McClure played a key role in the fighting of January 3rd but was modest in describing his deeds. He wrote:

Sgt. Wesley Calahan and I were wounded in a shootout with a rather sizeable force of Germans. However, tanks on January 3, 1945 were rather reluctant to help us. All the enemy vehicles I saw destroyed were the result of action by Company 'E' men.

When asked if he remembered borrowing a luger from medic "Cleto" Leone, McClure responded:

Yes, I did have Cleto Leone's luger and Calahan had an M1 when he picked a fight with those Germans who wounded us on January 3rd. I discarded the luger for something more effective, like the 20mm cannon on the knocked-out German half-track that Lt. MacGregor and some of his people had put out of action earlier. I don't remember much after I rolled out of that vehicle when it exploded . . .

As a replacement officer for "E" Company, 1Lt. Bernard A. Jordan had this praise for S/Sgt. McClure and the men of his platoon. He wrote:

On the 3rd of January our company saw heavy action northeast of Bastogne. 1Lt. Joe MacGregor and I were 1st Platoon, 'E' Company officers. One of our rocket launcher crews was knocked out of action and Joe and I manned the launcher and knocked out an enemy half-track. Afterwards, I boosted S/Sgt. Frank McClure over into the back of a disabled half-track and he manned the gun and killed a number of enemy – this helped turn the enemy back. McClure was put in for a Silver Star.

1Lt. Bernard A. Jordan sent along a copy of a commendation 1st Platoon received for their actions of January 3, 1945. It read as follows:

---

[176]Cleto Leone added to his story: "Three days later, we were ordered to retake the woods. As we were going across the field, Cpl. Johnny Altick exclaimed, 'Hey, look what I found!' It was a muddied luger. I said, 'If it has a serial number of 3689 – that is the one I gave McClure the other day!' Believe it or not – I still have the luger!"

1st Platoon of 'E' Company, 501st Parachute Infantry Regiment, is hereby commended for heroic achievement in action 3rd January 1945. During a determined enemy counterattack northeast of Bastogne, Belgium, the 1st Platoon was committed when the enemy succeeded in penetrating the Battalion flank. Although harassed by enemy artillery and automatic weapons fire, they succeeded in reaching the right flank of the enemy. With only three rocket launchers at its disposal, the bazooka teams knocked out one tank and two half-tracks. Setting up an anti-tank gun, the platoon knocked out 3 more tanks and 2 hostile half-tracks, repulsing the enemy counterattack. The platoon took advantage of the then demoralized enemy, mounted the abandoned enemy vehicles and turned the enemy guns on the retreating forces. After completely overrunning the enemy, the platoon evacuated its wounded and then covered the reorganization of the regiment. Their actions were in accordance with the highest tradition of the military service.

The remainder of the *S-2 Periodic Report* for 3 January 1945 gives an overview of the actions which took place for 2nd Battalion that day:

Intense artillery continued. The enemy employed his tanks, artillery, mortars and nebelwerfer fire against our front lines and rear installations.

While we were attacking, the enemy pushed a strong counterattack against this unit's lines with tanks, then proceeded to attack our exposed flank and rear. Their attack was generally down the road at 605615 (map coordinates). This action on the part of the enemy caused us to pull back and defend the gap prior to reaching the regimental objective.[177]

---

[177]*S-2 Periodic Report.* op. cit.

# 17. JANUARY 4, 1945

Unit commanders wondered just how much more powerful the enemy attacks on the 101st perimeter might have been on January 4 had it not been for the enemy prisoner "spilling the beans" at the time of his interrogation during the previous night. Still wondering if the prisoner had actually been a plant, the Division commanders went ahead with a plan to devastate the locations from which the prisoner said the German attacks of the 4th were to be launched.

As the actions developed during the morning, the enemy activity was indeed on a smaller scale, but still, the killing went on.

The private credited with the capture of the enemy runner becomes a casualty when he seeks shelter to clean his tommy gun.

On the western perimeter, an enemy attack is launched at 0400 against the glider infantry battalion which had just replaced units of 1st Battalion of the 502nd Regiment.

Troops of 3rd Platoon of "A" Company of the 502nd are called on to counterattack over the same ground they had previously defended. The loss of a close buddy is a lasting impression for one of the soldiers.

The story of a strange attack by a solitary enemy soldier on an outpost position has left one soldier wondering just what the purpose of the move had been.

Over in the 501st area, a mortar sergeant relates a story of a happy ending to a situation that had been declared hopeless by a medic.

## A NEED TO CLEAN A WEAPON

After the prisoner who would "spill the beans" was marched off to 2nd Battalion Headquarters by Sgt. Reggie Davies, the machine gun team of the corporal and the private felt some maintenance had to be carried out on the tommy gun. The chore went to Pvt. Lincoln Bethel while the corporal stayed alert in the two-man foxhole. Pvt. Bethel continues his story in the third person:

> Meanwhile, back at the foxhole, the private had decided something must be done about cleaning his ice-encrusted tommy gun if things were to continue along these lines. Thrusting his newly captured, brand new loaded and cocked Luger pistol into his belt, he wormed his way – now crouching and crawling – to an abandoned farm building on their left flank made visible in the early morning mists.
>
> Reaching the building, he entered through a broken window and proceeded into the half above ground cellar made of one-foot thick stone

walls. Assorted farm animals had taken refuge here also. Removing his belt, outer coat, helmet – placing his newly-won Luger handily near by, he proceeded to restore the tommy gun for eventual use.

One of the Kraut tank crews must have observed his entrance into the barn as an ear-shattering noise was heard and a two-foot round hole was made in one of the walls facing the German lines.

'That son-of-a-bitch probably thinks he got me!' the private gloated. He hurriedly assembled his gear – tucked the Luger in his belt – reached down for the tommy gun when the bastardly German gunner sent another 88 shell through the opening made by the first shell.

This one crashed into the opposite wall and sprayed everything in the room with deadly fragments. Down went the private, blood spurting from both legs, left hand and right shoulder. (He later remembered thinking it had taken two 88mm shells to stop him!) How long he laid there seemed like eternity, but along came medics and he was doused with Sulfa powder and shot with morphine and carted off to Regimental Headquarters where, he thought it was Chappie Hall, gave him a belt of good whiskey.

It was not until days later, he would wonder which of those life-saving medics had relieved him of that beautiful, hard-earned, brand new German Luger.[178]

Upon being contacted about the above incident, Reginald Davies replied he had mistakenly been credited for a deed which should have cited his friend, H. Lincoln Bethel. The Silver Star that Davies had been awarded was for actions in Holland.

## 327TH ON CHAMPS PERIMETER

1st Battalion of the 327th Glider Infantry Regiment replaced 1st Battalion of the 502nd Parachute Infantry on the Champs perimeter on January 3rd. It was a situation in which the glider infantrymen had not seen the terrain in daylight and had to do their foxhole digging in total darkness with no opportunity to take advantage of terrain features.

After providing security for the Division Headquarters night command post at the Chateau Ile-la-Hesse and along with other 1st Battalion troops covering the MLR in front of Senonchamps, Capt. Walter L. Miller's Company "C" and

---

[178]The above is part of a narrative in which Lincoln Bethel related his Army experiences. He was cited for a Silver Star medal but at the time he wrote to retired Division commander, General Maxwell D. Taylor in 1980, he had not received it and the General felt the authorities turned down the request because too much time had elapsed.

Capt. Joseph B. Johnson's Company "A" were part of the move to the Champs area. Capt. Miller recalled the actions:

On the evening of January 3rd, I got orders to move to Champs to relieve the unit there. We arrived at approximately 0300 in the morning with no knowledge of fields of fire or other pertinent data about the area. I received some replacements at that time and, because of the depleted condition of my company, had to place them in the line. We took the crest of the hill and occupied the foxholes of the unit that had been there.

Platoon sergeant Jack Williamson of "A" Company describes his part in the January 3rd move to Champs and felt it was a bad situation with little support from heavy weapons.

On the night of January 3rd, we were moved into a defensive position around Champs. There were no good foxholes, lots of snow and it was just a bad situation. We could hear tanks moving around out in front of us. We only had two .37mm anti-tank guns with us. That was after midnight.

As happened on numerous occasions during the Bastogne fighting, the enemy struck around 0300 in the morning. S/Sgt. Jack Williamson describes the early action:

I alerted everyone at 0400. It wasn't but ten minutes later and here came the Germans – tanks with steel attached to their sides – too thick for our 37mm guns. They ran over our front lines in nothing flat. They knocked out the two anti-tank guns. We were without any weapons to knock out those tanks now. Our front line was gone. Our mortar sergeant fired everything he had. I called back on the hand radio to Capt. J. B. Johnson, our company commander, and asked 'Should we fall back?' He said, 'No, hold what you have!' I said 'There is nobody here but PFC. Burt Wolverton and myself!' Johnson said, 'Stay where you are and some reinforcements will be there soon.'

Over on his sector of the perimeter, Capt. Walter Miller could see the enemy tanks as they approached. Fortunately, some mines placed along the road took care of a few of the enemy armored vehicles. Miller continues his story:

In the darkness, I could see the enemy tanks as they approached and they fired directly into the holes killing the men there. We pulled back over the crest – the enemy tanks came over the crest and came over toward the village of Champs. As they moved on my left flank they swung over on to the road and struck several mines that destroyed two or three of the tanks. As the men bailed out of the tanks, my reserves cut them down and the other tanks stopped on the hill.

Those tanks knocked out two anti-tank guns that they couldn't possibly have seen. I was convinced the Germans had some night scopes that they used to knock out targets which couldn't be seen with the naked eye. The tanks also fired a round into the building I had selected as my CP. I can remember the armor-piercing shell going completely through and flying off in the distance. I wondered who it would kill some distance away.

From the house in which they had sought shelter, S/Sgt. Williamson and PFC. Wolverton could see the big German tank outside. Fortunately, at that moment, they had some help from a friendly tank destroyer. Williamson related:

We were in this house and the Krauts had us zeroed in. Wolverton and I went out the back window. A big German tank was right there in front of the house and headed into Champs where one of the TD's had been coming out our way. It fired down the road and hit that tank. It took a good hit and had a big explosion and only one man got out. He was up in the turret and fell to the ground. He laid there in the snow and begged for help. At the time, we couldn't do anything for him. He froze stiff right there.

With the first enemy tanks to penetrate the perimeter defense, Capt. Walt Miller and one of his platoon leaders made an effort to stop one of them from the concealment of a hay stack. Miller related:

In an attempt to stop the German tanks, Lt. Carlock and myself ran to a haystack and fired a bazooka round at them. It had no effect. Carlock was wounded and a German followed us with fire into the haystack where we made juncture with friendly forces moving from that direction.

The undermanned troops of "A" Company got some assistance when "C" Company moved over to provide support. S/Sgt. Jack Williamson has an encounter with a German medic. He relates:

Then Capt. Walter Miller came up with 'C' Company. We finally set up a defensive line behind the house. There was a drop-off there and it made a good line for defense. They started firing and were careful not to hit me or Wolverton. Burt and I were behind the corner of the house when a German came around. He was clean and neat and he spoke English. He said, 'Don't shoot – I'm a medic!' He indicated there were some wounded soldiers out there. I asked, 'Amerikaner?' He said nothing. I said, 'Those are American soldiers out there.' I figured they'd be some of mine. He didn't say anything so I decided to go out with him. I told Wolverton, 'Put your rifle right on his back. If they shoot me, you shoot the German.' Burt said, 'OK.' Well, no one shot me and we ran into about 20 to 30 Germans. About that time, I heard some good old American cussing. I told Burt to stay with the Germans and I'm going out to see who that is. It turned out to be an American but he wasn't one of my soldiers. He was hit in one leg. I got hold of one of his arms and dragged him over the snow. I'm sure it was a rough trip for him. We got him back and there was a jump trooper over there and he said, 'I'll take him,' which he did.

PFC. Willis Rohr remembered that getting ammunition to the mortar gunners became a real problem with so many enemy soldiers milling around the Champs area. He wrote:

Three of the ammo bearers for our mortar squad went into Champs for resupplies and were unable to return because the Germans were overrunning the positions. I believe it was Joe Brennan, Ted Knapek and myself who went down. It was during this attack that 1Lt. Ron Mills was injured and the 1st sergeant was wounded.

PFC. Werner W. Jutzin was part of the mortar section of "C" Company. He remembered an action in which his group had support from several different units. He wrote:

I remember when 'C' Company was pinned down behind a deep embankment from an attack by a battalion-sized unit. Our mortars were firing without base plates – tube held by hands. Finally, 502nd paratroops opened up with 81mm mortars and the 81st anti-tankers knocked out three German tanks. The counterattack was successful.

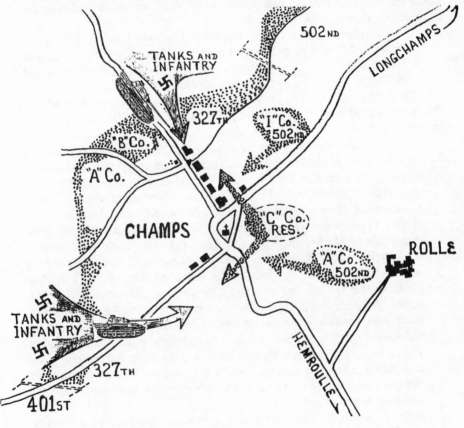

*Map 20*

Describing his role at Bastogne as a member of "C" Company, and a fellow mortarman, PFC. Andrew Thieneman wrote:

I was the 1st gunner on a 60mm mortar and, in this case, we used the bi-pod. I set the sights on 200, which was the closest you can level the sight. Then I cranked the tube one more turn and we fired to see where it landed. Then I turned it one more time until we saw it was effective and we captured quite a few.

With the arrival of daylight, Capt. Walter Miller could see the targets out to his front and around him. Using his radio, he called for artillery support. Miller added to his story:

As the enemy infantry approached, they were met by my men and cut down. With daylight, the enemy tanks remained on the hillside facing Champs. I lay in the snow on the hillside, calling for artillery fire to drive those tanks away but the fire was denied because we were inside the 'no fire' line.

Troops of the 1st Battalion of the 502nd Parachute Regiment arrived on the scene and were now attempting to drive the enemy soldiers from their previously held position. S/Sgt. Jack Williamson became a part of that counter-attack to retake the positions on the hillside. He relates:

Here came a jump unit up there. They lined up in a skirmish line to counter-attack back up that hill. Burt and I were standing there. They started up the hill. This old sergeant turned to us and said, 'You two fellas, move it on up!' I said we were not from their outfit. He then answered back, 'You're an American soldier aren't you?' He added, 'Move your ass!' As we were attacking up the slope, I noticed Wolverton kneeling down to help a German. My rage was great when I saw this happening. It turned out ole Burt was looking for food. He found it, too – bread, cheese, some sausage. He didn't say a word, just moved out with me. We went up the hill firing our guns and Wolverton eating as we went. But God, we were hungry!

Capt. Walter Miller goes on to describe the culmination of the day's action on the front southwest and west of Champs:

About 1100 in the morning, a lone Sherman tank approached from the right and fired at the German tanks and they withdrew over the crest of the hill and back toward their former location. We then reoccupied the top of the hill. A patrol by S/Sgt. Ernest Cummings moved forward to make contact and to learn the location of the enemy. During this time I also observed an artillery observer who manned a machine gun. We found the two-man crew of a 37mm anti-tank gun had been choked to death.

I have not mentioned the individual rifleman or machine gunner who stood in his foxhole and performed his duties. It was so cold, water in my canteen froze. All these men are great heroes. No one, but one who was there, knows the cold, shelling, fire and the privations they underwent to prevent the enemy from entering Bastogne. It is a tribute to the individual American soldier – all the way!

## 3RD PLATOON COUNTER-ATTACK

While 1st and 2nd Platoons and Company Headquarters were involved in the January 3rd action in support of 2nd and 3rd Battalions at Longchamps, 3rd Platoon of "A" Company of the 502nd was still on line west of Champs. PFC. Ted Goldmann was serving as platoon runner and positioned in a house in the village. On this occasion he was separated from his buddy, Pvt. Johnny Ballard, who was in action supporting 1st Battalion of the 327th Glider Infantry in repulsing the enemy attack. Goldmann describes the action on the 3rd Platoon front as it was related to him later by others:

In Champs, the 327th Glider Infantry relieved all 502nd troops the evening of the 3rd but they weren't fully organized and dug in for some reason or other and when the Germans hit there at 4 a.m., January 4th, the 327th retired to the Crucifix in the center of Champs. The 502nd troops (all 1st Bn.) were sent in to force the Germans back because we had to hold the hill to hold Champs and if we lost Champs, Longchamps and Monaville, occupied by the remainder of the 502nd would be cut off and lost, leaving the northern route to Bastogne open. The 3rd Platoon spearheaded this counter-attack and regained their previous position only to be pinned down by five tanks and they had no tank support of their own, although some was coming up. Johnny had a bazooka and Asay, taking my job, was loading for him. Having the only anti-tank weapon, they were firing it at the tanks but to no avail. Four rounds bounced off the thick armor. Just as Johnny was getting set to fire the 5th round, a mortar shell hit near by and the shrapnel from it killed Johnny instantly but left Asay untouched. But, another shell in the next few minutes seriously wounded him. Anderson got a bullet in the scalp, just above the temple, and jumped up crazily and ran around some before they could get him back down on the ground. Williams had been hit in the leg the evening before when the 327th came up to relieve them.[179]

During the counterattack of the 502nd 1st Battalion at Champs after the forward positions of "A" Company of the 327th Glider Regiment were overrun, Sgt. Charles Asay of "A" Company of the 502nd was involved in the action. He wrote:

We counter-attacked January 4th with my squad on point. When we crested the hill, we ran into tanks as well as infantry. I sent the squad around to set up flanking fire. I took the bazookaman, Pvt. John Ballard, with me

---

[179]Goldmann, op. cit.

to take on the tanks. They zeroed in and shell fire hit him and killed him. Another shell blew me out of the position and I woke up face down in the snow.[180]

When 3rd Platoon was relieved from attachment to the 327th near Champs during the evening of the 4th, platoon runner Pvt. Ted Goldmann was to learn of the death of his close friend. This is how he described it in his letter to the father of Johnny Ballard:

The evening of the 4th, the company had all gone (with the exception of the 3rd Platoon) to Monaville and Longchamps. I was still at a road junction in Longchamps waiting for the platoon to show them where to go. At this time, I knew nothing of their fight that morning, so when they came up, I yelled, 'Ballard!' and received no answer and then they told me what had happened. I had found a carbine for Johnny so he wouldn't have to carry the bazooka and a rifle too. But that meant nothing now. I took the fellows into a house where I had a fire so they could dry out and eat some food I had rustled up from an aid station. I sat down in the corner and cried; it all seemed so impossible and useless – that anything could happen to our 'invincible lucky squad' and never occurred to me after Christmas morning and when it did, I couldn't believe it. In a little while we moved on to Monaville, too. We got the remaining 18 men in a house and settled down. I went back to the CP where I spent the night relaying telephone messages for artillery concentrations and carrying mortar ammo up to a position which had just been hit by an enemy patrol.[181]

## WAS IT "KAMIKAZE?"

Over in the 2nd Battalion sector near Longchamps, PFC. Ray "Calfboy" Blasingame was on outpost duty. His story of a one-man "kamikaze" attack is related by his close friend, PFC. Emmert O. Parmley. Both men served with "F" Company.

On January 4, the morning following a tank attack which won him a Silver Star, Blasingame saw movement in front of our lines. It was still quite dark. There was a German helmet moving up and down. A German

---

[180]When Asay regained consciousness, he was shocked. He wrote: "In and out of consciousness till Paris – when I came to, I was in a room alone and the only voices were German. I thought I was captured. An Army nurse came by some time later and I asked her where I was. She told me I was in a German POW ward. I told her who I was and they had to run a check before they brought a gurney in and took me out. When I was carried off the line, I had been stripped of everything but my dog tags. I was blue-eyed, blonde and had a scar on my cheek – a perfect Aryan. Also, I was unconscious and couldn't converse."

[181]Goldmann, op. cit.

soldier was creeping and crawling directly toward Blasingame and he could see only the helmet. When so close that he could not miss from 30 feet, he fired five or six shots into the helmet with his carbine. After it was light enough to see there were no more Germans, Blasingame crawled out to examine the German. Being shot in the head, it was hard to tell his age but he seemed to be an older fellow. He was infantry and not a tanker from one of the four dead tanks in front of the line. He was carrying a machine pistol (we called them burp guns). In the left pocket of the ragged overcoat he was wearing was a cheaply made civilian automatic pistol. Blasingame took the burp gun and pistol back to his hole to examine them. There were only eight rounds in the burp gun. The pistol had only one shell. 'Calfboy' pointed the burp gun in the air to see if it would fire. It responded with a 'burp'. There was also an immediate response on the line. The sound of a German gun brought a response when fired on the front lines. Calfboy had sounded reveille for 'F' Company.

There were no more Germans seen that morning. What this German had in mind or where he was going was a mystery. If he was a deserter or wanted to surrender, his approach to the line would have been different. With only eight shots in his machine pistol, he could not have put up much of a fight anywhere.

## A HIT BY A SNIPER

Fierce fighting had been in progress in the Bois Jacques at the same time the 502nd troops were involved in the battles with tanks and infantry in the Longchamps area. Mortar sergeant Ahzez Karim of 2nd Battalion Headquarters Company of the 501st Regiment was making his second move in as many days. He describes an incident which had a strange and satisfying end. He wrote:

The next day, we moved again. Lt. Phipps took squads 3 and 4 and Capt. Homan moved out with squads 1 and 2. I didn't understand the reason for moving us across some open fields. This never made sense to me but we followed the captain until we came to a dead end. Now, as we had forest on three sides of us, and with the Germans somewhere ahead of us, the captain said to dig in along the edge of the forest. Then with the two troopers, he went back the way he came. Now, we thought, what the hell is this? Two 81mm mortars with no outposts and nothing to fire at. I had a map. I opened it, spread it out on the ground to find out where we were and which way the Germans were located. A couple of the guys knelt next to me on my left and one to the right. We were looking at the map when a single shot rang out. It hit the trooper to my right. The bullet hit him square in the chest. He fell forward on top of the map I had laid out.

At the sound of the shot, all the troopers hit the ground, put a tree between them and where the shot came from and tried to spot the sniper but in vain.

I went back to the wounded trooper, rolled him over, looked at the wound, called for a medic. The medic came up, looked at him and said, 'There isn't a thing I can do for him!' I said, 'The hell there isn't – get him on that jeep and to the aid station!' We put him on a stretcher and on the jeep. The medic drove off with him.

That sniper must have had a scope on his rifle, to pick out a target through all those trees. Grogan said, 'That's a hard way to find out where the Germans are!'

One of the troopers came over to me and said he saw several soldiers with white capes walking across the field. He picked them out with his field glasses. He saw them, but they did not spot him. We figured we had Germans on every side of us – surrounded again! There was one helluva fire fight to the right of us, maybe five or six hundred yards away. It was hard to tell. The sound of rifles, machine guns and direct tank fire was coming through the forest.[182]

---

[182]Later in the campaign, Sgt. Karim happened to pass the medic who had taken the wounded man toward the aid station in the jeep. He was called over and told that he (medic) had a good story for Karim. He said he was driving the jeep back toward the aid station when a half dozen German soldiers with white capes stepped in front of the jeep and captured him. He said they took him to a German field hospital where they put him to work and they had a surgeon who operated and removed the bullet from the trooper's chest. That saved his life. The medic said that a couple days later the advancing 101st captured the field hospital and he returned to the 501st. He thanked me for not giving up on the wounded trooper. That made me feel good, having something to do with saving the life of one of our brave warriors.

# 18. A RESPITE

## JANUARY 5

The period of January 5th through the 8th was relatively quiet with no major moves taking place on the 101st perimeter. There was sporadic shelling, especially of the town of Bastogne. Enemy bombers continued the nightly missions over the city whenever the weather permitted. There was a heavy snowfall during this period. Friendly divisions continued to move up on the left and right of the Bastogne perimeter. The campaign to pinch off the enemy salient was doing better from the north than from the south.

## A TRUCK LOAD OF MINES

There are so many instances in wartime when one can recall a "what if" situation when one had been in a life-threatening situation and to have moved out of harm's way just before such an occurrence. This was the case for PFC. Rudy Wedra and 1Lt. Lee Bowers on January 5th at the 501st Regimental command post in Bastogne. Wedra related:

I was in a large room in a school building or seminary. The ceiling was high. Outside the door was a corridor or hallway. The message center was here with 'Pappy' Colvin and Pat Winters. Right straight out the door was a courtyard where the truck was located. They loaded this truck (with mines) and I was back here in the building – probably goofing off. 1Lt. Lee Bowers came in saying, 'Damn it, I forgot my map dispatch case' and he walked back into the corridor and, just as he got in there, and I was standing nearby – that thing went off. We thought at first it must have been an aerial bomb because shells don't make that kind of racket. Colvin was in a daze for several days. After the dust settled, we went out in the courtyard. There was nothing left of the truck, the mines or the personnel who had been loading it.

A member of the Intelligence Section of the 501st who recalled the explosion of the mine-laden truck was Cpl. David M. Smith. He recalled:

The truck load of mines which blew up out in the courtyard left its mark. The courtyard wall is still blackened (witnessed on the 1989 trip) from the explosion. We lost some good men on that one.

The truck load of mines had been scheduled for deliverance to the front line troops of the 501st Parachute Regiment. A total of twelve members of the Demolitions Platoon and the truck driver died in the blast.

## General McAuliffe Promoted

On the 7th of January, word reached the 101st Airborne Division that General A. C. "Tony" McAuliffe had been promoted and assigned as commander of the 103rd Infantry Division as a reward for the superb manner in which he handled the 101st Division at Bastogne.

There was a "spur of the moment" farewell party for him by his fellow officers as they came to say goodbye to him. As a departure gift and as a reminder that he was leaving a division of booted paratroopers and glidermen, his fellow officers presented him with a gift of canvas leggings as a memento that he was now a "leg".

## Continued Shelling of the Division CP

Because of the continued shelling of the command post, it was felt the enemy had the caserne zeroed in. VIII Corps commander, General Troy Middleton arrived to pay a call during the day and while he was present, the command post was shelled again with several of the men being killed or wounded. The Corps commander was unhurt. The incident spurred Division to move out of the facility to another at Ile-le-Pre about a mile and a half southwest of Bastogne.

One of the lasting memories Major William Ferguson, assistant engineer officer for the Division Headquarters, has of the Bastogne campaign illustrates the point made above about the continuous shelling. He wrote:

Both the 326th Engineers and the 81st AA & AT Battalion had adjacent headquarters in barracks at the compound where Division HQ was located. One morning during the siege, I was outside our HQ talking to Major Kemm of the 81st when we both heard the unmistakable sound of an artillery shell coming in. We both hit the snow. The shell landed some 100 yards away and when the shrapnel quit flying, we both arose, brushed ourselves off and Kemm announced, 'You know Ferg, there must be an Army camp around here. I've been seeing a lot of soldiers lately'. It would be difficult to find a better example to illustrate the morale of the 101st under rather trying circumstances. I have never forgotten this episode.

## Goldmann Wounded

The 7th of January was the last day of the Bastogne fighting for PFC. Ted Goldmann as he was injured in an accidental explosion. He describes the day's events leading up to his injury:

From then until the evening of January 7th (Sunday), activity was limited to the usual barrages and the 3rd Platoon had a two-man guard at night to pull on a knocked-out German tank 150 yards in front of us. Here we had the only white uniform (sheets) I saw up there. During the night, some Germans came up in front of us several times laying mines. We fired at them several times during the night but after a while they kept coming back. Visibility was so limited it was hard to distinguish anything.

At 8 p.m. on the 7th, a blizzard started and continued until nearly daybreak – in all about 16 inches. Visibility was nil but every man was on guard about five hours in it. Trench foot was becoming prevalent because of the bad weather. During the blizzard the MG's fired every 30 to 45 minutes to keep the belts from freezing up. Just at daybreak, Sgt. Zweibel came up and told about two-thirds of us to go down in town and cook our breakfasts and I started back. He fired the gun to check it and the third bullet hit a mine and it went off; I caught a piece of it in the wrist as I walked along. It knocked me to my knees but I started running for cover because I didn't know what it was then and thought more might be coming.[183]

Goldmann walked back to the CP where he was treated and then evacuated to Battalion and then on to Regiment. His first hand reporting ended at this time. However, later actions were reported to him when he returned from hospitalization and recuperation. His letters written in June of 1945 are what have kept the memories of those actions alive.

---

[183]Goldmann, op. cit.

# 19. ON THE OFFENSIVE

## JANUARY 9

The morning of January 9 found the 1st Army forces within seven miles of Houffalize in their drive south. On that day 3rd Army, of which the 101st was a member, broke the quiet in that sector with an attack past Recogne to seize Noville which had been a principle objective of the 101st since mid-December. The 6th Armored Division was on the right of the 101st while the 17th Airborne Division was on the left.

The 501st had the assignment of taking Recogne. The attack was made with "F" Company as the point unit. The center of the small farm community was reached by 1335. The accompanying TD's chased two tanks out of town and these fled toward Noville. With the help of "E" Company, the town was cleared by 1700. Enemy casualties were heavy while the 2nd Battalion forces lost 25 enlisted men and 3 officers.

One of the major losses of the day was the wounding of Colonel Julian Ewell, regimental commander of the 501st who was then replaced by LTC. Robert Ballard who remained in that position throughout the remainder of the war.

The day was dull with snow falling thickly through most of the day. There was no air support. The tracked vehicles had difficulty in movement with much slipping and sliding.

The 506th Regiment, along with Team Cherry, attacked northeast through the Fazone Woods toward Noville.

3rd Battalion had been relieved and moved into a forward assembly area in woods south of Sonne Fontaine. The 2nd Battalion led the attack toward Noville after the artillery battered the woods in front of them. Ten minutes later 3rd Battalion moved to the left flank position. This is when they were hit hard. The 3rd Battalion Headquarters Company took a heavy battering from enemy mortar and artillery shelling. Twenty of its members were wounded, among them the commanding officer, Captain James G. Morton.

## HEADQUARTERS COMPANY BATTERED

As commander of 3rd Battalion Headquarters Company, Captain James Morton was in the thick of the fighting on January 9. This would be his last day with the 101st Division in World War II. He wrote:

On January 9 we began a big attack to reduce the German bulge. We attacked all day. Headquarters 3rd was caught in a woods by a mortar barrage and my men dropped at every quarter. Webb went out of his mind. Beard, now a lieutenant, was shot in the arm. Lundquist was killed . . . Kopala, my runner, was hit at my side. A mortar shell hit the trees above us. Fragments wounded Kopala severely, but I was unscathed. I was blown off my feet twice, a most unpleasant experience . . .

That night, as we were digging in on the objective, Tiger tanks came through the snow and shelled the woods. I was hit by the first round. It nearly severed my ankle. I bled like a stuck hog. Gibson, the medic, raced to my assistance and got hit by the next round. I, too, was wounded again. Barney Ryan has written to me that 156 men were killed or wounded that terrible night. The next morning, says Ryan, there were fifteen dead bodies sprawled about the aid set-up. Blood trails, he said, marked in the snow where our wounded had dragged themselves in futile effort to find shelter or medical aid. Ryan writes: 'Never have I lived through such a nightmare. All night long, shells screamed into the woods, direct fire from tanks. It was nearly impossible to evacuate the wounded. They were dying like flies. Through the whole night we heard the screams of the wounded and the moans of the dying.'[184]

Though he had undergone many harrowing experiences in Normandy and Holland as a surgeon for 3rd Battalion of the 506th Parachute Infantry Regiment, Capt. Bernard J. Ryan found the situation near Foy and Noville to be far worse. He wrote:

The worst time of my Army career was the afternoon and night of January 9, 1945. During the afternoon and night as we attacked towards Cobru, we had 156 battle casualties in our battalion. They had to be evacuated several miles over a road broken through the woods by tanks and in about two feet of snow. There were artillery barrages all night and an enemy infantry attack during the night. Major Charlie Shettle was also wounded. He gave me his British tanker coveralls saying, 'Doc, you're going to need these more than I will.'

While pulling a wounded soldier out of his foxhole in the edge of the woods, looking toward Cobru, I said to Medic Harold Haycroft, who was helping me, 'Listen to that German tank out there!' He said, 'Yes, look at it.' I said horsecollar to myself but turned around to see a German Panther threshing up the snow and practically looking right down our throats. Just

---

[184]The above material is from a letter which Capt. James S. Morton wrote to his friend 1Lt. William E. Reid of the 3rd Battalion Mortar Platoon while recuperating in a stateside hospital in 1947. Copy sent by Helen Briggs Ramsey, former Red Cross "Doughnut Dolly" for 3rd Battalion.

as we pulled the wounded man away, the Panther put a round in where we had just been, evidently having seen us.

On the morning of January 10, dead were piled everywhere.

In an action which occurred near Recogne, PFC. James H. Martin recalled the bravery of a medic who was looking after the needs of the men of his platoon. Martin wrote:

Our 2nd Platoon was dug in a couple hundred yards from a little village called Recogne. Regiment asked for information about guns and positions in front of our position. It was decided to send an 'H' Company patrol out through our position to draw fire. The first scout started out of our grove of trees onto the crusted snow. A machine gun opened up from Recogne and he was hit a glancing blow on the breast bone. His lieutenant sent him right back out and he was hit again. On being hit again, he went down and stayed down. After a short wait, the whole patrol went out in groups of two and three. About a hundred yards out to the right of Recogne they were fired upon again and several went down. The Mexican-American medic who was left behind with us started to take off his pack and I asked what he was doing. He said, 'I'm the medic. It's my job to go after them.' I said, 'Hell, you'll get killed, you can't help that way!' He ignored me and went out to the farthest man, got him on his shoulder and started shuffling back. He went down several times but finally made it back. All this amid heavy small arms fire. He didn't seem to think he'd done anything unusual though I felt that this was an incredibly brave thing to do.

## MEDIC GIBSON'S ORDEAL

Medic John W. Gibson served his regiment as a medic from way back in the early days at Camp Toccoa in Georgia in 1942. He was about to experience his most trying day in a combat situation near the small town of Foy. He describes the events of that memorable day:

We left our positions near Foy, Belgium on January 9, 1945. We had been there three weeks but it was not exactly like leaving home. There were no buildings and a cold blizzard had hit. We were dug in well but a medic can't stay in those safe foxholes. We had to be out where and when we were needed. We walked out of that area and trudged along in the snow in a sweeping movement toward Noville. Noville is a small town but certainly one to remember. We were to narrow the gap and push the German lines back.

Part of the time we walked in open areas but were protected from view by the overcast weather. We stopped along a small road through the edge of some pines. A jeep came slowly by in the snow and hit a mine with the left front tire. Parts of the engine and dash board hit the driver, PFC. Herbert A. Derwig, in the chest. I was forty feet away and went quickly to help. Derwig was dead within seconds and his passenger was badly shaken. He was trembling and pale but seemingly uninjured.

We moved on and there was some shelling up ahead. In crossing an open field, I found a trooper with his leg off below the knee. He was in a sitting position holding both hands on his knee, which kept the stub of his leg from dragging in the snow. I got out a large compress bandage and some sulfanilomide powder and he refused treatment. He asked me to find his shoe. It was about 20 feet away. I put it at his side. His foot and part of his leg were in the shoe. He was pale and near shock. He requested a cigarette so I got one from his pocket and lit it. He again refused treatment. Several people came near and I noticed a couple medics in the group. I told them he needed immediate attention and that I had to move on to catch up. I walked a ways across the field and looked back. He was holding his leg and fighting with the medics.

As I moved on into the forest toward Noville, the shelling was more intense. The shrapnel was picking our men off. Three troopers lay face down in the snow. I turned their heads for identity. I knew a couple of them. When I caught up with the main force, I reported the loss. It came as a shock to one of the officers. It was hard for him to accept the loss. They must have been close friends from the same unit.

As darkness drew closer, we dug harder on our foxholes. It has been decided that we'd dig in there for the night. I dug hard and fast and worked up a sweat in spite of the cold weather. Shells roared in and I hit that foxhole. More shells hit and I heard calls for a medic. I made my way through the trees and found Capt. James Morton, Headquarters Company commander, injured rather severely in the ankle. He was face down. I straddled over him and cut his clothes so I could get to the wound. As I attempted to patch him up, the shells came closer. I couldn't leave him, so I ignored them. One struck a few yards away and it killed T/5 Robert Y. Evans, one of our 3rd Battalion medics. Suddenly, an 88mm shell from a German tank hit in a tree above our heads and drilled me thoroughly in the back. A piece went through my right lung, diaphragm and lodged in my liver. I laid down on Morton and yelled for a medic. It was a while, but one came. It could have been John Eckmann who placed wide tape over the holes. Before being taped, I could hear the blood bubbles when I exhaled. I thought I might be a goner. It felt like my entire right lung was ripped open and exposed. I felt the blood run down my spine.

Pretty soon Morton and I were put on a jeep that had stretchers. Seems like there were at least four of us wounded put on that jeep. We slowly made our way out of the forest and eventually reached the Regimental aid station in Bastogne. Major Kent was there as was Medic Owen Miller. Several were there but I distinctly remember those two. I don't know what they did with Morton, as I never saw him again.

Over in the 1st Battalion area, Major Robert Harwick, its commander, and his executive officer, Captain Knut Raudstein, were lost when a shell hit the command post. Captain Charles Shettle assumed command of 1st Battalion but he, too, was wounded the following day and was replaced by Captain Clarence Hester from the regimental staff.

## JANUARY 10

The day was cold and cloudy though air support did appear on call when the clouds broke up from time to time. For those waiting in the woods for the continuing attack, the temperature never rose above freezing and at night hovered near the zero mark.

The 326th Airborne Engineers cut logs to cover foxholes and, in some cases, used explosives to blast holes in the frozen ground.

The 101st mission for the day continued to be the seizure of Noville. Action began at 0230 when an enemy combat patrol of two platoons supported by heavy artillery hit the newly won positions at the edge of the Fazone Woods. The attack was turned back but the heavy artillery caused the 1st Battalion of the 506th Regiment, which was in reserve behind 2nd Battalion to pull back three-quarters of a mile. Casualties from that shelling were 126 men from the 506th Regiment. Those casualties occurred during the night of January 9 and early morning of the 10th.

As a member of "H" Company of the 3rd Battalion, PFC. Guy D. Jackson was in on the attack on the 10th. That was the night he lost his closest buddy during an extremely heavy shelling. Jackson wrote:

We were dug in that night on a reverse slope facing south. Evidently, the Germans knew we were there and had already zeroed in their guns. They started shelling us that night and every one of them was on target. The thing happened here. You couldn't dig in the ground – it was frozen and I just had a lil ole trench, more or less. That night, my best buddy was killed – PFC. Charles Kieffer – and one of my buddies didn't have a hole at all and he came over and tried to jump over in front of me. It seemed like the shelling went on for at least 30 minutes. You can't go by time in combat. Anyway, if the guys hadn't had half of the holes dug there probably would have been a lot more casualties that night. The next day, we had to go through this big woods and the snow was on the ground about a foot deep. I guess my platoon, the 3rd, was on the point. There was a German tank, no more than 100 yards away and he opened up. He just missed me but the guy in front of me was wounded. The tank fired that one time and took off. Going through those woods – that was the only fire we got.

In on the same action that night was PFC. Ewell B. Martin of "G" Company who remembered the cold night and how men got tangled in their sleeping bags during inopportune moments when an enemy patrol was passing the line of foxholes.

Some of the heaviest shell fire I remember occurred one cold night in January. We were dug in at a point of woods. Jack Luce and I had the squad's machine gun and were swapping two hour watches. Jack suddenly shook me awake after seeing a German patrol in snow suits get into the woods behind us. We took the machine gun and tried to catch up with them; however, as I heard later, one of the men down the line was zipped up in his sleeping bag – saw the patrol go by him – couldn't get his 'fart sack' unzipped so he started firing his .45. The Kraut patrol got out in a hurry before we could spot them again. We exchanged machine gun fire with the Krauts who had begun firing from their point of woods opposite us. They did no damage and I doubt that we did, either.

During that same night, PFC. William N. Chivvis of "I" Company was on outpost duty, which he never seemed to mind. He recalled a situation when one of the new replacements died – probably because he couldn't make up his mind whether he should fire while he had the drop on an approaching enemy soldier. Chivvis wrote:

We had a new guy named Pvt. Eugene A. Smith who must have been shipped to us after the fight started. He had been raised by his mother and was such a NICE guy that there was some doubt in his mind as to whether he could pull the trigger. I heard that he confronted the enemy and was shot down while still trying to decide.

3rd Battalion was withdrawn from its forward position on the night of January 10 with Battalion Headquarters moving all the way back to the small village of Savy. Medical captain Barnie Ryan remembered worrying about an impending attack. He wrote: "The following night, January 10, we retired from the position which it had cost us so dearly to take and spent January 11th in Savy."

The coordinated moves of neighboring divisions never took place so the 101st was forced to withdraw from the positions they had gained over a period of a day and a half. The continuing fight to take Noville would involve battling to gain the lost ground.

## JANUARY 11

During mortar and artillery barrages, the platoon medic is called on to go to the aid of his wounded comrades. Sometimes his move saves him from death or serious danger. T/5 Leon Jedziniak cites such an experience:

Eddie Kelley and I were in a pre-dug foxhole in the woods. The Germans started laying down a mortar barrage. The call 'Medic' came up. My kit was in a log and dirt covered bunker several yards from the foxhole. As I got to the top of the hole, a concussion knocked me down. I got to the dugout and got my kit.

After ministering to the men who had received wounds as the result of the mortar barrage and saw to their evacuation, he returned to the dugout to return his first aid kit. While there, he learned of the loss of his foxhole mate. Jedziniak wrote: "I returned to the dugout and a trooper told me that Ed Kelley took a direct hit in the foxhole I was in a few minutes earlier."

As executive officer for "A" Company of the 501st Regiment, 1Lt. Joseph B. Schweiker remembered that his commander, Captain Stanfield Stach had been evacuated with a painful ankle wound and his replacement, 1Lt. Charles Seale, was killed in an accidental shooting and was replaced by 1Lt. Hugo Sims. Schweiker was very saddened with the loss of an enlisted man who had just shown him pictures of his family. The pictures had arrived with the latest mail call:

I can remember very clearly PFC. Edgar Kelley, one of our BAR men, had just received some mail and he was showing me pictures of his family. Shortly after, Kelley was killed by a direct hit on his foxhole.

## JANUARY 12

The 12th of January was very cold and, fortunately, little offensive action was in the offing for this day. The only aggressive move in the direction of the enemy was conducted by troops of the 501st Regiment. These troops were to make a limited advance which would provide a better line of departure for the 327th Glider Infantry which would move through those positions on the 13th. The 501st made a limited attack at 1405 to take and stabilize along the Foy-Mageret road about 500 yards in front of the regimental MLR.

Nothing has appeared in the text about the men of "I" Company of the 501st since the fighting on December 19 at Wardin. In his narrative, *D-Day to Bastogne*, S/Sgt. Robert Houston provides a detailed story of the actions of his

platoon in this action in the Bois Jacques bordering the Bastogne to Bourcy
railroad line.[185]

It was a very cold morning – somebody at company HQ said the
temperature was 6 degrees. We crawled out of our foxholes at daybreak and
ate a hot breakfast that had been brought out from the battalion kitchen. Lt.
Bill Morgan called the officers and platoon sergeants together to go over the
plan of attack. My German map was the most detailed, so we all studied
that. We were to attack through the woods about 500 yards to a small road
that ran from Foy through Le Bois Jacques and across the railroad. The
502nd Regiment was now on the other side of the track and had an outpost
line up to the road on that side.

We collected a full load of ammo, including two extra boxes for the
machine guns, and explained the attack plan to the men. Our platoon was on
the extreme right against the railroad, with the rest of 'I' Company about 50
yards to the left and other companies of the 501st to the left of them. The
Battalion CP would move up to our line of departure after we started
forward. Lt. Morgan told us to keep the line of advance even, so that nobody
would be too far in front in the thick woods and in the line of fire of our
troops.

We moved out at about two o'clock and went forward about two hundred
yards before bumping into a German patrol in a small clearing. Shear shot
one and we captured two others. One got away in the woods beyond the
clearing. Mortar shells began falling around us. Lt. Vaishvilla caught a
piece of shrapnel in his arm. The medic put a bandage on it and the
lieutenant told me to take over while he went back to the aid station.

We went on through the thick woods again, over the rough ground near
the tracks; I was carrying a box of machine gun ammo in addition to my
tommy gun and everybody else had a full load. The trees in this part of the
forest were small, only six to eight inches around, and close together. It was
impossible to walk among the trees without hitting branches and dumping a
load of snow down on our heads. Our platoon, down to eight men now,
along with our first aid man, whom everybody called *Medic*, seemed isolated
in the dark woods. Troopers of the 502nd were supposed to be across the
tracks to our right, but we didn't see or hear anything of them. We could
hear rifle and machine gun fire on our left – it was hard to tell how close it
was.

A burp gun fired directly in front of us and we hit the ground. Crawling
forward, we saw a clearing along a trail that must be our objective. There
was rifle fire coming from a group of foxholes, but the Germans were all
down in their holes, and the fire was going over our heads. I crouched on my

---

[185]Houston, 128-132.

knees behind a little tree and fired two bursts from the tommy gun. Something hit my helmet and knocked me over backwards – one of the Germans must have been aiming. I grabbed the helmet from the snow and saw a bullet hole almost dead center, but just high enough so that the bullet had deflected up, making just one long hole. The helmet liner had broken and cut my scalp a little.

I straightened the liner and put my helmet back on. By that time Crotts and Shear had a machine gun firing from behind the bank that sloped down to the railroad. When *Medic* saw the hole in my helmet and blood dripping down my forehead he said, 'Are you hurt, Sergeant?' 'No, just mad. Let's get them out of there!' I told Crotts to continue spraying the foxholes while two men with the other machine gun circled around to the left. They started to set up the second gun, but I told them to fire from the hip and keep moving. It was hard to aim, but a light machine gun could be fired this way and throw a lot of lead in the general direction that we wanted. The two men kept moving around until their fire was going in toward the foxholes at 90 degrees to our other gun on the railroad bank. I took another box of ammo over to them and told them to set the gun up and fire in bursts skimming the foxholes.

No fire was coming back at us now, so I told Crotts to stop firing while *Medic*, who could speak a little German, shouted at them to surrender because they were surrounded. In a little while, we could see a white handkerchief being waved from one of the foxholes. Some of us shouted to them in our 'good' German 'Kommen zee hier, mit der hands hoche, macht schnell!'

We heard 'Kamerad, Kamerad,' and two men appeared with their hands up. *Medic* shouted at them that everyone had to come out or we would begin firing immediately.

More white handkerchiefs and 'Kamerads' and in a few minutes there were twelve standing with their hands on their heads. We searched them for pistols and then, while Crotts covered the group with his machine gun, the rest of us raced across the trail, firing at dugouts we could see among some bigger trees. Franklin and I ran up to what looked like a big covered dugout; he started to throw a grenade into the opening. I shouted to him, 'Stop, don't throw a grenade in there – we will use that dugout tonight and don't want blood all over it!'

A burst of tommy gun bullets and the 'Kommen zee hier' routine brought four men scurrying out. Three of them had big, red crosses on their arms. That seemed like too many first aid men for one dugout and, when we went in the dugout, we found three rifles.

Shear and the other men had rounded up five more Krauts from along the bank of the railroad cut, so we had a total of 21 prisoners. There would be a problem getting them back through the thick woods to Battalion HQ. Mel Ponder suggested marching them back down the tracks, so he took my tommy gun and stood on the bank while they lined up in single file and set out with hands on top of their heads.

Crotts set four men in foxholes along the bank at the edge of the trees, while the platoon medic, Shields, Berry and I went into the big dugout. It was 'just like home' with blankets on the floor, a roof of logs covered with dirt, and some candles set in shelves dug into the wall. It was way below freezing outside so we were glad that the Germans had built a good home for us.

As I came out of the dugout, I heard a man calling for help from the woods ahead of us. *Medic* and I went to check it out and found a German officer shot through both legs. He had probably been hit when the machine guns were spraying bullets around. We picked him up and carried him to our dugout and then decided to take him to the battalion CP.

We sat him on a German rifle held between us and started back, with our passenger complaining all the way. It was very hard going through the snow and over the rough ground with our heavy load, but we made it after threatening to throw the German on the railroad track if he didn't keep quiet. About half way along we met Ponder coming up after having delivered the other 21 prisoners.

Battalion HQ was set up where we had started from earlier in the day. We were told to stay in the positions we had taken and to expect a company from the 327th to go through the next day.

*Medic* and I picked up a five-gallon thermos can marked for 3rd Platoon, 'I' Company, and started our return trip. The can was easier to carry than the wounded man, but it was dark now, so again the going was slow. We came to the clearing where we had captured the first 12 Krauts and had started across when we saw a flash from across the tracks ahead of us. We hit the ground and 'Whissht-bang!' The explosion followed almost instantly on the whistle of the shell.

We lay in the snow for a minute and then got up to start on with our can of food. We had gone only a few steps when there was another flash with the shell whistling right over us. The 502nd was supposed to be on the other side of the tracks, but apparently they weren't up that far. It was dark, but when we started across the open space the enemy could see us against the snow. We were only about 25 yards from the trees by our dugout, so we made a dash for it while another shell whistled and exploded behind us.

We were concealed by the trees now and got the can into our dugout. *Medic*, Berry and Shields filled their mess kits with warm chilli while I went to tell Crotts to send men into the dugout one at a time. His foxhole was at the edge of the woods, so I lay in the shadows to talk to him. He said that there was a tank across the tracks; they had seen it come in before dark. Another flash and 'Whissht-bang' and the shell exploded against the side of the foxhole, throwing dirt all over me. I ran to the dugout and got *Medic* to help me check on the wounded men. Crotts and another man were killed, but Shear, Franklin and Ponder were okay.[186]

There was nothing to do about it now, so we settled down with two men to stay on watch in the foxholes while the rest slept in the dugout.

On the morning of January 13, what was left of Houston's platoon, and the rest of "I" Company, would be relieved by the men of "Ace" Company of the 327th. The glidermen would attack through the "I" Company positions.

## JANUARY 13TH

This day would find elements of each of the four infantry regiments on the move to the northeast. Guiding on the railroad, headed toward Bourcy, the 502nd Parachute Regiment, led by 1st Battalion, was moving up the east side of the railroad. On the west side, the troops of 1st Battalion of the 327th Glider Infantry Regiment would sweep to the northeast.

The open terrain, with a snow depth ranging from one to two feet, and the heavy enemy machine gun and small arms fire supported by tank fire of the well dug-in and concealed Germans made the going slow for the regiment with its left flank up against the elevated railroad grade in that sector. The 502nd jumped off on time at 0830.

The troops of the 327th had moved from their reserve quarters at Champs and had experienced much difficulty in reaching the jump-off point assigned to them. The guides assigned to lead them were unfamiliar with the terrain and had become lost as they led the glidermen to the positions. However, once they had launched their drive, the troops moved along rapidly.

Descriptions of the actions on the 502nd drive are provided with the morning report account of the "A" Company actions as recorded by the first sergeant Ted Beishline.

0715 – Alerted for attack at 0830. 0830 – Able 1 on left, Able 2 on right supported by Able 3 and four tanks crossed LD. Keepsake Blue (3rd Bn of 327th Glider Regiment) on left, Baker Red on right. 0945 – Reached

---

[186]It wasn't until 1993 that Michael Finn of "I" Company learned that the second man with Crotts in the foxhole was not killed but was seriously wounded. PFC. Charles Galvin's family was notified he had been killed in action. It wasn't until nine months later that he was able to communicate with doctors as to who he was. His family now learned he was indeed alive. Galvin spent two and a half years more in the hospital where a metal plate was inserted in his head. Finn learned from Galvin's family that he had been awarded a Silver Star for knocking out a tank at Wardin on December 19 during the first hours of combat.

phase line one. Intermediate shelling. <u>1000</u> – Enemy opposition heavy. Much small arms and mortar fire received. Casualties inflicted both upon enemy and our own forces. Able 3 moved on line. <u>1300</u> – Advanced to phase line 2. Able 1, 2 and 3 on line. <u>1410</u> – Reached phase line 3. Defense set up and EM dig in. Maintain sound and sight contact throughout night. <u>2400</u> – Casualties this date: Dagostino and Lenz KIA. Lt. Wise, Graham, Smoot, Kessel, Taylor, Lyons, Shaw, Tippins, Lee, Ciriaco, Koeller, Merlano, Baker H. W., Soliz, Bergeron WIA. Grosvenor MIA later reported KIA, Bergeron, MIA later reported WIA. Kehoe, Lemos MIA.

One of those casualties listed above was 1Lt. Albert J. Wise whose platoon was now at squad strength, described his part in the action of the 13th:[187]

The 2nd Platoon was down to nine men, including me, on Jan. 13th. Our mission was to take a patch of woods occupied by the Jerries approximately two hundred yards to our front and up a slight rise. Two tanks were assigned to assist. I split the 'platoon' – gave four men to Terwilliger to move to the left flank approximately 50 to 100 yards and try to take the woods, or at least distract the Jerries, while my three men and I tried to make it straight ahead with the tank support. About half way out (100 yards) into the clearing, am sorry to report the lead tank stopped and refused to go any closer to the woods, claiming he couldn't go into them. I tried to persuade the tank commander (a captain) to at least lower his tube and fire his 76mm as low as possible into the woods – anything to cover us. I was up by his bogey wheel sighting for targets when I was hit. So for me, I'm sorry to report, the fight ended by 0800 that morning – was shot through the mouth, jaw and shoulder. Merlano saw the whole action as he was right behind me.

Mortar sergeant Lou Merlano was in on the action with 1Lt. Albert Wise and this is his recollection of the action:

Early Jan. 13th, Lt. Wise, who was now my 2nd in command in 1st Platoon, and I were given the duty to go out with him and we had two tanks to cut through the barbed wire entanglement outside the area toward Houffalize at 0830 in the morning. We were caught in this move by several Tiger tanks which turned around and destroyed the first two tanks. I saw Lt. Wise get hit in the face with a shell and I moved on through the barbed wire entanglement and proceeded to lose fifty percent of my men. I was then hit again – for the third time, in the right arm and hung in there until late that evening when I lost all mobility in the arm.

We took a pasting but we held our ground, I am proud to say. The boys, despite the odds, hung in there. I was evacuated and sent back to Paris and placed in a hospital and that ended my episode back at Bastogne.

---

[187]Wise, op. cit.

In a letter he had written to his friend, Lloyd Brazell, with whom he had served in World War II, Cpl. Elmer G. Nicks, a machine gunner with the 1st Battalion of the 502nd, relates his experiences of the drive on January 13th and 14th when he lost a close friend:

After General Patton broke through the ring around Bastogne, we had expected to be relieved but apparently things were a lot worse than we knew. We were regrouped and put in the spearhead to attack the Germans that had surrounded us. Companies were down to 25 men or less and our machine gun platoon was like two squads, but they were expected to cover the same amount of ground. We had attacked and moved into positions alongside a high railroad embankment with a dirt road running along both sides and with heavy planted forest on both sides of the railroad. The fighting in the planted forest brought a lot of terrifying experiences. You never knew what you would meet as you pushed through the heavy foliage.

We had fought, up to a point, the night before (January 13) and we had taken over some German positions. My hole was a typical German dugout, very deep with a place to sit and stand, with only your head and shoulders barely out of the hole. It had been a rough day and a miserable night. Sub-zero weather, snow was waist deep – constant mortar and artillery shelling. No food and only a fool would light a fire or smoke a cigarette. My feet had been killing me but I noticed the next morning they didn't hurt any more. I didn't know until the next day the reason they didn't hurt was because they were frozen.[188]

The coldest part of the winter was now upon the troops as will be described by several of the troops in their accounts. Pvt. Gerald B. Johnston of "C" Company relates what he witnessed and experienced during this attack. He wrote:

The odd thing is we found a dead trooper in a foxhole, wearing a tan jump suit and galoshes. Everyone else was wearing green. How did this man get into the cold weather wearing a jump suit? The galoshes were new to us; no one in our crowd had them. They were Lt. Wall's size so Hollingsworth and another fellow wrestled them off the frozen body and they were put to some use – he didn't need them anymore. The snow was deep. Running was not possible so it was just a matter of a slow slog across a field towards a wood line, wondering when the first shots would greet us. There were a few shells but no small arms fire. The great dilemma was whether to take your glove off to free your trigger finger (and freeze your hand) or leave it on and hope you could get it off quick enough should you need to shoot.

---

[188]From a letter Elmer Nicks wrote to Lloyd Brazell on January 3, 1984 when Brazell was writing to Congress to encourage them to provide an award of the Congressional Medal of Honor, posthumously, for his buddy, Sgt. Leo Pichler.

God, it was cold! My overcoat got full of moisture from body heat one night and I took it off to dig. When we moved out at dawn, it was frozen, still in a folded shape. It was too awkward to carry, with the ammo and other stuff, so I just had to leave it.

All the German bodies we came across were frozen solid and often stripped of their outer clothing, some even to bare legs. One was wearing American galoshes stuffed with straw to try to escape the cold. By this time my feet were board-like, numb.

## THE DRIVE INTO BOIS JACQUES

The ranks of Companies "A" and "C" of 1st Battalion of the 327th Glider Infantry Regiment had been badly decimated in the January 3rd and 4th enemy attack northwest of Champs. Now they were being called on to be a part of the attack toward Cobru and Noville on January 13 as the troops of the 101st were to drive through the Bois Jacques. Capt. Joseph B. Johnson of "A" Company describes what was done to make a more effective unit:

After the defense of Bastogne was successfully completed, we went on the offensive. Walter Miller was the commander of 'C' Company at Bastogne and between my Company 'A' and his 'C' Company our unit strength was only about 40 percent of what the TO provided. In order to be more effective, we merged 'A' and 'C' Companies and it was called 'Ace' Company and we fought as that unit until our offensive was completed and we were withdrawn from offensive combat.

The attack through the Bois Jacques (Jack's Woods) was to be the third and final action in the Ardennes campaign for "C" Company, led by Capt. Walter L. Miller. He related:

We remained in Champs until I received orders to attack through another unit in the woods with the objective being Bois Jacques. Most important for the Bois Jacques attack was that 'A' and 'C' Companies had been combined due to the lack of man power and we were now called 'Ace' Company. The company now consisted of roughly 120 men, with many being cooks and supply personnel. They did a magnificent job in accomplishing their mission.

The guards provided to lead us, got lost and I phoned in that we would be late and received orders to attack within a half hour. An artillery barrage would be laid and I was to get off or else!

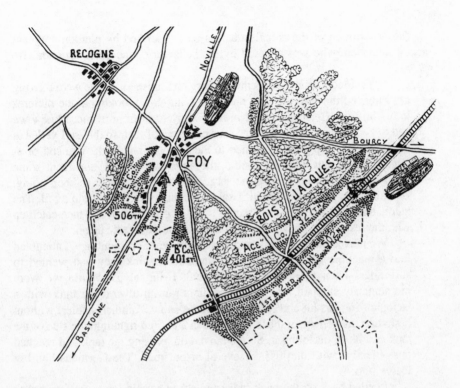

*Map 21*

The segment of "Ace" Company which was composed of "A" Company men had few topgrade non-coms left. S/Sgt. Jack (Eleopoulos in wartime) Williamson was trying to ease the tensions of his men before the actual attack through the area toward Noville took place. He related:

We were rounded up from several different units. We were to attack toward the town of Noville. We needed to break the line so the tanks of General Patton's outfit could roll on through. There was one other sergeant and myself. I turned to the other sergeant and said, 'You bring up the rear and make sure no one runs off.' He was lying there in the snow. He had his billfold out and was looking at some pictures. I decided to walk back forward to encourage the troops who were scattered about, some were smoking a last cigarette. I believe they cheered me up more than I cheered them. One soldier said, 'Sergeant, I want to do a good job but I'm scared. I wish I could be like you and not be scared.' If the truth was told, I was more scared than he was. I held out my hands and they were not shaking but I guess, after a time, I had reached the point where I could hold it within me. It is damn sure I was shaking on the inside.

The description of the actual attack is best described by platoon sergeant Jack Williamson, who was angered by the behavior of the other sergeant. He related:

We started moving out as the artillery had finished. As we were moving up, I noticed the sergeant who had been lying down looking at the pictures in his billfold. He shot himself in the foot right in front of me. I knew we had to keep going before the Germans came out of their foxholes. I yelled at the troops to keep going. I turned to the sergeant and said, 'You son-of-a-bitch!' About that time our medic, the only one we had, and from some other outfit, came up to help the sergeant. I told the medic to keep going. He said, 'I've got to help him!' I said, 'The hell with him' to no avail. The medic had to help him. As we parted I said, 'You help him and then catch up with the rest of us.' I never saw that sergeant or that medic again.

We moved on up. The Germans were the best at camouflage. I stumbled into a machine gun nest – three Germans – I think they had wanted to surrender. Then there was a small tank firing at us. While we were momentarily stopped, one of our soldiers ran up toward the tank with a bazooka. He was hit and rolled over in the snow. Another soldier, without hesitation, moved up, grabbed the bazooka and fired right into the side of the tank and hit it, disabling it. So we moved on, passing the tank and reached our objective with the loss of several of our men. The Germans had big losses, too.

I called back on the pack radio and asked permission to go forward to our second objective. It wasn't that I was so damned brave but the artillery was firing right on top of us. I got that permission. We were moving forward and my good friend, Pvt. James A. Poynter, was hit and went down. He yelled, 'Jack – Jack!' I looked back and saw him with blood on that white snow – God knows I wanted to go back and see him but if I had stopped to go back, my men would have stopped, so I went on.[189]

I was way out in front and I was firing at a German sergeant and my submachine gun misfired – nothing was happening. The German sized up the situation and came back after me. The troops were catching up and one of my men with a BAR leveled on that sergeant and dropped him right in his tracks.

Here I had a machine gun that was no good and a shell came in, exploding over our heads. There was a man standing there with a submachine gun. I guess he got a concussion with blood coming out of his

---

[189]Jack Williamson was pleasantly surprised when James Poynter showed up at the annual reunion of the 101st Airborne Division Association in 1991. It was their second meeting since 1945. They met once 30 years ago.

mouth. He died. I got his submachine gun and he had a canvas bag of clips. I picked that up and moved up further.

We got up to a wooded area and there was an opening where I waved four Germans in to surrender. One wanted to know if he could go to New York. Another said 'War fini!' We sent them all back.

We moved on up and got into the woods and set up a defensive position. The Germans attacked us. We jumped up and attacked them. Then they retreated and went around our right flank and started in. I ordered all up to attack except a couple who were wounded. They were in a big German dugout. We moved out up to the Germans and mixed it up with them. One of my very brave soldiers, who hadn't been up in the front lines very long, got killed right there. A couple got wounded and ran off toward the rear. I didn't try to stop them. I hope they got back. We captured four more German soldiers, brought them back and stuck them in one of the German dugouts with a guard. We settled down for the night.

Meanwhile, over on the "C" Company segment of "Ace" Company, Captain Walter L. Miller took advantage of some abandoned equipment and remembered losing a good friend as the result of the terribly cold weather. Miller related:

During this attack, we had picked up an abandoned half-track and transported our heavy equipment on it. Unfortunately, the truck slipped off the road and we had to abandon it.

There were units to my right and left which attacked at the same time but they did not make it. We were glad to move forward as the tree bursts were deadly. 1Lt. Joe Carpenter was wounded and died because the plasma would not flow – it had frozen in the bottle and tube.

We advanced, hollering and shouting through the woods, chasing out the Germans, and arrived at the Bois Jacques to find well-emplaced bunkers in which we took shelter from the tree bursts that we were receiving. We could see the enemy infiltrating behind us. We established a perimeter defense and beat off the Germans who approached through the woods to our left. We were aided by an artillery ('1776') concentration. We were isolated here for a couple days till the companies adjacent to us moved forward and established contact.

I had informed 1st Battalion of the enemy troops between us and the Kraut lines behind us. In an effort to reach us, Colonel Salee was wounded along with PFC. Hugo Dobberstein, his radio operator.

A member of the mortar section of Captain Miller's segment of "Ace" Company, PFC. Werner W. Jutzin, had this recollection of the actions in the drive northward:

Company 'C' was involved in a counterattack to take three objectives in three days. We were flanked by jumpers on our left and Company 'A' on our right. However, we moved so fast all opposition was overrun the first day and we were out ahead of our supporting companies. We remained in this wooded area for two days, using German foxholes well covered with logs and camouflage. We ran out of rations and existed on potatoes we found in the foxholes. We were attacked several times by Germans wearing white sheets but held our positions. We captured 10 to 12 Polish-speaking Germans who were interrogated by Sgt. Gus Orleansky.

Though they had jumped off three-quarters of an hour late, much to the annoyance of General Taylor, 1st Battalion of the 327th had reached the northern edge of the Bois Jacques by 1600 hours. They had taken a patch of woods between Bois Jacques and Bourcy. Having moved faster than the 502nd troops on the right flank, enemy troops in company strength had been able to move in behind "Ace" Company and the neighboring 502nd troops were being fired on from three sides. This certainly was a major factor in the 502nd not reaching their first day objective. LTC. Ray Allen and his 401st Glider Battalion was then brought forward to root out the enemy troops between "Ace" and the 502nd.

## 2ND BATTALION ATTACK ON FOY

The 506th had begun its part of the coordinated attack at 0900 when "E" Company attacked along the western edge of Foy, astride the road. The company fought into the edge of Foy, meeting increasing resistance and at 1015 Company "I" was sent up the road to help. Company "H" was also called into the fray and later in the afternoon "F" Company would join them. They were followed by "B" Company of the 401st on the right flank.

Shortly after the new year began, the snow fall had increased and the temperature sank lower and hovered around the zero reading. Captain Dick Winters was now commanding 2nd Battalion and it was his troops which led the attack on Foy this day. He did some reading before daylight and then had the following description of the actions:

The night before, I sat in my foxhole reading (by candlelight) the *Infantry Manual on Attack*. When I think about that – lugging an infantry manual off to Bastogne – I should have taken a Hershey chocolate bar. I had that manual memorized, but this time that manual wasn't advanced enough for the situation for which I was preparing. It just seemed too elementary.

At early dawn, I had 1Lt. Frank Reis, 2nd Bn. HQ. Co., set up two sections of LMG's on the edge of the woods facing Foy. They were to provide covering fire as 'E' Company moved through the snow across approximately 250 yards of open field to the village.

The attack jumped off. The covering fire was working but each time an MG had to change a belt, I held my breath through the lull of fire. The

Germans fired only a few random rifle shots from an outpost on the west edge of the village. It was tough going for the men through that snow in a skirmish formation, but the line was keeping a good formation and moving at a good pace. Then, suddenly, the line stopped about 75 yards from the edge of the village. Everybody hunkered down in the snow and stayed there for no apparent reason. I could not get any response from Lt. Dilke (company commander) on the radio. The company was a bunch of sitting ducks out there in the snow. I turned around and 1Lt. Ronald Speirs was standing behind me. I ordered him to move out, take over Company 'E' and move that attack. He did! The attack went off as planned. In the house to house fighting, we lost three men killed and several wounded.

First sergeant Carwood Lipton sheds further light on the replacement of his company commander and describes the fighting in Foy. Lipton wrote:

Lt. Dilke had managed to stay out of trouble since the shelling of 'E' Company on Jan. 3rd, but in the attack on Foy, he fell apart. The attack had hardly begun when he had one platoon stationary in an open position with no covering fire, and it was obvious he had no real plan for the attack. Captain Winters relieved him immediately and put 1Lt. Ronald C. Speirs from 'D' Company in command of 'E'. Lt. Speirs proved to be a fearless, capable combat commander and leader.

In the attack on Foy, we had three men killed – Herron, Mellett and Carl Sawosko, and several men wounded. Mellett's death was an infuriating one. A German hid in a building and, after the fighting had carried on beyond him, he shot Mellett through the heart as he was walking in the door of the building. Alley caught Mellett as he fell. We didn't take many prisoners after that. One of the wounded men, 'Burr' Smith, was hit in the leg close to me by a sniper. The sniper kept us pinned down for awhile. Then 'Shifty' Powers, one of our best rifle shots, saw the sniper in a building and put a bullet right in the middle of his forehead. 'Popeye' Wynn', Shifty's buddy, looked at me and said, 'You know, it just doesn't pay to be shootin' at 'Shifty' when he's got a rifle'.

## BREAK-IN ON COMMUNICATIONS

For the Ardennes campaign, 1Lt. Peter Madden had been assigned as the 81mm mortar section officer for 3rd Battalion. His men were to support the attack on Foy and, during the actions, he became suspicious of the directions he was receiving over his radio. Madden related:

Colonel Patch had told me the night before that the 3rd Battalion was going to make the attack in the morning with 'I' Company on the left going into Foy and he needed cover from the high ground, just beyond Foy, and there were about three different enemy machine guns that had good commanding fire over the whole one side of the road and the little buildings in Foy. The attack started and I was waiting for radio silence to be broken and I kept waiting for the call from Colonel Patch to go ahead and deliver the fire. We had all the sites numbered and coded. There didn't seem to be any call at all. I got one call stating, 'Stand by. We'll be in touch with you.' About a minute later, I got a call which I was not able to identify as the regular radio operator for Colonel Patch and he spoke about like the rest of the people in there and, of course, we weren't in there analyzing voices at that time.

We were watching very closely the movement of 'I' Company at this time. I got this call back, identifying himself as 'Kidnap Blue' stating 'Hold your fire!' I asked, 'What target do you want me to hit first?' There was a pause and then 'Just hold your fire. It is not necessary now.' By that time, I noticed there were little puffs of smoke up in the woods and I couldn't quite figure this out. I called back again and that operator said, 'I said hold your fire and that is a direct order!' That sort of alerted me and I said, 'Identify yourself!' There was no answer.

I called all four batteries in on the target in the direction the fire was coming from and said, 'Fire for effect!'

That night after we regrouped, Colonel Patch came over to me and said, 'Pete, that was right on time!' He added, 'It really cut down on that machine gun fire. We were really getting it heavy in there for awhile.'

I told him what happened and he said I had to send that back to regimental headquarters and let them know that the enemy had a pretty good break-in to our communications system.

## A DECIMATED "I" COMPANY

Though "I" Company's numbers were way down by January 13, they were still called on to take part in the bitter fighting at Foy. Pvt. Albert Cappelli describes his limited role in the actions:

At 0900 hours January 13th, it was supposed to be our last day in Foy. I had the bazooka and was sixth in line down the road. The first scout was pinned down by a Tiger tank in the curve of the road. I was called up and was stopped about 25 yards before the barn on the left. I laid on the side of a bank and felt heat on my left knee – saw two holes in my pants with red stuff. Got up and ran across the road to the side of the house on the right. I was told to go behind the house – down the pathway to see how close I could get to the tank. I hit the tank and it lost power. Before I could get another shot at it, I took a P-38 slug just six inches above my first wound.

Richie Shinn helped carry me into the barn where Joe Madona was killed by a sniper. I got out of the barn about 5 p.m. that evening. The tank was captured when it ran out of gas.

Captain Bernard J. Ryan, the 3rd Battalion surgeon, describes the attack of January 13 to retake Foy for the third time:

'Easy' Company of the 2nd Battalion and 'I' and 'H' of the 3rd attacked on the morning of January 13. I was the only medical officer available for the attack. Immediately, the Germans put a barrage into our positions. I followed 'I' Company into Foy, going down beside the main road. 'I' Company was held up on its way in by Germans in windows and cellars, firing automatic weapons.

There were many wounded already and transportation could not be brought in as the road was mined and was under small arms fire. The engineers could not pull the mines.

There were several casualties scattered about the second house on the left side of the road going into town so I decided to use that house as an aid station. With the help of T/3 Walter Pelcher and T/5 Eugene Woodside, several casualties were brought into the house. German equipment – grenades and a panzerfaust – were lying in the kitchen. Several of the wounded were put on mattresses which the Germans had been using. S/Sgt. Joe Madona, a platoon sergeant in 'I' Company, and I went to the rear of the house to survey the situation. We heard Captain Gene Brown telling Battalion that Company 'I' had hit a hornet's nest.

Sgt. Madona and I were standing by the back door, peering out, when suddenly I staggered sideways and had the sensation of being hit in the chest with an axe. Sgt. Madona hit the floor like a ton of bricks, stone dead. A German 7.92 machine pistol had been fired into the doorway in which we were standing and had ricocheted off the stone door jamb, hitting us both. I know the caliber as I still have the bullet which was removed from my lung at the 60th Field Hospital. Another bullet had gone through my chest. Sgt. Madona, being short, was hit in the head.

I felt myself breaking out into a sweat and getting weak but I was able to go into the room where the other wounded were collected and lie down. The blood was trickling down my back and Woodside applied a Carlisle bandage. I knew perfectly well what was going on; had practically no pain and told Woodside not to give me any morphine. I sent word across the street to Captain Gene Brown to notify Regiment that another medical officer would be needed. I then started to cough up blood, thought 'this was it' and said an Act of Contrition.

Pelcher came in shortly thereafter. Someone heard noises in the cellar and, looking down, said 'My God, the cellar is full of Heinies!' I could just picture them spraying the wooden floor from beneath with several helpless wounded lying on their backs above them.

However, in about 30 seconds, four Germans came out of the cellar with their hands high. Someone said, 'Let's shoot the bastards!' I said, 'Hell no – we'll use them to carry the wounded back!' no doubt thinking of myself. Pelcher put them to work hand carrying the litter wounded up the ditches, through the snow, to a point where the jeeps could come. As I heard later, Captain Brown stumbled out of Foy that night with eleven riflemen left in his company.[190]

One of those rare infantrymen of "I" Company who came through the actions unscathed was Pvt. Bill Chivvis who described how men made choices when offered platoon assignments:

Going into the attack one day, we were given a man named Florenzio Valenzuela. He was offered the job of 2nd scout behind me, (Bob Chouvan had been wounded) or the job of machine gunner (Dave Dillen was wounded). His response was that he was not interested in either job as he had heard what happened to scouts and the enemy was sure to zero in on machine gunners. So he was made a runner. The next thing you can guess – a shell came over and hit him point blank. Jim Meade took over the machine gun and he and I continued the war, unscathed.[191]

In a letter he wrote to his friend 1Lt. William E. Reid of the Mortar Platoon of 3rd Battalion, Captain James S. Morton relates what happened to another friend, Captain Bernard J. Ryan, from the same battalion:

Barney Ryan got two 'burp gun' slugs through the left chest on January 13, four days after I was hit. Joe Madona, a sergeant in 'I' Company, was standing next to Ryan and caught the same burst in the head. He fell stone dead.[192]

After "I" Company had been committed to the fight for Foy and experiencing more casualties to its limited numbers, "H" Company was ordered into the fight. The action of his platoon is described by 1Lt. Alex Andros as his men took advantage of the mortar fire put down by Lt. Pete Madden's 81mm men:

I don't know what the purpose of the attack was. I think they wanted us to take Foy so they could push some armor through there, which never happened. Actually, 'H' Company wasn't leading the attack. 'I' Company

---

[190]Material is from a letter written by Captain Bernard J. Ryan to Major Louis Kent, surgeon for the 506th Parachute Infantry Regiment while he was recuperating from his wounds after Bastogne.

[191]Florensio Valenzuela is listed as KIA on January 13, 1945 in Piet Pulles' book, *Honored Dead of WW2* published in Eindhoven, Holland.

[192]Morton letter to 1Lt. William E. Reid.

was in front of us. We were in support. They got close to Foy and got sort of bogged down. I think Captain Walker told me he got ordered by Patch to do a flanking movement with 3rd Platoon, which we did. We went around to the right of the road, or east of the outskirts of Foy, through the snow. It was pretty deep and hard going. When we got half way around, we got four or five rounds coming from the far distant woods. It was German tanks or SP guns – we really couldn't tell. As soon as we got close to the buildings, that fire stopped. I don't think anyone got hit at that time. As soon as we had enveloped them, about twenty or thirty of them surrendered. Sgt. Sam Hefner was near me and I think he can verify this.

I told Sam to take his squad and go a little bit north of town because you always have to be ready for a counterattack – typical military doctrine. I remember going back and stripping the Germans of their military equipment.

After that, they took us and sent us to the left side of the road. We were in the village then. It was about 1000 or 1100 a.m. when those guys surrendered. They were sent to the rear and we were sent over to the west side of the road. 'I' Company was across the road.

The small village of Foy changed hands numerous times. It was a town which could not easily be defended. Sgt. Sam Hefner describes one of the forays into the town which occurred in January:

Sometime in January, we took Foy for about the third time and were mopping up and I had a Thompson with me so I busted out the window to the basement and sprayed it real good – out came these Krauts, hands behind their heads. One smart-ass young kid was among them. I told them to double time over to the compound we had set up for POW's. Medic Irving 'Blackie' Baldinger could speak German, though the enemy soldiers didn't know it. The kid was shouting at me and Blackie yelled, 'Hey Sarge, he's cussing you out real good!' I jerked the bolt back on that Thompson and sprayed the ground in front of his feet. He moved fast. That was the closest I have come to committing murder. That kid double-timed!

It was understandable that the enemy artillery would cease firing when Lt. Andros' platoon got in among the houses. German troops were still in some of those houses, some hidden but others were firing.

In the afternoon, Major Dick Winters was left in a sour mood because of two incidents which occurred during the day. He had asked Colonel Sink to relieve one of his replacement company commanders for cowardice in the face of the enemy and a second episode had to do with the antics of two photographers. Winters wrote:

One more memory of that day and that attack deserves to be remembered. It, too, left me in a foul mood. As the men were carrying the wounded back from Foy, I was suddenly aware of two photographers standing beside me, taking pictures of this detail. I am not sure where they came from or who they belonged to – I am only sure I'd never seen them before.

When the detail reached about 20 to 25 yards from the woods, well out of danger by this time of any possible fire from Foy, one photographer put down his camera and dashed out to grab hold of the soldier to help carry him. He grabbed him in such a way and manner that he got as much blood on the sleeve and front of his nice, new, clean, heavily-fleeced jacket as possible. Then this guy turned toward his buddy, who was still taking pictures, and put on a big act of being utterly exhausted as he struggled across those final few yards to the woods. At that point, he immediately dropped out of the picture. What a phony! This just topped off my day for phonies!

Troops from 3rd Battalion of the 327th Glider Regiment (1st Battalion of the 401st) were also in Foy in the afternoon for mopping up operations. A surprise awaited S/Sgt. Roger Seamon's men once they had set up a command post in one of the buildings. PFC. Ted Rhodes describes his experience:

We entered the small town of Foy approximately five miles northeast of Bastogne in the afternoon. Tony Casel was number 1 scout leading the column up the left side of the main street and I, number 2 scout, led the column up the right side. Tony would fire at the upstairs windows on the right and I would fire at the windows on the left.

From time to time, a German soldier would come out with hands over head and we would signal for him to walk down the middle of the street, toward the rear of our column. As we approached the other end of the town, Sgt. Seamon sent a roadblock team to set up a station a few hundred yards up the road. He chose the building at the edge of the town for our quarters for the night.

'Red' Leveille and I pulled the first watch behind the building overlooking a cleared area and the beginning of the wooded section. We had no sooner positioned ourselves when we heard a rumble like a tank toward the front of the house. I told 'Red' that I would go and investigate the noise. As I approached the front of the house, a German half-track pulled up in front of the house we had chosen for our quarters. From my position I could see the back of the half-track and the rear doors opened and I saw two pairs of legs below the door. I proceeded to advance toward the rear of the half-track where I came face to face with two big German soldiers. I looked into the half-track and saw the silhouettes of a number of German helmets. I said to the German nearest me, about six inches from my shoulder, 'You wait right here, I'll be back!' I was hoping he didn't understand English. I went into the house and, as I was warming my hands over the stove, I told S/Sgt. Seamon that we had visitors. 'There's a German half-track out front full of cold and hungry German soldiers.' Seamon said, 'You're kidding!' I said, 'Come on, I'll show you.' Sgt. Seamon opened the front door and took one glance outside and closed the door real fast. He said, 'Damn!' He told the men to get their rifles, that we had a problem. He led the men out the side door and we surrounded the half-track and, after we explained the situation to the Germans, they cooperated to the fullest.

PFC. Oliver Bryant had taken his rifle apart to clean and when Seamon said, 'Let's go!', Bryant picked up his entrenching tool. When I was relieved on watch and I started to break down my rifle to clean it, I received the surprise of my life. The last round I had fired while taking the town of Foy, the shell had jammed in the chamber and I would have been very embarrassed if I had to use it while we were engaged in the diplomatic relations.

## "Fox" Company Enters Foy

S/Sgt. John H. Taylor then describes how his platoon from "F" Company of the 506th Regiment apparently replaced the 401st troops on the east side of Foy in the afternoon. He related:

Somewhere around 4 o'clock that afternoon we moved into Foy. We moved through those people who were down there to the far side of Foy with 2nd Platoon and to the right side of the road. I know 'Easy' Company pulled out of there and 'I' and 'H' Companies stayed, though they had very few men left. We got down there and started setting up. Jake's squad went over to the right – the town wasn't very big. Back to the left a bit, was Olanie and his mortar squad. Facing east was the house we set up as platoon headquarters. We had the rest of the platoon scattered around the area. There was a cellar in this house and we were trying to get communications back to company headquarters which was back over on the other edge of town.

We had gotten everything pretty well set by dark. We didn't have any food that night. They brought food up but 1/Sgt. Charles Malley said 'No – take it back.' Really, you have to expect a counterattack or something like this. That is what Charley had in mind.

## January 14: Pre-dawn Counterattack

The first attempt to retake the town from the Americans in Foy occurred at 0415 when six enemy tanks and 75 infantrymen attacked. The 506th units holding the town were supported by four TD's, two of which were in the village and the other two up on the ridge west of Foy. The regimental reserve, 2nd

Battalion (minus "E") moved up behind Foy but wasn't committed. The attack was repulsed but the enemy came on again with a force of 14 tanks and a battalion of infantry. The defenders were forced to withdraw to the ridge west of the village. A heavy artillery barrage was placed on the enemy-occupied town. By 0900, Company "I" was back in town.

In describing his role in the predawn fighting, S/Sgt. John H. Taylor had a narrow escape when the enemy burst into the house his platoon was using as a command post. He related:

About this time, Lt. Williams from the 3rd Platoon came up with several men. I know Oakley was one of them. They were going through our position to see if they could contact the 327th. We were in the cellar talking about it. I was supposed to direct him out through Jake's forward position. We got the men together and there was a long hall all the way through the house. As you went out of the house, you turned left where Olanie was at the corner of the village. At the end of the street, there was a hill leading out of town. Lt. Williams and the patrol and I got up to the front door when heavy .50 caliber fire from the hill started coming down the street. Williams said, 'We're gonna have to wait until this fire lifts.' He sent the two or three men he had with him down into the cellar. Down in that cellar was Shaefer and little Joe Gillespie. I believe there was a sergeant from 'I' Company who was trying to use our communication to get back to 3rd Battalion. Lt. Williams and I were standing in the door of this house, watching as the fire was hitting Jake's house.

All of a sudden, there was a lull in the firing. For some reason, or by instinct, I said, 'I hear a tank!' I ran through the hall of that house and looked out back. About 30 to 40 yards from the house I could see this tank – I knew it was German – in the snow, coming up over a little bank and quite a few foot soldiers on either side. I ran back and told Lt. Williams 'we have a damn tank in back of us'. He said, 'I'll get the men out of the cellar.' This all happened. I ran to the back door again. I saw the tank move on to the left side of the house while the troops went around to either side of the house. I stepped back from the rear door and could see one man come nearly to the rear door. I stepped back into another room that had the windows blown out. I was standing by the door when one of the enemy soldiers started through the blown out window right toward the door and he couldn't see me. I knew he was going to run over me if I didn't do something. I shot him and jumped back into the hall. Just as I jumped back, I heard one of two men fire down the hall toward me. I heard someone scream. I remember turning my head, momentarily. The two guys in the front door threw their hands up and fell. Almost at the same time they fired down the hall, Lt. Williams came up the stairs and cut them down with a submachine gun.

We knew that tank was out there setting beside the house. I think Lt. Robertson came out of the cellar. He yelled, 'Let's get out of here!' We went out of the back door, firing from the hip. I remember Oakley and I went out about the same time and I ran over a roll of barbed wire, turned a flip and we went down behind a church building. Another column was coming down the street and Luke Atkins cut down on them with an M1. He fired it like an automatic weapon. We got organized down there and moved back up a little side street and got into another house. Couldn't find Lt. Cook. We crawled along a high bank which was beside the street. Got back up there and about 40-50 yards from the house, crawling through the snow, I heard someone say, 'You German or American?' There was Lt. Cook. He had been hit pretty bad through the hip and leg. We pulled him back and got him out of there.

Meanwhile, at another "F" Company position, Lt. Ben Stapelfeld was with members of his platoon. One of its members was Pvt. John B. Himelrick, a replacement who had just returned to his unit on the 10th of January, after being hospitalized in England. He had been painfully burned when a gasoline stove had exploded when two men were cooking a meal on the Island in Holland. Pvt. Himelrick describes his piece of the action:

We went into town and I was out on outpost, slightly to the north of Foy and probably to the east a bit. Myself and another trooper were in a previously dug foxhole. It was covered with a wooden sled over which earth had been thrown. It was a long, narrow slit trench. There was barely enough room for the two of us. The sled was over the center of it and we could look out either side. The hole was aligned parallel to the front, facing the enemy. One had to watch out from one side and one from the other. We were there for several hours.

Early in the morning, sometime between midnight and 0400, there was a German attack on Foy by several tanks accompanied by infantry and the person in the hole with me became extremely frightened and refused to get out of the hole, or even to look out. It was a very safe thing to do, as the tracers were passing a few feet over our heads and spraying the walls of the building behind us. Tank fire was being directed at the buildings. While they were approaching, they had apparently hit the town from other directions also, because a runner came up and told us we were pulling back to the center of town, to move the line back. When I got out of the hole, the other fellow was at the bottom of the hole, at the other end, and would not get out. The runner and I literally dragged him out of that hole. He disappeared that night. He was suffering from combat fatigue and I don't think he saw any more service with the outfit. He had reached his wits end and this is not said in a derogatory way. It happened to lots of us and some of us went over the edge, some teetered on it and some never approached it.

We pulled back into the center of town. I would assume my squad had gone into some sort of reserve. I remember that I was in a building. It was getting warm. Someone came after me to go on a contact patrol. There was a big question as to whether the outfits on either side of us had pulled back. If they had gone back into the hills outside of Foy, we didn't want to be left sticking out there by ourselves so we tried to make contact that night.

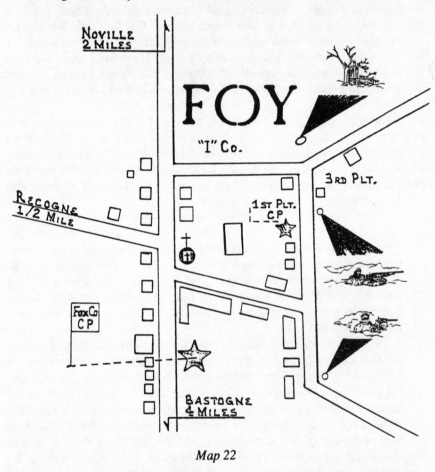

*Map 22*

*The material above was copied from two pages of a combat journal which was kept by Lt. Ben Stapelfeld of "F" Company of the 506th Parachute Infantry Regiment during the Bastogne campaign. Stapelfeld kept accurate records of his platoon (and "F" Company). Material was sent to Richard D. Winters by Dorothy Stapelfeld after her husband died. Winters, in turn, sent copies for this narrative with permission of Mrs. Stapelfeld.*

Lt. Ben Stapelfeld was on the contact patrol with me and one other person. I believe it was Sullivan, our radioman. The three of us went across some open fields, made contact with the unit on our right and started back. It was just getting light and we felt it was not safe to go back across those same open fields. We took a route back around the hill where the armor was lined up. We were climbing that hill toward an armored half-track or tank destroyer weapon – a tracked vehicle of some sort and a person stepped out from behind that vehicle, possibly from the 11th Armored. We used double passwords, sign and countersign. He called out the first part of the password. I was leading, coming up the hill, and I responded with the proper countersign just as he fired. It took me a moment to realize I had been hit in the right arm and hip. The bullet went completely through my right arm and hip and came through several layers of clothing before lodging at a point where my pants were bloused into my boots.

Lt. Stapelfeld called to me and asked if I was hurt. I told him I had been hit. They came over and examined the damage and it wasn't that severe. I was able to walk and could do everything else. We went on to the top of the hill. The man shot me with a .45. Lt. Stapelfeld told me the man began crying and was really upset about what he had done. I knew where the aid station was, having passed it on the way into the outfit.

When the fighting had ended on the 13th, the remnants of "I" Company and "H" Company were in positions along the north and west perimeters of Foy. 1Lt. Alex Andros was sleeping in a barn. He added to his story.

That night I was sleeping in one of the barns and one of the outposts came and wakened me saying, 'There's some tanks out there!' We went out and we could hear three or four German tanks but they were all confused. They started firing their machine guns but they were way over us. I don't know where they thought we were. It was very confusing. Just before dawn we got orders to move back to the top of the hill. I was lagging behind to make sure all my men got out and I turned to look back and here came Pat Fitzmaurice – somebody had forgotten to tell him we were moving back – slogging up the hill. They didn't fire on us. They must have moved out before dawn. I have no idea what happened to them.

Over on the northeast side of Foy, S/Sgt. John Taylor and his men moved to another location. He describes how the situation developed in his area during the early morning hours after the first tank had appeared beside the house in which they had set up temporary quarters:

The tank had apparently set fire to one of the houses. We had gotten a phone back in communication and we had to move to another house. The enemy had come through 'H' and 'I' Companies and were up on our rear side. We didn't know what the situation was. Along with Lt. Robertson and about 15 men, we didn't know who else was in there. So we stayed in there until just before daylight. Finally, just before dawn, word came down by runner for us to pull back on the high ground. We started sending the men up the hill.

As a member of "Dog" Company, PFC. Paul Z. Martinez stated that the fighting at Foy on January 13 and 14 was his most memorable experience in the Bastogne area. The actions occurred in the early morning hours when an enemy tank had set several houses on fire. He wrote:

The night Captain, Joe McMillan, was chasing a Tiger tank with a bazooka to get a clear shot at it in the then burning town of Foy is still my vivid recollection. We had very heavy fighting in support of 'Fox' Company.

After S/Sgt. John Taylor saw to it that all of his men were out of Foy, he himself moved out as the last man. The tank that Captain McMillan was chasing may be the same one involved in Taylor's continuing story. He added to his account:

I thought I had everybody from my bunch moving back up that hill and I started crawling in the ditch back to the main road and back up the hill. I had gone about 150 yards up the hill and I heard a tank coming up the main road. I could see this German tank coming pretty fast from the far outskirts up through the main intersection. All of a sudden, about the time it reached that main intersection, something exploded almost over my head. One of our TD's was setting up there on the bank. It was camouflaged and it fired on the tank. The tank exploded and flames shot up all around it. I saw someone jump out of it and run. We moved back up the road and went over to the left side of it. I tell you we were beat. We were told to hold right there – we'd be getting some tanks. Sure enough, there came the 11th Armored Division. They moved up. They were new. They lined the tanks up on the hill and brought up a couple companies of armored infantry. This was the way to fight a war with tanks. They lined those tanks up on the hill – guess there must have been eight or ten of them. The tanks fired on the village with the big stuff and the fifty calibers for a few minutes and then the armored infantry took off. All they had to do was walk down there. They got the village secured. Lt. Robertson and I decided to go back down into Foy because we had left all of our stuff down in that cellar. Back down there, sure enough, there was a dead German in the room, some in the doorway, some in the yard. We got our stuff and went back. That afternoon, about 3 o'clock, we got word to move to our left and do a flanking movement and attack Noville.

The heavy artillery barrage called down on the shattered remains of Foy and the appearance of the 11th Armored Division tanks with their supporting infantry, was enough for the Germans. As mentioned earlier, they pulled out by

0900 and 3rd Battalion troops moved back into any buildings which still provided shelter.

## ON TO NOVILLE

The next order Captain Dick Winters received didn't sit well with him. The fighting wasn't over for 2nd Battalion on the 14th. He was ordered to get his troops ready to move on Noville. They had spent the past night in Foy, being driven out by a concerted tank and battalion-sized infantry attack. Now they were to move on Noville from whence 1st Battalion and Team Desobry had withdrawn on December 20. Winters wrote:

When word came down for this attack it pissed me off. I could not believe that after what we had gone through and done, after all the casualties we had suffered, they were putting us into an attack. It just had the flavor of an ego trip for General Taylor, a play to show General Eisenhower that now that Taylor's back, his troops will get off their asses and go into the attack.

The scheduled hour of attack also angered the battalion commander. Capt. Winters was bitter with the order to move out at mid-day.

2nd Battalion moved forward at 1200. That's another point of not using good judgment by regiment or division command. Why 1200? Why do you send men across one and a half miles of wide open fields to Recogne-Cobru-Noville, through snow almost knee deep, in the middle of a bright, sunny day? The Germans were sitting on the high ground with tanks hidden by the cover of buildings. Why not early morning – first light of day, so we would have had the cover of darkness for at least part of the time?

That day I earned my pay! Before we started, I recognized that our salvation just might be that there was a fairly deep shoulder in the terrain on the southwest side of Noville and if I sent the column straight for it, I could pick up more and more cover as we got closer to Noville. (The 1st Battalion took advantage of the same terrain feature on the 20th of December when they withdrew from Noville.) We were lucky. They did not have any strong point on the shoulder and the plan worked. I had to put the whole battalion in single file to cut through that snow. It was a dangerous formation.

The 1st Battalion was about 400 yards to our left and slightly to the rear of our column. From time to time I'd glance over to see how they were doing. They were being cut up by direct fire from the 88's on those tanks in Noville. The fire was hitting into their lines; men were flying through the air. Years later, in the Movie *Dr. Zhivago*, I saw troops crossing snow-covered fields being shot into by cannon from the edge of the woods and men flying through the air. Those scenes seemed very real to me. I sure could relate that with Bastogne.

We worked very hard getting across those fields and getting snuggled up to the underside of that shoulder by about 1530. By dark I had worked the Battalion around to a draw on the southeast corner of town. To do that we had to go through the fire from machine guns in Noville that were covering the draw. To take care of this we set up a couple of LMG's of our own. The Germans would fire, we would give them a return burst and, at the same time, send a group of eight or ten men across the draw and a stream to the other side. It became a cat and mouse game. It took a lot of patience, but we did it without any casualties. By dark, we were in position for the attack the next day.

One of the infantrymen of "E" Company, Pvt. Anthony Garcia, remembers that move and falling into a small stream in that bitter cold weather. He wrote:

While trying to jump across a small stream, carrying personal equipment and six mortar rounds during the advance toward Noville several hundred yards distant, I broke through the ice soaking the front of myself and by the time we entered Noville, my clothes were frozen, making a crackling sound as I walked. This turned out in my favor because the ice, strangely enough, kept me warm that night while in my foxhole and because of the noise the ice made, I did not have to go on an all-night patrol which never made contact with its intended (another 101st unit).

When Foy was cleared on the 13th, "E" Company was pulled back to prepare for the attack on Noville. They were moved up to within a few hundred yards of the town. 1st/Sgt. Carwood Lipton added to his story:

That evening, the officers were briefed on the attack and the general situation. After the briefing, Lt. Speirs told me that he wanted me to take command of the 2nd Platoon for the attack which was to be led by the 2nd Platoon to the left of the road through the town and the 3rd Platoon to the right of it. We were also told that there were friendly tanks to our right rear, although it was not known when or even if, they would join us. Some of them were said to be a new tank, the M-26 as I remember, which had a long gun with a muzzle brake and a low silhouette so that it resembled the German tanks.

When I pulled the 2nd Platoon together to brief them on Noville and the attack into it to take place the following morning, Captain Winters, not Lt. Speirs, stood by to listen in. He apparently approved of all that I said except that he corrected my estimate of how far the edge of the town was from our attack line. I had estimated it too low.

As darkness set in, I put the platoon along a fence row facing Noville several hundred yards to our front. It was not a completely dark night and we could faintly see some of the buildings on the outskirts of town. It was, however, a bitter cold night.

I was uneasy about leading the platoon in the attack without knowing more about what lay ahead of us so I decided to go forward, under cover of the darkness, to some of the buildings that I could see ahead. I took the radioman with me. The first building we reached was a barn. We went in through a door in the back and felt our way through to where a door opened onto a courtyard that was by the main road through Noville. I could dimly see several Sherman tanks so I talked with Lt. Speirs again to ask him if he had any late information on where our friendly tanks were. He had none and I told him that I could see some of our tanks ahead and that it looked like our tankers had already moved into Noville.

We moved more confidently up the road, but when we got to the tanks I could see that they were knocked out. There were a number of American bodies, their former crews, on the ground around them. It was obvious that they had been left there when armored Team Desobry and the 1st Battalion of the 506th had withdrawn from there on December 20th. The Germans still definitely held Noville and my radioman and I were right in the middle of it.

We pulled back as quickly and as silently as we could to the barn and I told Lt. Speirs what I had seen. The attack the next morning would still be necessary.

After the 11th Armored Division had moved in to mop up Foy, "F" Company had moved to the left flank of the 2nd Battalion positions. S/Sgt. John Taylor remembered the cold and the wakefulness as his group waited out the night. He added to his story:

During the night the enemy fired some screaming meemies. They went over us and hit in the Headquarters Company area. I think they lost some people that time. We had some TD's with us. Oh, it was cold! Bitter cold! We went through two towns – Recogne and Cobru. We got through both of them and there was a draw and just getting dark that night. We were told to go across a draw onto the high ground on the other side. We did. I think "D" Company was with us. It was cold. I'm sure it was zero. The snow was swirling. It was hard. You couldn't dig in. We set up a hasty defense around the area. Sometime during the night, Sgt. Jack Borden and I were just walking around, swinging our arms and trying to keep warm. They had roving guards out there. The password that night was 'Whizz'. This new guard came by – you didn't take any chances in giving the password. The countersign was 'Wiper'. The password that night was 'Whizz - Wiper' and this new guard came by. I remember Borden challenged with 'Whiz!' and the kid on guard duty got excited and said, 'Windshield wiper – Windshield Wiper!' That was one miserable night. It was so cold – bitter!

That miserable, cold night is a lasting memory for 2nd Battalion commander Dick Winters who also remembers harboring thoughts of ordering a night attack. He wrote:

That night was the coldest, I repeat, the coldest night of my life and I think the same goes for every other man in the outfit. As I mentioned earlier, we had worked hard all afternoon and we were wringing wet with sweat. Then, after the sun went down, it got bitter cold. All you could do was shiver. At one point during the night, I tried to lie down on a little knoll of ground. In no time, I had just shivered myself down that knoll to the bottom. I soon gave up trying to get any sleep.

Without sharing this thought with anyone, at one point I considered making a night attack rather than standing there all night freezing to death, for I just had the feeling they had pulled out. But I eliminated the night attack idea, realizing that the chances were too great that we could end up shooting some of our own men in the dark.

It wasn't the cold so much that bothered Sgt. Louis E. Truax of "Dog" Company as the German nebelwerfer that pounded them during the night. He wrote:

We had moved to the east side of the Bastogne-Noville road. It was in a valley here that I experienced the worst indirect fire. In that valley, a nebelwerfer came in. I hit the ground and rolled under a fallen tree. I looked up and could see hot, smoking shrapnel protruding from Bill Batchelder's back. We must have lost five or six guys to that one nebelwerfer. We called them 'screaming meemies'.

Some people might think you would stop at this point and render assistance to the wounded. Believe me, you don't. I moved quickly up to the hill where I had heard the nebelwerfer firing. Halfway up the hill was a low spot. I fell into it to catch my breath. I've never been a religious person but, right there, I kinda said a little prayer that I was still there.

Guess what – that nebelwerfer was gone, but the tracks of it were there along with a piece of burlap. The Krauts had wrapped the hooves of a team of horses which towed that thing out of there. That's the way they moved it around at night – quietly.

## A TRAGIC BOMBING

In the 502nd sector where the troops of 1st Battalion had been attacking up the side of the railroad track leading to Bourcy, a misdirected attack by friendly aircraft caused heavy casualties among the troops who were already suffering from the bitter cold and having to attack through heavy snow.

The extreme cold of January 14 is also remembered by PFC. John E. Fitzgerald who felt that getting something warm on the inside provided a feeling of warmth in the body. He found a new use for "C-2". He wrote:

Our basic weapon against enemy tanks was the rocket firing bazooka but there were never enough of them to go around. To help offset this shortcoming, the English had given us a new weapon called the 'Gammon Grenade'. It was made of a putty-like substance called Composition C-2 and came wrapped in a sack-like cloth. When activated and thrown at a tank, it would usually slow it down or stop it completely. It had a tremendous explosive force. When our canned sterno began to run out, someone discovered that small pieces of C-2 would burn fiercely. We used it to dry out wet gloves and socks and thaw out the rifle bolts that would constantly freeze. The biggest benefit was that we now had another way to make instant coffee and bullion that came with our K-rations. The only problem was that any further use of the grenades against targets proved less effective as the C-2 continued to decrease in size.

As mentioned earlier in the text, the rifleman and machine gunner on the front line never knew what the grand strategy of the commanders was on the various moves made in combat situations. When relief was made, it was not always with men of one's own battalion and thus there was confusion on the part of Cpl. Elmer Nicks when he describes the unit moving through his position. I am sure there were liaison personnel from the 6th Armored Division attached to the 3rd Battalion of the 502nd as it moved through the positions of 1st Battalion on the morning of January 14. Nicks continues his account as the day brings disaster to the elements of 1st and 3rd Battalions of the 502nd Regiment:

Sgt. Pichler was the squad leader and gunner and I was assistant gunner. His hole was also a German takeover. The best I can remember his hole was between mine and the railroad. The next morning, the 6th Armored Infantry started moving up through us. They were apparently getting the point and attack job. I think it was a battalion headquarters company because there were several officers and I believe one major that were killed by the bomb.

As they were moving through our position, I was trying to heat a cup of water into which I had chipped shavings from a chocolate bar and thawing out a can of K-rations. I was burning the wax-coated K-ration box cut into tiny pieces to do the heating. Several of the 6th Armored Infantry men, plus one or two of our men, were crowded around my hole and the tiny fire. They were trying to soak up all the heat to warm up a cup of water for coffee when I got through. (I saved the wax cartons as I found that they were really priceless many times for a small fire to heat water or thaw out cans of food).

I was aware of the big explosions, bombing and strafing that were going on over on the other side of the tracks to our right rear. After a while, you don't pay too much attention unless it is affecting you. Then the bomb hit. When I regained my senses, I found a blown-off tree in my hole and bodies on top of me. By the time I got out of my hole, I could see a huge crater, trees blown down and many casualties, mostly dead, everywhere. I noticed something I had never seen before. Some of the men's faces were blown out like toy balloons. I started helping with the wounded with tourniquets and morphine. We could not use most of the morphine as it had frozen.

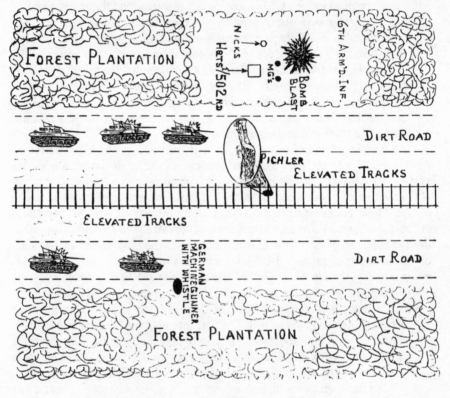

*Map 23*
*Area where bomb was misdropped on the troops of the 502nd on January 14. (Map provided by Cpl. Elmer Nicks.)*

I asked one of the survivors where Pichler was and I was told he had gone up on the railroad tracks with a panel to signal the P-47's. I climbed up cautiously and found him sprawled on the railroad track. I checked him and he did not seem to have any outward wounds but with all the layers of clothes, wounds would not show unless they were really severe. I rolled him off the track and he felt like a sack of coal. Then I noticed several holes in his uniform. We had been close together in combat. We had learned to make the best of every situation. He was a leader and he always knew that I was right with him at all times. It was an unspoken feeling that we could always depend on each other. When he went up on that track he knew that he would be shot at by the Germans and a plane diving at 400 mph. could not tell an American from a German but somebody had to get the identification panel up there so the planes would know and not finish us off.[193]

The officers who were killed by the bomb blast included the commander of 3rd Battalion which was passing through the 1st. Another was a liaison officer, 1Lt. Edward Mitchell, from the 377th Parachute Field Artillery Battalion which always served as the support group for the 502nd Regiment.

As the medic who was assigned to the pathfinder team of the 101st in the combat jumps into Normandy and Holland, PFC. Raymond "Snuffy" Smith missed the first ten days of the Bastogne operation as the pathfinder teams not used for the resupply drop were in England. However, he was sent forward and was assigned to Lt. Col. John F. Stopka, commander of 3rd Battalion on January 14 near Bizory. Smith describes the actions that resulted in the heavy loss of life and wounding of so many of the others:

I was with LTC. John F. Stopka, commander of 3rd Battalion of the 502nd. A few miles outside of Bastogne we were advancing through a pine forest and on one side of a railroad which was built up 15 to 20 feet above the surrounding ground level. German tanks were on the other side of the roadbed. Someone requested air power to knock out the tanks. Our own planes strafed and bombed the 3rd Battalion and killed Col. Stopka and about thirty of our men and wounded forty or more. As a medic, I was the one to treat and tag these men. It was the most horrifying experience I had from D-Day through all the 101st battles.

1Lt. Ray Brock was also involved in the January 14th action when part of a major 101st Division attack to the northeast toward Noville as the mortar platoon leader for 3rd Battalion of the 502nd. He recalled the attack by our fighter planes on our own troops. He wrote:

We were attacking along the railroad tracks toward Bourcy and had become somewhat mingled with the 1st Battalion. As we were trudging up alongside the tracks in the deep snow, a sergeant from 'A' Company, 1st Battalion, called 'Lieutenant Brock – here is one of your men!' I wondered how one of my men got ahead of me and up on the bank. I climbed up and looked. It was Cpl. Leo Pichler from HQ. Co. 1st Bn. I had spent half of my 502nd time in that unit so knew Leo well. He had been killed and was lying there in the snow. I always admired Leo as he was such a neat person and always looked so sharp when going out on pass. He was an outstanding

---

[193]Nicks, op. cit.

fighter on the regimental boxing team and an excellent soldier. It saddened me to see Leo's life end this way.

After the fighter planes had completed their jobs and actions had quieted down that evening, PFC. Elmer Nicks went over to check on the other side where most of the heavy strafing and bombing had taken place. He wrote:

> That evening as we were withdrawing, we crossed over on the other side. I could see the knocked-out Sherman tanks, the anti-tank gun, many dead Germans and Americans and the wrecked equipment. I noticed a German sitting hunched over in a machine gun emplacement. A second look and I could see that the back of his head was gone. He was defending the large anti-tank gun that was dug in the side of the embankment and was also the lookout. He had a whistle in his hand and apparently would use it for a signal to the anti-tank gun. I walked over and took the whistle out of his hand. Only the planes with bombs could have knocked out the defenses the Germans had built without severe casualties.[194]

1Lt. Henry Barnes and T/5 George Whitfield continued their role as a medical evacuation team. They had worked together throughout the Holland campaign and continued their work with the 502nd Regiment. On this occasion they were on the scene of the mistaken bombing episode.

After the Division changed from defensive to offensive maneuvering, the soldiers became much more cautious and wanted the medics near them at all times, as was observed by Lt. Barnes who also remembered being on the scene after the bombing:

> The spirit of the soldiers changed. They wanted the medics to stay with them and not follow the other attacks. There was a general letdown and an unwillingness to take extra risks. I grew more cautious. I remember digging a hole for the night behind one of the battalions when three of our P-47 fighters came roaring in at tree height. I sensed danger and dove into the hole. The bombs blew off the head of one of the colonels and killed other members of his staff. Apparently, according to the rumor, we had requested aid to knock out a tank and then radioed a cancellation, and only the first message had been received by the Air Force.

The memory T/5 George Whitfield has of the actions involving 3rd Battalion is being called to pick up two forward observer casualties and rush them to the aid station. He wrote:

> While working with 3rd Battalion, I was ordered up the hill to pick up two forward observers. One had lost his right arm and the other had a wound in his chest. While carrying him to our jeep, he thrashed about, trying to breathe. That evening I talked to the man with the missing forearm. He

---

[194]ibid.

asked about his buddy. I didn't tell him he had died earlier but said he had been evacuated.

The morning report prepared by First sergeant Ted Beishline of "Able" Company presents this picture of the 1st Battalion actions for January 14th and then provides the casualty report at day's end:

0830 – Able alerted to move forward. Charley on right, Baker on left. Able guiding on railroad leading to Bourcy. Phase line 3 cleared 0900.

1015 – While advancing toward phase line 4, our Air Corps failed to identify our lines and subjected us to strafing and aerial bombardment. Casualties suffered.

1620 – Phase line 4 taken. Defense set up, Able 2 on left, Able 1 on right, Able 3 in center.

2400 – Casualties this date: Vondress KIA, Jemiolo, Heath, Egic, Sheppard, Holliday, Ray WIA. Enemy this date: Killed 51, captured 17.

The attack by 1st and 3rd Battalions of the 502nd had halted at 1800, still short of its objectives. Contact had been made with the troops of "Ace" Company of the 327th on the left and with the 320th Armored Infantry on the right. Most of the day's casualties were the result of misdirected bombing which cost 37 men, 12 of whom had been killed, including the 3rd Battalion commander, LTC. John P. Stopka. The command went over to Major Cecil Simmons, who had been serving as executive officer. The medical detachments of the attacking regiments suffered numerous casualties to the medics who were killed or wounded while tending casualties.

## "ACE" COMPANY ACTIONS

The glider infantrymen of the 1st Battalion of the 327th were now into their second day of isolation from the neighboring troops of the 502nd. Now in among the captured and abandoned enemy positions, S/Sgt. Jack Williamson describes the terrible shelling inflicted on them and his considering the thought of surrendering his surrounded troops. He wrote:

The enemy threw some big artillery at us. They hit those trees and made toothpicks of them – scared the hell out of us. This time we were surrounded for good. We had pushed out too far. I entertained the idea of surrendering. I remember being told to never surrender because our forces knew where we were and they would come to the rescue. As I was in this big German dugout with some of the wounded men, I was thinking of Private Mayer, who had been hit in the face and chest. He had a hard time talking but he turned to the others and said, 'I know one thing – we've got the best darned sergeant in the whole outfit!' And he kept braggin on me. So I stepped outside and made up my mind that if we had to go, we'd go down fighting. We wouldn't surrender. Pvt. Arthur C. Mayer was a brave soldier. He showed bravery in France. He missed the Holland operation and came back into Bastogne and there he again showed bravery. He got the Distinguished Service Cross and the Silver Star.

Those wounded soldiers needed to be moved out of the shell-torn area. PFC. Willis Rohr of "A" Company remembered the attack had three objectives, which were taken the first day. However, "Ace" Company was cut off for a couple days. The wounded needed to be taken out. Rohr related his role:

> We had wounded that needed to be taken out. I was chosen to get help to bring four stretcher cases and four walking wounded out and bring back water and ammunition. I remember walking along the edge of a woods, under the gun of a tank on the way out.

# 20. MOPPING UP

## JANUARY 15

The morning was cloudy and cold (as mentioned earlier by Captain Winters and S/Sgt. Taylor). On the highway leading from Bastogne to Houffalize, the attacking force on the west side of the road was the 1st Battalion of the 506th with 1st Battalion of the 501st attached. At 1030 hours, the 1st and 2nd Battalions of the 506th attacked simultaneously. The 1st struck east out of the Fazone Woods and advanced almost a mile over open fields to take the high ground north of Cobru. At the same time, 2nd Battalion attacked from south of Noville, moved in and took the village, being in position with a perimeter defense set up by 1145. The resistance was limited to small groups of enemy soldiers and a tank or two which made up a rear action force.

After enduring the bitter cold of the previous night, S/Sgt. John Taylor remembered a surprise appearance of the mess section with hot food before the final assault was made on Noville from the south. He related:

Next morning, it was overcast. Just at the crack of dawn, a runner came scurrying to our positions to tell us they had some hot food for us but we'd have to come and get it. It didn't take us long to get there. Sure enough, it was hot food. We got it back to the men. We had hot oatmeal with pineapple in it, a whole can full of fried eggs, some bread and coffee. That was a life saver. I don't know who or how someone was able to get that stuff to us. I will always remember that nothing ever tasted any better.

So we jumped off in the attack up this draw, right into Noville. Not too much of a problem but, as we came through the open areas in the snowcovered fields, you could see the tanks all out up the hillsides and see the troops and the firing. Everything that was involved in fighting a battle was there that morning. We went ahead and took Noville that day. We held up in Noville overnight. Not much took place that night.

Lt. Ben Stapelfeld's journal provided another sketch map of the actions which involved his 1st Platoon troops as they moved to the left side of Noville. The comments which accompanied his sketch of the village are as follows: "Hot chow after dark, Jan. 13. Attack at 'H' Hour tomorrow. Aebisher in overshoes. No casualties. Pinned down by MG at pig pen. Thought I had it. Stone put mortar on enemy tank and it withdrew. Return to MLR. Check Aebisher on ammo. Check Aebisher on rations."

As a member of "Dog" Company, Sgt. Louis E. Truax remembers January 15 as the day he lost another buddy. He was also a participant in the capture of several enemy soldiers. Truax wrote:

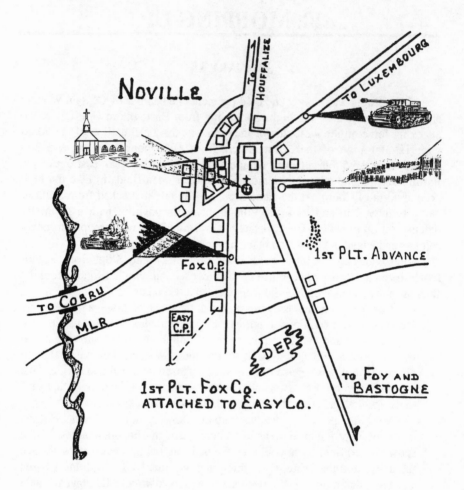

NOVILLE

TO LUXEMBOURG

HOUFFALIZE

1ST PLT. ADVANCE

FOX O.P.

TO COBRU

MLR

EASY
C.P.

DEP

1ST PLT. FOX CO.
ATTACHED TO EASY CO.

TO FOY AND
BASTOGNE

*Map 24*

I was standing in Noville. This town had been taken and retaken before but for me, it was a brand new experience and everything I could see, I was in control of. Roy Austin had just been killed down the street.

I think it was here that Alvin Quimby and I chased five Krauts into a pig sty. He had a BAR and I had an M1. He had a 20-round clip and I had an 8. We put 'em through the thick wooden door top to bottom. Guess what – those Krauts came out of there with their hands behind their heads. Not a scratch on them. I started to pull their wrist watches and loot 'em, but just then two P-47's came over with all their wing guns firing.

## MISTAKEN IDENTITY

As a member of 3rd Platoon of "Easy" Company, Cpl. James H. Alley was in on the move into Noville but from a different part of the perimeter to the small farming town. He has a vivid memory of a mistaken identity as he approached an idling tank. He wrote:

It was during the attack on Noville and we moved up and occupied some burned-out buildings as members of 3rd Platoon. We set up some positions in the ruins and were waiting for further orders when, over the radio came a message, 'Friendly armor on our right'.

Lt. Ed Shames and I were together when the message came through. Very shortly after that, I heard motors running not far away so assumed it was our tanks. Anxious to get the show on the road, I decided to link up with our armor, so I told Lt. Shames I was going to go over to the tanks and proceeded to move off. I had gone but a short distance when Lt. Shames joined me. We moved by several burned out buildings and rounded a corner into the main road. Up ahead, between two buildings, part way out, was our objective. I proceeded to approach the tank until I was ten or fifteen feet away. The tank commander was standing in the turret looking the other way so I shouted to him over the roar of the engines – 'This way!' He turned and it dawned on me – I had made a serious mistake (as had Lt. Shames); this was a Tiger tank! The tank commander immediately started traversing his 88mm turret gun.

Without another word spoken between Lt. Shames and myself, we took off. The tank took off after us. We ran around the corner of a building with Lt. Shames in the lead and me hot on his heels. Lt. Shames saw a window in a burned-out building as we were passing so he sailed through head first. I ran ten feet or so past him and jumped into a doorway with my gun ready, for I was sure infantry soldiers were with the tank and this was where I'd make my stand. The tank followed our tracks, turned the same corner we had just turned, knocking down half the building in the process. It roared past our positions without a shot being fired at him, out to the main road.

1st/Sgt. Carwood Lipton was leading 2nd Platoon of "Easy" Company during the attack. His platoon was approaching along a different route. He has this description of an encounter with a tank, possibly the same one that was chasing Alley and Shames.

The attack jumped off as planned and the 2nd Platoon had less resistance on our side of the road than the 3rd Platoon had on the right. We were well past the center of the town and the first knocked-out Sherman tanks when, suddenly, a German tank roared out from behind a building on the 3rd Platoon side of the road and raced up the road toward us, firing its machine gun as it came. I learned later from Jim Alley of the 3rd Platoon that he had walked up to the tank behind a house, thinking it was one of ours, and that he had only seen his mistake when he yelled greetings to the tanker, who had his hatch open and then saw that the tanker was wearing the German black-billed cap.

We in the 2nd Platoon jumped behind the buildings and dived under the knocked-out Shermans. The German tank then stopped dead and, swivelling its turret, put a shell into each of the knocked-out tanks to prevent anyone from using their guns to put a shell into him as he went by. When these shells hit the Shermans it felt to us under them that they jumped a foot in the air.

That didn't save the German tank, though. When it roared on out of town and reached the higher ground north of town, we saw one of our P-47 fighter planes strafe it and drop a 500-pound bomb on it, finishing it off.

Cpl. Jim Alley added to his account concerning the tank and echoing what 1st/Sgt. Lipton had related about its demise:

Someone radioed to P-47's overhead. Though the sky was partly overcast, one spot opened up and out shot a P-47 and caught the tank on top of the hill and knocked it out. All this happened so fast it didn't seem real!

Battalion commander Dick Winters sent his troops out in mid-morning and found the resistance was light as he had suspected it would be. Most of the enemy had pulled out during the night. He wrote:

I jumped the attack off on Noville. The resistance was light. The Germans had pulled out, leaving nothing more than a rear guard.

We picked up a few prisoners. Among them were two junior officers. Lt. Ed Thomas, my S-2 by this time, tried to get some worthwhile information with no success.

Noville was now back under Division control. It had been an objective since the first day and now its shattered buildings were hardly considered a prize at this stage of the game.

## "ACE" COMPANY OF THE 327TH

To the east of 2nd Battalion of the 506th, troops of the 327th continued to move northeast. The trapped men of "Ace" Company, with S/Sgt. Jack Williamson, were elated when a group from the 502nd broke through to them but Williamson was surprised to find that his men would spearhead the attack that mounted when daylight arrived. He recalled:

Sometime in the night a combat patrol from one of the jump outfits broke through to us. They gave us each a K-ration and some ammo. Early the next morning, the lieutenant in charge of that group called me and said we were to attack and that I and my men were to lead. I figured they wouldn't be satisfied until we were all killed. We lined up in a skirmish formation and, when he gave the word, we went forward howling like Comanche Indians. That did the trick because the Germans ran to their rear and we captured several. Then we stopped for the night. We set up a defensive position – a big, wide hole in the ground with straw on the bottom and laid down and went to sleep.

Late that night, there was a big thud beside my head – which woke me up. I jumped up, scared, and there stood the biggest darn horse I'd ever seen. Those big, oversized hooves – the Germans had been using horses to haul their big guns. If that horse had hit my head, he'd have squashed it like a pumpkin. Wouldn't that have been a helluva way to get killed in a war! That dugout hole, with the hay in it, had been where they kept that horse.

## MAIL CALL!

Mail call is very important to the GI and sometimes it occurred in very surprising surroundings. Pvt. Alden Todd remembered one such occasion. He wrote:

Around January 13, our company moved forward in the forest toward Bourcy, being held up on occasion by enemy resistance to other company units of our regiment on the left and right. We heard behind us someone shouting 'Mail call!' several times. We were amazed, one man after the other, when the men behind us started passing forward dozens of letters from home – the first mail we had received since December 15th. What was amusing about this for me was that each envelope had the name of the soldier, serial number and 'Company F, 502nd Parachute Infantry Regiment' as the address. We had been taught since we entered the Army that at the battle front we should not carry on us anything that might identify our military unit. But now, almost every man was carrying in his pockets several letters marked with exact identification of the company and regiment. We burst out laughing. Mail call at last, after almost a full month![195]

## THE MILLION DOLLAR WOUND

The wound, which is not serious, that gets a soldier out of a combat situation, at least temporarily, is another memory of PFC. Alden Todd. He wrote:

---

[195]From a paper, *Memories of my first visit to Bourcy – January 1945*, by Alden Todd, November 1986. Copy provided by Walter F. Zagol.

Things were fairly quiet during that day and a half of waiting, but we knew that the attack on Bourcy was imminent. We did receive a number of presents from the enemy, both incoming artillery shells and some screaming meemies, the whistling mortar shells that were supposed to frighten the people in the target area. Unfortunately, the radio operator of 'F' Company was wounded in one arm. I still remember Cpl. Walter Zagol, a lively fellow from Chicago, making his way back to the rear, holding up his bleeding arm and calling out with a big smile: 'At last, I got it! A million dollar wound!' This was the comic pose of the guy who got hit; a wound that took him to the hospital, but which was not very serious. Zagol was a good young fellow and he rejoined us after a few weeks.[196]

## JANUARY 16

In the 502nd sector (right flank), the 2nd Battalion had moved into position in the northeast section of the Bois Jacques about midnight on the 14th and at 0830 on the 15th passed through 3rd Battalion. Now on the 16th, 2nd Battalion would lead the drive into Bourcy.

With the capture of Captain Earl Hendricks and a fellow officer, along with 47 members of a platoon on January 3 in an enemy tank attack on Longchamps, command had gone over to Captain Raymond "Whispering" Smith who had lost his radio operator, Cpl. Walter Zagol, who had picked up his "million dollar wound". Needing a replacement, Smith had selected Pvt. Alden Todd to fill the void. Todd had no working knowledge of the SCR-300 radio or communication procedures. He did realize the radio was heavy when carried around on the back (42 pounds) with an antenna which projected nine feet above the set. Radio operators were often targets of enemy snipers. Another soldier had given Todd ten minutes of operating instructions. Todd relates that first experience:

After the elementary instructions, I was on my own. My job was to transmit the orders and queries between Captain Smith and the battalion command post and to receive the replies. We were supposed to use code words for the units and the commanders to keep the enemy from understanding our messages.[197] But in fact, I used only a few of those codes – very few. I really was not fully trained.

The attack on Bourcy was scheduled to jump off at 0830. It was being preceded by a thunderous artillery barrage. Captain Smith was supposed to move

---

[196]ibid.

[197]Code names were assigned to all regiments. The 502nd was "Kickoff" while the 1st, 2nd and 3rd Battalions were "Red", "White" and "Blue" respectively. In the above case, "F" Company was "Fox".

his troops forward at 0830 and he was becoming extremely nervous wondering if the barrage would let up so the shells wouldn't land on his advancing troops. Pvt. Alden Todd continues his story:

Suddenly he shouted at me in that thunderous tone of voice for which he was well known: 'Todd! Tell them to lift the artillery. Stop the artillery!'

Obediently, I called into the radio mouthpiece: 'Captain Smith says to lift the artillery!' A second later, thinking that perhaps the word 'lift' had not carried clearly by radio, I repeated the message, using every useful word that came to my mind: 'Stop the barrage – Do not fire any longer!'

Eight-thirty – a whistle sounded, the signal for the attack. Suddenly, the thundering shells stopped falling. Silence.

With some apprehension, not having any idea of what might happen, we crossed the ridge, every man now being an excellent target for the enemy in Bourcy, if he wanted to take aim at us. We moved forward in a strange silence, sinking deep into the snow, moving downhill toward the village. Then Captain Smith and his neophyte radio operator found a track in the snow made by a German Tiger tank that had gone up our hill a couple days earlier and then back toward Bourcy. The Tiger, with its great weight, had flattened the snow so as to form two perfect walkways, each one about two feet wide. Smith, being the commanding officer, took the left-hand path to make it easier to cross this enemy terrain. The radio operator, who, of course, had to stay near the captain, took the right-hand track. Then several other men in the company, seeing how easily we got out of the deep snow, fell in line behind us in the two Tiger tracks – and then the captain saw them.

'Get out of those tracks!' he shouted in his angry 'whisper'. 'You are a perfect target!' Of course, he was right. The other men, somewhat annoyed, spread out to the right and left in the snow, moving forward with difficulty, one heavy step following the other. Fortunately, there was not a single rifle or machine gun shot from the direction of Bourcy – at least, not so far.[198]

PFC. Robert T. Harrison was in on the same action as a member of the 3rd Battalion Headquarters Company. He remembers it was a real struggle through the snow. It was tough on the "ole man" of his unit. Harrison describes the action:

After we were relieved, we went on the offensive and moved up the highway. Bastogne was on our right and before we were to kick off, Captain Frank Lillyman asked me to cover a machine gun in a tank but I wasn't too happy to get in that thing so Chuck Clites took it. They were short a gunner. We had a man in our outfit, one of the first to go through jump school. His name was Nick Vignovich. He was much older than most of us. We called

---

[198]Todd, op. cit.

him 'the ole man' or 'Dad'. I think he was about 32 years old. We had to cross a field one at a time. It was open and the snow was pretty deep. When my turn came, I got out in the middle of the field. Nick was lying there and couldn't go anymore so I got him up, took his equipment and got him over and under cover just in time for we were on the receiving end of another artillery barrage.

T/5 Richard J. Kazinski was a member of a bazooka team with 2nd Battalion Headquarters Company of the 502nd Regiment. He was in on the attack toward Bourcy and remembered some large enemy tanks facing his position and being told by a tanker to forget about making an attempt to stop one of them with his bazooka. Kazinski wrote:

*The final days of the Bastogne campaign had to be fought through the heavy snow. In some open areas the snow lay almost two feet deep. (Photo from collection of Richard Winters.)*

One morning I remember, we were to attack a town in a valley. As we approached the top of the hill, we saw five Tiger Royals waiting for us. Our Sherman tanks were no match for them. Our tank shells bounced off the Royals like ping-pong balls. It was quite a show when the Air Corps came in to take care of them. We had front row seats for the performance.

I remember the tanker who gave me a pair of gloves and a word of advice – 'Take your bazooka and get your ass the hell away from that tank,' for he knew that neither he nor I stood a chance against the Tiger Royal.

Out of small arms range, one of the Division Artillery Piper Cub L-4 planes was observing the battles for Bourcy and Rachamps, looking for enemy tanks and hidden artillery positions. The pilot, 1Lt. George Schoeneck and his aerial observer were shot down when their plane ran into the path of a friendly artillery shell reportedly fired by one of the units moving down from the north to close the gap. The explosion blew the small plane and its occupants from the sky.

When the troops arrived in Bourcy, they found the enemy was gone. The few civilians who peeked furtively from the doorways informed the paratroopers that the enemy left the night before. The enemy artillery fire had been directed at the advancing troops from beyond the confines of the small village.

## MOPPING UP IN RACHAMPS

After the seizure of Noville had occurred, S/Sgt. John H. Taylor had one more action that his group was to perform before they could be relieved of their combat duties on the Bastogne front. He related:

About noon the next day, we moved out some distance along the main road to Noville and did a right flank and attacked up a slope, a snow-covered hill to a little village called Rachamps. This little village couldn't be seen from the slope as the town was a half mile away and on the reverse side of the slope. We drew mortar and artillery fire, not heavy but scattered. We moved up toward the village, formed a little bit to the right and hit the road that led into the village. As we were moving into the village, I heard a shell coming. It was coming close. We hit the ditch. The shell hit up on the head-high bank among the trees which lined the road. We were showered with snow and broken tree limbs. It scared the daylights out of us.

Sgt. Louis Truax of "Dog" Company remembered they had some shelling on the attack into Rachamps and again he lost a few close buddies. He wrote:

After Noville, we moved up the road toward Houffalize. I think Meehan, Blankenship, Werbela and Van Every were with me. Slightly below us, about 300 to 400 yards, was the village of Rachamps. Just then an American tank destroyer, located back on the road behind us, put a 90mm shell through the church steeple. First 90mm I'd seen or heard. Much better than 75's. Lying prone on top of a spud cellar, I could see all kinds of Kraut tanks and infantry going up a hill behind Rachamps. I could hear incoming 88's landing behind me. Some of them must have killed Blankenship and Sherbon. We saw Krauts entering the town. We opened fire and then shifted to a ridge farther away. The company moved around to the left and the town was ours.

Among the first to enter Rachamps from his unit, Sgt. Duane L. Tedrick was posted with his Browning Automatic Rifle. He wrote:

I was the first man into Rachamps from Company 'D' and remained on the edge of the town covering our right flank with the BAR as the company attacked through the town. A German tank came up over a ridge to my right and traversed its gun toward the house I was in and I turned to get into the basement and that is all I remember until I regained consciousness in the company CP. Joe Powers found me walking down one of the streets dragging my BAR by the barrel. Someone said the tank fired and the shell went through the door and hit the kitchen stove. So you can say my stay in Bastogne ended with a bang. I was not wounded but had a black and blue belly and thighs for a while.

Returning to platoon sergeant John H. Taylor's story, he was now entering the village. He relates:

We took off on the double into the village. We got some mortar fire in there – hardly any small arms. We were moving down the street. A civilian – a man – ran out from somewhere into the street, hollering 'Bosche!' and pointing to a house where we got four or five Germans out of there in a cellar. We moved on into the town and were still drawing some fire from east of Rachamps and I believe Captain Dick Winters, now with Battalion, came up saying, 'Bring your men and come with me.' I remember Lt. Robertson and our 2nd Platoon and some other people took off back up the street, now knowing what was taking place. We left this road and went on to some open ground about five or six hundred yards back. There were some heavy woods on the left side and quite a few troops were approaching from that direction toward us. We could not tell if they were friend or foe – not from that distance. I guess this is what Dick Winters got word of. We positioned some machine guns and set off smoke. They kept coming toward us. We soon realized it was some of our people. They suddenly did a flanking movement toward the woods on their right. Quite a few Germans came running out of the woods with their hands in the air and gave themselves up.

This was taken care of and it had quieted down some. Got ourselves set up for the night. Our platoon CP was in a barn which was set up as a typical rural building with a barn and house attached on our edge of the small village and had our positions set up on the crest of a little rise or ridge and it was still bitter cold. That night we dug in, got our OP's out.

The move to take Rachamps was rather easy for "E" Company as described by 1st/Sgt. Carwood Lipton, who had led his platoon successfully in his first effort after having been assigned as platoon leader by the new company commander, 1Lt. Ronald Speirs. Lipton wrote:

We had one more attack, though, and that was to take the town of Rachamps, east of the road and north of Noville. Rachamps was in a valley with the ground covered with snow, sloping gently down to it from all sides, giving an effect similar to attacking from the rim of a saucer toward its center. That attack was next day and we moved in a widespread attack formation so that artillery and small arms fire and the white phosphorus shells the Germans threw at us on the way in, would have minimal effect. We didn't have a man hit. The town was quickly cleared. The Bastogne campaign was over for us.

## WILLIAMSON AND HIS "ACE" TROOPS

As the morning of January 16 dawned, S/Sgt. Jack Williamson was sure he and his men would be called on to lead another attack. He didn't think it would be possible to come out of that mess alive. He got another surprise:

The next morning the lieutenant ordered me to report to him. I was sure he was gonna order me to lead another attack but I had just about given up ever getting out of that mess. To my surprise, he told me 'Get what troops you have left, leave and go back to the rear.' We did, just as fast as we could shuffle. We slept that night in the woods, on the ice and snow. That was cold, cold, cold! My time in Bastogne was over. I was alive. I had walked through hell with my eyes open to the Lord.[199]

## ANTICIPATED!

When the 327th troops arrived late at the line of departure for the first attack on the 13th, General Taylor had threatened to fine each of the company officers a hundred dollars if they did not reach the objective by 1630 that day.[200] Captain Walter Miller had stated earlier that "Ace" Company had been lost in the thick woods because the men sent to direct them were unfamiliar with the ground. After the attack was completed three days later, Miller was ordered to report to the commanding general. Miller describes the brief meeting:

Following the last attack, I was called before General Taylor to explain the delay (our late arrival for the Bois Jacques attack). I told him we got lost. His answer was, 'You should have anticipated that!' End of conversation.

---

[199]S/Sgt. Jack Williamson of "A" Company, 327th Glider Infantry Regiment, received a battlefield commission shortly after the Ardennes campaign was completed.

[200]Instead of fines being levied against the 1st Battalion officers, the glidermen received a case of Scotch for each battalion which participated in the mission.

## CCB RETURNS TO THE 10TH ARMORED DIVISION

After serving beside the 101st Airborne Division almost a month, Combat Command B was ordered to return to the 10th Armored Division. The two units had worked well together as a cohesive unit along with the members of the 705th Tank Destroyer Battalion.

Throughout the hundreds of responses received for this account from the veterans of the 101st Division, a common thread ran through them with praise for the men of CCB and the 705th TD's. To a man the Screaming Eagles felt the achievements at Bastogne were the result of team effort.

As his troops moved to the south, CCB commander Colonel William L. Roberts had this final message for the commanders and troops of the 101st Division.

For nearly a month CCB, 10th Armored Division, has been associated with your fine division in an action which may become historic. After the first two days this unit was attached to your division. In behalf of the officers and men of CCB, I wish to inform you that it has been a pleasure to serve with the splendid corps of officers and with the fine fighting men of the 101st and, if ever in the future there is a choice of divisions to fight with, we choose the 101st and in turn we hope that CCB may be again associated with you and your division.

Your General Staff and your Special Staff have been generous, fair and solicitous in all matters. They have made my troops feel as if they belonged to the 101st instead of being the usual attached orphans. Your regimental and battalion commanders and my team commanders have worked together with a singleness of purpose that is seldom attained and is only possible where there is wholehearted cooperation on both sides. Many of our enlisted men have expressed the highest admiration of your soldiers and a willingness to go along with them anywhere the going is tough.[201]

---

[201]Rapport and Northwood, p. 662.

# EPILOGUE

## JANUARY 17

The troops of the 101st Division were informed on the previous afternoon that tankers of the 11th Armored Division driving up from the southern end of the bulge had met armored units and infantrymen of the 2nd Armored Division fighting their way down from the north. The 101st troops at Bourcy, Rachamps and Marigny had a rather easy night of it in the barns and houses out of the cold foxholes – except for those who did their stints out on the observation posts.

Dawn of January 17 brought a pleasant surprise for S/Sgt. John H. Taylor as he stood at the barn door enjoying the last part of a cigarette. He had just sent one of the men back to notify the company CP that he had pulled in his OP's if it became necessary to fire artillery to their front. Taylor relates:[202]

Early the next morning as dawn was breaking, I sent Shaefer back to the company CP to let them know we had moved our OP's in so if we needed artillery fire they could drop it in front of us without fear of hitting our men on the OP's. If we were gonna get an attack it would be at daybreak. I had one-half of a cigarette, standing in the barn door, looking back up the street into the village. I was smoking this last butt when a door opened and I looked around at the house attached to the same barn. A little old lady came over to me and gave me some bread and a wooden bowl of hot milk. I certainly welcomed that. I've never forgotten.

The notation in T/3 George Koskimaki's diary has a terse summary of the day's actions:

January 17, 1944 – The Division is being relieved today. We are to go into Corps reserve somewhere to the rear. It is cold and snowy. Our regiments captured Bourcy before they were relieved.

Platoon sergeant John Taylor remembered how his battalion was relieved without too much warning. He closed his taped narrative with this comment:

That night without too much forewarning, we were relieved around ten or eleven o'clock. It was the 17th Airborne Division people who came up and relieved us. We retraced our steps through Noville and the area where we had dug the deep holes a week or so before. We spent the night there. We

---

[202]John H. Taylor added: "When I went back to Europe in 1969 and 1974, I found the same barn and through an interpretor found the man who lived there. He looked to be 65 to 70 years old. He told me, 'Yes, this was the home of the woman who had given that bread and hot milk' – that was his mother. He asked, through the interpretor, if I recalled anyone in the village pointing out where there were some Germans in a cellar and I said 'Yes'. He said, 'That was me!' He had been the burgomeister of the village at that time. I thought that was quite a coincidence."

got word – would you believe – we were going to be trucked out of Bastogne!

On this day, 1st/Sgt. Carwood Lipton reverted back to his former assignment in "Easy" Company headquarters. He closed his Bastogne experiences with this story:

I went back to company headquarters as first sergeant and we moved into a convent or girl's school, our first stay inside a building since we arrived at Bastogne, to await being relieved. In our first night there, the nuns and teachers brought a group of girls, who were about twelve or thirteen years old, into the large hall where we were. They sang a serenade for us, including their French and Belgian songs. Several were sung in English and, surprisingly, they sang the German marching song, 'Lili Marlene'.

## AWARDS CEREMONY

On the 18th of January in a ceremony in front of the shattered city hall of Bastogne, General Maxwell D. Taylor turned over to Lt. General Troy Middleton, commander of VIII Corps, the shattered remains of Bastogne and its perimeter defense network.

At the time the 101st Airborne Division history, *Rendezvous with Destiny* was published in 1948, the casualty figures were not yet finalized. The KIA's cited in the "Honored Dead" listing for the Bastogne campaign totaled 482. After years of careful research, hunting through all the available files, Dutch researcher, Piet Pulles, came up with a figure of 982. Many of those added men had previously been listed as missing in action.[203]

During the award ceremony in the town square, a total of five hundred Screaming Eagles passed the reviewing stand after several of the division troopers were presented with Silver Star awards for their deeds.

Reviewing the troops were VIII Corps commander Lt. General Troy Middleton, Division commander Maxwell D. Taylor, 11th Armored Division commander Brig. General Charles S. Kilburn and ADC of the 101st Division Brig. Gen. Gerald J. Higgins.

---

[203]Pulles, op. cit.

*Lt. Gen. Troy Middleton, Maj. Gen. Maxwell D. Taylor, Brig. Gen. Charles S. Kilburn and Brig. Gen. Gerald J. Higgins.*

## NO RETURN TO BASE CAMP

After a brief stay in the towns between Bastogne and Neufchateau, the mentally and physically beat troops of the 101st Airborne Division learned they would not be returning to Mourmelon. After receiving additional winter gear, the Division was ordered to move to the Alsace-Lorraine region of the U.S. 7th Army Front. The distance of 160 miles with convoys slipping and sliding on treacherous snow and ice-covered roads was completed in a few days. Mid-winter was still venting its fury on the fighting fronts.

The threat of another German offensive on that front failed to materialize. The 101st spent the last week of January to February 25 on the 7th Army front. They were now going back to Mourmelon. However, they did learn their comfortable barracks had been turned over to U.S. Army hospital units. The troops would be quartered in squad tents.

Due to the fact that airborne divisions are not as well equipped with motorized transport as are infantry and armored units, many of the men had to return to Mourmelon via 40 et 8 box cars attached to slow moving steam engines.

During the month of March at Mourmelon, after having been involved in front line actions for the better part of three months with little relaxation, and with the Division once more demanding spit and polish, there was a marked show of resentment on the part of many of the troops. The various regimental stockades found 139 members confined for "activities unbecoming a soldier".

On March 15, the entire division assembled on a large parade ground near Mourmelon where they were presented the Presidential Unit Citation by General Dwight D. Eisenhower, the first full division ever to receive this prestigious award.

## MUCH TRAVELING

At the end of March, the Division was sent north to the Ruhr Pocket to participate in an action to secure the surrender of 350,000 enemy troops who no longer had egress to flee deeper into Germany.

The 501st Parachute Regiment did not participate in this move. They were held back at Mourmelon and closeby marshaling areas with the intent of parachuting combat teams into Nazi prisoner of war camps to rescue soldiers who might be in danger of being liquidated by their captors before they, too, fled into the heartland of Germany. That mission was never undertaken.

On April 20, the Division was ordered to move south from the Ruhr Pocket. They were to rejoin 7th Army in southern Germany. Again, many of the men had to board 40 et 8 box cars pulled by the same type of cranky engines as was their experience on the earlier ride. The trains detoured and backtracked as those operating them hunted for usable sections of track which headed in a southerly direction.

From then on, it was a race into Bavaria with as much as two hundred miles between the advance elements and those following in the rear with the heavier equipment.

During the trip south, the convoys passed hundreds of thin bedraggled concentration camp victims, trudging toward their homelands, wearing nothing more than their striped camp uniforms but lacking footwear.

Still remembering his experience of witnessing these victims of war, so happy to be liberated, T/3 George Koskimaki wrote:

> I remember seeing hundreds of these concentration camp victims and displaced people, with thighs no bigger around than our arms, plodding down the roads near the numerous camps we passed. We tossed out cases of

10-in-One rations to them. We knew we'd pick up additional supplies down the road. I'm sure many of them became very ill, putting all that rich food into their shrunken stomachs.

As "Charley" Company of the 506th Regiment arrived at the site of one of the concentration camps, they were ordered to stop. They mounted a guard on the nearby town and the concentration camp. After General Taylor inspected the camp with its dead piled in ditches and scattered about the grounds, he viewed the gas ovens. Returning to the "C" Company command post, he gave orders to the commander to have his men round up all the citizens of the town, young and old. These German people were then forced to march through the camp, viewing the remains of the decomposing victims. Hundreds of them came out, vomiting, visibly upset at what they had seen, shaking their heads at what was witnessed – man's inhumanity to man. The troops guarding them wondered how many of these people had known what was taking place on the outskirts of their town. They were sure many of the adults had known what was going on.

Further down the road, as the troops approached "Hitler's Hideout" near Berchtesgaden, T/3 George Koskimaki remembered sending a message to the 506th Regiment, which was leading the chase. He wrote:

In keeping a diary of all of my days in the war, my memories of certain incidents has stayed with me. I recall a message Division Headquarters had me transmit to the 506th troops out in front of us. The comment for May 6 was 'The German army group in front of our division has surrendered. I sent the 506th a message to stop their advance.'

The remnant of German Army Group "G" expressed the wish to surrender to the 101st. That surrender was taken by troops of Colonel Robert F. Sink's 506th Parachute Regiment.

On May 7th, the day the war was officially ended in Europe, the Screaming Eagles were perched at Hitler's Hideout, the "Eagles Nest" overlooking the beautiful little city of Berchtesgaden.

# BIBLIOGRAPHY

Astor, Gerald. *A Blood-Dimmed Tide.* New York: Donald T. Fine, 1992.

Dank, Harlan. *The Glider Gang.* Philadelphia: J. B. Lippincott, 1977.

440th Troop Carrier Group. *DZ Europe, The Story of the 440th Troop Carrier Group.* Extract.

Gilmore, Lawrence J. & Lewis, Howard J. *History of the 435th Troop Carrier Group.* Greenville, S.C. 1946.

Greindl, Countess Rene. *Christmas 1944 at Isle-la-Hesse.* Bastogne, 1965.

Hanlon, John. *Is That All You Write, One Story a Day?.* Providence, R.I.: Providence Journal, 1983.

Houston, Robert J. *D-Day to Bastogne.* New York: Exposition Press, 1979.

Koskimaki, George E. *Hell's Highway.* Sweetwater, TN: 101st Airborne Division Association, 1989.

Marshall, S. L. A. *Bastogne, The First Eight Days.* Washington, D.C.: Infantry Journal Press, 1946.

McKenzie, Fred. *The Men of Bastogne.* New York: David McKay Co., Inc., 1968.

Minick, Robert. *Kilogram.* Hobart, IN: Private Printing. 1979.

Mrazek, James. *The Glider War.* New York: St. Martin's Press.

Rapport & Northwood. *Rendezvous with Destiny.* The History of the 101st Airborne Division, Sweetwater, TN: 101st Airborne Division Association, 3rd Printing, 1980.

Sampson, Francis L. *Look Out Below!* Sweetwater, TN: 101st Airborne Division Association, Reprint, 1989.

Van Horn, William R. *Currahee.* Austria: 506th Parachute Infantry Regiment, 1945.

Wolfe, Martin. *Green Light.* Philadelphia: University of Pennsylvania Press, 1989.

# PERIODICALS

Agnew, John. "Experiences as Bastogne Pathfinder." *Newsletter of 9th Troop Carrier Command Pathfinder Association:* Vol. I, No. 4.

Ferretti, Fred. Interview of Schuyler Jackson, *Stars and Stripes.* August 8, 1984.

Fourth Armored Division Association Newsletter. "A Special Christmas Issue." *Rolling Along.* 1985.

Hanlon, John. "A Bell Rings in Hemroulle." *Readers Digest.* Pleasantville, 1962.

Harwick, Robert. "Christmas for Real!" *The Magazine of the Gulf Companies:* Nov.-Dec. 1945.

Marshall, S. L. A. "Men Against Armor." *Armored Cavalry Journal.* May-June, 1950.

Martin, Darryl R. "Unexpected Trap for Panzers." *Military History.* December, 1988.

McKenzie, Fred. "Christmas in Bastogne." *The Detroit Free Press.* January 18, 1945.

Peniche, Eduoard. "Mad Minute at Longchamps." *Military:* April 15, 1985.

Prior, John T. "The Night before Christmas - Bastogne 1944." *Onendago County Medical Society Bulletin:* December, 1972.

Small, Collie. "Bastogne: American Epic." *The Saturday Evening Post:* February 17, 1945.

Taylor, Maxwell D. "3,000 Miles to Bastogne." *The Washington Post:* op. ed. December 18, 1984.

# LETTERS

Block, Gordon L. Letter to a magazine editor for renewal, May 19, 1945.

Boggess, Charles. Letter to William Dwight. 1972.

Bostwick, Richard V. Memories of World War II. 1946.

Corwin, Carleton W. Letter to William H. Horn. July 15, 1977.

Davis, Walter E. Letter to author. April 20, 1966.

Dickinson, Carl E. Letter to Peter Hendrikx. July 13, 1985.

Goldmann, Ted. Letters to parents of Johnny Ballard. June 15 and 22, 1945.

Meason, Richard P. Letter to James Morton. 1947.

Morton, James S. Letter to William E. Reid. 1947.

Nicks, Elmer G. Letter to Lloyd Brazell. Jan. 3, 1984.

Pangerl, Joseph. V-Mail letter to parents. Dec. 29, 1944.

Patching, 2Lt. Ted. Letter to Melvin Davis. 1945.

Ryan, Capt. Beranrd J. Letter to Major Louis Kent. 1945.

Schmidt, Rene A. Letter to H. Lincoln Bethel. Oct. 19, 1980.

Sherburne, Thomas L. Letter to LTC. John T. Cooper. Dec. 25, 1944.

Taylor, Gen. Maxwell D. Letter to H. Lincoln Bethel. 1980.

Todd, Alden. Letter to Walter Zagol. "Memories of my first visit to Bourcy – January 1945, November 1986.

Turner, Ernest. Letter to Colonel Charles H. Young. March 11, 1981.

Wise, Albert J. Letter to Major Ivan G. Phillips. June 19, 1948.

# ORAL TAPES

| | | |
|---|---|---|
| Alex Andros | Charles W. Hogan | Harry Rosinski |
| Park Appler | Lloyd Jones | William G. Sefton |
| Robert Barger | Charles Kocourek | James Sherriff |
| Henry DeSimone | Anaclete Leone | Cecil H. Simmons |
| Joseph Dominguez | Peter Madden | Robert Stroud |
| Bert Ellard | Howard Matthews | John H. Taylor |
| Jim D. Ferguson | Walter L. Miller | Rudy Wedra |
| Willis Fowler | George K. Mullins | Jack Williamson |
| Edward Hallo | Floyd F. Phillips | Gordon Yates |
| Robert J. Hartzell | Alfred J. Regenburg | Michael Zorich |

PFC. Jerald Abrahamson (DivArty)
CPL. Paul V. Abroze (HQ1/506)
T/5 Fred C. Adams (Svc/501)
PFC. George E. Adams (A/321)
PFC. John Agnew (Pfdr/506)
1Lt. Roger Airgood (79TCS)
Sgt. James H. Alley (E/506)
Sgt. Thomas H. Alley (F/506)
PFC. Amos J. Almeida (B/502)
Capt. Charles Althoff (Med/502)
T/5 Sam J. Amico (326Med)
Pvt. Carl R. Anderson (HQ1/501)
1Lt. Everett Andrews (HQ/377)
1Lt. Alex Andros (H/506)
PFC. Park Appler (G/506)
Sgt. Charles Asay (A/502)
P-38 Association
LTC. Richard W. Ayars (USAF)
PFC. Douglas M. Bailey (B/463)
T/4 Rod Bain (E/506)
T/5 Albert S. Baker (C/377)
F/O Herbert W. Ballinger (439/93)
PFC. Robert Barger (326Med)
1Lt. Henry Barnes (326Med)
Sgt. Robert F. Barnes (A/502)
SSgt. Clive B. Barney (C/501)
PFC. Luther E. Barrick (B/907)
T/4 Joe W. Barringer (502/Band)
F/O Albert S. Barton (439/93)
PFC. Allen D. Bastian (F/327)
Sgt. Paul Bebout (HQ1/501)
SSgt. Earl M. Bedwell (B/907)
Roger Bell (Brit Hist)
Pvt. Nicholas Bellezza (B/463)
1Lt. Harry Begle (H/506)
Sgt. Jack C. Behringer (HQ/502)
PFC. Wayne Bengel (E/501)
PFC. James M. Beresford (B/401)
Pvt. Gordon M. Bernhardt (B/463)
Pvt. Albert Bernier (HQ2/502)
Cpl. Joseph Berra (HQ/326Eng)
PFC. Seth O. Berry (HQ1/501)
PFC. H. Lincoln Bethel (HQ/502)
Pvt. John Bettencourt (C/501)
Cpl. Bruce M. Beyer (HQ2/501)
Pvt. Roy H. Biffle (B/501)
SSgt. Arthur Bittner (A/326Eng)
Sgt. Layton Black, Jr. (C/502)
T/5 George Blain (Pfdr/506)
PFC. Ray Blasingame (F/502)
F/O Fred E. Bliss (438/88)
Capt. Gordon Block (326Med)
Cpl. Wilson Boback (G/501)
2Lt. Charles Boggess (C/37Armd)
Sgt. John Boitano (B/506)
SSgt. Michael Bokesch (HQ1/327)

Pvt. John Bortolon (A/327)
PFC. Richard V. Bostwick (B/401)
Pvt. John J. Bouska (E/501)
SSgt. Robert M. Bowen (C/401)
T/5 Glenn Braddock (Pfdr/502)
Pvt. Lloyd Brazell (HQ1/502)
1Lt. Eugene D. Brierre (F/501)
Sgt. Donald Brininstool (A/506)
PFC. Ottie Brock (C/81AT)
1Lt. Raymond Brock (HQ3/502)
PFC. Charles R. Brookman (HQ/501)
Sgt. Chester Brooks (HQ1/501)
Pvt. Charles E. Brown (B/501)
Maj. William E. Brubaker (HQ/377)
1Lt. Austin J. Buchanan (438/90)
PFC. Donald Burgett (A/506)
PFC. Lawrence Burgoon (I/501)
PFC. James Cadden (C/506)
PFC. Samuel R. Caiazzo (A/463)
SSgt. Erminio Calderan (I/501)
Pvt. Joseph Callahan (B/463)
1Lt. Derwood Cann (G/506)
Pvt. Albert P. Cappelli (I/506)
Pvt. Michael J. Caprara (HQ/501)
Capt. Charles Carlsen (Svc/501)
F/O Pershing Y. Carlson (439/94)
PFC. Edward Carowick (B/326Eng)
PFC. Keith L. Carpenter (HQ/506)
2Lt. Vincent Carroll (HQ2/501)
PFC. Carl H. Cartledge (HQ/501)
Sgt. Donald Castona (G/501)
Pvt. John G. Cavaluzzo (D/501)
T/3 Charles D. Chapman (101Sig)
Pvt. William Chivvis (I/506)
PFC. Joseph N. Christman (I/501)
PFC. Leonard Cinquanta (HQ/501)
Doug Clanin (Ind His Soc)
SSgt. William E. Clark (DivHQ)
SSgt. Stanley Clever (G/506)
Jan Coolen (Dutch)
LTC. John T. Cooper, Jr. (HQ/463)
Capt. Charles H. Corwin (440/96)
SSgt. Earl L. Cox (F/501)
PFC. Charles D. Cram (HQ2/506)
1Lt. R. W. Creamer (435TCG)
1Lt. Laurence Critchell (HQ/501)
PFC. Robert A. Crowe (HQ3/501)
Pvt. Harold Curry (A/502)
Capt. Lewis A. Curtis (HQ/435TCG)
Sgt. Anthony D'Angelo (705TD)
PFC. Everett M. Daugherty (I/501)
T/5 Reginald E. Davies (HQ2/502)
Pvt. Walter E. Davis (G/501)
SSgt. William G. Davis (HQ1/501)
F/O Warren deBeauclair (440/95)
Pvt. Patrick DePerna (Med/501)

1Lt. Gordon DeRamus (Pfdr/502)
T/5 Glen A. Derber (HQ2/501)
PFC. Raymond Derosier (C/377)
Pvt. Henry DeSimone (E/501)
Maj. William R. Desobry (10CCB)
SSgt. Carl E. Dickinson (F/327)
Capt. Robert S. Dickson (E/502)
Sgt. Frank A. Digaetano (C/326Eng)
Capt. Anthony A. DiGiovanni (DivArty)
1Lt. Charles A. Disney (HQ1/502)
Pvt. Joseph Dominquez (E/506)
Pvt. William Druback (D/501)
PFC. Angelo Dukelis (HQ1/506)
PFC. Robert Dunning (HQ3/506)
Sgt. Edward C. Eaton (B/326Eng)
PFC. Bert Ellard (F/502)
Pvt. Carroll Ellis (A/501)
Cpl. James L. Evans (DivArty)
1Lt. Jim D. Ferguson (E/81)
Maj. William A. Ferguson (HQ/326Eng)
Pvt. Angelo Ferrera (HQ2/502)
Sgt. Michael Finn (I/501)
PFC. Charles H. Fisher (HQ2/327)
1Lt. Frank Fitter (HQ1/501)
PFC. John E. Fitzgerald (HQ3/502)
Pvt. James W. Flanagan (C/502)
Cpl. Robert A. Flory (B/506)
Sgt. Edward E. Ford (C/81AT)
PFC. Albert C. Foster (A/907)
Cpl. Willis Fowler (A/502)
PFC. Willie Ray Fox (C/501)
PFC. Donald E. Frederick (Med/327)
PFC. Bradford C. Freeman (E/506)
2Lt. Joseph Fry (439/91)
1Lt. Everett Fuchs (A/377)
PFC. Charles Galvin (I/501)
Sgt. Joseph Gambino (101Sig)
Sgt. William D. Gammon (B/377)
PFC. Anthony C. Garcia (E/506)
PFC. James T. Gardner (B/401)
Pvt. Warren H. Gardner (A/506)
Maj. Victor E. Garrett (HQ/463)
PFC. John R. Garrigan (B/506)
SSgt. Kenneth Garrity (HQ/502)
LTC. Robert Gates (438/85)
SSgt. John L. Ghiardi (HQ2/501)
Cpl. John W. Gibson (Med3/506)
1Lt. Howard Gielow (I/501)
Sgt. Donald Gill (101Sig)
T/5 Richard E. Gilmore (Svc/501)
Pvt. Carmen Gisi (B/401)
PFC. Donald P. Glaspey (G/501)
Sgt. James A. Goble (C/327)
Pvt. George Goldberg (DivHQ)
PFC. Ted Goldmann (A/502)
Pvt. Kenneth Gong (HQ3/501)

Cpl. Walter S. Gordon (E/506)
1Lt. Henry B. Gorman (HQ/326Eng)
Pvt. John M. Graham (326Med)
Pvt. Albert Gramme (A/377)
PFC. James O. Grant (HQ/326Eng)
PFC. Wilford J. Grant (HQ2/506)
T/5 Charles R. Grauel (HQ/321)
Cpl. Millard B. Green (101Sig)
Capt. Frank Gregg (E/501)
Countess Rene Greindl (Bastogne)
PFC. Marshall Griffith (B/401)
Capt. Alphonse G. Gueymard (B/81AT)
PFC. Frank Guzy (I/501)
Capt. David Habif (326Med)
Pvt. Richard Hahlbohm (I/501)
F/O David Hakala (435/75)
Cpl. Donald B. Hall (101Sig)
PFC. Edward Hallo (A/501)
Capt. W. L. Hamilton (440/95)
F/O Jack Hamm (436/80)
Sgt. Jack Hampton (D/501)
Maj. John Hanlon (HQ1/502)
Capt. Fred Hancock (HQ/a502)
Pvt. Harold R. Hanson (A/401)
PFC. Russell Hardeman (HQ1/327)
1Lt. William Hardie (HQ/377)
PFC. Leslie Harris (I/501)
Pvt. Alfred K. Harrison (E/502)
PFC. Robert T. Harrison (HQ3/502)
PFC. Robert J. Hartzell (I/502)
Pvt. Duane K. Harvey (HQ1/501)
Maj. Robert Harwick (HQ1/a506)
LTC. Carl Hash (438/88)
Pvt. Lester E. Hashey (E/506)
1Lt. Albert M. Hassenzahl (C/506)
Capt. James J. Hatch (HQ/502)
PFC. Hargus Haygood (C/463)
PFC. Gus Hazzard (B/463)
Sgt. Sam D. Hefner (H/506)
1Lt. Clark Heggeness (H/506)
PFC. Louis F. Henson (HQ1/501)
PFC. Kenneth Hesler (D/463)
Cpl. Leonard Hicks (F/506)
2Lt. John D. Hill (439/91)
PFC. John B. Himelrick (F/506)
PFC. Jack W. Hinton (G/327)
Sgt. Ted C. Hintz (C/506)
Pvt. Morris Hoffman (101Sig)
PFC. Charles W. Hogan (B/907)
F/O E. H. Hohman (434/74)
Capt. Jean Holstein (I/506)
Sgt. Tom Holmes (10CCB)
F/O William K. Horn (435/78)
SSgt. Robert Houston (I/501)
Pvt. Bobby G. Hunter (D/501)
PFC. Ernest C. Hurt (HQ1/501)

F/O Frank J. Hynes (439/92)
Pvt. Guy D. Jackson (H/506)
Sgt. Schuyler Jackson (HQ/502)
Pvt. James Jacobsma (B/501)
T/5 Leon Jedziniak (Med/501)
PFC. Robert Jessup (HQ/327)
T/4 Frank Jobe (326Med)
Capt. Joseph B. Johnson (A/327)
PFC. Eugene E. Johnson (H/506)
Sgt. Robert W. Johnson (A/705TD)
Pvt. Gerald B. Johnston (C/502)
Pvt. Lee Jones (HQ1/401)
Sgt. Lloyd Jones (A/501)
1Lt. Bernard A. Jordan (E/501)
Cpl. Werner W. Jutzin (C/327)
PFC. Donald F. Kane (G/501)
Capt. Steve Karabinos (DivHQ)
Sgt. Ahzez Karim (HQ2/501)
PFC. Jay Karp (B/463)
Pvt. Richard J. Kazinski (HQ2/502)
Pvt. Leo E. Kelley (A/501)
PFC. George M. Kempf (C/327)
1Lt. Robert I. Kennedy (A/501)
SSgt. Joseph Kenney (E/501)
Pvt. Joseph Kettering (F/502)
T/4 Richard Ketzdever (I/501)
Pvt. John Kilgore (G/506)
Pvt. Ralph G. King (H/506)
Col. Harry W. O. Kinnard (Div HQ)
SSgt. Richard Klein (HQ3/501)
PFC. Kenneth K. Knarr (B/326Eng)
Pvt. Frank Kneller (H/506)
Sgt. Kenneth Kochenour (C/502)
T/4 Ernest L. Koenig (101Sig)
Sgt. John Kolesar (HQ/377)
T/5 Steve Koper (B/377)
T/3 George E. Koskimaki (101Sig)
LTC. William E. Kuhn (HQ/327)
PFC. William A. Kummerer (D/463)
Sgt. Ludwig Labutka (E/502)
PFC. Richard Ladd (HQ/502)
T/5 Charles Laden (101Sig)
PFC. William P. Laidlaw (463PFA)
Sgt. Lawrence C. Lamb (D/506)
Cpl. Ernest A. Lambert (B/501)
T/5 Malcolm B. Landry (HQ/506)
Cpl. Frank Lasik (D/501)
Sgt. Bud Lauer (B/907)
SSgt. Walter T. Leamon (C/401)
PFC. Charles Lenzing (101Sig)
PFC. Anaclete Leone (Med2/502)
Norbert Lhote (Belgian)
Sgt. Saul Levitt (YANK)
Pvt. Elias Lingenfeld (Svc/502)
1/Sgt. Carwood C. Lipton (E/506)
Capt. William S. Lockman (C/81AT)

PFC. Mickey B. Long (326Med)
Cpl. Frank Lopez (B/502)
PFC. Werner K. Lunde (A/502)
PFC. Lamar C. Lutz (B/501)
1Lt. Joseph W. Lyons (B/463)
PFC. Robert L. MacNaughton (D/502)
1Lt. Peter Madden (HQ3/506)
T/4 William B. Magruder (101Sig)
PFC. Norman P. Maine (HQ/321GFA)
PFC. Frank J. Malik (H/506)
T/5 Richard Mandich (HQ/506)
T/5 John F. Marohn (E/501)
Capt. Donald N. Martin (HQ/463)
Pvt. Ewell B. Martin (G/506)
PFC. James H. Martin (G/506)
PFC. Paul Z. Martinez (D/506)
Pvt. Mike Marquez (HQ/506)
Sgt. Howard Matthews (F/502)
1Lt. Henry D. Mavis (D/502)
Pvt. Arthur C. Mayer (A/327)
T/4 William C. McCall (101Sig)
T/5 Charles McCallister (HQ2/506)
PFC. James McCann (H/506)
SSgt. Frank McClure (E/501)
Pvt. John F. McElfresh (A/501)
Pvt. Christopher C. McEwan (A/501)
1Lt. Bernard McKearney (E/502)
Capt. Willis P. McKee (326Med)
Pvt. Ford McKenzie (HQ1/502)
PFC. William R. McMahon (I/501)
PFC. Dennis P. McManus (Svc/501)
PFC. George R. McMillan (Pfdr/506)
PFC. Melton McMorries (G/501)
Pvt. Merle W. McMorrow (B/464)
1Lt. Bill McRae (HQ/377PFA)
Capt. Richard P. Meason (A/506)
Pvt. Joel Mehall (HQ3/502)
1Lt. Edward Mehosky (C/506)
PFC. Frank Menard (D/81AA)
Sgt. Louis P. Merlano (A/502)
Andre Meurisse (Belgian)
PFC. Bruce Middough (C/463)
Pvt. Clarence W. Miller (326Med)
T/4 Joseph W. Miller (A/94Sig)
T/5 Owen E. Miller (Med1/506)
Capt. Walter L. Miller (C/327)
2Lt. Willie Miller (H/506)
PFC. James T. Milne (Med2/502)
Robert Minick (B/907 Kin)
2Lt. Charles A. Mitchell (B/506)
T/5 Hiram Mitchell (Svc/502)
Sgt. Lionel C. Mitchell (HQ/502)
PFC. Christie Mite (C/326Eng)
Pvt. John E. Mockabee (D/463)
Sgt. Charles F. Monroe (HQ1/506)
PFC. John B. Moore (101Rcn)

LTC. Ned D. Moore (DivHQ)
Capt. Bill Morgan (I/501)
Capt. James Morton (HQ3/506)
Pvt. Herman Moulliet (HQ1/506)
PFC. George K. Mullins (C/327)
PFC. Hubert N. Mullins (A/463)
Cpl. Walter P. Murphy (C/377)
Cpl. Lloyd A. Nace (B/327)
PFC. John Nasea (B/321GFA)
T/4 Keith E. Natalle (326Med)
PFC. David Nelson (8010rd)
PFC. Norman A. Nelson (H/501)
1Lt. Ralph K. Nelson (A/401)
Sgt. Forrest J. Nichols (B/502)
Cpl. Elmer G. Nicks (HQ1/502)
1Lt. Thomas J. Niland (HQ2/327)
Pvt. Memphis E. Nixon (HQ1/502)
Pvt. James W. Norene (G/502)
SSgt. Vincent Occhipinti (F/506)
1Lt. Robert P. O'Connell (E/501)
Sgt. Donald Oldham (10CCB)
T/5 James A. Oleson (DivHQ)
SSgt. Kenneth V. Oliver (Med/501)
Cpl. Daniel C. Olney (DivHQ)
1Lt. Donald Orcott (440/95)
Sgt. Joseph P. O'Toole (C/81AT)
Sgt. Ben Ottinger (B/401)
Cpl. Cleon Overbay (C/401)
F/O E. B. Paige (439/92)
Cpl. Bernie Palitz (C/377)
SSgt. Frank Palys (HQ/506)
Capt. Joseph Pangerl (HQ/502)
PFC. Ben P. Panzarella (B/81AT)
Sgt. Arthur Parker (HQ/377)
Sgt. Hurschel Parker (C/327)
Pvt. Kenneth Parker (C/506)
Col. William Parkhill (441TCG)
PFC. Emmert O. Parmley (F/506)
2Lt. Ted Patching (A/506)
Sgt. Harold L. Paulson (C/501)
PFC. Edward A. Peniche (C/81AT)
PFC. Walter Peplowski (B/463)
Capt. Joseph K. Perkins (HQ/321GFA)
PFC. Floyd F. Phillips (G/506)
Capt. Ivan G. Phillips (HQ/502)
PFC. Willard C. Phillips (B/907)
Pvt. Steve Polander (A/506)
Sgt. Sam R. Pope (HQ2/501)
PFC. Ernest Porter (C/463)
2Lt. Huber C. Porter (B/506)
1Lt. Jack A. Price (A/377PFA)
T/5 Oryn L. Pride (B/401)
Capt. John T. Prior (Med/20Armd)
T/4 Hugh Pritchard (D/506)
Sgt. Robert J. Rader (E/506)
F/O Case Rafter (439/91)

Helen Briggs Ramsey (ARC3/506)
1Lt. Bill E. Reed (HQ1/506)
2Lt. Joseph R. Reed (C/506)
1Lt. John H. Reeder (HQ/506)
1Lt. Alfred J. Regenburg (G/327)
PFC. David Reich (Rcn/6Armd)
Capt. Jack Reiss (326Med)
PFC. Roswell Reusser (HQ/502)
SSgt. Robert Reynolds (Med1/501)
Sgt. Ted Rhodes (B/401)
1Lt. John C. Rice (C/326Eng)
PFC. Donald J. Rich (G/327)
Sgt. Charles E. Richards (H/506)
SSgt. Robert C. Richards (435/75)
PFC. George Ricker (HQ1/501)
Sgt. Bruce Robinson (101Sig)
1Lt. James A. Robinson (B/377)
Sgt. Dominick Rochetto (C/377)
PFC. Willis F. Rohr (A/327)
Pvt. Robert T. Romo (C/377)
PFC. Harry Rosinski (G/327)
PFC. Ben H. Rous (HQ2/506)
T/5 Richard C. Rowles (E/501)
PFC. Leo Rozman (I/501)
Pvt. Tony Rubino (H/506)
Capt. Bernard J. Ryan (Med3/506)
SSgt. Robert W. Salley (HQ/326Eng)
Capt. Francis Sampson (HQ/501)
PFC. Victor Sauerheber (HQ/321GFA)
PFC. Rene A. Schmidt (HQ2/502)
PFC. Wallace J. Schoen (B/327)
PFC. Julius J. Schrader (I/501)
2Lt. Deford R. Schwall (B/907)
1Lt. Joseph B. Schweiker (A/501)
SSgt. Roger Seamon (B/401)
Maj. Stuart Seaton (HQ/463PFA)
1Lt. William G. Sefton (D/501)
T/4 John Seney (HQ2/502)
1Lt. H. Rex Shama (313TCG)
Pvt. Kerman A. Sheckler (B/506)
F/O Mike Sheff (439/91)
Col. Thomas L. Sherburne (DivHQ)
Cpl. Jack Sherman (G/327)
PFC. Harry Sherrard (A/326Eng)
SSgt. James Sherriff (G/327)
Capt. Charles G. Shettle (HQ3/506)
Cpl. Charles Shoemaker (A/506)
Pvt. William J. Shorter (B/326Eng)
Pvt. Louis E. Siegle (A/326Eng)
1Lt. David H. Sill (439/92)
Maj. Cecil Simmons (HQ3/502)
SSgt. Paul Slevey (B/327)
T/4 Matthew Slifstein (HQ/502)
1/Sgt. Claude D. Smith (B/463)
PFC. David M. Smith (HQ/501)
PFC. Fred Smith (B/327)

Pvt. Lester D. Smith (326Med)
Sgt. Raymond Smith (Med/502)
PFC. Robert W. Smith (Med1/501)
Pvt. Peter A. Sorci (I/501)
Capt. Robert Speer (HQ/502)
2Lt. Ben Stapelfeld (F/506)
PFC. Stanley Stasica (H/506)
Pvt. Edward H. Stein (E/506)
Cpl. Bernard A. Stevens (D/501)
Neil Stevens (British)
PFC. William J. Stone (B/321)
Cpl. Clayton E. Storeby (C/326Eng)
Pvt. Donald B. Straith (A/506)
LTC. Robert L. Strayer (HQ2/506)
1Lt. Wallace Strobel (HQ/502)
1Lt. Robert Stroud (H/506)
F/O Charles F. Sutton (440/98)
Capt. Wallace A. Swanson (A/502)
PFC. Leonard Swartz (HQ/502)
SSgt. John H. Taylor (E/506)
Cpl. Ted Teach (101Sig)
Pvt. John Thach (B/377PFA)
PFC. Andrew C. Thieneman (C/327)
Capt. Eber H. Thomas (Svc/501)
PFC. Walter W. Tibbets (B/377PFA)
Pvt. Stanley R. Tiller (DivHQ)
Pvt. Alden Todd (F/502)
Capt. Victor J. Tofany (F/463)
PFC. A. J. Tower (D/463)
Sgt. Joseph Toye (E/506)
F/O David H. Trexler (315/34)
PFC. John C. Trowbridge (HQ1/501)
Sgt. Louis Truax (D/506)
PFC. William True (F/506)
F/O David A. Truman (436TCG)
1Lt. Ernest Turner (439TCG)
Cpl. Richard Turner (B/506)
PFC. Newman L. Tuttle (HQ/502)
T/5 Arie Van Dort (HQ/326Eng)
Capt. Charles Van Gorder (326Med)
Cpl. Edward Vetch (G/506)
Pvt. John Vlachos (HQ/506)
1Lt. Wally H. Wagner (435/75)
PFC. William Wakeland (B/907)
Cpl. E. B. Wallace (F/506)
Capt. Ted Wallace (Svc/502)
F/O Ben Ward (436/81)
1Lt. Jack Washishek (DivArty)
Sgt. Elmer Weber (101Rcn)
1Lt. William Wedeking (HQ3/506)
PFC. Rudy Wedra (HQ/501)
T/5 David Weintraub (101Sig)
PFC. Paul West (A/401)
SSgt. Maurice C. White (I/501)
Capt. Thomas J. White (HQ/321)
T/5 George Whitfield (326Med)

Pvt. Robert M. Wiatt (C/506)
PFC. Robert I. Wickham (HQ1/501)
PFC. John J. Wielkopolan (G/502)
PFC. George E. Willey (E/501)
1Lt. Shrable D. Williams (Pfdr/506)
SSgt. Jack Williamson (A/327)
F/O Douglas Wilmar (438TCG)
1Lt. Robert Wing (C/326Eng)
SSgt. Ted Wingstrom (B/463PFA)
Capt. Richard D. Winters (HQ2/506)
1Lt. Albert J. Wise (A/502)
2Lt. Leonard Witkin (I/501)
1Lt. George B. Woldt (DivHQ)
PFC. Marvin C. Wolfe (I/501)
PFC. Crit B. Womack (HQ1/506)
Sgt. Donald J. Woodland (A/501)
Capt. Rufus Woody (31PhotoRcn)
1Lt. Ben F. Wright (HQ/463)
Cpl. Richard M. Wright (Pfdr/506)
T/4 Gordon Yates (H/506)
Col. Charles H. Young (439TCG)
1Lt. Harold E. Young (C/326Eng)
PFC. Raymond O. Zabriskie (C/81AT)
PFC. Walter Zagol (F/502)
T/4 Gerald Zimmerman (101Sig)
Pvt. Michael Zorich (I/501)